Management, Technology, and Economic Growth in Smart and Sustainable Cities

Jorge A. Ruiz-Vanoye
Universidad Politécnica de Pachuca, Mexico

IGI Global
PUBLISHER of TIMELY KNOWLEDGE

A volume in the Advances in Finance, Accounting, and Economics (AFAE) Book Series

Published in the United States of America by
IGI Global
Business Science Reference (an imprint of IGI Global)
701 E. Chocolate Avenue
Hershey PA, USA 17033
Tel: 717-533-8845
Fax: 717-533-8661
E-mail: cust@igi-global.com
Web site: http://www.igi-global.com

Library of Congress Cataloging-in-Publication Data

Names: Ruiz Vanoye, Jorge, 1975- editor.
Title: Management, technology, and economic growth in smart and sustainable cities / Jorge Ruiz Vanoye.
Description: Hershey, PS : Business Science Reference, [2023] | Includes bibliographical references and index. | English; one contribution in Spanish. | Summary: "This book will be the basis for the understanding and advanced and optimal management of smart and sustainable cities. With this reference book readers will learn how to identify or achieve international recognition of a city as a smart and sustainable city, as well as the most advanced topics that enable optimal management of cities"-- Provided by publisher.
Identifiers: LCCN 2023034554 (print) | LCCN 2023034555 (ebook) | ISBN 9798369303733 (hardcover) | ISBN 9798369303740 (paperback) | ISBN 9798369303757 (ebook)
Subjects: LCSH: Smart cities. | Sustainable urban development.
Classification: LCC TD159.4 .M36 2023 (print) | LCC TD159.4 (ebook) | DDC 307.1/416--dc23/eng/20231018
LC record available at https://lccn.loc.gov/2023034554
LC ebook record available at https://lccn.loc.gov/2023034555

This book is published in the IGI Global book series Advances in Finance, Accounting, and Economics (AFAE) (ISSN: 2327-5677; eISSN: 2327-5685)

British Cataloguing in Publication Data
A Cataloguing in Publication record for this book is available from the British Library.

For electronic access to this publication, please contact: eresources@igi-global.com.

Advances in Finance, Accounting, and Economics (AFAE) Book Series

Ahmed Driouchi
Al Akhawayn University, Morocco

ISSN:2327-5677
EISSN:2327-5685

Mission

In our changing economic and business environment, it is important to consider the financial changes occurring internationally as well as within individual organizations and business environments. Understanding these changes as well as the factors that influence them is crucial in preparing for our financial future and ensuring economic sustainability and growth.

The **Advances in Finance, Accounting, and Economics (AFAE)** book series aims to publish comprehensive and informative titles in all areas of economics and economic theory, finance, and accounting to assist in advancing the available knowledge and providing for further research development in these dynamic fields.

Coverage

- Economics Geography
- International Trade
- Auditing
- Theoretical Issues in Economics, Finance, and Accounting
- Applied economics
- E-Accounting
- Economics of Risks, Uncertainty, Ambiguity, and Insurance
- Accounting Standards
- Economic Theory
- Applied Accounting

The Advances in Finance, Accounting, and Economics (AFAE) Book Series (ISSN 2327-5677) is published by IGI Global, 701 E. Chocolate Avenue, Hershey, PA 17033-1240, USA, www.igi-global.com. This series is composed of titles available for purchase individually; each title is edited to be contextually exclusive from any other title within the series. For pricing and ordering information please visit http://www.igi-global.com/book-series/advances-finance-accounting-economics/73685. Postmaster: Send all address changes to above address.

Titles in this Series

For a list of additional titles in this series, please visit: http://www.igi-global.com/book-series/advances-finance-accounting-economics/73685

Optimizing Energy Efficiency During a Global Energy Crisis
Meltem Okur Dinçsoy (Trakya University, Turkey) and Hamit Can (Trakya University, Turkey)
Business Science Reference • © 2023 • 408pp • H/C (ISBN: 9798369304006) • US $240.00

Theory and Practice of Illegitimate Finance
Abdul Rafay (University of Management and Technology, Pakistan)
Business Science Reference • © 2023 • 389pp • H/C (ISBN: 9798369311905) • US $295.00

The Sustainable Fintech Revolution Building a Greener Future for Finance
Kuldeep Singh (Faculty of Management Studies, CMS Business School, Jain University (Deemed), Bengaluru, India) Rebecca Abraham (Huizenga College of Business and Entrepreneurship, Nova Southeastern University, Fort Lauderdale, USA) and Prasanna Kolar (Koneru Lakshmaiah Education Foundation, India)
Business Science Reference • © 2023 • 358pp • H/C (ISBN: 9798369300084) • US $250.00

Sustainable Growth and Global Social Development in Competitive Economies
Andrei Jean Vasile (Petroleum-Gas University of Ploiesti, Romania & Romanian Academy, National Institute for Economic Research "Costin C. Kiriţescu", Romania) Mile Vasić (European Marketing and Management Association, Banja Luka, Bosnia and Herzegovina) and Predrag Vukovic (Institute of Agricultural Economics, Belgrade, Serbia)
Business Science Reference • © 2023 • 331pp • H/C (ISBN: 9781668488102) • US $250.00

The Impact of AI Innovation on Financial Sectors in the Era of Industry 5.0
Mohammad Irfan (NSB Academy Business School, India) Mohammed Elmogy (Information Technology Department, Faculty of Computers and Information, Mansoura University, Egypt) M. Shabri Abd. Majid (Faculty of Economics and Business, Syiah Kuala University, Banda Aceh, Indonesia) and Shaker El-Sappagh (Department of Artificial Intelligence and Machine learning, Sungkyunkwan University, South Korea)
Business Science Reference • © 2023 • 320pp • H/C (ISBN: 9798369300824) • US $275.00

Concepts and Cases of Illicit Finance
Abdul Rafay (University of Management and Technology, Pakistan)
Business Science Reference • © 2023 • 273pp • H/C (ISBN: 9781668485873) • US $250.00

The Importance of Entrepreneurship in Fostering Economic Progress
Mohammed El Amine Abdelli (University of Western Brittany, France) Naima Bentouir (Ain Temouchent University, Algeria) and Esra Sipahi Döngül (Aksaray University, Turkey)
Business Science Reference • © 2024 • 300pp • H/C (ISBN: 9781668471272) • US $240.00

IGI Global
PUBLISHER of TIMELY KNOWLEDGE

701 East Chocolate Avenue, Hershey, PA 17033, USA
Tel: 717-533-8845 x100 • Fax: 717-533-8661
E-Mail: cust@igi-global.com • www.igi-global.com

Table of Contents

Detailed Table of Contents

Humans have always sought a place for safe living with the comforts and facilities to do decent work and for the family's healthy growth. This chapter aims to guide understanding smart and sustainable cities by presenting a survey of chronological aspects, elements and components of smart cities, smart cities' indicators, solutions to city problems, and other aspects related to smart cities. The authors also propose a Smart and Sustainable Cities Puzzle that contains the main components of a smart city to which various pieces of the puzzle can be added depending on the characteristics and needs of the city, indicators of smart cities; the idea is that trafficking in a city with technological elements allows citizens to better their quality of life, but that there must be optimum management (minimisation and maximisation) of all components involved in the city order to optimise time, money, and effort. This chapter can serve as a basis for experts' academic knowledge and professional practice in sensors and decision-makers.

Globalization driven by the development of information and communication technologies has triggered a context of competition and competitiveness in all areas of social and economic life. Smart cities have taken advantage of this situation to generate new conditions in health and employment. However, it is important to identify the needs of the population in smart cities to reduce poverty rates and the consequences that could be generated in the context of social life. Currently, several smart cities have proposed different ways to reduce poverty rates, so this chapter aims to analyze the poverty scenario in smart cities, raising questions such as Will it be possible to build smart jobs to maintain competitiveness in the global context and strengthen local development? What competitiveness alternatives can be used in the face of technological development in smart cities? What treatment do smart cities give to poverty areas seeking to incorporate them into urban and technological development?

Several technologies are available to help citizens, and government officials perform their daily activities in a city. The current state-of-the-art technologies to help citizens and government officials exist wireless sensor networks, RFDI technology, combinatorial optimisation, machine learning, big data, data visualisation, internet of government things, big-data analytics, and others to enhance the quality of the government. The authors have collected the relevant literature published during 2001-2021 by searching and browsing all the major digital libraries and publisher websites. The findings show the importance of the smart government's technology-assisted (electronic government, management of the economy, open data, civil works, tourism, management of the disasters, healthcare systems, and others). This chapter aims to determine how smart government components improve the activities in a city of the citizens and government officials. This paper also presents a survey of the characteristics, taxonomy, smart government indicators, history, and future trends.

Electronic voting is a topic that has been developing with the idea of applying technology and facilitating the process, however, the main objective has always been the reliability and confidentiality of the vote. The possibility of applying an emerging technology such as Blockchain has been visualized due to its characteristics such as immutability, that is, it cannot be changed or altered, however, some studies have found challenges for its implementation. This chapter addresses the state of the art of electronic voting, the strategy of electronic voting in Smart-Government, the security and transparency of electronic voting through Blockchain, as well as the structure of the blockchain. In addition, the operation of smart contracts as a tool for implementation and important concepts such as consensus algorithms are explained.

The tourist cities that apply technology help to strengthen and to facilitate the communication of the tourists with the sporting, cultural, and scientific aspects of a city. This chapter aims to be a guide for understanding smart tourism components by presenting a survey of the characteristics, history and future trends. Smart tourism is the innovation and the adoption of information and communication technologies in tourism. Smart tourism additionally must consider natural attractions, cultural (music festival), accessibility of transportation, amenity characteristics, ancillary services (banks, hospitals), innovative hubs for electric vehicles with a mobile app to check the availability status of charging cars, and the infrastructure of professional sports. The smart tourism is the optimal administration of the personnel or object related to the tourism by using technology like the internet of tourism things, data-mining, artificial intelligence, combinatorial optimization, machine learning, and others to enhance the quality of the tourism.

The concept of safe cities is relatively new and is addressed as an outcome of Crime Prevention Environmental Design (CPTED). Safe cities use technology to help governments, communities, and businesses reduce the likelihood of crime and create an environment where people feel safe and comfortable. In this context, the house of quality (HoQ) presents itself as a valuable tool to ensure the design of safe cities and respond to community needs. The HoQ is a graphical matrix that establishes the relationship between citizens' demands and design features. By applying the HoQ in the context of safe cities, priority areas for the implementation of safety measures can be identified, as well as understanding community expectations and needs in terms of safety. This methodology provides a systematic approach to urban planning and design, helping to improve security and promoting safer and more livable urban environments.

The study analyzes the use of digital technologies as a platform for the integration of adults aged 60 and over to smart cities and proposes policies and strategies to governments that allow the reduction of the prevailing backwardness in digital literacy. The results show the existence of significant inequalities in the use, access, modality, and frequency of ICT by this age group; the gap is deepened by age, level of education, social stratum and gender. Some other factors of perception hinder the adoption of technology use, such as lack of knowledge, lack of access to ICTs, lack of knowledge about the use of ICTs, lack of access to ICTs, lack of knowledge about the use of ICTs, and lack of access to ICTs, lack of interest or feeling that they do not need to use ICTs, the latter factors have been identified as the main obstacles to associating the usefulness of these tools to their benefit.

This chapter examines the transformative impact of integrating smart technologies – encompassing the internet of things (IoT), artificial intelligence (AI), and data analytics – into urban agriculture. By addressing challenges like limited arable land and traditional practices, smart technologies offer enhanced resource efficiency, increased productivity, and improved sustainability. Real-time monitoring, circular resource systems, intelligent irrigation, and controlled environments all contribute to these advancements. While acknowledging potential challenges such as costs and technology dependence, the study emphasizes collaboration and education for successful implementation. Ultimately, the integration of smart technologies in urban agriculture has the potential to reshape urban food systems, ensuring greater sustainability and resilience.

Urban agriculture has made it possible to move vegetable production from rural to densely populated areas, for which it uses different approaches to achieve its mission: food sufficiency. Approaches range from open-sky plantations to controlled environments. Open sky plantations, such as community gardens or roof gardens, offer social rather than economic welfare; it is the controlled environments that offer profitable productions in abandoned spaces or built in a special way. In this chapter, the advantages and disadvantages are mentioned as well as techniques that can improve the performance of this growing area of food development.

In recent years, as a result of the recent events that humanity has experienced due to the arrival of the pandemic situation by COVID-19, it has led to the increase in the use of various information and communication technologies, changes in various limits related to the way of interacting, work, learn, and teach. Collaborative tools, smart boards, educational platforms, massive courses, web development platforms, and the internet of things are examples of some technologies that support education. The purpose of this section is to present various technologies or tools that can support education in sustainable and sustainable cities.

Nowadays, potable water supply has become a problem, involving different aspects such as water quality, pollution, pipes' quality, supply and demand of drinking water, water leaks, and supply cuts, among other aspects that have complicated the efficient use of potable water in urbanized regions. The objective of this chapter is to define potable water distribution network (PWDN) optimization as a complex problem, from the perspective of an NP-Hard problem, and the complexity as a variant of water distribution network optimization. The main result of the proposal is the definition of a problem that identifies the main variables involved in the supply of quality potable water as a global problem where each researcher can solve the main problem as one or propose solutions for different parts. The proposal simulation is oriented to present a brief solution related to the supply and demand of drinking water as a part of the PWDN.

The implementation of artificial intelligence (AI) has greatly improved the effectiveness and sustainability of conserving drinking water resources. Through the utilization of AI, real-time data is collected and analyzed, leading to the optimization of water distribution and delivery while minimizing unnecessary waste. Additionally, AI enables timely emergency responses and provides accurate predictions for future water demand.

This chapter offers a comprehensive study on the impact of artificial intelligence (AI) in the sustainable energy industry. It aims to provide a detailed analysis of the potential applications, challenges, and opportunities that AI presents in the energy sector. To be able to accomplish this goal, a literature review was conducted on twelve papers directly or indirectly related to the subject. Their aims, methods, and main findings were included in the fourth section. A conclusion was reached by examining these contents. The findings indicate that AI has demonstrated significant advantages in the sustainable energy industry. It increased the efficiency of sustainable energy systems and had been used to improve their performance in different ways and tasks. Future opportunities of AI in this sector and a guideline for better use of AI were also included in the contents of this paper. Lastly, the limitations of this study and recommendations for future research were shared in the discussion.

The sugar industry's contribution towards the production level is a substantial negative externality and "trade-off" caused by the industrial sector due to trade-off on the environmental front and genuine concern. This chapter is application-oriented to a precise environmental management system in a simple way of demonstration in a combination of enhancing management systems like recycling, reusing, green chemistry, energy and quality management system, acceptable housekeeping practices. This environmental management system reinforces a holistic approach with different data survey cross-check list in the manufacturing industry. Methods used are in a qualitative and quantitative to: 1. Interview schedule method, and 2. Calculate net savings and payback, saving cost, and environment advantages per year. EMS in developed countries like India is still in the rudimentary stage.

To speak of smart cities is interpreted as the exclusive use of information technologies for the development of the daily activities of a population, however, this chapter develops the analysis of a smart city in the area of mobility and the factors involved for an efficient development of the existing relationship of society-infrastructure-sustainability, so that they converge within a single space that positively impact the quality of life of people. Through different international organizations, evaluation metrics for smart cities are established, where key indicators are valued for the development of a city with the perception of its inhabitants, emphasizing sustainable, safe and intelligent mobility. Therefore, data from 2019 to 2023 are rescued with the exception of 2022 (due to the Covid-19 pandemic), for the analysis of Mexico City regarding quality of life-technology-sustainability, directing its resources to the development of smart mobility, through an efficient management of its resources so that there is a permanent interconnectivity and care for the environment. In this sense, a proposal for improvement is made by taking advantage of communication technologies and the existing infrastructure for the implementation of means that allow connectivity between means of transportation and resources to collect data and thus manage them according to the needs of users.

In this research, the use of Alexa for monitoring patients with asthma anxiety attacks was evaluated. Twenty-seven dates in the current year were randomly selected and the duration of anxiety attacks in seconds was recorded, as well as their severity on a Likert scale ranging from 1.00 to 7.00. The results showed that the duration of anxiety attacks ranged from 47 to 287 seconds, with a mean of 163.7 seconds. In addition, a positive correlation was found between the duration of anxiety attacks and severity according to the Likert scale. These findings suggest that Alexa monitoring could be a useful option for the evaluation and treatment of patients with asthma anxiety attacks. Based on these findings and suggestions, the authors propose the integration of a mechatronic system that uses the conjunction of mechanical, computer, electronic, and electrical systems to monitor the possible most recurrent symptoms of anxiety-induced asthma, in addition to the analysis of ergonomic factors that contemplate the satisfaction of the people to whom the proposal is addressed. This monitoring is aimed at reducing

Preface

Welcome to *Management, Technology, and Economic Growth in Smart and Sustainable Cities*, a comprehensive reference book dedicated to exploring the intricate realm of smart and sustainable urban development. In a world where cities are at the forefront of innovation and change, understanding their dynamics, challenges, and potential is more critical than ever.

Cities are the epicenters of human activity, hubs of creativity, and engines of economic growth. Yet, they face numerous complex issues – from environmental sustainability to efficient resource management, from the well-being of their citizens to the creation of vibrant, inclusive communities. It is within this multifaceted context that this reference book seeks to make a meaningful contribution.

Authored by Jorge A. Ruiz-Vanoye and a consortium of experts, this book delves into the heart of smart sustainable cities, those urban centers that leverage Information and Communication Technologies (ICTs) and other innovative approaches to enhance the quality of life, streamline urban operations, and maintain a competitive edge while safeguarding the interests of both present and future generations across economic, social, environmental, and cultural dimensions.

Our aim with this volume is to provide a rich tapestry of insights and practical knowledge that will serve as a compass for anyone interested in the management and administration of smart and sustainable cities. Whether you are a seasoned researcher, a forward-thinking professional, or an executive responsible for guiding your community or organization towards a smarter and more sustainable future, this book has something valuable to offer.

The diverse array of topics covered within these pages encompasses mathematical modeling, Artificial Intelligence, and various technology-driven solutions that optimize city management across different sectors. From smart government and healthcare to energy, transportation, and education, we explore the multifaceted aspects that underpin the success of modern cities.

The breadth of subjects covered in this book aligns with the vision of a holistic smart and sustainable city. You will discover insights into smart open data, advanced transportation systems, energy efficiency, digital security, and much more. By delving into these topics, you'll gain a comprehensive understanding of the intricate web of elements that constitutes a city's vitality and resilience.

We have designed this book with a diverse readership in mind. It caters to professionals and researchers from a wide spectrum of disciplines, including smart government, healthcare, education, agriculture, environment, and beyond. Regardless of your area of expertise, our goal is to empower you with the knowledge needed to drive positive change in your respective field and contribute to the evolution of your city towards a smart and sustainable future.

In closing, we extend our gratitude to the contributors who have shared their expertise, experiences, and insights to create this valuable resource. We hope that *Management, Technology, and Economic*

Growth in Smart and Sustainable Cities will serve as an indispensable reference for years to come, guiding us all towards a brighter, more sustainable urban future.

CHAPTER OVERVIEW

Chapter 1: Smart and Sustainable Cities

This chapter provides a comprehensive survey of the fundamental aspects of smart and sustainable cities. It takes you on a journey through the chronological evolution, core elements, and critical components that define smart cities. Additionally, it explores the key indicators used to measure the smartness of a city and presents solutions to some of the most pressing urban challenges. The chapter introduces the concept of the "Smart and Sustainable Cities Puzzle," which serves as a framework for understanding the intricate components of a smart city. It underscores the importance of technological elements in improving citizens' quality of life while emphasizing the need for optimal management of all city components to maximize efficiency.

Chapter 2: Smart Cities: Complexity in the Economic Growth Versus Poverty

This chapter delves into the complex relationship between smart cities, economic growth, and poverty reduction. It explores how globalization and Information and Communication Technologies (ICTs) have transformed urban environments, creating both opportunities and challenges. The chapter examines strategies employed by smart cities to reduce poverty rates and enhance local development. It raises thought-provoking questions about maintaining competitiveness, addressing technological advancements, and incorporating poverty areas into the urban and technological fabric.

Chapter 3: Smart Government and Future Trends

Chapter 3 explores the realm of smart government and the technologies that empower citizens and officials in urban settings. It provides insights into the current state-of-the-art technologies, such as Wireless Sensor Networks and Big Data Analytics, that enhance the quality of government services. The chapter also surveys the history and future trends of smart government, shedding light on its significance in modern city management.

Chapter 4: Smart Government and e-Voting: Opportunities and Challenges in the Implementation of Electronic Voting With Blockchain

This chapter delves into the intricate world of electronic voting, especially focusing on its implementation with Blockchain technology. It explores the quest for secure and confidential voting processes, emphasizing the immutability and challenges associated with Blockchain technology. The chapter presents the state of the art in electronic voting, the security and transparency benefits of Blockchain, and the operation of smart contracts in this context.

Chapter 5: Smart Tourism: Technologies to Improve Tourism

Chapter 5 serves as a guide to understanding Smart Tourism, showcasing how technology enhances tourist experiences. It explores the integration of Information and Communication Technologies into the tourism sector, emphasizing their role in promoting natural attractions, cultural experiences, and accessibility. The chapter also highlights the importance of smart tourism for improving the quality of the tourism industry.

Chapter 6: House of Quality for Safe Cities

This chapter introduces the concept of safe cities and how technology is used to enhance security and reduce crime. It explores the House of Quality (HoQ) methodology as a tool for designing safe cities and aligning community needs with urban planning. The chapter demonstrates how HoQ can systematically improve urban planning, making cities safer and more livable.

Chapter 7: Older Adults in Mexico, Their Inclusion in ICTs and Smart Cities

Chapter 7 analyzes the integration of older adults into smart cities through digital technologies. It addresses the digital divide among older adults, exploring factors such as age, education, and gender that affect their use of ICTs. The chapter seeks to propose policies and strategies to reduce this digital divide and empower older adults to benefit from technology.

Chapter 8: The Role of Smart Technologies in Urban Agriculture, A Comprehensive Review

This chapter examines the transformative impact of smart technologies, including the Internet of Things and artificial intelligence, on urban agriculture. It explores how these technologies increase resource efficiency, productivity, and sustainability in agriculture. The chapter highlights real-time monitoring, controlled environments, and other advancements that reshape urban food systems.

Chapter 9: Using the Smart Cities Infrastructure for Urban Farming and Z-Farming

Chapter 9 explores the integration of urban agriculture into smart cities' infrastructure. It discusses various approaches to urban agriculture, from community gardens to controlled environments, emphasizing their role in achieving food sufficiency. The chapter also examines techniques for improving the performance of urban agriculture in densely populated areas.

Chapter 10: Tools and Technologies for Smart Education in Sustainable Smart Cities

Chapter 10 focuses on technology's role in smart education within sustainable smart cities. It highlights various tools and technologies that support education, including collaborative tools, smart boards, educational platforms, and the Internet of Things. The chapter discusses how these technologies enhance learning and teaching in the modern era.

Chapter 11: Potable Water Distribution Network Optimization

This chapter delves into the optimization of potable water distribution networks. It addresses the challenges related to water quality, supply, and demand, as well as leaks in distribution networks. The chapter defines Potable Water Distribution Network Optimization as a complex problem and explores potential solutions to improve the efficient use of drinking water in urbanized regions.

Chapter 12: Description of Artificial Intelligence Models in Sustainable Water Resource Management

Chapter 12 explores the application of Artificial Intelligence (AI) in sustainable water resource management. It discusses how AI collects and analyzes real-time data to optimize water distribution, reduce waste, and respond to emergencies. The chapter emphasizes the role of AI in preserving water resources and ensuring access to quality water.

Chapter 13: Artificial Intelligence (AI) in the Sustainable Energy Industry

Chapter 13 provides a comprehensive study of the impact of Artificial Intelligence (AI) in the sustainable energy industry. It analyzes the potential applications, challenges, and opportunities that AI presents in the energy sector. The chapter highlights how AI increases the efficiency of sustainable energy systems and improves performance.

Chapter 14: Comprehensive Environmental Management System Report in Specific Sugar Mill, India

This chapter presents a case study focused on environmental management within a sugar mill in India. It discusses the economic and environmental accountability of the industry, considering factors like recycling, green chemistry, and quality management. The chapter aims to reinforce a holistic approach to environmental management, emphasizing the importance of data analysis and cross-checking.

Chapter 15: Mobility Management in Smart Cities, Exploratory Analysis in Mexico

Chapter 15 explores mobility management within the context of smart cities in Mexico. It analyzes factors that contribute to efficient urban development, emphasizing the interplay between society, infrastructure, and sustainability. The chapter evaluates metrics used to assess smart cities' impact on quality of life, technology, and sustainability, with a specific focus on smart and sustainable mobility solutions.

Chapter 16: Use of an Intelligent Voice Recognition Device to Monitor and Mitigate Children with Anxiety-Induced Asthma Attack

This research-oriented chapter investigates the use of intelligent voice recognition devices, such as Alexa, for monitoring and mitigating anxiety-induced asthma attacks in children. It presents findings related to the duration and severity of anxiety attacks and highlights the potential utility of voice recognition technology in evaluating and treating asthma-related anxiety. The chapter proposes the integration of mechatronic systems to enhance monitoring and analysis while considering ergonomic factors for user satisfaction.

IN SUMMARY

As we conclude this preface, we reflect on the diverse and insightful chapters that make up *Management, Technology, and Economic Growth in Smart and Sustainable Cities*. The collective effort of our esteemed authors has illuminated the multifaceted landscape of smart and sustainable urban development. Through these chapters, we've embarked on a journey through the intricacies of modern cities, where technology, innovation, and sustainability converge.

From the foundational exploration of smart city elements in Chapter 1 to the examination of AI's transformative impact on sustainable energy in Chapter 13, this book has provided a rich tapestry of knowledge and insights. We've ventured into the domains of governance, tourism, agriculture, education, water resource management, and much more, uncovering the pivotal roles played by technology and innovative approaches.

Our authors have delved into critical issues such as poverty reduction, accessibility for older adults, and the pursuit of safer urban environments. They've examined the potential of emerging technologies like Blockchain for secure voting and the integration of voice recognition devices for healthcare applications.

In this collection, we've not only explored the current state of affairs but have also peered into the future of smart and sustainable cities, where technologies like IoT, AI, and Big Data will continue to shape urban landscapes and improve the quality of life for all citizens.

The contributions from our authors have gone beyond mere descriptions and analyses; they have paved the way for actionable insights and real-world solutions. Whether you are an academic researcher, a city planner, a government official, an urban innovator, or a concerned citizen, this book offers you a wealth of knowledge to draw upon in your quest for smarter, more sustainable cities.

We extend our sincere gratitude to the authors who have shared their expertise, experiences, and vision for a brighter urban future. *Management, Technology, and Economic Growth in Smart and Sustainable Cities* is a testament to the collective efforts of those dedicated to improving the quality of life in urban environments. We hope this book serves as a valuable resource, guiding you toward informed decisions and innovative solutions as we collectively navigate the complex landscape of modern cities.

As we look ahead, we are confident that the insights contained within these chapters will continue to shape the discourse on smart and sustainable urban development. Together, we can work toward the realization of cities that are not just smart but also sustainable, inclusive, and resilient, ensuring a prosperous and harmonious future for generations to come.

Warmest Regards,

Jorge A. Ruiz-Vanoye
Universidad Politécnica de Pachuca, Mexico

Chapter 1
Smart and Sustainable Cities

Jorge A. Ruiz-Vanoye
https://orcid.org/0000-0003-4928-5716
Universidad Politécnica de Pachuca, Mexico

Ocotlán Diaz-Parra
Universidad Politécnica de Pachuca, Mexico

Francisco Marroquín-Gutiérrez
Universidad Politécnica de Pachuca, Mexico

Blas Manuel Rodríguez-Lara
Tecnológico de Monterrey, Mexico

Jaime Aguilar-Ortiz
Universidad Politécnica de Pachuca, Mexico

ABSTRACT

Humans have always sought a place for safe living with the comforts and facilities to do decent work and for the family's healthy growth. This chapter aims to guide understanding smart and sustainable cities by presenting a survey of chronological aspects, elements and components of smart cities, smart cities' indicators, solutions to city problems, and other aspects related to smart cities. The authors also propose a Smart and Sustainable Cities Puzzle that contains the main components of a smart city to which various pieces of the puzzle can be added depending on the characteristics and needs of the city, indicators of smart cities; the idea is that trafficking in a city with technological elements allows citizens to better their quality of life, but that there must be optimum management (minimisation and maximisation) of all components involved in the city order to optimise time, money, and effort. This chapter can serve as a basis for experts' academic knowledge and professional practice in sensors and decision-makers.

DOI: 10.4018/979-8-3693-0373-3.ch001

I. INTRODUCTION

The purpose of a smart city is to achieve efficient management in all areas of the city (urban planning, infrastructure, transportation, services, education, health, public safety, energy, among others), satisfying the needs of the city and its citizens, based on the principles of sustainable development set out in Agenda 21 of the United Nations, and considering technological innovation and cooperation between economic and social agents as the main engines of change (Enerlis and Young, 2012).

A smart sustainable city is an innovative city that uses ICTs and other means to improve quality of life, efficiency of urban operation and services, and competitiveness, while ensuring that it meets the needs of present and future generations with respect to economic, social, environmental as well as cultural aspects.

This paper aims to guide understanding smart cities by presenting a survey of smart cities' characteristics, taxonomy, and history. Section 2 presents the history of smart cities, Section 3 presents smart cities and future trends, and the last section presents the conclusions.

II. HISTORY OF THE SMART CITIES

For the concept of the knowledge society, Drucker (1959) proposed the term "initial knowledge workers"; later, Drucker (1969) proposed that knowledge replaces the work, mentions that the material resources and capital are the main production source, and allows growth and social differences, which gave rise to the term "knowledge society". Financial information and knowledge society are addressed in the global work implications of the information's society (Porat, 1978). Bell (1999) proposes a postindustrial society as the combination of encoding theoretical knowledge and the relationship with the science of technology.

The safe city concept is practically new and is handled as a result of crime prevention through environmental design (CPTED). This was a term used for the first time in 1971 by the criminologist Clarence Ray Jeffery. In 1989, external CERN network connections gave rise to the Internet that we currently know. Howard (1965) proposes the term garden city; this may be the first reference to a green city in history. Howard proposes this city planning for some 30 new towns in the United Kingdom.

Brambilla (1992) mentions that urbanisation is the process whereby a sufficiently large number of people is concentrated in a specific area of land and prepares citizens with the infrastructure needed to fulfil activities and provide the largest possible comfort. Douligeris (1993) proposes the term intelligent home systems. Motiwalla, Yap, and Ngoh (1993) propose the term intelligent island by proposing a national information infrastructure (NII) and Singapore's national information technology (IT).

The Kyoto Protocol was created to limit CO2 emissions, protect the global environment, and influence modern and industrialised cities.

Soong (1997) presents a vision of an Intelligent Island of the future (Singapore) in situating information technology and Intelligent Island discourse within the discourses of postcoloniality, techno-capitalism, late modernity and globalisation.

Newman and Kenworthy (1999) comment on the urban aspects of sustainability and how it applies to cities and manages transportation or automobile dependence.

Kevin Ashton spoke for the first time in 1999 on the concept of the Internet of Things, but this was not published in a journal until 2009 (Ashton, 2009).

OECD (1999) mentions that the term 'learning' in 'learning cities' covers both individual and institutional learning. Individual learning refers to acquiring knowledge, skills and understanding for individual people, whether formally or informally.

Baird (1999) mentions some aspects of compact cities (combining the organic freedom Jacobs was advocating with some clear municipal planning to protect the public rather than corporate interests) and greenback cities. The Internet brought e-services to healthcare, energy, education, environmental management, transportation, mobility and public safety in 2000. The Internet brings the strengthening of innovative cities, wired cities, creative cities and cultural cities.

Hall (2000) mentions that a city that monitors and integrates conditions of all of its critical infrastructure, including roads, bridges, tunnels, rails, subways, airports, seaports, communications, water, power and even major buildings, can better optimise its resources, plan its preventive maintenance activities, and monitor security aspects while maximising services to its citizens.

Paquet (2001) mentions the first definition of smart communities. Schuler (2001) mentions that a virtual city concentrates on digital representations and manifestations of cities.

The California Institute (2001) says that a knowledge city is a city that aims for knowledge-based development by encouraging continuous creation, sharing, evaluation, renewal and update of knowledge; this comes through the continuous interaction between its citizens, and between them and other cities' citizens. The California Institute (2001) proposes that a smart community is a community that has used information technology to transform the life and work of the people's community.

Komninos (2002) attempts to delineate the intelligent city and mentions that intelligence lies in solving these communities' problems; it is linked to the transfer of technology to know when an issue is resolved.

Geller (2003) exposed the smart growth movement to build, work, live and promote health and well-being.

Smart Tourism can be seen as the innovation, and the technological orientation of the industry and the consumers were laid early with the extensive adoption of information and communication technologies in tourism (Buhalis, 2003).

Cook and Das (2004) mention that a smart environment is a small world where all smart devices are working continuously to make inhabitants' lives more comfortable.

In 2005, UNESCO (2005) defined a knowledge society as the ability to produce and access, produce and integrates information, knowledge and practical knowledge. The Agency of the Nations United International Telecommunications Union (ITU) published the first study on the Internet of Things in 2005.

Kickbusch and Sakellarides (2006) mentioned public health and the role of health promotion to prevent a possible pandemic situation in smart cities, where the authors consider the empowerment of citizens as crucial in dealing with the threat.

Komninos (2006) mentions that some intelligent cities are territories with a high capacity for learning and innovation, their knowledge creation institutions, and their digital infrastructure for communication and knowledge management.

The New York Academy of Medicine (NYAM) proposed the Age-Friendly New York City project in 2007 to apply the WHO initiative (Finkelstein, 2008).

Giffinger et al. (2007) mention that smart community citizenship ensures citizens' interaction with government data to permit participation in decisions about municipal aspects.

Saugata and Masud (2007) mention that electronic governance or e-governance is the application of information and communications technology (ICT) for delivering government services, the exchange of information, communication transactions, the integration of various stand-alone systems, and services for government-to-citizen (G2C), government-to-business (G2B), government-to-government (G2G) and government-to-employee (G2E) relationships.

Smart cities measurement indicators were created in 2007 (Giffinger and Pichler-Milanović, 2007): smart economics indicators, indicators of smart mobility, indicators of the smart environment, indicators of smart people, indicators of smart life, and indicators of smart government.

Hollands (2008) mentions that a wired city / smart city contains urban life, urban planning, sustainable development, environment, energy grid, economic development, technologies and social participation.

In 2008, IBM noted the concept of the smart planet (an instrumented, interconnected and intelligent planet in which leaders in business, government and civil society around the world could use big data to transform enterprises and institutions through analytics, mobile technology, social business and the cloud) to have a good quality of life and to improve the city.

Komninos (2008) mentions that a digital city denotes an area that combines broadband communication infrastructure with flexible, service-oriented computing systems to ensure citizens' better services.

In 2008, a group of companies created the IPSO Alliance, aiming to promote Internet protocol networks of intelligent objects and make the Internet of Things possible.

Smart city concept was created in 1994, but it was popularised when the European Union started to use smart technology in 2010 to qualify sustainability projects and actions in the urban space.

A knowledge city or knowledge-based development strategy (Ergazakis, Metaxiotis, and Ergazakis, 2010) is a city where intellectual people from universities, research institute, companies and citizens support the formulation of a strategy to improve communication networks, city's infrastructure and citizens' education level.

Anthopoulos et al. (2010) propose a new definition of a ubiquitous city (U-City) as a further extension of digital city concept or as a city or region with ubiquitous information technology.

Anthopoulos et al. (2010) propose the definition of the information city as a digital environment that collects official and unofficial information from local communities and delivers it to the public via web portals.

OECD (2010) proposes the concept of the green city. The green city concept follows green growth, a new paradigm that promotes economic development while reducing greenhouse gas emissions and pollution, minimising waste and the inefficient use of natural resources and maintaining biodiversity.

IBM (2010) defined a smart city as using information and communication technology to sense, analyse, and integrate core systems' key information in running cities.

WHO (2010) proposed creating the global network of friendly cities for the elderly, formed initially by 33 member cities.

Zhang (2010) proposes the smart planet and smart city's interpretation as the Internet plus the Internet of Things to equal a smart planet.

Cohen (2011) proposed a holistic framework (Smart Cities Wheel) to consider all key components (smart economics, smart government, intelligent people, smart habitat, intelligent mobility and intelligent environment) that make that a city smart.

Caragliu et al. (2011) propose that a smart city is when the government invests in human capital, social capital, traditional transport, modern communication infrastructure, sustainable economic growth, high quality of life, and the wise management of natural resources.

Su et al. (2011) propose that a smart city is the digital city's product combined with the Internet of Things.

A smart valley (Allwinkle and Cruickshank, 2011) is a decentralised valley of innovations that bring together investors, projects, and experts in the professional community's closed ecosystem.

Cohen (2012) performed a process to identify and select 100 indicators and then narrow the list to 28 indicators to measure and compare different world cities.

Setis-Eu (2012) proposes that a smart city is a city that offers a better life to their citizens and reduces the environmental impact through water recycling, advanced energy grids and mobile telecommunications.

Herrera (2012) shows the importance of water and mentions the supply and sanitation of water as the main structures in smart cities' operation.

Dameri (2013) proposes that a smart city is a geographical area governed by rules and policy to create benefits for citizens through logistic, energy production, environmental quality, intelligent development and technologies.

Healthier cities (an extension of smart cities) are proposed to improve the quality of life-based on implementing IoT-driven services to generate big data analytics systems. The World Health Organization (WHO) proposes the Healthy Cities Network and associated national networks to improve local populations' health (Kamel-Boulos and Al-Shorbaji, 2014).

Garbage collection is one of the services offered in smart cities. A type of waste generated by residential centres is waste plants, which must be delivered and processed by special waste management treatment plants, as in the city of St. Petersburg, Russia (Anagnostopoulos, 2015).

Smart home is a residence with household appliances capable of communicating from any room in the home, from any location in the world through the phone or Internet (Jin et al., 2016).

Bonola et al. (2016) raise the problem of obtaining information from various distributed things on all streets an intelligent city; it is difficult not to have a mechanism that obtains information from such small devices (and have no direct link with the smart city).

The National Academy of Sciences (NAS) of the United States notes that more than 1,000 million people living in cities will probably live with less than 100 litres of water a day. In contrast, more than 3,000 million will not have water for between one month and one year. To provide a solution for the technology of reuse and the conscious use of water, exemplary regions in water management can be taken as an example: Singapore for the reuse of water and desalination and Nassau for the detection and management of water losses (Bouskela, 2016).

Coro (2016) developed a prototype wireless IPV6 and IoT that allows more efficient monitoring to check water quality in real-time Smart Cities.

A Smart city must cover six conditions: energy, integration, public services, mobility, smart construction and water; this also implies reuse and all liquid supplies, which is an imminent challenge for human settlements in cities (Great realities, 2017).

Smart Water Santander is an application that allows the supervision and monitoring of water in Santander, Spain, which reflects data for users in real-time of information taken from meteorological data, network data, stations critical (sensors) and remote readings (González, 2017).

Brovko et al. (2017) present a system (Smart Clean City) that combines calculations, algorithms, devices and trash bins; it allows the optimisation of the contenders and traffic generated in the collection of garbage and waste dumps (Borozdukhin, 2016).

Oralhan (2017) designed trash bins with sensors that measure the level of garbage, temperature and level of carbon dioxide in the container, with the intention of optimising garbage collection in large cities and the effect of pollution on the environment by using the Internet of Things technologies, ant colony optimisation and a data mining algorithm.

Vu and Kaddoum (2017) propose a sensor model that allows the detection and measurement of the volume of waste, the geolocation of trash bins and serial numbers, to predict the amount of waste, sorting waste and optimisation of the routes that trucks follow.

Muyunda et al. (2017) propose using sensors based on Arduino to a garbage collection management system.

Vasagade (2017) focused on the automated management of solid waste through verification and alert waste deposits levels.

Chris Clague (2017) produced a report in 60 cities analysed by 49 indicators to assess digital security, health and safety, infrastructure security and personal safety.

Joong Hoon Kim (2018) refers to smart technologies that help create a better lifestyle through technological advancements such as intelligent mobility, smart homes, health and intelligent education.

Yigitcanlar and Kamruzzaman (2018) investigate smart mobility from the angle of sustainable commuting practices in the context of smart cities.

Yigitcanlar et al. (2018) developed a systematic review of the literature on smart cities that reveals three types of drivers of smart cities—community, technology, policy—which are linked to five desired outcomes—productivity, sustainability, accessibility, well-being, liveability, governance.

III. SMART CITIES AND FUTURE TRENDS

A smart city is a city that uses the optimum management of water, city technology, energy, mobility, public transportation, distribution of transport routes, road network safety management, the construction of homes / offices / transportation structure, industry / jobs, education, healthcare, public safety, government, civil protection, food, environmental pollution, and solid, hazardous and special waste. To be considered a smart city, the city should also be self-sustaining (sustainable energy production, sustainable water production, and sustainable food production), reduce the cost to private operators, reduce the cost to municipalities, and improve quality of life for citizens. Each service provided by the smart city must solve a problem that could be considered complex.

There are several categories of the complexity of problems in the world, as well as methods and methodologies to solve them. The problems vary between two extremes (Checkland, 1990), which include defined problems, such as situations in which the "what" and the "how" are defined clearly. Some examples of hard problems are maximising corporate profits, minimising production cost for the company, changing a tire on a car, preparing a chocolate cake, and constructing a building. Some methodologies related to defined problems are systems theory, operations research, decision theory and systems analysis, among others. Soft problems are those situations where the "what" is very difficult to define and the "how" is difficult to solve. Some examples of soft problems are defining the business mission, solving poverty in a country, implementing a quality programme in a company to develop an information system for decision making, and implementing a strategic change in the company, among others.

A smart city also has two kinds of problems and ways to resolve them:

- City-Hard problems. All issues where there can be optimised (maximisation or minimisation) of the city's resources. The problems of transportation representation and TSP are NP-hard problems.
- City-Soft problems. A fuzzy concept used to drive specific political agendas.

The elements or components of smart Cities are below:

A. Smart government. The smart government is an electronic government organised around the management and use of information. The smart government provides open government information (Smart Open Data) available to the citizens (Coates, 2001; Alcock and Lenihan, 2001). Additionally, we define the smart government as the electronic government with open data that optimised the budget (smart management of the economy of the city, or smart economics, and the relationship between government and enterprises) for civil works (smart infrastructure) and priority services for the well-being of citizens; and the smart government must consider smart disasters and smart tourism.

Smart infrastructure includes systems that manage, communicate and integrate different types of intelligent infrastructure such as energy grids, transport network, water and waste management systems and telecommunications. Smart disasters optimise human resources to address disaster impact assessments, prevention and mitigation investment planning, shelter location, evacuation planning, relief delivery, casualty transportation, stakeholder coordination, recovery operations, refugee camp location, coordination and management, refugee resettlement, big data for disaster management, disaster information systems, resilient land use and agriculture, epidemics control and supply chain management.

Smart tourism (e-tourism) is the innovation and the adoption of information and communication technologies in tourism (Buhalis, 2003). Smart tourism additionally must consider natural attractions, cultural (music festival), accessibility of transportation, amenities characteristics, ancillary services (banks, hospitals), innovative hubs for electric vehicles with a mobile app to check availability status of charging cars, and the infrastructure of professional sports.

E-government is a form of relationship of the state with its citizens, businesses and other organisations. It consists of e-administration and e-management. E-management is the application of the Internet, information technologies, and telecommunications in the state's areas, activities, and processes. E-administration includes international trade, online justice online, tax administration and e-procurement, among others (Coe, 2001). E-government activities are the policies of the various levels of government in relation to their constituencies. E-government includes electronics democracy, virtual parliament and electronic voting (Coe, 2001).

International trade provides electronic documentation (departure, transit, insurance, letters of credit, permits entry of goods, among others) in custom systems. Online justice is computerised courts that contains tables of input virtual legal issues, where it is feasible to undertake a legal study from anywhere where there the Internet is available. Tax administrations are systems or mechanisms that allow the electronic fulfilment of tax obligations.

E-procurement is systems that allow government providers to carry out recruitment, trading, and payment of supplies. Tenders will be known by citizens, which allows knowing the financial resources of the government are used. Electronic democracy is a decentralised means of access infrastructure to provide public information and electronic services to citizens.

Virtual parliament and electronic voting allow citizens to participate, along with the state's different powers (deputies, senators, mayors), in the analysis of social, economic problems and the creation of legislation measures to regulate life in society. This allows the citizen to be informed on the subjects promised in the campaign. E-voting is the suffrage of the citizens via the Internet, thereby avoiding going to polling places. Electronic voting allows you to streamline the voting, counting of votes, voting from anywhere in the world, decreasing bureaucracy, and offering a lower cost for the election, among others.

B. Smart energy / smart grid. Smart energy uses digital technology such as advanced meter infrastructure (AMI), distribution grid management, high voltage transmission systems, and demand responses to the intelligent and integrated transmission and distribution of power. Additionally, in this article, we define smart energy as the optimised energy transfer by smart grid communication infrastructures with a minimum production cost to citizens.
C. Smart healthcare. Smart healthcare is the use of electronic-health, mobile-health intelligent systems to connect medical devices. It also involves implementing policies that encourage health, wellness and well-being of citizens, and health monitoring and diagnostics as opposed to treatment. Additionally, in this paper, we defined smart healthcare as the influence of information and communication technology to improve the quality (optimisation) of healthcare services and a focus on better diagnostic tools, better treatment for patients, and devices to improve quality of life.
D. Smart transportation. Smart transportation is also known as the Intelligent Transportation System (Advanced Transportation Management Systems, Advanced Transportation Pricing Systems, Advanced Public Transportation Systems, and Advanced Traveller Information Systems). The systems are coupled with communications and sensors to ensure real-time management to improve environment protection, traffic management, public transport, freight management, automotive telematics, road safety and security, parking management and road user charging. It is a transportation structure that offers safe transport services and secures Transport management systems using artificial intelligence and information technology. Additionally, smart transportation minimise the transportation services cost to the citizens and government, with the objective to improve the well-being of citizens.
E. Smart building / smart home. Smart buildings and homes are advanced automated infrastructures that manage the lighting and temperature, security and energy consumption into buildings and homes, and streetlights.
F. Smart mobility. Smart mobility (Wi-Fi, 5G) enables intelligent mobility for connect the home, office, mobile phone and car on a single wireless IT platform. Smart technology includes the adoption of smart grid systems, smart home solutions, high-speed broadband connections, and roll out of 5G technology.
G. Smart society / smart people / smart digital citizens. The smart society possesses an interest in embracing embrace smart and green solutions in the day-to-day work schedule. Citizens are more proactive in adopting smart concepts and smart products, which includes making smart lifestyle choices. The smart society must have digital citizenship, smart education, the affinity for lifelong learning, social and ethnic diversity, flexibility, creativity, cosmopolitanism, and participation in public life.

Smart education is the influence of digital technologies to enhance the quality of education and generate ubiquitous learning. We also consider smart education as the process of optimally managing human, economic, and technology resources from educational institutions and research centres.

There are various types of affinity for lifelong learning: home schooling (home education), adult education, continuing education, knowledge work and personal learning environments. Learning can be through massive open online courses (MOOC), assistive technology, the Web and workplace learning.

Performing exercises for the brain lessens mental decline (Grady, 2012), which allows lower expenditures for treatments related to Alzheimer's disease and degenerative diseases of the brain.

H. Smart production of foods / smart farming (Agriculture, livestock and fisheries). A city must be sustainable in food production. This means that they must produce food from agriculture, livestock and fisheries to feed the city without relying on other cities. In addition, food production should use certain technologies to save water, energy and food waste. In other words, smart food production is the optimal administration of the sowing, harvesting and distribution of products derived from agriculture, livestock and fisheries.
I. Smart industry / smart manufacturing. Smart industry is related to entrepreneurship (rate workers, local self-employment), the city's importance as the centre of decision-making, productivity, the flexibility of the labour market, and international roots.
J. Smart environment. A smart environment can control devices remotely or automatically, using technologies to communicate with other devices, acquiring and disseminating information from intelligent sensor networks (Wireless Sensor Networks), and enhancing services through intelligent devices (Cook and Das, 2004).

Additionally, the smart environment must optimise (minimise the cost of management) water (smart water) and waste (smart waste). The smart environment has the ability to control devices remotely or automatically related to smart water, smart waste, attractive natural conditions, pollution, animal protection, and the sustainable management of the resources by wireless sensor networks and intelligent devices.

Smart water is the optimal use of water used in the smart city. The city uses water savings in the toilets (dry toilets), showers, the optimised irrigation of plants or vertical gardens of buildings, and the optimised water used in the fields. Smart waste is the optimal management of solid, special, dangerous, electronic and electrical waste.

Attractive natural conditions have a relationship with many sunshine hours, and the number of spaces with green areas. Pollution is the system to monitor the level of suspended particles in the air, damage to the ozone layer, people with respiratory illnesses caused by pollution. Animal protection is participation in individual and group actions or associations for animal protection. Sustainable management includes the resources for water, efficient use of electricity, and rescuing contaminated soils.

K. Smart life. This component provides (with technology or without) peace and labour and emotional stability for citizens to live with dignity. Smart life contains smart age-friendly, smart security (safe city includes digital security, health security, security infrastructure, personal safety), cultural facilities, and social cohesion.

A smart city must contain all elements or components, not just some. In this document, we propose the idea components as parts of a jigsaw puzzle, where each piece of the puzzle is an important and unique element that interacts to form the smart city comprehensively. This puzzle (Figure 1) can be updated and improved as time and generations change, to obtain better smart cities.

Figure 1. Smart city puzzle

Quantification depends on the indicators used and the weighting and relevance of each. The result of knowing if a city is more intelligent than others depend on the values of the indicators. In addition, a key factor is that each city can operate different models; there is no single successful model. Each city must set their lines of action to be smart by relying on external models but adapting to their reality. In this article, we propose these following indicators to determine whether or not a city is smart. We propose the indicators based on the work of (Giffinger and Pichler-Milanović, 2007), and improved with the idea to allow citizens a better quality of life, but that there must be optimum management (minimisation and maximisation) of all components involved in the city order to optimise time, money and effort.

Table 1. Indicators of smart government

Indicators of Smart Government	
Smart economics	Smart decision / participation in decision-making, smart service / public and social services.
Smart open data (transparent government)	Open government information available to the citizens,
Smart infrastructure	Energy grids, transport network, water and waste management systems and telecommunications, civil works, and priority services for the well-being of citizens.
Smart disasters	Prevention and mitigation investment planning, shelter location, evacuation planning, relief delivery, casualty transportation, stakeholders' coordination, recovery operations, refugee camp location, coordination and management, refugee resettlement, big data for disaster management, disaster information systems, resilient land use and agriculture, epidemics control supply chain management.
Smart tourism	Total natural attractions, total cultural (music festival) in a year,accessibility by transportation, amenities characteristics, ancillary services (bank, package shipping services, hospitals), innovative hub for electrical vehicles with app mobile to check all the availability status of vehicle's charging cars, the infrastructure of professional sports.
E-Government	International trade, justice online, tax administration, E-procurement, electronics democracy, virtual parliament, electronic voting.
Indicators of Smart Energy	
Energy infrastructure	Advanced meter infrastructure (AMI), distribution grid management, high voltage transmission systems and for demand response to the intelligent and integrated transmission and distribution of power, solar farm to reduce carbon emission.
Indicators of Smart Healthcare	
Conditions and health services	Electronic-health, mobile-health Intelligent systems to connected medical devices, policies that encourage health, wellness and well-being of its citizens and health monitoring and diagnostics as opposed to treatment.
Indicators of Smart Transportation	
Transportation services	Environment protection, traffic management, public transport, freight management, automotive telematics, road safety and security, parking management and road user charging, intelligent transportation system (advanced transportation management Systems - ATMS, advanced transportation pricing systems - ATPS, advanced public transportation systems (APTS) and advanced traveler information systems (ATIS)), secure transport management systems using artificial intelligence and information technology.
Indicators of Smart Building / Home	
Advanced automated infrastructure	Manages the lighting and temperature, the security and the energy consumption into the buildings / homes and in the light of the streets.
Indicators of Smart Mobility	
Innovative and integrated technologies	Low emission cars and multimodal transport systems, the home, office, mobile phone and car's connectivity on a single wireless IT platform, the adoption of the smart grid system, smart home solutions, high-speed broadband connection, and roll out of 5G technology.
Indicators of the Smart Society / Smart People / Digital Citizens	
Smart education	The affinity for lifelong learning, social and ethnic diversity, flexibility, creativity, cosmopolitanism and participation in the public life, citizen science, technology and innovation system, e-learning, highly trained human capital formation, open science, important scientific infrastructure.
Indicators of the Smart Foods Production / Smart Farming	
Food production	Technology to save water, energy and food waste, optimal administration of sowing, harvesting and distribution of products derived from agriculture, livestock and fisheries.
Indicators of the Smart Industry / Manufacturing	

Continued on following page

Table 1. Continued

Enterprises services	Rate workers local self-employment, GDP per person employed, regional unemployment rate, the proportion of the labour market in part-time, companies based in the city are listed at the national level in the stock market, the number of passenger operations, the number of operations in air freight.
Indicators of the Smart Environment	
Smart water	Uses technology for the water saving in the toilets (dry toilets), showers, optimised irrigation of plants or vertical gardens of buildings, optimised irrigation of water used in the fields.
Smart waste	Uses technology for the optimal management of the solid, special, dangerous, electronic and electrical Waste.
Attractive natural conditions	Hours of sunshine, and the number of spaces with green areas.
The pollution	To monitor the level of suspended particles in the air, damage to the ozone layer, people with respiratory illnesses caused by pollution
Animal protection	Participation in individual and group actions or associations of animal protection.
Sustainable management	Management of the resources of water, efficient use of electricity, rescue to contaminated soils.
Indicators of the Smart Life	
Smart age-friendly	Banks more resistant and durable in public areas, such as bus stops, and hospitals, focusing especially on the areas with a higher concentration of the elderly population. Traffic lights with countdown clocks and increased the time of crossing for pedestrians. In the metro signs with larger font sizes, older persons did not have difficulties reading them. Agreements with the city gyms so announced discounts on registration and free fitness classes for seniors. Establishment of timetables for seniors in the pools. Courses affordable and accessible for seniors in the universities so that the elders enjoy ongoing training and learning. Campaigns to combat discrimination by age at work. Each train stop is less than a 10-minute walk from anywhere in the nursing home. Stops of public transportation, close to all clinics and other similar services. The elderly travelling by bus can ask the driver to stop where want to within the residential areas.
Smart security (safe city)	Social prevention, actions, or policies (educational, cultural, urban) aimed at improving an area's quality of life. Environmental or situational prevention, actions aimed at reducing crime opportunities (administrative criminology), create nice, clean surroundings, illuminated (it has been confirmed that the environment is one of the factors that most affect the feeling of insecurity). Neighbourhood watch.
Cultural facilities	A number of cinemas, theatres.
Social cohesion	End of poverty; zero hunger; health and welfare; quality education; gender equality; clean water and sanitation; affordable energy and pollution; decent work and economic growth; industry, innovation and infrastructure; reduction of inequalities; cities and sustainable communities; production and responsible consumption; climate action; underwater life; life of terrestrial ecosystems; peace, justice and strong institutions.

VII. CONCLUSION

This article sought to guide understanding smart cities and the components, indicators, and history of the concepts that gave rise to smart cities. We proposed a smart cities puzzle that can be improved as the needs of the city change, but without losing the main objective of a smart city, which is to have a place to live safely and with the comforts and facilities to do decent work, and with the best city technology.

We present a taxonomy of two types of problems in smart cities: City-Hard and City-Soft problems. We proposed that the city has technology that will allow citizens to improve their quality of life, but that there must be optimum management (minimisation and maximisation) of all components involved in the city to optimise time, money, and effort.

REFERENCES

Alcock, R., & Lenihan, D. G. (2001). Opening the e-government file: Governing in the 21st Century. *Changing Government, 2001*, 2.

Allwinkle, S., & Cruickshank, P. (2011). Creating smarter cities: An overview. *Journal of Urban Technology, 18*(2), 1–16. doi:10.1080/10630732.2011.601103

Anagnostopoulos, T., Zaslavsy, A., Medvedev, A., & Khoruzhnicov, S. (2015). Top — k Query Based Dynamic Scheduling for IoT-enabled Smart City Waste Collection. *16th IEEE International Conference on Mobile Data Management.*

Anthopoulos, L., & Fitsilis, P. (2010). From digital to ubiquitous cities: Defining a common architecture for urban development. *2010 Sixth International Conference on Intelligent Environments.* 10.1109/IE.2010.61

Arup. (2010). *Smart Cities: Transforming the 21st-century city via the creative use of technology.* Arup.

Ashton, K. (2009). That 'Internet of things' thing. *RFID Journal, 22*(7), 97–114.

Baird, V. (1999). Green cities. *New Internationalist, 313.* Retrieved March 19, 2018, from https://newint.org/features/1999/06/05/keynote

Bătăgan, L. (2011). Smart cities and sustainability models. *Informações Econômicas, 15*(3), 80–87.

Bell, D. (1999). The Coming of Post-industrial Society (Reissue edition). Basic Books.

Bloomberg. (2009). *Age-friendly NYC: Enhancing our city's livability for older New Yorkers.* The City of New York Office of the Mayor.

Bonola, M., Bracciale, L., Loreti, P., Amici, R., Rabuffi, A., & Bianchi, G. (2016). Opportunistic communication in smart city: Experimental insight with small-scale taxi fleets as Data Carriers. *Ad Hoc Networks, 43*, 43–55. doi:10.1016/j.adhoc.2016.02.002

Borozdukhin, A., Dolinina, O., & Pechenkin, V. (2016). Approach to the garbage collection in The "smart clean city" project. *2016 4th IEEE International Colloquium on Information Science and Technology (CiSt).* 10.1109/CIST.2016.7805019

Bose, S., & Rashel, M. R. (2007). Implementing e-governance using OECD model (Modified) and Gartner model (modified) upon agriculture of Bangladesh. *2007 10th International Conference on Computer and Information Technology.* 10.1109/ICCITECHN.2007.4579410

Brovko, A., Dolinina, O., & Pechenkin, V. (2017). Method of the management of garbage collection in The "smart clean city" project. *Communications in Computer and Information Science, 718*, 432–443. doi:10.1007/978-3-319-59767-6_34

Buhalis, D. (2003). eTourism: Information technology for strategic tourism management. Pearson Education.

California Institute. (2001). http://smartcommunities.org/concept.php

Caragliu, A., Del Bo, C., & Nijkamp, P. (2011). Smart cities in Europe. *Journal of Urban Technology, 18*(2), 65–82. doi:10.1080/10630732.2011.601117

Cats-Baril, W., & Thompson, R. (1995). Managing information technology projects in the public sector. *Public Administration Review, 55*(6), 559. doi:10.2307/3110347

Checkland, P. B. (1989). Soft systems methodology. *Human Systems Management, 8*(4), 273–289. doi:10.3233/HSM-1989-8405

ChillonP. S. (2012). *Urban 360*. http://urban360.me

Coates, B. E. (2001). SMART government on Line, not in line: Opportunities, challenges, and Concerns for Public Leadership. *Public Management, 30*(4), 37–40.

Coe, A., Paquet, G., & Roy, J. (2001). E-governance and smart communities. *Social Science Computer Review, 19*(1), 80–93. doi:10.1177/089443930101900107

Cook, D., & Das, S. K. (2004). *Smart Environment: Technology, protocols and applications* (Vol. 43). John Wiley&Sons. doi:10.1002/047168659X

Coro, Y., & Elizabeth, S. (2016). *Diseño e implementación de un prototipo inalámbrico IPv6 que permita comprobar la calidad de agua en smartcities*. Bachelor'sthesis, Escuela Superior Politécnica de Chimborazo.

Couclelis, H. (2004). The construction of the digital city. *Environment and Planning. B, Planning & Design, 31*(1), 5–19. doi:10.1068/b1299

Dameri, R. P. (2013). Searching for smart city definition: A comprehensive proposal. *International Journal of Computers and Technology, 11*(5), 2544–2551. doi:10.24297/ijct.v11i5.1142

Danziger, J. N., & Dutton, W. H. (1983). *Computers and politics: High technology in American local governments*. Columbia University Press.

Douligeris, C. (1993). Intelligent Home Systems. *IEEE Communications Magazine, 31*(10), 52–61. doi:10.1109/35.237984

Drucker, P. F. (2011). *Landmarks of tomorrow: A report on the new*. Transaction Publishers.

Dutton, W. H., Blumler, J. G., & Kraemer, K. L. (1987). *Wired Cities: Shaping the future of communications*. GK Hall &Co.

Enerlis, E., & Young, F. (2012). *Libro Blanco. Smart cities. Madrid Network.*

Ergazakis, K., Metaxiotis, K., & Ergazakis, E. (2010). Exploring Paths Towards Knowledge Cities Developments: A Research Agenda. Encyclopedia of Knowledge Management, 288–297. doi:10.4018/978-1-59904-931-1.ch028

Finkelstein, R., Garcia, A., Netherland, J., & Walker, J. (2008). *Toward an age-friendly New York City: A findings report*. New York Academy of Medicine.

Fritts, C.E. (1883). On a new form of selenium cell, and some electrical discoveries made by its use. *American Journal of Science, s3-26*(156), 465–472. . doi:10.2475/ajs.s3-26.156.465

Fujdiak, R. (2016). Using genetic algorithm for Advanced Municipal Waste Collection in smart city. *2016 10th International Symposium on Communication Systems, Networks and Digital Signal Processing (CSNDSP)*. 10.1109/CSNDSP.2016.7574016

Geissbühler, A., Demongeot, J., Mokhtari, M., Abdulrazak, B., & Aloulou, H. (2015). *Inclusive Smart Cities and e-Health*. In Lecture Notes in Computer Science. Springer. doi:10.1007/978-3-319-19312-0

Geller, A. L. (2003). Smart growth: A prescription for livable cities. *American Journal of Public Health, 93*(9), 1410–1415. doi:10.2105/AJPH.93.9.1410 PMID:12948954

Giffinger, R., Fertner, C., Kramar, H., Kalasek, R., Pichler-Milanovic, N., & Meijers, E. (2007). *Smart cities – Ranking of European medium-sized cities*. Centre of Regional Science. https://www.smart-cities.eu/download/smart_cities_final_report.pdf

Giffinger, R., & Pichler-Milanović, N. (2007). *Smart cities: Ranking of European medium-sized cities*. Centre of Regional Science, Vienna University of Technology.

Grady, D. (2012). Exercising an aging brain. *New York Times*.

Hall, P. (2000). Creative cities and economic development. *Urban Studies (Edinburgh, Scotland), 37*(4), 633–649. doi:10.1080/00420980050003946

Hauber-Davidson, G., & Idris, E. (2006). Smart water metering. *Water (Basel), 33*(3), 38–41.

Hiramatsu, K., & Ishida, T. (2001). An augmented web space for digital cities. In *Applications and the Internet, 2001. Proceedings. 2001 Symposium on* (pp. 105-112). IEEE. 10.1109/SAINT.2001.905173

Howard, E. (1965). *Garden cities of tomorrow* (Vol. 23). MIT Press. https://northstream.se/white-paper/archive

Iacob, V. S. (2013). The wastewater–a problem of integrated urban water management. *Procedia Economics and Finance, 6*, 436–443. doi:10.1016/S2212-5671(13)00160-3

IBM. (2010). *Smarter thinking for a smarter planet*. IBM.

Jessop, B. (1990). Regulation theory in retrospect and prospect. *Economy and Society, 19*(2), 153–216. doi:10.1080/03085149000000006

Jin, M., Bekiaris-Liberis, N., Weekly, K., Spanos, C. J., & Bayen, A. M. (2016). Occupancy detection via environmental sensing. *IEEE Transactions on Automation Science and Engineering*.

Jordan, B. (2011). *Corbin ball associates*. www.corbinball.com

Kamel-Boulos, M. N., & Al-Shorbaji, N. M. (2014). On the Internet of Things, smart cities and the WHO Healthy Cities. *International Journal of Health Geographics, 13*(1), 10. doi:10.1186/1476-072X-13-10 PMID:24669838

Kamel Boulos, M. N., & Al-Shorbaji, N. M. (2014). On the Internet of Things, smart cities and the WHO Healthy Cities. *International Journal of Health Geographics, 13*(1), 10. doi:10.1186/1476-072X-13-10 PMID:24669838

Kamel-Boulos, M. N., Rocha, A., Martins, A., Vicente, M. E., Bolz, A., Feld, R., Tchoudovski, I., Braecklein, M., Nelson, J., Laighin, G. O., Sdogati, C., Cesaroni, F., Antomarini, M., Jobes, A., & Kinirons, M. (2007). CAALYX: A new generation of location-based services in healthcare. *International Journal of Health Geographics*, *6*(1), 9. doi:10.1186/1476-072X-6-9 PMID:17352802

Kamel-Boulos, M. N., & Yang, S. P. (2013). Exergames for health and fitness: The roles of GPS and geosocial apps. *International Journal of Health Geographics*, *12*(1), 18. doi:10.1186/1476-072X-12-18 PMID:23561306

KamelBoulos, M.N., Tsouros, A.D., & Holopainen, A. (2015). Social, innovative and smart cities are happy and resilient: insights from the WHO EURO 2014 International Healthy Cities Conference. *Int J Health Geogr., 14*(3). 10.1186/1476-072X-14-3

Kickbusch, I., & Sakellarides, C. (2006). Flu City—Smart City: Applying health promotion principles to a pandemic threat. *Health Promotion International*, *21*(2), 85–87. doi:10.1093/heapro/dal014 PMID:16714297

Komninos, N. (2002). *Intelligent Cities: Innovation, knowledge systems and digital spaces*. Taylor and Francis.

Komninos, N. (2006, July). The architecture of intelligent cities. In *Conference Proceedings Intelligent Environments* (*Vol. 6*, pp. 5-6). Academic Press.

Komninos, N. (2008). *Intelligent cities and globalisation of innovation networks*. Routledge. doi:10.4324/9780203894491

Komninos, N. (2009). Intelligent cities: Towards interactive and global innovation environments. *International Journal of Innovative Research and Development*, *1*(4), 337–355. doi:10.1504/IJIRD.2009.022726

Kristanto, S., Yashiro, T., Koshizuka, N., & Sakamura, K. (2016, May). Dynamic Polling Algorithm for Low Energy Garbage Level Measurement in Smart Trash Bin. In *Proceedings of the Second International Conference on IoT in Urban Space* (pp. 92-94). ACM. 10.1145/2962735.2962748

Motiwalla, J., Yap, M., & Ngoh, L. H. (1993). Building the intelligent island. *IEEE Communications Magazine*, *31*(10), 28–34. doi:10.1109/35.237979

Musso, J., Weare, C., & Hale, M. (2000). Designing web technologies for local governance reform: Good management or good democracy? *Political Communication*, *17*(1), 1–19. doi:10.1080/105846000198486

Muyunda, N., & Ibrahim, M. (2017, November). Arduino-based smart garbage monitoring system: Analysis requirement and implementation. In *Computer and Drone Applications (IConDA), 2017 International Conference on* (pp. 28-32). IEEE.

Newman, P., & Kenworthy, J. (1999). *Sustainability and Cities: Overcoming Automobile Dependency*. Island Press.

OECD Observed. (1999). *Learning cities: the new recipe in regional development*. OECD.

OECD. (2010). *Green Cities Programme*. https://www.oecd.org/gov/regional-policy/49318965.pdf

Oralhan, Z., Oralhan, B., & Yiğit, Y. (2017). Smart City Application: Internet of Things (IoT) Technologies Based Smart Waste Collection Using Data Mining Approach and Ant Colony Optimization. *The International Arab Journal of Information Technology, 14*(4).

Paquet, G. (2001). Smart communities. *LAC Carling Government's Review, 3*(5), 28–30.

Polèse, M., & Stren, R. E. (Eds.). (2000). *The social sustainability of cities: Diversity and the management of change*. University of Toronto Press. doi:10.3138/9781442682399

Porat, M. U. (1978). Global Implications of the Information Society. *Journal of Communication, 28*(1), 70–80. doi:10.1111/j.1460-2466.1978.tb01565.x

Qi, L., & Shaofu, L. (2001). Research on digital city framework architecture. In *Info-tech and Info-net, 2001. Proceedings. ICII 2001-Beijing. 2001 International Conferences on* (Vol. 1, pp. 30-36). IEEE.

Ramaswami, A., Russell, A. G., Culligan, P. J., Sharma, K. R., & Kumar, E. (2016). Meta-principles for developing smart, sustainable, and healthy cities. *Science, 352*(6288), 940–943. doi:10.1126cience.aaf7160 PMID:27199418

Reddy, P. S. N., Naik, R. N., Kumar, A. A., & Kishor, S. N. (2017, February). Wireless dust bin monitoring and alert system using Arduino. In *Electrical, Computer and Communication Technologies (ICECCT), 2017 Second International Conference on* (pp. 1-5). IEEE. 10.1109/ICECCT.2017.8117960

Rogerson, S. (1997). *A prospectus for the electronic delivery of government services*. Centre for Computing and Social Responsibility.

Schiewe, J., Krek, A., Peters, I., Sternberg, H., & Traub, K. P. (2008). HCU research group "Digital City": developing and evaluating tools for urban research. Digital earth summit on geoinformatics.

Schuler, D. (2001, October). Digital cities and digital citizens. In *Kyoto Workshop on Digital Cities* (pp. 71-85). Springer.

Setis-Eu. (2012). setis.ec.europa.eu/implementation/technology-roadmap/European-initiative-on-smart-cities

Shim, E., Kim, D., Woo, H., & Cho, Y. (2016). Designing a sustainable noise mapping system based on citizen scientists smartphone sensor data. *PLoS One, 11*(9), e0161835. doi:10.1371/journal.pone.0161835 PMID:27626273

Shin, D. H. (2009). Ubiquitous city: Urban technologies, urban infrastructure and urban informatics. *Journal of Information Science, 35*(5), 515–526. doi:10.1177/0165551509100832

Su, K., Li, J., & Fu, H. (2011). Smart city and the applications. *IEEE International Conference on Electronics, Communications and Control (ICECC),* 1028-1031. 10.1080/13604810802479126

Turner, A. J., Willetts, J. R., Fane, S. A., Giurco, D., Chong, J., Kazaglis, A., & White, S. (2010). *Guide to demand management and integrated resource planning* (Update on Original 2008 Guide). Academic Press.

Van Bastelaer, B. (1998, October). Digital Cities and transferability of results. In *4th EDC Conference on digital cities* (pp. 61-70). Academic Press.

Van der Meer, A., & Van Winden, W. (2003). E-governance in cities: A comparison of urban information and communication technology policies. *Regional Studies, 37*(4), 407–419. doi:10.1080/0034340032000074433

Vasagade, T. S., Tamboli, S. S., & Shinde, A. D. (2017, March). Dynamic solid waste collection and management system based on sensors, elevator and GSM. In *Inventive Communication and Computational Technologies (ICICCT), 2017 International Conference on* (pp. 263-267). IEEE. 10.1109/ICICCT.2017.7975200

VomBrocke, J., Simons, A., Niehaves, B., Riemer, K., Plattfaut, R., & Cleven, A. (2009, June). Reconstructing the giant: On the importance of rigour in documenting the literature search process. In ECIS (Vol. 9, pp. 2206-2217). Academic Press.

Vu, D. D., & Kaddoum, G. (2017). *A Waste City Management System for Smart Cities Applications*. IEEE. doi:10.1109/RTUWO.2017.8228538

Werthner, H., & Klein, S. (1999). *Information technology and tourism: a challenging relationship*. Springer-VerlagWien. doi:10.1007/978-3-7091-6363-4

Yigitcanlar, T., & Kamruzzaman, M. (2018). Smart cities and mobility: Does the smartness of Australian cities lead to sustainable commuting patterns? *Journal of Urban Technology*. Advance online publication. doi:10.1080/10630732.2018.1476794

Yigitcanlar, T., Kamruzzaman, M., Buys, L., Ioppolo, G., Sabatini-Marques, J., Costa, E., & Yun, J. (2018). Understanding 'smart cities': Intertwining development drivers with desired outcomes in a multidimensional framework. *Cities (London, England), 81*, 145–160. Advance online publication. doi:10.1016/j.cities.2018.04.003

Yovanof, G. S., & Hazapis, G. N. (2009). An architectural framework and enabling wireless technologies for digital cities and intelligent urban environments. *Wireless Personal Communications, 49*(3), 445–463. doi:10.100711277-009-9693-4

Chapter 2
Smart Cities:
Complexity in the Economic Growth vs. Poverty

Alejandro Fuentes-Penna
https://orcid.org/0000-0002-4303-3852
El Colegio de Morelos, Mexico

Raúl Gomez Cardenas
El Colegio de Morelos, Mexico

ABSTRACT

Globalization driven by the development of information and communication technologies has triggered a context of competition and competitiveness in all areas of social and economic life. Smart cities have taken advantage of this situation to generate new conditions in health and employment. However, it is important to identify the needs of the population in smart cities to reduce poverty rates and the consequences that could be generated in the context of social life. Currently, several smart cities have proposed different ways to reduce poverty rates, so this chapter aims to analyze the poverty scenario in smart cities, raising questions such as Will it be possible to build smart jobs to maintain competitiveness in the global context and strengthen local development? What competitiveness alternatives can be used in the face of technological development in smart cities? What treatment do smart cities give to poverty areas seeking to incorporate them into urban and technological development?

INTRODUCTION

The urban space (city) is the place of emergence and dissemination of new ideas, technologies, and innovative initiatives. Urbanization is a characteristic of contemporary civilization and the process of urban development itself is conditioned by several factors, including globalization and technological progress. Research on the development of cities indicates factors of city transformation:

- The knowledge-based economy

DOI: 10.4018/979-8-3693-0373-3.ch002

- Digital technology
- Green approach
- Smart cities

The factors that serve as a foundation for the development of urban centers are Social capital, knowledge, and advanced technologies. Today, development and advanced technologies are indispensable for the management of city management and administration processes. Technologically advanced cities stand out as smart cities or simply smart cities.

Local authorities face a challenge and must answer the question: how to make the city smarter and what does this mean in reality? It is accepted that the concept of smart cities is oriented towards sustainable development, i.e. a long-term functioning of the city, based on factors, conditions, and instruments that guarantee an improvement of the living conditions of the local society and ensure a lasting development of the city, both on a local and regional scale.

In recent years, the implementation of programs related to the reduction of operating costs of cities and programs for saving resources, particularly energy resources, has been a particularly important element of European Union policy. Consequently, the idea of a smart city, allowing for a more comfortable, more economical, and safer life, should be considered when determining the direction of development of urban areas.

The smart city idea deals with urban development holistically, although it refers to the multidimensional characteristics of cities. However, this causes difficulties in explicitly and precisely defining what a smart city is. smart city. Researchers who have been working on this problem for almost twenty years emphasize different aspects of smart cities. different aspects of the smart city have been emphasized by researchers who have been working on this problem for almost twenty years.

The concept of a smart city has been gaining importance and great relevance in the design and implementation of public policies worldwide, given the development and population growth of urban centers.

The idea of the smart city is relatively new and has been strengthened in the last decade; therefore, it is evolving and is characterized by being a broad concept since, in general, it is made up of a complex combination and interaction of social, political, technological and economic factors.

The application of the smart city concept follows very varied paths depending on specific policies, objectives, financing, and the scope of each city according to its particular context. This concept arises from the need to rationalize and optimize through technologies the use of resources, mainly common resources understood as shared exhaustible facilities susceptible to social dilemmas (infrastructure, water, energy, among others) that present, as a consequence, problems that threaten their availability, such as congestion, pollution, and overexploitation.

This paper is presented in three sections:

a) Smart city concept and model
b) Economic growth in smart cities
c) Poverty context in smart cities

SMART CITY CONCEPT: A COMPLEX SUBJECT

A contemporary city is not only its physical structure, it is also a huge network of cyber-connections focused on optimizing the consumption of resources and processes of preventing negative external effects in line with the idea of sustainable development.

In the last decade, concepts aimed at saving resources have emerged. One of these concepts is smart growth, which is a method of special planning of transport networks, to avoid increased costs resulting from territorial expansion of cities. Technologically advanced cities are highlighted as smart cities that strive to save all kinds of resources (including financial resources), time, or energy (Parysek, Mierzejewska, 2016).

The smart city concept (intelligent city) seems to be very fashionable in the political arena of the last decade. In its basic aspect, it should provide public authorities with solutions that allow turning the city into a welcoming and respectful environment, making life easier for all users. The authorities stress the importance of ICT (information and communication technologies) infrastructure in the life and development of cities. However, they also stress the importance of human and social capital, a clean natural environment, and efficient transportation as the main factors in the development of urbanized areas. development of urbanized areas.

The literature on the smart city concept includes discussions on the role of innovative technologies in urban life. In the last twenty years, national and local politicians in different regions of the world have tried to define standards that promote the use of ICT to assess the development of urban areas.

Tranos (2013) described the lack of standard criteria that allow differentiating a smart city from a less smart one. The availability and quality of advanced technologies are unique factors to grant a city the attribute of a *smart city*. Some researchers apply to this concept the relationship between teleinformatics infrastructure and economic performance (Roller & Waverman 2001). Others emphasize that the problems associated with the growth of urban agglomerations are often solved by creative means, stakeholder cooperation, human capital, and innovative ideas - in other words, by resorting to "smart" methods. Consequently, smart cities should focus on skillful solutions that allow modern cities to develop, through qualitative and quantitative improvement of their productivity (Caragliu, Del Bo & Nijkamp, 2011).

The European smart city approach is based on actions linked to the reduction of carbon dioxide emissions and actions whose objective is the efficient use of energy, in each area of activity of the city together with the simultaneous improvement of the quality of life of the inhabitants. Following this common European vision, the functioning of a smart city is based on cooperation, to stimulate progress in areas where energy generation, distribution and use, mobility and transport, and modern technologies are closely related and offer an improvement in the quality of life of the inhabitants. Modern urban technologies are considered to make a relevant contribution to the sustainable development of European cities (Sikora-Fernández, 2017).

The main priorities of the European Union, applicable to cities, include support for an integrated urban policy that favors the sustainable development of urban areas to increase the role of cities in the new integration policy. This strategy focuses on four areas (Sikora-Fernández, 2017):

- Economy's Innovation based on knowledge.
- Freedom of financial, energy, transport, and telecommunication markets.
- Stimulation of the entrepreneurial spirit, through actions to create and manage the business activities.

- A new model of social assistance based on social integration.

Sikora-Fernández (2017) described the objective of the Europe 2020 Strategy as oriented to achieve an intelligent, sustainable and socially inclusive development, sustainable and socially inclusive development. In this field, three main initiatives have been identified:

1. European digital agenda based on high-speed data transmission connections.
2. Innovation, innovation process optimization, and use of research and development activities aimed to reduce the major problems in the social and economic areas.
3. Mobile youth: increasing the attractiveness of European university centers and better access to foreign universities and higher education institutions.

Smart development is based on positive outcomes in education, training, scientific research, and innovation, together with the research and innovation, together with the effective use of ICT techniques.

Although there is no common definition of smart cities, researchers agree on the number of dimensions included in this concept (Lombardi et al., 2012). It is admitted that cities can be defined as smart or intelligent cities if they possess the following elements (Figure 1):

- Smart Economy
- Smart Mobility
- Smart Environment
- Smart People
- Smart Living
- Smart Governance

These dimensions of smart cities are linked with traditional and neoclassical theories of growth and development of urban areas based on the theory of competitiveness of cities and regions, social capital, governance, and new public management, inscribing the use of advanced technologies, among the different elements. Indeed, this concept goes well beyond the use of innovative technologies for efficient use of energy resources, and the reduction of CO_2 emissions and encompasses other aspects of urban life and the functioning of public administration.

Figure 1. Smart cities requirements
Source: Lombardi et al. (2012)

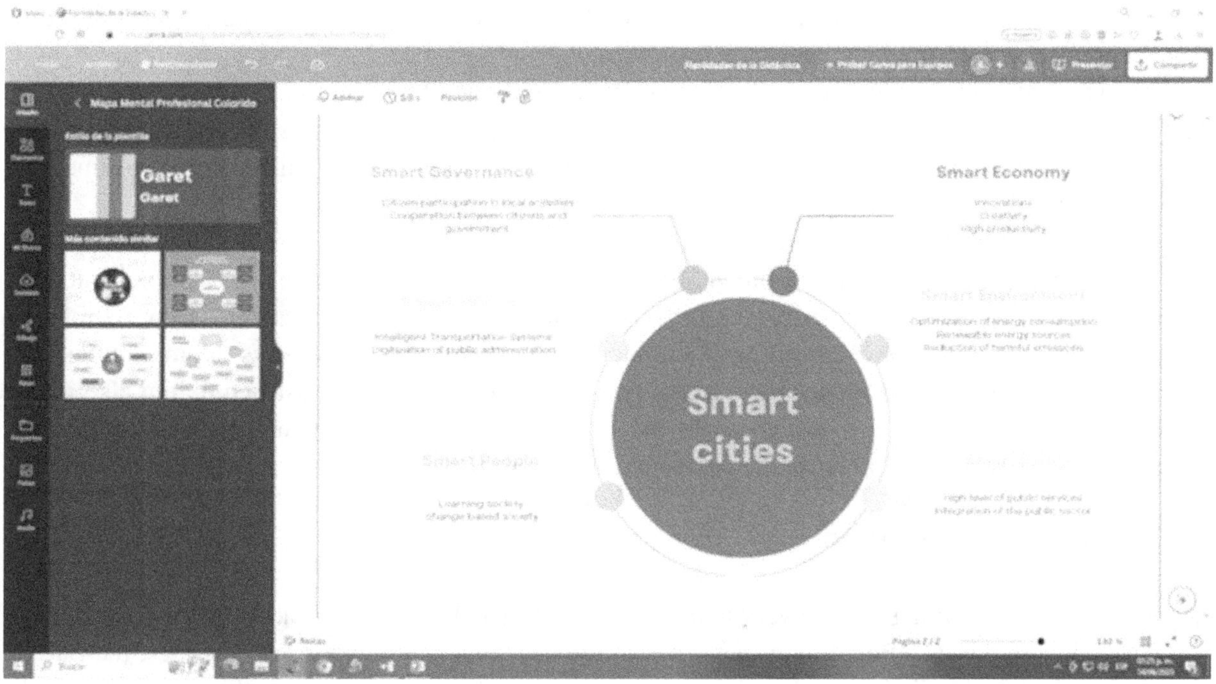

The main questions that arise when classifying a city as a smart city refer to the stage of development:

- Can a city be considered a smart city if it has actions described in only one field?
- Is it possible to consider a smart city a city with actions described in a single field?
- Should the smart city concept be considered only globally and applied only to a city that meets the requirements in the six dimensions?
- What is the state to which cities should aspire?

The smart city concept is a complex concept, which explains the essence and importance of many aspects related to city development.

A smart city is a city that uses advanced technologies, among other things, to create more efficient systems of transportation and communications, heating, public lighting, ensuring safety in public places, waste management, more effective water use, communication and information exchange between the users of urban space, etc. Modern materials and technologies are used in the construction of the city to reduce energy consumption.

A city managed according to the guidelines of the smart city concept also means that people think creatively and can absorb their activity's technical innovations and technology and the use of techniques commonly known as ICT.

It is common in these cities the presence of digital telecommunications networks. Digital networks are compared in the concept of a smart city with the nervous system where they play the role of brain devices that control the system by the information collected by the network of sensors (sense organs).

The smart city is a broad concept, covering many areas of the city. However, it should not be forgotten that the city is not only smart technology and its achievements, it is not only ICT systems, above all it is people, intelligent, capable of environmental solutions, caring for the environment, able to plan and manage urban space optimally manage the urban space.

The evolution and development of information technologies have brought about a new way of conceiving cities and urban spaces. Smart cities are a trend that is being massively promoted to take advantage of the use of ICTs to envision service-centered cities through a significant improvement in the relationship with the citizen.

In terms of literature, it is a growing academic field in the last decade, which shows that it is an area in constant evolution and development given its novelty and the development of implementation experiences in Europe and Asia as pioneers and where Latin America is betting heavily. Information and communication technologies are becoming a fundamental element for the success of smart cities, but it should be noted that it is not enough to invest only in the provision of infrastructure, but also in the provision of innovative services in such a way that they allow the establishment of a dynamic, flexible and collaborative relationship between citizens and government entities.

The Model of Smart Cities

At present, we are adapting to the overwhelming changes that flow from the accelerated communication derived from the ICT Revolution that leads to the fact that, as innovation accelerates, the rate of economic, social, and political change accelerates even more; this does not escape the way of living and coexistence of society, which necessarily requires processes of adaptation and change.

In this sense, smart cities, more than a dream of the future, are a possible reality, but above all a necessary one to face the challenges of growing urbanization, where ICTs undoubtedly play a preponderant role due to their capacity to provide solutions that permeate the economic, environmental and social spheres.

Accelerated urbanization adds pressure to the resource base, and increases the demand for energy, water, and sanitation, as well as for public services, education, and health. And, consequently, the various social, economic, and environmental issues have become strongly connected, hence the need to address them holistically.

Vegara (2009) described the main challenge faced by large cities is to boost competitive advantages, which implies the build of efficient urban structures, appropriate training programs specific infrastructures and facilities, appropriate training programs, improvement of urban quality of life and quality of life, strategic alliances, etc. It is clear that more and more citizens, as well as companies, need to be aware of events and conditions in the city and its surroundings. increasingly, citizens, like businesses, need to be aware of events and conditions in the broad context in which they operate. and this calls for new working methods and tools in urban planning and spatial planning. tools in urban and regional planning).

The term smart city has some points of coincidence from different authors, where they present the smart city as the conception of a complex system, where different actors and several factors converge to achieve its functionality, such as interconnection, adaptation, organization, and especially feedback.

The Smart city's basic model necessarily implies an intensive and extensive use of ICT where these technologies play a central role as a factor of dynamism of the new model, driving a set of techno-scientific, organizational, social, and institutional innovations, and generating new opportunities for economic and social return in the most varied activities (Lastres and Cassiolato, 2007). In this case, the authors present ICT as a vehicle for technical progress and for reducing inequality in society, particularly in developing countries.

In this way, territorial evolution and, therefore, the development of a Smart City model requires new forms of organization and interrelation, considering that new technologies and systems (economic and social) evolve in new logics based on the active interrelation of several actors, both in the social, environmental, economic and governmental spheres.

Therefore, there is an urgent need to generate strategies for planning and adapting the environment in favor of urban inclusion and participation with benefits for the environment, the economy, and society in general. The necessary environments (smart and sustainable) are possible under the current ICT paradigm.

Smart cities propose innovative strategies as:

- ICTs to improve decision-making, operational efficiency, urban service delivery, and competitiveness.
- Improve the current and future generations based on the economic, social, and environmental aspects
- Improve the inventive activity (creativity), the generation/dissemination of knowledge sustained with networking, i.e., economic, social, educational and environmental economic, social, educational, and governmental actors.
- A smart city places people (citizens) at the center of development, where it seeks to promote integrated and sustainable development, where cities become more innovative, competitive, attractive, and resilient.
- Improve the quality of life of the population

The challenge for cities or territories is to reach levels of "intelligence", through the extensive use and integration of ICTs in those strategic sectors and activities such as education, health, energy, water, waste management, security, economy, etc.; all of them aligned to the principles of equity, sustainable development, and innovation, which would imply the growth of infrastructure and its efficiency.

In the model proposed by Alvarado López (2018), he determines that the central point is inclusive innovation, greater social integration and equality, greater access to different public services, programs for environmental care, mobility, and economic competitiveness. In turn, the author highlights that cities play an important role in providing a series of requirements for a successful business, especially for innovation and quality-based competition. Among the challenges of today's society is that of moving towards spaces of coexistence and development that make it possible to meet the growing demands of citizens without having to exert greater pressures on the environment or limit the dynamics of economic growth and social welfare (Figure 2).

Figure 2. Axes and factors of a smart city
Source: Alvarado López (2018).

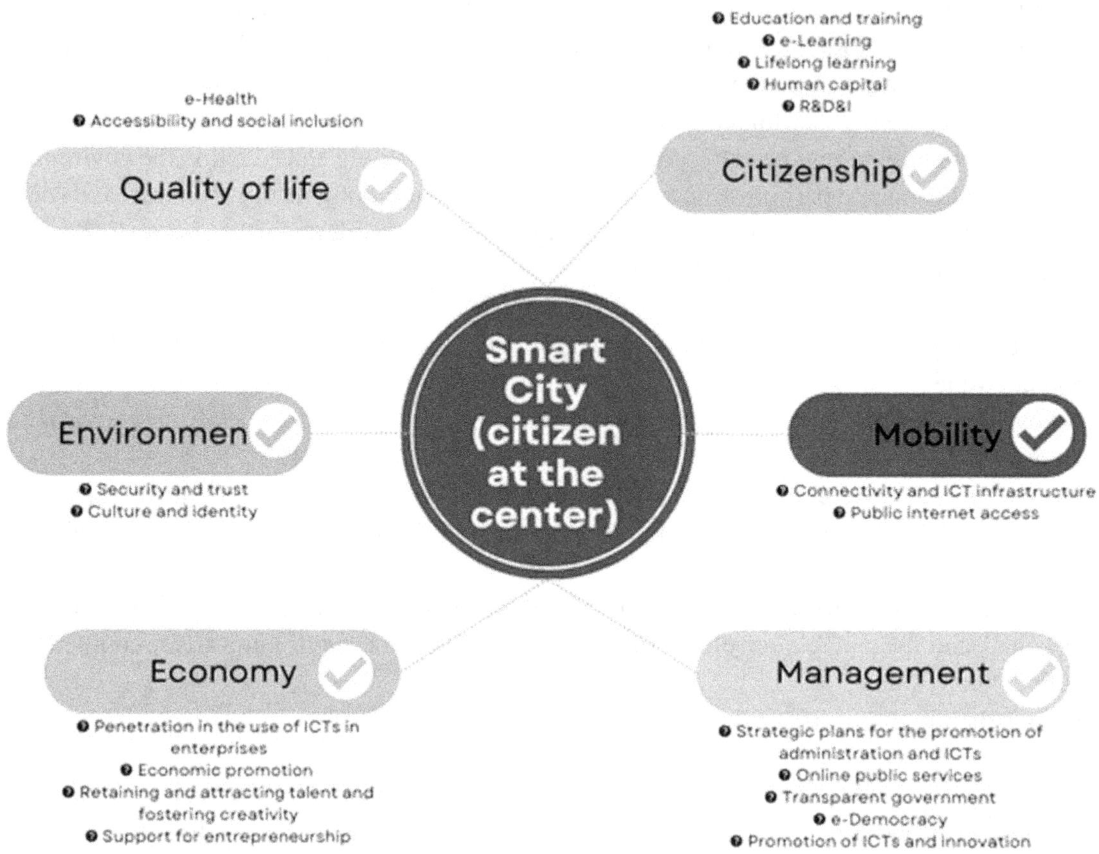

Given the broad scope of smart cities and the transversality of the model, Villarejo Galende (2015) mentions the following legal implications:

- Good governance, transparency, and e-Government.
- Municipal competencies, local public services, and effective cost of services.
- Smart public procurement: new approaches to service provision.

ECONOMIC GROWTH IN SMART CITIES

Within the framework of the smart city development concept, Barcelona is implementing 200 projects within 22 major initiatives in different areas of city operation. The actual implementation effects of different projects are presented in Figure 3.

Figure 3. Barcelona is a smart city

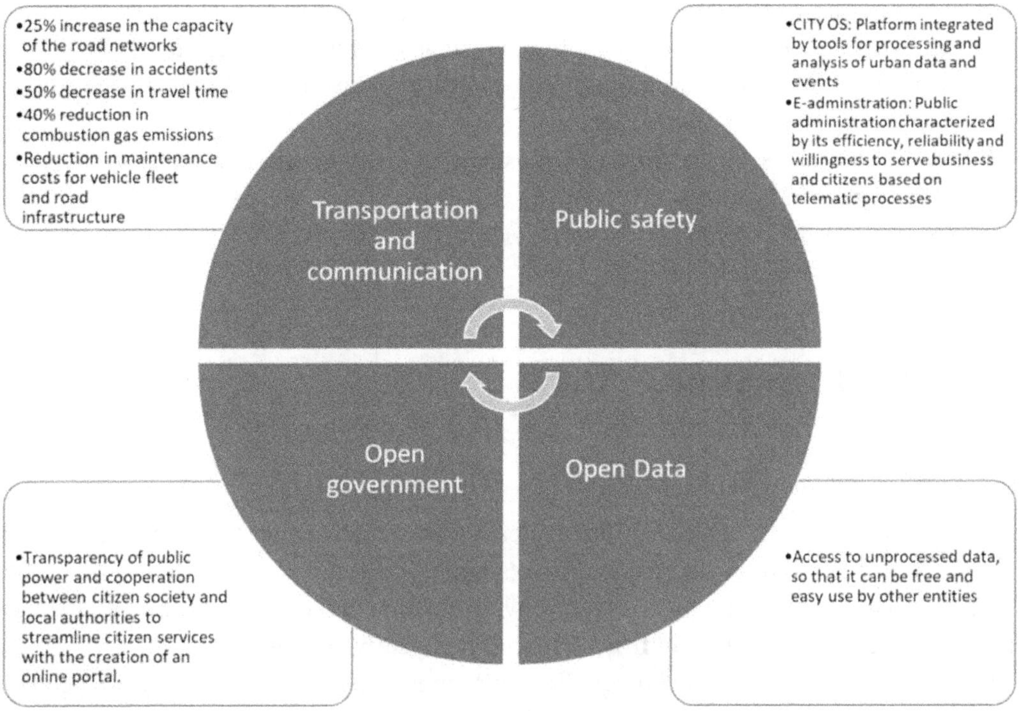

Albino Berardi & Dangelico (2015) presented research related to the identification of projects oriented to the development of smart cities, where it can be highlighted that, at the beginning of 2013, 143 smart city projects were proposed:

- North America had 35 projects:
  - Ottawa's "Smart Capital" project to improve business, local government, and the community through the use of Internet resources
  - Quebec City government launched a public-private partnership to support a growing multimedia sector and high-tech entrepreneurship.
  - Riverside, California improved traffic flow and replaced antiquated water, sewer, and electrical infrastructure through a technology-driven transformation.
  - San Diego and San Francisco proclaim themselves as the City of the Future based on ICTs.
- Europe 47 projects:
  - Several cities in the European Union: Barcelona, Amsterdam, Berlin, Manchester, and Edinburgh.
  - United Kingdom: Southampton is a smart city based on multi-application smart cards for public transport, leisure, and leisure-related transactions. Tallinn bases on a large-scale digital skills training program, extensive e-government, and an award-winning smart ID card.
- Asia 50 projects:
  - 6 provinces and 51 cities as Smart Cities over the Pearl and Yangtze River Deltas, Bohai Rim, and the Midwest area.

  - The first smart cities Beijing, Shanghai, and Shenzhen.
  - Masdar City as an eco-city paradigm and smart city.
  - Other examples are Singapore (Intelligent Island), Taiwan (E-Taoyuan and U-Taoyuan for creating e-governance and ubiquitous possibilities), and Hong Kong promoting economic growth through smart city programs.
  - Songdo in Korea as a smart city (telepresence in every apartment to create an urban space) and 13 projects in progress
- South America with 10 projects;
- the Middle East and Africa 10 projects.

POVERTY CONTEXT IN SMART CITIES

Poverty

Poverty is multidimensional in nature. Different definitions indicate that there is a certain consensus that poverty is the deprivation of the essential assets and opportunities to which all human beings are entitled such as vulnerability, inequality, marginality, exclusion, and discrimination, are examined, and the specific forms that poverty takes on from a gender perspective are analyzed.

It is now recognized that poverty and inequality are growing phenomena that have not been overcome in the Latin American region; these concepts continue to be elusive objectives of our development and have been hit hard in recent years by our macroeconomic vulnerability.

Poverty processes are aspects of broader phenomena that are related to the development models and strategies implemented. These models and strategies delimit trade and financial openness options, macroeconomic and microeconomic policies that are mediated by institutions, norms, and practices that together define the access of individuals and their families to the use and control of resources and, specifically, access to the labor market and income. It derives from restricted access to property, low income and consumption, limited social, political, and labor opportunities, insufficient educational attainment, health, nutrition, access, use, and control over natural resources, and other areas of development.

A person is poor if he or she lacks the necessary resources to carry out a certain minimum of activities (Sen, 1992). Social Watch (1997) proposed five basic and necessary capabilities, poverty is linked to people's rights to a decent life that meets their basic needs, i.e., to the so-called economic, and social. and cultural rights.:

- The ability to stay alive and enjoy a long life;
- The ability to ensure biological and cultural intergenerational reproduction;
- The ability to enjoy a healthy life;
- The ability to interact socially (social capital); and
- The ability to have knowledge and freedom of expression and thought.

It is also argued that poverty is complex, relational, and multidimensional in nature. The characteristics of poverty differ from one country to another and the interpretation of the precise nature of poverty depends on cultural, social, and cultural factors. of poverty depends on cultural factors, such as gender, race, and ethnicity of gender, race, and ethnicity, as well as the economic, social, and historical context.

Challenges in Smart Cities

Growing urbanization presents a myriad of challenges for local governments, which must develop their policies for the future with the growing number of urban dwellers in mind. Sustainable urbanization requires cities to generate better income and employment opportunities; expand the necessary infrastructure for water and sanitation, energy, transportation, information, and communications; ensure equal access to services; reduce the number of people living in slums; and preserve natural assets in and around the city.

In the study of smart cities, several relevant challenges have been identified for their analysis. Among the challenges to be highlighted is that better coordination is required either for the actors and sectors to focus the idea of technology in the cities with the specific needs of their inhabitants or to prioritize the applications of greater social and economic impact when these projects are implemented, thus focusing on the real issues and problems. Fernández Güell (2015) presents a list of challenges and challenges that at a practical or conceptual level have Smart Cities:

- Develop comprehensive management systems to obtain a global interpretation of the urban system.
- Real-time comprehensive management to evaluate the performance of urban services and take corrective measures on a realistic basis.
- Analyze the interconnection between urban systems.
- Establish interoperability between sectoral technology platforms through the use of information gateways.
- Leverage the value of data, its analysis, and systemic thinking to generate information that benefits citizens.

In Europe, the current economic context represents a strong conditioning factor for the definitive boost of smart initiatives in our cities (EOI, 2015):

- The private sector is facing economic and financial restrictions to address R&D&I investment projects.
- The public sector is subject to budgetary constraints, especially local entities, which should be the main drivers of the smart model.
- The reduction in tax collection caused by the economic crisis in recent years, municipal budgets have been drastically reduced, which, together with the increase in financing costs, has made it difficult to undertake transformational projects in cities. These budgetary difficulties are forcing cities to seek new formulas to transform themselves and provide urban services more efficiently.

Figure 4. Challenges in smarty city dimensions
Source: Ontiveros, Vizcaíno, and López Sabater (2016)

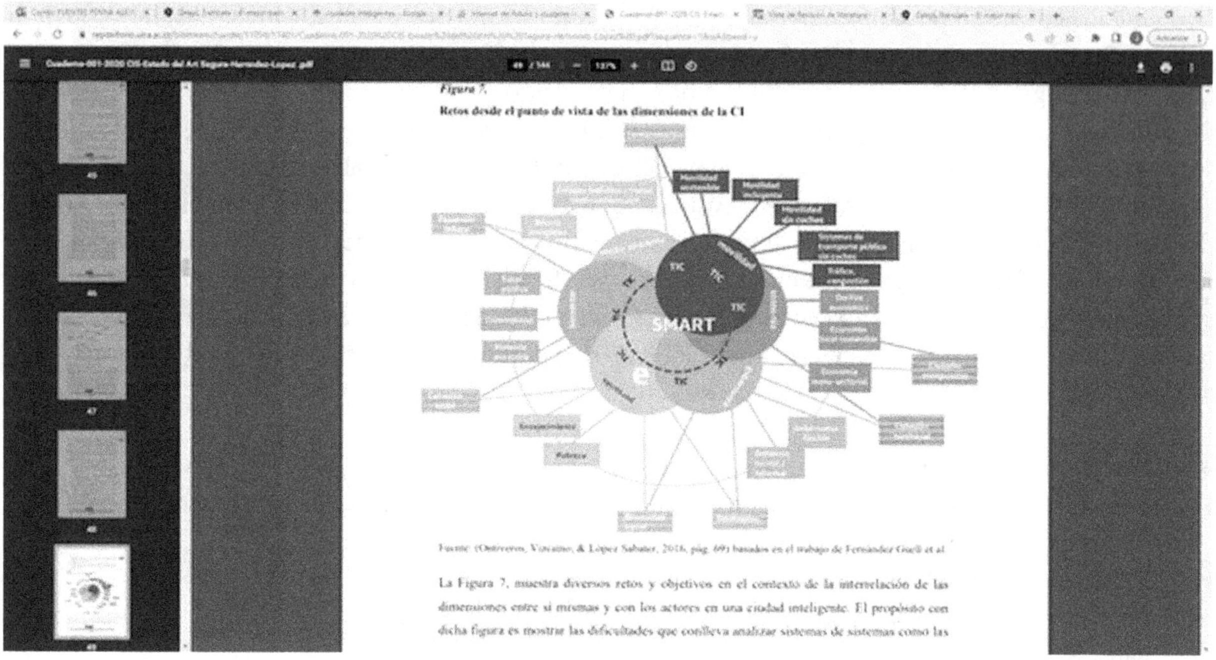

Figure 4 shows several challenges and objectives in the context of the dimensions among themselves and with the stakeholders in a smart city. This figure shows the difficulties involved in the analysis of systems in a smart city.

In emerging countries, the discourse of the failure of cities has gained strength, as we are faced with a large shapeless mass that must be controlled to ensure the safety and smooth flow of flows. However, some examples make it clear how proposals for the smartization of the city can contribute directly to widening rather than solving the already profound economic and social differences in these contexts.

There is the prospect that smart cities will become walled cities, ruled by powerful corporations that can bypass local laws and governments to keep the poor out, ensuring a smart life for the rich and a life of alienation, misery, and exclusion for the poor, a scenario that we can already observe in the major capitals of countries in the so-called Global South, long before smart cities.

Given the challenges associated with increasing European urbanization, as well as the broader agenda to address economic recovery, unemployment, and environmental damage, the Europe 2020 Strategy incorporates a commitment (European Commission, 2010)12 to promote the development of smart cities across Europe and to invest in the necessary ICT infrastructure and the development of human and social capital.

The European 2020 Strategy and the Horizon 2020 Program

Villarejo Galende (2015) presented the European strategy and the horizon program where the European Union believes that cities, based on digital technologies, can become laboratories for a more dynamic and digital economy in which to experiment with innovative measures capable of generating growth and employment, resulting in economic and social benefits for citizens, and contributing to the industrial and socioeconomic renaissance of the European Union.

Through the Europe 2020 Strategy, the European Union has promoted a strong financial commitment to the development of initiatives that enable smart growth of territories. The Europe 2020 Strategy promotes smart cities throughout Europe by investing in ICT infrastructures, in the conviction that they can contribute to meeting the objectives derived from the three priority areas proposed in the Strategy: smart growth, through the development of an economy based on knowledge and innovation; sustainable growth, based on a greener economy, more efficient in the management of resources and more competitive; and inclusive growth, aimed at strengthening employment, social and territorial cohesion (European Commission, 2010).

The inclusion of funding tools for smart cities is aimed at achieving clear objectives: contributing to the sustainability of urban environments, improving the efficiency of urban services, reducing the carbon footprint of cities, and stimulating the creation of an innovative environment for the development of technology-based companies.

Although the commitment to the development of smart cities was boosted through the Europe 2020 Strategy, where the Community Funding Framework (2014-2020) was incorporated:

- The VII Framework Program (2007-2013) was launched, and approved by agreement of the European Council on June 10, 201013, where an investment of 1,900 million euros was contemplated for the development of Smart initiatives.
- The economic support of the European Union to smart cities was increased in the Multiannual Financial Framework (2014-2020).
- For the 2014-2020 period, the Horizon 2020 program foresaw 16 billion euros, which implies an eightfold increase in the funding foreseen for the previous period (EOI, 2015).
- previous period.
- The European Regional Development Fund (ERDF) is appropriate for the promotion of smart cities.
- The Operational Program for Smart Growth 2014-2020, which is the document that specifies the strategy and objectives of intervention of the General State Administration (AGE) co-financed with the ERDF fund intending to contribute to the improvement and recovery of the competitiveness of the Spanish economy, through the promotion of a smarter growth model, supported by research, innovation, and ICT, with special attention to the needs and potential of SMEs.

In the context of Villarejo Galende (2015) article make a review of the National Smart Cities Plan where the European commitment to smart cities has received strong support at the national level, which has been embodied in the so-called National Smart Cities Plan, approved in March 2015 by the Secretary of State for Telecommunications and the Information Society of the Ministry of Industry, Energy and Tourism. The Plan has an initial budget of 153 million euros for the 2015-2016 biennium, co-financed with ERDF Funds. The purpose of the National Smart Cities Plan is to contribute to economic development, as established in the Digital Agenda for Spain: maximize the impact of public policies in ICT to improve productivity and competitiveness; and transform and modernize the Spanish economy and society through efficient and intensive use of ICT by citizens, companies, and Administrations.

The National Smart Cities Plan contemplates the achievement of the following objectives and the Plan is structured in five axes (Figure 5):

- Increase the contribution of ICTs to the industrial sector's GDP
- Improve the effectiveness and efficiency of Local Entities in the provision of public services through the use of ICTs, to advance the governance of the smart cities system and to promote the standardization, regulation, and norms of smart cities.

Figure 5. 5 axes of the National Smart Cities Plan

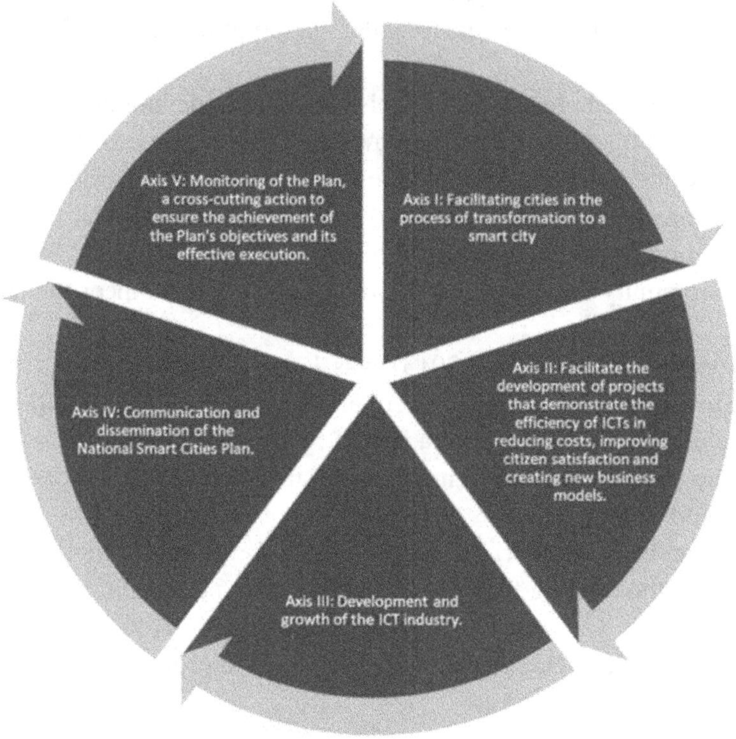

Eco-Cities and Smart Cities

Recent technological advances have boosted economic growth, consumption, and wealth, leading to an unprecedented demographic explosion, concentrated mainly in cities. However, all this has brought with it serious environmental and social consequences that threaten humanity and the health of the planet, such as global warming, high pollution, congestion, urban sprawl, widespread urban poverty, etc. Thus, from the point of view of urban designs and approaches, different city models have emerged that have tried to respond to these evils, some based on ecological logic, others considering technology as the only one capable of providing an effective solution.

Currently, the idea is spreading that achieving a truly sustainable and livable city means embracing the ecological concepts that make it possible to achieve sustainability while putting technology at the service of citizens to achieve these goals. There are many examples of projects that are being built or have already been executed following the conceptions of some of these models. models, it is enough to know if their approaches have been able to effectively solve these problems. effectively solve these problems.

González Izquierdo (2016) presented a description of two smart cities:

- Sociopolis in Valencia and
- Eco-city of Sarriguren in Navarra,

Both projects are new urbanization projects, although their development is based on the respect of pre-existences (Sociopolis) or the development of an already existing historical nucleus (Sarriguren). On the other hand, it will be observed that the intentions of the Sarriguren project are more systematized concerning some key guidelines for the planning and project of an ecocity, while Sociopolis leaves many variables to the choice of the designer, as different teams of architects are in charge of proposing the buildings of the eco-neighborhood, according to a series of general requirements set out in the project. Sociopolis.

Another difference in general terms between the eco-neighborhoods is that Sarriguren is a project that has been built almost as soon as possible. Subsequently, a comparative analysis of the two eco-neighborhood projects is carried out in terms of the two eco-neighborhood projects in terms of the sustainability criteria.

Concerning public space and habitability, it is observed that Sociopolis does not have the system of streets and squares of traditional urban planning. However, it could be said that the pedestrian walkways inside the central area and the open areas that function as public squares on the plots of some of the proposed buildings generate quality public space, although the lack of information in this area means that it is not possible to rule on such a question.

Sustainable mobility has been taken into consideration in both projects. However, the car-free central area in Sociopolis is conducive to avoiding parking on the streets, but not in the case of Sarriguren, which, although it has large parking lots on the outskirts of the eco-city, the presence of cars is higher. Regarding functional diversity and urban complexity, both projects have an attractive mix of uses, with the presence of economic activities that promote employment in the case of Sarriguren (Sarriguren Park). of Sarriguren (Parque de la Innovación).

In the case of Sociópolis, the hybrid buildings, with cultural and sports facilities, favor social interaction. and sports facilities, favor social interaction and urban complexity. However, in Sarriguren there is a so-called spatial monofunctionality, since one plot groups together economic activities, others the residential areas, and another the single-family residential area. residential areas, for single-family residential, and others for facilities. other the equipment areas. In addition, the design of the road network does not favor contact between the different functional parts, but rather separates them, isolating these uses and preventing a real mix of uses. and preventing a real mix on a pedestrian scale. Similarly, the sports facilities are located on the edge and do not favor the personal exchange between residents and visitors.

Smart Tourist Destinations: A Strategy for Local Development in Poor Countries?

Castro Álvarez, González Rodríguez, & Maldonado Duarte (2017) described that globalization is based on (ICT) and this has triggered a new context of competition and competitiveness in all areas of social and economic life. Tourism has not escaped the new conditions of postmodern life, originating the concept of smart tourist destinations, which has been positioning itself, particularly in developed countries. The authors analyze the panorama that smart tourism can reduce poverty in developing countries, raising questions such as: Will it be possible to build smart tourist destinations in poor countries to maintain competitiveness in the global context and strengthen local development, what alternatives for competitiveness can be used in the face of the technological development of intelligent destinations in developed countries?

IUIT (2015) mentioned that Smart Cities can be considered smart tourism destination (STD); however, there are also tourist destinations in rural areas or in integrated territories that differ in their structures from those of cities. It is therefore relevant to analyze which regions, destinations, or territories can be adapted to the original concept of STD. IUIT (2015) described the phases to becoming a STD by changing traditional tourist destinations to STDs should be considered to analyze the cost-benefit and therefore the advisability of the investments involved in this effort, especially in areas where the needs are great and it is necessary to rationalize the use of scarce resources. In this sense, it is proposed that SITDs should be promoted under the following considerations:

- The configuration of an STD should respond to the needs of each destination and the benefits it can bring to it.
- The STD must establish a new framework of relations in local tourism management through greater involvement and co-responsibility of the private sector.
- Although there are already proven experiences in urban areas, the configuration of STDs has a high experimental component, so the deployment of initiatives associated with ITDs should be previously tested in proofs of concept and pilot projects to ensure the viability of investments and guarantee the continuity of the projects.

It is possible to create Smart Tourism Destinations (STD) in poor or developing countries, by sifting the original concept through adaptation to the characteristics of the contexts where their destinations are developed, taking advantage of ICT's as a mechanism for generating collective intelligence, knowledge, and innovation, taking care of the resources and values that will be the distinctive differentiating feature on which competitiveness in the global tourism market can be sustained.

CONCLUSION

This article presents the context and complexity of the meaning of an increasingly popular concept: the smart city. An in-depth review of the literature reveals that the meaning of a smart city is multifaceted. Descriptions of smart cities include qualities of people and communities, as well as the use of ICT as a foundation, however, it is necessary to analyze the orientation of the term smart city towards poverty reduction and towards addressing the 2030 agenda. An analysis of the existing literature reveals a large number of elements and dimensions that characterize a smart city.

The debate that technology has opened up in our society is here to stay, as it concerns not only cities but also the relations between cities and their inhabitants. not only in cities but also in the human relations that will be generated from now on. human relations that will be generated from now on. On the other hand, trying to bring together ecology and technology in the same sustainability equation could prove difficult when technology difficult when technology is put at the service of economic interests. economic interests.

In the present analysis, we identify the complexity regarding the measurement of a smart city. However, this document does not intend to define a framework for the evaluation of the intelligence of a city, but rather to focus on identifying the social and economic aspects that allow for a better quality of life.

Cities around the world have begun to use ICT to promote themselves under the label smart. So-called smart cities incorporate innovation and technology into basic infrastructures (transportation, energy, water, waste management, telecommunications, etc.) to develop a more efficient, flexible, and less costly city. Behind the smart city movement, there is a certain e-topia in that it aims to achieve the ideal city through the digital revolution.

Smart cities cannot simply be considered a fad, an attractive slogan, or an opportunistic financing strategy. They undoubtedly represent a business opportunity for innovative and service companies, but they are also an opportunity to develop cities economically and to improve the quality of life of their inhabitants. The citizens must be the epicenter of the model. If cities want to be smart, they will have to approach a transition, focusing on the citizens and the communities in which they are integrated, and take advantage of the potential of new technologies to contribute effectively to greater social, environmental, and cultural development.

REFERENCES

Albino, V., Berardi, U., & Dangelico, R. M. (2015). Smart Cities: Definitions, Dimensions, Performance, and Initiatives. *Journal of Urban Technology, 22*(1), 1, 3–21. doi:10.1080/10630732.2014.942092

Alvarado López, R. A. (2018). Ciudad inteligente y sostenible: hacia un modelo de innovación inclusiva. *PAAKAT: revista de tecnología y sociedad, 7*(13).

Caragliu, A., Del Bo, Ch., & Nijkamp, P. (2011). Smart cities in Europe. *Journal of Urban Technology, 18*(2), 65–82. doi:10.1080/10630732.2011.601117

Castro Álvarez, U., González Rodríguez, J. Á., & Maldonado Duarte, L. M. (2017). Destinos Turísticos Inteligentes: ¿Estrategia para el Desarrollo Local en Países Pobres? *Revista Turydes: Turismo y Desarrollo, 22*. https://www.eumed.net/rev/turydes/22/destinos-turisticos-inteligentes.html

EOI. (2015). *El ecosistema SMART en Andalucía. Retos y oportunidades para la colaboración público-privada*. Escuela de Organización Industrial. Madrid. http://a.eoi.es/andalsmart

European Commission. (2010). *Europa 2020: Una estrategia para un crecimiento inteligente, sostenible e integrador, COM(2010) 2020 final, Bruselas, 3.3.2010.* https://eurlex.europa.eu/legal-content/en/ALL/?uri=CELEX:52010DC2020

ISSN. 1988-5261

IUIT. (2015). *Destinos Turísticos Inteligentes. Manual operativo para la configuración de destinos turísticos inteligentes. Universidad de Alicante, Instituto Universitario de Investigaciones Turísticas*. IUIT.

Lombardi, P., Giordano, S., Farouh, H., & Yousef, W. (2012). Modelling the Smart City Performance. *Innovation (Abingdon), 25*(2), 137–149. doi:10.1080/13511610.2012.660325

Ontiveros, E., Vizcaíno, D., & López Sabater, V. (2016). *Las Ciudades del Futuro: inteligentes, digitales y sostenibles*. Ariel.

Parysek, J., & Mierzejewska, L. (2016). Spatial structure of a city and the mobility of its residents: Functional and planning aspects. *Bulletin of Geography. Socio-Economic Series*, *34*(34), 91–102. doi:10.1515/bog-2016-0037

Roller, L., & Waverman, L. (2001). Telecommunication Infrastructure and Economic Development: A Simultaneous Approach. *The American Economic Review*, *91*(4), 909–923. doi:10.1257/aer.91.4.909

Sen, A. (1992b). Pobreza: identificación y agregación. In L. Beccaria y otros (Ed.), *América Latina: el reto de la pobreza. Conceptos, métodos, magnitud, características y evolución.* Programa de las Naciones Unidas para el Desarrollo (PNUD).

Sikora-Fernández, D. (2017). Factores de desarrollo de las ciudades inteligentes. *Revista Universitaria de Geografía*, *26*(1), 135–152.

Tranos, E., & Gertner, D. (2012). Smart networked cities? *Innovation (Abingdon)*, *25*(2), 175–190. doi :10.1080/13511610.2012.660327

Vegara, A. (2009). Territorios inteligentes. *Ambienta*, (89), 34-58. https://www.revistaambienta.es/WebAmbienta/marm/Dinamicas/secciones/articulos/Vegara.htm

Villarejo Galende, H. (2015). Smart cities: una apuesta de la Unión Europea para mejorar los servicios públicos urbanos. *Revista de estudios europeos*, (66), 25-51.

Chapter 3
Smart Government and Future Trends

Jorge A. Ruiz-Vanoye
https://orcid.org/0000-0003-4928-5716
Universidad Politécnica de Pachuca, Mexico

Ocotlán Díaz-Parra
Universidad Politécnica de Pachuca, Mexico

Francisco Marroquín-Gutiérrez
Universidad Politécnica de Pachuca, Mexico

Blas M. Rodríguez-Lara
Tecnológico de Monterrey, Mexico

Alejandro Fuentes-Penna
https://orcid.org/0000-0002-4303-3852
Colegio de Morelos, Mexico

Ricardo A. Barrera-Cámara
https://orcid.org/0000-0002-3170-4671
Universidad Autónoma del Carmen, Mexico

Julio C. Ramos-Fernández
Universidad Politécnica de Pachuca, Mexico

Juan M. Xicoténcatl-Pérez
Universidad Politécnica de Pachuca, Mexico

Jaime Aguilar-Ortiz
Universidad Politécnica de Pachuca, Mexico

ABSTRACT

Several technologies are available to help citizens, and government officials perform their daily activities in a city. The current state-of-the-art technologies to help citizens and government officials exist wireless sensor networks, RFDI technology, combinatorial optimisation, machine learning, big data, data visualisation, internet of government things, big-data analytics, and others to enhance the quality of the government. The authors have collected the relevant literature published during 2001-2021 by searching and browsing all the major digital libraries and publisher websites. The findings show the importance of the smart government's technology-assisted (electronic government, management of the economy, open data, civil works, tourism, management of the disasters, healthcare systems, and others). This chapter aims to determine how smart government components improve the activities in a city of the citizens and government officials. This paper also presents a survey of the characteristics, taxonomy, smart government indicators, history, and future trends.

DOI: 10.4018/979-8-3693-0373-3.ch003

1. INTRODUCTION

Smart government (a Smart City component) has become a popular term around the world (Gil-Garcia et al., 2014). Smart, intelligent or e-government is characterised by the adoption of information and communication technologies in conjunction with strategic management as a tool to achieve better government (Rivera Urrutia, 2006; OECD, 2003a).

One of the trends to overcome smart governance challenges is the design and implementation of business architectures as the cutting edge practice to provide better services in government offices. (Maestre & Nieto, 2017). In recent years, governments in different parts of the world have adopted technology and implemented strategies for Electronic Government and Digital Government, producing different types of innovations and achieving different types of impact on their organisations and citizens' quality of life (Esévez &Twjanowski, 2015).

This paper aims to determine how smart government components improve or not the citizens' activities and government officials in a city. This paper presents a survey of the characteristics, taxonomy, smart government indicators, history and future trends. Section 2 presents Smart Government and future trends, and the last section presents the conclusions.

2. SMART GOVERNMENT AND FUTURE TRENDS

The smart government is an electronic government organised around the management and use of information (Coates, 2001; Alcock and Lenihan, 2001).

Additionally in this paper, we define the smart government as the electronic government with open data that optimised the budget (smart management of the economy of the city, or smart economics, and the relationship between government and enterprises) for civil works (smart infrastructure) and priority services for the well-being of citizens; and the smart government must consider smart disasters and smart tourism. In other words, the smart government is the process of optimally managing human resources, economic and technology from government institutions.

We also consider the Smart Government as the influence of diverse technologies (Combinatorial Optimization, Machine Learning, Big Data, data visualisation, Internet of Government Things, Big-Data Analytics, and others) to enhance the service quality of government-objects.

The Technology Components of Smart Government are (Figure 1):

- Internet of Government Things (IoGT). The IoGT is a digital interconnect of not computational and computational government objects using sensors and RFID technology with the Internet.
- Smart economics. Establish the policy of prices, and with the help and participation of local authorities, monitor their compliance, particularly in what refers to items of consumption and widespread usage, and set rates for the provision of those services in the public interest. Regular, guide and stimulate consumer protection measures. Standard and register the property industrial and commercial and regular and direct foreign investment and technology transfer. Establish and monitor standards of quality, weights and measures necessary for commercial activity and standards and industrial specifications, among other functions. Set budget to the other department of the government.

- Smart open government. The smart open government engages in a constant conversation with citizens to hear what they say and requested, taking decisions based on their needs and preferences, which facilitates the collaboration of citizens and officials in the development of services that provides and communicates all that decides and makes open and transparent collaboration and participation using diverse technologies.
- Smart infrastructure. Smart infrastructure manages, communicates, and integrates different types of intelligent infrastructure such as energy grids, transport networks, water and waste management systems, and telecommunications.
- Smart disasters. Smart disasters optimise human resources to address disaster impact assessments, prevention and mitigation investment planning, shelter location, evacuation planning, relief delivery, casualty transportation, stakeholder coordination, recovery operations, refugee camp location, coordination and management, refugee resettlement, big data for disaster management, disaster information systems, resilient land use and agriculture, epidemics control and supply chain management.
- Smart Tourism (e-tourism). Smart tourism is the innovation and the adoption of information and communication technologies in tourism (Buhalis, 2003). Smart tourism considers natural attractions, culture, accessibility of transportation, amenities characteristics, ancillary services, and professional sports infrastructure.
- E-Government. E-government is a form of relationship of the state with its citizens, businesses and other organisations. It consists of e-administration (International trade, online justice online, electronic democracy, virtual parliament, electronic voting, tax administration and e-procurement, among others) and e-management (the Internet application, information technologies and telecommunications in the areas, activities and processes of the state).
- Data Science. The Smart Government uses Big-Data analytics to make a policy decision based on the information government (Crime prevention and investigations, Traffic and pollution, Healthcare, Tourism, and other public services).
- Smart Government Policy. The Smart Government Policy are public policies by the governments that have sustainability and adaptability, and the constitutional, legal, and practical limitations of government.

Figure 1. Components of the smart government

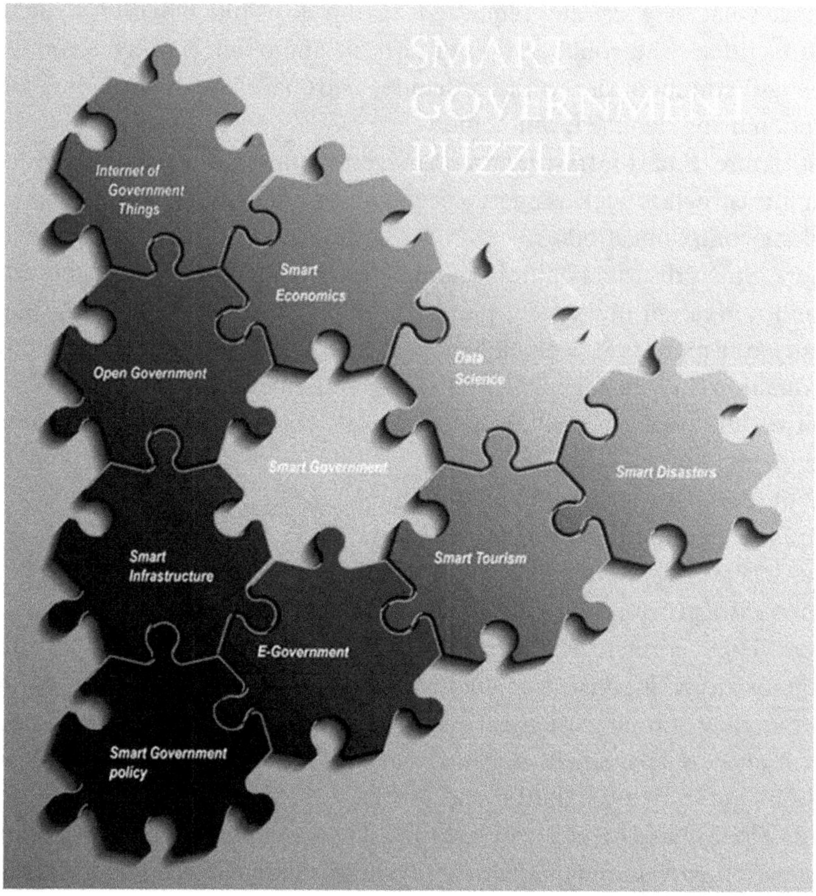

The Government-objects could be:

- For all the citizens: Police patrol, fire truck, the box of votes, control traffic lights, surveillance cameras, bicycles, public transportation, registration of motorists, potable water, public parking, bridges, railway tracks, cameras urban, monitors the proper functioning of its structures as well as more flexibly adapt their operation to new events. Environmental or situational prevention, actions aimed at reducing crime opportunities (administrative criminology), creating beautiful, clean surroundings, illuminated (it has been confirmed that the environment is one of the factors that most affect the feeling of insecurity). Neighbourhood watch. Some cinemas, theatres. End of poverty; zero hunger; health and welfare; quality education; gender equality; clean water and sanitation; affordable energy and pollution; decent work and economic growth; industry, innovation and infrastructure; reduction of inequalities; cities and sustainable communities; production and responsible consumption; climate action; underwater life, and others.
- For the elderly population: Banks are more resistant and durable in public areas, such as bus stops, and hospitals, focusing primarily on the areas with a higher concentration of the elderly population. Traffic lights with countdown clocks and increased the time of crossing for pedestrians. In

the metro signs with larger font sizes, older persons did not have difficulties reading them. Each train stop is less than a 10-minute walk from anywhere in the nursing home. Stops of public transportation, close to all clinics and other similar services. The elderly travelling by bus can ask the driver to stop where want to within the residential areas. Social prevention, actions, or policies (educational, cultural, urban) aimed at improving an area's quality of life. Agreements with the city gyms so announced discounts on registration and free fitness classes for seniors. Establishment of timetables for seniors in the pools. Courses are affordable and accessible for seniors in the universities so that the elders enjoy ongoing training and learning. Campaigns to combat discrimination by age at work.

Smart Government in a Smart City has three general kinds of problems and ways to resolve them:

- Government-Hard problems. The government-hard problems can be optimised (from Combinatorial Optimization: maximisation or minimisation) of the government's resources. The Smart Government-Hard Problems in the management of the Government with Technology to optimise or monitor in real-time by the Internet of Thing Technology the physical infrastructure, aspects related to government institutions.
- Government-Soft problems. The government-soft problems are a fuzzy concept used to drive specific government agendas and others. The Smart Government-Soft Problems are the government problems that handle information inaccurate or incomplete, with uncertainty and ambiguity, volatile, poorly understood and dynamics (government public policy, administration, decision-making, government reforms).
- Government-wicked problems. The complex, intractable, open-ended and wicked government problems are a problem that is difficult or impossible to solve because it presents incomplete, contradictory and changing requirements that are generally difficult to recognise. This problem requires deliberation and debate; for example, the social policy, urban planning, environmental and natural resource policy, child protection policy and service systems, Self-harming unhealthy (drugs, smoking, alcohol, junk food) behaviours, urban transport planning and services, overcoming indigenous disadvantage, policy responses to climate change, and others.

To assess whether a government is smart, it is necessary to use indicators to evaluate the government's services. Table 1 shows the smart government indicators used to determine if the smart city has a Smart Government.

Table 1. Smart government indicators

Indicators of smart government	
Smart economics	Smart decision/participation in decision-making, smart services / public and social services.
Smart open government (transparent government)	Open government information is available to the citizens.
Smart infrastructure	Energy grids, transport network, water and waste management systems and telecommunications, civil works, and priority services (smart security: safe city includes digital security, health security, security infrastructure, personal safety) for the well-being of citizens, cultural facilities and social cohesion.
Smart disasters	Prevention and mitigation investment planning, shelter location, evacuation planning, relief delivery, casualty transportation, stakeholders' coordination, recovery operations, refugee camp location, coordination and management, refugee resettlement, big data for disaster management, disaster information systems, resilient land use and agriculture, epidemics control supply chain management.
Smart tourism	Total natural attractions, total cultural (music festival) in a year, accessibility of transportation, amenities characteristics, ancillary services (bank, package shipping services, hospitals), an innovative hub for electrical vehicles with app mobile to check all the availability status of the vehicle´s charging cars, the infrastructure of professional sports.
E-government	International trade, justice online, tax administration, E-procurement, electronics democracy, virtual parliament, electronic voting, take decisions and the online consultations of aspects of the government, application of the technologies of information and communication (ICT) to provide information and improve the provision of public services, Happiness Meter of citizenships.

3. SURVEY METHODOLOGY

For collecting the relevant literature published in the years (2001-2023), the authors searched and browsed Google Scholar, Springer, Science Direct and Web of science. We try different search queries including "e-government", "Smart Government", "Technology for government", "Smart Economy", "Smart Tourism", "Smart Healthcare", among others related to technology applied to the government. If deemed relevant, then the paper's full text was downloaded to apply our eligibility criteria, and the manual inspections of the references list of the selected papers to identify other related papers.

Our eligibility criteria consider research publications that:

- Enhance the use of the technology to the government, for example, Geographical information system, sensor networks, information and communication technologies, and others.
- Mathematical Models or Combinatorial Optimization applied to government problems.
- Smart decision/participation in decision-making, smart service/public and social services.
- Smart services of waste management, intelligent public transportation, sustainable government buildings, smart lighting, data and green government economy, and so on.
- Prevention and mitigation investment planning, shelter location, evacuation planning, relief delivery, casualty transportation, stakeholders' coordination, recovery operations, refugee camp location, coordination and management, refugee resettlement, big data for disaster management, disaster information systems, resilient land use and agriculture, epidemics control supply chain management.

- Total natural attractions, total cultural, accessibility of transportation, amenity characteristics, ancillary services, an innovative hub for electrical vehicles with app mobile to check all the availability status of the vehicle´s charging cars, the infrastructure of professional sports.
- Smart open data and Open government information are available to the citizens.
- Energy grids, transport networks, water and waste management systems and telecommunications, civil works, and priority services for the well-being of citizens.

We adopted the PRISMA checklist (Moher et al., 2009) from the search to the papers' final selection to include in the literature review. The results obtained from the search, are included in the identification of research trends and future research opportunities.

4. SUMMARY OF KEY OBSERVATIONS

4.1. Technology to Government Objects

Vlacheas et al. (2003) mentioned the integration of the Internet of Things to support the sustainable development of smart cities. The proposal is based on identifying the main issues of IoT (cognitive management framework) as a crucial role in smart government. The framework is focused on the 4th axes: Plan the heterogeneity of connected objects, ensure resilience, instruct systems to assess proximity, and use cognitive technologies. The proposal introduced 3 application domains: smart health, public safety and smart transport. In this case, the Virtual Object in the medical centre can be presented as the health's monitoring and the environmental conditions; in police departments for traffic jam monitoring and smart vehicles for smart transportation on the city streets.

Ji and Anwen (2010) presented the concept of sensing China based on IoT as China's national strategy. The IoT application at China government starts from the city security and emergency management applications, where the pilot projects are focused on the Emergency Management Systems.

Washburn and Sindhu (2010) proposed the definition of a smart city as a collection of Smart Computing technologies oriented to improve the critical infrastructure components and services. The authors mentioned the main areas to be improving in smart cities: City administration (Streamlinemanagement), Smart Education (Increase access, improve quality, and reduce costs), Healthcare(Increase the availability and provide more rapid, accurate diagnosis), Public safety (use real-time information to respond rapidly to emergencies and threats), real estate (Reduce operating costs, increase the value, and improve occupancy rates), transportation (Reduce traffic congestion while encouraging the use of public transportation), utilities (deliver only as much energy or water as is required while reducing waste).

Bueermann (2012) mentioned the need for police officials to shift to the science of controlling crime. According to criminologist Lawrence Sherman, that model is called evidence-based policing, and it represents the field's most powerful force for change. The police officials can implement Evidence-based policing, implement and evaluate proactive crime-fighting strategies.

AlAwadhi and Scholl (2013) documented the Smart City initiatives in Seattle local government oriented to make the greater urban space.

Barone et al. (2014) proposed research-oriented Parking as an expensive resource and limited availability in urban traffic congestion. This problem can be presented as managing public parking spots. In this proposal, the authors mentioned that industrial automation progresses based on: wireless networks, sensor communication, smart devices and financial transactions in mobile payment.

Mohammed et al. (2014) oriented the research to the applications of Unmanned Aerial Vehicles (UAVs) in smart cities. UAV applications in smart cities like environmental hazards monitoring, traffic management, and pollution monitoring are oriented to contribute the smart cities' development. In this paper, the authors presented a review of the opportunities and challenges of UAVs.

Djahel et al. (2015) mentioned the need to optimise people's mobility, resulting in many challenges for road traffic management, accidents management, and air pollution. The authors presented a review of up-to-date technologies related to Traffic Management Systems and the potential of smart cars and social media to optimise traffic congestion detection and mitigation.

Celani, Sperling and Juarez (2015) mentioned the Internet as the base of communication and promotor of social, technological and economic changes. The IoT base on several developments is a big data collector, where this information can benefit government services. IoT application can be seen in the Operation Center of Rio de Janeiro building as a monitor of flood and rain problems. The data can support a lot of government agencies like civil defence, security forces, police departments, fireman departments, transit departments, urban cleaning, and so on. The proposal is focused on sharing in real-time the data and images between these agencies share. The Operation Center has access to satellites, land sensors, a special google map to cross the information, meteorology sensors, etc. Detecta is a software based on the Security Program Digital Awareness System developed by Microsoft and New York Police Department; this system can identify thousands of crime patterns and track suspects, read a car"s license plate, image algorithms to search suspects, and so on. The smart meter (water, energy and gas) is another government management system to optimise this kind of energy.

Gharaibeh et al. (2017) mentioned the smart city as integrating embedded devices and heterogeneous systems. The proposal survey is focused on a data-centric perspective (security, interoperability, reusability, consistency and granularity) and the data management techniques.

4.2. Hard, Soft, and Wicked Government Problems

There are several works on Government-hard problems: For example, Municipal waste problem transportation, Medical waste medical transport, Municipal Water Networks, Municipal Wastewater, and others.

Sharholy et al. (2008) described Municipal Solid Waste Management (MSWM) as the major environmental problem of Indian cities. They provide a comprehensive review of the characteristics, generation, collection and transportation, disposal and treatment technologies of MSWM practised in India.

Zhang et al. (2010) overview the problem of Municipal Solid Waste (MSW) generation and composition in China by analysing the existing problems related to MSW: collection, separation, recycling and disposal.

Cheng and Hu (2010) analysed the problem of Municipal Solid Waste in China and proposed a solution based on Waste-to-energy incineration, where the aim is to recover the energy from discarded Municipal Solid Waste and produces electricity and steam for heating.

Tabasová et al. (2012) review the thermal treatment methods for waste-to-energy, their performance, and environmental impact. The research is oriented to analyse the waste treatments and legislation by the European Communities.

Daelman et al. (2012) focused their research on analysing the use of methane as a greenhouse gas. The methane gas generated by the treatment plants can achieve sustainable urban water management.

This research study uses methane emission from fullscale municipal wastewater facilities with sludge digestion into the greenhouse.

Marshall and Farahbakhsh (2013) mention Solid Waste Management (SWM) issues and the correlation with health and environmental pollution. The authors make a review of the practices, policies and the relation to climate change and health.

Lotti et al. (2014) proposed to remove the Autotrophic nitrogen from municipal wastewater to develop energy autarkic wastewater treatment plants. The authors evaluate the anammox process in a granular sludge fluidised bed lab-scale reactor.

Jouhara et al. (2017) reviewed the available waste management systems for households. In this research, the authors analyse the Biological methods and physicochemical methods related to the householder's waste usage.

Malinauskaite et al. (2017) reviewed the municipal waste management systems and wasted energy in the context of the circular economy in Europe. The authors proposed the use of waste as a source of energy. The proposal is based on the Waste-to-energy with incineration. In this case, the authors considered the conversion of waste into energy as the main key to a circular economy.

Several works on Government-soft problems: Soft System Methodology can address problems related to stench or property titration systems and the situation under which these systems are used (Barry and Fourie, 2002). Soft Systems Methodology solves wicked problems in managing construction projects (Maqsood, Finegan, & Walker, 2003). Soft and hard methodologies are applied for strategic planning problems of information systems in the Australian public sector (Pollack, 2009).

Martin and Guarneros-Meza (2013) discuss the types of local public service associations that are self-governing to address public policy issues and the government's external influence as a means of support or as an obstacle. Soft leadership is essential for establishing and mobilising partnerships.

Gharehgozli, Mileski, Adams, & von Zharen (2017) propose a framework related to the ports' resilience that supports managers to carry out their operations before adverse weather factors.

Intuitive logic methods with soft OR methods are analysed and used for planning IL scenarios that support strategic decision-making. Six desirable attributes were identified with a basic IL scenario method proposal (Wright, Cairns, O'Brien, & Goodwin, 2019)

de Abreu & de Andrade (2019) developed a framework based on public, collaborative and adaptive governance approaches to solving problems in ecological partner systems affected by industrial disasters. The model is circularly represented by transitions that show that long-term recovery requires time and resources.

Tzezana (2017) develops a framework for studying possible futures of crimes and terrorist attacks that depend on IoT. This, presents its possible motives, methods and objectives, with these elements presenting real scenarios that allow anticipating possible crimes or attacks.

There are several works on Government-wicked problems: Head (2008) sketches some key aspects of wicked problems, and illustrates the discussion with two contemporary Australian examples – recent attempts to address the causes and possible solutions to Indigenous disadvantage; and policy responses to climate change.

Mileski, Clott, and Galvao (2018) address the "wicked problem" of maritime cybersecurity breaches by trying to identify any inconsistencies in two AIS receiver systems used by ships through a unique methodology known as "Ask, JOAN." JOAN is the acronym for Joint Operational Authenticity Network. A wicked problem is one where the planning for adverse events such as a security breach is impossible to solve because of incomplete, contradictory, and changing requirements that are often difficult to recognise (Mileski, Clott, and Galvao, 2018).

4.3. Smart Economics

There are several works on Smart economics (Smart decision/participation in decision-making, smart service/public and social services).

Harsh and Ichalkaranje (2014) proposed e-government as a government using the Internet to improve its decision-making. The emergence of social media, mobile apps, big data analytics and mashup technologies empower citizens to connect their issues with government solutions. In this paper, the authors showed South Australian Government's steps to transform itself into a smart government based on Open data, modern public services, community engagement and co-production, financial investment, automation, collaboration, and governance.

Gil-Garcia et al. (2014) proposed the term smart government as a characterisation of activities to invest in emerging technologies with innovative strategies to agile the government structures and governance infrastructures.

Janowski (2015) mentioned the evolution of digital government divided into a four-stage framework: Digital Government Evolution Model Comprising Digitization (the first stage, where the government adopts private technology gaps to improve the efficiency of public information services), transformation (the second stage consists of interconnect and integrate the agencies to improve the public services and government programs based on digital technologies. In this stage, some technologies have emerged like: business process integration – reengineering, information and services shared, government management, and so on), engagement (the third stage is focused on the use of technology to facilitate citizens exercise their civil and political rights, and the use of social web and the semantic web), contextualisation (in the last stage, the technology is oriented to support the self-governance for local communities and to enable personalised public services through government-to-citizen or even citizen-to-citizen co-production; and stimulating the development of the main sectors based on technology).

Anthopoulos (2017) mentioned that to improve the local information performance, the government need to explore a new infrastructure deployed in the city to enhance its ability to create the smart services of waste management, intelligent public transportation, sustainable government buildings, smart lighting, data and green government economy, and so on. These changes prompted a new role for government and citizens, where the government has to govern the communities with a decreasing amount of resources and new challenges (poverty, climate change, and so on).

Aguilera et al. (2017) considered the smart city framework to use Open Government Data and sensor networks to ease the generation of citizen-centric apps to exploit the data based on the IoT network architecture and an algorithm for Media-based Surveillance System.

Sangki (2018) analysed the social paradigm (information society) shift can be modified by the new Information Technologies, where the main proposal is related to new e-government named as E-Government Maturity Model based on Social-political Development where the levels are based on the social maturity of the e-democracy and the maturity level of civic society with statistic model.

Witanto et al. (2018) mentioned the use of data and information to improve the services provided to the citizen (Smart government). In this case, the authors mentioned the importance of planning the city's events, proposing a city event's prediction with a map-based visualisation using the crowdsourced geodata from the citizen's report.

Lv et al. (2018) exposed the Government affairs service platform based on 3D Geographical Information System (GIS) and cloud computing, where the government services like an urban disaster and environmental protection, intelligent transportation, and others can be optimised.

Kiss and Muha (2018) mentioned some needs for the government's proper operating like complex IT infrastructure versus cyber-attacks. This kind of attack can influence the operations of an organisation. The authors proposed some suggestions and afterwards based on the smart government's security capability to prevent these attacks.

Mechant and Walravens (2018) introduced the thematic e-government and smart cities, where the authors discussed data, governance and participation linked to e-government and smart cities.

Viale-Pereira et al. (2018) reviewed smart governance. The authors aim to provide the basic definitions of smart governance and the concepts like smart and electronic government: Application of emerging information and communication technologies (ICT), Intelligent use of ICT to improve decision-making, social media, complex interactions between governments, citizens and other stakeholders.

4.4 Smart Open Data

Several works on the Smart open data (transparent government) and the Open government information available to the citizens.

Góngora and Nieto Bernal (2015) propose a general model for the management of information technology for a smart Government that considers the technological trends, enterprise architecture, collaboration and technology management services. The use of open data is linked and good use, allowing Governments and people management simple and clean data in the city for later use (Emaldi, Pena, Lazaro, and Lopez-de-Ipina, 2015). Through open data available in the network of smart cities Spanish tourism-related information is obtained to raise policy better and make this activity more attractive (Celdran-Bernabeu, Mazon, and Sanchez, 2018). Citizen participation is a key element in the use and effect of open data in smart cities of municipalities in Canada (HivonandTitah, 2017).

Dong et al. (2017) comment on the availability of open data and the problems posed by seven cities in Canada regarding the data that the Council considers are essential to citizens, as well as the development of applications and tools by citizens or companies that support the access to these data. Urbansense is a tool to make connections between citizens and Governments, so they use open data is easy and free by creating various services and products for the Government (Gagliardi et al., 2017).

4.5. Smart Infrastructure

There are several works on the Smart infrastructure (Energy grids, transport network, water and waste management systems and telecommunications, civil works, and priority services for citizens' well-being).

Wickramasuriya, Ma, Berryman, and Perez (2013) mentioned that one of the problems that arise in Australia is the missing interconnection of networks of public and private infrastructure, the use of SMART Infrastructure Dashboard can help solve this problem.

Edmondson et al. (2018) propose to use various sensors placed in the UK sewer network allows the monitoring and prediction in real-time from possible flooding.

In (Naik et al., 2019), it was shown a smart public transportation network where electric buses were used for mass transportation in Guwahati, India. Algorithm-based controllers were used to regulate the power of the buses. In the stations it was used fuzzy logic with the same application, the study was simulated for all seasons of the year in different circumstances and the main idea was to expand electrified transportation. With the control of the buses, the electric energy must be reduced in its consumption and with a solar plant and a model about irradiation according to the season of the year, more energy can be saved. This proposition seems to be a benefit for the ordinary citizen, and it is sustainable.

Similar work was presented by Lin et al. (2019), who did a location-based service, it is a topic that has obtained more attention with the Internet of things, and the main idea was to report driver's location to avoid traffic jams in smart transportation. For information security, they proposed homomorphic encryption and a signature. In this work, it was used the location without loss of privacy and also fuel can be saved with this application, it was developed for smartphones with Android, and the information is in the cloud. Thus the cloud centre gives information about driver's locations, road conditions, and traffic jam events.

4.6. Smart Disasters

There are several works on smart disasters (Prevention and mitigation investment planning, shelter location, evacuation planning, relief delivery, casualty transportation, stakeholders' coordination, recovery operations, refugee camp location, coordination and management, refugee resettlement, big data for disaster management, disaster information systems, resilient land use and agriculture, epidemics control supply chain management).

The smart systems are also used for smart hospitals, (Thakare and Khire, 2014) where various kinds of sensors and smartphones are used in a network communication as a service for the user in a hospital. The paper mentioned above analyses the information system to find areas of opportunity. This application was possible thanks to the wireless sensors, they are connected to a central unit, and the users can access the information with smartphones or tablets, thus different events can be monitored from a remote location, for example in need of certain kind of blood and according to the priority, the bank blood can take action immediately and precisely.

For example, for smart cities development, the planning projects are very important, an interesting application in a Swedish city was presented by Axelsson and Granath (2018), they developed a framework to take into consideration the stakeholders and the dimensions for urban construction regarding the consequences and the complexity of the city development, an interesting case of study is the use of stakeholder theory with the smartness dimension to identify the stakeholder's involvement in the city's projects.

Ragini et al. (2018) analysed the information from social media to measure customer satisfaction, and this result can be extrapolated for the disaster response due social media give many emergency responses in case of disaster, this information needs to be processed to have a decision for being useful. To classify the disaster, they used machine learning, in this case, SVM. It is important for rescue personnel and government actions. The information on social media was obtained from Twitter, and text processing was used to classify as positive or negative. The tweets were analysed for the SVM to feed the sentiment strength in each sentence. Finally, the needs of the people can be obtained from big data processing.

The crowdsourced social media was presented by Ogie et al. (2019), their application was for flood mapping, this article shows the results of the project PetaJakarta applied for three years, this project takes into consideration the authorities of Jakarta and the errors of the crowdsourced flood maps were minimised, and the project will be used in other Indonesian cities as Surabaya, Bandung and Semarang.

4.7. Smart Tourism

There are several works on smart tourism (Total natural attractions, total cultural (music festival) in a year, accessibility of transportation, amenity characteristics, ancillary services (bank, package shipping services, hospitals), an innovative hub for electrical vehicles with app mobile to check all the availability status of the vehicle´s charging cars, the infrastructure of professional sports).

For example, Varfolomeyev et al. (2015) used historical data to promote historical and cultural tourism by recommending trips, events and services. This contribution was made in multi-agents to process the integrated information into an ontology that can be updated continuously.

Wang et al. (2016) explored a methodological approach for the smart tourism attraction, they used the factor analysis for the evaluation about smart tourism and then with fuzzy logic the classification of this evaluation was made, finally by using analytic hierarchy was applied for the case of the Hongshan Zoo an attraction in China, a limitation in this paper was the sample used in the study because they were used 400 interviews and more of them were with people around 60 years old.

Another example is shown by Sikora-Fernandez (2018). It was noted the development of urban areas in Poland. Now the question is to know if the urbanisation can be named a smart city, even to what degree the city can be considered smart. One point to be bear is the communication and information technology present in the city, it is mentioned that only "dressing" the city of technology is not enough, it is important the quality of life, for example, the smart environment was not possible to describe entirely because of the lack of stations to measure the smog levels, and the existence of public administration for applications online payments is only one point. However, the cities also need smart transportation where online payment and smart environment can be reached.

4.8. E-Government

Jeong (2006) stresses the importance of e-government by referring to the transformation process to reach the information society and in the same way describes that predicting the course of technology not only allows setting objectives and direction for technological development, but also for generating medium and long term plans for IT applications such as e-government.

It should be mentioned that public officials currently have a more significant number of capacities to carry out projection and organisation tasks since they have the information of external agents that interact with public administrations in real-time allowing them guarantees of increasingly reduced costs (Dunleavy, Margetts, Bastow, and Tinkler, 2006).

The use of information and communication technologies shows a complex process in public administrations at the time they are adopted and applied as they were issues that were not taken into account or not considered at the time of applying the e-government, due to efficiency, productivity and effectiveness in adopting technologies within public administrations (García and Helbig, 2006).

For the OCDE cited in (CEPAL, 2010) which says in its letter: electronic government, is the use of Information and Telecommunications Technologies, particularly the Internet, as a tool to achieve good governance. The above, to manage government procedures, deliver transparency and accountability, and citizen participation.

The remarkable thing is that the evidence mentioned the support that the coordination between public dependencies has a margin of improvement using the organisations' true technological immersion.

Public policies are updated and transformed by using information and communication technologies, in their different classes, faces and environments. (Purón-Cid and Gil-García, 2012).

E-government is already a priority of public administrations to improve administrative intelligence in the design of public policies. It should be clear that the repercussions or benefits of e-government are not the exclusive use of information and communication technologies. The e-government also involves a political and organisational construction that requires various factors (García, 2012).

E-government is essential to generate benefits in public administrations due to information and communication technologies in different sectors of public action. As an example, one can cite the interoperability between intergovernmental relations that have revealed the different opportunities generated by the implementation of e-government that has allowed a better exchange of information data between different government agencies (Gascó, 2005). This allows generating several certain public services through interoperable platforms to provide better collaboration between the agents included in the process, this yields that better services for citizens are generated as defined (Luna-Reyes, 2013).

As part of the seventeen objectives set out in the 2030 agenda for sustainable development published by the United Nations Organization in 2015, objective 16 explicitly states. Among its goals is creating at all levels of active and transparent institutions that are accountable and expand and strengthen the participation of developing countries in global governance institutions (ONU, 2015).

In the results of the 2018 electronic government survey published by the United Nations, the electronic government development index of the member states is established (It is a weighted average of standardised scores in the three most important dimensions of electronic government). The three main ones are Denmark, Australia and the Republic of Korea, hence the United Kingdom, Sweden, Finland, Singapore, New Zealand, France and finally Japan (UNITED NATIONS, 2018).

4.9. Technology's Challenge on Smart Cities

There are several technological challenges to applying Smart Government in Smart Cities correctly. The author Eynon (2007) mentions obstacles to improving European Public Services: Economic and financial barriers (cost of the development of e-services, cost of the provision of services in multiple channels, costs of implementing laws and regulations related to e-government, difficulty of demonstrating the long-term benefits), Barriers to access and use of new technologies (low level of access to new technologies, ability to manage citizens' ICTs, ability to manage ICT by officials, concern regarding information privacy, concern about the security of online services, Lack of motivation to use electronic services), Ethnic design barriers (multilinguals, access mechanisms for non-seers and persons with other disabilities, difficulty use of e-government applications, lack of secure identification and authentication mechanisms, no standards for identification electronics, lack of interoperability of systems), legal barriers (differences in laws and regulations at the national level, inadequate freedom of information policies, public concern about public-private collaboration, employment laws that limit the creation of e-jobs, unclear regulations on protection and shared access to information22Lack of citizens' rights to communicate electronically with public authorities, limitations concerning intellectual property and the re-use of information, risks associated with the legal responsibility), Organisational and administrative barriers (differences in administrative traditions and internal processes to the public sector, resistance to change by government officials, coordination between national, regional and local levels, lack of political support for e-government).

GEALC NETWORK (2008) in the collection of working documents on e-government called "From theory to practice: how to successfully implement electronic government", lists the main barriers of e-government, economic and financial, access and use of new technologies, of technical, legal, organisational and administrative design.

Johnston (2010) discussed about the interaction between technology and society to design participation-based governance.

Chourabi et al. (2012) identified the Smart cities' critical factors initiatives, where the technology is part of the main factors.

Townsend (2013) mentioned the challenge of technology and data combined with the actual and new infrastructure, the architecture issues, everyday objects and the incorporation of new objects, and even our bodies to address social, economic, and environmental problems.

Vanolo (2016) mentioned the need for technology usage by citizens in smart cities. In this scenario, the citizens will be subjugated by technologies because they need this leverage.

Dameri and Benevolo (2016) proposed that Smart City Governance is a processual interplay among stakeholders (roles and responsibilities), the support decision systems driven and facilitated by technology and data, and so on, but this challenge needs a certain type of legislation, policies and exchange arrangements.

According to the report (Manyika et al., 2017) 60% of occupations, one third will be able to automate. Hence, 50% of the activities for which people are paid can be automated using technology. Therefore, it is estimated that 30% of the hours worked may be automated by 2030. However, the impact of automation depends on three factors: income level, demography and industry structure. Within the sectors threatened by automation in Spain, education is the least affected, in which it can end 24% of the occupation. 37% of professionals, scientists and very technical services, and 39% are medical services, social assistance, art and entertainment. (Nieves, 2017)

Perveen et al. (2017) mentioned the urban growth of technology usage in smart cities as a negative impact on the society and the environment like the greenhouse gas (GHG) emissions (e.g. Carbon dioxide), the increase of global warming (Yigitcanlar and Dizdaroglu, 2015) and the climate change with negative implications on health (Deilami et al., 2018).

Ruhlandt (2018) mentioned the lack of research about the smart cities components like stakeholders, processes and technology & data. The Smart City concept's substantial potential can be predicted, but the implementation requires strategic and technical challenges, which made it difficult for cities to capture the promising benefits. There are many factors to affect Smart Cities e.g. technological factors, etc. (Bolivar & Meijer, 2016).

Praharaj, Han, and Hawken (2018) mentioned the lack of appropriation of arrangements for the governance, where this situation can be seen as the most serious obstacle for their effective transformation into being smart. Coupled with this problem, the technology-driven developments affect the cities, because there is an irrespective investment in incorporating the Smart City concept into their governance agenda (Cosgrave et al., 2014). Smart Cities' basis is the technology and data, but their implementation deals with the usage of new technologies to support or enable particular activities.

Fernandez-Anez (2018) mentioned some initiatives to respond to challenges facing smart cities. The smart city is based on technology mainly, however, the technology adoption needs a lot of changes in infrastructure, people's perception, and the governance and stakeholders' involvement at the core of strategies. Smart City's challenges about the new technology implementation can differ from stakeholders' opinions and the society.

Lim et al. (2018) mentioned the smart city's key factors are the urban big data usage from stakeholders and physical objects (technology, mainly). The authors mentioned the challenge of data-based smart city transformation with a large-scale initiative for change where the move to a smart city is not easy. This challenge depends on using urban big data and infrastructure implementation.

Randed (2018) points out that according to the United Nations, in 2020 they will have 50 billion devices connected to the Internet, which means it can be a focus of attention for a cyber attack. In these aspects, such as traffic lights or public lighting, power grid, water service, communications, among others.

Camboim et al. (2019) presented the smart city concept as an urban innovation ecosystem based on knowledge flows between stakeholders to create wealth and support a digital (green) infrastructure and a functional urban design. However, if the cities want to become smarter, they should upgrade the techno-economic activity elements.

5. CONCLUSION AND FUTURE TRENDS

This article proposes determining how smart government components improve the activities in a city of the citizens and government officials, the characteristics, taxonomy, indicators and future trends. Smart cities seek to be the cleanest and happiest cities globally by using Artificial Intelligence, autonomous cars, smart living (by excellent public services), and a sense of collective happiness.

However, Green (2019) mentions that Smart cities, where technology is used to solve every problem, are hailed as futuristic urban utopias. Smart cities promised that apps, algorithms, and artificial intelligence would relieve congestion, restore democracy, prevent crime, and improve public services. Green (2019) describes a smart city as a livable city, a democratic city, a just city, a responsible city, and an innovative city, in other words, the technology into a holistic vision of justice and equity.

Then, the smart cities in the future should consider the positives of the use of technologies in smart cities. The problems arising from the overuse of technology should also be considered. Chronic diseases derived from the use of technology, ethics in the development of service robotics (who is to blame for a programming error in e.g. service medical robots?), the percentage of determination of the probability of death in a self-driving car accident, pollution by discarded E-waste devices, elimination of jobs by the use of service robots, among others.

REFERENCES

Aguilera, U., Peña, O., Belmonte, O., & López-de-Ipiña, D. (2017). Citizen-centric data services for smarter cities. *Future Generation Computer Systems*, *76*, 234–247. doi:10.1016/j.future.2016.10.031

AlAwadhi, S., & Scholl, H. J. (2013, January). Aspirations and realisations: The smart city of Seattle. In *2013 46th Hawaii international conference on system sciences* (pp. 1695-1703). IEEE.

Anthopoulos, L. G. (2017). *Understanding Smart Cities: A Tool for Smart Government or an Industrial Trick?* (Vol. 22). Springer. doi:10.1007/978-3-319-57015-0

Axelsson, K., & Granath, M. (2018). Stakeholder's stake and relation to smartness in smart city development: Insights from Swedish city planning project. *Government Information Quarterly*, *35*(4), 693–702. doi:10.1016/j.giq.2018.09.001

Barone, R. E., Giuffrè, T., Siniscalchi, S. M., Morgano, M. A., & Tesoriere, G. (2013). Architecture for parking management in smart cities. *IET Intelligent Transport Systems*, *8*(5), 445–452. doi:10.1049/iet-its.2013.0045

Barry, M., & Fourie, C. (2002). Wicked problems, soft systems and cadastral systems in periods of uncertainty: South African experience. *Survey Review*, *36*(285), 483–496. doi:10.1179re.2002.36.285.483

Bolívar, M. P. R., & Meijer, A. J. (2016). Smart governance: Using a literature review and empirical analysis to build a research model. *Social Science Computer Review*, *34*(6), 673–692. doi:10.1177/0894439315611088

Bueermann, J. (2012). Being smart on crime with evidence-based policing. *NIJ Journal*, *269*, 12–15.

Camboim, G. F., Zawislak, P. A., & Pufal, N. A. (2019). Driving elements to make cities smarter: Evidences from European projects. *Technological Forecasting and Social Change*, *142*, 154–167. doi:10.1016/j.techfore.2018.09.014

Celani, G., Sperling, D. M., & Franco, J. M. S. (Eds.). (2015). Computer-Aided Architectural Design: The Next City–New Technologies and the Future of the Built Environment. *16th International Conference, CAAD Futures 2015, São Paulo, Brazil, July 8-10, 2015. Selected Papers* (*Vol. 527*). Springer.

Celdran-Bernabeu, M. A., Mazon, J. N., & Sanchez, D. G. (2018). Open Data and tourism. Implications for tourism management in Smart Cities and Smart Tourism Destinations. *Investigaciones Turísticas*, (15), 49–78. doi:10.14198/INTURI2018.15.03

CEPAL. (2010). *Gobierno electrónico: indicadores. Comisión Económica para América Latina y el Caribe (CEPAL)*. Instituto Latinoamericano y del Caribe de Planificación Económica y Social (ILPES). https://www.cepal.org/ilpes/noticias/paginas/0/40660/alejandra_naser_INDICADORES.pdf

Cheng, H., & Hu, Y. (2010). Municipal solid waste (MSW) as a renewable source of energy: Current and future practices in China. *Bioresource Technology*, *101*(11), 3816–3824. doi:10.1016/j.biortech.2010.01.040 PMID:20137912

Chourabi, H., Nam, T., Walker, S., Gil-Garcia, J. R., Mellouli, S., Nahon, K., Pardo, T. A., & Scholl, H. J. (2012, January). Understanding smart cities: An integrative framework. In *2012 45th Hawaii international conference on system sciences* (pp. 2289-2297). IEEE.

Cosgrave, E., Doody, L., & Walt, N. (2014). Delivering the smart city–governing cities in the digital age. *Arup, Liveable Cities, UCL, Smart City Expo, London*.

Daelman, M. R., van Voorthuizen, E. M., van Dongen, U. G., Volcke, E. I., & van Loosdrecht, M. C. (2012). Methane emission during municipal wastewater treatment. *Water Research*, *46*(11), 3657–3670. doi:10.1016/j.watres.2012.04.024 PMID:22575155

Dameri, R. P., & Benevolo, C. (2016). Governing smart cities: An empirical analysis. *Social Science Computer Review*, *34*(6), 693–707. doi:10.1177/0894439315611093 de Abreu, M. C. S., & de Andrade, R. D. J. C. (2019). Dealing with wicked problems in socio-ecological systems affected by industrial disasters: A framework for collaborative and adaptive governance. *The Science of the Total Environment*, *694*, 133700. doi:10.1016/j.scitotenv.2019.133700 PMID:31398643

Djahel, S., Doolan, R., Muntean, G. M., & Murphy, J. (2014). A communications-oriented perspective on traffic management systems for smart cities: Challenges and innovative approaches. *IEEE Communications Surveys and Tutorials*, *17*(1), 125–151. doi:10.1109/COMST.2014.2339817

Dong, H., Singh, G., Attri, A., & Saddik, A. E. (2017). Open Data-Set of Seven Canadian Cities. *IEEE Access : Practical Innovations, Open Solutions*, *5*, 529–543. doi:10.1109/ACCESS.2016.2645658

Dunleavy, P., Margetts, H., Tinkler, J., & Bastow, S. (2006). *Digital era governance: IT corporations, the state, and e-government*. Oxford University Press. doi:10.1093/acprof:oso/9780199296194.001.0001

Edmondson, V., Cerny, M., Lim, M., Gledson, B., Lockley, S., & Woodward, J. (2018). A smart sewer asset information model to enable an 'Internet of Things' for operational wastewater management. *Automation in Construction*, *91*, 193–205. doi:10.1016/j.autcon.2018.03.003

Emaldi, M., Pena, O., Lazaro, J., & Lopez-de-Ipina, D. (2015). Linked Open Data as the Fuel for Smarter Cities. In F. Xhafa, L. Barolli, A. Barolli, & P. Papajorgji (Eds.), *Modeling and Processing for Next-Generation Big-Data Technologies: With Applications and Case Studies* (Vol. 4, pp. 443–472). Springer Int Publishing Ag. doi:10.1007/978-3-319-09177-8_18

Estévez, E.C., and Janowski, T. (2016). Gobierno digital, ciudadanos y ciudades inteligentes. *Bit & Byte, 2*.

Eynon, R. (2007). Breaking Barriers to eGovernment: Overcoming obstacles to improving European public services. DG Information Society and Media. European Commission.

Fernandez-Anez, V., Fernández-Güell, J. M., & Giffinger, R. (2018). Smart City implementation and discourses: An integrated conceptual model. The case of Vienna. *Cities (London, England)*, *78*, 4–16. doi:10.1016/j.cities.2017.12.004

Gagliardi, D., Schina, L., Sarcinella, M. L., Mangialardi, G., Niglia, F., & Corallo, A. (2017). Information and communication technologies and public participation: Interactive maps and value added for citizens. *Government Information Quarterly*, *34*(1), 153–166. doi:10.1016/j.giq.2016.09.002

Gascó, M. (2005). Exploring the e-government gap in South America. *International Journal of Public Administration*, *28*(7-8), 683–701. doi:10.1081/PAD-200064235

Gharaibeh, A., Salahuddin, M. A., Hussini, S. J., Khreishah, A., Khalil, I., Guizani, M., & Al-Fuqaha, A. (2017). Smart cities: A survey on data management, security, and enabling technologies. *IEEE Communications Surveys and Tutorials*, *19*(4), 2456–2501. doi:10.1109/COMST.2017.2736886

Gharehgozli, A. H., Mileski, J., Adams, A., & von Zharen, W. (2017). Evaluating a "wicked problem": A conceptual framework on seaport resiliency in the event of weather disruptions. *Technological Forecasting and Social Change*, *121*, 65–75. doi:10.1016/j.techfore.2016.11.006

Gil-García, J. R. (2007). Exploring e-government benefits and success factors. In *Encyclopedia of digital government* (pp. 803–811). IGI Global. doi:10.4018/978-1-59140-789-8.ch122

Gil-Garcia, J. R. (2012). *Enacting electronic government success: An integrative study of government-wide websites, organisational capabilities, and institutions* (Vol. 31). Springer Science & Business Media. doi:10.1007/978-1-4614-2015-6

Gil-Garcia, J. R., Helbig, N., & Ojo, A. (2014). Being smart: Emerging technologies and innovation in the public sector. *Government Information Quarterly*, *31*, I1–I8. doi:10.1016/j.giq.2014.09.001

Góngora, G. P., & Nieto Bernal, W. (2015). Factores Clave en la Gestión de Tecnología de Información para Sistemas de Gobierno Inteligente. *Journal of Technology Management & Innovation*, *10*(4), 109–117. doi:10.4067/S0718-27242015000400012

Góngora, G. P. M., & Bernal, W. N. (2017). Gestión de tecnología de información para gobiernos inteligentes: Un enfoque de arquitectura empresarial. *Gestion*, *38*(42), 14–24.

Grande, J. I. C. (2016). Las administraciones públicas en la era del gobierno abierto. Gobernanza inteligente para un cambio de paradigma en la gestión pública. *Revista de Estudios Políticos*, (173), 245–275.

Green, B. (2019). *The Smart Enough City: Putting Technology in Its Place to Reclaim Our Urban Future*. MIT Press. doi:10.7551/mitpress/11555.001.0001

Harsh, A., & Ichalkaranje, N. (2015). Transforming e-government to smart government: A South Australian perspective. In *Intelligent Computing, Communication and Devices* (pp. 9–16). Springer. doi:10.1007/978-81-322-2012-1_2

Head, B. W. (2008). Wicked problems in public policy. *Public Policy*, *3*(2), 101.

Hivon, J., & Tita, R. (2017). Conceptualising citizen participation in open data use at the city level. *Transforming Government: People. Process and Policy*, *11*(1), 99–118. doi:10.1108/TG-12-2015-0053

Janowski, T. (2015). *Digital government evolution: From transformation to contextualisation*.

Jeong, K. H. (2006). *E-government, the road to innovation; Principles and Experiences in Korea*. Gil-Job-E Media.

Ji, Z., & Anwen, Q. (2010, November). The application of Internet of things (IOT) in emergency management system in China. In *2010 IEEE International Conference on Technologies for Homeland Security (HST)* (pp. 139-142). IEEE.

Jimenez, C. E., Solanas, A., & Falcone, F. (2014). E-government interoperability: Linking open and smart government. *Computer*, *47*(10), 22–24. doi:10.1109/MC.2014.281

Johnston, E. (2010). Governance infrastructures in 2020. *Public Administration Review*, *70*(s1), s122–s128. doi:10.1111/j.1540-6210.2010.02254.x

Jouhara, H., Czajczyńska, D., Ghazal, H., Krzyżyńska, R., Anguilano, L., Reynolds, A. J., & Spencer, N. (2017). Municipal waste management systems for domestic use. *Energy*, *139*, 485–506. doi:10.1016/j.energy.2017.07.162

Jouhara, H., Czajczyńska, D., Ghazal, H., Krzyżyńska, R., Anguilano, L., Reynolds, A. J., & Spencer, N. (2017). Municipal waste management systems for domestic use. *Energy*, *139*, 485–506. doi:10.1016/j.energy.2017.07.162

Kiss, M., & Muha, L. (2018). The Cybersecurity Capability Aspects of Smart Government and Industry 4.0 Programmes. *Interdisciplinary Description of Complex Systems: INDECS, 16*(3, 3-A), 313–319. doi:10.7906/indecs.16.3.2

Lim, C., Kim, K. J., & Maglio, P. P. (2018). Smart cities with big data: Reference models, challenges, and considerations. *Cities (London, England), 82*, 86–99. doi:10.1016/j.cities.2018.04.011

Lin, J., Niu, J., Li, H., & Atiquzzaman, M. (2019). A secure and efficient location-based service scheme for smart transportation. *Future Generation Computer Systems, 92*, 694–704. doi:10.1016/j.future.2017.11.030

Lorenzo, S., and César, C. (2010). *Open government: gobiernoabierto*. Jaén, España: AlgónEditrores MMX, 2010.

Lotti, T., Kleerebezem, R., van Erp Taalman Kip, C., Hendrickx, T. L. G., Kruit, J., Hoekstra, M., & van Loosdrecht, M. C. M. (2014). Anammox growth on pretreated municipal wastewater. *Environmental Science & Technology, 48*(14), 7874–7880. doi:10.1021/es500632k PMID:24927034

Luna-Reyes, L. F. (2013). Trust and Collaboration in Interorganizational Information Technology Projects in the Public Sector. *Gestión y Política Pública*, 22.

Lv, Z., Li, X., Wang, W., Zhang, B., Hu, J., & Feng, S. (2018). Government affairs service platform for smart city. *Future Generation Computer Systems, 81*, 443–451. doi:10.1016/j.future.2017.08.047

Malinauskaite, J., Jouhara, H., Czajczyńska, D., Stanchev, P., Katsou, E., Rostkowski, P., Thorne, R. J., Colon, J., Ponsa, S., Al-Mansour, F., Anguilano, L., Krzyzynska, R., Lopez, I. C., Vlasopoulos, A., & Spencer, N. (2017). Municipal solid waste management and waste-to-energy in the context of a circular economy and energy recycling in Europe. *Energy, 141*, 2013–2044. doi:10.1016/j.energy.2017.11.128

Malinauskaite, J., Jouhara, H., Czajczyńska, D., Stanchev, P., Katsou, E., Rostkowski, P., Thorne, R.J., Colón, J., Ponsá, S., Al-Mansour, F., Anguilano, L., Krzyżyńska, R., López, I.C., Vlasopoulos, A., Spencerk, N. (2017). Municipal solid waste management and waste-to-energy in the context of a circular economy and energy recycling in Europe. *energy, 141*, 2013-2044.

Manyika, J., Lund, S., Chui, M., Bughin, J., Woetzel, J., Batra, P., Ko, R., & Sanghvi, S. (2017). *Jobs lost, jobs gained: Workforce transitions in a time of automation*. McKinsey Global Institute. http://hdl.voced.edu.au/10707/444873

Maqsood, T., Finegan, A. D., & Walker, D. H. (2003). A soft approach to solving hard problems in construction project management. Digital Connections. https://digitalcollections. qut. edu. au/1661/.

Marshall, R. E., & Farahbakhsh, K. (2013). Systems approaches to integrated solid waste management in developing countries. *Waste Management (New York, N.Y.), 33*(4), 988–1003. doi:10.1016/j.wasman.2012.12.023 PMID:23360772

Martin, S., & Guarneros-Meza, V. (2013). Governing local partnerships: Does external steering help local agencies address wicked problems? *Policy and Politics, 41*(4), 585–603. doi:10.1332/030557312X655819

Mechant, P., & Walravens, N. (2018). E-Government and Smart Cities: Theoretical Reflections and Case Studies. *Media and Communication*, *6*(4), 119–122. doi:10.17645/mac.v6i4.1848

Memos, V. A., Psannis, K. E., Ishibashi, Y., Kim, B. G., & Gupta, B. B. (2018). An efficient algorithm for media-based surveillance system (EAMSuS) in IoT smart city framework. *Future Generation Computer Systems*, *83*, 619–628. doi:10.1016/j.future.2017.04.039

Mileski, J., Clott, C., & Galvao, C. B. (2018). Cyberattacks on ships: A wicked problem approach. *Maritime Business Review*, *3*(4), 414–430. doi:10.1108/MABR-08-2018-0026

Mohammed, F., Idries, A., Mohamed, N., Al-Jaroodi, J., & Jawhar, I. (2014, May). UAVs for smart cities: Opportunities and challenges. In *2014 International Conference on Unmanned Aircraft Systems (ICUAS)* (pp. 267-273). IEEE. 10.1109/ICUAS.2014.6842265

Moher, D., Liberati, A., Tetzlaff, J., & Altman, D. G. (2009). Preferred reporting items for systematic reviews and meta-analyses: The PRISMA statement. *Annals of Internal Medicine*, *151*(4), 264–269. doi:10.7326/0003-4819-151-4-200908180-00135 PMID:19622511

Naik, M. B., Kumar, P., & Majhi, S. (2019). Smart public transportation network expansion and its interaction with the grid. *International Journal of Electrical Power & Energy Systems*, *105*, 365–380. doi:10.1016/j.ijepes.2018.08.009

Nieves, V. (2017). *Economista*. elEconomista.es. https://www.eleconomista.es/economia/noticias/8128422/02/17/Donde-la-maquina-sustituira-al-hombre-los-empleos-mas-amenazados-en-Espana-por-la-automatizacion.html

Ogie, R. I., Clarke, R. J., Forehead, H., & Perez, P. (2019). Crowdsourced social media data for disaster management: Lessons from the PetaJakarta.org project. *Computers, Environment and Urban Systems*, *73*, 108–117. doi:10.1016/j.compenvurbsys.2018.09.002

ONU. (2015). Organizaci6n de las Naciones Unidas. Retrieved 08 21, 2019, from: http://www.onu.org.mx/wp-content/uploads/2017/07/180131_ODS-metas-digital.pdf

Pereira, G.V., Parycek, P., Falco, E., and Kleinhans, R. Smart governance in the context of smart cities: A literature review. *Information Polity*, 1-20.

Perveen, S., Yigitcanlar, T., Kamruzzaman, M., & Hayes, J. (2017). Evaluating transport externalities of urban growth: A critical review of scenario-based planning methods. *International Journal of Environmental Science and Technology*, *14*(3), 663–678. doi:10.100713762-016-1144-7

Perveen, S., Yigitcanlar, T., Kamruzzaman, M., & Hayes, J. (2017). Evaluating transport externalities of urban growth: A critical review of scenario-based planning methods. *International Journal of Environmental Science and Technology*, *14*(3), 663–678. doi:10.100713762-016-1144-7

Pollack, J. (2009). Multimethodology in series and parallel: Strategic planning using hard and soft OR. *The Journal of the Operational Research Society*, *60*(2), 156–167. doi:10.1057/palgrave.jors.2602538

Praharaj, S., Han, J. H., & Hawken, S. (2018). Towards the right model of smart city governance in India. *International Journal of Sustainable Development and Planning*, *13*(2), 171–186. doi:10.2495/SDP-V13-N2-171-186

Puiu, D., Barnaghi, P., Tonjes, R., Kumper, D., Ali, M. I., Mileo, A., Parreira, J. X., Fischer, M., Kolozali, S., Farajidavar, N., Gao, F., Iggena, T., Pham, T. L., Nechifor, C. S., Puschmann, D., & Fernandes, J. (2016). Citypulse: Large scale data analytics framework for smart cities. *IEEE Access : Practical Innovations, Open Solutions*, *4*, 1086–1108. doi:10.1109/ACCESS.2016.2541999

Purón-Cid, G., & Gil-García, J. R. (2012). Gobierno abierto, tecnologías de información y análisis de políticas públicas: oportunidades y retos para América Latina y el Caribe. In *XVII Congreso Internacional del clad*. Cartagena de Indias.

Ragini, J. R., Anand, P. M. R., & Bhaskar, V. (2018). Big data analytics for disaster response and recovery through sentiment analysis. *International Journal of Information Management*, *42*, 13–24. doi:10.1016/j.ijinfomgt.2018.05.004

Randed. (2018, 05 11). randed.com. Retrieved 08 23, 2019, from https://randed.com/smart-city-riesgos-y-beneficios/

RED GEALC, S.-O. I. (2008, 10). De la teoría a la práctica: cómo implementar con éxito el gobierno electrónico.

Rivera Urrutia, E. (2006). Concepto y problemas de la construcción del gobierno electrónico Una revisión de la literatura. *Gestión y Política Pública*, *15*(2), 259–305.

Ruhlandt, R. W. S. (2018). The governance of smart cities: A systematic literature review. *Cities (London, England)*, *81*, 1–23. doi:10.1016/j.cities.2018.02.014

Sangki, J. (2018). Vision of future e-government via new e-government maturity model: Based on Korea's e-government practices. *Telecommunications Policy*, *42*(10), 860–871. doi:10.1016/j.telpol.2017.12.002

Sharholy, M., Ahmad, K., Mahmood, G., & Trivedi, R. C. (2008). Municipal solid waste management in Indian cities–A review. *Waste Management (New York, N.Y.)*, *28*(2), 459–467. doi:10.1016/j.wasman.2007.02.008 PMID:17433664

Sikora-Fernandez, D. (2018). Smarter cities in post-socialist country: Example of Poland. *Cities (London, England)*, *78*, 52–59. doi:10.1016/j.cities.2018.03.011

Tabasová, A., Kropáč, J., Kermes, V., Nemet, A., & Stehlík, P. (2012). Waste-to-energy technologies: Impact on environment. *Energy*, *44*(1), 146–155. doi:10.1016/j.energy.2012.01.014

Thakare, V., & Khire, G. (2014). Role of emergency technology for building smart hospital information system. *Procedia Economics and Finance*, *11*, 583–588. doi:10.1016/S2212-5671(14)00223-8

Townsend, A. M. (2013). *Smart cities: Big data, civic hackers, and the quest for a new utopia*. WW Norton & Company.

Tzezana, R. (2017). High-probability and wild-card scenarios for future crimes and terror attacks using the Internet of Things. *foresight*, *19*(1), 1-14.

United Nations. (2018). *E-Government Survey. Department of Economic and Social Affairs*. UN. publicadministration.un.org

Vanolo, A. (2016). Is there anybody out there? The place and role of citizens in tomorrow's smart cities. *Futures*, *82*, 26–36. doi:10.1016/j.futures.2016.05.010

Varfolomeyev, A., Kozun, D., Ivanovs, A., Soms, H., & Petrina, O. (2015). Smart space based recommendation service for historical tourism. *Procedia Computer Science*, *77*, 85–91. doi:10.1016/j.procs.2015.12.363

Vlacheas, P., Giaffreda, R., Stavroulaki, V., Kelaidonis, D., Foteinos, V., Poulios, G., Demestichas, P., Somov, S., Biswas, A. R., & Moessner, K. (2013). Enabling smart cities through a cognitive management framework for the Internet of things. *IEEE Communications Magazine*, *51*(6), 102–111. doi:10.1109/MCOM.2013.6525602

Wang, X., Li, X., Zhen, F., & Zhang, J. (2016). How smart is your tourist attraction?: Measuring tourist preference of smart tourism attractions via FCEM-AHP and IPA approach. *Tourism Management*, *54*, 309–320. doi:10.1016/j.tourman.2015.12.003

Washburn, D., Sindhu, U., Balaouras, S., Dines, R. A., Hayes, N., & Nelson, L. E. (2009). Helping CIOs understand "smart city" initiatives. *Growth*, *17*(2), 1–17.

Wickramasuriya, R., Ma, J., Berryman, M., & Perez, P. (2013). Using geospatial business intelligence to support regional infrastructure governance. *Knowledge-Based Systems*, *53*, 80–89. doi:10.1016/j.knosys.2013.08.024

Witanto, J. N., Lim, H., & Atiquzzaman, M. (2018). Smart government framework with geo-crowdsourcing and social media analysis. *Future Generation Computer Systems*, *89*, 1–9. doi:10.1016/j.future.2018.06.019

Wright, G., Cairns, G., O'Brien, F., & Goodwin, P. (2018). Scenario analysis to support decision making in addressing wicked problems: Pitfalls and potential. *European Journal of Operational Research*, *278*(1), 3–19. doi:10.1016/j.ejor.2018.08.035

Yigitcanlar, T., & Dizdaroglu, D. (2014). Ecological approaches in planning for sustainable cities: A review of the literature. *Global journal of environmental science and management, 1*(2), 159-188.

Zhang, D. Q., Tan, S. K., & Gersberg, R. M. (2010). Municipal solid waste management in China: Status, problems and challenges. *Journal of Environmental Management*, *91*(8), 1623–1633. doi:10.1016/j.jenvman.2010.03.012 PMID:20413209

Chapter 4
Smart Government and E-Voting:
Opportunities and Challenges in the Implementation of Electronic Voting With Blockchain

Evangelina Lezama-León
https://orcid.org/0000-0003-0818-0897
Universidad Autónoma del Estado de Hidalgo, Mexico

Edgar Pérez Pineda
Alfasistemas TI, Mexico

Sandra Luz Hernández Mendoza
Universidad Autónoma del Estado de Hidalgo, Mexico

Alonso Ernesto Solís Galindo
Universidad Autónoma del Estado de Hidalgo, Mexico

ABSTRACT

Electronic voting is a topic that has been developing with the idea of applying technology and facilitating the process, however, the main objective has always been the reliability and confidentiality of the vote. The possibility of applying an emerging technology such as Blockchain has been visualized due to its characteristics such as immutability, that is, it cannot be changed or altered, however, some studies have found challenges for its implementation. This chapter addresses the state of the art of electronic voting, the strategy of electronic voting in Smart-Government, the security and transparency of electronic voting through Blockchain, as well as the structure of the blockchain. In addition, the operation of smart contracts as a tool for implementation and important concepts such as consensus algorithms are explained.

DOI: 10.4018/979-8-3693-0373-3.ch004

INTRODUCTION

Technological improvement projects in elections always pose challenges and require careful deliberation and planning, which is why the introduction of electronic voting (also called e-vote) is probably the most difficult improvement, since this technology touches the essence of the entire electoral process, in the casting and counting of votes, this electronic tool significantly reduces the control and direct human influence on this process, Likewise, the social challenges inherent to the e-vote are considerable since it lacks transparency for the voters and even for the electoral bodies, as well as the technological challenges, such as the complexity of the technology itself, the privacy of the voters and the need for an intuitive and accessible user interface.

Therefore, blockchain technology today is an ally of integrity in electoral processes when applied logically in an institutional context.

A blockchain is generally considered a distributed ledger (distributed transaction log) in which a transaction between two entities can be recorded efficiently and in such a way that it can be verified at any time by a peer-to-peer network (De Ávila, 2019).

With the use of blockchain, the efficiency of an electoral process could be improved in terms of security, time and verification in a decentralized and distributed way; in such a way that it is transparent and secure; as well as a decrease in the delivery time of results, for a transparent and secure electoral process. In addition, Blockchain technology has been hailed as one of the most innovative since the invention of the Internet, due to its versatility and its potential to disrupt in financial services, supply chain management, finance, healthcare among others.

As mentioned by (Ching Li, Chen, Jiang, & Bertino, 2019), the main characteristic of Blockchain technology is that what has already been recorded cannot be erased or repeated, this property is known as "immutability", this is reflected when an action is performed through this technology when it is transmitted and recorded by all the nodes of the network, which allows all participants to have all the information permanently updated. This technology allows the storage of votes as cryptographically linked blocks, which guarantees the integrity of the data.

Blockchain technology is a trend in terms of transaction security, as it is one of the characteristics with which it has become associated.

Blockchain is a decentralized distributed database that keeps records of all transactions made by individuals and it is not possible to delete it, that is, it complies with one of the principles of information security, the "non-repudiation", this is an important aspect of the transactions recorded by the blockchain, likewise, in this transaction there are no intermediaries. Any change or new entry will be recorded, identifying the person making the change. It is not possible to modify or delete any entry, likewise, if an attempt is made to go against the rules of the system, no one would trust it (Moorkattil, 2022).

Blockchain being a distributed blockchain that stores specific information for which the blockchain has been designed, it maintains a decentralized record of transactions, generating trust and security without requiring an intermediary. The blocks contain specific information that is exchanged between the nodes of the participants in a P2P (peer-to-peer) network, i.e. the users' computers, and each block is connected to the previous block because it contains the hash of the block.

Any information that is exchanged between participants will be broadcast to all nodes, the block will not be published every second, rather the record will be stored on all nodes until the block is proposed, i.e. until the cryptographic hash function is solved. The node that solves the hash function proposes the block on the existing blockchain network, i.e., the miners who must show a proof of work based on the calculation of hashes (Nakamoto, 2008) once for each block.

Bitcoin is one of the use cases of Blockchain, it was the first to be raised by the same creator of this structure in order to dispense with intermediaries for the management of money such as banking institutions, however, over time new use cases have been created, for the security it offers. In the aspect of electronic voting, some questions arise such as Do the votes in total form a block? How can the vote be registered with Blockchain technology, are the nodes created or are the votes only joined to the network that already exists, and finally, how is it possible to implement an electronic voting system with Blockchain technology?

E-voting is a system that allows citizens to cast their votes electronically, rather than through paper ballots at a physical polling station. While this technology has the potential to improve the accessibility and efficiency of the electoral process, it also presents significant challenges, such as the security and privacy of votes.

Blockchain technology, for its part, offers potential solutions to address some of these challenges. In particular, its decentralized nature and its ability to guarantee data integrity can help ensure the security and transparency of the electoral process.

One possible way to implement e-voting with Blockchain technology is through the use of a network of decentralized nodes, each of which can verify the authenticity of each vote cast. Each vote would be recorded on the Blockchain and would be available for public verification, ensuring the transparency of the electoral process.

However, the implementation of e-voting with Blockchain technology also presents significant challenges. First, voter privacy must be protected at all times. It is also necessary to ensure the integrity of the blockchain and prevent vote manipulation by malicious actors. In addition, there must be a reliable system for voter authentication and identification.

In summary, e-voting with Blockchain technology presents a number of interesting possibilities for improving the electoral process. However, challenges in terms of privacy, security and reliability must be adequately addressed before widespread implementation.

STATE OF THE ART OF ELECTRONIC VOTING (E-VOTING)

Electronic voting has advanced significantly in recent decades, offering new possibilities for improving the voting process, however, its implementation must address key challenges related to security, public trust and digital inclusion, in addition to seeking solutions that balance the convenience and efficiency of e-voting with the protection of fundamental democratic principles.

Electronic voting, also known as e-voting, refers to the use of information and communications technology to facilitate the voting process in elections and as technology continues to advance and society becomes more digitized, electronic voting has emerged as a potential alternative to traditional paper-based voting, which is why the current state of e-voting, highlights the technological advances, challenges and key considerations related to its implementation (Alvarez 2016).

Background of Electronic Voting (e-Voting)

Electronic voting (e-voting) has been the subject of study and research for several decades. The first attempts to implement e-voting systems date back to the 1960s, when mechanical voting machines were used in some jurisdictions. Since then, advances in information technology have allowed the development of more sophisticated systems, such as online voting and voting through electronic voting machines.

Also in the 1970s, the first commercial electronic voting machines were developed, such as the Direct Recording Electronic (DRE) in the United States, which allowed voters to select their choices on a screen and recorded the votes electronically.

In the 1990's e-voting pilot tests were conducted in several countries, including the Netherlands, France and Canada, these tests were conducted in both political elections and union elections, and it was until 2000 where the use of e-voting became widespread in several countries (Election Commission of India, 2018).

Rivest (2009), renowned cryptographer and computer scientist points out that the integrity of the electoral process is fundamental and that any electronic voting system must be reliable and resistant to cyber threats, likewise he has defended the need for electronic voting systems that can be audited and that use cryptographic techniques to ensure the security and anonymity of the vote.

On the other hand, Dill (2016) professor of computer science and founder of Verified Voting, has raised concerns about the lack of transparency and auditability in e-voting systems, he advocates the use of e-voting systems that allow independent verification and are capable of producing a paper record that can be audited and used in case of dispute.

The state of the art of e-voting has experienced significant advances in recent years, in many countries, pilot projects have been carried out and e-voting has been implemented at different levels, from local elections to national elections. However, the degree of adoption and acceptance varies widely in different regions of the world due to several challenges associated with this technology.

However, there are also concerns and challenges associated with e-voting. Security is one of the most critical aspects, as it is essential to guarantee the integrity and confidentiality of the votes. E-voting systems must be robust and protected against possible cyber-attacks, ensuring the authenticity of voters and the impossibility of altering the results.

Types of Electronic Voting (e-Voting)

There are different approaches and technologies used in e-voting, some of them are:

- Online voting: allows voters to cast their votes through the internet, using computers or mobile devices. Online voting systems can vary in terms of security and privacy, but generally involve voter authentication and encryption of voting data to ensure the integrity of the process.
- Electronic voting machines: devices specifically designed to facilitate the voting process, these machines may have touch screen or keypad interfaces and store votes in digital form.
- Email voting: allows voters to send their vote via email to the election authorities, this approach poses additional challenges in terms of authentication and security, as votes must be sent securely and protected against tampering.

Advantages of Electronic Voting (e-Voting)

Electronic voting (e-voting) offers several potential advantages compared to traditional paper-based voting

- Increased efficiency and speed

E-voting can streamline the voting process, reducing the time needed to cast, count and tabulate votes, which can allow for faster results to be published and more timely decision-making.

- Increased accessibility

Electronic voting (e-voting) can make the voting process more accessible to people with disabilities or physical limitations, because e-voting systems can provide accessible interfaces and voting options tailored to the needs of each individual.

- Reduces errors

Electronic voting (e-voting) has the potential to reduce errors associated with manual vote counting, such as misinterpreted or miscounted votes, where e-voting systems can incorporate automated validations and verifications to minimize human error.

Challenges and Considerations of Electronic Voting (e-Voting)

Despite the potential advantages, the implementation of e-voting also presents significant challenges (Panizo, 2007).

- Security

Security is a fundamental concern in e-voting; e-voting systems must be secure and protect the integrity and confidentiality of votes and strong authentication, encryption and protection against cyber-attacks are critical aspects to take into account.

- Public trust

Public trust in e-voting systems is essential for their acceptance and success, where citizens must have confidence in the security and transparency of e-voting systems, as well as in the fairness and integrity of electoral processes.

- Digital inclusion

The implementation of e-voting poses challenges related to digital inclusion so it is important to ensure that all voters have access and sufficient skills to use e-voting systems, this involves addressing the digital divide and ensuring that no one is excluded due to lack of access to technology.

- Verification and auditability

The ability to verify and audit election results is fundamental to ensure confidence in the electronic voting system, where independent verification mechanisms and transparency in the process are key elements to address any doubts or controversies that may arise.

E-VOTING AS A STRATEGY IN SMART-GOVERNMENT

The use of technology has given way to new definitions and one of them is the so-called "smart government", which refers to the use of smart services by a government. Smart government refers to the execution of business processes and implicit IT capabilities; it promotes innovations in the use of data and that allow data to flow consistently through government processes and its projects to provide high quality services to citizens (Harsh & Ichalkaranje, 2014).

Some governments have made implementations where they use electronic processes, but it is important to assimilate that in order to make a real transition to a smart government, data should be freely available without restrictions. Therefore, in the process of implementing e-voting as a smart government strategy, it is essential that information flows naturally and transparently. Blockchain technology can provide the necessary characteristics to give credibility and security to all the agents involved in the voting process, and although it is best known in its application in the so-called cryptocurrencies, it can also be used in the voting process and in the action plans of governments at their different operational levels (Harsh & Ichalkaranje, 2015).

At the international level, there are three countries that have mainly carried out the most research on topics related to electronic voting and government, and according to a bibliometric analysis executed with the bibliometrix tool (Aria & Cuccurullo, 2017), from a search of 323 items in the Scopus database, it was obtained as a result that these countries are India (137 documents), United States(66 documents) and United Kingdom (62 documents) (Figure 1).

Figure 1. Scientific production on the topics of electronic voting and government by country
Source: Scopus (2023)

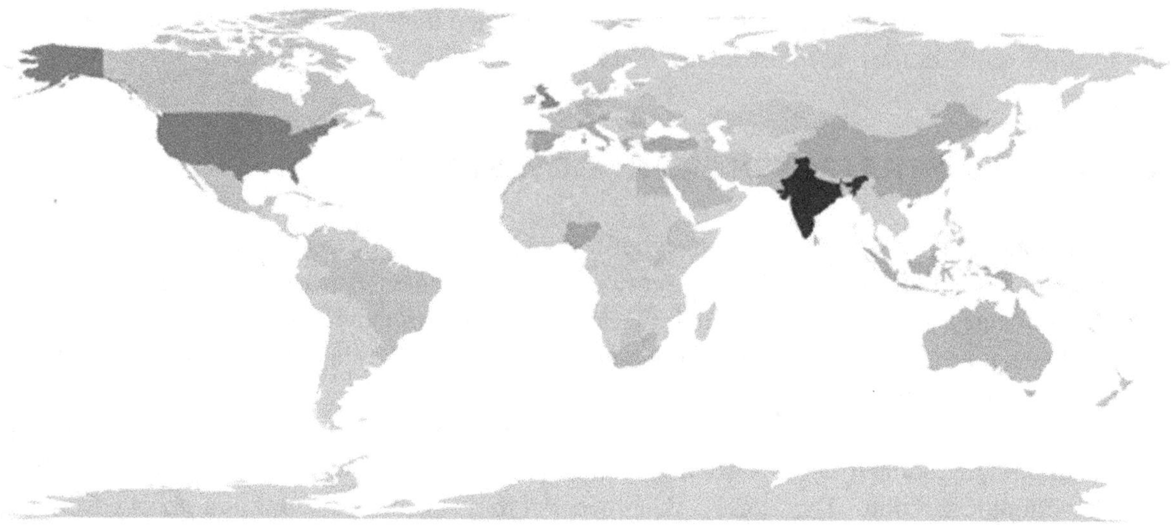

Increased accessibility and the use of Internet-based technologies in everyday activities have leveled the path towards e-governance and e-administration. Various administration-related services can now be accessed online, and increasing attention has been paid to implementing electronic voting in election processes and overcoming barriers that have limited its application in specific cases. It should be noted that electronic voting significantly reduces the cost of these operations on a larger scale and facilitates the process for senior citizens or citizens with some disability, and also reduces the level of stress and hassle, which are often associated with traditional elections along with the benefits. However, many drawbacks have limited its application, such as lack of trust and concerns about security and privacy of information, leading many governments to avoid its application during general elections or limit e-voting to specific situations of certain population sectors (Esposito & Choi, 2023).

Figure 2. Number of articles per year
Source: Scopus (2023)

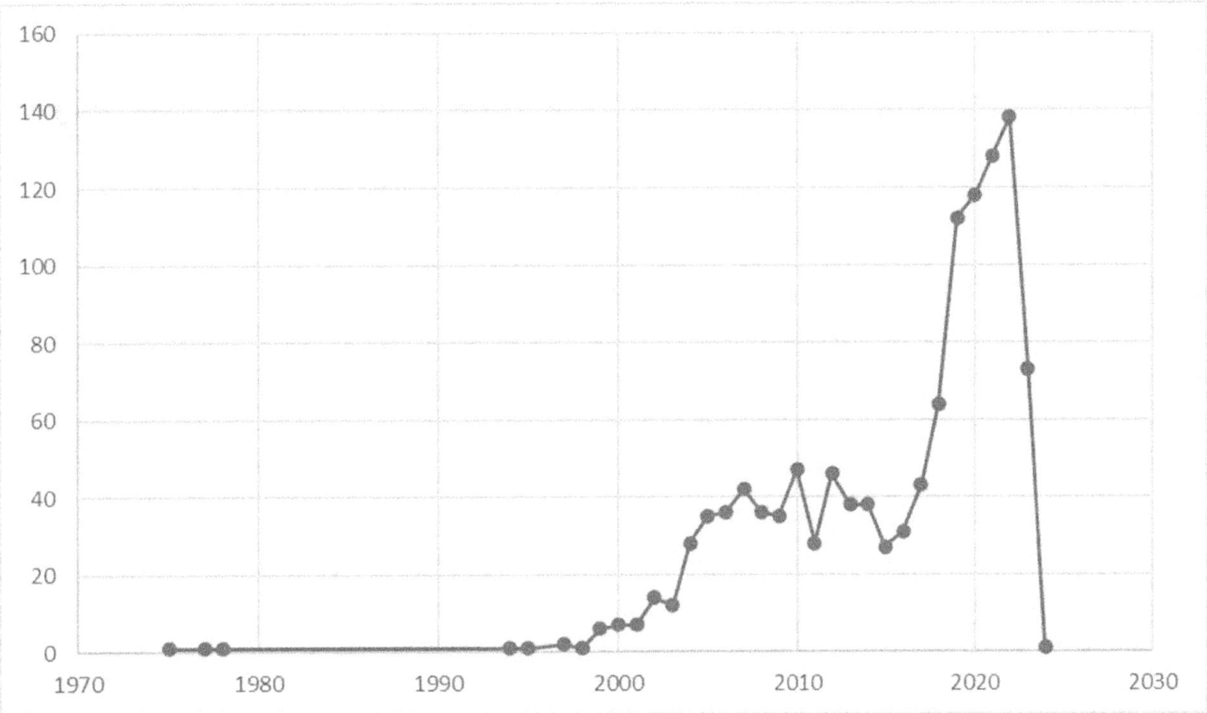

As shown in Figure 2, according to the analysis carried out by means of the bibliometrix tool, there is a positive trend in the study of e-voting with blockchain, and as of 2019 there is a significant increase in the number of articles published per year.

Figure 3. Most relevant words
Source: Scopus (2023)

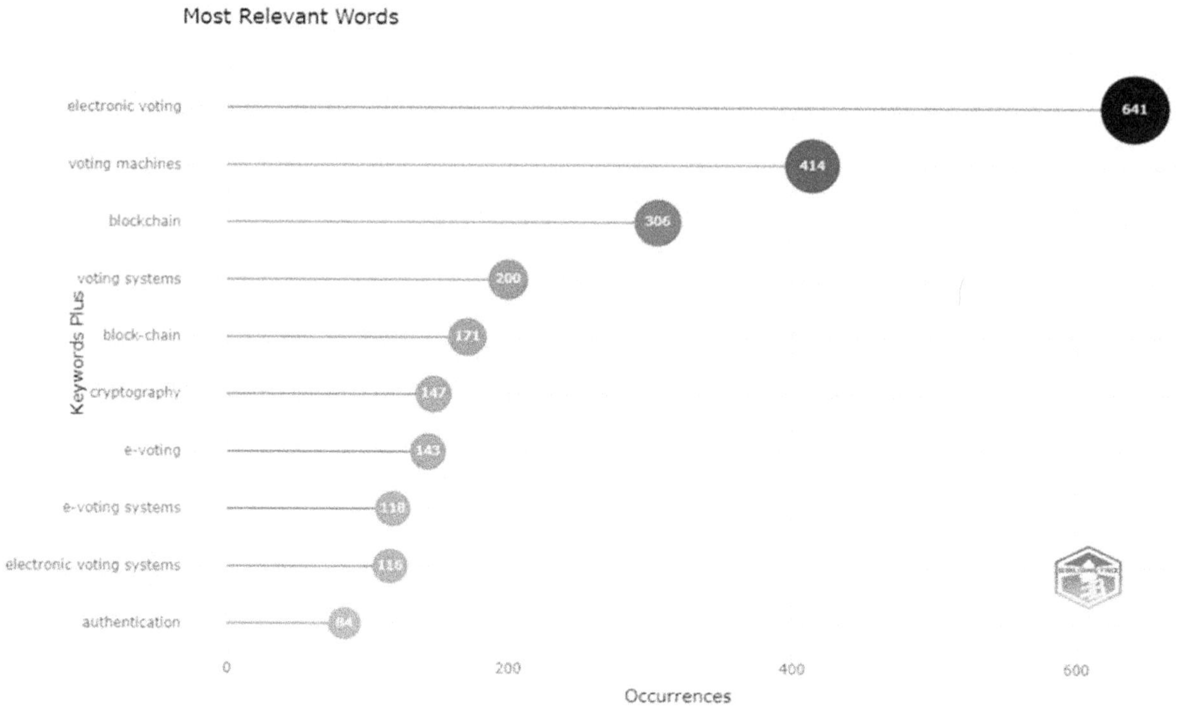

Figure 3 shows the results of the analysis according to the most relevant words, where electronic voting is the most mentioned word with a total of 641 times. In conclusion, these graphical analyses give us the necessary confidence to continue our research work on a relevant and current topic on which there is still much to discover.

In addition to the interest of researchers in electronic voting, there are companies that offer services to carry out electronic voting processes, one of which is EVOTING, whose motto is "Leader in electronic democracy". This company has 1077 clients with a total of 2644 votes and regional offices in Perú, México, Argentina, Colombia, among others, data on its website at the time of the consultation (Evoting, 2021). This company offers voting services for small and medium sized companies and even for Universities, it offers security through a voting software under an encryption scheme that ensures the secrecy of the vote, a transparent process and efficiency reducing the costs of the voting process.

Countries like Estonia, Norway and Switzerland have used electronic voting systems for national election processes, which according to Daramola and Thebus (2020) are centralized and therefore susceptible to distributed denial of service (DDOS) attacks.

SECURITY AND TRANSPARENCY OF E-VOTING THROUGH BLOCKCHAIN

E-voting security is a crucial issue in the development of modern election systems. Blockchain technology has emerged as a potentially promising solution to address e-voting security challenges. Through the use of blockchain, it seeks to ensure integrity, transparency, and privacy in the voting process.

According to Berke (2020) it is important to implement data encryption and anonymization mechanisms to protect voter confidentiality. His study is based on the analysis of an electronic voting system called Helios and explores its security and privacy in the context of elections. This system was created in 2008 and has been used in several elections and popular consultations.

Helios is based on cryptographic principles and uses homomorphic cryptography and independent verifiability techniques to ensure the confidentiality of the vote and the integrity of the results. Its design focuses on protecting voter privacy and enabling public verification of the accuracy of election results.

This is how it can be exemplified how through Blockchain technology it addresses voter privacy and the challenges involved, with the possibility of preventing votes from being tracked.

The researchers examine in detail the architecture of the Helios system and the cryptographic mechanisms used to ensure voter privacy. Potential vulnerabilities of the system are addressed and possible improvements are proposed to strengthen its security and privacy. The challenges and limitations observed in Helios, forces consideration of different threat scenarios and the need for comprehensive privacy assessments to ensure system reliability.

Similarly, Taş and Özgür (2020) also address the problems associated with e-voting systems and propose solutions using technologies such as cryptography and blockchain. Cryptography is used to protect the confidentiality of voter data and ensure the integrity of the results. Blockchain technology, meanwhile, provides an immutable and transparent record of all transactions, which reduces the possibility of manipulation and fraud.

According to Taş and Özgür (2020), the fundamental concerns related to security in electronic voting systems, voter authenticity, vote integrity, information confidentiality, and protection against malicious attacks. Addressing these concerns requires addressing them through cryptography, authentication protocols, data protection and robust system design.

The importance of ensuring trust and transparency in electronic voting systems is essential to guarantee the integrity of the electoral process. And for this it is necessary to implement robust security mechanisms, independent audits and verifiability of results to strengthen voter confidence and the validity of the results.

Taş & Özgür (2020) highlights the challenges that arise with the implementation of electronic voting systems, where they identify those that have to do with accessibility, scalability and acceptance by citizens and electoral authorities, which can be addressed through robust security measures and adequate auditing practices.

According to Hjálmarsson, et al. (2018), the use of Blockchain technology can be used to implement it in electronic voting systems. Said authors address the challenges of security and reliability in electronic voting systems. The inherent security and privacy features of blockchain technology, is presented in the immutability of records and decentralization. The decentralization of the blockchain increases the resilience of the system against malicious attacks. Therefore, they enable the creation of a voting system that is resistant to manipulation and protects voter confidentiality.

Employing Blockchain technology in e-Voting results in votes being recorded in blocks on the blockchain in an encrypted and anonymous way. The integrity of the votes is guaranteed by the immutable nature of the blockchain, which prevents votes from being altered or deleted once recorded. On the other hand, the decentralization of the blockchain ensures that there is no single point of failure and that the system is resistant to malicious attacks.

With blockchain technology, transparent and audible verification mechanisms can be provided for voters and observers. This helps to increase confidence in the electoral process and in the accuracy of the results.

The advent of blockchain technology in e-voting can improve the security, integrity and reliability of election systems. However, there are also additional challenges and considerations, such as scalability and citizen participation, that need to be addressed for a successful implementation, according to (Hjálmarsson, et al. 2018).

On the other hand, (Enguehard 2008) focuses on the analysis of different transparent electronic voting systems, including those based on Blockchain technology. A key element in voting systems is transparency, as it is a key factor in generating confidence in election results. Transparency allows voters and observers to verify the accuracy and validity of votes cast. Blockchain technology can be a solution to achieve this transparency. The blockchain provides a public, decentralized record of all vote transactions, allowing voters and observers to openly access information and verify the integrity of the results.

That is why transparent electronic voting systems based on Blockchain technology offers security and privacy features, thus ensuring the confidentiality of votes and the protection of voters' identities. Blockchain is a mechanism that can allow the anonymization of votes while maintaining the integrity of the system.

On the other hand, Enguehard (2008) highlights the benefits of verifiability and auditability of votes, as well as the resistance to manipulation of the results when using Blockchain technology. However, the author also recognizes the concerns about scalability, accessibility and citizen participation that must be addressed in the implementation of these systems.

E-voting is a use case of blockchain technology that can prevent many security attacks, internal vote manipulation and promote transparency, however voter validation and security of the blockchain architecture are potential weaknesses that need to be addressed (Daramola & Thebus, 2020).

Daramola & Thebus (2020) describe the layers of security in blockchain implementation under the Hyperledger Fabric platform which is an application foundation with modular architecture that offers components, consensus and membership services to satisfy a wide range of use cases. Hyperledger Foundation is open source software created as a Linux project.

Other authors have proposed e-voting solutions based on a customised blockchain architecture, however, Kovačević & Kečo (2023) noted some challenges or problems to overcome in such proposals, e.g. establishing the ownership of the blockchain, finding out whether there is assurance that proprietary entities are not acting maliciously, Likewise, another question is whether they will be exempt from a 51% attack, which is a technique that aims to fork a chain to make a double spending, if you control more than half of the total hash power could perform this attack, in the case of cryptocurrencies in this type of attack would be spending the same currency twice.

Sayeed, S. & Marco-Gisbert, H. (2019) identified other attacks such as:

- Long-range attack
- Distributed Denial of Service (DDoS) attack
- P+Epsilon attack
- Sibyl attack
- Equilibrium attack
- Border gateway protocol hijacking

In conclusion, e-voting security through the implementation of blockchain technology is a constantly developing area of research. The aforementioned literature references provide a solid foundation for understanding the security issues related to e-voting and how blockchain technology can address them. Through cryptography, transparency and decentralization, the blockchain offers a potential solution to ensure the integrity and reliability of e-voting systems. However, it is important to continue researching and evaluating new proposals and approaches in this field to achieve secure and reliable e-voting systems.

STRUCTURE OF THE BLOCKCHAIN

Transactions can be a purchase, a vote or a contract. For a transaction to be attested to have happened, it will be written to a distributed database that is built, where all nodes keep a real-time copy of that database that is being built collectively. That P2P shared database is the blockchain which is a growing list of chronologically linked records, where the information is immutable, ordered and can only be added to if there is an agreement between the majority of the nodes. Transactions are written in a block that will be encrypted and connected to another, each node is connected to another and so on. Each transaction is verified in consensus by all participants.

In a blockchain network only the hash codes of the data are seen, the hashes are grouped in blocks and are joined to the next block of data. In order to verify that the data has not been altered, a digital fingerprint is obtained from the data set by means of hash algorithms.

Each block has a header that includes the hash of the previous block and the information or transactions of the block itself, in addition to data such as the timestamp which is a piece of data in each block that is used to determine the exact time the block was mined, Nonce a random number to vary the input to a cryptographic hash function "number used once", Merkle roof that allows validating the integrity of the data, target difficulty is a numerical data that controls the mining time of the block and version. Finally, the hash of the block is obtained, so they are completely intertwined. Each hash of a block is the input of the next block. Figure 4 shows this process, representing the header that includes the block hash with a color that identifies each encrypted block (fingerprint).

Figure 4. Representation of encryption (cryptographically sealed)
Source: Own elaboration based on course notes Strategic vision of the digital ecosystem (De la Mata, 2021).

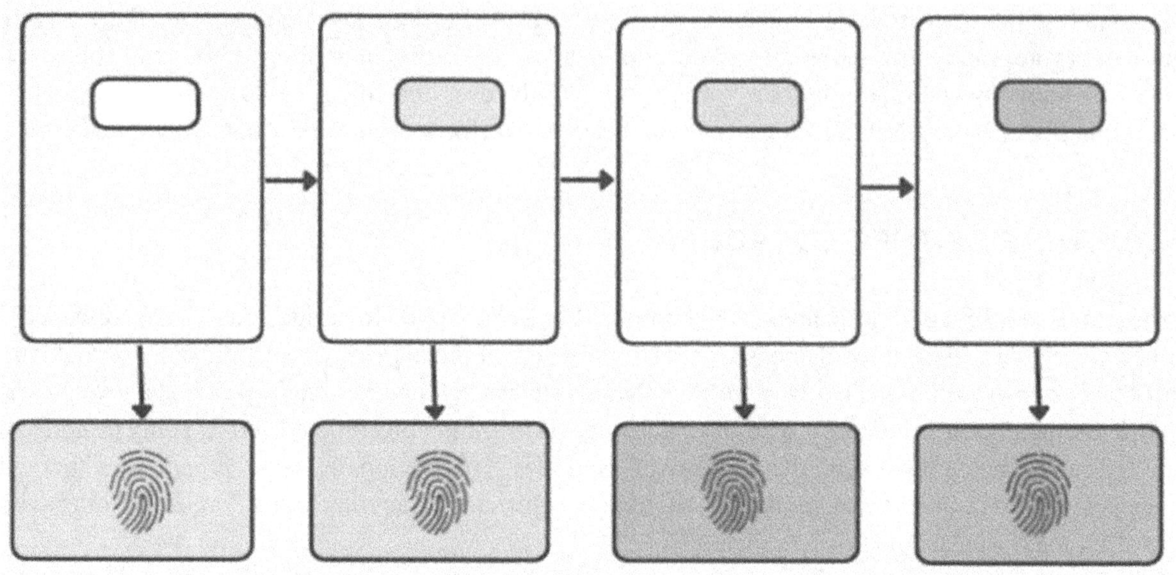

A hash algorithm produces encrypted data that cannot be decrypted. In order to verify that the data has not been tampered with, a fingerprint is obtained from the data set by means of hash algorithms.

In the process of generating the hash or fingerprint of a block, encryption algorithms are used, for example, SHA256, used by Bitcoin as well as being one of the most widely used. In this case, if we enter the value of a letter h (Figure 5), it will result in the string:

aaa9402664f1a41f40ebbc52c9993eb66aeb366602958fdfaa283b71e64db123

Figure 5. SHA256 online hash function example one
Source: https://emn178.github.io/online-tools/sha256.html

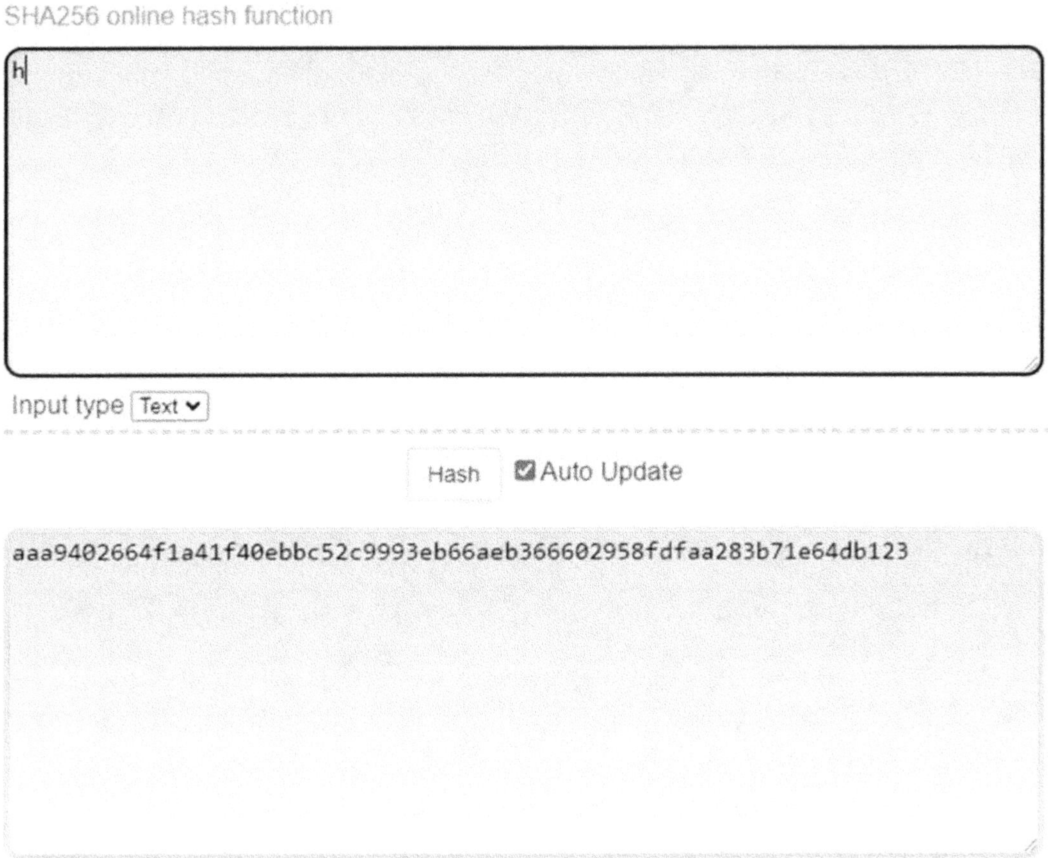

If, as a variant, we add a dot to the letter h (Figure 6), the result offered by the SHA256 algorithm will be the string:

be780ffeb9371ba70e5ced2322a2b179af8dfd53b1b8ae4411c7c9b4601acd71

This is a completely different sequence. These variants that are added in the hash machine in real life represent the encrypted data of the corresponding block.

Figure 6. SHA256 online hash function example two
Source: https://emn178.github.io/online-tools/sha256.html

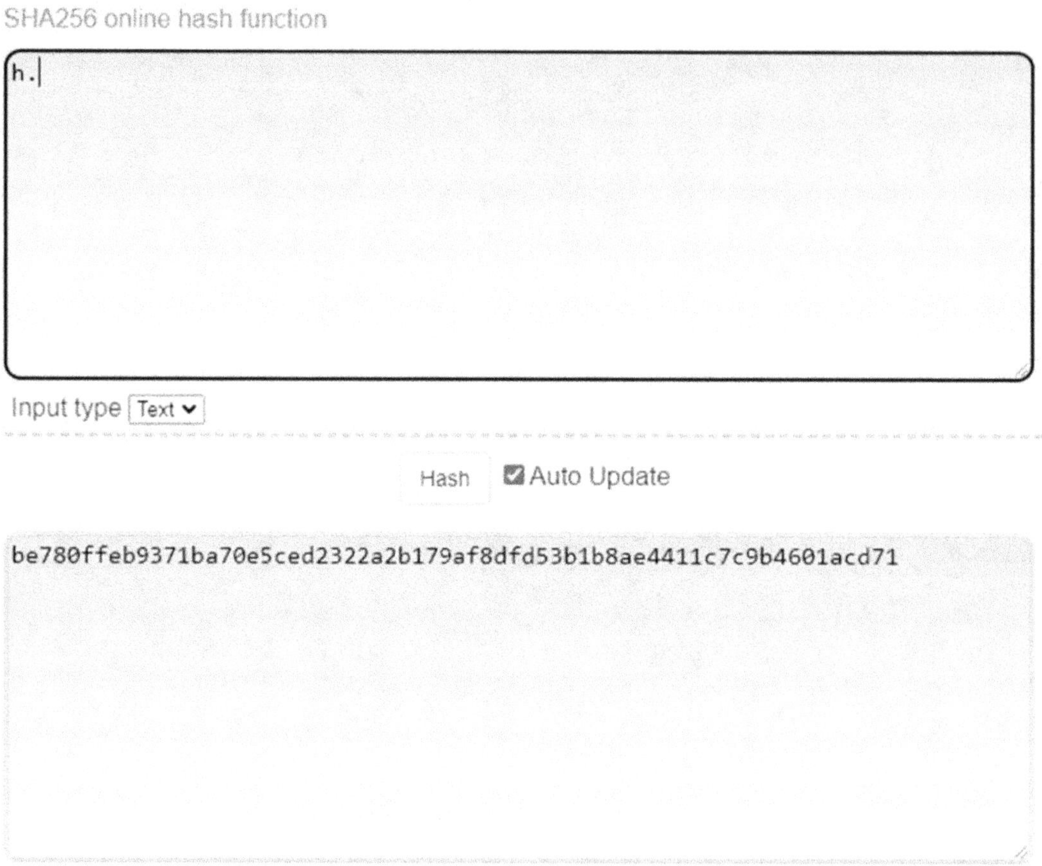

Similarly, if the exercise is performed (Figure 7) considering that blockchain is composed of several blocks, it is possible to check by means of the hash algorithm, when any value or characteristic of any block has been modified once the mining process has been performed (Figure 8). This is of vital importance to preserve the integrity, availability and confidentiality of the information.

Blockchain is a distributed network with solid and stable structures to obtain functionalities such as immutability and with the possibility of exchanging value. Each block has its transactions in the form of a hash, each block has its hash and each following block has its hash with its transactions, plus the hash of the previous block giving rise to a specific footprint. If a simple piece of data is changed in any of the blocks, this action will give rise to a totally different footprint with an effect on the entire block chain (De la Mata, 2021).

Figure 7. Blockchain blocks mined.
Source: https://demoblockchain.org/blockchain

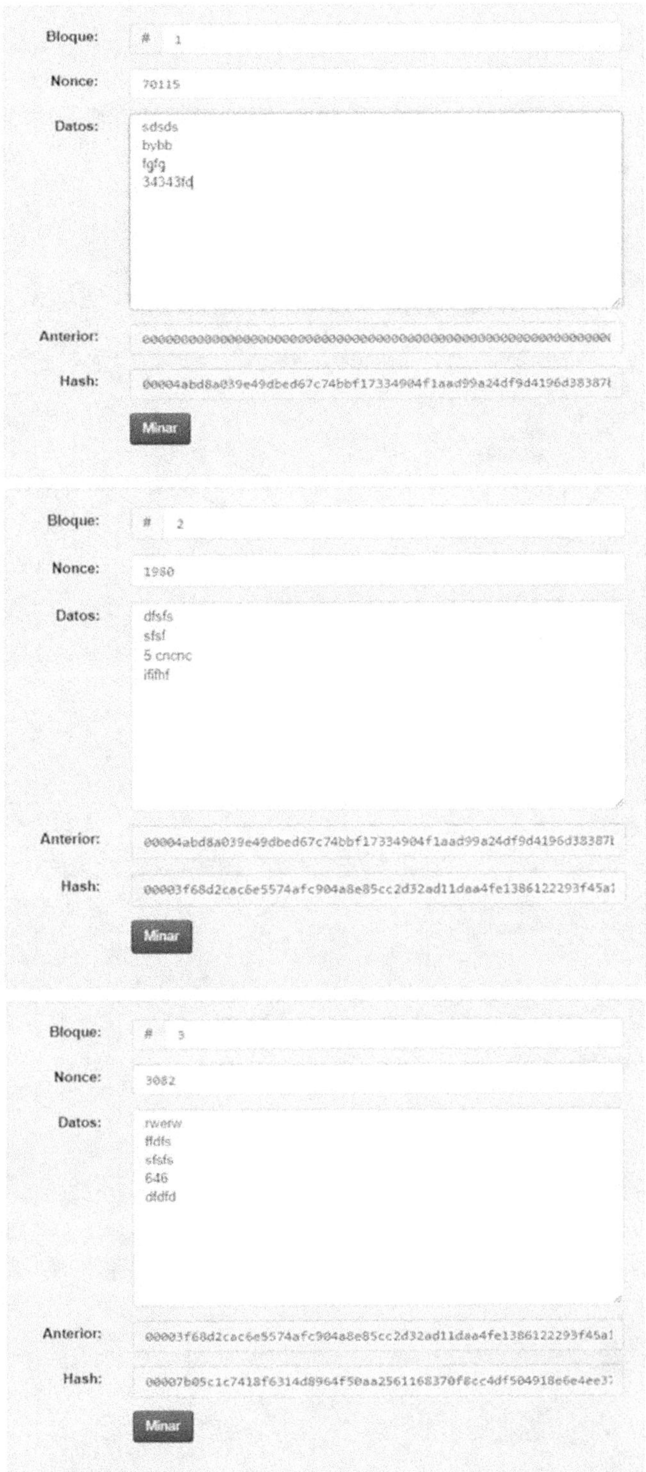

Figure 8. Blockchain blocks with modified data in block no. two
Source: https://demoblockchain.org/blockchain

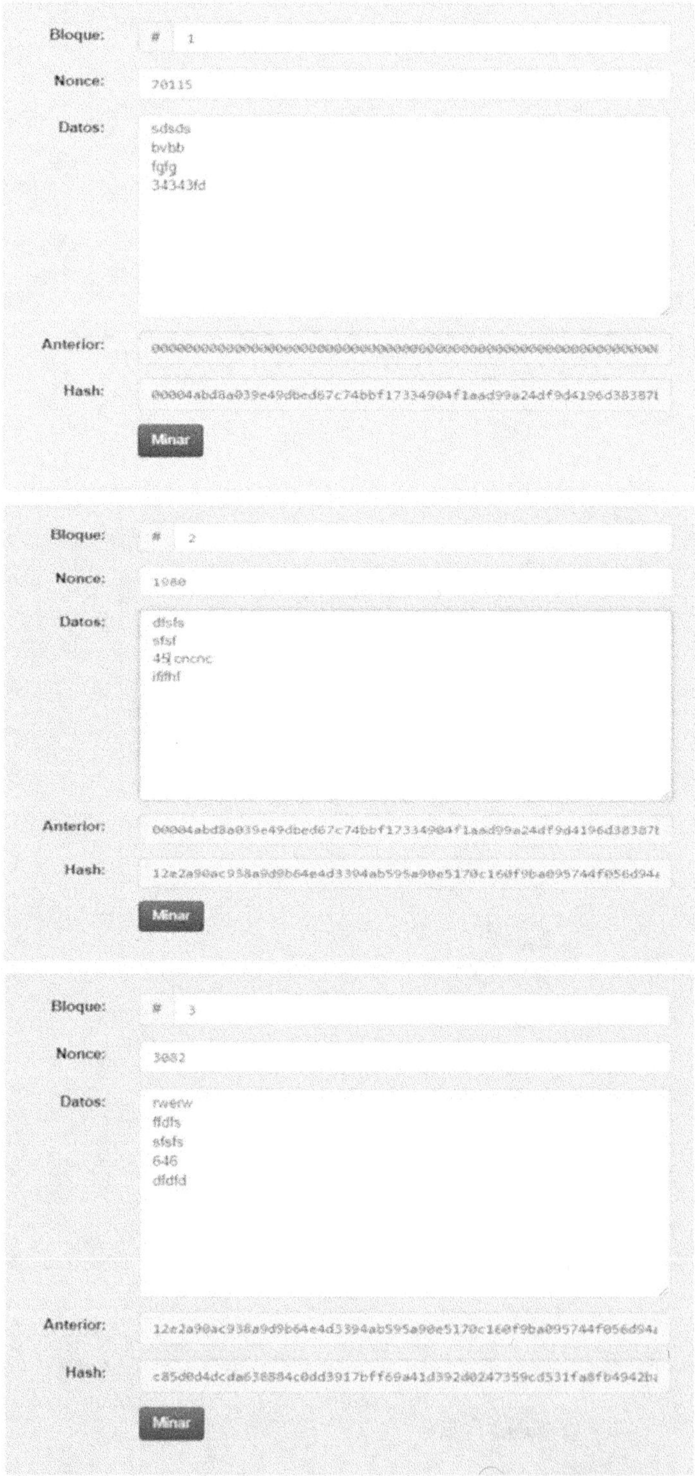

Hash functions are known as asymmetric algorithms. Asymmetric algorithms are based on mathematical relationships that are easy to solve in one direction, but very complex to perform in the reverse direction, unless the corresponding key is known.

SMART CONTRACTS

This term refers to the automation of legal contracts and has recently been used to refer to low-level code scripts running on a Blockchain platform. Smart contracts are embedded procedures that are stored with data on which they act (Bragagnolo, 2018).

Since the emergence of Bitcoin, Blockchain technology has enabled the development of decentralized systems as was the case with Ethereum, created in 2014 which is a cryptocurrency like Bitcoin. The difference lies in that Ethereum was designed to store and execute code, which gave rise to smart contracts. These smart contracts are agreements between two or more parties that are executed autonomously in a system that is not controlled by third parties which avoids costs and saves time. Smart contracts in Ethereum offer the security of a public and private key that allows online transactions to be carried out anonymously, which is why it has been extended to electoral processes (Giraldo, et al. 2020).

Other applications of smart contracts are, for example, crowdfunding, which is a financing mechanism, where there are many participants who contribute to the capital of a company as shareholders.

Examples of e-voting where Ethereum-based smart contracts are implemented is McCorry, et al.(2017) who proposed a system for counting votes with maximum privacy for voters, as well as Hjálmarsson et al. (2018) who evaluated the application of distributed e-voting on a national scale with Iceland as a case study using a private Ehereum blockchain supported by an authentication company to ensure the verification of voter identity.

In the study by Zou (2019), the challenges that smart contracts have are described, in this an interview was applied to 232 professionals working in smart contracts finding in their analysis that there is no effective way to ensure the security of the smart contract code, coupled with this, They concluded that the tools that exist for development are still very basic, as well as programming languages and virtual machines still have a number of limitations, performance issues are difficult to handle in an execution environment with limited resources, and online resources such as advanced documents and community support are also limited.

CONSENSUS ALGORITHMS

Preventing voting fraud to establish democracy is a motivation for virtually all countries and several have chosen to implement electronic voting. Most of these implementations have used the consensus proof-of-work (PoW) method. Consensus means that data agreed upon throughout the network will be verified by storing a copy at each node. This agreement between nodes is similar to the political electoral system, where, normally a person can cast one vote, to avoid that a person votes more than once the voting unit must be the computing power for the case of proof-of-work consensus algorithms, for proof. of.stake is the number of tokens owned.

Since 2015, some countries have made implementations of electronic voting with Blockchain, this has meant a challenge in all countries because the PoW method they have used has a deficiency which is energy consumption (Rezvani & Khani, 2019).

Consensus algorithms are important elements of Blockchain networks as they maintain their integrity and security, they are mechanisms by which Blockchain reaches consensus. The first algorithm developed for a cryptocurrency was called proof of work.

Blockchain is made up of distributed nodes that must agree on the validity of transactions by means of consensus algorithms that ensure that the rules of the protocol are complied with. The protocol is defined as the primary rules of a Blockchain, it is what the Blockchain network is built on and defines the way the system works, examples of protocols are bitcoin and Ethereum. A consensus algorithm is a mechanism through which the rules will be followed.

Proof of work was the first consensus algorithm that is a crucial part of the mining process used by Bitcoin and other cryptocurrencies. Proof of work involves numerous hashing attempts and ensures that miners only validate a new block of transactions and add it to the Blockchain, this is achieved if the distributed nodes of the network reach consensus and accept the miner's hash block, likewise Proof of work is considered the best algorithm resistant to Byzantine or 51% attacks which is a type of cyber-attack performed by a person or organization targeting a blockchain with the goal of getting more than 51% of its computational power (Nogales, 2019). Within cryptocurrencies, Bitcoin, Ethereum and Litecoin are more susceptible to this type of attack, however, this type of attack requires a high investment exceeding even the profit that would be obtained from it (Rus, 2022,). Another algorithm proposed as an alternative to proof of work is proof of stake. This was developed in 2011 to replace proof of work mining by validating blocks according to Stake. Stake is the amount of coins accumulated. The importance of consensus algorithms is that they maintain the security and integrity of a Blockchain network and provide the means for nodes to reach a consensus as to which version of the blockchain is real.

In Du, et al.(2020) the following are mentioned in addition to POW and POS

- Delegated Proof of Stake (DPoS) or digital democracy algorithm. In this, network nodes vote for delegated nodes for their participation and these select a leader who takes responsibility for decision making. It is considered the most robust, reliable and efficient in Blockchain networks and is very popular among DAPPS (Decentralised Application Platforms) developers.
- Delegated Byzantine Fault Tolerance (dBFT), a DPoS algorithm with PBFT.
- Proof of Activity (PoA). The proof of activity algorithm was developed in 2012 as an evolution of PoW, being a combination of PoW and PoS.
- Proof of Burn (PoB). This allows the new block to be created and connected to the chain to the nodes that have spent the most in the network itself; it does not allow for forks to exist, thus preventing double-spending attacks.
- Proof of Capacity (PoC). This is based on storage; the greater the storage capacity, the greater the node's chances of winning.
- Proof of Elapsed Time (PoET). Any node that wants to join the network has to identify itself and be authorised. The algorithm looks for a fair way to distribute the possibilities among the nodes that compose it.
- Proof of Assignment (PoA). It is an algorithm that seeks to improve the deficiencies in other consensus algorithms in memory management.

- Proof of CheckPoint(PoC). The checkpoint consensus algorithm is based on the PoW algorithm. In this algorithm, the winning node is in charge of creating and chaining the block.
- Ripple Protocol Consensus. It is a low latency algorithm that is used for monetary transactions between banks.

BLOCKCHAIN IN E-VOTING

Blockchain was introduced to manage Bitcoin and has since found potential applicability in numerous secure distributed applications.

It involves the use of a decentralized, trusted network that enables the transfer of valuable digital assets (currency or data). A blockchain is a digital database shared across a large public network of interconnected nodes, in which each entry (block) is cryptographically linked to the previous one. Each block within the blockchain contains a "block hash", a value that combines the hash of the previous block with the respective data of the current block. For the network to accept a new block, its calculated hash must use the hash of the previous block as an input parameter and, by extension, the hashes of all previous blocks, creating a valid chain.

Each time an update, or a "transaction" (from any node) is made to the database, the communicating nodes must agree that the transaction is valid in a group agreement process called "consensus". There are several methods for reaching consensus on a blockchain, the most common being the byzantine fault tolerance algorithm, the proof-of-work algorithm, the proof-of-stake algorithm and the delegated proof-of-stake algorithm. Each node on the blockchain maintains its own copy of the distributed ledger that contains the information about the blockchain.

All transactions entering the blockchain must be authorized with a valid digital signature, or they will be rejected by the network. Blockchain uses the principles of public key (or asymmetric) cryptography, which uses two mathematically related, but not identical, keys: the private key and the public key. Blockchain is mainly based on ECC or elliptic curve cryptography.

Having considered the above, instead of creating a bespoke Blockchain network, it is possible to use the VoteChain system: which is a system that integrates with one of the large existing blockchain networks, Bitcoin Cash (Kovačević & Kečo, 2023).

Bitcoin Cash (BCH) is a decentralized peer-to-peer e-money system that implements the blockchain protocol with the proof-of-work (PoW) consensus algorithm. The main reason why BCH can be used is due to faster and cheaper transactions compared to Bitcoin, and support for a digital token protocol (SLP). Bitcoin Cash allows for the exchange of other virtual assets (such as stocks, gift cards, etc.), with the added reliability of a blockchain system. Simple Ledger Protocol (SLP) implements a system of virtual tokens on BCH, making it easy to create, manage and send tokens on the Bitcoin Cash Blockchain and costing only a minimal amount of spendable BCH for each authenticated (non-manipulated) transaction.The SLP protocol recognizes three different types of transactions: GENESIS, SEND and MINT transactions. The GENESIS transaction is the first transaction in the life of a token, which defines the properties of the token, the metadata (name, ticker symbol, URL, etc.) and the initial amount. A SEND transaction is used to transfer tokens from one or several outlets with tokens to other addresses. MINT transactions are used to increase the supply of tokens by spending the output of the mint token stick (created in a GENESIS transaction or in a previous MINT transaction). If no token is provided, the minting capability is permanently lost, so no new tokens of that type can be created in the future (Kovačević & Kečo, 2023)..

In a Blockchain-backed e-voting system, we could consider the casting of a vote as a "transaction". The inputs to the transaction would be the ballots distributed to citizens, while the outputs could be votes digitally signed and sent to the public addresses of election candidates. In this way, votes "cast" to a candidate's address would be easily verifiable, accountable and permanently stored on the blockchain. Moreover, it could easily be demonstrated that each voter would have cast only one vote, based on the number of transactions associated with a particular address. Thanks to transaction traceability, votes entered could be traced back to a government-sourced address to prove that they are official and have not been redistributed or modified by a malicious third party. Moreover, the only parameter that would "identify" a voter would be his or her public address, which is nothing more than a "random" hash stored in the blockchain. Although the address and its transactions are visible on the blockchain, a casual observer has no way of knowing who the address belongs to.

The ledger is distributed over a network of computers, which eliminates a single point of failure. Since elections are a crucial process that requires maximum availability, having a distributed system with no central point of failure would be essential.

Chain integrity would prevent the removal of votes or the addition of new fraudulent votes, while digital signatures would guarantee that the vote has been cast by an authenticated voter (no tampering).

REFERENCES

Aria, M., & Cuccurullo, C. (2017). Bibliometrix : An R-tool for comprehensive science mapping analysis. *Journal of Informetrics, 11*(4), 959–975. doi:10.1016/j.joi.2017.08.007

Avila Bula, M. A. D. (2019). *Sistema de votaciones con blockchain.* Uniandes. https://repositorio.uniandes.edu.co/handle/1992/44085

Berke, A. (2020). Crypto Voting + US Elections: Reality. *MIT Media Lab.* https://www.media.mit.edu/posts/crypto-voting-us-elections-reality/

Bragagnolo, S., Rocha, H., Denker, M., & Ducasse, S. (2018). SmartInspect: solidity smart contract inspector. *International Workshop on Blockchain Oriented Software Engineering (IWBOSE),* Campobasso, Italy. 10.1109/IWBOSE.2018.8327566

Daramola, O., & Thebus, D. (2020). Evaluación centrada en la arquitectura del voto electrónico por contrato inteligente basado en blockchain para elecciones nacionales. *Informatica (Vilnius), 7*(2), 16. doi:10.3390/informatics7020016

De la Mata, A. (2021). *Visión estratégica del ecosistema digital., Apuntes del módulo 5 Innovación y emprendimientos digitales, Conferencia "El ecosistema Blockchain".* Faculty Led Verano Universidad Politécnica de Madrid.

Dill, S. David (2016). Stanford *INGENIERÍA: Por qué votar en línea es un peligro para la democracia.* Seguridad, Tecnología y Sociedad. https://engineering.stanford.edu/magazine/article/david-dill-why-online-voting-danger-democracy

Du, M., Chen, Q., & Ma, X. (2020). MBFT: A new consensus algorithm for consortium blockchain. *IEEE Access : Practical Innovations, Open Solutions, 8*, 87665–87675. doi:10.1109/ACCESS.2020.2993759

Election Commission of India. (2018). *Electronic Voting Machines and the Election Process.* ECI. https://eci.gov.in/faqs/election-machinery/faqs-election-machinery-r13/

Enguehard, C. (2008). *Transparency in Electronic Voting : the Great Challe*nge. IPSA International Political Science Association Conference on "E-democracy - State of the art and future agenda, Stellenbosch , South Africa. https://www.researchgate.net/publication/32221266_Transparency_in_Electronic_Voting_the_Great_Challenge

Esposito, C., & Choi, C. (2023, March). Design and Implementation of a Blockchain-based e-Voting system by using the Algorand platform. *In Proceedings of the 38th ACM/SIGAPP Symposium on Applied Computing* (pp. 715-723). ACM. 10.1145/3555776.3577750

EVoting communications. (2021). *Evoting 2021: Entering the big league field.* Evoting. https://www.evoting.com/2021/12/30/z-evoting-2021-entrando-a-la-cancha-de-las-grandes-ligas/

Giraldo, F. D., Milton, B., & Gamboa, C. E. (2020). Electronic Voting Using Blockchain And Smart Contracts: Proof Of Concept. IEEE Latin America Transactions, 18(10). https://doi:10.1109/TLA.2020.9387645

Harsh, A., & Ichalkaranje, N. (2015). Transforming e-government to smart government: A South Australian perspective. *In Intelligent Computing, Communication and Devices: Proceedings of ICCD 2014,* Volume 1 (pp. 9-16). Springer India.

Hjálmarsson, F. Þ., Hreiðarsson, G. K., Hamdaqa, M., & Hjálmtýsson, G. (2018). Blockchain-Based E-Voting System. *2018 IEEE 11th International Conference on Cloud Computing (CLOUD), EUA*, (pp. 983-986). IEEE. 10.1109/CLOUD.2018.00151

Iza, X. C., Zumba, X., & Cardoso, S. M. (2021). *Análisis comparativo de Métodos de Consenso sobre plataformas Blockchain Comparative analysis of Consensus Methods on Blockchain platforms* (Vol. 33). Revista Tecnológica Espol–RTE.

Kohad, H. W., Kumar, S., & Ambhaikar, A. (2023). Design of a Novel Side Chaining Model for Improving the Performance of Security Aware E-Voting Applications. In *Mobile Radio Communications and 5G Networks: Proceedings of Third MRCN 2022* (pp. 13-28). Singapore: Springer Nature Singapore.

Kovačević, A., & Kečo, D. (2023, June). VoteChain-A Blockchain-Based Voting Platform. In *2023 XXIX International Conference on Information, Communication and Automation Technologies (ICAT)* (pp. 1-6). IEEE.

Li, K. C., Chen, X., Jiang, H., & Bertino, E. (Eds.). (2019). *Essentials of blockchain technology*. CRC Press. doi:10.1201/9780429674457

McCorry, P., Shahandashti, S. F., & Hao, F. (2017). A smart contract for boardroom voting with maximum voter privacy. In *Financial Cryptography and Data Security: 21st International Conference, FC 2017*, (pp. 357-375). Springer International Publishing. 10.1007/978-3-319-70972-7_20

Michael, A. R. (2016). *Título: Electronic Elections: The Perils and Promises of Digital Democracy.* Editorial Princeton University Press.

Moorkattil, X. (2022). Blockchain White Paper. *SSRN.* doi:10.2139/ssrn.4176506

Nakamoto, S. (2008). Bitcoin: A peer-to-peer electronic cash system. *Decentralized business review.* https://assets.pubpub.org/d8wct41f/31611263538139.pdf

Nogales, B. (2019). ¿Qué es un ataque de 51% de la Blockchain? *Bitcoin.es.* https://bitcoin.es/criptomonedas/que-es-un-ataque-de-51-de-la-blockchain/

Panizo, A. Luis (2007). *Aspectos tecnológicos del voto electrónico.* Oficina Nacional de Procesos Electorales (ONPE) Perú Editor. https://www.researchgate.net/publication/259668840_Aspectos_tecnologicos_del_voto_electronico

Rezvani, M. H., & Khani, H. (2019). e-Voting over Blockchain Platforms: A Survey. *Journal of Network Security and Data Mining, 2*(3), 1–14. doi:10.5281/zenodo.3463190

Rivest, L. Ronald (2009). *A Method for Obtaining Digital Signatures and Public-Key Cryptosystems.* ACM. https://dl.acm.org/doi/abs/10.1145/359340.359342

Rus, A. (2022). Ataque del 51%. *Economipedia.* https://economipedia.com/definiciones/ataque-del-51.html

Sayeed, S., & Marco-Gisbert, H. (2019). Assessment of Blockchain consensus and security mechanisms against the 51% attack. *Applied Sciences (Basel, Switzerland), 9*(9), 1788. doi:10.3390/app9091788

Taş, R., y Özgür Tanrıöver, Ö. (2020). A Systematic Review of Challenges and Opportunities of Blockchain for E-Voting. *208 MDPI Journals Awarded Impact Factor.* doi:10.3390/sym12081328

Zou, W., Lo, D., Kochhar, P. S., Le, X. B. D., Xia, X., Feng, Y., Chen, Z., & Xu, B. (2019). Smart contract development: Challenges and opportunities. *IEEE Transactions on Software Engineering, 47*(10), 2084–2106. https://ieeexplore.ieee.org/abstract/document/8847638. doi:10.1109/TSE.2019.2942301

Chapter 5
Smart Tourism:
Technologies to Improve Tourism

Ocotlán Díaz-Parra
Universidad Politécnica de Pachuca, Mexico

Alejandro Fuentes-Penna
https://orcid.org/0000-0002-4303-3852
El Colegio de Morelos, Mexico

Francisco Marroquín-Gutiérrez
Universidad Politécnica de Pachuca, Mexico

Blas Manuel Rodríguez-Lara
Tecnológico de Monterrey, Mexico

Julio C. Salgado Ramírez
Universidad Politécnica de Pachuca, Mexico

Francisco R. Trejo-Macotela
https://orcid.org/0000-0003-2133-3456
Universidad Politécnica de Pachuca, Mexico

Jaime Aguilar-Ortiz
Universidad Politécnica de Pachuca, Mexico

ABSTRACT

The tourist cities that apply technology help to strengthen and to facilitate the communication of the tourists with the sporting, cultural, and scientific aspects of a city. This chapter aims to be a guide for understanding smart tourism components by presenting a survey of the characteristics, history and future trends. Smart tourism is the innovation and the adoption of information and communication technologies in tourism. Smart tourism additionally must consider natural attractions, cultural (music festival), accessibility of transportation, amenity characteristics, ancillary services (banks, hospitals), innovative hubs for electric vehicles with a mobile app to check the availability status of charging cars, and the infrastructure of professional sports. The smart tourism is the optimal administration of the personnel or object related to the tourism by using technology like the internet of tourism things, data-mining, artificial intelligence, combinatorial optimization, machine learning, and others to enhance the quality of the tourism.

DOI: 10.4018/979-8-3693-0373-3.ch005

INTRODUCTION

The tourist has more and more information to plan their trips obtained from websites or mobile applications. To provide the information the tourist cities or Smart Tourism (part of the smart city) use the Robotics, Big Data, Artificial Intelligence (chatbots, deep Learning, machine learning), Virtual reality and augmented reality, 3d printing, Internet of things, blockchain, gamification and cybersecurity.

The tourist cities that apply technology help to strengthen and to facilitate the communication of the tourists with the sporting, cultural, and scientific aspects of a city. This chapter aims to be a guide for understanding Smart Tourism components by presenting a survey of the characteristics, history and future trends.

BACKGROUND

Main and O'Connor (1998) propose the concept of Smart hospitality; they mention that the hospitality and tourism industry fails to take advantage of the marketing intelligence gathered during visitor stays.

Camacho, Borrajo, and Molina (2001) present Intelligent Travel Planning (ITP), a multiagent planning system to solve Electronic Web problems in the Web, whose main goal is to search for useful solutions in the electronic-Tourism domain to system users. Godart (2001) uses the Travelling Salesperson Problem (TSP) as a starting point to plan trips.

Buhalis and Deimezi (2004) to examine the e-Tourism developments in Greece as a country that is gradually embracing eCommerce. They examine the level of ICT diffusion in Small and Medium-sized Tourism Enterprises (SMTEs) as well as whether the level of online presence is sufficient to cover for the lack of Destination Management System (DMS).

Maruyama et al. (2004) present a personal navigation device that calculates tourist routes called P-Tour.

Adomavicius and Tuzhilin (2005) propose Intelligent Tourism recommender systems. Ten Hagen et al. (2005) propose a collection of Tour Building Blocks (sights, restaurants, and others).

The medical tourism consists of patients travel overseas for cosmetic surgery, and medical treatment (Connel, 2006).

Lee, Kang and Park (2007) present a tourism tour planning system for a province in Korea. Vansteenwegen and Oudheusden (2007) use the OP to solve Tourist Trip Design Problems (TTDP).

Castillo et al. (2008) present a multiagent-based system for planning tourist visits. Lee, Chang, and Wang (2009) present a recommendation system that allows planning, personalized travel routes to Tainan City, China. Yu and Chang (2009) developed a framework for the personalized recommendation of hotels, restaurants, and POIs.

Sebastia et al. (2009) mention that the e-Tourism is a tourist recommendation and planning application to assist users in the organization of a leisure and tourist agenda.

Kawai, Zhang, & Kawasaki (2009) propose an advanced tour recommendation system, which includes the extraction of famous spots from the Web and route search based on the visibility of scenery along a route. Kawai, Zhang, and Kawasaki (2009) propose an efficient tourist route search system which not only recommends the path simply connecting several tourist spots, but also recommends the path with beautiful scenic sights.

Souffriau and Vansteenwegen (2010) demonstrate how existing models from the field of Operations Research fit the tourist trip planning problem, and enable a wide range of tourist trip planning functionalities.

Chakraborty, Hashimoto, and Chakraborty (2012) presented a computational framework of multiple route generation technique for a pedestrian navigation system incorporating user's preference based on computational intelligence approach, Particle Swarm Optimization (PSO), an evolutionary algorithm, has been used for generation of multiple routes with different characteristics.

The Smart Tourism Destinations (Buhalis and Amaranggana, 2013) aim is to utilize the system to enhance tourism experience and improve the effectiveness of resource management towards maximizing both destination competitiveness and consumer satisfaction while also demonstrate sustainability over an extended time frame.

The tourist trip design problem refers to a route-planning problem for tourists interested in visiting multiple points of interest. Gavalas et al. (2014) survey models, algorithmic approaches and methodologies concerning tourist trip design problems.

Smart tourism is a social phenomenon arising from the convergence of information technology with tourism experience (Hunter et al., 2015).

Hunter et al. (2015) introduce the constructivist paradigm and associated research methodologies as another toolbox for interpreting how smart tourism works as a form of soft power. The implications revealed by constructivism are that through smart tourism ecosystems, destination commoditization, experience and image formation. Smart tourism is defined as tourism supported by integrated efforts at a destination to collect and aggregate/harness data derived from the physical infrastructure, social connections, government/organizational sources and human bodies/minds in combination with the use of advanced technologies to transform that data into on-site experiences and business value-propositions with a clear focus on efficiency, sustainability and experience enrichment.

Lu et al. (2015) mention that the tourism recommender systems are programs which attempt to recommend the most suitable items (products or services) to particular users (individuals or businesses) by predicting a user's interest in an item based on related information about the items, the users and the interactions between items and users.

Koo et al. (2015) mention that the role of IT in tourism has evolved from the wired (connected through the Internet) to the wireless (connected via mobile devices), and smart technology (connected through sensors and data clouds) defines a new era of tourism.

Shiraishi et al. (2005) propose a personal navigation system which computes and shows the best route to the next destination and facilitates the composition of a schedule for visiting those destinations taking account of various requirements such as relative importance among destinations, time restrictions, travel expenses, and so on.

Kawai, Zhang, and Kawasaki (2009) propose an advanced tour recommendation system, which includes the extraction of famous spots from the Web and route search based on the visibility of scenery along a route.

Fernandes (2012) deployed a prototype of a Serious Game for Android to enable the study of the effects on tourists of an application

Gul and Topcu (2015) develop a touristic suggestion model (Analytic Hierarchy Process and Technique for Order Preference by Similarity to Ideal Solution TOPSIS multi-attribute decision-making methods) for tourist candidates with regards to their expectations and preferences about tourism.

Boes, Buhalis and Inversini (2016) explores the core components of smartness in the context of smart cities and smart tourism destinations and propose a framework to demonstrate how smartnes scan support tourism destination competitiveness.

Cacho et al. (2016) describe a smart city initiative presenting a mobile tourist guide developed for Natal, Brazil.

Sukhbaatar (2016) proposed the Iterated Local Search Algorithm to tackle the Time-Dependent Multi-Constraint Team Orienteering Problem with Time Windows and they applied the model and algorithm to mobile tourist tour recommendation system (UBTourPlanner) that enables to plan a tour for Ulaanbaatar city.

Scott et al. (2017) provides a review of eye-tracking as a technique for measurement of attention and discusses its theoretical basis, advantages and disadvantages, data collection procedures, analysis methods, and application in tourism and hospitality.

Micera and Crispino (2017) propose a framework for the analysis of the destination image-building process, where the sentiment analysis is integrated with social network analysis tools and social media analytics, making them accessible and functional for destination management choices.

Tüzünkan (2017) mention that the Smart tourism provides the adaptation of smart technologies with tourism, the internet, cloud computing, mobile communication technologies, artificial intelligence, fast wireless communication, Geographic Information System and Virtual Reality.

Tripathy et al. (2018) present a viable Internet of Things (IoT)-based solution framework (iTour) for independent tourist mobility.

Wu, and Cheng (2018) examine the relationships among technology attachment, the dimensions of experiential relationship quality, experiential risk and experiential sharing intentions by using structural equation modeling (SEM) and hierarchical regression analysis (HRA) of a convenience sample of 525 guests during check out from the LINQ Hotel & Casino in Las Vegas. They assist smart hotel management in developing and implementing market-oriented service strategies to increase the dimensions of technology attachment and the dimensions of experiential relationship quality, decrease experiential risk and create experiential sharing intentions.

Matsuda et al. (2018) propose a tourist emotion- and satisfaction-estimation system (EmoTour) to estimate the emotional status and satisfaction level of users susceptible to rating their activities (e.g., tourists during sightseeing from Germany and Japan). EmoTour employs the combination of behavioural cues and audiovisual data collected by an eye-gaze tracker, physical-activity sensors, and a smartphone. In detail, the following high-level features were derived from each modality and fused to build a final classifier: eye movement, head tilt, and footsteps from behavioural cues; and vocal and facial expressions from audiovisual data.

Dorcic, Komsic, & Markovic (2019) provides a systematic review of the most recently published academic research on mobile technologies and applications in smart tourism.

Farsani, Ghotbabadi, and Altafi (2019) investigate that the tourists are interested in agri-tours (agritourism) and both tangible and intangible agricultural heritage from the perspective of tourists.

Qin et al. (2019) uses the Big Data technology and the Call Detail Record data with the mobile phone real-time location information to monitor the tourist flow and analyse the travel behaviour of tourists in scenic areas.

Guo et al. (2019) present a framework of IoT-based intelligent tourist attractions and recognize specific intelligent functions brought by IoT techniques to tourist attractions.

Matsuda et al. (2018) propose a tourist emotion- and satisfaction-estimation system (EmoTour) to estimate the emotional status and satisfaction level of users susceptible to rating their activities (e.g., tourists during sightseeing from Germany and Japan). EmoTour employs the combination of behavioural cues and audiovisual data collected by an eye-gaze tracker, physical-activity sensors, and a smartphone. In detail, the following high-level features were derived from each modality and fused to build a final classifier: eye movement, head tilt, and footsteps from behavioural cues; and vocal and facial expressions from audiovisual data.

Dorcic, Komsic, & Markovic (2019) provides a systematic review of the most recently published academic research on mobile technologies and applications in smart tourism.

Farsani, Ghotbabadi, and Altafi (2019) investigate that the tourists are interested in agri-tours (agri-tourism) and both tangible and intangible agricultural heritage from the perspective of tourists.

Qin et al. (2019) uses the Big Data technology and the Call Detail Record data with the mobile phone real-time location information to monitor the tourist flow and analyse the travel behaviour of tourists in scenic areas.

Guo et al. (2019) present a framework of IoT-based intelligent tourist attractions and recognize specific intelligent functions brought by IoT techniques to tourist attractions.

Xiang, Zhang, Du, & Li (2019) conducted a study on the integration of social media and smart tourism destinations. They explored the use of social media platforms, such as Instagram and Facebook, as tools for enhancing tourists' experiences and promoting smart destinations. The findings revealed the importance of leveraging user-generated content, social media analytics, and personalized recommendations to create engaging and interactive experiences for tourists.

Zhang, Wang, Li, & Zhang (2020) focused on the application of artificial intelligence (AI) in smart tourism. They investigated how AI technologies, such as machine learning and natural language processing, can be employed to analyze large volumes of tourist data, automate processes, and provide personalized recommendations. The study highlighted the potential of AI in enhancing the efficiency and personalization of tourism services.

Li, Liu, Song, & Chen (2020) examined the role of blockchain technology in smart tourism. They explored the use of blockchain for secure and transparent transactions, identity verification, and data management in the tourism industry. The study highlighted the potential benefits of blockchain, such as reducing fraud, enhancing trust, and improving data privacy, in shaping the future of smart tourism.

Wang, Zhang, & Li (2020) investigated the application of virtual reality (VR) in smart tourism destinations. They explored how VR technologies can provide immersive and interactive experiences for tourists, allowing them to virtually explore destinations, historical sites, and cultural attractions. The study emphasized the potential of VR in enhancing tourists' engagement and understanding of a destination's heritage and unique features.

Gao, Pan, Li, & Wang (2020) focused on the use of chatbots in smart tourism services. They examined how chatbot technologies can provide instant and personalized assistance to tourists, offering information, recommendations, and support throughout their journey. The study highlighted the efficiency and convenience of chatbots in improving the overall tourist experience and reducing the workload of tourism service providers.

Li, Pan, Xie, & Liang (2020) conducted research on the integration of Internet of Things (IoT) and smart tourism. They explored the use of IoT devices, such as smart sensors and wearable devices, to collect real-time data and provide personalized services to tourists. The study emphasized the potential of IoT in enabling seamless connectivity, smart resource management, and enhanced safety and security in tourism destinations.

Liu, Li, & Wang (2020) examined the role of big data analytics in smart tourism. They investigated how big data can be used to analyze tourist behavior, preferences, and trends, enabling destination management organizations to make data-driven decisions and provide personalized services. The study emphasized the importance of harnessing the power of big data to enhance destination competitiveness and tourist satisfaction.

Chen, Huang, & Li (2020) focused on the use of augmented reality (AR) in smart tourism experiences. They explored how AR technologies can overlay digital information, such as historical facts, navigation guides, and interactive elements, onto the physical environment, enriching tourists' experiences and engagement. The study highlighted the potential of AR in transforming the way tourists explore and interact with destinations.

Huang, Li, Xiang, & Huang (2020) conducted a study on the impact of smart tourism on destination competitiveness. They investigated the relationship between smart tourism development, destination image, and tourist satisfaction. The findings revealed that smart tourism initiatives, such as advanced technologies and personalized services, positively influence destination competitiveness and tourists' perceptions and satisfaction.

Wang, Li, & Zhang (2021) examined the role of gamification in smart tourism experiences. They explored how gamification techniques, such as rewards, challenges, and interactive elements, can engage and motivate tourists, making their experiences more enjoyable and memorable. The study highlighted the potential of gamification in fostering tourists' participation and exploration of a destination's attractions and activities.

Wang, Xiang, Zhang, & Li (2021) conducted research on the use of social robotics in smart tourism. They investigated how social robots can interact with tourists, providing information, recommendations, and assistance in a friendly and engaging manner. The study emphasized the potential of social robotics in enhancing the quality of tourist services and creating unique and memorable experiences.

Li, Xiang, Wang, & Du (2021) focused on the application of geospatial technologies in smart tourism destinations. They explored how Geographic Information Systems (GIS) and location-based services can provide tourists with real-time navigation, personalized recommendations, and location-specific information. The study highlighted the importance of geospatial technologies in improving tourists' spatial awareness and exploration of a destination.

Zhang, Xiang, Du, & Li (2021) conducted research on the adoption of smart tourism technologies by destination management organizations. They examined the factors influencing the adoption and implementation of smart tourism initiatives, such as organizational readiness, stakeholder collaboration, and technological infrastructure. The study provided insights into the challenges and opportunities associated with the integration of smart technologies in destination management.

Wang, Li, & Zhang (2021) explored the concept of smart destinations and its implications for sustainable tourism development. They discussed how smart technologies can contribute to the economic, environmental, and social sustainability of tourism destinations. The study emphasized the need for a holistic and integrated approach to smart destination development, considering the interests and well-being of both tourists and local communities.

Xie, Li, Li, & Liu (2021) focused on the application of machine learning algorithms in smart tourism recommendation systems. They investigated how machine learning techniques can analyze tourists' preferences, behavior, and historical data to provide personalized recommendations for attractions, accommodations, and activities. The study highlighted the potential of machine learning in improving the accuracy and relevance of tourist recommendations, enhancing the overall travel experience.

SMART TOURISM

The components of Smart Cities are: smart government (Smart economics, Smart open data, Smart infrastructure, Smart disasters, Smart tourism, E-Government), Smart energy, smart healthcare, smart transportation, Smart building / home, Smart mobility, smart society / smart people / digital citizens, Smart education, smart foods production / smart farming, smart industry / manufacturing, smart environment, Smart water, Smart waste, smart life, Smart security (Secure city) (Ruiz-Vanoye et al., 2019). So that a city can be considered as Smart must comply with various elements, components or metrics.

Smart tourism is the innovation and the adoption of information and communication technologies in tourism. Smart tourism additionally must consider natural attractions, cultural (music festival), accessibility of transportation, amenity characteristics, ancillary services (banks, hospitals), innovative hubs for electric vehicles with a mobile app to check the availability status of charging cars, and the infrastructure of professional sports. The smart tourism is the optimal administration of the personnel u object related to the Tourism by using technology like the Internet of Tourism Things, data-mining, artificial intelligence, combinatorial optimization, Machine Learning, and others to enhance the quality of the Tourism.

The Technology Components of Smart Tourism are (Figure 1):

- Information and Communication Technologies for Tourism (ICTT). ICTT is the technology used in tourism. For example Internet of Tourism Things, data-mining, artificial intelligence, combinatorial optimization, machine learning, software engineering, and others. Internet of Tourism Things (IoTT) is a digital interconnect of not computational and computational Tourism-Objects (Museum, theatre, statues, monuments, temples, serene mountain area, waterfalls, spring pools, Islands, beach, mall, parking facilities, airports, bus stations, train, subway, hospitals, emergency services, park, universities, and others) using Wireless Sensor Networks, RFID technology, GPS, cell phones, sports devices, and all tourism devices with the Internet.
- Data Science. Data Science analyzes the behaviour of the data obtained from the technology devices applied to the tourism objects, extracting value from stored data, and formulating predictions through the patterns observed in order to serve for decision-making of the Smart Tourism.
- Environmental Impact. The Environmental Impact is the tourism impacts that affect the area, vegetation, air, water, land, animals, and all the environments (Briassoulis, 2000).
- Tourism Policy. Tourism policy is a set of discourses, decisions, and practices driven by governments, sometimes in collaboration with private or social actors, to achieve diverse objectives related to tourism (Velasco, 2016).
- Smart Hotel. A smart hotel is an intelligent hotel with a range of information technologies working together to let the guests have an honourable and convenient vacation environment. It allows guests to have a profound image of not only the hotel, but also the city and the country (Wu and Cheng, 2018). The elements of a smart hotel are: intelligent rooms (Leonidis et al., 2013), food (smart restaurant, smart kitchen), drinks (smart bar), entertainment, maintenance department,

department of administrative services, department of Personnel Service, smart laundries, smart public areas (terraces, balconies, Pools).

- Smart tourism destinations. Smart Tourism Destinations cored in massive tourism resource data centre, supported by the Internet of Things and Cloud Computing, focused on enhancing tourists experience through intelligent identification and monitoring (Buhalis and Amaranggana, 2013).
- Smart Government Services for Tourism. The smart government is the electronic government with open data that optimized the tourism budget for civil works (smart infrastructure) and priority services for the well-being of tourism. Smart healthcare, Secure cities, and others.

Figure 1. Smart tourism puzzle (components)

Smart Tourism in a Smart City has two kinds of problems and ways to resolve them:

- Tourism-Hard problems. All issues where there can be optimized (maximization or minimization) of tourism's resources. The Smart Tourism-Hard Problems is the management of the Tourism with Technology to optimize or monitor in real-time by the Information and Communication Technologies the physical infrastructure, aspects related to the tourism objects.
- Tourism-Soft problems. A fuzzy concept used to drive specific government tourism agendas and others. The Smart tourism-Soft Problems are the tourism problems that handle information inaccurate or incomplete, with uncertainty as well as being Ambiguous, volatile, poorly understood and dynamics (public tourism policy, administration, decision-making, tourism reforms).

Table 1. Smart tourism indicators

Smart tourism Indicators	Description
Total natural attractions	Astronomy (Solar eclipses, Midnight sun, Northern Lights), Beaches, Biomes and ecosystems, Bird watching, Botanical tourism, Caves, Exotic wildlife, Geographic records, Hot springs, space (Zero-G, Edge of space, Sub-orbital flight, Orbital flight, Trans-orbital flight), Karst, Mountain ranges, National parks, Outdoor life, Paleontology, Science tourism, UNESCO Global Geoparks Network, UNESCO World Heritage List, UNESCO World Network of Biosphere Reserves, Volcanoes, Waterfalls, Waterways, Whale watching.
Total cultural (music festival) in a year	Religion (Buddhism, Christianity, Churches of Ethiopia, Hinduism, Islam, Judaism, Sikhism, Zoroastrianism, Painted Monasteries, Sacred sites of the Indian sub-continent, Cemeteries, Imperial tombs of the Ming and Qing dynasties), Architecture (Castles, Delta Works, Florida lighthouses, Fortifications, Chicago skyline guide, New Mexico Pueblos, Le Corbusier World Heritage), Art (Visual arts, European art, Modern and contemporary art, Murals and graffiti, Art and antiques shopping), History (Archaeological sites, Old towns, Ghost towns, Industrial tourism, History of justice, Pioneer villages, UNESCO World Heritage List, Nuclear tourism, Military tourism, Indigenous peoples of North America, Military museums, Mining tourism, Spies and secrets), Ethnic groups (Celts, Sami culture in northern Scandinavia, Roma culture in Europe, Indigenous heritage, Indigenous Peoples Trail in Nepal, Indigenous cultures of North America, Indigenous cultures of South America, Minority cultures of Russia, New Mexico Pueblos), Spectator sports (American football, Australian football, Baseball in the United States, Basketball in North America, Cricket, Football in Europe, Handball in Europe, Ice hockey in North America, Motor sport, Olympic Games, Rugby football), Fiction tourism (Assassin's Creed Tour, Game of Thrones tourism, Horror fiction, James Bond tourism, Literary travel, Breaking Bad Tour, The Wire Tour, X-Files tourism), Music (European classical music, Jazz, Music festival circuit, Music in Britain and Ireland, Nordic music, Rock and roll, Salsa dancing in Latin America), Games (Chess, Xiangqi), Holidays (Christmas and New Year travel, Easter travel, Christmas markets, Halloween, Day of the Dead, Chinese New Year/Golden Week holidays in China, Travelling during Ramadan), Others (Alcoholic beverages, Art and antiques shopping, Big things in Australia, Cryptozoology, Fringe phenomena, Japan's Top 3, Monarchies, The Most Beautiful Villages of France, Museums, Musicals, Nightlife, Off the beaten track in Japan, Ohio State Parks, Places with unusual names, Reenactment and LARP, Touring prestigious and notable universities in the U.S., Trams in Melbourne, Signs, Steam power, Stand-up comedy, UFOs, Underground works, UNESCO Creative Cities, UNESCO Intangible Cultural Heritage, United Nations).
Accessibility of transportation	speaking buses, accessible apps, braille labels on the stop buttons, high-contrast features, talking elevator controls, room keys that make it easy to tell which end goes in first, central call center, hotels with screen reader or software for zooming, screen reader or software for zooming, guided tour, large history and art museums sometimes hold special hands-on tours for blind and visually impaired people, gift shop, dog guide, deaf or hard of hearing (HOH) may benefit from some specific features, such as lights on fire alarms, restaurants and stores have employees that use sign language, public services to be accessible by wheelchair, coins are intentionally designed to be easily recognizable by touch.
Amenities characteristics	High-Speed Internet, Walk-in Closet, Soundproof Walls, Balcony or Patio, In-Unit Washer and Dryer, parking, pool, fitness center, secured community access, recycling, Walkability (to easily walk to nearby amenities and locations like shopping centres or schools, striking or unique design).
Ancillary services	Bank, package shipping services, hospitals.
Innovative Hubs	An innovative hub for electric vehicles with app mobile to check all the availability status of the vehicle´s charging cars.

CONCLUSION

Smart tourism considers natural attractions, cultural (music festival), accessibility of transportation, amenity characteristics, ancillary services (banks, hospitals), innovative hubs for electric vehicles with a mobile app to check the availability status of charging cars, and the infrastructure of professional sports.

In order for a Smart City to be considered as such, it is necessary to contemplate the fundamental component called Smart Tourism and to comply with all the indicators that integrate this component.

The integration of these indicators in a smart city is essential to ensure that tourists' needs and expectations are met. The availability of natural attractions and cultural events contributes to the diversity of experiences that can be offered, while transport accessibility facilitates tourists' mobility and enhances their travel experience.

Amenity features and complementary services, such as electric vehicle charging infrastructure and the availability of banking and healthcare services, are key factors in providing comfort and security for tourists. Innovation hubs also foster creativity and collaboration in the tourism industry, promoting the adoption of innovative technologies and solutions. Smart tourism is an essential component of a smart city and plays a key role in enhancing the tourism experience.

REFERENCES

Adomavicius, G., & Tuzhilin, A. (2005). Toward the next generation of recommender systems: A survey of the state-of-the-art and possible extensions. *IEEE Transactions on Knowledge and Data Engineering*, *17*(6), 734–749. doi:10.1109/TKDE.2005.99

Boes, K., Buhalis, D., & Inversini, A. (2016). Smart tourism destinations: Ecosystems for tourism destination competitiveness. *International Journal of Tourism Cities*, *2*(2), 108–124. doi:10.1108/IJTC-12-2015-0032

Briassoulis, H. (2000). Environmental impacts of tourism: a framework for analysis and evaluation. In *Tourism and the Environment* (pp. 21–37). Springer. doi:10.1007/978-94-015-9584-1_2

Buhalis, D., & Amaranggana, A. (2013). Smart tourism destinations. In *Information and communication technologies in tourism 2014* (pp. 553–564). Springer. doi:10.1007/978-3-319-03973-2_40

Buhalis, D., & Deimezi, O. (2004). E-tourism developments in Greece: Information communication technologies adoption for the strategic management of the Greek tourism industry. *Tourism and Hospitality Research*, *5*(2), 103–130. doi:10.1057/palgrave.thr.6040011

Cacho, A., Mendes-Filho, L., Estaregue, D., Moura, B., Cacho, N., Lopes, F., & Alves, C. (2016). Mobile tourist guide supporting a smart city initiative: A Brazilian case study. *International Journal of Tourism Cities*, *2*(2), 164–183. doi:10.1108/IJTC-12-2015-0030

Camacho, D., Borrajo, D., & Molina, J. M. (2001). Intelligent travel planning: A multiagent planning system to solve web problems in the e-tourism domain. *Autonomous Agents and Multi-Agent Systems*, *4*(4), 387–392. doi:10.1023/A:1012767210241

Castillo, L., Armengol, E., Onaindía, E., Sebastiá, L., González-Boticario, J., Rodríguez, A., Fernandez, S., Arias, J. D., & Borrajo, D. (2008). samap: An user-oriented adaptive system for planning tourist visits. *Expert Systems with Applications*, *34*(2), 1318–1332. doi:10.1016/j.eswa.2006.12.029

Chakraborty, B., Hashimoto, T., & Chakraborty, G. (2012, November). Fuzzy-PSO based route recommendation for user aware pedestrian navigation system. In *TENCON 2012 IEEE Region 10 Conference* (pp. 1–6). IEEE. doi:10.1109/TENCON.2012.6412292

Chen, M., Huang, Z., & Li, X. (2020). Augmented reality in tourism: A review of literature. *Journal of Travel Research, 59*(1), 3–19.

Connell, J. (2006). Medical tourism: Sea, sun, sand and… surgery. *Tourism Management, 27*(6), 1093–1100. doi:10.1016/j.tourman.2005.11.005

Dorcic, J., Komsic, A., & Markovic, I. (2019). Mobile technologies and applications in smart tourism: A systematic literature review. *Journal of Hospitality and Tourism Technology, 10*(2), 343–367.

Dorcic, J., Komsic, J., & Markovic, S. (2019). Mobile technologies and applications towards smart tourism–state of the art. *Tourism Review, 74*(1), 82–103. doi:10.1108/TR-07-2017-0121

Farsani, N. T., Ghotbabadi, A. R., & Altafi, A. (2019). Agri-tourism as a sustainable form of rural tourism: A systematic literature review. *Journal of Hospitality and Tourism Management, 41*, 218–232.

Farsani, N. T., Ghotbabadi, S. S., & Altafi, M. (2019). Agricultural heritage as a creative tourism attraction. *Asia Pacific Journal of Tourism Research, 24*(6), 541–549. doi:10.1080/10941665.2019.1593205

Fernandes, R. P. A. (2012). *Towards a collaborative tourist system using serious games*. UNIVERSIDADE DOPORTO.

Gao, L., Pan, B., Li, X., & Wang, D. (2020). Chatbots in tourism: A review of recent studies. *Journal of Hospitality and Tourism Management, 44*, 154–163.

Garcia, A., Linaza, M. T., Gutierrez, A., & Garcia, E. (2019). Gamified mobile experiences: Smart technologies for tourism destinations. *Tourism Review, 74*(1), 30–49. doi:10.1108/TR-08-2017-0131

Gavalas, D., Konstantopoulos, C., Mastakas, K., & Pantziou, G. (2014). A survey on algorithmic approaches for solving tourist trip design problems. *Journal of Heuristics, 20*(3), 291–328. doi:10.100710732-014-9242-5

Godart, J. M. (2001). Combinatorial optimisation for trip planning. *Belgian Journal of Operations Research, Statistics and Computer Science, 41*(1-2), 59–68.

Gretzel, U., Sigala, M., Xiang, Z., & Koo, C. (2015). Smart tourism: Foundations and developments. *Electronic Markets, 25*(3), 179–188. doi:10.100712525-015-0196-8

Gul, S., & Topcu, I. (2015). A Multi-Attribute Decision Support Model for the Selection of Touristic Activities. *International Journal of the Analytic Hierarchy Process, 7*(3). Advance online publication. doi:10.13033/ijahp.v7i3.354

Guo, L., Wu, H., Li, Z., Wu, W., & Zhang, C. (2019). An IoT-based intelligent tourist attraction framework: Concepts, technologies, and applications. *IEEE Access : Practical Innovations, Open Solutions, 7*, 10458–10467.

Huang, Z., Li, X., Xiang, Z., & Huang, D. (2020). Smart tourism destination competitiveness and tourist satisfaction: An empirical study. *Journal of Travel Research, 59*(6), 1090–1107.

Hunter, W. C., Chung, N., Gretzel, U., & Koo, C. (2015). Constructivist research in smart tourism. *Asia Pacific Journal of Information Systems, 25*(1), 105–120. doi:10.14329/apjis.2015.25.1.105

Kawai, Y., Zhang, J., & Kawasaki, H. (2009, June). Tour recommendation system based on web information and GIS. In *2009 IEEE International Conference on Multimedia and Expo* (pp. 990-993). IEEE. 10.1109/ICME.2009.5202663

Kurata, Y. (2009, June). Challenges in user-adaptive tour planning systems. In *AGILE Workshop on Adaptation in Spatial Communication* (pp. 19-26).

Lee, C. S., Chang, Y. C., & Wang, M. H. (2009). Ontological recommendation multi-agent for Tainan City travel. *Expert Systems with Applications*, *36*(3), 6740–6753. doi:10.1016/j.eswa.2008.08.016

Lee, J., Kang, E., & Park, G. L. (2007, August). Design and implementation of a tour planning system for telematics users. In *International Conference on Computational Science and Its Applications* (pp. 179-189). Springer, Berlin, Heidelberg. 10.1007/978-3-540-74484-9_16

Leonidis, A., Korozi, M., Margetis, G., Grammenos, D., & Stephanidis, C. (2013, December). An intelligent hotel room. In *International Joint Conference on Ambient Intelligence* (pp. 241-246). Springer, Cham. 10.1007/978-3-319-03647-2_19

Li, X., Liu, H., Song, H., & Chen, J. (2020). Blockchain in tourism and hospitality: A systematic review. *Journal of Travel Research*, *59*(7), 1244–1263.

Li, X., Pan, B., Xie, K., & Liang, Z. (2020). Internet of things and smart tourism: A systematic review of literature and future directions. *Journal of Travel Research*, *59*(2), 215–231.

Li, X., Xiang, Z., Wang, D., & Du, Q. (2021). Geospatial technologies in smart tourism destinations: A systematic review. *Journal of Travel Research*, *60*(2), 436–453.

Liu, H., Li, X., & Wang, D. (2020). Big data analytics in tourism and hospitality: A literature review. *Tourism Management*, *74*, 103961.

Lu, J., Wu, D., Mao, M., Wang, W., & Zhang, G. (2015). Recommender system application developments: A survey. *Decision Support Systems*, *74*, 12–32. doi:10.1016/j.dss.2015.03.008

Main, H. C., & O'Connor, P. (1998). The use of smart card technology to develop a destination based loyalty/affinity scheme for SMES in tourism and hospitality. In *Information and communication technologies in tourism 1998* (pp. 7–15). Springer. doi:10.1007/978-3-7091-7504-0_2

Maruyama, A., Shibata, N., Murata, Y., Yasumoto, K., & Ito, M. (2004, March). A personal tourism navigation system to support traveling multiple destinations with time restrictions. In *18th International Conference on Advanced Information Networking and Applications, 2004. AINA 2004.* (Vol. 2, pp. 18-21). IEEE. 10.1109/AINA.2004.1283747

Matsuda, Y., Fedotov, D., Takahashi, Y., Arakawa, Y., Yasumoto, K., & Minker, W. (2018). EmoTour: Estimating Emotion and Satisfaction of Users Based on Behavioral Cues and Audiovisual Data. *Sensors (Basel)*, *18*(11), 3978. doi:10.339018113978 PMID:30445798

Matsuda, Y., Sugiyama, O., & Yagi, Y. (2018). EmoTour: A tourist emotion- and satisfaction-estimation system using multimodal sensing and machine learning. *IEEE Transactions on Multimedia*, *20*(12), 3307–3319.

Micera, R., & Crispino, R. (2017). Destination web reputation as "smart tool" for image building: The case analysis of naples city-destination. *International Journal of Tourism Cities, 3*(4), 406–423. doi:10.1108/IJTC-11-2016-0048

Qin, S., Man, J., Wang, X., Li, C., Dong, H., & Ge, X. (2019). Applying Big Data Analytics to Monitor Tourist Flow for the Scenic Area Operation Management. *Discrete Dynamics in Nature and Society, 2019*, 2019. doi:10.1155/2019/8239047

Qin, X., Liu, Z., Chen, Y., Li, Z., Wang, Z., & Li, Z. (2019). Monitoring tourist flow and travel behavior in scenic areas using big data and CDR data. *Tourism Management, 75*, 345–357.

Scott, N., Zhang, R., Le, D., & Moyle, B. (2017). A review of eye-tracking research in tourism. *Current Issues in Tourism*, 1–18.

Sebastia, L., Garcia, I., Onaindia, E., & Guzman, C. (2009). e-Tourism: A tourist recommendation and planning application. *International Journal of Artificial Intelligence Tools, 18*(05), 717–738. doi:10.1142/S0218213009000378

Shiraishi, T., Nagata, M., Shibata, N., Murata, Y., Yasumoto, K., & Ito, M. (2005). A personal navigation system with functions to compose tour schedules based on multiple conflicting criteria. *IPSJ Digital Courier, 1*, 528–536. doi:10.2197/ipsjdc.1.528

Souffriau, W., & Vansteenwegen, P. (2010, July). Tourist trip planning functionalities: State–of–the–art and future. In *International Conference on Web Engineering* (pp. 474-485). Springer, Berlin, Heidelberg. 10.1007/978-3-642-16985-4_46

Sukhbaatar, U. (2016). *A model simulation for trip planning recommendation system in Tourism* [Doctoral dissertation, Université Grenoble Alpes].

Ten Hagen, K., Kramer, R., Hermkes, M., Schumann, B., & Mueller, P. (2005). Semantic matching and heuristic search for a dynamic tour guide. In *Information and Communication Technologies in Tourism 2005* (pp. 149–159). Springer. doi:10.1007/3-211-27283-6_14

Tripathy, A. K., Tripathy, P. K., Ray, N. K., & Mohanty, S. P. (2018). iTour: The future of smart tourism: An IoT framework for the independent mobility of tourists in smart cities. *IEEE Consumer Electronics Magazine, 7*(3), 32–37. doi:10.1109/MCE.2018.2797758

Tüzünkan, D. (2017). The Relationship between Innovation and Tourism: The Case of Smart Tourism. *International Journal of Applied Engineering Research: IJAER, 12*(23), 13861–13867.

Vansteenwegen, P., & Van Oudheusden, D. (2007). The mobile tourist guide: an OR opportunity. *OR insight, 20*(3), 21-27.

Velasco, M. (2016). Tourism Policy. In A. Farazmand (Ed.), *Global Encyclopedia of Public Administration, Public Policy, and Governance*. Springer. doi:10.1007/978-3-319-31816-5_2674-1

Wang, D., Li, X., & Zhang, J. (2021). Gamification in tourism: A review of literature. *Journal of Travel Research, 60*(1), 104–124.

Wang, D., Li, X., & Zhang, J. (2021). Smart destination and sustainable tourism development: A review of literature. *Journal of Sustainable Tourism, 29*(3), 291–309.

Wang, D., Xiang, Z., Zhang, J., & Li, X. (2021). Social robots in tourism and hospitality: A review of current research. *Journal of Hospitality and Tourism Management, 48*, 139–151.

Wang, D., Zhang, J., & Li, X. (2020). Virtual reality for tourism: A systematic review. *Tourism Management, 82*, 104202.

Wu, H. C., & Cheng, C. C. (2018). Relationships between technology attachment, experiential relationship quality, experiential risk and experiential sharing intentions in a smart hotel. *Journal of Hospitality and Tourism Management, 37*, 42–58. doi:10.1016/j.jhtm.2018.09.003

Wu, H. C., & Cheng, C. C. (2018). Relationships between technology attachment, experiential relationship quality, experiential risk and experiential sharing intentions in a smart hotel. *Journal of Hospitality and Tourism Management, 37*, 42–58. doi:10.1016/j.jhtm.2018.09.003

Xiang, Z., Zhang, D., Du, Q., & Li, G. (2019). Understanding social media data for smart tourism destination: An integrated approach. *Journal of Travel Research, 58*(9), 1656–1670.

Xie, K., Li, X., Li, X., & Liu, H. (2021). Machine learning in smart tourism recommendation systems: A systematic review. *Journal of Travel Research, 60*(4), 933–952.

Yu, C. C., & Chang, H. P. (2009, September). Personalized location-based recommendation services for tour planning in mobile tourism applications. In *International Conference on Electronic Commerce and Web Technologies* (pp. 38-49). Springer, Berlin, Heidelberg. 10.1007/978-3-642-03964-5_5

Zhang, J., Wang, D., Li, X., & Zhang, W. (2020). Artificial intelligence in smart tourism: A review. *Journal of Hospitality and Tourism Management, 44*, 103–116.

Zhang, J., Xiang, Z., Du, Q., & Li, X. (2021). Adoption of smart tourism technologies by destination management organizations: A systematic review. *Journal of Travel Research, 60*(3), 674–690.

Chapter 6
House of Quality for Safe Cities

Ocotlán Díaz-Parra
Universidad Politécnica de Pachuca, Mexico

Alejandro Fuentes-Penna
https://orcid.org/0000-0002-4303-3852
Colegio de Morelos, Mexico

Francisco Marroquín-Gutiérrez
Universidad Politécnica de Pachuca, Mexico

Julio C. Ramos-Fernández
Universidad Politécnica de Pachuca, Mexico

Blas Manuel Rodríguez-Lara
Tecnológico de Monterrey, Mexico

Ricardo A. Barrera-Cámara
https://orcid.org/0000-0002-3170-4671
Universidad Autónoma del Carmen, Mexico

Miguel Angel Ruiz-Jaimes
https://orcid.org/0000-0002-2585-9896
Universidad Politécnica del Estado de Morelos, Mexico

Evelyn Valeria V. Tafoya
Universidad Politécnica de Pachuca, Mexico

ABSTRACT

The concept of safe cities is relatively new and is addressed as an outcome of Crime Prevention Environmental Design (CPTED). Safe cities use technology to help governments, communities, and businesses reduce the likelihood of crime and create an environment where people feel safe and comfortable. In this context, the house of quality (HoQ) presents itself as a valuable tool to ensure the design of safe cities and respond to community needs. The HoQ is a graphical matrix that establishes the relationship between citizens' demands and design features. By applying the HoQ in the context of safe cities, priority areas for the implementation of safety measures can be identified, as well as understanding community expectations and needs in terms of safety. This methodology provides a systematic approach to urban planning and design, helping to improve security and promoting safer and more livable urban environments.

DOI: 10.4018/979-8-3693-0373-3.ch006

INTRODUCTION

The safe city concept is practically new and is handled as a result of Crime Prevention Through Environmental Design (CPTED). Safe City is an idea in a community that uses technology to help governments, communities and businesses reduce the possibility of crime and provide an environment where people feel safe and comfortable (Smith, 2020). We also consider the safe city as the influence of diverse technologies (combinatorial Optimization, Machine Learning, Big Data, data visualisation, Internet of Things, Big-Data Analytics, software and others) to enhance the service quality of security objects. Secure city in a Smart City has three general kinds of problems and ways to resolve them:

- Security-Hard problems. The Security-hard problems can be optimised (from Combinatorial Optimization: maximisation or minimisation) of the public security's resources.
- Security-Soft problems. The security-soft problems are a fuzzy concept used to drive specific security government agendas and others. The security-Soft Problems are the security problems that handle information inaccurate or incomplete, with uncertainty and ambiguity, volatile, poorly understood and dynamics (security public policy, administration, decision-making, security government reforms).
- Security-wicked problems. The complex, intractable, open-ended and wicked security problems are a problem that is difficult or impossible to solve because it presents incomplete, contradictory and changing requirements that are generally difficult to recognise. This problem requires deliberation and debate.

The components of a safe city are (Figure 1). In this document, we propose the idea components as parts of a jigsaw puzzle, where each piece of the puzzle is an important and unique element that interacts to form the secure city comprehensively. This puzzle can be updated and improved as time and generations change, to obtain better secure cities:

- Edge computing devices— Edge Computing encompasses industries such as transportation, healthcare, manufacturing, agriculture and Smart Farms, Energy, security, and others; an environment where everything is connected to everyone: Vehicle to Pedestrian (V2P), Vehicle to Vehicle (V2V), Vehicle to Infrastructure (V2I), Vehicle to Network (V2N), Vehicle to Everything (V2X).
- Safe cities framework—The Safe Cities Index is a global, policy benchmarking tool developed to measure urban safety. Score draws on personal, infrastructure, health, digital and environmental security.
- Data Science. Secure cities use Big-Data analytics to make a policy decision based on the information government (Crime prevention and investigations, and other public services).
- Smart Security Policy—Smart Security policies are agreements or laws (regulations and agreements) governmental related to security.
- Internet of Security Things (IoST) —The IoST is a digital interconnect of security objects using sensors and RFID technology with the Internet. The security-objects could be Police patrol, fire trucks, control traffic lights, surveillance cameras, intelligent public transportation, potable water, waste, parking, bridges, railway tracks, cameras urban, and others.

- Smart Government—The smart government is the electronic government with open data that optimised the budget for civil works and priority services for the well-being of citizens; and the smart government must consider smart disasters and security.
- Smart Healthcare— Smart Healthcare is the influence of diverse technologies (Combinatorial Optimization, Machine Learning, Big Data, data visualisation, Internet of Healthcare Things, and others) to enhance the quality of HealthCare. Smart healthcare is the use of electronic-health, mobile-health intelligent systems to connect medical devices. It also involves implementing policies that encourage health, wellness and well-being of citizens, and health monitoring and diagnostics as opposed to treatment.
- Smart Infrastructure—Smart infrastructure includes systems that manage, communicate and integrate different types of intelligent infrastructure such as energy grids, transport networks, water and waste management systems and telecommunications, police networks, and others related to the security of a city.
- Smart Life—This component provides (with technology or without) peace and labour and emotional stability for citizens to live with dignity. Smart life contains smart age-friendly, smart security (safe city includes digital security, health security, security infrastructure, personal safety), cultural facilities, and social cohesion.
- Smart Environmental—The smart environment must optimise (minimise the cost of management) water (smart water) and waste (smart waste). The smart environment can control devices related to smart water, smart waste, attractive natural conditions, pollution, animal protection, and the sustainable management of the resources.

Figure 1. Components of the secure cities; figure (puzzle) 1 shows the technology components of secure cities

The Security-objects could be Police patrol, fire truck, a box of votes, control traffic lights, surveillance cameras, public transportation, potable water, public parking, bridges, railway tracks, cameras urban, monitor the proper functioning of its structures as well as more flexibly adapt their operation to new events, the network of electric power, transformers, high voltage lines, ambulances, emergency rooms, intensive care rooms, hazardous waste, actively monitor the patients an outpatient basis and non-invasive, train, subway, truck, helicopter, the processes and activities educational, research, administrative and other aspects related to the institutions of higher education as strategies for teaching and learning, smart campus), smart classroom, and the smart education, atmospheric, meteorological, sensors and seismic systems, and others.

To assess whether a city is secure, it is necessary to use indicators to evaluate the security's services. There are security indicators (Safe Cities Index 2021 framework) used to determine if the smart city is a Secure City, see Table 1: Digital security (assesses the ability of urban citizens to freely use the internet and other digital channels without fear of privacy violations, identity theft and malicious online attacks). Health security measures how cities fare on the level and quality of healthcare services and infrastructure in the city. Infrastructure security considers the built physical environment, measuring the availability, quality and sufficiency of existing city infrastructure and its vulnerability to man-made and natural disasters. Personal security considers how at-risk citizens are from crime, violence, terrorist threats, natural disasters and economic vulnerabilities. Environmental security considers how the city has incorporated sustainability parameters into its urban planning to reduce carbon emissions and manage climate risks.

According to the research by Ginting et al. (2020), since its formalization in the 1960s and 1970s, Quality Function Deployment (QFD) techniques have helped various public and industrial sectors to ensure product quality in different stages of creation. To establish the relationship between customer needs and technical characteristics of the product, the House of Quality (HOQ) is used, where weighted values are assigned to ensure that services or products align with customer desires.

Sahin and Demirtas (2020) utilized the QFD technique, providing a HOQ based on a DSS (Decision Support System), on a proportional scale, to determine customer and technical requirements in the banking sector and understand the desires and expectations in the use of credit cards for university students. The study found, as one of the results, that the relative weights in internet shopping security are the highest. Finally, it highlights the potential future work to integrate it as a mathematical model for the optimization of target values.

Spasova and Raiu (2022) demonstrated the use of the HOQ method to evaluate quality within software engineering, as this tool is often more commonly used in product and service development. They evaluated two template engines, Twig and Blade, to assess their functionality and performance based on customer feedback. This helped developers understand customer needs and avoid making mistakes when working with them.

Barad (2019) implemented a structured framework based on Quality Function Deployment (QFD) in his research for future investigation on improving cybersecurity in the healthcare industry. He referred to the House of Quality as a foundation and represented it through two corresponding matrices. One matrix translated the strategic needs for improving the healthcare system, while the other focused on enhancing cybersecurity procedures.

Lombardi et al. (2020) applied the knowledge of the House of Quality to adapt it to the context of security engineering. As they mention, the QFD method was developed as a tool to assist in the design of products and services, supported by the use of House of Quality matrices. The approach they adopt is to utilize this tool to create the so-called House of Security (HoS), expanding the concept to information physical security.

HOUSE OF QUALITY FOR SECURE CITIES

The Quality Function Deployment concept appeared in Japan in the 1960s decade and quickly spread due to several factors. The construction of the QFD instrument makes use of a graphical method that determines the relations between the demands of customers and the characteristics of the design. In the matrix structure, customer expectations (attributes) are contrasted with the design characteristics (Sullivan, 1986; Hauser & Clausing, 1988; Cohen, 1995).

The House of Quality applied to Secure City is a framework to convert the city's needs into a set of specifications to improve the security of a Smart City. The House of Quality for the Secure City (Figure 2) includes:

- Requirements of the Secure City. It is one of the House of Quality inputs, and it defines the analysis, interviews, assessing risks and vulnerabilities in the Smart City.
- The relationship matrix. This is the dimension where requirements correspond or match with the characteristics or specifications of the improvement of security.
- Secure City Characteristics. Product features or specifications to improve the secure city.
- Correlation matrix. This stage is classified as strongly positive, positive, negative, strongly negative and none.
- Competitive benchmark. The result of the relationship matrix is compared with the security products available on the market. And is used to enhance weaknesses identified in the comparison.
- Technical Details. In this section, the matrix relationship begins to analyse and measure the city's needs related to the times, costs and difficulties.
- Technical Benchmark. This is the assessment of the improvements to the needs of the Cities and the specifications or City characteristics.
- Goals. Herein determining the goals that must be obtained to improve the needs of the city.

Figure 2. The methodology of house of quality applied to secure cities

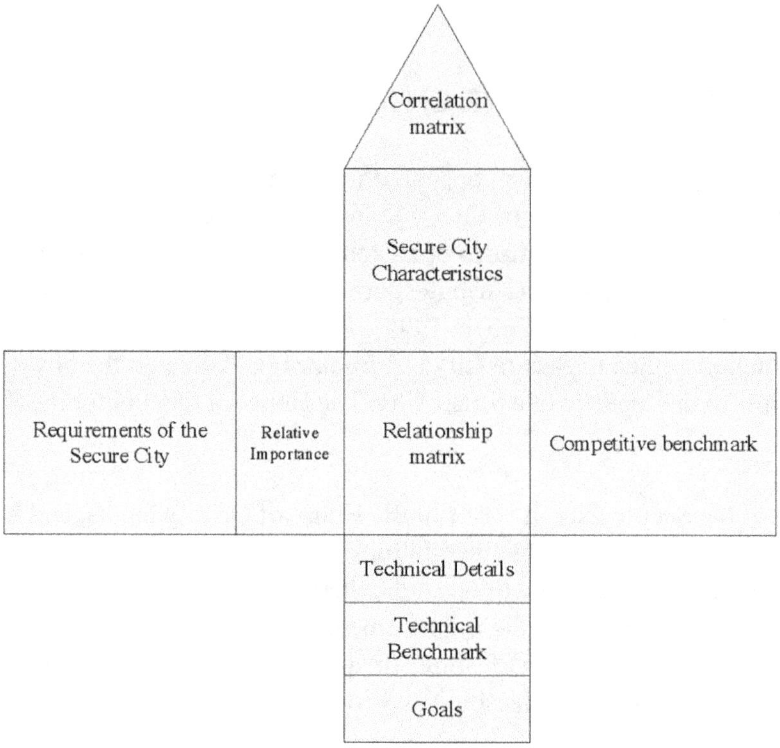

In this section, the House of Quality applies to analyse strategies to improve a Secure city. The House of Quality is applied to the city of Cuernavaca, México. The process for making the House of Quality for Secure City consists of the following steps

1. -Make a list or select needs of the secure City (from Table 1). And the ranks assigned section for the needs of the Secure City (Table 2). It also determines the relative importance (RI) of each of the needs with values between 0 (unimportant) to 10 (very important).

Table 1. Security indicators (Safe Cities Index 2021 framework)

Areas	Indicators
Digital security	Privacy policy, Citizen awareness of digital Threats, Cybersecurity preparedness, Percentage with internet access, Secure internet servers, Risk of attacks, IT infrastructure risk, Percentage of computers Infected from online attacks.
Health security	Universal healthcare coverage (No. of beds per 1,000, No. of doctors per 1,000, Quality of private healthcare Provision, Quality of public healthcare provision), Access to safe and quality food, Policy on substance abuse / drug use, Pandemic preparedness, Mental health, Emergency services in the city, Life expectancy years, Infant mortality, Cancer mortality, Lifestyle-related disease burden, Mental health burden, pandemic mortality.
Infrastructure security	Enforcement of transport safety, Pedestrian friendliness, Disaster management/business continuity plan, Water infrastructure, Hazard monitoring, Road traffic deaths, Deaths from climate-related disasters, Transport infrastructure: Air transport facilities, Road network, Rail network. Power network, Catastrophe insurance, Disaster-risk informed Development, Percentage living in slums, Percentage of Homeless Population.
Personal security	Use of data-driven techniques for crime, Gun regulation and enforcement, Threat of terrorism, Threat of military conflict, Threat of civil unrest, Police personnel per capita, Prosecution personnel per capita, Professional judges or magistrate, Expenditure on social security, Laws on domestic violence, Laws on sexual harassment, Prevalence of petty crime, Prevalence of violent crime, Organised crime, Severity of terrorist attacks, Deaths from substance use disorders, Level of corruption, Income inequality levels, Share of population in vulnerable employment, Female homicide rates, Prevalence of domestic violence.

After conducting analyses, interviews and risk and vulnerability assessments, we identified the following requirements:

Table 2. Needs of the smart city (Cuernavaca)

# Rows	RelativeImportance	Requirements of the Smart City
1	9.0	Constant surveillance and monitoring of public areas.
2	10.0	Rapid and efficient response to emergencies.
3	9.0	Adequate and safe lighting in public spaces.
4	9.0	Prevention of crime and suspicious activities.
5	9.0	Effective communication between security services and citizens.

Others possible needs that you can consider: Effective law enforcement and crime prevention measures, Robust surveillance and monitoring systems, Quick emergency response and effective disaster management, Adequate street lighting and well-maintained public spaces, Secure and reliable transportation infrastructure, Accessible and secure public facilities (e.g., parks, schools, hospitals), Strong cybersecurity measures to protect digital infrastructure, Active community engagement and involvement in safety initiatives, Effective measures to combat organized crime and terrorism, and Reliable and efficient communication systems for emergency situations.

2.- Determine City Characteristics (CC) that focus on how you should implement the city's aspects. And assigns in the columns for the features section of the city (Table 3).

Tabla 3. Secure city characteristics

#Column	City Characteristics
1	Equip police vehicles with advanced communication systems.
2	Implement surveillance cameras in police cars.
3	Provide first aid equipment in police vehicles.
4	Install high resolution cameras in strategic locations.
5	Implement real-time video analysis systems.
6	Integrate cameras with the centralised monitoring system.
7	Install efficient and high quality LED lighting in public spaces.
8	Implement motion sensors for automatic lighting.
9	Carry out regular maintenance of existing lights.
10	Develop an intuitive and user-friendly interface for crime and emergency reporting.
11	Integrate the app with emergency response systems
12	Provide real-time updates on safety and security in the city.

Other possible city characteristics: Efficient transportation infrastructure, Well-planned urban design and layout, Sustainable energy and waste management systems, Accessible and inclusive public spaces, Advanced technology and digital infrastructure, Integrated public transportation systems, High-quality healthcare facilities, Reliable and efficient public services (water, electricity, etc.), Affordable housing options for all income levels, Strong community engagement and participation, Vibrant cultural and recreational amenities, Effective urban security and crime prevention measures, Sustainable and green building practices, Educational institutions and lifelong learning opportunities, and Promoting economic growth and entrepreneurship.

3. - Develops the evaluation corresponding to the matrix of relationship. Assigns Θ to the strong relationship (9), O moderate relationship (3), or ? weak relationship (1) where the needs corresponding or match the City characteristics (Table 4). In this stage, we assessed the correlation between the requirements and the characteristics. We used categories such as "strongly positive", "positive", "negative", "strongly negative" and "none":

Table 4. The matrix of relationship

	Peso Importancia relativa		CITY CHARACTERISTICS / Requeriments of the Secure City(1)	Equip police vehicles with advanced communication systems.	Implement surveillance cameras in police cars.	Provide first aid equipment in police vehicles.	Install high resolution cameras in strategic locations	Implement real-time video analysis systems.	Integrate cameras with the centralised monitoring system.	Install efficient and high quality LED lighting in public spaces.	Implement motion sensors for automatic lighting.	Carry out regular maintenance of existing lights.	Develop an intuitive and user-friendly interface for crime and emergency reporting.	Integrate the app with emergency response systems.	Provide real-time updates on safety and security in the city.
1	19.6	9.0	Constant surveillance and monitoring of public areas.	⊙	⊙	⊙	O	O	O	O	O	O	O	O	O
2	21.7	10.0	Rapid and efficient response to emergencies.	⊙	⊙	⊙							O	O	O
3	19.6	9.0	Adequate and safe lighting in public spaces.	O	O	O				⊙	⊙	⊙			
4	19.6	9.0	Prevention of crime and suspicious activities.	O	O	O	O	O	O				O	O	O
5	19.6	9.0	Effective communication between security services and citizens.	O	O	O	O	O	O	O	O	O	⊙	⊙	⊙

4.- Assigns 5-10 to City products on the market at competitive benchmark section (Table 5). City products will serve to improve the weaknesses identified in the city. Rate 0 to 5, where 0 is the worst rating of the product that solves the city's weaknesses and 5 is the best.

Table 5. Competitive benchmark

Benchmark competitivo
(0=Worst, 5=Best)

ENTERPRISE 1	ENTERPRISE 2	ENTERPRISE 3	ENTERPRISE 4	ENTERPRISE 5	ENTERPRISE 6
				3	4
				2	5
4	3	3			
4	4	4			
3	3	3	5		
4	4	4	5		
			5		
				4	4
				4	4
				5	5

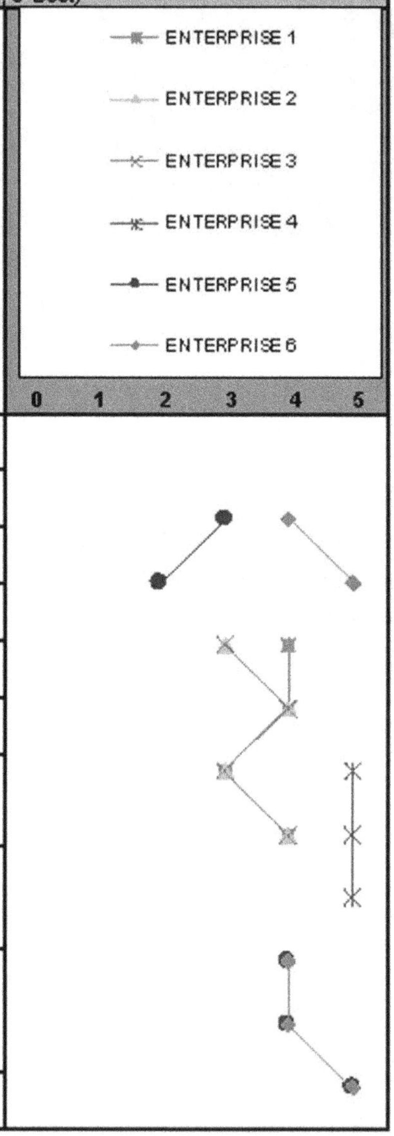

5. - Determines the time and computational costs of each solution, and the difficulty required to implement the business plan according to the city in the technical details section. Assign between 0 to implementation that is easy to perform and 10 if it is extremely difficult (Table 6).
6. - Calculate the importance of improving the aspects of the city and allocate in the section technical benchmark from 0 (unimportant) to 10 (very important), (Table 6).
7. - Determine the goals to be fulfilled at the time of improving the Smart City and assigned them to the goals section (Table 6).

Table 6. Technical details, technical benchmark, and goals

Technical Details (Time, Cost)	3 MONTH, 80,000 USD	2 Months, 50,000 USD	1 WEEK, 100 USD	2 MONTHS, 5,000 USD	1 WEEK, 2,000 USD	6 MONTHS, 200,000 USD	2 MONTHS, 100,000 USD	1 WEEK, 10,000 USD	1 WEEK, 10,000 USD	1 WEEK, 10,000 USD	1 WEEK, 10,000 USD	1 YEAR, 2,500,000 USD
Difficulty	4	4	3	9	1	9	7	8	9	9	8	9
Technical Benchmark (Importance)	4	4	3	4	2	5	4	4	5	4	4	3
Goals	Infrastructure	Infrastructure	Report	Software	Services	Infrastucture	Infrastucture	Software	Software	Software	Software	Infrastucture

Goals	Description
Goal 1:	Reduce the overall crime rate by a 20 percentage in two years.
Goal 2:	Enhance the effectiveness of law enforcement and emergency response systems to ensure quick and efficient interventions.
Goal 3:	Improve public perception of safety and security by implementing visible security measures and promoting community engagement.
Goal 4:	Enhance the physical infrastructure of the city to deter criminal activities and create a secure environment.
Goal 5:	Establish a comprehensive surveillance system to monitor critical areas and detect potential security threats.
Goal 6:	Enhance the lighting infrastructure to improve visibility and deter criminal activities in public spaces.
Goal 7:	Implement proactive measures for disaster management and emergency preparedness.
Goal 8:	Strengthen cybersecurity systems to protect critical infrastructure and digital assets from cyber threats.
Goal 9:	Foster collaboration between law enforcement agencies, community organizations, and residents to create a cohesive security network.
Goal 10:	Promote education and awareness programs to empower individuals with the knowledge and skills to contribute to the safety of the city.
Goal 11:	Develop and implement policies and regulations that support the prevention and reduction of crime.
Goal 12:	Establish effective communication channels between authorities and the public to disseminate information and receive feedback.
Goal 13:	Ensure equitable access to security resources and services across different neighborhoods and communities.
Goal 14:	Improve data collection and analysis to identify patterns and trends in criminal activities for better decision-making.
Goal 15:	Continuously evaluate and update security measures based on emerging technologies and evolving threats.

8. - Rate the correlation between each of the City features and assign ++ to the strong positive correlation, + the positive correlation, ■ the negative correlation, ▼ if the objective is to minimise, ▲ if the objective is to maximise, *x* if the goal is only the fulfilment of the activity (Figure 3 and 4).

Figure 3. Correlations

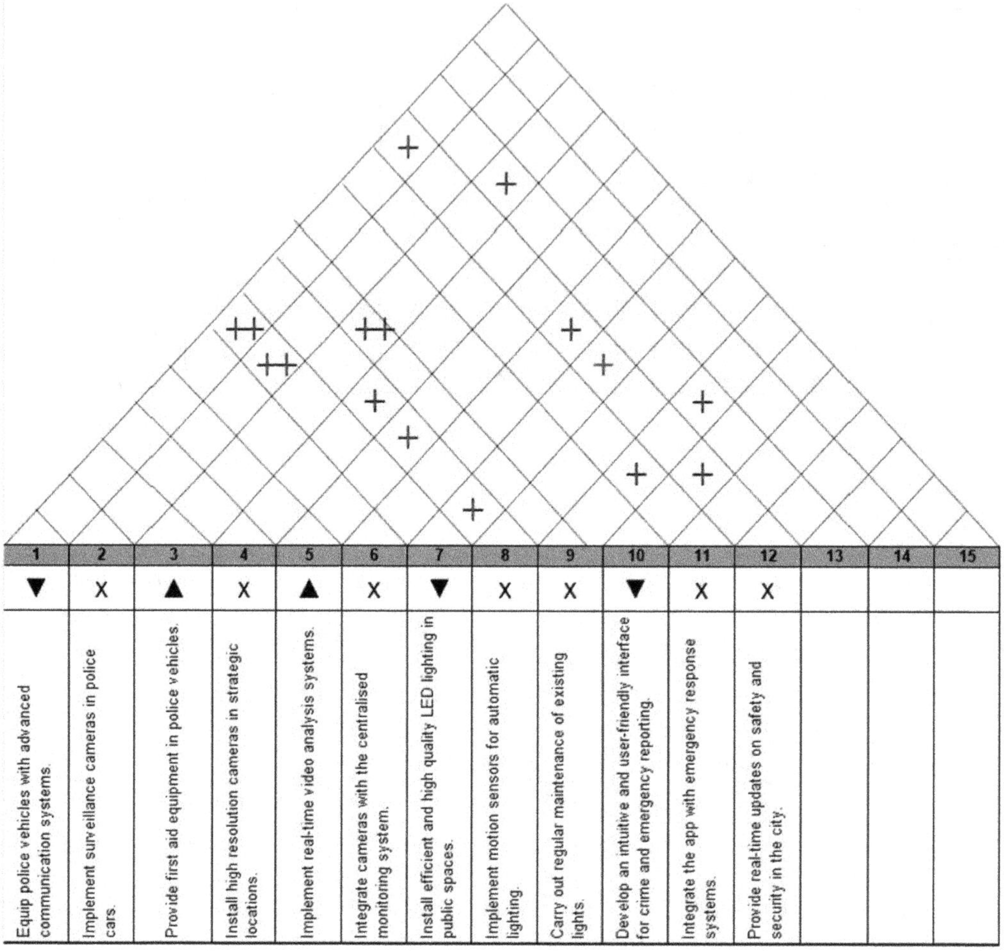

Figure 4. House of quality for the Cuernavaca City

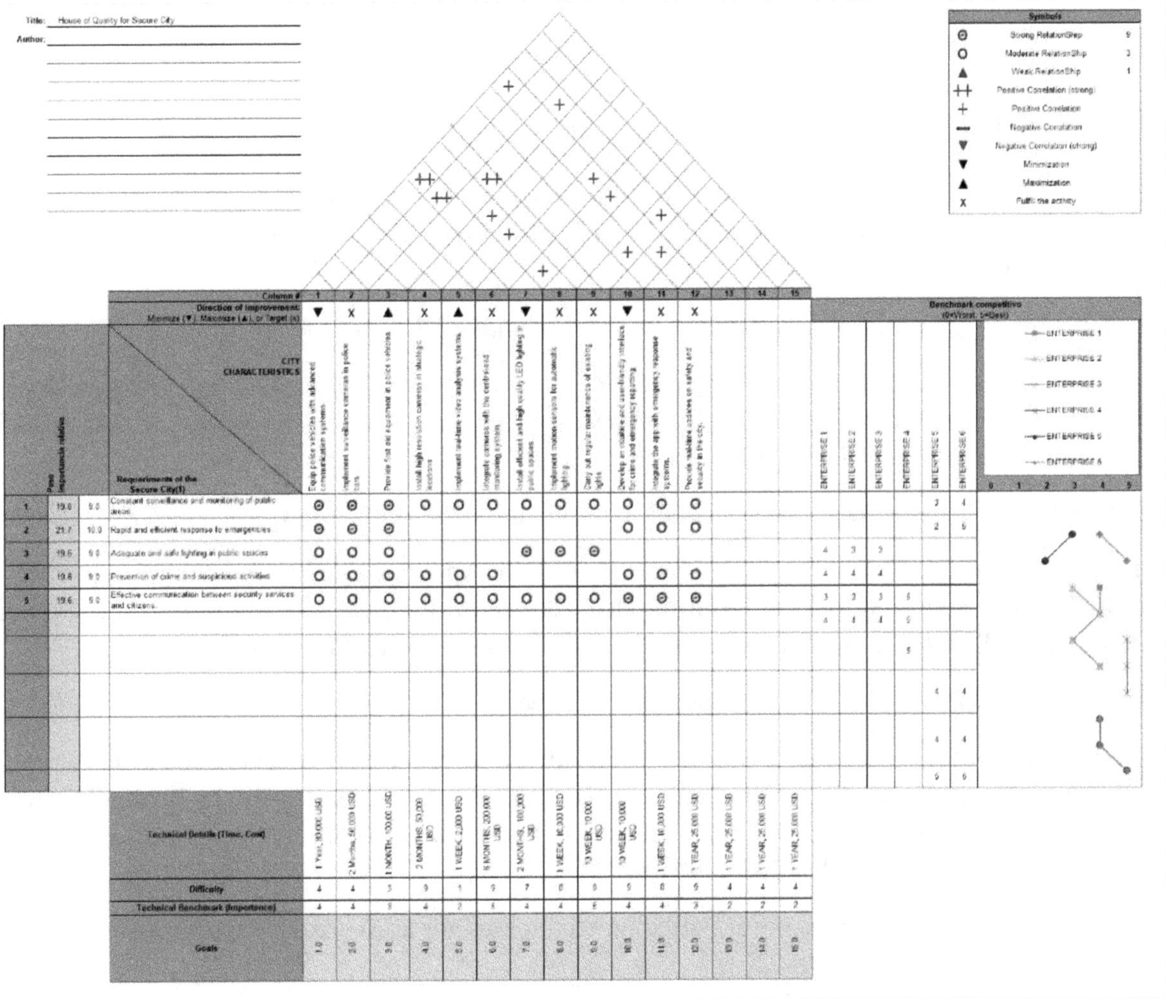

CONCLUSION

The House of Quality (HoQ) approach is a valuable tool for ensuring the design of safe cities and responding to community needs and expectations in terms of safety and security. The application of HoQ in the context of safe cities allows for the identification of priority areas for the implementation of safety measures to improve the quality of life of residents. The use of technology in safe cities is essential to strengthen crime prevention and provide safer and more comfortable urban environments. The combination of HoQ and technology helps governments, communities, and businesses to reduce the likelihood of crime and create a sense of security in the community.

The application of HoQ in the design of safe cities enables more effective and efficient urban planning. By understanding the demands of citizens and establishing relationships between these demands and design features, informed strategic decisions can be made and resources can be allocated more effectively. In conclusion, the application of the House of Quality in safe city design has the potential to improve safety, strengthen urban resilience and promote safer and more liveable urban environments. This systematic and community needs-based approach provides a sound basis for informed decision-making and effective implementation of security measures.

REFERENCES

Barad, M. (2019). Implementing Quality Function Deployment for improving cybersecurity in the healthcare industry: A structured framework. *Journal of Healthcare Informatics Research, 3*(2), 145–162. doi:10.100741666-019-00042-9

Cohen, L. (1995). *Quality function deployment: How to make QFD work for you*. Addison-Wesley.

Ginting, A., Napitupulu, A., Tumanggor, R., & Lumbanraja, P. (2020). Quality function deployment and its application in public services. *Journal of Physics: Conference Series, 1567*(2), 022038. doi:10.1088/1742-6596/1567/2/022038

Hauser, J. R., & Clausing, D. (1988). The house of quality. *Harvard Business Review, 66*(3), 63–73.

Lombardi, F., Rinaldi, C., Cirillo, F., & Russo, D. (2020). Applying Quality Function Deployment to Security Engineering: The House of Security (HoS). *Proceedings of the 15th International Conference on Availability, Reliability and Security (ARES)*, (pp. 1-10). ACM. 10.1145/3407023.3409231

Safe cities index. (2021). Safe Cities. https://safecities.economist.com

Sahin, E., & Demirtas, E. A. (2020). Utilizing the Quality Function Deployment technique and a proportional House of Quality for determining customer and technical requirements in the banking sector: A case study on credit card services for university students. *Journal of Business Economics and Finance, 9*(4), 203–218. doi:10.13189/jbef.2020.090401

Smith, J. (2020). The safe city concept: Utilizing technology for crime reduction and enhanced safety. *Journal of Urban Safety, 7*(2), 45–58.

Spasova, E., & Raiu, I. (2022). Evaluating quality in software engineering using the House of Quality method. *Informatics (MDPI), 9*(2), 31. doi:10.3390/informatics9020031

Spasova, V., & Raiu, O. (2022). Implementation of House of Quality Method for software tools evaluation. *Mathematical and Software Engineering, 8*(1-2), 10–18.

Sullivan, L. P. (1986). Quality function deployment: A system to assure that customer needs drive the product design and production process. *Quality Progress, 19*(9), 39–50.

Chapter 7
Older Adults in Mexico:
Their Inclusion in ICTs and Smart Cities

Miguel Angel Torres-González
Universidad Politécnica de Pachuca, Mexico

Zeús Salvador Hernández-Veleros
Universidad Autónoma del Estado de Hidalgo, Mexico

José Gonzálo Ramírez-Rosas
Universidad Politécnica de Puebla, Mexico

Lizbeth Elena Guzmán-Escorza
https://orcid.org/0009-0001-4953-1342
Universidad Politécnica de Pachuca, Mexico

ABSTRACT

The study analyzes the use of digital technologies as a platform for the integration of adults aged 60 and over to smart cities and proposes policies and strategies to governments that allow the reduction of the prevailing backwardness in digital literacy. The results show the existence of significant inequalities in the use, access, modality, and frequency of ICT by this age group; the gap is deepened by age, level of education, social stratum and gender. Some other factors of perception hinder the adoption of technology use, such as lack of knowledge, lack of access to ICTs, lack of knowledge about the use of ICTs, lack of access to ICTs, lack of knowledge about the use of ICTs, and lack of access to ICTs, lack of interest or feeling that they do not need to use ICTs, the latter factors have been identified as the main obstacles to associating the usefulness of these tools to their benefit.

DOI: 10.4018/979-8-3693-0373-3.ch007

INTRODUCTION

Contributing to Public Policies for the construction of Smart and Sustainable Cities is the objective of the public management of many governments. To achieve this, it is necessary to rethink the government from the digital transformation, enabling resources to innovate, be more efficient and better know the citizen to meet their needs and improve their quality of life.

However, not all cities that implement smart city projects follow an orderly plan or have governance designed for that purpose. Sometimes they follow opportunities that arise as they go along, step by step, starting with providing higher levels of connectivity and developing platforms that facilitate the management of transportation, security and health services, which originate from different internal areas, adjusting to the available budget.

Smart cities are drivers of innovation, set a course sometimes ahead of the rest of the country, and are therefore drivers of digitization.

(Alvarado-López Raúl Arturo, 2020a)proposes smart city development models based on the types of initiatives undertaken. This qualitative classification takes into account the level of development in terms of a more limited and select group of digital enablers, but allows to obtain some distinctive characteristics of the stage of evolution or path in which they are moving, proposes the existence of a specialized authority, levels of government coordination, citizen participation, maturity of an open data policy, data-based decision-making and use of cloud computing services.

There are many definitions and classifications of what is meant by a Smart City (Bouskela et al., 2016). proposes a definition of a Smart City based on six main characteristics:

- Generates integration, which in turn provides the public administration with necessary and transparent information.
- Resource optimization. Optimizes resource allocation.
- Performance indicators that are useful for measuring, comparing, and improving public policies.
- Attention to citizens. High degree of satisfaction of the inhabitants.
- Process efficiency. Common procedures that increase government efficiency.
- Citizen participation. Greater participation of civil society in the Administration.

These six characteristics imply many challenges of internal transformation in the management of cities, where innovation and sustainability must be transversal axes to the rest of the objectives or priorities that are outlined. Technologies are only tools that must be linked to the management process in order to offer better services, as well as to meet current and future citizen demands (see figure 1).

Figure 1. Six main characteristics of a smart city
Source: Adapted from Bouskela et. al. (2016). In the figure 1, the six characteristics of a smart city are shown below

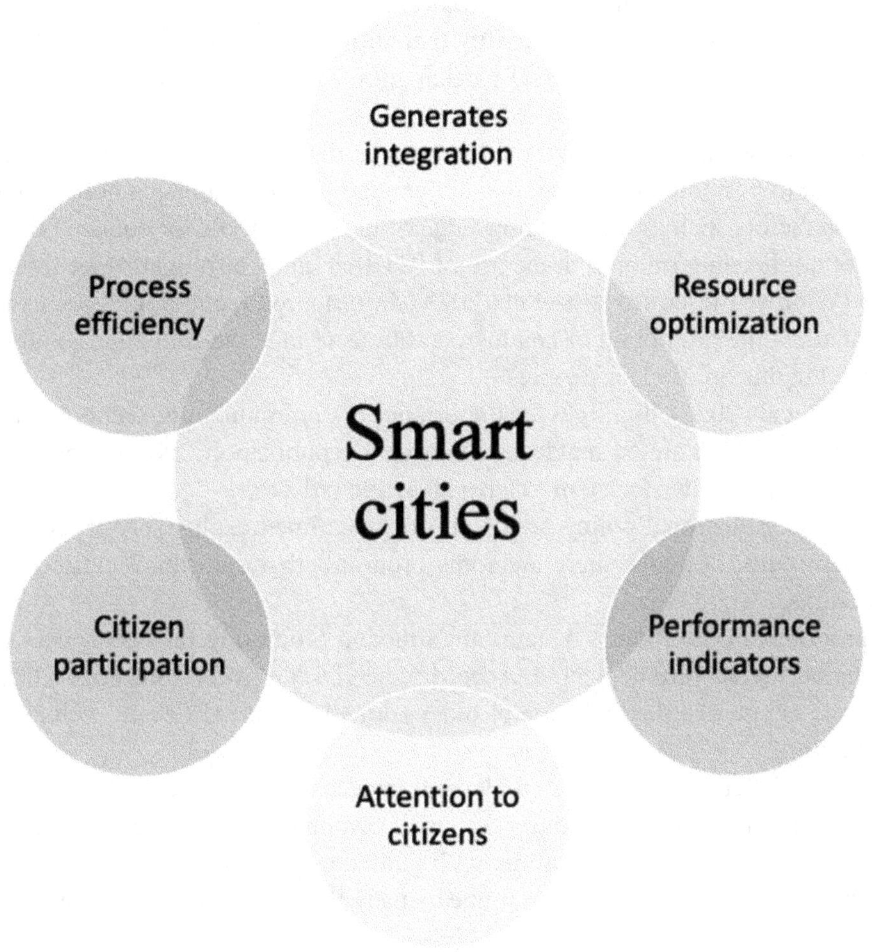

As noted (Pittaluga Lucia & Rivoir Ana, 2012), the smart city aims to improve the quality of life of citizens and, therefore, has increased its importance in both political and academic agendas.

The expansion and growth of cities have led to traffic problems, pollution, and social (Rocha et al., 2019). At this point, the knowledge and use of technologies play a fundamental role in their adoption. The integration of adults aged 60 and over into this vision of the future represents a real challenge for governments.

Mexico is in a stage of aging, although it is not yet an advanced process compared to other countries, the population over 60 years of age is expected to grow rapidly in the coming years, according to (Alvarado-López Raúl Arturo, 2020b), at 2038 the 20% of the population will be from this sector, the challenge is how to cope with their integration into Smart Cities, as older adults require communication, shopping or information search.

The concept of Smart Cities emphasizes the efficient use of ICTs, which are aimed at improving the quality of life of the population and, therefore, caring for the environment and reducing social inequality, actions that are in line with the definition of inclusive education, whose objective is to favor the least favored sectors of the population.

The inclusion of the elderly in smart cities should not be seen as a future or distant and unattainable option, but as a necessity to the current reality that allows facing the challenges of today's society, where the use of ICTs will have a transversal participation as an access tool that guarantees security and sustainability.

The objective of this work is to analyze the factors that determine the inclusion of older adults in Smart Cities, in order to promote this action, it is not enough just to establish a policy to offer services, there are perception factors such as lack of knowledge of the use of tools for connectivity, little interest or consideration of not needing training in the use of ICT that are determinants (see tables 8, 9 y 10)

According to (Widmer-lliescu Roxana et al., 2023), information technologies are essential to build environments that allow the promotion of healthy conditions to face the challenges of aging, becoming facilitators of social inclusion of older people.

At work, (Lozoya et al., 2022), highlight the importance of communication technologies in the implementation of learning programs aimed at older adults as well as public policies that promote technological literacy in this age group in order for them to have an active old age.

In Mexico, there is no national policy or social program aimed exclusively at reducing the digital divide among older adults, although there are some programs that contribute indirectly to the digital literacy of older adults.

Most of the programs in the country's states are aimed at promoting Internet access, but important factors such as digital literacy are neglected. According to (Di Virgilio & Serrati, 2022), new government policies should encourage the inclusion of older adults in Smart Cities, as well as the benefits to the general population.

The internet should be considered as a complement to access to ICT and not an imposition to use it, some older adults prefer traditional procedures, so small computer centers could be established in government offices and offer the procedure online, with guided assistance for the adult to experience and learn how to use it, thus motivating them to continue using these tools that will facilitate their integration into the digital age and smart cities.

Problem Statement and State of the Art

In the literature on determinants of digital exclusion, a change is visible in its main cause, which goes from the general to the personal, i.e., the main barriers to ensure that the entire population has access to ICTs, today are not the same as a few years ago, technology, having a very rapid evolution in its growth and progress in the frontiers of knowledge, generates that some major problems of the past cease to be so in the present.

The main problems for connectivity on the supply side are lack of access, lack of physical infrastructure to enable connectivity, price of the service and quality. On the demand side: people's income and their preference for these tools (Huerta-Wong Juan Enrique & Gómez García Enrique, 2013).

In spite of this, technological advances allow access to a backbone network via satellite or Wireless (a wireless communication system, where a physical connection is not required to bring connectivity to an area), helping the most remote rural communities or areas of difficult access (Alirio González-Bustamante et al., 2020)

In fact, there are several studies that seek to identify the determinants of digital exclusion, even when there is access to or the possibility of using some ICTs. The main results of this work confirm the idea of the perception proposed by (Estévez-Ortiz et al., 2016) and complements them with other sociodemographic factors of individuals. Specifically, among older adults, it has been identified that there is a great lack of motivation or interest in learning and using electronic devices or communication tools such as the Internet.

This lack of interest can be very related to the lack of experience, in terms of terms that during their adult stage does not exist these gadgets, so I know their advantages and can be tied to realize their activities trying to maintain the customs that acquired during their training. In reality, try to modify the behavior of an adult person is difficult, so by ensuring them access or provide them with access to community centers where they can use different tools would be a partial solution, and you need first a motivation.

Despite their motivation, adults face a second major problem in successfully engaging with technology: a lack of digital literacy, that is, an individual's ability to successfully perform tasks in a digital environment that requires reading and interpreting text, sounds and images, and reproducing data through the manipulation of information (Llorca Abad, 2012).

Evidently, the lack of skills or knowledge to use social networks, internet or other tools can not only demotivate older adults, but also limit those who use them, by restricting the potential benefits brought by their massive use.

The lack of digital literacy is highly correlated with the educational level of the elderly, especially in developing countries, where the elderly population is the one with the highest level of educational backwardness. To increase digital inclusion, it is necessary to think of an intuitive way of using these tools, to which in general, little attention has been paid.

Digital exclusion depends on socioeconomic characteristics, such as age, income and level of education, as well as some perception factors, such as lack of motivation, lack of interest or feeling that they do not need to use these tools. In fact, these last factors (perception) are the ones that have been identified as the main barriers for older adults to associate ICTs with their usefulness (Pino Juste et al., 2015).

According to (Huerta-Wong Juan Enrique & Gómez García Rodrigo, 2013), complementary actions were carried out in this sector, which had been highly monopolized, resulting in greater market penetration, lower prices and greater adoption of services related to Internet access and use.

However (Masanet et al., 2021), states that there is a digital lag in the elderly sector of the population. This digital divide includes important differences in the use and knowledge of ICTs.

Aging is the subject of different studies and perspectives that consider demographic, psychological, biological, cultural, and social processes. In the West, they associate old age as a process of decline, loss of functions and deterioration, derived from the emerging paradigm that points to greater freedom and the importance of the forms of a better aging with activity in social networks that allow its link with society (Casamayou & Morales González, 2018). Under the above context, the appropriation of technology in older adults can become an opportunity for the exercise of their rights and greater participation in the digital economy.

According to (Haub & Kaneda, 2011), social transformation in the world has occurred at different rates, some years ago communication was done through letters and calls to landlines; in today's society, social platforms or networks, video calls or email, provide opportunities to communicate anywhere in the world with family or friends, says that for the elderly, this becomes a complex gap, however, joining the ICT offers better opportunities and quality of life.

Many studies have been devoted to the relationship between the elderly and the use of technologies, as well as to the benefits and social advantages they can have, however, at present, the social dynamics, brings with it a marked use of ICTs for most of the daily activities, which generates a new challenge for this sector of society during this phase of industrialization and future modernization of countries that has been occurring at different rates in the world.

The smart city concept was introduced to the world in the late 2000s as part of the Agenda for a Smarter Planet. Since then, many countries have based their strategies on this concept, however, in spite of its great importance, and according to the conditions of developing cities, this transformation continues to be a little studied topic (Kuecker & Hartley, 2019).

Smart Cities focus on improving the quality of life of their inhabitants through the implementation of advanced technologies. The inclusion of older adults in these initiatives is essential to ensure that they benefit from the advantages offered by ICTs in terms of accessibility, services, and citizen participation (Coutinho et al., 2019).

According to (Pino Juste et al., 2015)there is a growing interest in the adoption of ICTs by older adults and their integration into smart cities, several barriers have been identified, such as lack of digital literacy, limited accessibility of technologies, lack of knowledge about their use, and privacy and security concerns.

For (Morales Romo, 2016), inclusion in technologies is essential to overcome the barriers that older adults currently face, such as access to services and communication. Intuitive interfaces must be designed, which can be adapted to individual needs and capabilities, thus focusing on the use of ICTs becomes a key aspect for the inclusion of older adults in smart cities.

METHODOLOGY AND DATA

The Case of Mexico

There is a growing concern about the digital inclusion of adults to ICT and its linkage to Smart Cities, as they will face the disruptive change that are generating the information and communication technologies, and have not been contemplated methods of integration for them, it is considered that this sector of the population, can still contribute to society as members in their families, active participants in the workforce and as volunteers (Abella et al., 2015).

The source of information for this study is the National Survey on the Availability and Use of Information Technology in Households 2022 (ENDUTIH, 2022), the selection of this survey is derived from the fact that the statistical data has the precision and reliability required for its treatment, in addition to the fact that it supports decision making in public policy matters, and offers elements of analysis to national and international studies.

Description of the Data

In the table 1, The evolution of the use of technologies from 2015 to 2022 can be observed, highlighting the increase in the use of internet and cellular telephony as a means of connectivity, with a significant decrease in the use of computers to carry out ICT-related activities. In the figure 1, shows the trend of the indicators for the period.

Table 1. Information technology users, period 2015 to 2022

Year	Computer Users		Internet users		Cellular Telephone Users	
	Absolutes	%	Absolutes	%	Absolutes	%
2015	54,73,584	51.2	61,358,202	57.4	76,369,882	71.4
2016	50,767,421	46.8	64,361,129	59.4	76,690,765	73.5
2017	49,826,347	45.2	70,289,609	63.7	79,587,494	72.1
2018	49,935,658	44.7	73,142,199	65.5	81,865,019	73.3
2019	48,362,012	42.4	79,489,450	69.6	85,549,900	74.9
2020	43,534,080	37.5	82,978,847	71.5	87,218,465	75.1
2021	43,844,751	37.4	88,562,249	75.6	91,731,856	78.3
2022	43,779,173	37.0	93,052,870	78.6	93,770,888	79.2

Source: Prepared by the authors.

In the figure 2, shows the trend of the ICT access indicators, in the period 2015 to 2022

Figure 2. Information technology users, period 2015 to 2022
Source: Prepared by the authors.

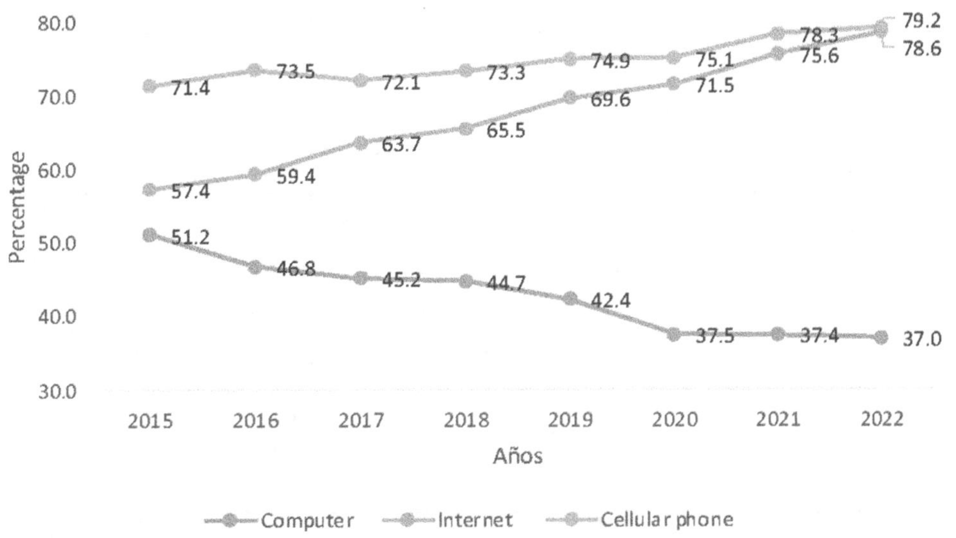

In the table 2, shows the adult population over 60 years of age by state. It can be seen that Mexico has the highest proportion of older adults with 13.08, followed by Colima with 10.25%, while Baja California Sur, Campeche, Chihuahua, Tlaxcala and Nayarit have the lowest adult population with 0.54, 0.56, 058, 0.82 and 0.96 percent respectively.

Table 2. Use of ICTs by the adult population aged 60 and over, by state

Estates	Freq.	Percent	Cum.
Aguascalientes	191,826	1.07	1.07
Baja California	473,422	2.65	3.72
Baja California Sur	96,476	0.54	4.26
Campeche	100,245	0.56	4.82
Chiapas	425,759	2.38	7.20
Chihuahua	103,865	0.58	7.78
Ciudad de México	617,271	3.45	11.23
Coahuila	473,535	2.65	13.87
Colima	1,833,479	10.25	24.12
Durango	209,910	1.17	25.29
Guanajuato	804,554	4.50	29.79
Guerrero	461,125	2.58	32.36
Hidalgo	377,312	2.11	34.47
Jalisco	1,201,642	6.71	41.19
México	2,341,000	13.08	54.27
Michoacán	610,003	3.41	57.68
Morelos	326,984	1.83	59.50
Nayarit	172,551	0.96	60.47
Nuevo León	860,977	4.81	65.28
Oaxaca	679,680	3.80	69.08
Puebla	874,659	4.89	73.96
Querétaro	321,283	1.80	75.76
Quintana Roo	200,464	1.12	76.88
San Luis Potosí	420,871	2.35	79.23
Sinaloa	482,892	2.70	81.93
Sonora	429,277	2.40	84.33
Tabasco	279,713	1.56	85.89
Tamaulipas	482,469	2.70	88.59
Tlaxcala	147,351	0.82	89.41
Veracruz	1,347,204	7.53	96.94
Yucatán	316,614	1.77	98.71
Zacatecas	230,939	1.29	100.00
Total	17,895,352	100.00	

Source: Prepared by the authors.

The table 3, represents older adults who are heads of household by gender, highlighting that 63.53% are male and 36.47% are female.

Table 3. Population of adults 60 years of age and older who are heads of household

Head of household	Freq.	Percent	Cum.	
Women	6,526,194	36.47	36.47	
Men	11,369,158	63.53	100.00	
Total	17,895,352	100		

Source: Prepared by the authors.

Table 4 shows that 63% of adults aged 60 and over use cell phones frequently, while 37% do not use them at all.

Table 4. Cellular telephone use by the adult population aged 60 and older

Cellular	Freq.	Percent	Cum.
No usa	6,603,508	0.37	0.37
Usa	11,291,844	0.63	100.00
Total	17,895,352	100.00	

Source: Prepared by the authors.

Table 5 shows that 88.5% of the population aged 60 years and over do not use a computer, while 11.5% use it regularly.

Table 5. Computer use by the adult population aged 60 years and older

Computer	Freq.	Percent	Cum.
No usa	15,838,919	0.885	0.885
Usa	2,056,433	0.115	100.00
Total	17,895,352	100.00	

Source: Prepared by the authors.

Table 6 indicates that 88.7% of the population aged 60 and over do not use the Internet, while 11.3% use it regularly.

Table 6. Internet use by the adult population aged 60 and over

Internet	Freq.	Percent	Cum.
No usa	15,874,803	0.887	0.887
Usa	2,020,549	0.113	100.00
Total	17,895,352	100.00	

Source: Prepared by the authors.

Table 7 shows the population 60 years of age and older according to the years of study attained. Forty-five percent have primary education, followed by 14.63 and 11.00 percent with high school and college degrees. It is clear that 14% have no studies and that the percentage of adults who have postgraduate degrees is incipient (0.34, specialty, 1.06% for master's degree and 0.33% for PhD).

Table 7. Adult population 60 years of age and older by level of education

Education level	Freq.	Percent	Cum.
00 None	2,599,047	14.52	14.52
01 Preschool or kindergarten	27,691	0.15	14.68
02 Primary	8,061,876	45.05	59.73
03 Secondary	2,618,649	14.63	74.36
04 Normal basic	104,974	0.59	74.95
05 Terminal technical study with high school	520,373	2.91	77.86
06 High school	1,195,071	6.68	84.53
07 Higher technical studies with completed high school	316,642	1.77	86.30
08 Bachelor's degree or engineering	1,969,162	11.00	97.31
09 Specialty	60,977	0.34	97.65
10 Master's Degree	189,290	1.06	98.71
11 PhD	59,093	0.33	99.04
99 Do not know	172,507	0.96	100.00
Total	17,895,352	100.00	

Source: Prepared by the authors.

In table 8, the reasons why adults over 60 years of age do not use cellular telephony are listed, noting that 38.33% corresponds to item 5 "Does not know how to use it", followed by 2. "Not interested or not needed" with 35.88%, 19.74%, referred to the lack of use is due to economic factors.

Table 8. Reasons why adults over 60 do not use cell phones

Reasons for not using cellular telephony	Freq.	Percent	Cum.
1. Due to lack of financial resources	1,303,260	19.74	19.74
2. Not interested or not needed	2,369,572	35.88	55.62
3. No service at your location (lack of infrastructure, network coverage)	47,657	0.72	56.34
4. For reasons related to privacy or security	16,321	0.25	56.59
5. Does not know how to use it	2,530,797	38.33	94.91
6. You are not allowed to use it	12,581	0.19	95.1
7. For physical or mental disability	206,628	3.13	98.23
8. Another reason	116,692	1.77	100
Total	6,603,508	100	

Source: Prepared by the authors.

Table 9 Regarding the use of computers by adults over 60 years of age. 62.18% responded that the reason is because they do not know how to use it, followed by 20.11% who stated that they are not interested or do not need it, only 5.84% referred to economic problems that prevent them from using it..

Table 9. Reasons why adults over 60 do not use a computer

Reasons for not using a computer	Freq.	Percent	Cum.
1. You do not have access to one, although you know how to use it.	859,383	5.51	5.51
2. Does not know how to use it	9,701,966	62.18	67.69
3. Not interested or not needed	3,138,281	20.11	87.8
4. Due to lack of financial resources	910,543	5.84	93.63
5. Uses his or her smart phone (Smartphone)	482,641	3.09	96.73
6. Ignorance of its usefulness	263,379	1.69	98.41
7. For physical or mental disability	209,342	1.34	99.76
8. Another reason	38,018	0.24	100
Total	15,603,553	100	

Source: Prepared by the authors.

Table 10 indicates that according to the questions asked in the ENDUTHI (2022), regarding the reasons why adults aged 60 years and older do not use the Internet, 66.85% responded that they know how to use it and 21.14% responded that they are not interested or do not need it. In this regard, 66.85% responded that they know how to use it and 21.14% responded that they are not interested or do not need it.

Table 10. Reasons why adults over 60 do not use the internet

Reasons for not using the Internet	Freq.	Percent	Cum.
1. Does not have access, but knows how to use it	390,929	3.67	3.67
2. Does not know how to use it	7,120,750	66.85	70.52
3. Not interested or not needed	2,251,501	21.14	91.66
4. Due to lack of financial resources	677,312	6.36	98.02
5. For physical or mental disability	163,844	1.54	99.55
6. For reasons related to privacy or security	11,073	0.1	99.66
7. You are not allowed to use it	1,110	0.01	99.67
8. Another reason	35,384	0.33	100
Total	10,651,903	100	

Source: Prepared by the authors.

THE MODEL

According to (Rokhman, 2016), the logit model is a basic tool for the analysis of binary dependent variables. to digital divide and other problems it is usual to use these binary response models (Botello-Peñaloza, 2015).

Based on the review of previous documents, we propose to estimate a logistic regression, where access to ICT is a function of observable household characteristics (internet, computer use and cell phone use), from these indicators, the variable "usotic" was constructed, that is, a dichotomous variable that takes the value zero for the population that does not have any electronic device that allows them to have access to ICT and value one for those who have and use at least one of them.

Whether ICT connectivity in the home is a function of other characteristics:

$$usotic = f(X)$$

Where X is a vector of observable variables, such as social stratum, age, geographic area, characteristics of the head of household, to name a few.

The regression equation would be:

$$usotic = \beta_0 + \sum_{j=2}^{k} \beta_j x_j + \varepsilon$$

Where: *usotic*: Dependent dichotomous variable that indicates whether the older adult makes use of ICTs and X_j is a vector of observable variables.

Table 11 shows a description of the variables, as well as the expected effect on the probability of ICT use.

Table 11. Description of variables and their effect

Variable	Description	Expected effect
usotic	Use of technology by adults aged 60 and over	Positive
estudios	Years of schooling of the older adult	Positive
escjefe	Schooling of the head of household	Positive
est_01	Social stratum (1-Low, 2-Lower Middle, 3-Upper Middle, 4-Upper)	Positive
zona	Zone of residence (0-Rural, 1 Urban)	Positive
edad	Age in years of the older adult	Negative
sexoadulto	Gender of head of household	Positive
edocivil	Marital status of head of household	Positive
adulhog	Number of older adults in the household	Negative

Source: Prepared by the authors.

Given the need to estimate a probabilistic model, the regression equation must be transformed to. A binary response model has the form of the equation:

$$P(y=1|X)=G(\beta_0+\beta_1x_1+\ldots+\beta_kx_k)=G(\beta_0+X\beta)=G(Z)$$

Note that: $X\beta= \beta 1x_{1} + \ldots + \beta kxk$

From the above equation, G is a cumulative distribution function that ensures that the predicted values of y are between zero and one (Wooldridge, 2012).

In the logit model, the distribution function G is a logistic distribution, so the equation becomes:

$$P(y=1\mid X)=\frac{1}{1+e^{-Z}}=\frac{e^{z}}{1+e^{z}}$$

Where $Z= \beta 0 + X\beta$

The coefficients β0 to βk should be estimated by maximum likelihood and then used in the distribution function of choice. The coefficients of both models are somewhat complex to interpret, which is why the best way to analyze the effect of the independent variables on the dependent variable is through changes in the estimated probabilities, i.e. the effect of X on the probability of success P(y=1 | X) in the face of a change in xj (Gujarati Damodar N. & Porter Dawn C., 2009).

The coefficient β_j associated with the variable x_j will not be interpreted directly, but the change in the probability of a change in the independent variable x_j must be calculated, the coefficient β_j represents the direction of the relationship between the variables, but not the magnitude.

Roughly speaking, in this model the coefficient of the slope of a variable indicates the change in the logarithm of the probabilities associated with a unit change in that variable, holding all other variables constant.

To obtain interpretations of the magnitude of the effect, the latent variable must first be constructed (y^*) using the estimated coefficients and the values of the dependent variables, such that:

$$y^* = \beta 0 + X\beta + e$$

$$y = 1 \; si \; y^*>0$$

The value obtained must be placed in terms of its probability density, so that it finally results in the probability of obtaining the adjusted dependent variable.

Determining the magnitude that a change in an independent variable x_j has on the probability of ICT use is known as the marginal effect of the independent variable on the dependent variable (Greene, 2003) and is equivalent to estimating the following derivative:

$$P(x) = P(y= 1|x)$$

$$\frac{\partial P(x)}{\partial x_j}=g(\beta_0+X\beta)x_j$$

Where:

$$g(z) = \frac{\partial G}{dz} z$$

Model Results

The results of the probabilistic model will give us an idea of the factors involved in the integration of older adults to ICTs and, consequently, the challenges they will face in their adoption of the smart cities model.

Table 12 shows the results of the application of the logistic model, highlighting that all the explanatory variables of technology use by adults aged 60 and over are significant.

Table 12. Results of the application of the logistic model to the ENDUTHI 2022 data

usotic	Coef.	Std. Err.	z	P>|z|	[95% Conf.Interval]	
estudios	0.000169	0.000070	2.42	0.0150	0.00003	0.00031
escjefe	0.506489	0.002505	202.18	0.0000	0.50158	0.51140
est_01	0.392677	0.001053	372.93	0.0000	0.39061	0.39474
zona	0.228899	0.001730	132.28	0.0000	0.22551	0.23229
edad	- 0.054695	0.000083	-658.7	0.0000	- 0.05486	- 0.05453
sexoAdulto	0.009515	0.002436	3.91	0.0000	0.00474	0.01429
edocivil	0.019332	0.000924	20.93	0.0000	0.01752	0.02114
adulhog	- 0.136093	0.000732	-185.88	0.0000	- 0.13753	- 0.13466
_cons	2.648452	0.006290	421.09	0.0000	2.63613	2.66078

Source: Prepared by the authors.

In Figure 3, we can see that the probability of older adults adopting the use of ICTs decreases as age increases.

Figure 3. Probability of ICT use in older adults by age
Source: Prepared by the authors.

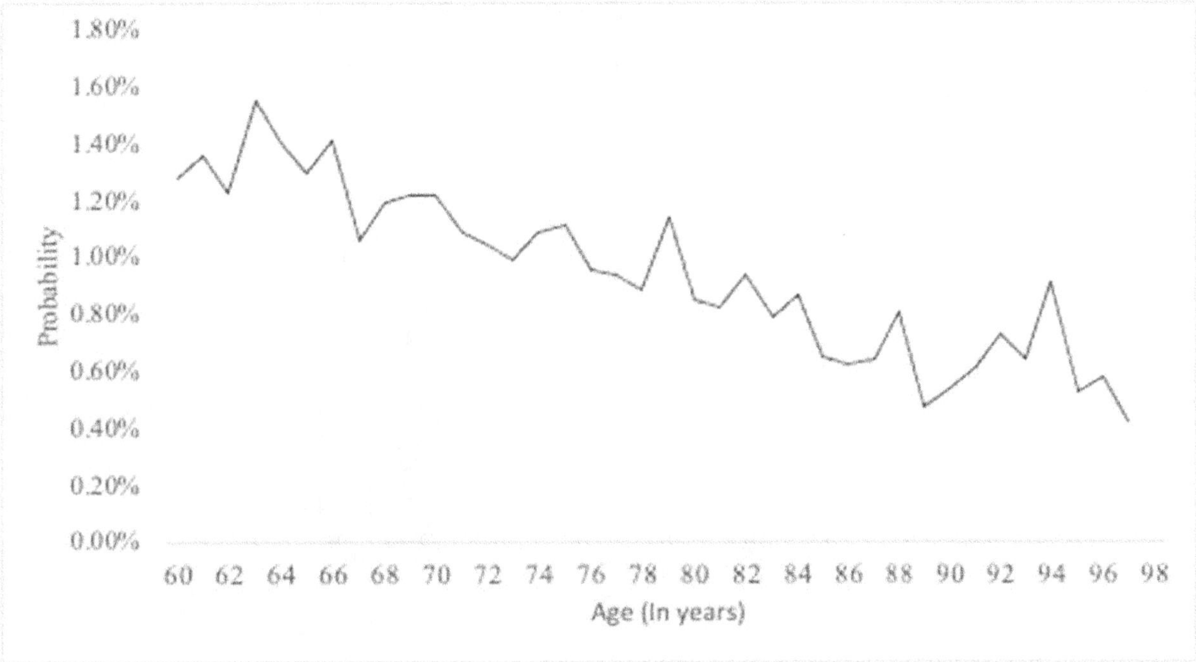

Figure 4 shows that older adults with basic education have a higher probability of using ICTs (2.93%) and those with no education have a probability of 0.60%.

Figure 4. Probability of ICT use by adults aged 60 and over by educational level
Source: Prepared by the authors.

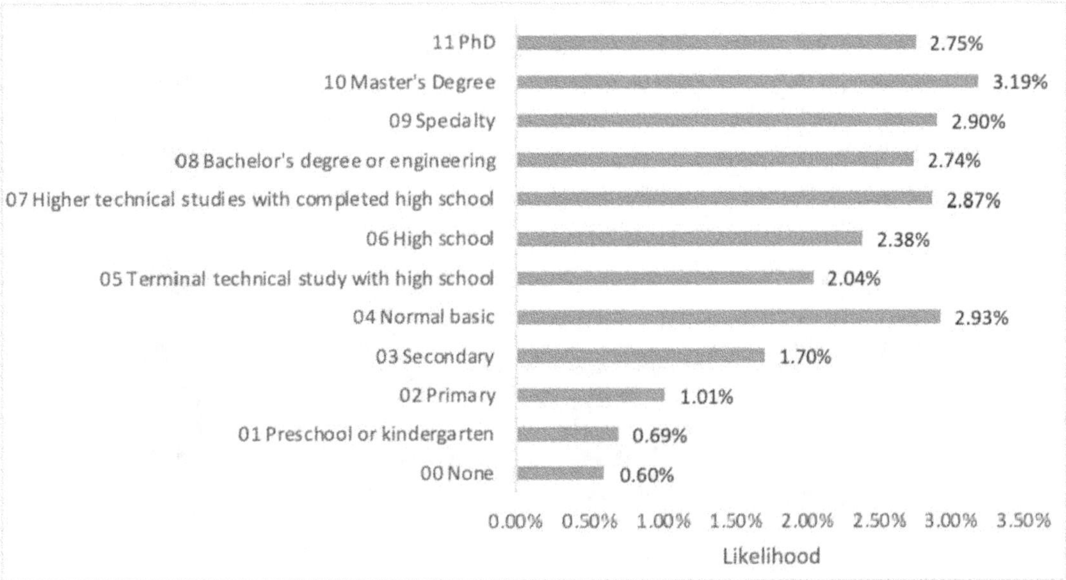

Figure 5 shows that there is a greater probability that adults aged 60 years and older are integrated to ICTs, compared to those living in rural areas.

Figure 5. Probability of ICT use by adults aged 60 years and older by area
Source: Prepared by the authors.

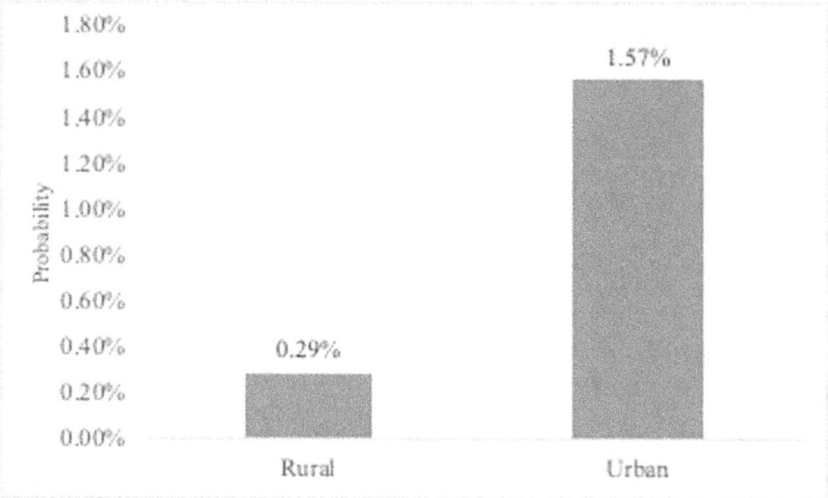

Figure 6 shows that the social stratum is an important determinant in the adoption of ICTs by older adults; the higher the social stratum, the higher the probability of adopting ICTs.

Figure 6. Probability of ICT adoption by older adults, according to social stratum

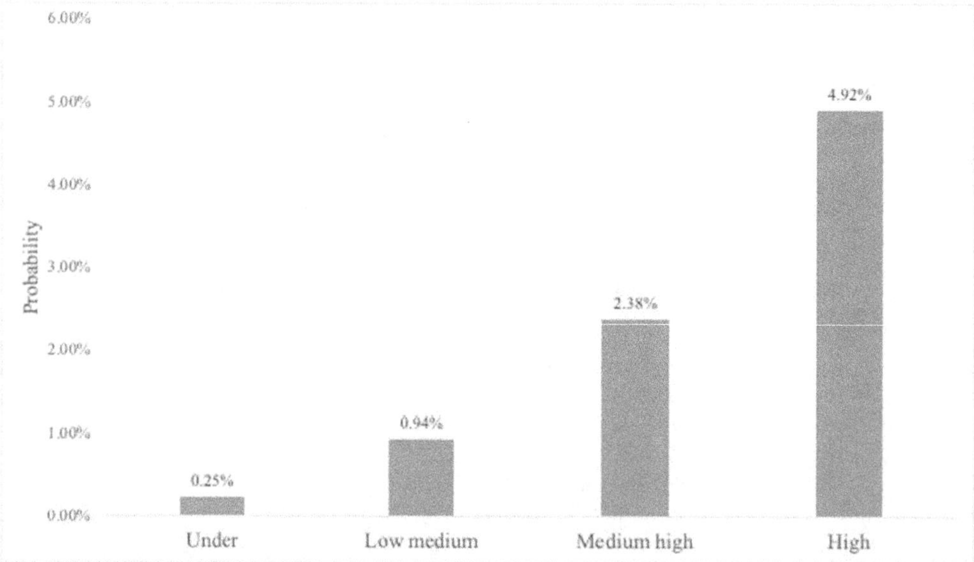

Figure 7 indicates that the probability of adopting ICTs by older adults increases if the head of household is male. 1.10% for men and 1.03% for women.

Figure 7. Probability of ICT use by adults over 60 years of age, by sex of the head of household
Source: Prepared by the authors.

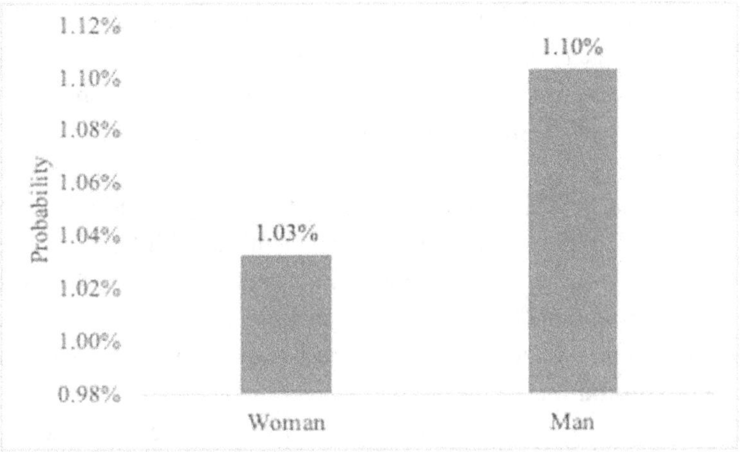

Figure 8 shows that adults aged 60 and over living in Nuevo León have the highest probability of adopting the use of ICTs (1.98%), while Oaxaca is the state with the lowest possibilities of adopting ICTs.

Figure 8. Probability of ICT use by adults aged 60 years and older by State
Source: Prepared by the authors.

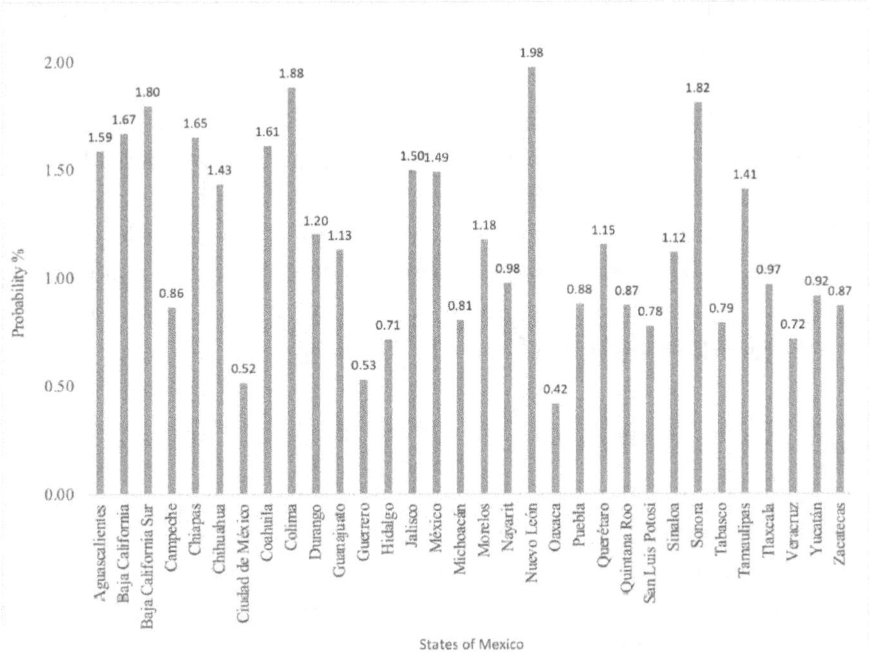

Analysis of Results

The descriptive analysis and the application of the logit econometric model, allowed us to reach relevant conclusions about the factors involved in the adoption of ICT by older adults, offering proposals for the generation of policies and strategies to facilitate their digital literacy and in the future their integration into Smart Cities.

The results of the study indicate that the use of ICT by the population of Mexico shows an increase in the period from 2015 to 2022 (see table 1), however, there is an increase in the use of mobile telephony and internet (7.8 and 21.2 percent, respectively) and on the other hand a decrease of 14.2% in the use of computer as a means of access to ICT, this phenomenon brings with it a problem of good use of devices for access to ICT.

On the other hand, the state with the largest population of adults aged 60 and over is Mexico with 2,341,000, representing 13.08% of the country, followed by Colima with 1,833,479 adults and 10.25%, on the other hand, Baja California Sur has 96,476 older adults representing 0.54%, followed by Campeche with 100,245 adults representing 0.56%. The above shows the great difference between the states with higher and lower age population, a condition that can be a determining factor when establishing public policies for the attention to digital literacy.

As expected, older adults living in rural areas are less likely to have access to the Internet than those living in urban areas (0.29% and 1.57%, respectively). This phenomenon is directly related to the still insufficient coverage and availability of telecommunications infrastructure, as there are still areas of difficult access, which prevent private investment or the existence of public or private service providers.

The social stratum and age variables have the expected sign. Both variables reflect the dynamics of ICT use, since when the stratum increases, the probability of ICT use increases, while when age increases, it decreases, reaffirming the importance of the area in which they live and age for the adoption of ICTs.

The indicators of ICT use by older adults (computer, cell phone and Internet) show that, in general, the lack of knowledge of the use of technology, that they are not interested or do not need it, leaving behind the economic condition as a limiting factor (see tables 8, 9 and 10, reasons for not using cell phone, computer and Internet).

Figure 7 indicates that in the city of Nuevo Leon, there is a greater probability of older adults adopting ICTs (1.98%), followed by Colima, Sonora and Baja California Sur, 1.88, 1.82 and 1.80 respectively. In contrast, Oaxaca, Mexico City and Guerrero are positioned as the States with the lowest possibilities of ICT integration by the elderly population (0.42, 0.52 and 0.53 percent, respectively).

Figure 3 shows that older adults with normal basic studies are the most likely to adopt ICTs, followed by master's degree, specialty, Higher technical studies with completed high school and phd with 2.93, 3.19, 2.90, 2.87 and 2.75 percent respectively. On the other hand, those with no studies, preschool or kindergarten and primary, represent 0.60, 0.69 and 1.01 percent.

CONCLUSION

Mexico is experiencing increasingly significant population growth, with consequences for sustainability, quality of life and competitiveness. Facing these challenges implies an evolution in the field of governance and decision making, as well as the increasingly efficient use of state resources, with a view to undertaking intelligent management.

As a result of their increasingly widespread use, Information and Communication Technologies (ICTs) have become a fundamental ally of this intelligent management. However, the use of these technologies must be understood as a means and not as an end.

The integration of the population to Smart Cities is not far away, however it is not enough to have them, it is also necessary to have trained citizens who can take advantage of the benefits that this entails. Therefore, people have a very important role as beneficiaries and participants of the transformations, from the active use of devices and mobile applications that increasingly facilitate the monitoring and collaboration with the policies of their rulers.

The development of Smart Cities brings with it various opportunities for older adults, for example in the area of health, new perspectives are opening up for the provision of medical services at home via computer, mobile applications for monitoring physical activities, wearable devices with sensors for monitoring vital signs, robotic exoskeletons to facilitate movement and emergency buttons connected to care centers are some of the countless benefits.

Considerations for the Integration of the Elderly Into ICTs

In accordance with (Frutos et al., 2012), an important stimulus for older adults to adopt ICTs is digital literacy, considering that this sector of the population has the highest educational lag and a steeper learning curve.

Following the strategy adopted by Brazil (Shirin Madon et al., 2009), the option of installing telecenters in government offices to provide personalized attention to the elderly to carry out any procedures they may need to perform, could be a viable option, since it would motivate them to use ICTs to solve their access problems.

Public policy proposals should focus on the development of skills and confidence in the use of ICTs by older adults, while at the same time seeking to ensure accessibility and capacity. At the same time, provide courses or workshops for the digital literacy of older adults and promote the creation of groups of guide advisors to provide advice either for the completion of any procedure or doubt in the management of any application.

Consideration should be given to encouraging the motivation of older adults to adopt the use of ICTs, since according to the indicators shown in tables 8, 9 and 10, the second most important indicator of non-use of cell phones, computers and the Internet is the lack of interest in their use and the perception that they do not need them, as well as improving the infrastructure in both rural and urban areas and promoting what they can do with the use of technologies through experiences in the use of different computer tools or applications.

ICT inclusion should be extended and encourage the use of technologies for older adults focused on their needs: health, safety, independence, mobility and participation, since according to Figure 2, age is a determining factor for the adoption of ICTs, which causes a wider digital divide at older ages.

One of the main challenges in the integration of older adults to the Smart Cities is their preparation and digital literacy, since according to Table 7, 45.05% have primary education, 14.63% have secondary education and 14.52% have no studies at all. This indicates that 74.20% of the adult population has basic education, and according to the forecasts made, the probability that they will adopt technologies is 1.70% for secondary, 1.10% for primary and 0.60% for those who have no studies (see Figure 3). This requires government strategies oriented to training plans that consider these indicators, while providing greater coverage of telecommunication services as well as the means for connectivity, for example, the design of software that considers options such as reminders and alerts about medications, exercise and diet programs, arranging medical appointments, allowing them to connect with public services and their family, as well as shopping at the supermarket without having to leave the house, among others. Similarly, consider programs to provide ICT access devices at no cost.

Government action is essential for the construction of Smart Cities that allow sustainability and support for the adult population, which is considered one of the most vulnerable, implementing public policies focused on reducing the digital divide and encouraging their future integration into smart cities that will bring them a better quality of life with self-sufficiency and active participation in their families in an increasingly digitized world.

REFERENCES

Abella, A., Ortiz-De-Urbina-Criado, M., & De-Pablos-Heredero, C. (2015). Informatio n reuse in smart cities ecosystems. *El Profesional de la Información*, *24*(6), 838–844. doi:10.3145/epi.2015.nov.16

Alirio González-Bustamante, R., Ferro-Escobar, R., & Vacca-González, H. (2020). Smart cities in collaboration with the internet of things Ciudades inteligentes en colaboración con internet de las cosas. *VISIÓN ELECTRÓNICA, 14*(2). https://doi.org/ doi:10.14483/issn.2248-4728

Arturo, A.-L. R. (2020a). Ciudades inteligentes y sostenibles: Una medición a cinco ciudades de México. *Estudios Sociales (Santo Domingo, Dominican Republic)*, *1*, 2–28. doi:10.836/es.v30i55.860

Arturo, A.-L. R. (2020b). Estudios Sociales. *Estudios Sociales (Santo Domingo, Dominican Republic)*, *1*, 2–28. doi:10.836/es.v30i55.860

Botello-Peñaloza, H. A. (2015). Determinantes del acceso al internet: Evidencia de los hogares del Ecuador. *ENTRAMADO*, *11*(2), 12–19. doi:10.18041/entramado.2015v11n2.22205

Bouskela, M., Casseb, M., & Bassi, S. (2016). *La ruta hacia las Smart Cities Migrando de una gestión tradicional a la ciudad inteligente.*

Casamayou, A., & Morales González, M. J. (2018). Personas mayores y tecnologías digitales: desafíos de un binomio Elderly people and digital technologies: a dual challenge Idosos e tecnologias digitais: desafios duplos. *Conocimiento y Sociedad*, *7*(2), 199–226.

Coutinho, S. M. V., Abilio, C. C. C., Da Penha Vasconcellos, M., & Netto, C. A. A. (2019). Smart cities indicators: The emergence of a new cliché. *Revista de Gestao Ambiental e Sustentabilidade*, *8*(2), 386–402. doi:10.5585/geas.v8i2.13574

Di Virgilio, M. M., & Serrati, P. (2022). Smart Cities, Digital Divide, and Space. Evidence from the Case of the Greater Buenos Aires Agglomerate. *Territorios*, *47*. doi:10.12804/revistas.urosario.edu.co/territorios/a.11635

Enrique, H.-W. J., & Enrique, G. G. (2013). Concentración y diversidad de los medios de comunicación y las telecomunicaciones en México. *Comunicación y Sociedad*, *19*, 113–152. https://www.scielo.org.mx/scielo.php?script=sci_arttext&pid=S0188-252X2013000100006

Huerta-Wong, E. & Gómez García, R. (2013). Concentración y diversidad de los medios de comunicación y las telecomunicaciones en México. *Comunicación y Sociedad, 19*(0188–252x), 113–152.

Estévez-Ortiz, F. J., García-Jiménez, A., & Glösekötter, P. (2016). An application of people's sentiment from social media to smart cities. *El Profesional de la Información, 25*(6), 851–858. doi:10.3145/epi.2016.nov.02

Frutos, E., Ruiz, M., Belén, A., Sánchez, M., & Escarbajal Frutos, A. Belén Mirete Ruiz, A., Maquilón Sánchez, J. J., Izquierdo Rus, T., Isabel López Hidalgo, J., Orcajada Sánchez, N., & Sánchez Martín, M. (2012). La atención a la diversidad: la educación inclusiva. *REIFOP, 15*(1), 135–144. https://www.redalyc.org/articulo.oa?id=217024398011

Greene, W. H. (2003). *Econometric analysis*. Prentice Hall. chrome-extension://efaidnbmnnnibpcajpcglclefindmkaj/http://www.mim.ac.mw/books/William%20H.%20Green%27s%20Econometric.pdf

Gujarati Damodar, N., & Porter Dawn, C. (2009). *Econometría*. Word Press. chrome-extension://efaidnbmnnnibpcajpcglclefindmkaj/https://fvela.files.wordpress.com/2012/10/econometria-damodar-n-gujarati-5ta-ed.pdf

Haub, C., & Kaneda, T. (2011). *PRB's 2011 World Population Data Sheet*. PRB. https://www.prb.org/resources/2011-world-population-data-sheet/

Kuecker, G. D., & Hartley, K. (2019). How Smart Cities Became the Urban Norm: Power and Knowledge in New Songdo City. In *Annals of the American Association of Geographers, 110*(2). https://www.tandfonline.com/doi/abs/10.1080/24694452.2019.1617102

Llorca Abad, G. (2012). Exclusión digital y límites de la comunicación mediada Digital exclusion and the limits of mediated communication. *Trípodos, 31*(1138–3305), 111–123. https://www.google.com/search?q=Llorca+Abad%2C+G.+(2012).+Exclusi%C3%B3n+digital+y+l%C3%ADmites+de+la+comunicaci%C3%B3n&oq=Llorca+Abad%2C+G.+(2012).+Exclusi%C3%B3n+digital+y+l%C3%ADmites+de+la+comunicaci%C3%B3n+&aqs=chrome.69i57.18327425j0j15&sourceid=chrome&ie=UTF-8

Lozoya, S. V. M., Guirado, M. A. Z., Zapata Gonzalez, A., & Lopez, A. B. M. (2022). Use of Technologies and Self-Efficacy in Older Adults. *IEEE-RITA, 17*(2), 125–130. doi:10.1109/RITA.2022.3166870

Lucia, P., & Ana, R. (2012). Ceibal Uruguay. *Edición Especial Bilingüe: Investigación Sobre TIC4D En Latinoamérica, 8*(4), 161–175. https://itidjournal.org/index.php/itid/article/view/962.html

Madon, S., Reinhard, N., Roode, D., & Walsham, G. (2009). Digital inclusion projects in developing countries: Processes of institutionalization. *Information Technology for Development, 15*(2), 95–107. https://onlinelibrary.wiley.com/doi/abs/10.1002/itdj.20108. doi:10.1002/itdj.20108

Masanet, M. J., Gómez-Puertas, L., & Pires, F. (2021). The risks of the gender digital divide among teenagers. *El Profesional de la Información, 30*(1), 1–15. doi:10.3145/epi.2021.ene.12

Morales Romo, N. (2016). El reto de la brecha digital y las personas mayores en el medio rural español. El caso de Castilla y León. *Fonseca. Journal of Communication, 13*(13), 165. doi:10.14201/fjc201613165185

Pino Juste, M. R., Soto Carballo, J. G., & Rodríguez López, B. (2015). Las personas mayores ante las Nuevas Tecnologías de la Información y Comunicación. Un compromiso para reducir la brecha digital social. *Pedagogia Social Revista Interuniversitaria*, *26*(26), 337. doi:10.7179/PSRI_2015.26.13

Rocha, A. . (2019). *2019 14th Iberian Conference on Information Systems and Technologies (CISTI) : proceedings of CISTI'2019 - 14th Iberian Conference on Information Systems and Technologies : 19 to 22 of June 2019, Coimbra, Portugal* (*Vol. 19*). Associação Ibérica de Sistemas e Tecnologias de Informação, & Institute of Electrical and Electronics Engineershttps://sigarra.up.pt/reitoria/pt/pub_geral.editora_view?pi_editora_id=378

Rokhman, A. (2016). The Case of Indonesia. *Journal of Computing E-Government Adoption in Developing Countries*. https://jurnal.asian.or.id/index.php/JIANA/article/download/44/37/Viewproject

Widmer-lliescu, R., Cristina, B., Simao, C. N., Mythili, M., & Chirs, L. (2023). El papel de las tecnologías digitales en el envejecimiento y la salud. In *El papel de las tecnologías digitales en el envejecimiento y la salud* (Vol. 1). Pan American Health Organization., doi:10.37774/9789275326558

Wooldridge, J. M. (2012). Introductory Econometrics. *Economics*. https://economics.ut.ac.ir/documents/3030266/14100645/Jeffrey_M._Wooldridge_Introductory_Econometrics_A_Modern_Approach__2012.pdf

Chapter 8
The Role of Smart Technologies in Urban Agriculture:
A Comprehensive Review

Marco Antonio Márquez-Vera
Polytechnic University of Pachuca, Mexico

Brenda Eguiluz-Ruiz
Polytechnic University of Pachuca, Mexico

Ricardo Calderón-Suárez
Polytechnic University of Tulancingo, Mexico

ABSTRACT

This chapter examines the transformative impact of integrating smart technologies – encompassing the internet of things (IoT), artificial intelligence (AI), and data analytics – into urban agriculture. By addressing challenges like limited arable land and traditional practices, smart technologies offer enhanced resource efficiency, increased productivity, and improved sustainability. Real-time monitoring, circular resource systems, intelligent irrigation, and controlled environments all contribute to these advancements. While acknowledging potential challenges such as costs and technology dependence, the study emphasizes collaboration and education for successful implementation. Ultimately, the integration of smart technologies in urban agriculture has the potential to reshape urban food systems, ensuring greater sustainability and resilience.

INTRODUCTION

Urban agriculture, encompassing practices such as rooftop farming, vertical farming, and hydroponics, has emerged as a promising approach to address the increasing demand for food in urban areas (Su et al., 2020). As the world's population continues to urbanize, the limited availability of arable land and the challenges associated with traditional agricultural practices pose significant obstacles to ensuring

DOI: 10.4018/979-8-3693-0373-3.ch008

food security in cities (Kasprzyk et al., 2022). However, the integration of smart technologies has the potential to overcome these challenges and optimize urban agricultural practices.

Smart technologies, including the Internet of Things (IoT), artificial intelligence (AI), and data analytics, are revolutionizing various industries, and urban agriculture is no exception. These technologies offer innovative solutions to enhance resource efficiency, improve productivity, and promote sustainability in urban farming (Pathmudi et al., 2023).

One of the key benefits of smart technologies in urban agriculture is the increased feasibility of food production in urban areas. Research conducted by Badami and Ramankutty (2015) suggests that urban agriculture is more feasible for growing basic daily vegetables for the urban poor in developed countries than in developing countries. By leveraging smart technologies, urban farming can be made more efficient and productive, making it a viable option for food production in resource-constrained urban areas.

Resource circularity is another area where smart technologies play a crucial role in urban agriculture. Weidner et al. (2019) highlight the potential of decentralized anaerobic digestion and vermicomposting, coupled with smart technologies, in utilizing organic waste for urban agriculture. By closing the loop and recycling organic waste, smart technologies contribute to a resource circular economy in urban farming, reducing the reliance on external resources and minimizing waste.

Water management is a critical aspect of urban agriculture, and smart technologies offer improved solutions in this regard. Mason et al. (2019) demonstrate the potential of intelligent irrigation systems, enabled by IoT and data analytics, to reduce water consumption while maintaining crop yield in smallholder farming systems. By integrating sensors, wireless communications, and data platforms, these systems provide real-time data for informed decision-making, enabling precise and optimized water management in urban agriculture.

In addition to resource efficiency, smart technologies also contribute to the environmental sustainability of urban agriculture. Jaramillo and Desyouni (2015) emphasize that the current food system contributes heavily to global environmental challenges such as biodiversity loss and climate change. However, smart urban farming practices, such as vertical farming and greenhouses, supported by smart technologies, offer controlled environments that reduce the need for land, water, and pesticides. This can help mitigate the negative environmental impacts associated with conventional agriculture.

While the integration of smart technologies in urban agriculture holds great promise, it is essential to address the challenges and considerations associated with their implementation. Benis and Ferrão (2018) highlight barriers such as high investment costs, narrow profit margins, and uncertain marketing channels that hinder the commercialization of rooftop farming. Moreover, the potential drawbacks of smart urban agriculture, including the dependence on technology and the exclusion of traditional farming practices, need to be carefully examined (Glaeser et al., 2021).

In conclusion, smart technologies have the potential to revolutionize urban agriculture by enhancing resource efficiency, improving productivity, and promoting environmental sustainability. Through the integration of IoT, AI, and data analytics, urban farming can overcome challenges associated with limited land availability, water scarcity, and environmental impact. However, it is crucial to consider the socioeconomic aspects, inclusivity, and long-term sustainability of smart urban agriculture initiatives.

Further research and collaboration are required to address existing knowledge gaps and develop scalable models for implementing smart technologies in urban agriculture. By harnessing the full potential of smart technologies, urban agriculture can contribute to sustainable and resilient food systems in the urban context (Miles et al., 2020; Petit, 2022; Singh and Sobti, 2022).

SMART URBAN FARMS

In recent years, the integration of smart technologies has revolutionized urban agriculture, enabling more efficient and sustainable farming practices. This section explores the role of electronics, sensors, the Internet of Things (IoT), and artificial intelligence (AI) in smart urban farms, highlighting their contributions to resource optimization, monitoring, and decision-making.

Electronics and Sensors in Smart Urban Farms

The use of electronics and sensors plays a crucial role in smart urban farms, enabling real-time monitoring and precise control over various farming parameters. He et al. (2022) describe an IoT-based urban agriculture container farm design that utilizes electronics and sensors for localized produce supply. This technology allows for continuous monitoring of temperature, humidity, light intensity, and nutrient levels, providing valuable data for optimizing plant growth conditions.

The combination of electronics and sensors with green Non-Orthogonal Multiple Access (NOMA) technology has also been explored in urban farming. Popli et al. (2021) propose a green NOMA-assisted NB-IoT system for urban farming in multistory buildings, which optimizes resource allocation and enhances connectivity for efficient data collection and monitoring.

IoT and Monitoring in Smart Urban Farms

The IoT plays a crucial role in smart urban farms by connecting various devices and systems to collect and analyze data, enabling real-time monitoring and decision-making. Li et al. (2020) present a decision support framework for the design and operation of sustainable urban farming systems, leveraging IoT technology for data integration, analysis, and optimization. This framework facilitates the monitoring of environmental parameters, crop growth, and resource usage, enabling informed decisions to enhance the overall performance of urban farms.

The Internet of Things, combined with autonomous control, has also been applied to vertical cultivation walls in smart urban farms, this kind of cultivation is shown in Figure 1. Halgamuge et al. (2021) review the use of IoT and autonomous control systems in vertical cultivation walls, highlighting their potential in creating smart food-growing environments. These systems utilize sensors and actuators to monitor and adjust environmental conditions, ensuring optimal growth for plants in urban settings.

Figure 1. Vertical farming

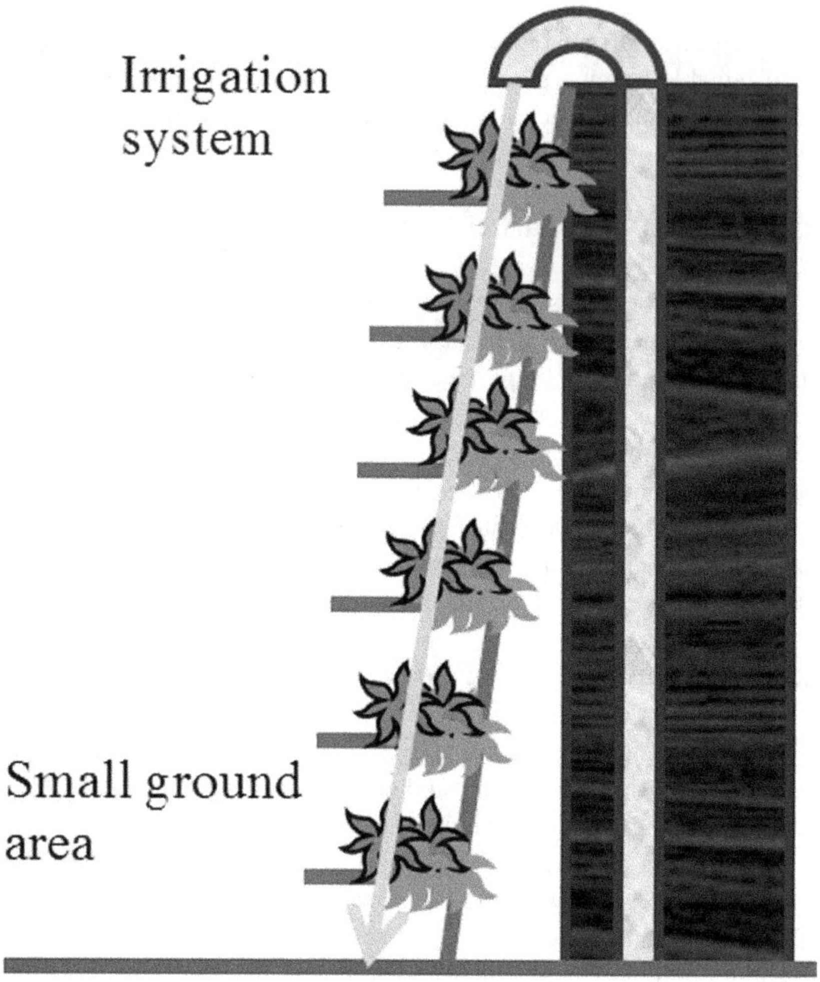

Artificial Intelligence in Smart Urban Farms

Artificial intelligence plays a significant role in smart urban farms by enabling advanced data analysis, prediction, and decision-making. Biswas et al. (2022) propose an IoT-based fuzzy logic-controlled mobile application for hydroponic farming, which utilizes AI algorithms to optimize nutrient supply and monitor plant health. This application incorporates machine learning techniques to provide real-time feedback and recommendations to farmers.

The use of deep learning algorithms in smart urban farms is another area of exploration. Mehmood et al. (2019) propose an object detection mechanism based on deep learning algorithms using embedded IoT devices for smart home appliances control in the context of urban agriculture. This technology enables the identification and monitoring of various objects and parameters, such as plant health, pests, and environmental conditions.

Smart urban farms also leverage AI in energy-efficient hydroponics systems. Khudoyberdiev et al. (2020) present an optimization scheme based on fuzzy logic control for efficient energy consumption in hydroponic environments, Figure 2 shown the use of rtificial neural networs to compute the heating, irrigation and ventilation control signals. This AI-based control system adjusts lighting, temperature, and nutrient supply to maximize energy efficiency and crop yield.

In summary, smart urban farms rely on the integration of electronics, sensors, IoT, and AI to optimize resource utilization, enable real-time monitoring, and facilitate data-driven decision-making. The use of these technologies enhances the efficiency, productivity, and sustainability of urban agriculture, contributing to the development of resilient and self-sufficient food systems in urban areas.

Figure 2. Smart farming using artificial neural networks

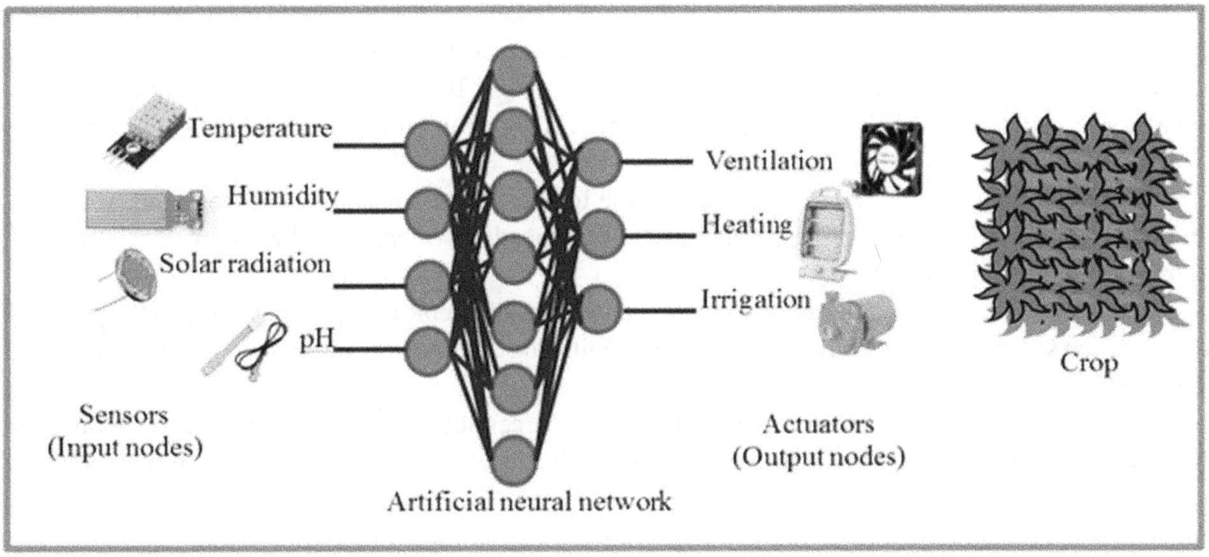

TECHNOLOGIES TO IMPROVE AGRICULTURAL EFFICIENCY AND PRODUCTIVITY

The use of different technologies and devices by various authors to improve crops and reduce energy and water consumption in agriculture is mentioned below.

Su et al., 2020: This study explores the use of a low-cost reflector-assisted two-layer hydroponic system for urban farming, aiming to increase vegetable yield and earnings.

Podder et al., 2021: The proposed IoT-based Smart AgroTech system utilizes sensors to monitor humidity, temperature, and soil moisture in urban farming, enabling efficient farming practices.

Mehra et al., 2018: This article discusses the application of hydroponics and aeroponics, coupled with Internet of Things (IoT), for smart farming. It emphasizes the benefits of automation and real-time control in hydroponic cultivation.

Miles et al., 2020: The use of Internet of Things (IoT) in agriculture is examined, focusing on its potential to improve decision-making, productivity, and resource conservation.

Priyanka et al., 2023: This research proposes a Region-based clustering and cluster-head election model to enhance the energy efficiency of IoT networks deployed in agriculture, particularly in smart farming applications.

Akkem et al., 2023: The review discusses various machine learning methods employed in crop selection and management, highlighting the role of AI in addressing agricultural sustainability challenges.

Fasciolo et al., 2023: The article presents a methodology based on IoT and AI for optimizing vertical farming, focusing on identifying parameters affecting plant growth and improving crop productivity.

URBAN AGRICULTURE AND NATURE-BASED SOLUTIONS

Ideas inspired by nature have also been used to solve different problems in agriculture, the most relevant works found are mentioned below.

Benis and Ferrão, 2018: This article addresses the challenges of commercializing rooftop farming and the potential of urban agriculture as a solution to reduce costs and enhance food security.

Kasprzyk et al., 2022: It discusses the importance of Nature-Based Solutions (NBSs) in urban areas, such as rain gardens and swales, to enhance ecosystem services and mitigate the effects of urbanization and climate change.

Nitoslawski et al., 2019: The study examines the integration of smart technologies, such as sensors and IoT, in urban forest management, emphasizing the need for effective utilization of social capital, entrepreneurship, and innovation.

Singh and Sobti, 2022: It explores the challenges faced by agriculture in urban areas and the potential of IoT-based solutions, particularly for irrigation monitoring and control, to enhance water management and crop productivity.

Moghayedi et al., 2022: This research investigates the perception and willingness of local African communities to engage in urban smart farms, emphasizing the benefits and barriers to their implementation.

INTEGRATION OF SMART TECHNOLOGIES IN URBAN MANAGEMENT

Regarding the implementation of intelligent technologies, it is worth mentioning the following articles.

Glaeser et al., 2021: The article discusses the role of information technology in smart cities, focusing on its impact on shared urban spaces and the potential for creative solutions in both private and public domains.

Oberascher et al., 2021: It explores the use of low-cost sensors and IoT technologies for decentralizing water infrastructure in smart cities, with a particular emphasis on the implementation of smart rain barrels. Figure 3 shows how different users can obtain information from certain crop and to control the actuators according to warnings of requeriments in the cultivation.

Petit, 2022: The paper highlights Nature-Based Solutions (NBSs) as a means to achieve urban resilience and sustainability, emphasizing their integration into urban planning and policies.

Gharaibeh et al., 2017: It addresses the concept of smart cities as an integrated approach for sustainable environments, quality of life, and cost of living.

Castañeda-Miranda and Castño-Meneses, 2020: The study focuses on smart sensors and artificial neural networks for frost protection in greenhouses, showcasing the potential of IoT systems in mitigating frost-related threats to agriculture.

Langendahl et al., 2022: The article explores smart urban agriculture initiatives, such as vertical farms and plant factories, emphasizing their potential role in sustainable food production in cities.

Oh and Lu, 2023: It discusses the challenges of land degradation and the importance of vertical farming and smart technologies, such as IoT and AI, in optimizing resource utilization and reducing environmental impact in agriculture.

Figure 3. IoT in smart farming

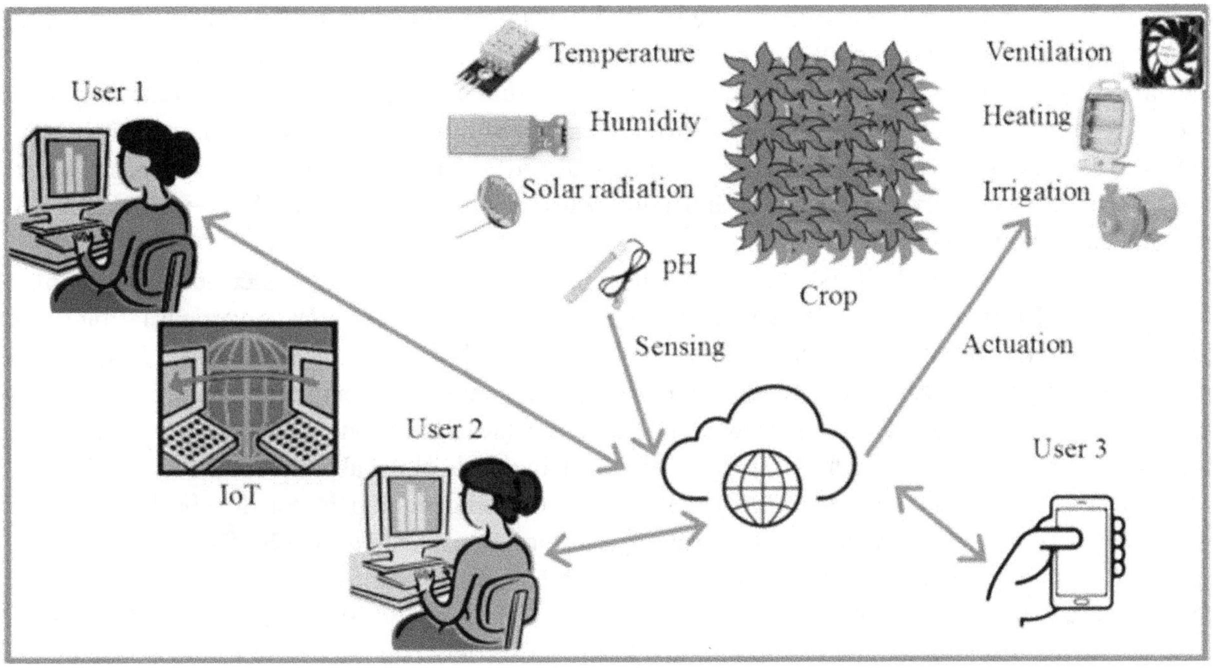

SOCIAL, ECONOMIC, AND POLITICAL ASPECTS OF SMART AGRICULTURE

An important point is the social impact, because the improvements made in agriculture are mainly for the producers. However, society benefits as mentioned by the following author.

Foster et al., 2023: This article critically examines precision agriculture and smart farming technologies, highlighting the need for an inclusive governance framework that ensures equitable benefit-sharing and avoids conflicts over labor and knowledge appropriation.

RESULTS

The implementation of smart urban farming practices, utilizing technologies such as IoT, AI, and data analytics, has shown promising results in improving various aspects of urban agriculture.

One significant result of employing smart technologies in urban farming is the increased feasibility of food production in resource-constrained urban areas. Studies by Badami and Ramankutty (2015) have demonstrated that smart urban farming can enhance the viability of growing basic daily vegetables, especially for the urban poor in developed countries. By optimizing resource utilization and implementing efficient farming techniques, smart urban farms have successfully addressed the challenges associated with limited arable land and enabled sustainable food production within urban environments.

Resource circularity has also been positively impacted by the integration of smart technologies. Weidner et al. (2019) highlight the success of decentralized anaerobic digestion and vermicomposting systems, coupled with smart technologies, in utilizing organic waste for urban agriculture. By implementing these circular systems, smart urban farms have achieved significant reductions in external resource dependency, minimized waste, and contributed to a more sustainable and self-sufficient farming approach.

Water management has seen substantial improvements through the implementation of smart technologies in urban agriculture. Mason et al. (2019) have shown that intelligent irrigation systems, driven by IoT and data analytics, have successfully reduced water consumption while maintaining optimal crop yields in smallholder farming systems. By utilizing real-time data and sensor-based monitoring, smart urban farms can precisely control and optimize water usage, leading to improved water efficiency and reduced environmental impact.

Environmental sustainability is another area where smart urban farming has yielded positive outcomes. Jaramillo and Desyouni (2015) emphasize that smart farming practices, such as vertical farming and greenhouses, supported by smart technologies, have significantly reduced the need for land, water, and pesticides compared to conventional agriculture. By creating controlled environments and employing advanced monitoring and management systems, smart urban farms have contributed to minimizing biodiversity loss, mitigating climate change impacts, and reducing the ecological footprint of food production.

However, it is important to acknowledge that there are challenges and potential drawbacks associated with the adoption of smart technologies in urban agriculture. Benis and Ferrão (2018) point out barriers such as high investment costs, narrow profit margins, and uncertain marketing channels that can hinder the commercialization of smart urban farming initiatives. Additionally, Glaeser et al. (2021) raise concerns about the potential exclusion of traditional farming practices and the overreliance on technology in smart urban agriculture. These factors highlight the need for careful consideration and comprehensive planning to ensure the long-term sustainability and inclusivity of smart urban farming initiatives.

Overall, the results obtained from employing smart urban farming practices have demonstrated their potential to address the challenges of urban agriculture. By improving feasibility, resource circularity, water management, and environmental sustainability, smart technologies have enhanced the productivity and sustainability of urban farming systems. Further research and collaboration are necessary to continue refining and scaling these technologies, as well as addressing the socioeconomic aspects and ensuring equitable access to the benefits of smart urban farming.

CONCLUSION

The implementation of smart technologies in urban farming has yielded significant results, addressing key challenges and enhancing the sustainability and productivity of food production in urban areas. Based on the findings from various studies, several important conclusions can be drawn:

Feasibility and Viability: Smart urban farming has demonstrated its feasibility and viability, particularly in resource-constrained urban environments. By optimizing resource utilization, employing efficient farming techniques, and utilizing smart technologies, urban farms have been able to overcome limitations such as limited arable land and meet the growing demand for food in urban areas.

Resource Circular Economy: The integration of smart technologies has facilitated the establishment of a resource circular economy in urban agriculture. Through the implementation of systems such as decentralized anaerobic digestion and vermicomposting, organic waste can be effectively utilized, reducing external resource dependency and minimizing waste generation. This closed-loop approach contributes to the sustainability and self-sufficiency of urban farming systems.

Water Management and Efficiency: Smart technologies have played a crucial role in improving water management in urban farming. The use of intelligent irrigation systems, enabled by IoT and data analytics, has resulted in significant reductions in water consumption while maintaining optimal crop yields. Real-time data monitoring and precise control mechanisms have enhanced water efficiency, reducing environmental impact and promoting sustainable water use in urban agriculture.

Environmental Sustainability: Smart urban farming practices have shown promise in mitigating environmental challenges associated with conventional agriculture. By creating controlled environments, employing advanced monitoring systems, and reducing the need for land, water, and pesticides, smart farms contribute to biodiversity conservation, climate change mitigation, and the reduction of the ecological footprint of food production.

To facilitate the successful implementation of smart urban farming, several factors are essential

1. Investment and Infrastructure: Adequate investment in smart technologies and the development of supporting infrastructure are critical for the widespread adoption of smart urban farming practices. Accessible funding, research, and development support can accelerate the implementation and scalability of these technologies.
2. Knowledge and Education: Building knowledge and providing training programs for farmers, entrepreneurs, and stakeholders is crucial for the successful integration of smart technologies in urban agriculture. This includes providing information on best practices, technical training on smart systems, and promoting awareness of the benefits and potential challenges associated with smart urban farming.
3. Collaboration and Partnerships: The success of smart urban farming relies on collaboration among diverse stakeholders, including farmers, researchers, policymakers, and technology providers. Building strong partnerships and fostering collaboration can lead to knowledge sharing, resource pooling, and the development of comprehensive frameworks for sustainable smart urban farming.

Looking ahead, there are several potential future applications and directions for smart urban farming:

1. Advanced Monitoring and Data Analytics: Further advancements in sensor technology, data analytics, and AI can enhance the monitoring and management of smart urban farms. Real-time data collection, analysis, and predictive modeling can enable more precise and optimized farming practices, leading to increased efficiency and productivity.
2. Integration of Renewable Energy: The integration of renewable energy sources, such as solar panels and wind turbines, can contribute to the energy self-sufficiency of smart urban farms. Combining smart farming practices with clean energy generation can further enhance the sustainability and reduce the environmental impact of urban agriculture.
3. Expansion of Vertical Farming: Vertical farming, which utilizes vertical stacking and controlled environments, has shown significant potential in maximizing space utilization and resource effi-

ciency. Expanding the application of vertical farming, supported by smart technologies, can further increase food production capacity in densely populated urban areas.

In conclusion, the implementation of smart technologies in urban farming has demonstrated its potential to address the challenges of food production in urban areas. By optimizing resource utilization, improving water management, and promoting environmental sustainability, smart urban farming offers a promising approach to achieving sustainable and resilient food systems. To realize the full benefits of smart urban farming, investments, knowledge sharing, and collaboration among stakeholders are essential. By embracing these opportunities and exploring future applications, smart urban farming can contribute to ensuring food security, promoting sustainable development, and building resilient cities.

REFERENCES

Akkem, Y., Biswas, S. K., & Varanasi, A. (2023). Smart farming using artificial intelligence: A review. *Engineering Applications of Artificial Intelligence*, *120*, 105899. doi:10.1016/j.engappai.2023.105899

Al-Kodmany, K. (2018). The vertical farm: A review of developments and implications for the vertical city. *Buildings*, *8*(2), 24. doi:10.3390/buildings8020024

Armanda, D. T., Guinée, J. B., & Tukker, A. (2019). The second green revolution: Innovative urban agriculture's contribution to food security and sustainability – A review. *Global Food Security*, *22*, 13–24. doi:10.1016/j.gfs.2019.08.002

Badami, M. G., & Ramankutty, N. (2015). Urban agriculture and food security: A critique based on an assessment of urban land constraints. *Global Food Security*, *4*, 8–15. doi:10.1016/j.gfs.2014.10.003

Benis, K., & Ferrão, P. (2018). Commercial farming within the urban built environment – Taking stock of an evolving field in northern countries. *Global Food Security*, *17*, 30–37. doi:10.1016/j.gfs.2018.03.005

Biswas, S., Deka, B., Dash, S., & Rout, K. (2022). IoT-based fuzzy logic-controlled novel and multilingual mobile application for hydroponic farming. In *AI* (pp. 31–42). Edge and IoT-based Smart Agriculture, Intelligent Data-Centric Systems. doi:10.1016/B978-0-12-823694-9.00027-X

Castañeda-Miranda, A., & Castaño-Meneses, V. M. (2020). Internet of things for smart farming and frost intelligent control in greenhouses. *Computers and Electronics in Agriculture*, *176*, 105614. doi:10.1016/j.compag.2020.105614

Demirkol, E. C. (2022). Impacts of modern agriculture on environment and sustainable agriculture. *Journal of Life Economics*, *9*(3), 171–182. doi:10.15637/jlecon.9.3.05

Fasciolo, B., Awouda, A., Bruno, G., & Lombardi, F. (2023). A smart aeroponic system for sustainable indoor farming. *30th CIRP Life Cycle Engineering Conference, 116*, (pp. 636-641). CIRP. 10.1016/j.procir.2023.02.107

Foster, L., Szilagyi, K., Wairegi, A., Oguamanam, C., & de Beer, J. (2023). Smart farming and artificial intelligence in East Africa: Addressing indigeneity, plants, and gender. *Smart Agricultural Technology*, *3*, 100132. doi:10.1016/j.atech.2022.100132

Gharaibeh, A., Salahuddin, M. A., Hussini, S. J., Khreishah, A., Khalil, I., Guizani, M., & Al-Fuqaha, A. (2017). Smart cities: A survey on data management, security, and enabling technologies. *IEEE Communications Surveys and Tutorials*, *19*(4), 2456–2501. doi:10.1109/COMST.2017.2736886

Glaeser, E., Kourtit, K., & Nijkamp, P. (2021). New urban challenges: Shared spaces in smart places – Overview and positioning. *Land Use Policy*, *111*, 105672. doi:10.1016/j.landusepol.2021.105672

Halgamuge, M., Bojovschi, A., Fisher, P. M. J., Le, T. C., Adeloju, S., & Murphy, S. (2021). Internet of Things and autonomous control for vertical cultivation walls towards smart food growing: A review. *Urban Forestry & Urban Greening*, *61*, 127094. doi:10.1016/j.ufug.2021.127094

He, L., Fu, L., Gravano, L., Fang, W., Sun, X., Suo, R., Li, G., Zhao, G., Yang, R., & Li, R. (2022). IoT-based urban agriculture container farm design and implementation for localized produce supply. *Computers and Electronics in Agriculture*, *203*, 107445. doi:10.1016/j.compag.2022.107445

Jaramillo, F., & Destouni, G. (2015). Local flow regulation and irrigation raise global human water consumption and footprint. *Science*, *350*(6265), 1248–1251. doi:10.1126cience.aad1010 PMID:26785489

Kasprzyk, M., Szpakowski, W., Poznańska, E., Boogaard, F. C., Bobkowska, K., & Gajewska, M. (2022). Technical solutions and benefits of introducing rain gardens – Gdańsk case study. *The Science of the Total Environment*, *835*, 155487. doi:10.1016/j.scitotenv.2022.155487 PMID:35483461

Khudoyberdiev, A., Ahmad, S., Ullah, I., & Kim, D. (2020). An optimization scheme based on fuzzy logic control for efficient energy consumption in hydroponics environment. *Energies*, *13*(2), 289. doi:10.3390/en13020289

Kullu, P., Majeedullah, S., Pranay, P. V. S., & Yakub, B. (2020). Smart urban farming (Entrepreneurship through EPICS). *Procedia Computer Science*, *172*, 452–459. doi:10.1016/j.procs.2020.05.098

Langendahl, P. A., Tunberg, M., & Kokko, S. (2022). Smart urban agriculture – Exploring its development in Sweden. *Future Food Reports, 18.*

Li, L., Fu, L., & Gravano, L. (2022). IoT-based urban agriculture container farm design and implementation for localized produce supply. *Computers and Electronics in Agriculture*, *203*, 107445. doi:10.1016/j.compag.2022.107445

Li, L., Li, X., Chong, C., Wang, C. H., & Wang, X. (2020). A decision support framework for the design and operation of sustainable urban farming systems. *Journal of Cleaner Production*, *268*, 121928. doi:10.1016/j.jclepro.2020.121928

Lin, F., Weng, Y., Chen, H., & Zhuang, P. (2021). Intelligent greenhouse system based on remote sensing images and machine learning promotes the efficiency of agricultural economic growth. *Environmental Technology & Innovation*, *24*, 101758. doi:10.1016/j.eti.2021.101758

Lovell, S. T. (2010). Multifunctional urban agriculture for sustainable land use planning in the United States. *Sustainability (Basel)*, *2*(8), 2499–2522. doi:10.3390u2082499

Marquez, G. P. B., Takeuchi, H., Montaño, M. N. E., & Hasegawa, T. (2020). Performance of rice straw as mono- and co-feedstock of Ulva spp. for thalassic biogas production. *Heliyon*, *6*(9), e05036. doi:10.1016/j.heliyon.2020.e05036 PMID:33015390

Marquez, G. P. B., Yuan, G. N., Deng, H., Iu, A., Fabella, M., Salonga, R. B., Ashardiono, F., & Cartgena, J. A. (2022). A review on urban agriculture: Technology, socio-economy, and policy. *Heliyon, 8*(11), e11583. doi:10.1016/j.heliyon.2022.e11583 PMID:36406682

Mason, B., Rufí-Salís, M., Parada, F., Gabarrell, X., & Gruden, C. (2019). Intelligent urban irrigation systems: Saving water and maintaining crop yields. *Agricultural Water Management, 226*, 105812. doi:10.1016/j.agwat.2019.105812

Mehmood, F., Ullah, I., Ahmad, S., & Kim, D. H. (2019). Object detection mechanism based on deep learning algorithm using embedded IOT devices for smart home appliances control in CoT. *Journal of Ambient Intelligence and Humanized Computing*. doi:10.100712652-019-01272-8

Mehra, M., Saxena, S., Sankaranarayanan, S., Tom, R. J., & Veeramanikandan, M. (2018). IoT based hydroponics system using Deep Neural Networks. *Computers and Electronics in Agriculture, 155*, 473–486. doi:10.1016/j.compag.2018.10.015

Miles, B., Bourennane, E., Boucherkha, S., & Chikhi, S. (2020). A study of LoRaWAN protocol performance for IoT applications in smart agriculture. *Computer Communications, 164*, 148–157. doi:10.1016/j.comcom.2020.10.009

Minaei, N. (2022). Critical review of smart agri-technology solutions for urban food growing. In *Digital Agritechnology* (pp. 199–217). Robotics and Systems for Agriculture and Livestock Production. doi:10.1016/B978-0-12-817634-4.00006-9

Moghayedi, A., Richter, I., Owoade, F. M., Kapanji-Kakoma, K. K., Kaliyadasa, E., Francis, S., & Ekpo, C. (2022). Effects of urban smart farming on local economy and food production in urban areas in African cities. *Sustainability (Basel), 14*(17), 10836. doi:10.3390u141710836

Nitoslawski, S. A., Galle, N. J., Van Den Bosch, C. K., & Steenberg, J. W. N. (2019). Smarter ecosystems for smarter cities? A review of trends, technologies, and turning points for smart urban forestry. *Sustainable Cities and Society, 51*, 101770. doi:10.1016/j.scs.2019.101770

Oberascher, M., Kinzel, C., Kastlunger, U., Kleidorfer, M., Zingerle, C., Rauch, W., & Sitzenfrei, R. (2021). Integrated urban water management with micro storages developed as an IoT-based solution – The smart rain barrel. *Environmental Modelling & Software, 139*, 105028. doi:10.1016/j.envsoft.2021.105028

Oh, S., & Lu, C. (2023). Vertical farming - Smart urban agriculture for enhancing resilience and sustainability in food security. *The Journal of Horticultural Science & Biotechnology, 98*(2), 133–140. doi:10.1080/14620316.2022.2141666

Pathmudi, V. R., Khatri, N., Kumar, S., Abdul-Qawy, A. S. H., & Vyas, A. K. (2023). A systematic review of IoT technologies and their constituents for smart and sustainable agriculture applications. *Scientific African, 19*, e01577. doi:10.1016/j.sciaf.2023.e01577

Petit, E. P. (2022). Smart City Technologies plus Nature-Based Solutions: Viable and valuable resources for urban resilience. In *Smart Cities Policies and Financing* (pp. 377–398). Approaches and Solutions. doi:10.1016/B978-0-12-819130-9.00001-2

Podder, A. K., Al Bukhari, A., Isalm, S., Mia, S., Mohammed, M. A., Kumar, N. M., Cengiz, K., & Abdulkareem, K. H. (2021). IoT based smart agrotech system for verification of Urban farming parameters. *Microprocessors and Microsystems*, *82*, 104025. doi:10.1016/j.micpro.2021.104025

Popli, S., Jha, R. K., & Jain, S. (2021). Green NOMA assisted NB-IoT based urban farming in multistory buildings. *Computer Networks*, *199*, 108410. doi:10.1016/j.comnet.2021.108410

Priynka, B. H. D. D., Udayaraju, P., Koppireddy, C. S., & Neethika, A. (2023). Developing a region-based energy-efficient IoT agriculture network using region-based clustering and shortest path routing for making sustainable agriculture environment. Measurement. *Sensors (Basel)*, *27*, 100734.

Salomon, M. J., & Cavagnaro, T. R. (2022). Healthy soils: The backbone of productive, safe and sustainable urban agriculture. *Journal of Cleaner Production*, *341*, 130808. doi:10.1016/j.jclepro.2022.130808

Singh, D. K., & Sobti, R. (2022). Long-range real-time monitoring strategy for Precision Irrigation in urban and rural farming in society 5.0. *Computers & Industrial Engineering*, *167*, 107997. doi:10.1016/j.cie.2022.107997

Song, S., Cheong, J. C., Lee, J. S. H., Tan, J. K. N., Chiam, Z., Arora, S., Png, K. J. Q., Seow, J. W. C., Leong, F. W. S., Palliwal, A., Biljecki, F., Tablaba, A., & Tan, H. T. W. (2022). Home gardening in Singapore: A feasibility study on the utilization of the vertical space of retrofitted high-rise public housing apartment buildings to increase urban vegetable self-sufficiency. *Urban Forestry & Urban Greening*, *78*, 127755. doi:10.1016/j.ufug.2022.127755

Su, Y. L., Wang, Y. F., & Ow, D. W. (2020). Increasing effectiveness of urban rooftop farming through reflector-assisted double-layer hydroponic production. *Urban Forestry & Urban Greening*, *54*, 126766. doi:10.1016/j.ufug.2020.126766

Weidner, T., Yang, A., & Hamm, M. W. (2019). Consolidating the current knowledge on urban agriculture in productive urban food systems: Learnings, gaps and outlook. *Journal of Cleaner Production*, *209*, 1637–1655. doi:10.1016/j.jclepro.2018.11.004

Yuan, G. N., Marquez, G. P. B., Deng, H., Iu, A., Fabella, M., Salonga, R. B., Ashardiono, F., & Cartgena, J. A. (2022). A review on urban agriculture: Technology, socio-economy, and policy. *Heliyon*, *8*(11), e11583. doi:10.1016/j.heliyon.2022.e11583 PMID:36406682

Zeunert, J., & Court, T. (2023). Translating unique agricultural precedents into public urban agriculture design. In *Urban and Regional Agriculture* (pp. 431–456). Building Resilient Food Systems. doi:10.1016/B978-0-12-820286-9.00002-9

Chapter 9
Using the Smart Cities Infrastructure for Urban Farming and Z-Farming

Juan Manuel Xicotencatl-Pérez
Universidad Politécnica de Pachuca, Mexico

Julio Cesar Ramos-Fernández
Universidad Politécnica de Pachuca, Mexico

Marco Antonio Marquez-Vera
Universidad Politécnica de Pachuca, Mexico

Ocotlán Díaz-Parra
Universidad Politécnica de Pachuca, Mexico

ABSTRACT

Urban agriculture has made it possible to move vegetable production from rural to densely populated areas, for which it uses different approaches to achieve its mission: food sufficiency. Approaches range from open-sky plantations to controlled environments. Open sky plantations, such as community gardens or roof gardens, offer social rather than economic welfare; it is the controlled environments that offer profitable productions in abandoned spaces or built in a special way. In this chapter, the advantages and disadvantages are mentioned as well as techniques that can improve the performance of this growing area of food development.

INTRODUCTION

FAO recognizes the importance of urban agriculture to solve famines in various parts of the world, in the same way it can help solve the problems of climate change, the problem of warming cities allows the reuse of resources and introduces biological diversity through the planting in or around cities of different varieties of plants and also provide sources of employment and psychological health. Urban

DOI: 10.4018/979-8-3693-0373-3.ch009

agriculture (UA) can occur in the following production environments: community gardens, municipal gardens, roof gardens, private gardens, greenhouses and vertical farming. Of which the first four correspond to open-field agriculture and the last two to controlled areas

Agriculture in the open field and in spaces with controlled environment has become a sector with a high degree of energy consumption, where directly the production of fertilizers, pesticides, herbicides, use of machinery and pumping water from its place of origin (underground well, reservoir or natural source) consumes 6.6% that the sector uses (Chou, L. et al, 2021). Additionally, it must be considered that indirectly energy consumption has to do with the packaging of production, refrigeration and transport. To try to minimize the energy consumption of the latter, it has been thought to move vegetable production activities to the urban environment (United Nations Report on the development of water resources in the world 4, 2012), where the dense population is in permanent search of fresh vegetables being in this way that you can save on the transfer of the same, Storage and refrigeration may be less due to shorter meal times on the road and packaging may also be skipped if consumers come directly to the production center within cities.

However, it should not be lost sight of the fact that one of the main problems of urban agriculture is not only the consumption of energy but the cost of its production, adding the cost of water, which leads to an additional consumption of energy so that water is used optimally, through reducing its use to those allowed by the crop and the expenditure of energy required for its recycling, since such water cannot be discharged into the drainage of the city directly.

Energy expenditure occurs differently for each of the different types of cultivation encompassed by urban agriculture: private gardens, communal gardens, municipal gardens, roof gardens, peri-urban crops, greenhouses, and finally vertical crops. The above crops can be divided into open-air crops, as are all types of gardens, as well as peri-urban crops and crops with controlled environment such as greenhouses and vertical crops.

Agriculture in controlled environments (CEA) is a technology that allows, in closed environments and through control and recycling techniques, the growth of plants independently of the type of soil, such as arid land or the absence of it, as in hydroponics or aquaponics. Given the current circumstances of the world regarding the food issue where fewer and fewer people are dedicated to farming and migrate to large cities, climate change, desertification and overexploitation of cultivated soils, the lack of drinking water (of which 70% (Windapo & Moghayedi, 2020) it is used for planting), population growth and soil depredation, for all these reasons the classic cultivation techniques have been exceeded and are already insufficient to sustain the current and future population.

Controlled agriculture techniques allow the planting and growth of vegetables independently of the climate and in some cases without the application of pesticides, herbicides or fertilizers and being a totally closed environment the plants thus obtained result in healthy plants and suitable for human consumption. Likewise, the use of monitoring, control and recycling systems allows the use of little water (up to 90% less water than traditional techniques (Benke & Tomkins, 2017)). Also artificial lighting can be controlled to achieve optimal vegetable growth and improve taste, generally controlling nutrients, lighting and temperature of plants can improve their food properties and generate high production rates by not depending on climate and sunlight as if open-air crops do.

Unfortunately, the high energy costs of CEAs are due to the higher cost of water, electricity, skilled labor, machinery, lighting technology, control technology, paperwork and permits before local authorities and mainly the value of urban properties compared to rural properties. according to Headrick (2019). The points in favor of CEAs are the elimination of the use of fossil fuels in transport and storage; the complete elimination of pesticides, herbicides, and fertilizers; the non-use of traditional field machinery and finally, more crops per year and the availability of healthy food.

Transport

Due to globalization, food travels great distances to reach the final consumer. Thus, in the United States, food travels 1350 miles on average from producers, both inside and outside the country, to the user, which implies that more energy is consumed in the form of fossil fuels to achieve such exchange and therefore, such a practice results in greater pollutants in the atmosphere (Li, M. et al. 2022), There is a study that found that 5 to 17 times more pollutants are produced on long journeys compared to local journeys, whether from rural areas to specific areas (Gwan-Gyu Lee et al. 2015). Additionally, the picture worsens if food transfers through air travel are considered, since these produce 50% more greenhouse gases than those produced by boat trips. Fortunately, 93% of international transfers are done by boat and 94% of local transfers are done by land. Moving food between the producer and the final consumer consumes 19% of all the energy involved in the food process (see figure 1).

Figure 1. Food energy use

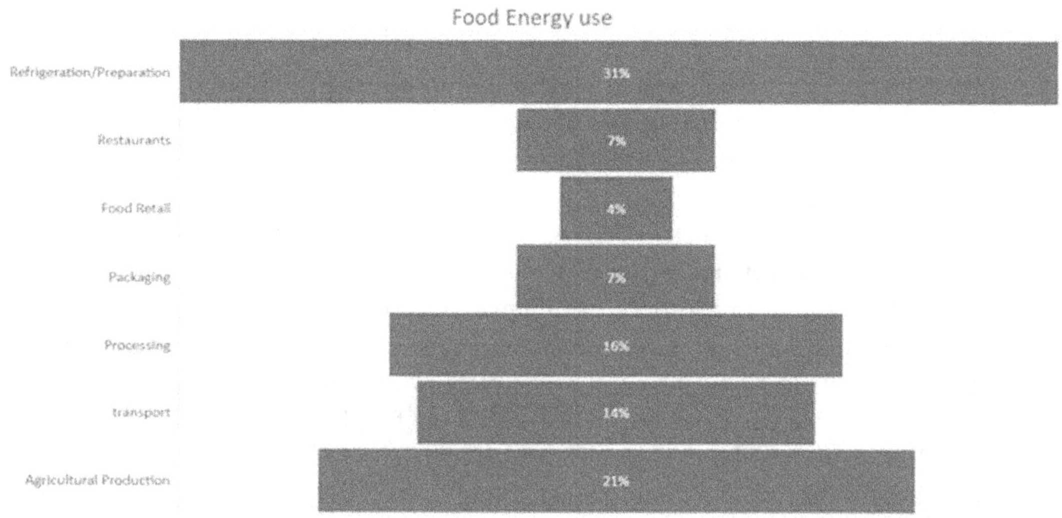

It is spoken in (Li, M. et al., 2022) about trade guaranteeing food security in poor countries, however, it is also shown that rich countries with only 12.5% of the world's population generate 46% of polluting emissions. Local production of vegetables in peri-urban areas is the most appropriate to significantly reduce greenhouse gas emissions.

Therefore, an additional benefit of vegetable production in urban environments is the distance traveled by transport vehicles, an example is the Korean government which promotes urban agriculture, where it is estimated that production by urban agriculture reduces 11668.53 tons of $CO2$ each year, which is equivalent to the annual emissions of the same gas of 1155 people based on the 2007 calculation of personal emissions. of 10.1 tons of $CO2$. (Gwan-Gyu Lee et al. 2015)

Water

Unfortunately, the water that reaches cities rarely comes from places close to them, because of this talking about water is also talking about energy (Sarker et al., 2016), where water generates energy in hydroelectric plants and this same energy is used to move or extract water by pumping or extraction. Water is indispensable for many human activities: in the extraction and conversion of materials, in the cooling of processes where water conducts 30 times more heat than air, in the synthesis of fuels separating hydrogen from water and combining it with CO2 from the atmosphere to produce methanol (Myers, 2022), in the generation of electricity in macro and microturbines, even the tidal force also makes use of water, agriculture and finally, human consumption. It is known that open-field agriculture uses 70% of the drinking water available on the planet, while hydroelectric energy generates 20% of the world's electricity worldwide, a proportion that may increase because it is estimated that by 2035 35% more energy will be required, while 85% more water will be used to generate it. Water from rivers, lagoons and other surface bodies of water needs up to 30% less energy for transport than groundwater or fossil water, the latter requiring prior steps for human consumption (Jin et al. 2019; Center for Sustainable Systems, University of Michigan, 2010).

The water-energy relationship is such that water is required for the exploration of energy-providing materials, the extraction, generation, and transmission of energy while energy is required for the extraction and drilling of wells, transportation to strategic reserves, distribution in municipal networks, treatment and use of water.

Wang et al. (2018) found that, of the total energy involved with water in urban environments, 10% is used for pumping and wastewater treatment. Wastewater can be used for open urban agriculture, with the health risks that come with it (Miller et al. 2017). CEAs use water from the municipal network but treat their waste from being dumped or reused in public gardens. Water treatment cannot be passive, requiring additional energy for some chemical processes to begin, so the water recycling process consumes energy in addition to that required to get the treated water to its destination (see figure 2).

Figure 2. Urban agriculture water cycle

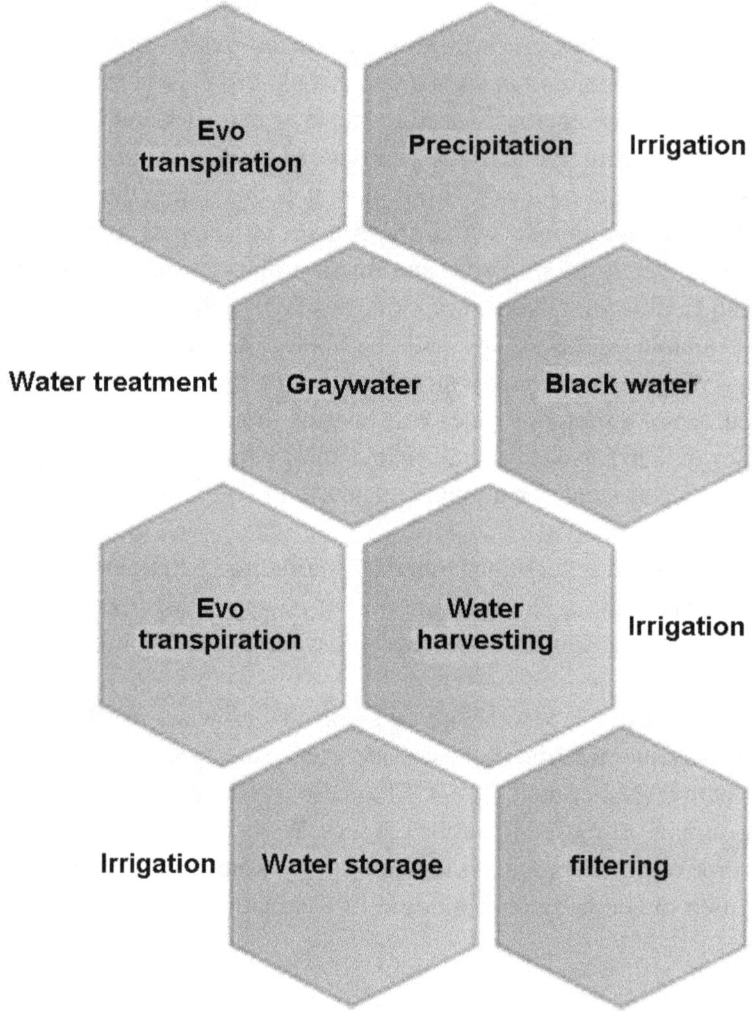

Although water treatment is an expensive process, alternatives to this and to the availability of clean water from the public network can be used: the use of rainwater, to treat gray water for reuse and to carry out a treatment of water for human consumption only in the proportion that is required. Additionally, the stored energy can be reused in the form of a potential difference between untreated and treated water, this energy can be recovered with heat pumps. This difference can be greater if the water that cools the LED lamps is used both at their entrance to their exit of the lighting system if the system has this type of artificial light. (Yu et al. 2012)

Microclimates

One of the great energy demands of a CEA are the climatic conditions that the environment must meet since they must perfectly adjust to the growth of crops within the construction or building, such environmental conditions consider the heating due to artificial lighting, temperature variations in the water that is supplied to the plants and the thermal insulation of the building. Climate control within a controlled environment such as a greenhouse or vertical farm involves the use of both water and air heaters, fans that move air in the environment, heat exchangers or heating with fossil fuels or natural gas, maintenance of thermal insulation and air filtration, as well as dehumidifiers. All the above has a consumption of energy that depends on the position within the city, the country where the city is located, the type of crop and even the type of energy supplied to the complex. These factors create a reliance on both skilled labor and maintenance-sensitive equipment and working conditions, which would likely increase the cost of moving technology in a non-urban environment.

The usual techniques to deal with energy expenditure to conserve microclimates within closed structures is to increase the degree of isolation of this with respect to the environment, where a wall exposed to the sun changes the conditions existing within the structure, in some parts of the world caves and even tunnels or abandoned bomb structures are used to fulfill this purpose (Kemp, 2020). However, it is not always fulfilled to have an underground structure available, so abandoned structures or built specifically for urban agriculture are used, being necessarily to isolate the structure or choose a better location.

An alternative to the use of gas heaters or heat pumps for both air and water, is the heating of water through LED lighting, LED lamps for crops have an efficiency of 80% to 95%, that is, 20% to 5% of the energy of the lamps is dissipated in the form of heat. With this method hot water can be pumped to the growing areas.

In greenhouses the use of LED lamps almost always comes from the ceiling thus allowing a means for air to move between the lamps and the ceiling, allowing a natural cooling, however, in vertical agriculture LED lamps are between trays, which heats the trays, having to be necessary some type of cooling so that the crops are not damaged (Koppes, 2023). For the purposes mentioned above, the heat generated by the power amplifiers must be added since LED lamps use AC to DC converters to perform their function (Oreon).

In greenhouses, the consumption of different types of fuel to achieve crop heating depends almost exclusively on non-renewable sources, although applications with charcoal or wood can also be found. The heating of the greenhouses is usually necessary in times where the environmental cold causes a drastic drop in the internal temperature of the greenhouses and seeks to compensate or minimize this fall, the above also depends on the type of plantation you have since some Plant varieties withstand significant temperature variations. Currently, the use of non-renewable fuels causes concern about the generation of greenhouse gases, which adds pressure to the research and development of alternatives for these materials. An alternative is the use of water heated during the day in tanks or solar heaters to give the stored energy at night, another is the use of heat pumps, which absorb heat from the atmosphere and transfer it to where it is required. Heat pumps represent an energy saving being more efficient than other heating systems. Each alternative should be analyzed and discussed since in hot countries a particularly energy-demanding heating system is not required, but things can change in a country further north, where the nights and seasons of the year are colder.

On the other hand, the use of biofuels can also be an alternative to non-renewable fuels, methane can be generated using the decomposition or composting of crop waste and can be used to generate heat at hours or days when required instead of being deposited in landfills. Biofuels can range from ethanol generated through the fermentation of some waste to hydrogen, although other biofuels such as bio-methanol, biodisel and biobutanol cannot be ruled out (Awogbemi & Kallon, 2022). It was found in one study that, during the colder months in some European countries, solar energy covered around 44-64% of the heating needs of an AEC, while in summer they were around 83-86% (Goldstein, et al. 2016).

Lighting

Currently the use of artificial lighting based on LED is the most popular due to energy consumption however sodium lamps are also used, although these have a luminous efficiency of 20% (GrowSpan, 2018), and the rest is dissipated in the form of heat. Similarly, the LED lamps have a duration of 15000 hours compared to the 8000 of the HID, on average the lamps must be on at least 8 hours daily plus 6 hours of natural light in the greenhouse to simulate a long day of 14 hours and thus stimulate the growth of crops, while in vertical agriculture the lighting of the lamps must be at least 15 to 18hrs. The place where the controlled environment is located must also be considered for energy costs given that in some countries of the European Union at least 6 cents are paid more than in the United States per KW / hour (Eurostat, Statistics Explained. 2023). That is why gardeners in the United States grow with 1000 W bulbs, while their European counterparts lean towards 600 W or 400 W bulbs. Additionally, in greenhouses the use of artificial light must compensate for the lack of natural light that varies as the seasons pass.

In the early stages of plant development and to minimize energy costs, fluorescent lamps are used which are less expensive compared to HID lamps and LEDs. Fluorescent lamps are initially suitable in crops within CEA since plants in their germination require more heat than light, then the replacement can be made by another type of lamps. Another alternative to energy consumption is to use fewer lamps at first and then increase the number as the plants mature.

Since the use of HIDs supposes more heat applied to the plants these respond transpired more which causes greater humidity in the environment and makes necessary the use of dehumidifiers to avoid the growth of mold.

Finally, in numbers, the electrical energy consumed by fluorescent lamps, heating equipment and additional equipment represent 63.6-71.3%, 25.9-16.9% and 10.5-11.8% of the total energy consumed in a controlled environment system (Yu Tong, et al 2013). Where between lighting, ventilation, and heating account for approximately 90% of the total cost of energy.

Automation

The sensors that can be found in a CEA and that are directly related to the development of plants are: CO2 sensors that help maintain carbon dioxide levels at acceptable levels for planting, light sensors to measure the light requirement in each part of the crop, temperature sensors since each type of plant has its own temperature needs, ambient humidity sensors that affect the perspiration rate of plants and soil moisture sensors, which measure whether water amounts are appropriate. In addition, sensors are required for the external part of the construction or building where the CEA is located, the mentioned sensors are placed to monitor the performance of the environment before the control of the variables, so intelligent algorithms carry out estimates and take the necessary actions to reduce diseases and efficiently control the microclimate of the CEA.

The operation of actuators occurs in the same way as sensors, the actuator control system can consist of valves and motors: valves for closing pipes or passage of nutrients and motors for closing vents or moving shadows in greenhouses. For vertical farming, motors can move grow tray structures for proper lighting.

Both sensors and actuators can benefit from IoT technologies (Bajer & Krejcar, 2015; Bhujel et al.2020), by making it possible to monitor the CEA from remote points or to exercise remote control and surveillance and even control in the cloud, which can even allow the application of computationally intensive controls calculated in the cloud and sent over the internet, simulate scenarios and propose mathematical models that can be checked in situ.

CONCLUSION

Energy is an aspect to consider in urban agriculture, being the most significant consumption the consumption of CEAs, in these controlled environments the air, water, climate and light, must be carefully measured and altered as appropriate. The rest of the places where urban agriculture is practiced have few energy demands, referring mainly to the pumping of water for plants and even the extraction of water through wells. Although only two aspects of controlled environment agriculture are significantly large in terms of energy, lighting and climate control, alternatives can be sought to minimize their impact on costs. One is the decomposition of solid waste from biomass plants, to obtain biofuels. Another is the use of a byproduct of lighting heat that can be channeled using ventilation that allows air to be recirculated. The water that although its use does not generate so much energy expenditure if it is impossible to do without it, since in the techniques of hydroponics, aquaponics and aeroponics turns out to be the vehicle of the nutrients that the plant requires, such waters cannot be discarded and sent to the public waste network, but must be treated to remove contaminants, being the degree of removal which will allow significant savings in energy consumption from recycling. Additionally, the temperature differences between the waters entering the controlled system and those leaving can be used for heating purposes. Finally, the greater the degree of crop isolation that seeks to increase climate independence and optimally use resources, the more investment and development will be needed, as well as research into improved techniques to address energy costs. You can think about the use of renewable energies, but in an urban environment perhaps resorting to a single source of energy probably does not meet all the needs of the system.

REFERENCES

Awogbemi, O., & Kallon, D. V. V. (2022, October 18). Valorization of agricultural wastes for biofuel applications. *Heliyon*, *8*(10), e11117. doi:10.1016/j.heliyon.2022.e11117 PMID:36303926

Bajer, L., & Krejcar, O. (2015). Design and Realization of Low Cost Control for Greenhouse Environment with Remote Control. *IFAC-PapersOnLine*, *48*(4), 368–373. doi:10.1016/j.ifacol.2015.07.062

Benke, K., & Tomkins, B. (2017). Future food-production systems: Vertical farming and controlled-environment agriculture. *Sustainability*, *13*(1), 13–26. doi:10.1080/15487733.2017.1394054

Bhujel, A., Basak, J. K., Khan, F., Arulmozhi, E., Jaihuni, M., Sihalath, T., Lee, D., Park, J., & Kim, H. T. (2020). Sensor Systems for Greenhouse Microclimate Monitoring and Control: A Review. *Journal of Biosystems Engineering*, *45*(4), 341–361. doi:10.100742853-020-00075-6

Center for Sustainable Systems, University of Michigan (CSS). (2010) U.S. water supply and distribution fact sheet. *Pub No. CSS05-17*. CSS. http://css.snre.umich.edu/css_doc/CSS05-17.pdf

Chang, Y., Li, G., Yao, Y., Zhang, L., & Yu, C. (2016). Quantifying the Water-Energy-Food Nexus: Current status and trends. *Energies*, *9*(65), 65. doi:10.3390/en9020065

Chou, L., Dai, J., Qian, X., Karimipour, A., & Zheng, X. (2021). Achieving sustainable soil and water protection: The perspective of agricultural water price regulation on environmental protection. *Agricultural Water Management*, *245*, 106583. doi:10.1016/j.agwat.2020.106583 PMID:33100487

Eurostat, E. E. (2023, April). Electricity price statistics. https://ec.europa.eu/eurostat/statistics-explained/index.php?title=Electricity_price_statistics

FAO (Food and Agriculture Organization of the United Nations). (2011). The state of the world's land and water resources for food and agriculture (SOLAW) – Managing systems at risk. Food and Agriculture Organization of the United Nations and London, Earthscan.

Firfiris, V. K., Fragos, V. P., Kotsopoulos, T. A., & Nikita-Martzopoulou, C. (2020). Energy and environmental analysis of an innovative greenhouse structure towards frost prevention and heating needs conservation. *Sustainable Energy Technologies and Assessments*, *40*, 100750. doi:10.1016/j.seta.2020.100750

Goldstein, B., Hauschild, M., Fernandez, J., & Birkved, M. (2016). Testing the environmental performance of urban agriculture as a food supply in northern climates. *Journal of Cleaner Production*, *135*, 984–994. doi:10.1016/j.jclepro.2016.07.004

GrowSpan. (2018, May 24). *Understanding Greenhouse Lighting*. GrowSpan. https://www.growspan.com/news/understanding-greenhouse-lighting/

Jin, P., Fang, D., & Chen, B. (2019, February). Water-energy nexus based on modified multiregional input-output model within China. *Energy Procedia 158*, 4092-4098.

Kemp, R. (2020). The Future Of Farming Is Inside This Bomb Shelter. Ten Stories Underneath London, Thousands Of Plants Are Growing. Popular Mechanics. https://www.popularmechanics.com/science/a34618094/future-farming-underground/

Koppes, S. (2023, February 20) New LED strategies could make vertical farming more productive, less costly. *Newsroom*. https://www.purdue.edu/newsroom/releases/2023/Q1/new-led-strategies-could-make-vertical-farming-more-productive,-less-costly.html

Leahy, S. (2018, June 7). Carbon Engineering Liquid Fuel Carbon Capture Neutral Science. *National Geographic*. https://www.nationalgeographic.com/science/article/carbon-engineering-liquid-fuel-carbon-capture-neutral-science

Li, M., Jia, N., Lenzen, M., Malik, A., Wei, L., Jin, Y., & Raubenheimer, D. (2022). Global food-miles account for nearly 20% of total food-systems emissions. *Nature Food*, *3*(6), 445–453. doi:10.103843016-022-00531-w PMID:37118044

Menardo, S., Bauer, A., Theuretzbacher, F., Piringer, G., Nilsen, P. J., Balsari, P., Pavliska, O., & Amon, T. (2012). Theuretzbacher, F.; Piringer, G.; Nilsen, P.J.; Balsari, P.; Pavliska, O.; Amon, T. Biogas Production from Steam-Exploded Miscanthus and Utilization of Biogas Energy and CO2 in Greenhouses. *BioEnergy Research*, *6*(2), 620–630. doi:10.100712155-012-9280-5

Miller-Robbie, L., Ramaswami A., & Amerasinghe, P. (2017, July 4). Wastewater treatment and reuse in urban agriculture: exploring the food, energy, water, and health nexus in Hyderabad, India. *Environmental Research Letters, 12*(7). doi:10.1088/1748-9326/aa6bfe

Myers, A. (2022, February 9). Stanford engineers create a catalyst that can turn carbon dioxide into gasoline 1,000 times more efficiently. *Stanford News.* https://news.stanford.edu/2022/02/09/turning-carbon-dioxide-gasoline-efficiently/#:~:text=captured%20co2%20can%20be,1%2c000%20times%20over%20existing%20methods

Oreon. (n.d.) *Water-Cooled Led Grow Lights.* Oreon. https://www.oreon-led.com/en/water-cooled-led-grow-lights

Pfister, S., Bayer, P., Koehler, A., & Hellweg, S. (2011, September). agriculture: Scenarios and related impacts. *The Science of the Total Environment, 409*(20), 4206–4216. doi:10.1016/j.scitotenv.2011.07.019 PMID:21840571

Ramaswami, A., Boyer, D., Singh Nagpure, A., Fang, A., Bogra, S., Bakshi, B., Cohen, E., & Rao-Ghorpade, A. (2017). An urban systems framework to assess the trans-boundary foodenergy-water nexus: Implementation in Delhi, India. *Environmental Research Letters, 12*(2), 025008. doi:10.1088/1748-9326/aa5556

Sarker, T., Kibler, K., & Reinhart, D. (2016). Concept mapping of food waste management alternatives within the food-energy-water nexus. *Proceedings of the World Environmental and Water Resources Congress.*

Semiat, R. (2008). Energy issues in desalination processes. *Environmental Science & Technology, 42*(22), 8193–8201. doi:10.1021/es801330u PMID:19068794

Tong, Y., Yang Q. C., Shimamura S. (2013, October). Analysis of Electric-Energy Utilization Efficiency in a Plant Factory with Artificial Light for Lettuce Production. *Acta Horticulturae 1037*(1037). . doi:10.17660/ActaHortic.2014.1037.32

Wang, S., Cao, T., & Chen, B. (2017). Urban energy–water nexus based on modified input–output analysis. *Applied Energy, 196*, 208–217. doi:10.1016/j.apenergy.2017.02.011

Weidner, T., & Yang, A. (2020). The potential of urban agriculture in combination with organic waste valorization: Assessment of resource flows and emissions for two european cities. *Journal of Cleaner Production, 244*(1), 118490. doi:10.1016/j.jclepro.2019.118490

Windapo, A. O., & Moghayedi, A. (2020). Adoption of smart technologies and circular economy performance of buildings. *Built Environment Project and Asset Management, 10*(4), 585–601. doi:10.1108/BEPAM-04-2019-0041

Yu, Tong & Kozai, T. & Nishioka, N. & Ohyama, Katsumi. (. (2012). Reductions in Energy Consumption and CO2 Emissions for Greenhouses Heated with Heat Pumps. *Applied Engineering in Agriculture, 28*, 401–406. doi:10.13031/2013.41488

Chapter 10
Tools and Technologies for Smart Education in Sustainable Smart Cities

Ricardo A. Barrera-Cámara
https://orcid.org/0000-0002-3170-4671
Universidad Autónoma del Carmen, Mexico

Alejandro Fuentes-Penna
https://orcid.org/0000-0002-4303-3852
El Colegio de Morelos, Mexico

Maria Beatriz Bernabe-Loranca
https://orcid.org/0000-0003-3014-4139
Benemérita Universidad Autónoma de Puebla, Mexico

ABSTRACT

In recent years, as a result of the recent events that humanity has experienced due to the arrival of the pandemic situation by COVID-19, it has led to the increase in the use of various information and communication technologies, changes in various limits related to the way of interacting, work, learn, and teach. Collaborative tools, smart boards, educational platforms, massive courses, web development platforms, and the internet of things are examples of some technologies that support education. The purpose of this section is to present various technologies or tools that can support education in sustainable and sustainable cities.

DOI: 10.4018/979-8-3693-0373-3.ch010

INTRODUCTION

The combination of technologies related to communications, computers, software, hardware, storage media that support the processing, storage or transmission of information are called information and communication technologies. Information and communication technologies (hardware and software) significantly support the teaching and learning process. Example of tools that support learning:

– Cloud storage: These are tools that use internet-based services to store and share files (Dropbox, Google drive, OneDrive, etc.).
– Plagiarism Detection: Prevention or detection of plagiarism in electronic documents available on the internet or in digital repositories (Plagium, Plagiarism Checker. Turnitin, etc.).
– Office: Set of tools to carry out office activities through the cloud or on portable or smart computers that include spreadsheets, word processors, graphic presenters, email clients (Google suite, Microsoft office, OpenOffice, etc.).
– Microlearning platforms: Platforms where the topics are presented in small modules and accessed at the time or schedule available to the student (Crehana, Edapp, GoSkills, HubSpot Academy, Luca, etc.).
– Integrated platforms: Set of free or commercial tools available on the internet that incorporate various technologies or applications for educational management or evaluation (Google Classroom, Microsoft Teams, etc.).
– Course Platforms: Also known as Learning Management Systems. They allow the administration and management of learning resources with various applications that are accessed through the network or internet (Blackboard Edmodo, Moodle, Schoology, TedEd, etc.).
– Presentations: Create or share non-sequential dynamic presentations with animations or movement using cloud services; share various types of documents or files (Emaze, Jamboard, Prezi, Padlet Slideshare, etc.).
– Social Networks: They allow communication and activities based on a group of interest or affinity (Facebook, Instagram, Telegram, Twitter, WhatsApp, etc.).
– Survey or evaluation systems: Used to administer surveys or exams under a network or local environment for free or paid (Google Forms, MS Forms, Survey Monkey, etc.).

Intelligent technology allows processing information and acquiring knowledge to certain objects based on data analysis, machine learning and artificial intelligence artificial (Thakur, 2022). This technology makes use of various devices connected to the internet, and cloud services. Some of the benefits of smart technologies are:

– Conserve and save energy (sustainability). The costs for the production, supply and use of energy have risen. With intelligent technology combined with various devices, energy automation, control and optimization is possible.
– Saving of resources. By having better control and monitoring of the resources and equipment used, instead of hiring staff, smart technology can help reduce expenses and support savings.
– Security. With the various applications and devices (sensors, alarms, cameras, etc.) unauthorized access to places or possible access attempts can be detected. Alert the authorities, people or security personnel about any behavior in the event of possible unauthorized access or attempted access. Also, the power to alert of possible gas leaks, fires, or failures in any equipment or device.

- Monitoring the health of people. With the sensors and applications that include biometric devices, it is possible to monitor patients or people with any disease or condition. This allows alerting family members, medical personnel, or emergency services.

A smart city is characterized by four elements (Silva et al., 2018): Sustainability (infrastructure and governance, energy and climate change, extraction and waste; social, economic and health); Quality of life (financial well-being, emotional well-being); Intelligence (Economic, Social, Environmental) and Urbanization (Technical, Infrastructure, Governance, Economic). A smart and sustainable city makes use of ICT with the intention of improving the quality of life, efficiency in the operation of services and with-it competitiveness, satisfying current and future needs in relation to the economic, social, environmental and cultural (Focus Group on Smart Sustainable Cities, 2015). In this sense, countries have been proposed to apply reforms in education systems, to apply smart technologies and environments efficiently that improve education for sustainable development (UNESCO, 2018).

The Qingdao declaration raises the use of information communication technologies to achieve sustainable development goal 4, which is linked to education (United Nations Educational, 2015). UNESCO proposes the use of a series of measures to consider in the use of artificial intelligence in education (United Nations Educational, 2019) and establishes a series of ethical recommendations for the use and implementation of artificial intelligence for the countries that form part of it. part of UNESCO (United Nations Educational, 2021). The UN within the 2030 agenda(United Nations, 2015), proposes a series of 17 objectives for the sustainable and prosperous development of people, planet, with the strengthening of justice and peace (Table 1). This framework considers a sustainable development goal called Goal 11 sustainable cities and communities. It "intends that settlements (cities) are safer, more inclusive, resilient and sustainable". Also, Objective 4 Linked to the quality of education.

Table 1. Sustainable development goals

Goal	Description
Goal 1: End of poverty	Eradicate any type of poverty in the world
Goal 2: Zero hunger	Put an end to hunger by ensuring sufficient and sustainable food access.
Goal 3: Health and well-being	To achieve sustainable development, it is essential to ensure healthy lives and promote well-being at all ages. This involves reducing mortality, eliminating epidemics, addressing well-being and mental health, and preventing and treating the use of addictive beverages or substances.
Goal 4: Quality education	Access to education regardless of the level of education, free of charge, inclusive, equitable and of quality. Whose learning is for life.
Goal 5: Gender equality	Achieve gender equality and empower all women and girls, eliminating discrimination, violence, practices of any kind. Create and apply laws that allow equality and empowerment.
Goal 6: Clean water and sanitation	Guarantee availability and access to water for all, improve water quality, sustainable management and sanitation for all.
Goal 7: Affordable and clean energy	Guarantee access to affordable, safe, sustainable and modern energy, increase the use of renewable energy, improve technological infrastructure and services in developing countries.
Goal 8: Decent work and economic growth	Promote inclusive (including disability) and sustainable economic growth, employment and decent work for all. Create and promote policies for productive activities, entrepreneurship and formalization of micro and small businesses.
Goal 9: Industry, innovation and infrastructures	Countries with less development increase the use of information technologies, providing them with economic, technical and technological support. Develop and promote industrialization through innovation with the people who dedicate themselves to research and development, and promote sustainable industrialization with resilient infrastructures.
Goal 10: Reduction of inequalities	Reduce inequalities and ensure that no one is left behind. Through the social, economic and political inclusion of people regardless of their demographic characteristics. Eliminating laws or practices that limit equal opportunities and decrease inequality.
Goal 11: Sustainable cities and communities	Settlements (cities) with more secure, inclusive, resilient and sustainable basic services. Protect and maintain cultural and natural heritage. Decrease deaths from water-related disasters.
Goal 12: Responsible production and consumption	Guarantee sustainable consumption and production modalities with the efficient use of natural resources. Reduction of food waste in production, supply and post-harvest losses. Development of sustainable tourism for the creation of sources of work, promotion of culture and local products.
Goal 13: Climate action	Take urgent measures to combat climate change and its effects. Measured in policies and strategies and plans. Education to raise awareness of climate change mitigation.
Goal 14: Life Underwater	Conserve and sustainably use the oceans, seas and marine resources. These are strongly linked to health and make the planet habitable. For this reason, pollution and damage to marine and coastal resources that are affected by polluting activities or excessively or illegally exploited operators must be avoided.
Goal 15: Life on land ecosystems	Sustainably manage forests, fight against desertification, stop and reverse land degradation, stop the loss of biodiversity caused by poaching and trafficking of protected species.
Goal 16: Peace, justice and strong institutions	Promote just, peaceful and inclusive societies. Eliminate any form of violence, mistreatment, exploitation, trafficking and torture; combat terrorism and crime, make accounts transparent at all levels of institutions.
Goal 17: Partnerships to achieve the goals	Revitalize the Global Partnership for Sustainable Development. Considering all types of institutions in the participation of alliances. The inclusive associations that cooperate have aspects such as: finance, Technology, Capacity building, trade, Systemic issues (Policy and institutional coherence, Multi-stakeholder partnerships and Data, monitoring and accountability).

Smart education describes a breakthrough in education supported by smart technology (Kaur & Bhatia, 2021). By incorporating smart technology, the abilities of those who teach are improved and it helps students learn in a more comfortable, flexible, effective and efficient way (Nanda & Randhawa, 2019).

A smart school is one that uses the Internet of Things to support its teaching and learning processes. It incorporates smart devices (phones, tablets, computers, laptop), IoT devices connected to the network (sensors, actuators), construction of decision systems (Smart Education, Smart Control) based on the analysis, processing, collection and storage of data, and support the monitoring of students, teachers, objects and equipment (Terzieva et al., 2022).

Smart schools are considered institutions that base the teaching and learning of students through information technologies (Omidinia et al., 2013). These contribute to urban governance in the formation of citizens' capacities to manage and optimize the city (Williamson, 2015).

The intelligent university incorporates technological infrastructure, the Internet of things, and big data to obtain educational objectives (Rico-Bautista et al., 2022). It is distinguished by incorporating new technologies such as e-learning, Internet of things, cloud computing, big data, Green-ICT, smart devices, Smart classroom, cybersecurity (Bakupa Mbombo & Nadire, 2021). It integrates the use of platforms and innovates in the way of working, learning and teaching in these platform spaces (Barn, 2020).

The combination of artificial intelligence with the internet of things makes personalized learning possible for each student, allows natural and human communication and receives feedback and help in real time (Kamruzzaman et al., 2023).

BACKGROUND

Related Work

Internet of things devices, smart connected devices and smart devices are discussed as part of the technologies and applications available to cities, and the use of these technologies as a means to achieve peace paz (Cheshmehzangi, 2022). The Internet of Things is used in many areas, such as education (school and smart education) supporting educational processes. This, through the use of various devices that are combined and that generate data for subsequent analysis (Terzieva et al., 2022).

Educational automation and improvement is applied in universities, campuses or schools in an intelligent way for the management and improvement of their educational resources and services educativos (Kassab et al., 2020). The use of the smart education concept, associated technologies and its development is analyzed as part of a study, the results show that learning must be supported in a more intelligent way (Kaur & Bhatia, 2021).Educational technology and intelligent education are considered the foundations in the training of engineers in the face of technology integration challenges (Diogo et al., 2023). Kaur (Kaur et al., 2022) analyzes various multidisciplinary works establishing a terminology and taxonomy, as well as research trends related to smart classrooms.

Smart technologies (smart campus, smart e-learning, e-matrix, educational network consortium) are innovative and intellectual tools that play a very important role in higher education systems (Lyapina et al., 2019).

TECHNOLOGIES AND TOOLS

There is a wide variety of technologies, tools, or devices applicable in intelligent education, among which the Internet of Things technologies stand out the most. An example of IoT Devices are smart devices, sensors, sports bands, wearable technologies, hearing aids, virtual or augmented reality glasses, robots, smart screens, lights, locks, smartphones, etc. Table 2 presents an adaptation (Terzieva et al., 2022) with examples of IoT devices and their possible location in schools.

Table 2. IoT devices

Device	Location								
	School	Classroom	Laboratory	Gym	Workplace	Students	Tools	Objects People	Teachers
Air quality analyzer	X	X	X	X					
Sports bands				X					
cameras	X	X			X	X			
Biomedical Devices				X		X			
RFID tags							X	X	
RFID readers	X	X			X	X			
Virtual or augmented reality glasses									
Smart displays		X	X						
Humidity sensor		X	X	X					
Motion sensor	X	X			X	X			
Noise sensor	X	X			X	X			
Temperature sensor	X		X	X					
Wearables						X			X

MOOC Platforms

MOOC or Massive Online Open are courses that are taught massively over the Internet to anyone, these generally have no limit on participants and are found in the Learning Management System. These can be free or paid access. Table 3 presents an exemplary list of platforms.

They are an academic and technological tool for sustainable education, in which students select their schedule and whose use is positive during the COVID 19 pandemic (Yang & Lee, 2021). They are educational strategies to educate and train communities in energy sustainability, obtaining good results on student learning and motivation (Carrera & Ramírez-Hernández, 2018).

MOOCs have generated great importance in sustainable education and, for this reason, a guide for policy developers has been formulated for countries that develop or intend to develop this modality of teaching. The intention is to cover the needs of access to education (UNESCO & Commonwealth of Learning, 2016). MOOC4ALL (Kasztelewicz et al., 2022), is an example of a project involving non-profit organizations from various organizations, it covers courses related to renewable energy, waste management and sustainable development supporting the 2030 agenda on sustainable development.

A strategy to raise awareness about sustainable lifestyles is the one developed by public and private institutions in Mexico and the United States, they used MOOCs to train, openly certify in terms of energy sustainability energética (Ramirez Montoya et al., 2022). There is a great diversity of platforms and applications aimed at offering massive or individual training, educational or job training services at various levels. Some are of free public access or subject to payment for training or the possible issuance of a certificate at the end of the education or training program (Table 3).

Table 3. Platforms and services MOOC

Platform	Description	Reference
ALISON	Free online education platform that grants diplomas and certificates available to anyone. The platform is aligned with various sustainable development goals.	(Alison.com, 2023)
Canvas	Platform oriented to competency-based education courses and that grants digital badges. Integrates Microsoft, zoom., Google, aws and nearpod applications.	(Instructure, 2023)
Coursera	It provides training or training services for people, businesses, universities or governments in a massive way in various areas or disciplines. Grants certificates, certificates or degrees. Some courses are free, most have to cover a fee.	(Coursera Inc, 2023)
EdX	It provides those interested in various courses and various disciplines, mostly free. Also training or training programs and academic degree programs that mostly have a cost.	(edX LLC, 2023)
FutureLearn	British platform for massive courses offered by undergraduate and postgraduate level universities.	(Global University Systems, 2023)
icourse163.org/	MOOC platform for higher education aimed at all those who wish to improve their education for free, obtain certificates or certificates.	(University of China, 2023)
iVersity	Online courses and conferences for higher and professional level. Most of the courses are paid and you get a certificate.	(iversity learning solutions GmbH, 2023)
Khan Academy	Free and non-profit courses WITH topics related to: mathematics (basic, undergraduate, college, university) science, economics, economics and finance, computing, arts and teacher training.	(Khan Academy, 2023)
MéxicoX	Initiative of the Mexican government to offer massive online courses. The courses are designed by various public or private institutions which in some cases grant a certificate with a fee. The platform provides free proof of participation.	(MéxicoX, 2023)
MOOC4ALL	Designed to offer massive and open online courses with the intention of educating and training people in basic environmental conservation issues. Supports the sustainability goals of the United Nations.	(MOOC4ALL, 2023)
Open2Study	Open platform of the University of Australia with free courses, and accreditation of courses at the vocational, undergraduate and postgraduate level.	(Open Universities Australia, 2023)
OpenLearning	Platform that offers MOOCs, paid or free courses, private courses and learning at the pace of the students.	(OpenLearning Limited, 2023)
OpenupEd	The aim is to collect, display and promote MOOC programs from European higher education institutions.	(OpenupEd, 2023)
Standford Online	It offers university education, educational certificates, master's degrees. Most of their programs have a cost, most of the free programs do not grant a certificate of completion.	(Stanford University, 2023)
Udacity	Commercial platform that offers course programs in various disciplines. They are oriented to people, groups, government, or companies. Free educational courses are free of charge and do not provide a certificate of completion.	(Udacity, 2023)
UDEMY	Massive courses in various disciplines, mostly in information technology. Courses with a fee grant a certificate of completion, and free courses do not grant recognition, only access to video.	(Udemy, 2023)

Smart Classroom

They are classrooms equipped with technology to contribute to teaching and learning with the integration of software, computers, learning technologies, communication networks with audiovisual technology and rapid response (Kuppusamy, 2019).

Smart classrooms should be built aware of the context of the smart campus, considering context awareness, technology integration and measures for their integration (Huang et al., 2019) .

User security, educational intelligence and technological accessibility, system diversity, interconnectivity, simplicity and sensitivity are attributes that influence the quality of smart classrooms from the perspective of higher education teachers (Alfoudari et al., 2023).

Infrastructure, sustainability content, evaluation-feedback and motivation are components for sustainable education, using smart classrooms as main agents for students and teachers (Angelaki et al., 2022).

Smart material, smart communication and participation, smart assessment, and smart physical environment are fields of the smart classroom taxonomy linked to experience and learning (Kaur et al., 2022).

The main characteristics of smart classrooms are (Iqbal et al., 2020) internet of things, Adaptation to smart equipment, consistent monitoring and analysis of performance, data detection and inference, awareness of collaborative learning, self-organization of communities of learning, anticipation of students' abilities, self-assessment tools, handling of big data in the digital cloud.

Interactive whiteboards or smart interactive whiteboards project the image on the whiteboard and it detects any touch or movement on the surface through some software application, these touches on the whiteboard become equivalent to click with additional functions (Isakova Mukhlisa Fakhriddin & Fayzullayev Sayfiddin Bakhadir, 2022).

SMART Classroom Suite is an example of a smart whiteboard software application designed for teachers and students. Which allows you to create classes, view and control student screens, students organize and schedule their activities, and tools that allow the teacher to create various assessments and monitor student (SMART Technologies ULC, 2009). Current versions (SMART Technologies ULC, 2023) SMART Board allows creating and scheduling classes in a simpler, more flexible and interactive way, and SMART Remote Management allows managing and controlling devices from any browser.

Green-ICT

Green information and communication technologies refer to the efficient and effective use of technologies with the intention of not harming or reducing damage to the environment (Deshpande & Unhelkar, 2011). Green classrooms and machine learning are combined as an educational strategy for a sustainable view (Pal et al., 2023).

Some countries consider that green technologies negatively affect the environment instead of being a means to obtain sustainability, they cause negative effects in higher education institutions (Moturi et al., 2016). An example of initiatives to protect the environment and student health in a short period is Go-Browm, and Go-Green in the long and medium term, also considering changes in infrastructure (Agarwal, 2023).

Blockchain Technology unites public and distributed database blocks securely and records network transactions. The Green Blockchain Technology helps with environmental social problems with an ecological perspective (Padmapriya & Sujatha, 2023).

Green Cloud Computing is a technology that refers to the use of technologies and services in the cloud with the intention of respecting and not harming the environment. Also to save energy resources and reduce costs by reducing the use of equipment. Green Hardware refers to ICTs that allow energy savings and respect the environment as a device and communication systems, storage, energy, cooling systems and facilities. Some technologies that are used in different areas are:

- Solar panels are technologies that use the sun's energy to be stored in batteries and equipment that transforms the energy received into energy necessary to supply energy and thereby activate lamps that illuminate.
- LED lights are used to illuminate any type of space because it is considered that energy consumption is considerably reduced and thus cost them for their consumption.
- The use of light sensors and their activation in places where there is constant movement of people or little movement, allows the activation of these only when passing through the area.
- The use of light and movement sensors allows the activation of lights or lighting with the stoppage of movement or their deactivation.

Chatbots

Chatbots are computer programs that use artificial intelligence and natural language processing with the intention of appearing to have a conversation with people, giving automatic responses based on data provided by users, and which have been previously established.

From the educational perspective, chatbots are used for computer support, language teaching, medical training, educational support for students (Lin & Yu, 2023). An example of its educational use is the improvement of students learning a second language using a digital storytelling chatbot or storybots (Bailey et al., 2021). The teaching of culture in secondary school students in English or French from public or private schools in France (Mageira et al., 2022). A great diversity of platforms, services or applications linked to chatbots are currently available, these can be free or with a fee available for multiple purposes (table 4).

Table 4. Platforms or services of chatbot

Nombre	Descripción	Referencia
AsasaraBot	Educational ChatBot to teach cultural content, its development is based on SnatchBot.	(Mageira & Pittou, 2020)
Character.ai	Chatbot that does not allow content for work but produces it. It allows interaction with favorite characters or the creation of custom characters which can converse.	(Character.ai, 2023)
Chatcompose	Conversation tools oriented to sales and support. It includes three versions: free, professional and company.	(ChatCompose, 2019)
ChatGPT	Based on GPT-4 built by OpenAI with intelligence. Some of the functions that it has developed at the prototype level are document synthesis, content generation, and various media publications on the Internet.	(OpenAI, 2023)
Cleverbot	Originally designed to learn foreign languages, however today it can be included in any web application.	(Carpenter, 2023)
Cliengo	Oriented to customer service using the figure of virtual assistant. It connects to various tools such as calendars, emails, various cloud technologies with a commercial focus.	(LEADAKI S.A, 2023)
Ernie Bot	Ernie (Enhanced Representation through Knowledge Integration) Bot from Baidu developed as an alternative to ChatGPT. In the demo he answered questions about a novel, created a video and a poem.	(Baidu, 2023)
Freudbot	Educational ChatBot aimed at philosophy students to learn about the theories, concepts and bibliography of Sigmund Freud.	(Athabasca University, 2023a)
Google Bard	Developed by Google as a conversational tool, based on LaMDA and as a competition to ChatGPT.	(Google, 2023)
HuggingChat	It is an artificial intelligence chat interface from the Hugging Face company, based on open assistant which responds to data input.	(Hugging Face, 2023)
Meta LLaMA	ChatLLaMA is a LLaMA (Large Language Model Meta AI) application based on Reinforcement Learning from human feedback. This was launched by Meta to answer questions and summarize documents.	(Meta AI, 2023)
Microsoft Chat Bing	It is part of the chatbot-type Microsoft Bing search engine, in which you write what you want to ask, it is still in a trial period.	(Microsoft, 2023c)
PiagetBot	Educational ChatBot aimed at philosophy students to learn about Jean Piaget's theories, concepts and bibliography.	(Athabasca University, 2023b)
SearchGPT	It is an implementation built into the Korean browser naver.	(NHN Corp, 2023)
Woebothealth	A conversational health chat is used as a means to offer therapy for the reduction of symptoms of depression and anxiety.	(Woebot Health, 2023)
YandexGPT	Service similar to chatGPT from the Russian company Yandex.	(Yandex, 2023)

The combination of artificial intelligence with the internet of things makes personalized learning possible for each student, allows natural and human communication and receives feedback and help in real time (Kamruzzaman et al., 2023)

IoT Platform

An Internet of Things platform considers facilities, applications, technologies that allow the connection of various devices. The storage, processing and analysis of data generated from the entire technological infrastructure. There are various types of Iot platforms, commercial platforms and open source or free platforms (Domínguez-Bolaño et al., 2022). The platforms by the type of use can be classified into connectivity management platforms, analysis platforms, IoT application development platforms, device management platforms. An example list of IOT platforms is presented in Table 5.

Table 5. IoT Platforms

Plataforma	Descripción	Referencia
Azure IoT	Service platform that manages the communication of IoT applications with linked devices. Applications are targeted at manufacturing, energy, healthcare, retail, transportation, and logistics.	(Microsoft, 2023b)
AWS IoT	Also called Amazon IoT, a platform that offers devices, control services and data analysis for various types of users and applications by combining artificial intelligence and machine learning.	(Amazon Web Services, 2023)
C3 IoT platform	Business platform for the development of artificial intelligence applications. It also offers infrastructure and management services for Iot and AI.	(C3.ai, 2023)
FarmBeats	IoT platform for agriculture that collects data from various sensors and makes it available.	(Microsoft, 2023a)
FIWARE	European open platform oriented to the development of future internet applications. Used in the development of smart agrifood, smart cities, smart energy, smart industry and smart water solutions.	(FIWARE Foundation, 2023)
HomeKit	Allows management of apple smart devices, as well as designing, locating devices	(Apple Inc., 2023)
IoTivity	An open source software framework based on the OCF open connectivity for Internet of Things devices.	(IoTivity, 2023)
openHAB	Open Home Automation Bus, open source and technology independent home automation platform.	(openHAB Foundation e.V, 2023)
sensiNact	IoT platform in which various devices exchange information and interact, data and information help improve the lives of citizens and carry out various applications.	(Eclipse Foundation, 2023)
Losant IoT	IoT platform that offers products and services for the development of IoT applications It offers visual tools for development, data analysis, administration.	(Losant IoT, 2023)
ThingWorx	IoT platform oriented to IIot that is to say to industrial applications. It allows the connection, creation, analysis, management and experimentation of IIot applications and devices.	(PTC, 2023)
ThingsBoard	Open source IoT platform oriented to collect, process, visualize and manage data.	(ThingsBoard, 2013)
IBM Watson IoT Platform	It allows the management, connectivity, communication of various devices and manage data.	(IBM, 2023)
WSO2 IoT Server	Platform that allows the connection, administration, development of applications, security of data and devices, as well as the visualization of sensors.	(WSO2 LLC, 2023)

Virtual Reality

Virtual reality (VR) allows for the design, modeling, and simulation of real environments or imagination simulating the physical presence and environment of the user. In the design of sustainable smart cities, they are tools that allow the integration of technologies, systems, equipment, etc. (Jamei et al., 2017).

The use of VR in the classroom allows students to participate in a virtual environment in an interactive way to walk through a work area and interact with all the elements of the environment, with the intention of analyzing and optimizing the work area (Krajčovič et al., 2022). It is also used as a means to promote and understand education for sustainable development, incorporating experiences and interactive models of immersion towards learning (Ebinger et al., 2022).

An area in which virtual reality is applied is in morality, in which it seeks to know if using virtual reality (through a story) would improve the morality of students (Shim, 2023).

Data visualization with 3D technologies, virtual reality and interactive screens allows for better visualization and monitoring of smart cities (Bouloukakis et al., 2019).

There is a wide variety of hardware devices and technologies, and software applications related to virtual reality are:

- Helmets or glasses. Devices that have an LCD or OLED type screen, allow to reproduce images where the eyes are very close to it. Some types have 2D and 3D vision. Other types of lenses are just a structure to insert a smartphone or other device. An example with lenses are PlayStation VR, VIVE Pro, Samsung Gear VR. With disgust or case: Samsung Gear VR, Google Cardboard, Daydream View.
- Position sensors: They are additional accessories to determine the location of the lenses in the space in which the device is located. Some new versions include these sensors in the lens or casing.
- Controllers: Devices that interact with the environment that is displayed, generally present in device buttons, or remote controls. These detect body parts or some position: Leap Motion, STEM System, PrioVR, Gloveone, PowerClaw)
- Software and content. The applications and contents developed for virtual reality make people feel effects that combine visual aspects, sounds, movements and even smells. Among the applications that stand out are entertainment, use of medical training, and use of military training. The applications depend a lot on the device or on which they are developed.

User Profile

A user profile is a set of characteristics, behaviors and information that make a user or users identifiable in some field. The use of adequate tools allows the orientation and personalized adaptability of the learning contents based on the needs and preferences and learning styles of the students (Bajaj & Sharma, 2018).

The combination of big data and deep learning on a MOOC platform makes it possible to design a system that makes personalized course recommendations to users (Li et al., 2023). User profiles play an important role in electronic guidance platforms that support professional and academic guidance that adapts to the characteristics of the students (Adib et al., 2022).

With the Internet of Behavior (IoB) you can obtain information on the interests and preferences of students and guide them in their educational training processes in a progressive manner when face-to-face education is not posible (Embarak, 2022).

User preferences enable better smart home comfort, made possible through smart home service automation and personalization (Schomakers et al., 2021). Citizen profiles are a type of user profile, these are generated and managed by platforms that also manage various services and information that is generated and shared in a city (Teslya et al., 2019).

With the information received by smartphone sensors, it is possible to customize certain activities and context-sensitive applications to identify the activities (Javed et al., 2021).

CONCLUSION

Sustainable smart cities integrate various devices, technologies and tools in the field of smart education. These elements, such as sensors, smartphones, smart medical devices, IoT platforms and devices, and artificial intelligence applications, improve education and training processes, as well as the generation of data for decision-making or reorienting the training process of people.

INTEREST CONFLICT

The authors declare that they have no conflict of interest in the publication of this chapter.

REFERENCES

C3.ai. (2023). *C3 IoT platform*. c3. https://c3.ai/c3-ai-platform/

Adib, J., Abdelouahid, R. A., Marzak, A., & Moutachaouik, H. (2022). Ontological user profile for E-orientation platforms. *Procedia Computer Science*, *198*, 417–422. doi:10.1016/j.procs.2021.12.263

Agarwal, S. M. (2023). Go-Brown, Go-Green and smart initiatives implemented by the University of Delhi for environmental sustainability towards futuristic smart universities: Observational study. *Heliyon*, *9*(3), e13909. doi:10.1016/j.heliyon.2023.e13909 PMID:36967932

Alfoudari, A. M., Durugbo, C. M., & Aldhmour, F. M. (2023). Exploring quality attributes of smart classrooms from the perspectives of academics. *Education and Information Technologies*. Advance online publication. doi:10.100710639-022-11452-3 PMID:37361782

Alison.com. (2023, 2023). Alison: Free Online Courses With Certificates & Diplomas. *AWS IoT*. https://aws.amazon.com/iot/?nc1=h_ls

Angelaki, M. E., Karvounidis, T., & Douligeris, C. (2022). Towards a Smart Classroom Enabled Sustainability Education: A Conceptual Model. In M. E. Auer & T. Tsiatsos, New Realities, Mobile Systems and Applications Cham. doi:10.1007/978-3-030-96296-8_45

Apple Inc. (2023, 2023). *HomeKit*. Apple. https://developer.apple.com/documentation/homekit

Athabasca University. (2023a). *FreudBot*. Athabasca University. https://psych.athabascau.ca/html/Freudbot/Freudbot.html

Athabasca University. (2023b). *PiagetBot*. Athabasca University. https://psych.athabascau.ca/html/Piagetbot/Piagetbot.html

Baidu. (2023, 2023). *Ernie Bot*. Baidu. https://yiyan.baidu.com/

Bailey, D., Southam, A., & Costley, J. (2021). Digital storytelling with chatbots: Mapping L2 participation and perception patterns. *Interactive Technology and Smart Education*, *18*(1), 85–103. doi:10.1108/ITSE-08-2020-0170

Bajaj, R., & Sharma, V. (2018). Smart Education with artificial intelligence based determination of learning styles. *Procedia Computer Science, 132*, 834–842. doi:10.1016/j.procs.2018.05.095

Bakupa Mbombo, A., & Nadire, C. (2021). Smart University: A University In the Technological Age. *TEM Journal, 10*(1). https://doi.org/DOI: doi:10.18421/TEM101-02

Barn, B. S. (2020). The Digital Enterprise as an Emerging Landscape for Universities and Their Operation. In V. Kulkarni, S. Reddy, T. Clark, & B. S. Barn (Eds.), *Advanced Digital Architectures for Model-Driven Adaptive Enterprises* (pp. 287–304). IGI Global. doi:10.4018/978-1-7998-0108-5.ch013

Bouloukakis, M., Partarakis, N., Drossis, I., Kalaitzakis, M., & Stephanidis, C. (2019). Virtual Reality for Smart City Visualization and Monitoring. In A. Stratigea & D. Kavroudakis (Eds.), *Mediterranean Cities and Island Communities: Smart, Sustainable, Inclusive and Resilient* (pp. 1–18). Springer International Publishing. doi:10.1007/978-3-319-99444-4_1

Carpenter, R. (2023, 2023). *CleverBot*. Cleverbot. https://www.cleverbot.com/

Carrera, J., & Ramírez-Hernández, D. (2018). Innovative Education in MOOC for Sustainability: Learnings and Motivations. Sustainability, 10(9), 2990. https://www.mdpi.com/2071-1050/10/9/2990

Character.ai. (2023). *Character.ai*. Character.AI. https://beta.character.ai/

ChatCompose. (2019). *ChatCompose Chatbot Platform for Sales and Support Automation*. Chatcompose. https://www.chatcompose.com

Cheshmehzangi, A. (2022). The Application of ICT and Smart Technologies in Cities and Communities: An Overview. In ICT, Cities, and Reaching Positive Peace (pp. 1-16). Springer Nature Singapore. doi:10.1007/978-981-19-3167-3_1

Corp, N. H. N. (2023). *Naver*. Naver. https://www.naver.com/

Coursera Inc. (2023, 2023). *Degrees, Certificates, & Free Online Courses*. Coursera. https://www.coursera.org/

Deshpande, Y., & Unhelkar, B. (2011). Information Systems for a Green Organisation. In B. Unhelkar (Ed.), *Handbook of Research on Green ICT: Technology, Business and Social Perspectives* (pp. 116–130). IGI Global. doi:10.4018/978-1-61692-834-6.ch008

Diogo, R. A., dos Santos, N., & Loures, E. F. R. (2023). 13 - Digital Transformation of Engineering Education for Smart Education: A systematic literature review. In M. Ram & L. Xing (Eds.), *Reliability Modeling in Industry 4.0* (pp. 407–438). Elsevier. doi:10.1016/B978-0-323-99204-6.00002-9

Domínguez-Bolaño, T., Campos, O., Barral, V., Escudero, C. J., & García-Naya, J. A. (2022). An overview of IoT architectures, technologies, and existing open-source projects. *Internet of Things, 20*, 100626. https://doi.org/https://doi.org/10.1016/j.iot.2022.100626

Ebinger, F., Buttke, L., & Kreimeier, J. (2022). Augmented and virtual reality technologies in education for sustainable development: An expert-based technology assessment. *TATuP - Zeitschrift für Technikfolgenabschätzung in Theorie und Praxis, 31*(1), 28-34. https://doi.org/ doi:10.14512/tatup.31.1.28

Eclipse Foundation. (2023, 2023). *Eclipse sensiNact*. Eclipse Foundation. https://projects.eclipse.org/projects/technology.sensinact

edX LLC. (2023, 2023). *edX Build new skills. Advance your career*. EDX. https://www.edx.org

Embarak, O. H. (2022). Internet of Behaviour (IoB)-based AI models for personalized smart education systems. *Procedia Computer Science*, *203*, 103–110. doi:10.1016/j.procs.2022.07.015

Focus Group on Smart Sustainable Cities. (2015, Octuber, 2015). *Smart Sustainable City*. Retrieved April 27, 2023 from

Global University Systems. (2023). *FutureLearn: Online Courses and Degrees from Top Universities*. Future Learn. https://www.futurelearn.com/

Google. (2023). *bard*. Google. https://bard.google.com/?hl=en

Huang, L.-S., Su, J.-Y., & Pao, T.-L. (2019). A Context Aware Smart Classroom Architecture for Smart Campuses. *Applied Sciences (Basel, Switzerland)*, *9*(9), 1837. https://www.mdpi.com/2076-3417/9/9/1837. doi:10.3390/app9091837

Hugging Face, I. (2023, 2023). *HuggingChat*. Huffing Face. https://huggingface.co/chat/

IBM. (2023, 2023). *IBM Watson IoT Platform*. IBM. https://internetofthings.ibmcloud.com/

Instructure. (2023, 2023). *CANVAS by Instructure*. Instructure. https://www.instructure.com/canvas

IoTivity. (2023, 2023). *IoTivity*. IoTivity. http://iotivity.org/

Iqbal, H. M. N., Parra-Saldivar, R., Zavala-Yoe, R., & Ramirez-Mendoza, R. A. (2020). Smart educational tools and learning management systems: Supportive framework. [IJIDeM]. *International Journal on Interactive Design and Manufacturing*, *14*(4), 1179–1193. doi:10.100712008-020-00695-4

Isakova Mukhlisa Fakhriddin, D., & Fayzullayev Sayfiddin Bakhadir, S. (2022). SMART LEARNING TECHNOLOGY. *British Journal of Global Ecology and Sustainable Development*, *10*, 178–183. https://journalzone.org/index.php/bjgesd/article/view/160

Jamei, E., Mortimer, M., Seyedmahmoudian, M., Horan, B., & Stojcevski, A. (2017). Investigating the Role of Virtual Reality in Planning for Sustainable Smart Cities. *Sustainability (Basel)*, *9*(11), 2006. https://www.mdpi.com/2071-1050/9/11/2006. doi:10.3390u9112006

Javed, A. R., Faheem, R., Asim, M., Baker, T., & Beg, M. O. (2021). A smartphone sensors-based personalized human activity recognition system for sustainable smart cities. *Sustainable Cities and Society*, *71*, 102970. doi:10.1016/j.scs.2021.102970

Kamruzzaman, M. M., Alanazi, S., Alruwaili, M., Alshammari, N., Elaiwat, S., Abu-Zanona, M., Innab, N., Mohammad Elzaghmouri, B., & Ahmed Alanazi, B. (2023). AI- and IoT-Assisted Sustainable Education Systems during Pandemics, such as COVID-19, for Smart Cities. *Sustainability (Basel)*, *15*(10), 8354. doi:10.3390u15108354

Kassab, M., DeFranco, J., & Laplante, P. (2020). A systematic literature review on Internet of things in education: Benefits and challenges. *Journal of Computer Assisted Learning*, *36*(2), 115–127. doi:10.1111/jcal.12383

Kasztelewicz, A., Tomaszewska, B., Rahner, S., Winter, I., & Voss, V. (2022). MOOC education for sustainable development. The Erasmus+ project experience [journal article]. *Polityka Energetyczna – Energy Policy Journal, 25*(4), 165-180. https://doi.org/ doi:10.33223/epj/156341

Kaur, A., & Bhatia, M. (2021, 4-5 Dec. 2021). Smart Education: A Systematic Survey and Future Research Directions. *2021 International Conference on Computing Sciences (ICCS).* ICCS. 10.1109/ICCS54944.2021.00042

Kaur, A., Bhatia, M., & Stea, G. (2022). A Survey of Smart Classroom Literature. *Education Sciences*, *12*(2), 86. https://www.mdpi.com/2227-7102/12/2/86. doi:10.3390/educsci12020086

Krajčovič, M., Gabajová, G., Matys, M., Furmannová, B., & Dulina, Ľ. (2022). Virtual Reality as an Immersive Teaching Aid to Enhance the Connection between Education and Practice. *Sustainability (Basel)*, *14*(15), 9580. https://www.mdpi.com/2071-1050/14/15/9580. doi:10.3390u14159580

Kuppusamy, P. (2019). Smart Education Using Internet of Things Technology. In Z. Ma & L. Yan (Eds.), Emerging Technologies and Applications in Data Processing and Management (pp. 385-412). IGI Global. doi:10.4018/978-1-5225-8446-9.ch017

Leadaki, S.A. (2023, 2023w). *Chatbot.* Cliengo. https://www.cliengo.com/chatbot

Li, B., Li, G., Xu, J., Li, X., Liu, X., Wang, M., & Lv, J. (2023). A personalized recommendation framework based on MOOC system integrating deep learning and big data. *Computers & Electrical Engineering*, *106*, 108571. doi:10.1016/j.compeleceng.2022.108571

Lin, Y. P., & Yu, Z. G. (2023). A bibliometric analysis of artificial intelligence chatbots in educational contexts. *Interactive Technology and Smart Education*. Advance online publication. doi:10.1108/ITSE-12-2022-0165

Lyapina, I., Sotnikova, E., Lebedeva, O., Makarova, T., & Skvortsova, N. (2019). Smart technologies: Perspectives of usage in higher education. *International Journal of Educational Management*, *33*(3), 454–461. doi:10.1108/IJEM-08-2018-0257

Mageira, K., Pittou, D., Papasalouros, A., Kotis, K., Zangogianni, P., & Daradoumis, A. (2022). Educational AI Chatbots for Content and Language Integrated Learning. *Applied Sciences (Basel, Switzerland)*, *12*(7), 3239. https://www.mdpi.com/2076-3417/12/7/3239. doi:10.3390/app12073239

Meta A. I. (2023, Feb 24, 2023). *Introducing LLaMA*. Meta AI. https://ai.facebook.com/blog/large-language-model-llama-meta-ai/

Microsoft. (2023a, March 30, 2023). *Azure FarmBeats*. Microsoft. https://learn.microsoft.com/en-us/azure/industry/agriculture/overview-azure-farmbeats

Microsoft. (2023b, 2023). *Azure IoT*. Microsoft. https://azure.microsoft.com/en-us/solutions/iot/

Microsoft. (2023c, 2023). *Bing Chat.* Microsoft. https://www.bing.com/search?form=MA13FJ&q=Bing+AI&showconv=1

MOOC4ALL. (2023, 2023). *MOOC4ALL.* MOOC4ALL. https://platform.mooc4all.eu/

Moturi, C., Ochieng, D., & Chepkoech, I. (2016). *An Assessment of Green ICT Effect on Sustainable Environment in Institutions of Higher Learning in Kenya.*

Nanda, M., & Randhawa, G. (2019). Smart Cities Project: Some Lessons for Indian Cities. In K. Saravanan, G. Julie, & H. Robinson (Eds.), *Handbook of Research on Implementation and Deployment of IoT Projects in Smart Cities* (pp. 80–95). IGI Global. doi:10.4018/978-1-5225-9199-3.ch006

Omidinia, S., Masrom, M., & Selamat, H. (2013). *An Examination of the Concept of Smart School: An Innovation to Address Sustainability.* CSE. doi:10.2991/cse.2013.73

Open A. I. (2023, 2023). *Chatgpt.* Open AI. https://openai.com/blog/chatgpt

OpenupEd. (2023). *OpenupEd.* https://www.openuped.eu

Padmapriya, V., & Sujatha, D. N. (2023). Impact of blockchain technology on the urban environment and climate change. In S. Krishnan, R. Kumar, & V. E. Balas (Eds.), *Green Blockchain Technology for Sustainable Smart Cities* (pp. 97–117). Elsevier. doi:10.1016/B978-0-323-95407-5.00016-5

Pal, S., Bhattacharya, S., Mustafi, S., & Mitra, S. (2023). Smart Green Classroom and Machine Learning to Promote Green Awareness for Sustainable Livings. *International Journal of Instructional Technology and Educational Studies*, *4*(1), 7–15. doi:10.21608/ihites.2021.107726.1081

PTC. (2023). *ThingWorx IIoT Platform.* PTC. https://www.ptc.com/en/products/thingworx

Ramirez Montoya, M. S., Martínez-Pérez, S., Rodriguez-Abitia, G., & Lopez-Caudana, E. (2022). Digital accreditations in MOOC-based training on sustainability: Factors that influence terminal efficiency. *Australasian Journal of Educational Technology*, *38*(2), 162–180. doi:10.14742/ajet.7082

Rico-Bautista, D., Guerrero, C., Collazos, C., Maestre, G., Sanchez, M., & Medina-Cárdenas, Y. (2022). *Universidad inteligente una mirada desde la adopción de tecnologías emergentes.*

Schomakers, E.-M., Biermann, H., & Ziefle, M. (2021). Users' Preferences for Smart Home Automation – Investigating Aspects of Privacy and Trust. *Telematics and Informatics*, *64*, 101689. doi:10.1016/j.tele.2021.101689

Shim, J. (2023). Investigating the effectiveness of introducing virtual reality to elementary school students' moral education. *Computers & Education: X Reality, 2*, 100010. https://doi.org/https://doi.org/10.1016/j.cexr.2023.100010

Silva, B., Khan, M., & Han, K. (2018). Towards sustainable smart cities: A review of trends, architectures, components, and open challenges in smart cities. *Sustainable Cities and Society*, *38*, 697–713. doi:10.1016/j.scs.2018.01.053

SMART Technologies ULC. (2009, 2019). *SMART Classroom Suite*. SMART. https://usermanual.wiki/m/0f5b7918aaa470a4cf118a8a208988be8d6263b84e27f1b85cf058d93af5d7db.pdf

SMART Technologies ULC. (2023, 2023). *SMART Technologies.* SMART. https://www.smarttech.com/en/education

Stanford University. (2023, 2023). *Stanford Online.* Stanford University. https://online.stanford.edu

Terzieva, V., Ilchev, S., & Todorova, K. (2022). The Role of Internet of Things in Smart Education. *IFAC-PapersOnLine, 55*(11), 108–113. doi:10.1016/j.ifacol.2022.08.057

Teslya, N. N., Ryabchikov, I. A., Petrov, M. V., Taramov, A. A., & Lipkin, E. O. (2019). Smart City Platform Architecture for Citizens' Mobility Support. *Procedia Computer Science, 150*, 646–653. doi:10.1016/j.procs.2019.02.041

Thakur, A. (2022). Sensor-Based Technology in the Hospitality Industry. In A. B. Waluyo & L. Tan (Eds.), *Mobile Computing and Technology Applications in Tourism and Hospitality* (pp. 24–43). IGI Global., doi:10.4018/978-1-7998-6904-7.ch002

ThingsBoard. I. (2023). *ThingsBoard IoT Platform.* ThingsBoard. https://thingsboard.io/

UNESCO. (2018). *Global Education Meeting 2018: Brussels Declaration.* UNESCO. https://unesdoc.unesco.org/notice?id=p:usmarcdef_0000366394_spa

UNESCO, & Commonwealth of Learning. (2016). *Making Sense of MOOCs: A Guide for Policy-Makers in Developing Countries.* https://doi.org/10.56059/11599/2356

United Nations. (2015). *Transforming our world: the 2030 Agenda for Sustainable Development.* UN. https://documents-dds-ny.un.org/doc/UNDOC/GEN/N15/291/89/PDF/N1529189.pdf?OpenElement

United Nations Educational. (2015). *Qingdao Declaration, 2015: Seize Digital Opportunities, Lead Education Transformation.* International Conference on Information and Communication Technology (ICT) and Post-2015 Education, Qingdao, China. https://unesdoc.unesco.org/notice?id=p:usmarcdef_0000233352

United Nations Educational. S. a. C. O. (2019). *Beijing Consensus on Artificial Intelligence and Education.* International Conference on Artificial Intelligence and Education 'Planning education in the AI era: Lead the leap', Beijing, Republic of China. https://unesdoc.unesco.org/notice?id=p:usmarcdef_0000368303

United Nations Educational. S. a. C. O. (2021). *Recommendation on the Ethics of Artificial Intelligence.* UN. https://unesdoc.unesco.org/notice?id=p:usmarcdef_0000381137

University of China. (2023, 2023). *icourse163-org.* University of China. https://www.icourse163.org/

Williamson, B. (2015). Educating the smart city: Schooling smart citizens through computational urbanism. *Big Data & Society, 2*(2), 2053951715617783. doi:10.1177/2053951715617783

Woebot Health. (2023). *Woebot.* Woebot. https://woebothealth.com/

WSO2 LLC. (2023, 2023). *WSO2 Iot.* WS02LLC. https://wso2.com/iot/

Yandex. (2023, 2023). *YadexGPT.* Yandex. https://cloud.yandex.ru/services/yandexgpt

Yang, Q., & Lee, Y.-C. (2021). The Critical Factors of Student Performance in MOOCs for Sustainable Education: A Case of Chinese Universities. *Sustainability (Basel), 13*(14), 8089. https://www.mdpi.com/2071-1050/13/14/8089. doi:10.3390u13148089

Chapter 11
Potable Water Distribution Network Optimization

Alejandro Fuentes-Penna
https://orcid.org/0000-0002-4303-3852
El Colegio de Morelos, Mexico

Ricardo A. Barrera-Cámara
https://orcid.org/0000-0002-3170-4671
Universidad Autónoma del Carmen, Mexico

Ileana Cruz-Sánchez
https://orcid.org/0000-0002-3354-8836
TecNM - CIIDET, Mexico

ABSTRACT

Nowadays, potable water supply has become a problem, involving different aspects such as water quality, pollution, pipes' quality, supply and demand of drinking water, water leaks, and supply cuts, among other aspects that have complicated the efficient use of potable water in urbanized regions. The objective of this chapter is to define potable water distribution network (PWDN) optimization as a complex problem, from the perspective of an NP-Hard problem, and the complexity as a variant of water distribution network optimization. The main result of the proposal is the definition of a problem that identifies the main variables involved in the supply of quality potable water as a global problem where each researcher can solve the main problem as one or propose solutions for different parts. The proposal simulation is oriented to present a brief solution related to the supply and demand of drinking water as a part of the PWDN.

INTRODUCTION

The demand and need for more water resources are creating water quality problems. Pollution is the main cause, as it causes changes in the physical, chemical, or biological composition of water through the introduction of unwanted substances or microorganisms that can become a risk to human health in

DOI: 10.4018/979-8-3693-0373-3.ch011

the short or long term. Sources of water pollution come from industrial, livestock, agricultural, urban, and even natural sources and can deteriorate water at its source, in catchments, in groundwater, or at other points in the supply area. Poor treatment not only leads to a reduction in quality but also presents health risks.

The quality of potable water is of utmost importance for health, which is why most countries have domestic legislation. These regulations serve to determine the responsibility of the different sectors involved in the production and distribution of drinking water, its monitoring, and control.

Countries also have regulations that define what is meant by potable water, i.e. the standards that must be followed for water to be safe for human health. Among these regulations is a very specific one, called the *Potable Water Quality Standard*. It states what substances may be present in the water and the concentrations in water and the maximum permissible concentrations that do not pose a health risk. to health.

All countries that set such national standards use the World Health Organization (WHO) Guidelines as the main benchmark for comparison. The WHO Guidelines for Potable Water Quality are used as the main parameter for comparison by all countries setting such national standards.

Water Quality

Determining the quality of water is a necessity for societies and industries in general. This vital liquid must meet chemical, biological, bacteriological, and other conditions, depending on its intended use, to be considered safe and adequate.

The indicators for measuring water quality are associated with the chemical, physical, biological, and radiological characteristics that this liquid should meet, according to the values established for its use. Measuring the quality of water for human consumption is not the same as measuring it for industrial uses, irrigation, or fish farming.

ISO 24510:2007

ISO (International Organization for Standardization) is a worldwide federation of national standards bodies (ISO member bodies). The work of preparing International Standards is normally carried out through ISO technical committees. Each member body interested in a subject for which a technical committee has been established has the right to be represented on that committee. International public and private organizations, in coordination with ISO, also participate in the work. ISO collaborates closely with the International Electrotechnical Commission (IEC) on all matters of electrotechnical standardization (ISO, 2023).

ISO International Standard ISO 24510 has been prepared by ISO Technical Committee ISO/TC 224, Service-related activities related to drinking water and wastewater supply systems - Service quality criteria and performance indicators. International Standard ISO 24510 is one of a series of standards dealing with water services. The complete series consists of the following International Standards:

- ISO 24510, Activities related to drinking water and wastewater services - Guidelines for the assessment and improvement of service to users.
- ISO 24511, Activities related to drinking water and wastewater utilities - Guidelines for the management of wastewater utilities and the assessment of wastewater services

- ISO 24512, Activities related to drinking water and wastewater utilities - Guidelines for the management of drinking water utilities and for the assessment of drinking water utilities

Objectives, Content, and Implementation of this International Standard

The objective of this International Standard is to provide relevant stakeholders with guidelines for assessing and improving service to users and guidelines for the management of water utilities, consistent with the overall objectives defined by the competent authorities and by the above-mentioned international intergovernmental organizations. This International Standard is intended to facilitate dialogue between interested parties, enabling them to develop a mutual understanding of the functions and tasks within the scope of water utilities.

The series of standards concerning water services consists of this International Standard (service-oriented), ISO 24511, and ISO 24512 (both management-oriented). This International Standard addresses the following topics:

- a brief description of the service components of the users;
    - The central objectives for the service, concerning the needs and expectations of the users;
    - Guidelines for meeting users' needs and expectations;
    - The evaluation criteria for the service to users according to the given guidelines;
    - Examples of performance indicators linked to the evaluation criteria that can be used to assess service performance.
    - ISO 24511 and ISO 24512 consider the following topics:
    - A brief description of the physical or infrastructure and managerial or institutional components of the water utilities;
    - The main objectives of the water utilities, considered globally relevant at the broadest level;
    - Guidelines for the management of water utilities;
    - Guidelines for the evaluation of water services with service evaluation criteria related to the objectives and performance indicators linked to these criteria.

The performance indicators shown in this International Standard, ISO 24511 and ISO 24512 are presented by way of example only, because the evaluation of service to users cannot be reduced to a single or universal set of performance indicators.

The scope formally excludes facilities located within the user's premises. However, attention is drawn to the fact that facilities within establishments may negatively impact the quality of the water supplied (or wastewater discharged) between the point of supply (or in the case of wastewater the point of collection) and the point of use (or in the case of wastewater the point of discharge). About this issue, some stakeholders such as competent authorities, owners, contractors, and users may have a role to play.

Since the organization of water service providers is within a country-specific legal and institutional framework, this International Standard does not recommend the respective roles of the various stakeholders nor does it define the internal organizations required for local, regional, or national bodies that may be involved in the provision of water services.

The guidelines given in this International Standard, ISO 24511 and ISO 24512 are focused on the needs and expectations of users and the water services themselves without imposing a means to meet those needs and expectations, the objective being to allow the widest possible use of this International Standard, ISO 24511 and ISO 24512, while respecting the cultural, socio-economic, climatic, health and legal characteristics of the different countries and regions of the world. It should therefore be understood that, in the short term, it may not always be possible to meet the expectations of local users. This may be due to factors such as climatic conditions, resource availability, and difficulties related to the economic sustainability of water services, particularly regarding financing and the ability of users to pay for improvements.

Environmental conditions may limit the achievement of some objectives or restrict the implementation of some recommendations in developing countries. However, this International Standard is drafted with these constraints in mind and therefore allows, for example, variable levels of fixed networks and the need for "on-site" alternatives.

Notwithstanding the need for flexibility in terms of engineering and hardware, many recommendations in this International Standard, such as consultation mechanisms, should be applied universally.

To evaluate and improve service to users and to ensure adequate follow-up of improvements, an appropriate number of performance indicators (PIs) or other methods can be established to verify compliance with requirements. The use of PIs is only one of the possible tools to support continuous improvement. Stakeholders may select PIs from the examples given or develop other relevant PIs considering the principles described in this International Standard, ISO 24511, and ISO 24512. The PIs are logically related to the objectives for which they were defined through evaluation criteria and are used to measure performance. They can also be used to define a set of required values or target values. This International Standard does not impose any specific indicators or minimum values or performance ranges. It respects the principle of adaptability to local contexts, facilitating local implementation.

This International Standards, ISO 24511 and ISO 24512, and more specifically the examples of performance indicators are not intended to be considered as a prerequisite or condition for the implementation of a water policy or the financing of projects or programs but may serve to assess progress towards policy goals and the objectives of financing programs.

The objective of these International Standards, ISO 24511 and ISO 24512 is not to establish systems of specifications that support direct certification of conformity but to provide guidelines for continuous improvement and service evaluation. Under ISO rules, the use of the International Standards, ISO 24511, and ISO 24512 is voluntary.

This International Standards, ISO 24511 and ISO 24512 are consistent with the principle of the PDCA (plan - do - check - act) approach: they propose a step-by-step process, from the identification of the components and the definition of the service provider's objectives to the establishment of performance indicators, with a feedback loop to the objectives and management, after having assessed performance.

46001:2019

ISO 46001:2019 is the new standard published by the international organization ISO. Its purpose is to enable efficient water management. This standard, like others, can be certified and is based on the high-level structure on which the latest standards published by ISO have been designed. This means that it can be integrated with the management systems of other standards such as ISO 14001 or ISO 9001.ISO 46001 is based on practices for monitoring, measuring, documenting, reporting, design, and procurement of equipment, systems, processes, and training for water efficiency management. The standard has 3 key fundamental aspects that coincide almost entirely with the 3Rs (reduce, recycle, and reuse) however, in this case, recycle is replaced by replace. Reduce: this point is intended to use accessories and equipment to use water efficiently, also to monitor its use, and detect leaks. Reuse: it simply consists of reusing water whenever possible and not wasting it once it has been used. Replace: there are cases in which it is not necessary to use drinking water, which is why we can simply replace it with seawater or rainwater.

Objective of the Model

The main objective of ISO 46001 is to improve water efficiency and aims to achieve the following results:

- Help organizations manage water correctly and optimize their water requirements.
- Establish water as an important framework for the organization's planning and budgeting.
- Seek continuous improvement in the use of this resource.
- Raise awareness among all members of the organization of the responsible use of this resource.
- Identify the impacts caused by water use not only to our organization but to our entire environment.

POTABLE WATER TREATMENT PROCESS

One of the great water challenges we face globally is to provide drinking water, sewerage, and sanitation services to the population, due, on the one hand, to accelerated demographic growth and, on the other, to the ever-increasing technical difficulties involved in doing so. Having these services in the home is a determining factor in the quality of life and integral development of families. In Mexico, the number of beneficiaries has been growing in recent years; however, the closer we get to universal coverage, the more complex the task becomes.

The Manual on Potable Water, Sewerage, and Sanitation proposed by CONAGUA (*Comisión Nacional del Agua)* is aimed at those who design, build, operate, and manage drinking water, sewerage, and sanitation systems in the country; it seeks to be a reference on criteria, procedures, standards, indexes, parameters, and success stories. This manual favors and guides decision-making by authorities, professionals, administrators, and technicians of water utilities in the Mexican Republic and the work of educational institutions (CONAGUA, n. d.).

Potabilization processes depend on the quality of the water in the catchment sources and can be as simple as disinfection, or involve various unit operations such as oxidation, coagulation, flocculation, sedimentation, filtration, and disinfection. In some cases, ion exchange, reverse osmosis, or adsorption with activated carbon, among other more specialized processes, may be required. These processes are integrated with unit operations and processes. In unitary operations, the removal of pollutants is done by physical forces. In unit processes the treatment is carried out by chemical and biological reactions.

The set of unit operations and unit processes is known as a treatment train or process train. The considerations to be considered when selecting a treatment train depend on the quality characteristics of the water supply. These include variations over time, the permissible limits in current regulations, the site conditions for plant construction, the available technology, the economics of the process, and many other factors.

The objective is to remove undesirable constituents in the source water, but also to properly dispose of the waste from the water treatment plant (AWWA, 2012). The basic factors that influence the selection of treatment processes are:

a) Treated water specifications b) Quality of the water supply and its variations
b) Particular economic and social conditions
c) d) Relative costs of the different treatment processes, concerning investment,
d) operation and maintenance

The selection of processes will be influenced primarily by effluent requirements and raw water quality and will be facilitated by field investigations and laboratory tests. If chemical coagulation is required, jar tests should be carried out to determine velocity gradients, optimum pH, the type of coagulants and dosage ranges, and the suitability of using adjuvants. In large-scale plants, it will be desirable to carry out pilot plant tests. Such plants should include models to determine the design parameters and design parameters and the type of particle size of the filter materials (Kawamura, 2000).

Figure 1 shows a general water treatment. The water purification process can be presented as a reference for describing the main process units.

Figure 1. General water treatment
Source: CONAGUA (n. d.)

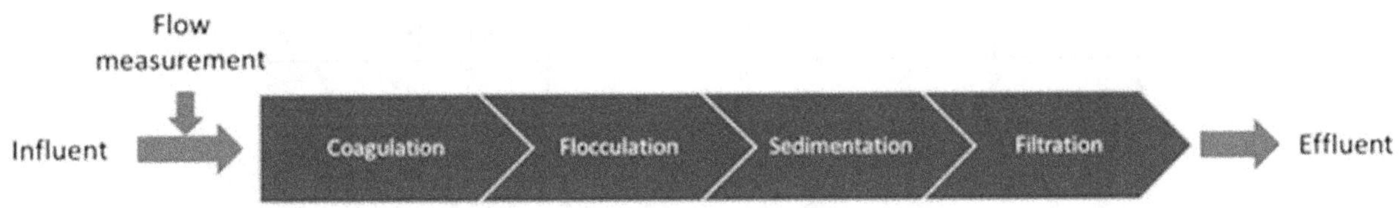

ALGORITHMS, PATENTS, AND SOLUTIONS OF POTABLE WATER DISTRIBUTION

Patentscope (2022) presents 5,100 patents related to potable water search. Table 1 presents some examples related to potable water patents.

Table 1. Potable water patents

Authors	Patent's title	Application
Haase Richard Alan (2022)	Potable water treatment system and method of operation thereof	Potable water treatment system
Haase Richard Alan (2007)	Potable water treatment system and apparatus	Potable water treatment system
Lee W. Froemke (2019)	Air temperature control using potable water	Potable Water Temperature control
Hou Guangrong, Li Zhiyuan, Wang Jing & Jiang Yanbin (2012).	Solar potable water preparation system and method for preparing potable water by using solar potable water preparation system	Potable Water Temperature control
Ikeda Sunao (2012).	Potable Water Remote Automatic Supply Control Unit and Potable Water Remote Automatic Supply Control System	Potable water treatment system
Haase, Richard Alan. (2001)	Potable water treatment system and method of operation thereof	Potable water treatment system
Haase, Richard Alan. (2000)	Potable Water Treatment System and Method of Operation Thereof	Potable water treatment system
Burd Peter John Leslie& Earce Nicholas James Wilton (2016).	Cruciform Water Distribution Valve for Aircraft Galley Plumbing System	Potable water treatment system
Cory Albers & Bernard Amell (2018).	System and Method for Producing Potable Water from Stormwater	Potable water treatment system
Palm Joseph M. & Semler Loren H. (2005).	Automatic Flushing System and Method for a Potable Water Station	Potable water treatment system
Lawrence D. Lansing, JR & Lawrence D. Lansing P.E. (2019)	Water Production Employing a Hydrogen Cycle	Potable water production
Palm Joseph M, SemlerLoren H & Schulz William E. (2005).	Potable water station sanitizing system and method	Potable water station sanitizing system

Table 2. Potable water management research

Authors	Research title	Application
Rao & Mamatha (2004)	Water quality in sustainable water management	Potable Water Quality
Grady, Weng & Blatchley, (2014)	Global potable water: Current status, critical problems, and future perspectives	Global Potable Water Perspective study
	A Review of China's rural water management	Potable Water Management
Yu,Geng, Heck & Xue (2015)	A Review of China's rural water management Sustainability	Potable Water Management Review
Molobela & Sinha (2011)	Management of water resources in South Africa: A review	Potable Water Management Review
Goosen & Shayya, (1999)	Water Management, Purification	Water Management, Purification
Bouwer (2002)	Integrated water management for the 21st century: problems and solutions	Potable Water Management Review
Biswas (1981)	Integrated water management: Some international dimensions	Potable Water Management Review
Makropoulos, Natsis, Liu, Mittas, & Butler (2008)	Decision support for sustainable option selection in integrated urban water management	Potable Water Management
Lee, Sarp, Jeon, & Kim, (2015)	Smart water grid: the future water management platform	Potable Water Management
Bouwer (2000)	Integrated water management: emerging issues and challenges	Potable Water Management Review
Abu-Mahfouz,Hamam, Page, Djouani & Kurien (2016).	Real-time dynamic hydraulic model for potable water loss reduction	Potable Water Management
Khan, & Siddique, (2000)	Urban water management problems in developing countries with particular reference to Bangladesh	Potable Water Management
Pingale, Jat & Khare (2014)	Integrated urban water management modeling under climate change scenarios.	Potable Water Management

POTABLE WATER DISTRIBUTION NETWORK OPTIMIZATION: AN NP-HARD DEFINITION

The potable Water Management Problem (PWMP) consists of maximizing the quantity and quality of drinking water from a location (or multiple locations (water treatment plants) to the households served. The PwMP is a combination/interrelationship of 2 different problems:

- Water Distribution Network Optimization (WDNO)
- Proposal of Potable Water Distribution Network Optimization (A variant of WDNO)

Introduction

A distribution system is a set of closed conduits that have the purpose of transporting water at a pressure that meets the demand of users in hours of maximum consumption that exist during the day and year. These users can be residential, commercial, public and private services, industries, etc., for public and private services, industries, etc.

The maximum and minimum pressures allowed to avoid damage to the network are 70 mca and 10 mca respectively, it is also important to maintain the range of minimum and maximum speeds within the pipe, for maximum speeds will be 4.5 m/s in the plastic pipe (PVC), speeds higher than these could cause erosion and subsequently breakage of the pipe and fittings, and for minimum speeds in the plastic pipe (PVC), it will be 0.45 m/s, speeds lower than these produce the accumulation of sediment and clogging of the pipe (SENAGUA, 2012).

The pipe should, as far as possible, form meshes without blind spots or open branches, commercial diameters similar to those calculated hydraulically should be used, the perimeter of the mesh should have ranges between 500-2000m, a parallel pipe should be located in case of having road widths greater than 20 m with diameters similar to those of the secondary branches, population growth rates and useful life of the hydraulic elements, perform a socioeconomic analysis of the population, supply and consumption (Mena, 2016).

The optimization of water distribution systems (WDS) has been mainly oriented toward the design, rehabilitation, and optimal operation of the drinking water system. This problem involves multiple objectives, but it has been approached from the computational complexity as a main objective; however, multi-objective approaches have been applied for its analysis, having as examples objectives oriented to:

- Operating costs
- Service Quality
- System reliability
- Water quality
- Design and rehabilitation of distribution networks
- Maximizing system reliability
- Water network robustness
- Water network rehabilitation costs
- Quality of service as a pressure deficit
- Minimization of pumping energy costs
- Trade-off between energy costs of pumping and pump maintenance

- Greenhouse gas emissions
- Among others.

The purpose of the present work is to propose an algorithm related to the loss of water quality based on the characteristics of the drinking water network. The parameters of the algorithm include:

- Measuring the quantity of drinking water.
- Identify the quality of drinking water in the network.

Mathematical Model

Zecchin et al. (2006) described the mathematical model of WDNO represented by the equations 1 – 4.

$$C(\Omega)=\sum_{i=1}^{n} L_i c(\omega_i) \tag{1}$$

Subject to

$$H_i^j(\Omega) \geq \underline{H_i^j} \forall i=1,\dots N_{node} \forall j=1,\dots N_{pattern} \tag{2}$$

$$DM_i^j + \sum_{k\epsilon \Theta_{out}^k(\Omega)} Q_j^k(\Omega) - \sum_{k\epsilon \Theta_{in}^k(\Omega)} Q_j^k(\Omega) = 0 \forall i=1,\dots N_{node} \forall j=1,\dots N_{pattern} \tag{3}$$

$$H_{i_{start}}^j(\Omega) - H_{i_{end}}^j(\Omega) = A \frac{L_i}{HW_i(\Omega)^a Di(\Omega)^b} Q_i^j(\Omega)^a \forall i=1,\dots N_{pide} \forall j=1,\dots N_{pattern} \tag{4}$$

Where the equations are:

- (1) the main objective
- (2) Design constraint
- (3) nodal continuity
- (4) head loss equation

Proposal of Potable Water Distribution Network Optimization

We present the Potable Water Distribution Network (PWDN) as an acyclic-directed graph G=(N, L) where N is the set of water sources nodes, potable water treatment plants nodes, and demand's nodes; L is the set of arcs integrated by pipes; and K is the temporal evolution of the distribution network. The mathematical model proposal is based on WaterModels (n.d.) updating the equations and the extension of the problem described below.

The potential nodes are denoted by $tp_i^k, i \in N$ where each tp_i^n represents the total of potable water treatment plants; each $tp^k \cong tp^{k'}$ can be seen as the temporal evolution for each *tp*, where $tp^{k'}$ indicates the degradation of materials with time; this natural process can reduce the potable water's quality.

Part of the potential nodes are the Potable Water source denoted by $ws_i^n, i \in N$ represents the total of water sources; each $ws^k \cong ws^{k'}$ can be seen as the temporal evolution for each *ws*, where $ws^{k'}$ indicates the degradation of the water source with time; in this case, the water source can change by contamination, droughts, water level reduction, etc.

The last part of the potential nodes is denoted by the demands identified by end customers where each demand has the constant q_i^m (demanded volumetric flow rate). In this case, the demand can be covered or uncovered by supply water management.

The pipes are denoted by $l_{ij}^k, i \in L$. The pipes can be seen as the main transportation water mean, because the water flows through pipes, where each l_i^k represents the pipe between the node *i* and node *j*.

The pipes do not have a constant flow, considering that the diameter of the pipes can vary, the amount of waste in the pipes, and the deterioration of the pipes, among other conditions that modify the flow of drinking water.

The constant water flow plus the conditions of the pipes and the environment cause evaporation. The factors that condition the evaporation rate are, on the one hand, those that characterize the state of the atmosphere around the evaporating surface, and on the other hand, factors that characterize the nature and state of this surface. As a form of correlation between evaporation and other meteorological factors that influence both media (water and air), Dalton (1802) proposes the following formulation:

$E = K(ps - pv), K = cte$

Where:

E: evaporation rate (L)

k: Evaporation constant $\left(plg^2 * \left(\frac{gal}{lb} \right) * 3.78541L \right)$

ps: saturated vapor pressure (psi)

Aging in distribution networks and the natural deterioration associated with it produces an increase in pipe failures, increasing physical losses over the years. This deterioration can be modeled to predict which pipes will be more prone to fail given their current conditions.

In this case, we adjust the PWDN as the sum of the main elements involved in the Potable Water supply and the elements involved in the Potable water's quality.

Objective Function

The objective function is determined by the flow of drinking water that is requested by several users and the determination of the quality of the drinking water.

$$Max\sum_{s1}^{S}\sum_{s2}^{S}\sum_{s3}^{S}PW_{s1}QW_{s2}FW_{s3} \tag{1}$$

Where:

PW – Potable Water
QW – Quality of the Water
FW - Flow of potable water
s1, s2, s3 – index

The potable water objective is oriented to meet the water quality needs of various user groups. This target is defined as the reduction of drinking water quality by increasing the pipe run and conditions concerning the required values, which are usually prescribed by sanitary guidelines and other regulations. The water quality requirements of different customer groups are represented as demand nodes. Each of these customer groups has different water quality requirements. The objective function is defined as the square of the deviations of the actual (modeled) constituent concentrations from the minimum and maximum required values (Equation 2).

$$\sum_{c=1}^{C}\sum_{d}^{D}\sum_{j}^{J}\left\{\left[0, c_{cdj}-c_{cd}^{min}, c_{cd}^{max}-c_{cdj}\right]\right\}^{2} \tag{2}$$

The aim objective function complies with the following principles:

- Measure the quantity of drinking water
- Identify the quality of drinking water in the network.

This type of problem becomes complex given the number of variables that can be involved; in general, partial solutions have been developed, where we can identify an orientation towards:

- Constant flow of drinking water
- Water quality at different points of the distribution network
- Quality of the materials used in the drinking water distribution network
- Potabilization processes

Restrictions

The main condition will be

$$Min\sum_{s4}^{S}\sum_{s5}^{S}WL_{s4}R_{s5} \tag{3}$$

Where:

WL – Water leaks

R – Resources (Time, Resources, Cost)
s4, s5 – index

In the scheme presented in Figure 2, we can identify different stages that make up the drinking water management problem which, as a whole, is an HP-hard problem given its characteristics.

Figure 2. Schematic potable water management

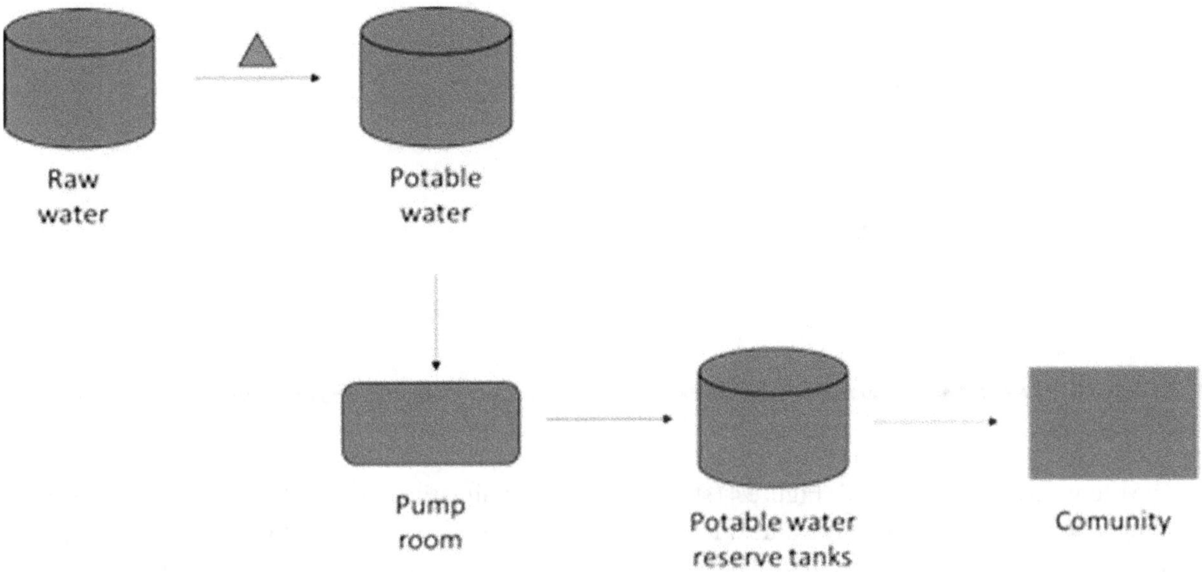

Supply and Demand of Potable Water Based on (PWNO)

This example implements a proposed potable water supply and demand model with uncertain water demand, covering a single period (figure 3). The problem is to determine the water capacities required to meet an increase in demand. However, future demand is uncertain and is modeled by proposing scenarios. This example builds on AIMMS support for dealing with uncertainty in the input data using methods such as scenario analysis and stochastic programming.

Figure 3. Input data

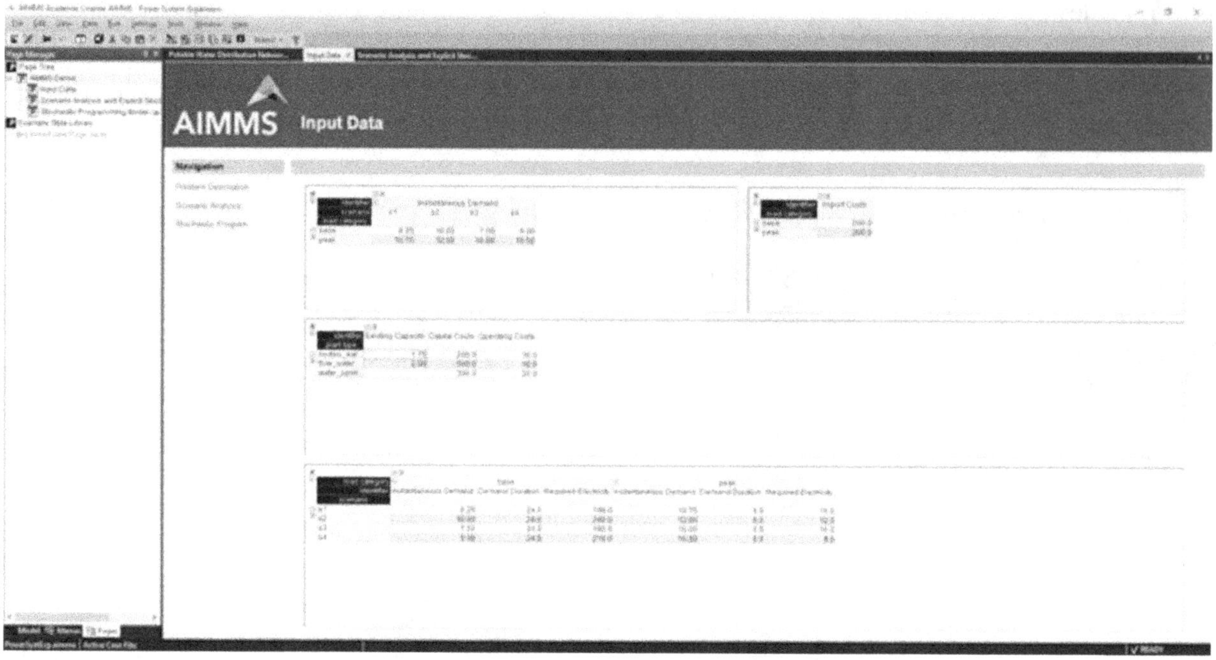

The scenario analysis method (Figure 4) starts from a deterministic model and examines its sensitivity to changes in uncertain parameter values. It is also called scenario analysis and is essentially a manual technique for dealing with uncertainty. The stochastic programming approach collects the inputs associated with an entire hypothetical analysis into a single model formulation. It seeks a capacity design that optimizes the overall expected costs by considering all scenarios (each scenario with a given weight). The stochastic model can be

- explicitly built as a stand-alone symbolic model within the AIMMS project, or it can be automatically
- automatically generated from the deterministic formulation.

The second approach is based on the special stochastic programming functions provided by AIMMS through the GMP library.

Figure 4. Scenarios

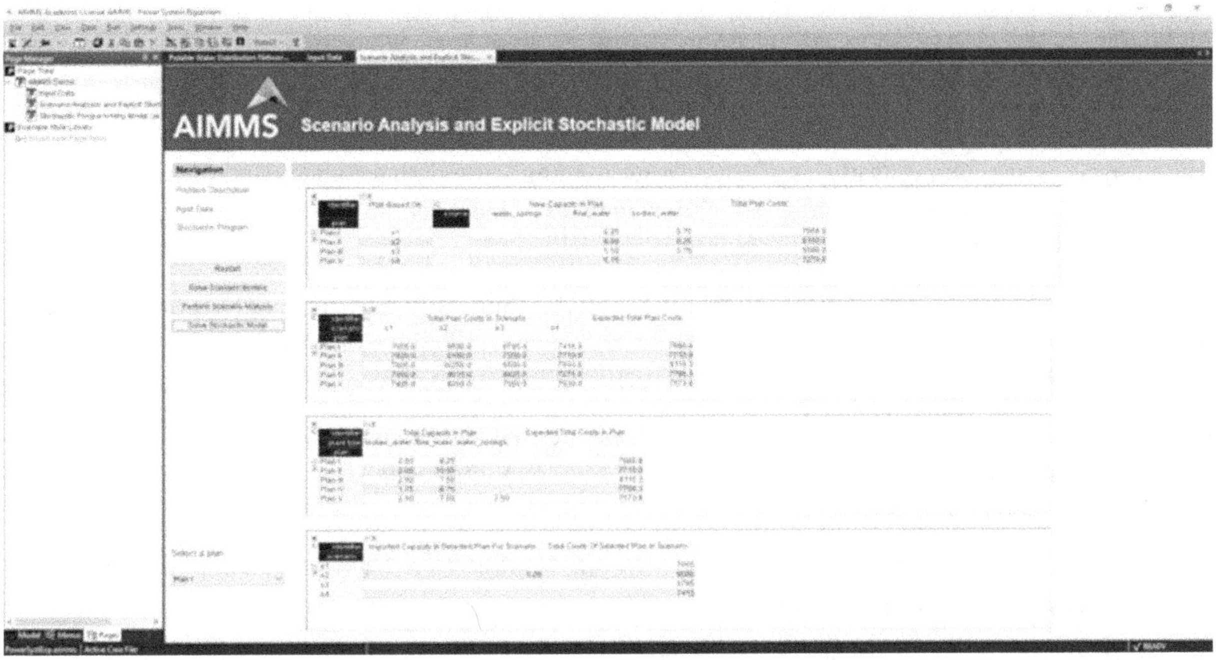

CONCLUSION

Water distribution networks are a fundamental part of the urban infrastructure of cities, towns and rural areas. This paper proposes a variant of potable water distribution network incorporating complementary elements for its optimization.

Potable water distribution networks are those whose purpose is to transport drinking water to users from the treatment plant. It is composed of a main network that is responsible for carrying water from the treatment plant to the various storage and compensation tanks located upstream of the supply sectors. And a set of secondary or minor distribution networks through which the potable water moves from the storage tanks to the user.

Many methods have been used to calculate flow rates in pipe networks, some include mathematical models or graphical methods. Numerous metaheuristics are currently being implemented to optimize these designs, reducing construction costs, or optimize the potable water flux.

ACKNOWLEDGMENT

The authors are grateful to CONACYT (National Council of Science and Technology) for its support. We thank Laboratorio Nacional en Vehículos Autónomos y Exoesqueletos (LANAVEX).

REFERENCES

Al-Mefleh, N. K., AlAyyash, S. M., & Bani Khaled, F. A. (2019). Water management problems and solutions in a residential community of Al-Mafraq city, Jordan. *Water Science and Technology: Water Supply*, *19*(5), 1371–1380. doi:10.2166/ws.2019.003

Alam, M. S., Sasaki, N., & Datta, A. (2017). Waterlogging, crop damage and adaptation interventions in the coastal region of Bangladesh: A perception analysis of local people. *Environmental Development*, *23*, 22–32. doi:10.1016/j.envdev.2017.02.009

An, Y., Zhang, F., He, J., Shi, F., Han, S., & Li, X. (2010). Saltwater intrusion analysis and trend forecast in the coastal plain of Laizhou Bay. 2010 International Conference on Computer Application and System Modeling (ICCASM 2010). IEEE. doi:10.100712665-018-7866-8

Apollonio, C., Delle Rose, M., Fidelibus, C., Orlanducci, L., & Spasiano, D. (2018). Water management problems in a karst flood-prone endorheic basin. Environmental Earth Sciences, 77(19), 676. doi:10.1007/s12665-018-7866-8

AWWA. (2012). Water Treatment Plant Design. Second Edition. Cap 5. USA: Coagulation and Flocculation-American Water Works Association (AWWA).

Brown, R. R., Keath, N., & Wong, T. H. (2009). Urban water management in cities: Historical, current and future regimes. *Water Science and Technology*, *59*(5), 847–855. doi:10.2166/wst.2009.029 PMID:19273883

Burd, P., Leslie, J., & Wilton, N. (2016). *Cruciform Water Distribution Valve for Aircraft Galley Plumbing System* [Patent]. https://patentscope.wipo.int/search/es/detail.jsf?docId=EP222931358&_cid=P12-L9MVZJ-64483-1

CONAGUA. (n. d.). *Manual de Agua Potable, Alcantarillado y Saneamiento. Evaluación Rápida de Plantas Potabilizadoras. Comisión Nacional del Agua*. CONAGUA.

Cory Albers & Bernard Amell. (2018). *System and Method for Producing Potable Water from Stormwater* [Patent]. https://patentscope.wipo.int/search/es/detail.jsf?docId=US213379733&_cid=P12-L9MVZJ-64483-1

Dalton, J. (1802). Experiments and observations to determine whether the quantity of rain and dew is equal to the quantity of water carried off by rivers and raised by evaporation; with an inquiry into the origin of the springs. *Manchester Philosophical Society Memories*, *5*, 346–372.

Haase, R. A. (2001). Potable water treatment system and method of operation thereof (Australia, Patent). OMPI. https://patentscope.wipo.int/search/es/detail.jsf?docId=AU180922058&_cid=P12-L9MVZJ-64483-1

Haase Richard Alan. (2007). *Potable water treatment system and apparatus*. Australia, Patent. OMPI. https://patentscope.wipo.int/search/es/detail.jsf?docId=US40239475&_cid=P12-L9MVZJ-64483-1

Hassan, A. G., Fullen, M. A., & Oloke, D. (2019). Problems of drought and its management in Yobe State, Nigeria. *Weather and Climate Extremes*, *23*, 100192. doi:10.1016/j.wace.2019.100192

Hateffard, F., Balog, K., Tóth, T., Mészáros, J., Árvai, M., Kovács, Z. A., Szűcs-Vásárhelyi, N., Koós, S., László, P., Novák, T. J., Pásztor, L., & Szatmári, G. (2022). High-Resolution Mapping and Assessment of Salt-Affectedness on Arable Lands by the Combination of Ensemble Learning and Multivariate Geostatistics. *Agronomy (Basel)*, *12*(8), 1858. https://www.mdpi.com/2073-4395/12/8/1858. doi:10.3390/agronomy12081858

Hou, G., Li, Z., Jing, W., & Jiang, Y. (2012). *Solar potable water preparation system and method for preparing potable water by using solar potable water preparation system* [China, Patent]. https://patentscope.wipo.int/search/es/detail.jsf?docId=CN85324013&_cid=P12-L9MVZJ-64483-1

Kawamura, S. (2000). Integrated Design and Operation of Water Treatment Facilities. United States of America: Second Edition; John Wiley & Sons, Inc.

Lawrence, D., Lansing, J. R., Lawrence, D., & Lansing, P. E. (2019) Water Production Employing a Hydrogen Cycle. https://patentscope.wipo.int/search/es/detail.jsf?docId=US279855441&_cid=P12-L9MVZJ-64483-1

Lee, W. Froemke (2019). Air temperature control using potable water [Patent]. https://patentscope.wipo.int/search/es/detail.jsf?docId=US238727825&_cid=P12-L9MVZJ-64483-1

Li, Q., Chen, L., & Xu, Y. (2022). Drought risk and water resources assessment in the Beijing-Tianjin-Hebei region, China. *The Science of the Total Environment*, *832*, 154915. https://doi.org/https://doi.org/10.1016/j.scitotenv.2022.154915. doi:10.1016/j.scitotenv.2022.154915 PMID:35364182

Matchaya, G. C., Tadesse, G., & Kuteya, A. N. (2022). Rainfall shocks and crop productivity in Zambia: Implication for agricultural water risk management. *Agricultural Water Management*, *269*, 107648. https://doi.org/https://doi.org/10.1016/j.agwat.2022.107648. doi:10.1016/j.agwat.2022.107648

Mehdipour, S., Nakhaee, N., Khankeh, H., & Haghdoost, A. A. (2022). Impacts of drought on health: A qualitative case study from Iran. *International Journal of Disaster Risk Reduction*, *76*, 103007. https://doi.org/https://doi.org/10.1016/j.ijdrr.2022.103007. doi:10.1016/j.ijdrr.2022.103007

Mena, M. (2016). *Diseño de la Red De Distribución De Agua Potable De La Parroquia El Rosario Del Cantón San Pedro De Pelileo,Provincia De Tungurahua.". Tesis de Ingeniería. UNIVERSIDAD TÉCNICA DE AMBATO*. AMBATO.

Mens, M., Minnema, B., Overmars, K., & van den Hurk, B. (2021). Dilemmas in developing models for long-term drought risk management: The case of the National Water Model of the Netherlands. *Environmental Modelling & Software*, *143*, 105100. https://doi.org/https://doi.org/10.1016/j.envsoft.2021.105100. doi:10.1016/j.envsoft.2021.105100

NOM. (1994). Norma Oficial Mexicana Nom-127-SSA1-1994, Salud Ambiental, Agua para Uso y Consumo Humano-Límites Permisibles de Calidad y Tratamientos a que Debe Someterse el Agua para su Potabilización. http://www.agrolab.com.mx/sitev002/sitev001/assets/nom-127-ssa1-1994.pdf

Palm Joseph, M., & Semler Loren, H. (2005). Automatic Flushing System and Method for a Potable Water Station [Patent]. https://patentscope.wipo.int/search/es/detail.jsf?docId=US40921905&_cid=P12-L9MVZJ-64483-1

Patentcope. (2022). *Patentscope search engine*. Patentcope. https://patentscope.wipo.int/search/es/search.jsf

Pingale, S. M., Jat, M. K., & Khare, D. (2014). Integrated urban water management modeling under climate change scenarios. *Resources, Conservation and Recycling*, *83*, 176–189. doi:10.1016/j.resconrec.2013.10.006

SENAGUA. (2012). *Normas para Estudio y Diseño de Sistemas de Agua Potable y Disposición de Aguas Residuales para Poblaciones Mayores a 1000 Habitantes (Norma CO 10.07 SENAGUA)*. Código Ecuatoriano de la Construcción de Parte IX Obras Sanitarias.

Si, F., Huang, T., Li, N., Li, K., Wen, G., Li, Y., & Zhang, H. (2022). Effects of flood discharge on the water quality of a drinking water reservoir in China – Characteristics and management strategies. *Journal of Environmental Management*, *314*, 115072. https://doi.org/https://doi.org/10.1016/j.jenvman.2022.115072. doi:10.1016/j.jenvman.2022.115072 PMID:35452880

Singh, A. (2018). Assessment of different strategies for managing the water resources problems of irrigated agriculture. *Agricultural Water Management*, *208*, 187–192. doi:10.1016/j.agwat.2018.06.021

Sunao, I. (2012). Potable Water Remote Automatic Supply Control Unit and Potable Water Remote Automatic Supply Control System [Patent]. https://patentscope.wipo.int/search/es/detail.jsf?docId=JP273350066&_cid=P12-L9MVZJ-64483-1

WaterModels. (n.d.). *Mathematical models in Watermodels*. Water Models. https://lanl-ansi.github.io/WaterModels.jl/latest/math-model.html

Zecchin, A. C., Simpson, A. R., Maier, H. R., Leonard, M., Roberts, A. J., & Berrisford, M. J. (2006, September). Application of two ant colony optimisation algorithms to water distribution system optimisation. *Mathematical and Computer Modelling*, *44*(5–6), 451–468. doi:10.1016/j.mcm.2006.01.005

Zvobgo, L., & Do, P. (2020). COVID-19 and the call for 'Safe Hands': Challenges facing the under-resourced municipalities that lack potable water access - A case study of Chitungwiza municipality, Zimbabwe. *Water Research X*, *9*, 100074. doi:10.1016/j.wroa.2020.100074 PMID:33089132

Chapter 12
Description of Artificial Intelligence Models in Sustainable Water Resource Management

Luis Amador Guzman
Universidad Politecnica de Pachuca, Mexico

Jaime Aguilar Ortiz
Polytechnic University of Pachuca, Mexico

José Miguel Liceaga Ortiz de la Peña
Polytechnic University of Pachuca, Mexico

ABSTRACT

The implementation of artificial intelligence (AI) has greatly improved the effectiveness and sustainability of conserving drinking water resources. Through the utilization of AI, real-time data is collected and analyzed, leading to the optimization of water distribution and delivery while minimizing unnecessary waste. Additionally, AI enables timely emergency responses and provides accurate predictions for future water demand.

INTRODUCTION

This paper aims to thoroughly assess a handful of AI models that look to make water management more reliable and efficient. We are talking algorithms designed for scrutinizing water quality, detecting leaks, anticipating floods, maximizing consumption and treating wastewater. As time goes on, these constructs will be bolstered by newer AI techniques. Mostly, we'll focus on refining existing systems to bring them up to speed.

Particularly, the artificial intelligence models described in this work are in the following topics:

DOI: 10.4018/979-8-3693-0373-3.ch012

- Artificial intelligence models to assess water quality
- Artificial intelligence models for the detection of water leaks
- Artificial intelligence models for flood management
- Artificial intelligence models to optimize water use
- Artificial intelligence models for wastewater treatment.

Water's essential for all life, and it's pervasive on our world– blanketing around 70% of Planet Earth. But even though it is plentiful, the availability of H2O varies across the globe, causing an imbalance in access. That is why this resource plays a big role in multiple scientific disciplines including biology, ecology, and environmental science. In this piece, we will examine some key figures and facts about water.

In this introduction, we are plunging into the fascinating realm of water statistics. Explore with us as we unveil significant key elements, such as the figures depicting usage and abundance, along with a glimpse into the fundamental principles tied to freshwater.

Based in a research of Koop and van Leeuwen (2017) are well aware of the daunting challenge of safeguarding our drinking water reserves. The scarcity of this vital resource combined with its frequent pollution from industrial waste and dilapidated urban infrastructure has created a colossal issue.

INTRODUCTION, WATER STATISTICS AND BASIC CONCEPTS

Water in the World and its Problems

From droughts to floods, contamination to shortages, the issues facing our global aqua reserves are both numerous and extreme. We have a crisis of water.

Every year sees a whopping 1.386 billion cubic kilometers of water added to the planet, but not all of it is fit for us to drink: 97.5% is salty ocean stuff. And when you narrow down the rest to only fresh liquid, 35 million cubic kilometers, almost 70 percent is not up for grabs either—it is tied up in snow and ice caps. Climate change isn't helping either; global warming causes glaciers to melt (Chen et al., 2019) and totally disrupts hydrological cycles (Livingstone et al., 2022).

Water– the lifeblood of our planet– is becoming a scarce commodity, with availability and quality on shaky ground. In deserts and semi-arid zones, water's especially endangered. The growing population and booming cities are just two of the contributing factors to its dwindling status and as if that weren't enough, climate change is not helping matters either (Kanyangarara et.al., 2017). Thornton & Herrero (2010) found that the situation was dire enough to require urgent action.

Besides an obvious lack of access to H2O, contamination has also become a pressing problem. This could lead to both serious health issues for people as well as damage the environment by ruining aquatic ecosystems used for drinking water or raising crops and sustaining wildlife (Sarker et al., 2021).

The fact that we're damaging the world with global warming is no secret. Temperatures are on a hot streak, rain isn't falling where it should, and floods and droughts have become more frequent (Hyandye et al., 2018). Not only humans are hurting, but entire ecosystems as well. To protect our water sources in these trying times, we need to step up and develop advanced plans for mitigating and adapting (Bellon et al., 2022).

Water and Urban Growth in the World

The correlation between cities growing and water consumption is direct. With more people, the need for freshwater grows exponentially. So, urban planners should take into account green sources of H2O when getting ready to build new developments.

It's an undeniable fact that cities are swelling at a shocking rate – two new city-dwellers every single second! Experts anticipate that 95% of urban growth in the next few decades will be in developing nations across Africa and Asia. This means that by 2030, their cities will have boomed to double the size they were back in 2000 a rather intimidating thought for those tasked with carrying out infrastructure maintenance and other essential services.

One in four city-dwellers– 789 million in total– lack access to even basics like improved sanitation. What's worse is that a whopping 497 million folks have to make do with shared facilities, a number which has ballooned since 1990 when it was just 249 million (Kanyangarara et al., 2021).

The harsh truth remains that a significant portion, approximately 27 percent, of individuals living in urban areas within developing nations lack access to fundamental necessities such as running water within their own homes. This single statistic serves as a compelling catalyst for the urgent need to implement essential reforms and advancements in water and sanitation within these specific regions (Gebremichael et al., 2020).

This large-scale movement of people from rural regions to metropolitan areas mainly comes from folks searching for better job chances and improved quality of life.

Water Pollution in Cities in the World

Water pollution is an alarming problem. Cars, businesses, and crappy waste management systems are all major contributors to the poisoning of our planet's liquid life source. This matters to us humans and all the critters out there too, so it is urgent that we act fast.

Tainted water is a major concern that affects many cities across the world. The root cause of this, unfortunately, is rapid urban expansion and industrial progress. This has caused an immense load on our water sources, which has led to their deterioration and even the extinction of various water-living species (Strokal et al., 2021).

City water pollution has numerous triggers, the main one being sewage draining without any proper handling. A significant number of metropolises don't possess proper sewer systems or wastewater treatment plants– resulting in raw wastewater being dumped into close-by water sources. This taints rivers, lakes and subterranean aquifers, endangering not only aquatic habitats but also the wellbeing of people (Strokal et al., 2021).

No shocker, wastewater isn't the only thing poisoning our water. Rain runoff from city surfaces like roads and rooftops can rush a variety of toxins into rivers and creeks. Chemicals, oils, and other rubbish are usually to blame here, making our urban H2O unsafe for consumption (Strokal et al., 2021).

It is a no-brainer that cities are in serious need of serious water safety solutions– and The governments, locals, and companies to implement effective wastewater treatments and sustainable practices. No doubt about it, a comprehensive approach is paramount for cities to guarantee access to clean H2O. (World Bank, 1999).

The planet's cities are in a disastrous state when it comes to water safety. We must to have initiatives like implementing sustainable wastewater management and setting up regulations regarding water access.

All in all, one comprehensive solution is required if our hopes of achieving freshwater for everyone are to be met (World Bank, 1999).

GENERAL DESCRIPTION OF ARTIFICIAL INTELLIGENCE ALGORITHMS

If you play your cards right, AI-powered algorithms can open up unimaginable possibilities. Activities that were thought to be beyond reach are now doable thanks to the technology. And, it goes without saying, these algorithms can give you access to several promising opportunities and advancements.

Figure 1. General process of artificial intelligence algorithms

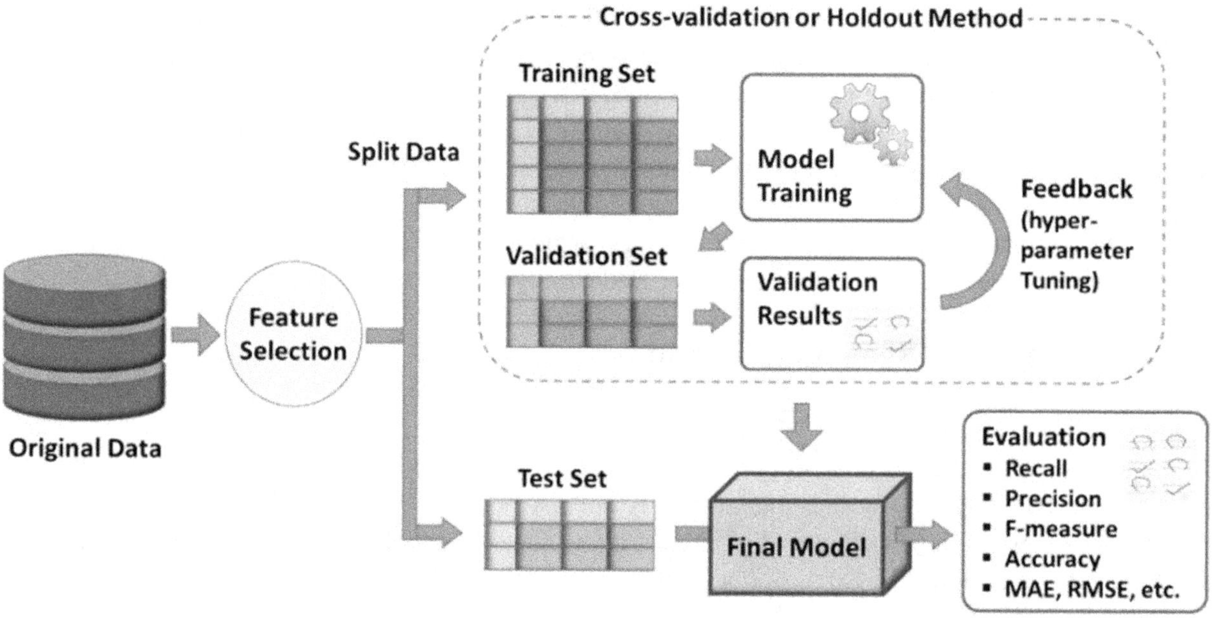

This section dives deep into the inner workings of AI algorithms. It paints a picture of their general structure and capabilities.

Artificial intelligence algorithms have a certain way of doing things. That is why we map the entire process (see Figure 1).

AI is a valuable asset when it comes to addressing urban water quality issues as mentioned by Najwa et al. (2022) in a study.

In Figure 2 we have regression model. It is a graphical interpretation of the associations between two or more variables, allowing us to better comprehend their correlations.

In the regression model we search a formula like $\hat{Y} = bX + a$, where X is an independent variable and Y is dependent on it. In other words, we want to find the equation that best equation to data.

Figure 2. Regression model

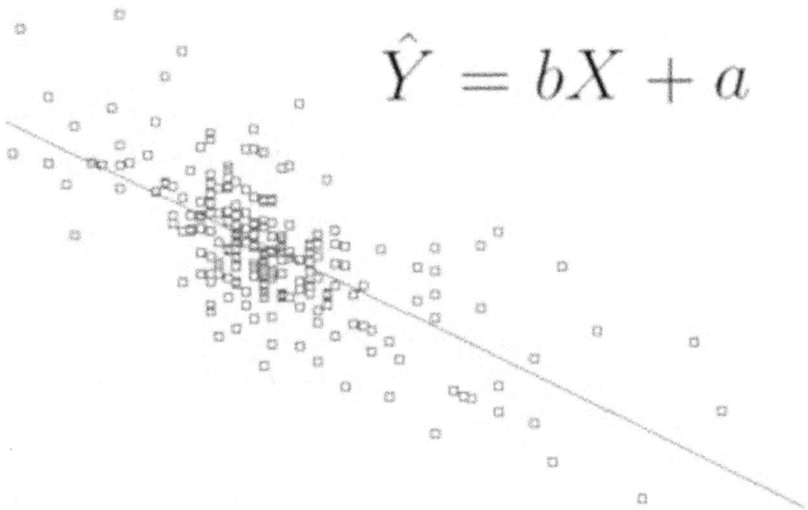

Figure 3. Artificial neural network model

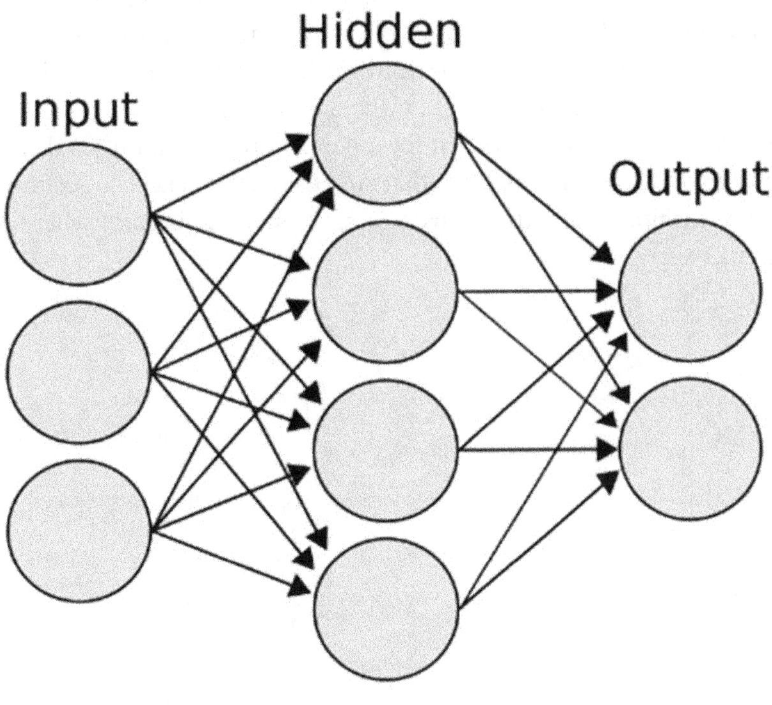

We implemented a neural network model to help us understand our data. This representation, as shown in Figure 3 allows us to better comprehend the relationships between our variables and draw meaningful conclusions.

The AI is a major game-player, especially when it comes to predicting water quality. To do this, we employ machine learning models like neural networks and regression models. With these models, we can to obtain the entire picture of any given environment, from monitoring parameters to environmental variables, and identify high-pollution zones preventatively (Najwa et al., 2022).

Some of the blueprints discussed in this paper are broad approximations of regression equations or artificial neural networks.

The Figure 3 contains components of a neural network model known as neurons, each one containing a w_i and b_j parameters list. This structure will minimize the loss function and manage to classify data into multiple categories.

Data-gathering is key when it comes to predicting water quality. Thus, we analyzed the concentration of pollutants, temperature, pH level, murkiness, and nutrient levels. With machine learning techniques at our disposal, we uncovered correlations between those variables and water quality (Najwa et al., 2022).

Regression models are algorithms that connect the dots between what goes in and what comes out of a water source. They allow you to take past data on cleanliness and extrapolate its future results. In particular, linear regression among other forms have been commonly used in this case (Najwa et al., 2022).

Neural networks draw inspiration from our brain's design to make sense of and learn from difficult data. Basically, each layer of connected neurons takes in info then outputs an understanding that guides the model. We're talking about predicting water quality here turns out these models can take previous data and accurately forecast future conditions (Najwa et al., 2022).

Machine Learning tech, like regression models and neural networks, can be great assistants in determining water contamination levels in cities. They help protect human health by monitoring ecosystems. Even though we've come a long way, we still need to work on refining the algorithms for more precise and dependable assessments (Chang et al., 2020; Grbčić et al., 2021).

Staying on top of water leakage is important for any network. Thankfully, AI has some great methods to identify pressure and flow abnormalities that suggest a leak. These algorithms can use anomaly detection and machine learning to identify signs of a problem and pinpoint where the issue is coming from (Grbčić et al., 2021).

Figure 4. Anomaly detected in a time series

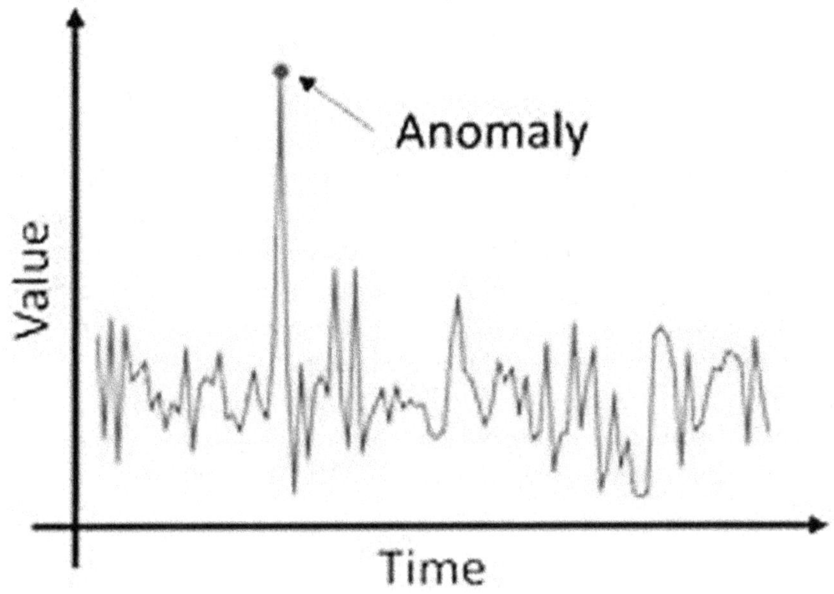

Figure 5. Anomaly detected in a boxplot

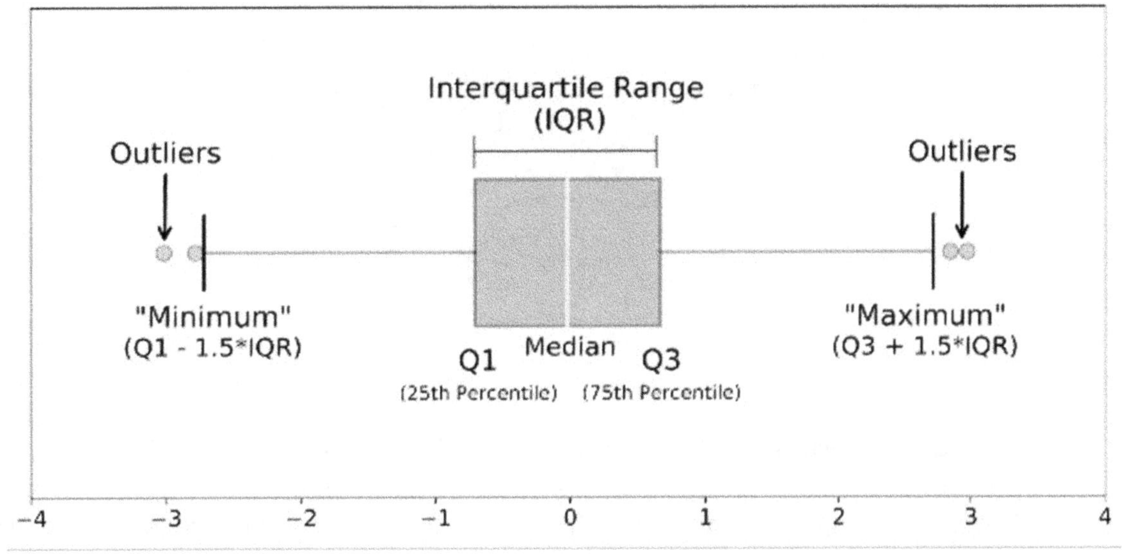

What about when we hear the phrase 'anomaly detection'? In this case, it is about uncovering leaky spots in a water distribution network. To do so, algorithms scan past pressure and flow information looking for irregular patterns that might suggest there's a problem with that area. Even an uptick in pressure or a dip in flow could be suspicious, and when they're found, operators receive an alert letting them know to investigate further. It may be hard to believe but tech can save gallons of water.

In Figures 4 and 5, we showcase two unique methods for identifying anomalies in a dataset of information over time and with a boxplot.

If we want to analyze water pressure and flow data to detect leaks, Artificial Intelligence (AI) is a possibility. Specifically, machine learning and anomaly detection models can be used to find patterns that suggest a leak, and even pinpoint where it is coming from Zhou et al. (2018). This could be done manually, but with artificial intelligence it can be done faster and better many times.

Anomaly-detection algorithms make it their mission to examine historical pressure and flow data in water networks, in search of irregular movements. Say, spikes in pressure in certain areas or drops in flow in others. Whenever such odd patterns are detected, these programs can send off alerts to network operators so they can investigate any potential leaks (Zhou et al., 2018).

When it comes to making sure the water supply is getting used properly, optimization algorithms are a must. They decide the most efficient and equitable way of giving out water in an area based on demand, restrictions, and performance goals (Zhou et al., 2018). It's vital for managing any water-related resources well.

Figure 6. Optimization process

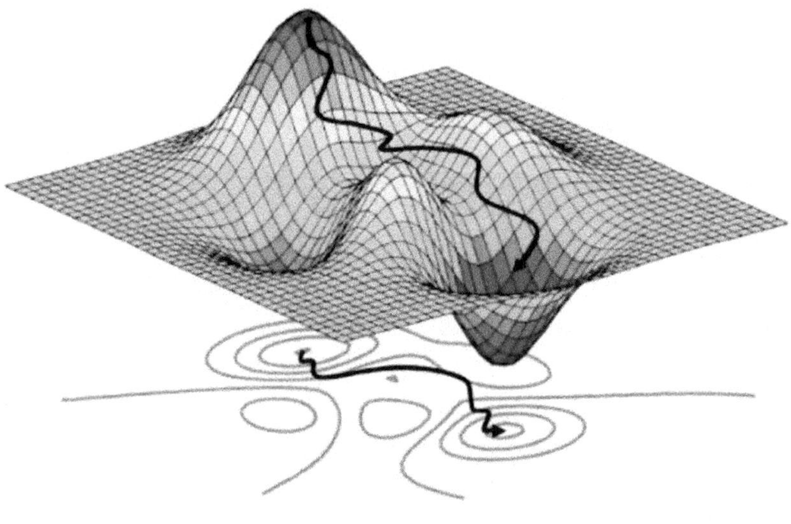

When it comes to water management, optimization algorithms can prove quite useful. By applying linear, nonlinear, or mixed programming formulas and models, these programs can take inventory of variables such as reservoir capacity, conduit infrastructure, contamination levels, and demands of users (households, businesses, farmers etc.). Basically, they are really great at finding the best balance between all of these elements (Munawar et al., 2018).

This paper examines several strategies that attempt to locate the lowest possible value, as illustrated in Figure 6, by following a downward path. We applied a range of tactics to get an accurate result.

Moreover, optimization algorithms can guide us in making the right decisions for water shortages. These programs can analyze a variety of scenarios and strategies; like water protection efforts, limitations when drought hits, or prioritizing water access for essentials. This helps make smarter, sustainable decisions about water accessibility during scarcity (Al-Jawad et al., 2019; Zhai et al., 2022).

Considering the ever-important goal of utilizing water efficiently, algorithms are becoming increasingly relied upon. These programs can be programmed to identify areas where losses in the distribution network can be cut back or irrigation practices in agriculture made more prudent. On top of that, algorithms are also being used to map out distribution infrastructures and pinpoint optimal locations for new reservoirs and pumping stations.

Water optimization also includes access to reliable data and ensuring its quality. If we want accurate results, a model must be calibrated with trustworthy information. Therefore, to have dependable monitoring and data collection systems are key in Yan et al. (2019).

AI algorithms have emerged as a powerful tool for optimizing water use. Using anomaly detection and machine learning models, these algorithms can detect when there's a leak - so you won't be throwing good money after bad. Plus, it helps reduce water waste and the financial costs associated with it, making the whole water distribution process much more efficient (Yan et al., 2023).

Optimization algorithms are true game-changers when it comes to water resource management. They help determine how to best allocate a region or existing water sources in a region, considering factors such as needs, constraints and efficiency goals. In other words, these algorithms ensure that each sector receives the required amount of water.

It can be a tough job to allot the amount of water needed. Fortunately, there's an algorithm to make this headache easier. This algorithm integrates mathematical models like linear and nonlinear programming in its process. Moreover, it takes into account aspects such as reservoir capacity, infrastructure, water quality, and demand of households, industries and agriculture (Kadenge et al., 2020). It makes life way simpler.

Maximizing the utility of limited water resources is paramount. To do this, algorithms can crunch the numbers by analyzing demands from different areas and sectors as well as limitations, like seasonal restrictions or purity levels. In doing so, it's possible to discover how much water should be allocated to each user or sector taking into account both efficiency and equity objectives (Kadenge et al., 2020).

Optimization algorithms come in handy when making tough decisions about water shortages. These can take into account and weigh multiple probability outcomes, such as initiating water conservation rules, limiting use during droughts, or targeting essential uses. All of this allows for informed and strategic choices that guarantee decent water availability even during hard times (Kadenge et al., 2020).

When it comes to flood management, Artificial Intelligence algorithms really hit the spot. A combination of real-time data, including weather patterns and water levels in rivers and these brainy algorithms makes it easier to foresee floods in urban areas, which then allows us to make rapid decisions like closing off floodgates, evacuating folks, and allocating emergency resources. It is a powerful tool that can benefit many people (Najwa et al., 2020).

The monitoring data can be aided by AI algorithms to detect anomalies and unusual events. Utilizing anomaly detection techniques, these algorithms can pinpoint noteworthy deviations from the usual patterns, signaling potential problems in the treatment procedures or incidents of contamination. Swift corrective actions and reduced risks to public health and the environment become possible with the timely detection of these anomalies (Czyczula et al., 2022).

Improving the operational efficiency of treatment plants is possible through wastewater management that utilizes AI algorithms. By optimizing various key processes such as dosing of chemicals, aeration control, and sedimentation, these algorithms enable energy savings and reduce operating costs (Czyczula et al., 2022). Additionally, AI contributes to the optimization of preventive and predictive maintenance schedules, resulting in minimized downtime and increased availability of treatment facilities.

In wastewater monitoring and management, the successful use of AI algorithms relies heavily on having precise and top-notch data (Nandal et al., 2022). The effective operation of these algorithms also requires the presence of appropriate infrastructure for data collection and monitoring (Mahbooba et al., 2021). Real-world implementation and enhancement of these algorithms necessitate the cooperation among wastewater treatment experts, data scientists, and treatment plant operators (Loftus et al., 2020).

By analyzing data from sensors and monitoring systems, AI algorithms have a pivotal function in the oversight and administration of wastewater. An optimized wastewater treatment, in terms of load and quality prediction, is achieved through these algorithms, resulting in efficient treatment processes and decreased operating expenses.

AI algorithms have a major effect on the management of water in urban areas. They provide innovative solutions for challenges like water quality, flood management, leak detection, wastewater monitoring, and optimizing water usage, resulting in improved efficiency and accuracy. This not only saves costs and resources but also has a significant impact on water management in cities (Himeur et al., 2023).

Machine learning algorithms and neural networks play a major part in predicting water quality. These tools grant us the ability to foresee water contamination using factors such as the environment and tracking data. In other words, we can now distinguish places and times with higher pollution rates, and take necessary steps accordingly. In fact, advanced AI systems can even estimate the Water Quality Index (WQI) plus Water Quality Classification (WQC).

The use of machine learning algorithms, such as Nearest Neighbor (K-NN) and Naive Bayes and artificial neural networks models of Nonlinear Autoregressive Neural Network (NARNET) and Long Short-Term Memory deep learning algorithm (LSTM), have been implemented for the purpose of predicting water quality indices (WQI) (Aldhyani et al. 2020).

AI algorithms are commonly employed in the wastewater treatment sector to evaluate data collected from sensors and monitoring systems. By doing so, these algorithms are capable of enhancing treatment procedures and projecting the load and quality of wastewater (Dehghani et al., 2021). Operating costs are lowered, and overall efficiency is heightened, thanks to the automatic adjustments made by these algorithms. A recent investigation capitalized on an artificial neural network technique to simulate and refine the absorption of a specific dye in wastewater, employing compost ash from municipal solid waste. The outcomes indicated that the adsorption process could be satisfactorily described by the pseudo-second order kinetic model and the Freundlich isotherm. This therefore suggests that AI algorithms have the potential to optimize wastewater treatment operations considerably (Dehghani et al., 2021).

Incorporating computer vision and language processing, artificial intelligence is designed to easily identify patterns in provided data, resulting in the automation of various processes. From playing chess to making purchase suggestions, forecasting weather to predicting sales, artificial intelligence engages in activities based on perfected patterns. The ultimate objective is to combine algorithms and techniques, enabling machines to possess human-like abilities such as logical reasoning, knowledge, planning, natural language processing, perception, and a broad sense of intelligence (Thierer et al., 2017).

Safder et al. (2022) pointed out that machine learning algorithms, a subset of Artificial Intelligence, have the ability to learn and enhance their performance through experience by analyzing extensive datasets, detecting patterns, and making precise predictions. Consequently, these algorithms have proven their utility in diverse fields, ranging from disease prognosis to optimizing resource allocation.

Deep learning has totally transformed the way machines learn. Taking its cues from the intricate brain workings of humans, artificial neurons are knitted together to form neural networks. These intelligent systems are unsurprisingly at the heart of deep learning, giving machines the power to improve on particular targets as they gain experience from data (Srinivasu et al., 2021).

ARTIFICIAL INTELLIGENCE MODELS FOR WATER QUALITY PREDICTION

AI knows how to make predicting water quality a cinch. We are talking about the whole physical, chemical, and microbiological characteristics that can influence whether it is safe to drink, use for industrial purposes, or even support aquatic life. But here is: 'good' water is not always a clear-cut option. It can change regularly due to human intervention and natural events. As Passos et al. (2019) explain, these properties are vital bits of information when assessing water quality. However, what you do with that info is all up to you.

22 different models of artificial intelligence exist for the purpose of "evaluating water quality". A brief description is available for every one of these models.

Figure 7. Red neuronal NARNET

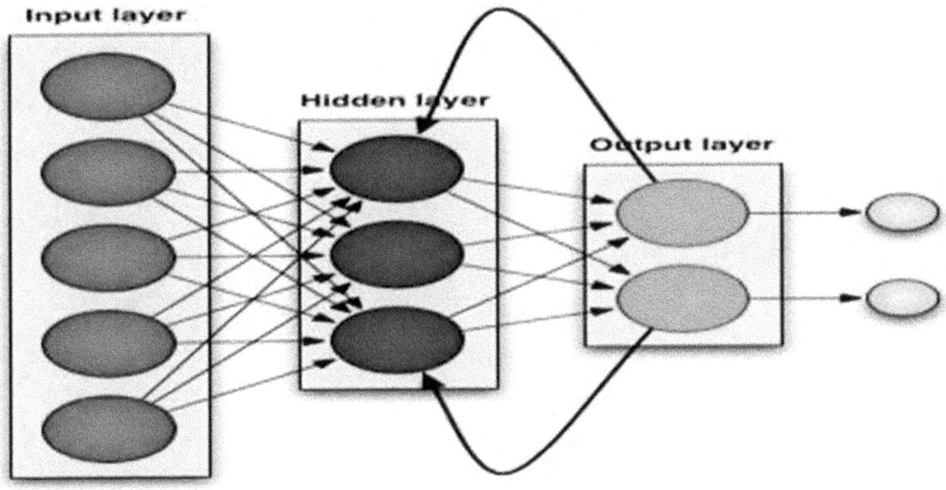

Figure 8. Red neuronal LSTM

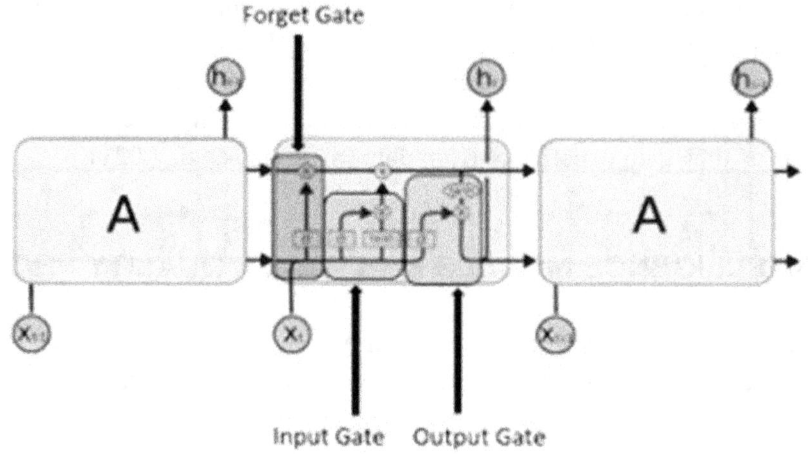

Models 1. The Water Quality Index (WQI) has been successfully predicted using the Nonlinear Autoregressive Neural Network (NARNET) model, as demonstrated by Aldhyani et al. in 2020.

Models 2. To predict the WQI, the LSTM algorithm, a deep learning approach, has been applied successfully (Aldhyani et al., 2020).

Figures 7 and 8 show the general structure of a NARNET and LSTM neural network, respectively. This allows us to highlight the memory property that many physical phenomena have. In both cases there is a stage of recurrence of the information..

Figure 9. Support vector machine

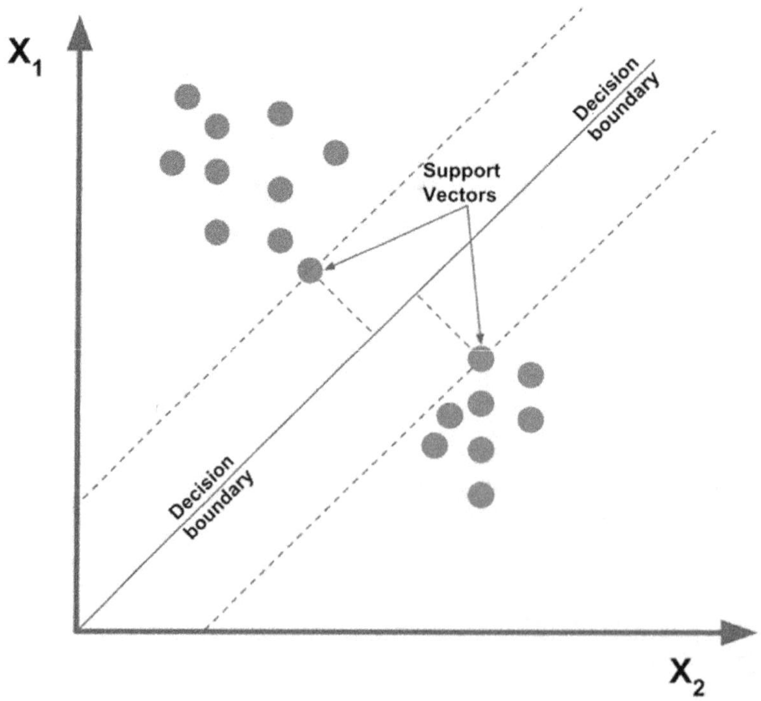

Figure 10. k-NEAREST neighbor

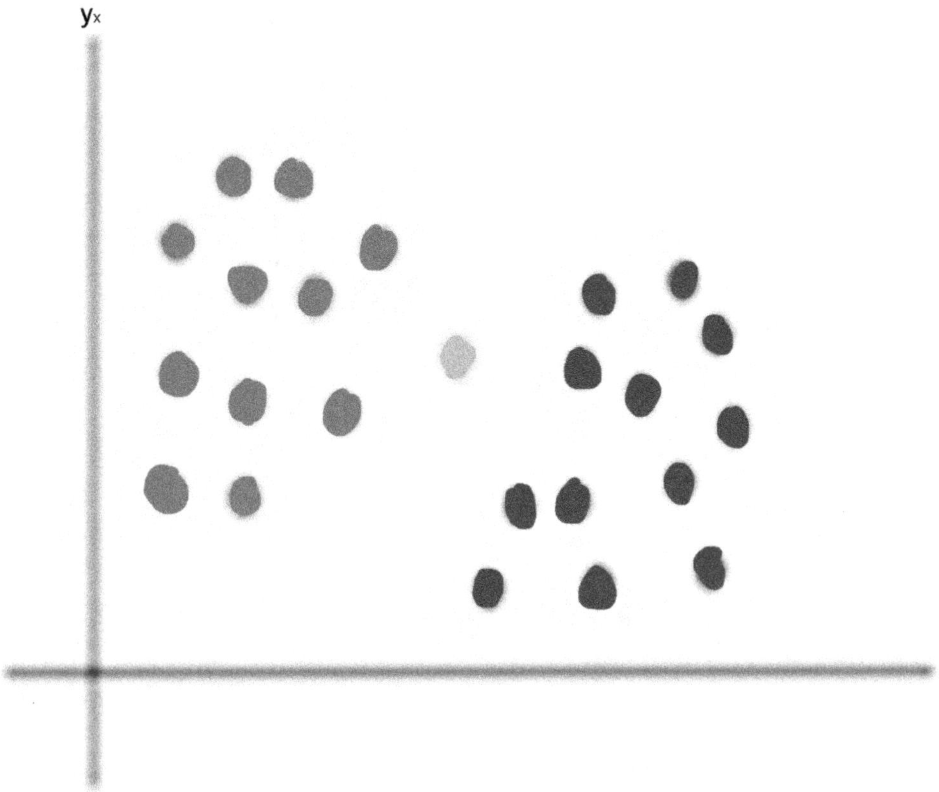

Water Quality Classification (WQC) has been a topic of interest for researchers. Aldhyani et al. (2020) explored the use of the Support Vector Machine (SVM) algorithm in predicting it.

Models 3. Used by Aldhyani et al. (2020) for predicting the WQC, the K-Nearest Neighbor (K-NN) algorithm is employed at a 1.4 rate.

Displayed in Figures 9 and 10, we can observe the configuration of two classification models that are commonly utilized for situations necessitating group formation. The initial model (Figure 9) demonstrates the Support Vector Machines algorithm, which aims to discover a suitably broad and appropriately slanted line to effectively classify data into 2 or more groups, as evidenced in the 2D illustration. This same process is also applicable to data with more than two dimensions. Conversely, Figure 10 introduces the commencing stages of the K-Nearest Neighbor model, wherein classifications of observations into multiple groups are determined by their respective degrees of proximity.

Models 4. Aldhyani et al. (2020), utilized the Naive Bayes algorithm for predicting the WQI.

Figure 11. Fuzzy logic model.

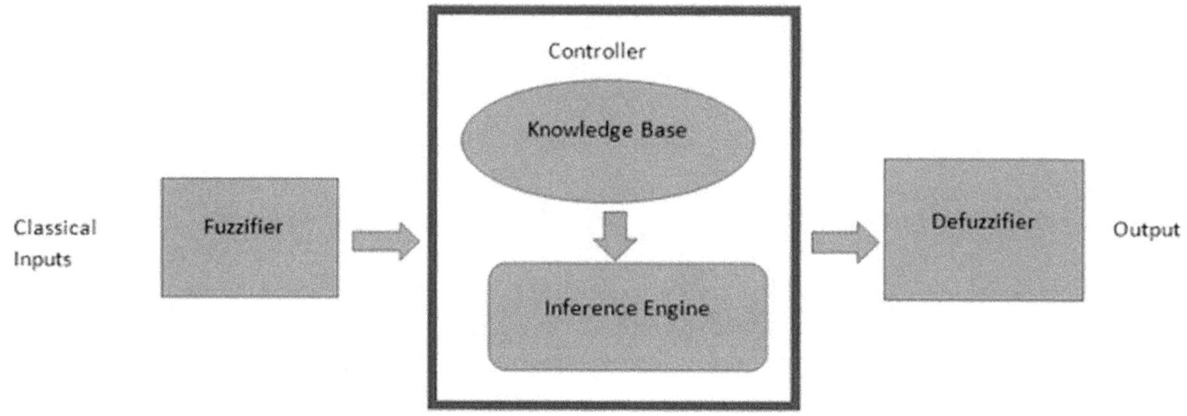

Figure 12. Neuro-fuzzy logic model

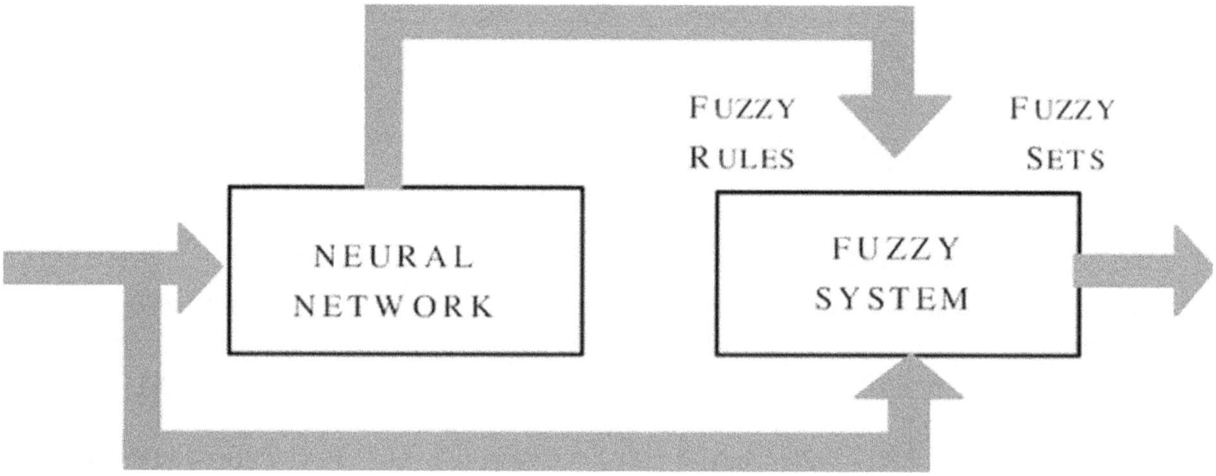

Mimicking human reasoning, a fuzzy logic algorithm is an artificial intelligence technique that deals with uncertainties and approximations. Specifically designed to handle problems with inherent vagueness, this method is widely used. According to Slashchova et al. (2023) (Figure 11), the stages of a fuzzy logic algorithm are as follows.

- It involves determining the degree of membership for each element in the input set. Fuzzification is the process of transforming crisp input values into fuzzy values. This is done by converting precise and distinct inputs into values that are not precise or are ambiguous.
- The decision-making process is guided by control rules, which consist of if-then statements. Fuzzy input values are applied with the rules to obtain a fuzzy output.

- Using control rules, the fuzzy input is mapped to the fuzzy output, resulting in a fuzzy set. This process is called inference.
- The area enclosed by the fuzzy set is where the centroid or the balance point is found during the defuzzification process. This process converts the fuzzy output set into a crisp value.

Models 5. Used by Hmoud et al. (2021), the Adaptive Neuro-Fuzzy Inference System (ANFIS) algorithm was employed to make predictions regarding the WQI.

You may have heard of something called an ANFIS, or a Neuro Fuzzy Logic algorithm before. It is a great tool for AI engineers of fuzzy logic and neural networks that helps tackle complicated issues with imprecision or uncertainty involved. We use ANFIS for all sorts of tasks, from data analysis and classification to modelling and control. To give you an idea, the diagram below shows how adding a neural network stage to the fuzzy logic process forms the stages of a Neuro Fuzzy Logic model.

An advantage of ANFIS, in comparison to conventional methods, is its capacity to predict output based on inputs and the rule base. Additionally, these systems offer the option to modify control system parameters (Vesović & Jovanovic, 2022).

Models 6. The FFNN, also known as a Feed-Forward Neural Network, has proven effective in the classification of water quality according to a study conducted by Hmoud et al. (2021).

Models 7. Used to estimate the WQI, the classic model of Multi Linear Regression (MLR) has been utilized (Gaya et al., 2020).

Models 8. The estimation of the WQI (Gaya et al., 2020) has utilized the Artificial Neural Network (ANN) model.

Models 9. These methods and models, known as Artificial Intelligence/Machine Learning (AI/ML), have been employed in enhancing, simulating, and streamlining vital processes involving the treatment of water and wastewater. Additionally, they have proven to be beneficial in monitoring and overseeing the operations of various natural systems and in the field of water-based farming, specifically hydroponics and aquaponics (Lowe et al., 2022).

Models 10. Chang et al. (2020) and Lv et al. (2023) presented an Artificial Neural Network (ANN) model designed to predict water quality in reservoirs.

Models 11. In 2020, Wu et al. developed a model called Support Vector Machine (SVM) to predict the quality of water in rivers.

Models 12. Water quality prediction was achieved by Agrawal et al. (2021) using a Naive Bayesian Classifier (NBC) and Particle Swarm Optimization (PSO) model.

Models 13. In aquaculture ponds, Nourani et al. (2018) developed an Artificial Neural Network (ANN) model to predict water quality.

Models 14. In 2022, Wu et al. developed a model called Artificial Neural Network (ANN) that can predict water quality in rivers.

Models 15. Groundwater quality in the Mazandaran plain in northern Iran was simulated using a hybrid model known as SVM-FFA. This unique approach combines the Firefly Algorithm with Support Vector Machine, as reported by Shiri et al. in 2021.

Models 16. Using a Naive Bayesian Classifier (NBC) and a Support Vector Machine (SVM) in conjunction, Agrawal et al. (2021) applied the Particle Swarm Optimization (PSO) algorithm to forecast the water quality index.

Models 17. As has been reported in Agrawal et al. (2021), the Naive Bayes Classifier (NBC) has been employed alongside Particle Swarm Optimization (PSO) for the purpose of water quality index prediction.

Models 18. Groundwater quality has been simulated using a self-organizing map (SOM), which is an artificial intelligence model (Gholami et al., 2021).

Models 19. Gholami et al. (2021) have utilized the Co-Active Neuro-Fuzzy Inference System (CANFIS) to replicate the quality of groundwater.

Models 20. To estimate the concentration of phycocyanin pigment, an indicator of water quality, the use of feedforward neural networks (FFNNs) has been implemented (Heddam et al., 2019).

Models 21. Used to estimate the concentration of phycocyanin pigment, Gene Expression Programming (GEP) is an artificial intelligence algorithm (Heddam et al., 2019).

Models 22. (Heddam et al., 2019) estimated the concentration of phycocyanin pigment using the Adaptive Neuro-Fuzzy Inference System with Grid Partition (ANFIS-GP) model.

ARTIFICIAL INTELLIGENCE MODELS FOR WATER LEAK DETECTION

For the detection of water leaks, there are 6 artificial intelligence models available.

Models 1. Using a combination of Artificial Neural Networks (ANN) and Genetic Algorithm (GA), this model effectively detects and locates leaks in the water distribution network by predicting the water pressure at the nodes and optimizing the ANN model parameters. This innovative approach was proven successful by Giustolisi et al. (2009).

Models 2. Using a combination of Artificial Neural Networks (ANN) and the Particle Swarm Optimization Algorithm (PSO), a successful model was developed that allows to identify, locate leaks and determine the correlation between water flow and pressure in the different nodes. within the distribution network and the parameters of the ANN model were optimized (Giustolisi et al., 2009).

Models 3. The detection and location of leaks in the water distribution network have been effectively achieved using a model that combines Artificial Neural Networks (ANN) and Ant Colony Optimization Algorithm (ACO). This unique approach utilizes the ANN to accurately represent the connection between water flow and pressure at different points in the network. The ACO algorithm is then employed to optimize the parameters of the ANN model. The success of this method has been demonstrated in previous research conducted by Giustolisi et al. in 2009.

Models 4. Using image analysis, a leak detection system is implemented in the water distribution network. Image processing techniques are applied to identify, analyze and process images for changes that could indicate the presence of a leak. This approach is presented by Negm et al. (2023.

Models 5. The Leak Detection System, which is built using deep learning techniques, has the capability to autonomously learn and enhance its accuracy by analyzing sensor data and identifying potential leak patterns (Fu et al., 2022).

Models 6. Using neural networks, the Leak Detection System is able to identify potential leaks by analyzing sensor data and recognizing patterns. These networks are highly effective for leak detection due to their ability to model intricate and non-linear relationships (Li et al., 2022).

ARTIFICIAL INTELLIGENCE MODELS FOR FLOOD MANAGEMENT

The adverse effects of floods in urban areas can be prevented or minimized through various measures and policies collectively known as flood management: Monitoring water levels, predicting floods, planning responses, and managing resources to protect communities and reduce damage. Flood management is a complex issue due to the presence of different sources of risk, including riverine, tidal, and coastal floods, as well as urban runoff and localized drainage disturbances. Cea and Costabile (2022) suggested various management strategies to analyze these risks.

For flood management, the following three artificial intelligence models can be used.

Models 1 Image-based Flood Alert System (IFAM): This system uses images to monitor water levels in real time. The images are processed and then flood risks are calculated using modules that estimate the water level (Ramos et al., 2007).

Models 2 Edge Detection in Images: This algorithm helps to find the edge points on the water surface and the point of the dam height. The algorithm has been useful for determining the water's edge. The system calculates the existing water level by comparing the edge pixel coordinate. If the water level rises, the pixel coordinate drops, resulting in altered segmentation. A warning system can be established using this method (Kumar et al., 2022).

Models 3 Detection of Significant Landmarks in Images: Researchers are focusing on extracting landmarks present on the ground, such as bridges, roads, houses, and buildings. These features can be further processed using image processing techniques to assist in disaster response (Munawar et al., 2021).

CONCLUSION

Using artificial intelligence (AI) models can be valuable for water management. Several models have been showcased in this study.

As AI usage, we're able to make hydration efficiency and sustainability a priority. With the technology's capacity to compile and inspect current data in real-time, supply chain optimization is becoming increasingly feasible. Thanks to AI is rapid emergency response and precise forecasting capabilities, we can walk into the future with confidence.

The properties of water: the physical, chemical, and microbial; determine its quality. Depending on how 'good' it is this will decide whether it's viable for human intake, industry use, or even aquatic living. But take note that water quality isn't a fixed concept as it can be altered from natural forces and man-made actions. To get a better handle on this idea we looked different AI models including NARNET, LSTM, SVM, K-NN, Naive Bayes, ANFIS, FFNN, MLR and ANN. All of these have something to contribute in understanding the nuances of water quality.

When it comes to gauging water quality, Artificial Intelligence models like NARNET and LSTM can compute the Water Quality Index. And for classifying water quality, SVM, K-NN and Naive Bayes are what you need. AI/ML is also used to help manage natural systems, optimize wastewater treatment and monitor hydroponic and aquaponic agriculture. Not to mention, AI has created algorithms that measure the potency of water in areas such as reservoirs, rivers, aquaculture ponds and groundwater.

Hunting for water leaks is of paramount importance in a water supply system – even a tiny trickle can have devastating consequences. That's why AI is an absolute godsend. It examines pressure and flow data to locate any signs of leaks without delay. In short, AI amplifies the entire process – making it swifter, more effective, and thriftier.

We present six AI models to detect water leaks. They have coupled Artificial Neural Networks with Genetic Algorithms, Particle Swarm Optimization, and Ant Colony Optimization to pinpoint the pressure at distribution nodes and refine ANNs. Plus, they are leveraging image processing and deep learning to recognize leakage in the water distribution system. Ultimately, these systems can analyze sensor data and spot patterns indicating a leak– getting better all the time.

Controlling floods is no easy feat. Taking into account things like water levels, potential flooding events, forward-thinking and resource administration are just a few of the necessities for success in this endeavor. Urban areas have quite a challenge when it comes to water management due to rivers overflowing, coasts being overwhelmed and drainage systems unable to cope with all the pressure. So, producing a strategic plan that utilizes multiple methods is key.

We have present three AI-driven solutions for flood management. The first is IFAM: a real-time system that uses images to follow water levels and determine potential flooding threats. We also have an algorithm that pinpoints the edges of the water, as well as the height of a dam– super useful for gauging the liquid depth. All in all, these clever models can really help us stay on top of floods. Moreover, scientists are expending the majority of their energy on recognizing the land's focal points– including roads, bridges, and homes. Subsequently, we can use picture control techniques to further refine this data to help during crisis times.

Making the most of water resources, that is the objective of 'Optimization of Water Use'. When you have a limited supply but still need to meet demands, you've got to get creative. Especially during months when water demands are especially high, like for agriculture. To tackle this problem head-on, a collective approach is recommended that balances aquifers and meets max needed water based on available resources and their restrictions.

We have managed to compile a list of ten AI models that can help us manage water use more efficiently. We've got robotic sensors tracking temporal changes in rivers and lakes, Adaptive Neuro-Fuzzy Inference Systems (ANFIS) with Cultural Algorithms (CA), Bees Algorithms (BA) and Invasive Weed Optimization (IWO) helping us locate flood dangers, Human Learning Optimization (HLO) algorithms to get the most out of concrete tech, Support Vector Regression models, Gaussian Process models, Sequential Allocation techniques and the cleverly named eSIP algorithm for robot navigation. Finally, we've got Stepwise Weight Assessment Ratio Analysis models and AI driven desalination tech.

Tracking down wastewater and its components is as important as it sounds. To understand how to treat wastewater, engineers must measure and comprehend all the variables associated with it. That includes nutrient contents from the start of processing through when it's released back in the wild or reused. By running a set of physical, chemical, and biological procedures, we can reduce toxins in wastewater before it does any harm.

Diving into wastewater monitoring, there are 18 artificial intelligence models that can help us out. ANFIS predicts the water quality index, while KNN and FFNN both classify it. We're also able to use ML and AI to bring about more safety and efficacy in our algorithms. But the real time data collection doesn't stop there. IoT comes into play for wastewater quality and evaluating treatment processes. Furthermore, FFNN, ANFIS, SVM, and MLR all work together to ascertain a wastewater treatment plant's efficiency.

FUTURE LINES OF WORK TO BE EXPLORED

According to the articles analyzed for each of the five topics on water, presented in this work document, which only represent a small part of all the existing literature on the subject, there are great possibilities of generating new applications that use different methods. artificial intelligence aimed at solving water problems.

Exploration into the enhancement of leak detection systems can lead to improved accuracy and efficiency by integrating additional variables and real-time data. While current models are effective, there is still room for improvement.

Smart cities can optimize water use by implementing better AI models. This involves researching ways to optimize water use in urban settings. For instance, AI can be utilized to enhance the management of irrigation systems in parks and gardens or reduce water consumption in public and residential buildings.

Wastewater treatment, where AI can be utilized, aims to eliminate emerging contaminants, known as emerging contaminants. These contaminants cause growing concern in wastewater. AI models are being explored to maximize the elimination of these substances.

We are trying to explore the possibility of including AI models into large water systems, for more effective and lasting water management. It is being established that AI can be useful in certain circumstances, but there's still room to assess how they could make their way into this kind of infrastructure.

REFERENCES

Afzaal, H., Farooque, A. A., Abbas, F., Acharya, B., & Esau, T. (2020). Computation of evapotranspiration with artificial intelligence for precision water resource management. *Applied Sciences (Basel, Switzerland)*, *10*(5), 1621. doi:10.3390/app10051621

Agrawal, P., Sinha, A., Kumar, S., Agarwal, A., Banerjee, A., Villuri, V. G. K., Annavarapu, C. S. R., Dwivedi, R., Dera, V. V. R., Sinha, J., & Pasupuleti, S. (2021). Exploring artificial intelligence techniques for groundwater quality assessment. *Water (Basel)*, *13*(9), 1172. doi:10.3390/w13091172

Al-Jawad, J. Y., Al-Jawad, S. B., & Kalin, R. M. (2019). Decision-making challenges of sustainable groundwater strategy under multi-event pressure in arid environments: The Diyala River Basin in Iraq. *Water (Basel)*, *11*(10), 2160. doi:10.3390/w11102160

Aldhyani, T. H. H., Al-Yaari, M., Alkahtani, H., & Maashi, M. (2020). Water quality prediction using artificial intelligence algorithms. *Applied Bionics and Biomechanics*, *2020*, 1–12. doi:10.1155/2020/6659314 PMID:33456498

Allaire, J. J. (2018). *Deep learning with R*. Manning Publications.

Bartram, J., Brocklehurst, C., Fisher, M. B., Luyendijk, R., Hossain, R., Wardlaw, T., & Gordon, B. (2014). Global monitoring of water supply and sanitation: History, methods and future challenges. *International Journal of Environmental Research and Public Health*, *11*(8), 8137–8165. doi:10.3390/ijerph110808137 PMID:25116635

Bartram, J., & Cairncross, S. (2010). Hygiene, sanitation, and water: Forgotten foundations of health. *PLoS Medicine*, *7*(11), e1000367. doi:10.1371/journal.pmed.1000367 PMID:21085694

Bayu, T., Kim, H., & Oki, T. (2020). Water governance contribution to water and sanitation access equality in developing countries. *Water Resources Research*, *56*(4), e2019WR025330. Advance online publication. doi:10.1029/2019WR025330

Bellon, M., Aligishiev, Z., & Massetti, E. (2022). Macro-fiscal implications of adaptation to climate change. *Staff Climate Notes*, *2022*(002), 1. doi:10.5089/9798400201608.066

Błaziak, M., Urban, S., Wietrzyk, W., Jura, M., Iwanek, G., Stańczykiewicz, B., Kuliczkowski, W., Zymliński, R., Pondel, M., Berka, P., Danel, D., Biegus, J., & Siennicka, A. (2022). An artificial intelligence approach to guiding the management of heart failure patients using predictive models: A systematic review. *Biomedicines, 10*(9), 2188. doi:10.3390/biomedicines10092188 PMID:36140289

Brandt, S. A. (2016). Modeling and visualizing uncertainties of flood boundary delineation: Algorithm for slope and DEM resolution dependencies of 1D hydraulic models. *Stochastic Environmental Research and Risk Assessment, 30*(6), 1677–1690. doi:10.100700477-016-1212-z

Cea, L., & Costabile, P. (2022). *Flood risk in urban areas: Modelling, management and adaptation to climate change.* A review. *Hydrology, 9*(3), 50. doi:10.3390/hydrology9030050

Chang, D.-L., Yang, S.-H., Hsieh, S.-L., Wang, H.-J., & Yeh, K.-C. (2020). Artificial Intelligence methodologies applied to prompt pluvial flood estimation and prediction. *Water (Basel), 12*(12), 3552. doi:10.3390/w12123552

Chen, M., Wang, C., Wang, X., Fu, J., Gong, P., Yan, J., Yu, Z., Yan, F., & Nawab, J. (2019). Release of perfluoroalkyl substances from melting glacier of the Tibetan plateau: Insights into the impact of global warming on the cycling of emerging pollutants. *Journal of Geophysical Research Atmospheres*, 2019JD030566. . doi:10.1029/2019JD030566

Cosgrove, W. J., & Rijsberman, F. R. (2014). *World water vision: Making water everybody's business.* Routledge. doi:10.4324/9781315071763

Crini, G., & Lichtfouse, E. (2019). Advantages and disadvantages of techniques used for wastewater treatment. *Environmental Chemistry Letters, 17*(1), 145–155. doi:10.100710311-018-0785-9

Czyczula Rudjord, Z., Reid, M. J., Schwermer, C. U., & Lin, Y. (2022). Laboratory development of an AI system for the real-time monitoring of water quality and detection of anomalies arising from chemical contamination. *Water (Basel), 14*(16), 2588. doi:10.3390/w14162588

D'Amore, G., Di Vaio, A., Balsalobre-Lorente, D., & Boccia, F. (2022). Artificial intelligence in the water–energy–food model: A holistic approach towards Sustainable Development Goals. *Sustainability (Basel), 14*(2), 867. doi:10.3390u14020867

Dehghani, M. H., Salari, M., Karri, R. R., Hamidi, F., & Bahadori, R. (2021). Process modeling of municipal solid waste compost ash for reactive red 198 dye adsorption from wastewater using data driven approaches. *Scientific Reports, 11*(1), 11613. doi:10.103841598-021-90914-z PMID:34078966

Deng, L., Guo, S., Yin, J., Zeng, Y., & Chen, K. (2022). Multi-objective optimization of water resources allocation in Han River basin (China) integrating efficiency, equity and sustainability. *Scientific Reports, 12*(1), 798. doi:10.103841598-021-04734-2 PMID:35039583

Dewitte, S., Cornelis, J. P., Müller, R., & Munteanu, A. (2021). Artificial Intelligence revolutionises Weather Forecast, Climate Monitoring and Decadal Prediction. *Remote Sensing (Basel), 13*(16), 3209. doi:10.3390/rs13163209

Dondeynaz, C., Carmona Moreno, C., & Céspedes Lorente, J. J. (2012). Analysing inter-relationships among water, governance, human development variables in developing countries. *Hydrology and Earth System Sciences*, *16*(10), 3791–3816. doi:10.5194/hess-16-3791-2012

Du, J., Wen, Y., Wang, L., Zhang, P., Fei, M., & Pardalos, P. M. (2022). An adaptive human learning optimization with enhanced exploration–exploitation balance. *Annals of Mathematics and Artificial Intelligence*. doi:10.100710472-022-09799-x

Dumitrascu, O., Dumitrascu, M., & Dobrotă, D. (2020). Performance evaluation for a sustainable supply chain management system in the automotive industry using artificial intelligence. *Processes (Basel, Switzerland)*, *8*(11), 1384. doi:10.3390/pr8111384

Famiglietti, J. S. (2014). The global groundwater crisis. *Nature Climate Change*, *4*(11), 945–948. doi:10.1038/nclimate2425

Feng, Z. (2011). *Research on water-saving irrigation automatic control system based on internet of things. 2011 International Conference on Electric Information and Control Engineering*. IEEE. do10.1109/ICEICE.2011.5778297

Fereidooni, Z., Tahayori, H., & Bahadori-Jahromi, A. (2021). A hybrid model-based method for leak detection in large scale water distribution networks. *Journal of Ambient Intelligence and Humanized Computing*, *12*(2), 1613–1629. doi:10.100712652-020-02233-2

Fu, G., Jin, Y., Sun, S., Yuan, Z., & Butler, D. (2022). The role of deep learning in urban water management: A critical review. *Water Research*, *223*(118973), 118973. doi:10.1016/j.watres.2022.118973 PMID:35988335

Gaya, M. S., Abba, S. I., Abdu, A. M., Tukur, A. I., Saleh, M. A., Esmaili, P., & Wahab, N. A. (2020). Estimation of water quality index using artificial intelligence approaches and multi-linear regression. *IAES International Journal of Artificial Intelligence (IJ-AI)*, *9*(1), 126.. doi:10.11591/ijai.v9.i1.pp126-134

Gebremichael, S. G., Yismaw, E., Tsegaw, B. D., & Shibeshi, A. D. (2021). Determinants of water source use, quality of water, sanitation and hygiene perceptions among urban households in North-West Ethiopia: A cross-sectional study. *PLoS One*, *16*(4), e0239502. doi:10.1371/journal.pone.0239502 PMID:33886565

Gholami, V., Khaleghi, M. R., Pirasteh, S., & Booij, M. J. (2022). Comparison of self-organizing map, artificial neural network, and co-active neuro-fuzzy inference system methods in simulating groundwater quality: Geospatial artificial intelligence. *Water Resources Management*, *36*(2), 451–469. doi:10.100711269-021-02969-2

Giustolisi, O., Savage, D. A., & Capellan, Z. (2009). Pressure-Driven Demand and Leakage Simulation for Water Distribution Networks. *Journal of Hydraulic Engineering*, *134*(5), 383–391. doi:10.1061/(ASCE)0733-9429(2009)135:5(383)

Goralski, M. A., & Tan, T. K. (2020). Artificial intelligence and sustainable development. *International Journal of Management Education*, *18*(1), 100330. doi:10.1016/j.ijme.2019.100330

Grbčić, L., Kranjčević, L., & Družeta, S. (2021). Machine learning and simulation-optimization coupling for water distribution network contamination source detection. *Sensors (Basel), 21*(4), 1157. doi:10.339021041157 PMID:33562175

Grigoras, G., Bizon, N., Enescu, F. M., Lopez Guede, J. M., Salado, G. F., Brennan, R., O'Driscoll, C., Dinka, M. O., & Alalm, M. G. (2018). ICT based smart management solution to realize water and energy savings through energy efficiency measures in water distribution systems. *2018 10th International Conference on Electronics, Computers and Artificial Intelligence (ECAI).* IEEE. 10.1109/ECAI.2018.8679012

Heddam, S., Sanikhani, H., & Kisi, O. (2019). Application of artificial intelligence to estimate phycocyanin pigment concentration using water quality data: A comparative study. *Applied Water Science, 9*(7), 164. doi:10.100713201-019-1044-3

Himeur, Y., Elnour, M., Fadli, F., Meskin, N., Petri, I., Rezgui, Y., Bensaali, F., & Amira, A. (2023). AI-big data analytics for building automation and management systems: A survey, actual challenges and future perspectives. *Artificial Intelligence Review, 56*(6), 4929–5021. doi:10.100710462-022-10286-2 PMID:36268476

Hmoud Al-Adhaileh, M., & Waselallah Alsaade, F. (2021). Modelling and prediction of water quality by using artificial intelligence. *Sustainability (Basel), 13*(8), 4259. doi:10.3390u13084259

Hyandye, C. B., Worqul, A., Martz, L. W., & Muzuka, A. N. N. (2018). The impact of future climate and land use/cover change on water resources in the Ndembera watershed and their mitigation and adaptation strategies. *Environmental Systems Research, 7*(1), 7. doi:10.118640068-018-0110-4

Icke, O., van Es, DM, de Koning, MF, Wuister, JJG, Ng, J., Phua, KM, Koh, YKK, Chan, WJ y Tao, G. (2020). Mejora del rendimiento de los procesos de tratamiento de aguas residuales mediante la aplicación de aprendizaje automático. *Water Science and Technology: A Journal of the International Association on Water Pollution Research, 82*(12), 2671–2680. . doi:10.2166/wst.2020.382

Islam, SMD-U., Mondal, PK, Ojong, N., Bodrud-Doza, M., Siddique, MAB, Hossain, M. y Mamun, MA (2021). Prácticas de agua, saneamiento, higiene y eliminación de desechos como estrategia de respuesta al COVID-19: perspectivas de Bangladesh. *Desarrollo y sustentabilidad ambiental, 23*(8), 11953–11974. . doi:10.1007/s10668-020-01151-9

Jawad, J., Hawari, A. H., & Javaid Zaidi, S. (2021). Artificial neural network *modeling of wastewater treatment and desalination using membrane processes: A review. Chemical Engineering Journal (Lausanne, Switzerland: 1996), 419*(129540), 129540. https://doi.org/. doi:10.1016/j.cej.2021.129540

Jones, J. A. A., Vardanian, T. G., & Hakopian, C. (Eds.). (2009). *Threats to global water security.* Springer Netherlands., doi:10.1007/978-90-481-2344-5

Jury, W. A., & Vaux, H. Jr. (2005). The role of science in solving the world's emerging water problems. *Proceedings of the National Academy of Sciences of the United States of America, 102*(44), 15715–15720. doi:10.1073/pnas.0506467102 PMID:16249337

Kadenge, J., Mandel, N., Mkandawile, M., & Grace Masanja, V. (2020). Multi-criteria decision making and numerical optimization approaches for optimizing water loss management strategies in water distribution system - A case of urban water supply and sanitation authorities in Tanzania. *International Journal of Mathematical Sciences and Computing*, *6*(1), 10–24. doi:10.5815/ijmsc.2020.01.02

Kanyangarara, M., Allen, S., Jiwani, S. S., & Fuente, D. (2021). Access to water, sanitation and hygiene services in health facilities in sub-Saharan Africa 2013-2018: Results of health facility surveys and implications for COVID-19 transmission. *BMC Health Services Research*, *21*(1), 601. doi:10.118612913-021-06515-z PMID:34172045

Karam, A., Zaher, K., & Mahmoud, A. S. (2020). Comparative studies of using nano zerovalent iron, activated carbon, and green synthesized nano zerovalent iron for textile wastewater color removal using artificial intelligence, regression analysis, adsorption isotherm, and kinetic studies. *Air, Soil and Water Research*, *13*, 117862212090827. doi:10.1177/1178622120908273

Karaouzas, I., Theodoropoulos, C., Vardakas, L., Kalogianni, E., & Th. Skoulikidis, N. (2018). A review of the effects of pollution and water scarcity on the stream biota of an intermittent Mediterranean basin. *River Research and Applications*, *34*(4), 291–299. doi:10.1002/rra.3254

Kayhomayoon, Z., Milan, S. G., Arya Azar, N., Bettinger, P., Babaian, F., & Jaafari, A. (2022). A simulation-optimization modeling approach for conjunctive water use management in a semi-arid region of Iran. *Sustainability (Basel)*, *14*(5), 2691. doi:10.3390u14052691

Khan, M. R., Voss, C. I., Yu, W., & Michael, H. A. (2014). Water resources management in the Ganges basin: A comparison of three strategies for conjunctive use of groundwater and surface water. *Water Resources Management*, *28*(5), 1235–1250. doi:10.100711269-014-0537-y

Kim, J., Lee, J., & Park, M. (2022). Identification of smartwatch-collected lifelog variables affecting body mass index in middle-aged people using regression machine learning algorithms and SHapley additive explanations. *Applied Sciences (Basel, Switzerland)*, *12*(8), 3819. doi:10.3390/app12083819

King, D. A. (2004). The scientific impact of nations. *Nature*, *430*(6997), 311–316. doi:10.1038/430311a PMID:15254529

Koop, S. H. A., & van Leeuwen, C. J. (2017). The challenges of water, waste and climate change in cities. *Environment, Development and Sustainability*, *19*(2), 385–418. doi:10.100710668-016-9760-4

Krishnan, S. R., Nallakaruppan, M. K., Chengoden, R., Koppu, S., Iyapparaja, M., Sadhasivam, J., & Sethuraman, S. (2022). Smart water resource management using Artificial Intelligence—A review. *Sustainability (Basel)*, *14*(20), 13384. doi:10.3390u142013384

Li, L., Pan, C., Ling, S., & Li, M. (2022). Ecological efficiency of urban industrial land in metropolitan areas: Evidence from China. *Land (Basel)*, *11*(1), 104. doi:10.3390/land11010104

Li, Q., Shi, Y., Lin, R., Qiao, W., & Ba, W. (2022). *A novel oil pipeline leakage detection method based on the sparrow search algorithm and CNN*. Measurement. *Measurement*, *204*(112122), 112122. doi:10.1016/j.measurement.2022.112122

Lin, L., Yang, H., & Xu, X. (2022). Effects of water pollution on human health and disease heterogeneity: A review. *Frontiers in Environmental Science, 10*, 880246. doi:10.3389/fenvs.2022.880246

Liu, Y., Ramin, P., Flores-Alsina, X., & Gernaey, K. V. (2023). *Transforming data into actionable knowledge for fault detection, diagnosis and prognosis in urban wastewater systems with AI techniques: A mini-review.* Process Safety and Environmental Protection : Transactions of the Institution of Chemical Engineers. *Process Safety and Environmental Protection, 172*, 501–512. doi:10.1016/j.psep.2023.02.043

Livingstone, S. J., Li, Y., Rutishauser, A., Sanderson, R. J., Winter, K., Mikucki, J. A., Björnsson, H., Bowling, J. S., Chu, W., Dow, C. F., Fricker, H. A., McMillan, M., Ng, F. S. L., Ross, N., Siegert, M. J., Siegfried, M., & Sole, A. J. (2022). Subglacial lakes and their changing role in a warming climate. *Nature Reviews. Earth & Environment, 3*(2), 106–124. doi:10.103843017-021-00246-9

Loftus, T. J., Tighe, P. J., Filiberto, A. C., Efron, P. A., Brakenridge, S. C., Mohr, A. M., Rashidi, P., Upchurch, G. R. Jr, & Bihorac, A. (2020). Artificial intelligence and surgical decision-making. *JAMA Surgery, 155*(2), 148–158. doi:10.1001/jamasurg.2019.4917 PMID:31825465

Lowe, M., Qin, R., & Mao, X. (2022). A review on machine learning, artificial intelligence, and smart technology in water treatment and monitoring. *Water (Basel), 14*(9), 1384. doi:10.3390/w14091384

Lv, M., Niu, X., Zhang, D., Ding, H., Lin, Z., Zhou, S., & Zhu, Y. (2023). A data-driven framework for spatiotemporal analysis and prediction of river water quality: A case study in Pearl River, China. *Water (Basel), 15*(2), 257. doi:10.3390/w15020257

Mahbooba, B., Timilsina, M., Sahal, R., & Serrano, M. (2021). Explainable Artificial Intelligence (XAI) to enhance trust management in intrusion detection systems using decision tree model. *Complexity, 2021*, 1–11. doi:10.1155/2021/6634811

Martinez Silva, A. (2022). *Análisis y presentación de información para el área de población y desarrollo del Fondo de Población de las Naciones Unidas (UNFPA).* Universidad de los. *Andes (Salta).*

Mashhadi, N., Shahrour, I., Attoue, N., El Khattabi, J., & Aljer, A. (2021). Use of machine learning for leak detection and localization in water distribution systems. *Smart Cities, 4*(4), 1293–1315. doi:10.3390martcities4040069

Montesinos-López, O. A., Montesinos-López, A., Pérez-Rodríguez, P., Barrón-López, J. A., Martini, J. W. R., Fajardo-Flores, S. B., Gaytan-Lugo, L. S., Santana-Mancilla, P. C., & Crossa, J. (2021). A review of deep learning applications for genomic selection. *BMC Genomics, 22*(1), 19. doi:10.118612864-020-07319-x PMID:33407114

Munawar, H. S., Ullah, F., Qayyum, S., Khan, S. I., & Mojtahedi, M. (2021). UAVs in disaster management: Application of integrated aerial imagery and Convolutional Neural Network for flood detection. *Sustainability (Basel), 13*(14), 7547. doi:10.3390u13147547

Najwa Mohd Rizal, N., Hayder, G., Mnzool, M., Elnaim, B. M. E., Mohammed, A. O. Y., & Khayyat, M. M. (2022). Comparison between regression models, support vector machine (SVM), and artificial neural network (ANN) in river water quality prediction. *Processes (Basel, Switzerland), 10*(8), 1652. doi:10.3390/pr10081652

Nandal, N., Singh, A., Kumar, M., & Tanwar, R. (2022). Healthcare based financial decision making system using artificial intelligence. [IJHS]. *International Journal of Health Sciences*, 11255–11267. doi:10.53730/ijhs.v6nS2.8025

Nasiri, H., Mohd Yusof, M. J., & Mohammad Ali, T. A. (2016). An overview to flood vulnerability assessment methods. *Sustainable Water Resources Management*, *2*(3), 331–336. doi:10.100740899-016-0051-x

Negm, A., Ma, X., & Aggidis, G. (2023). Review of leakage detection in water distribution networks. *IOP Conference Series. Earth and Environmental Science*, *1136*(1), 012052. doi:10.1088/1755-1315/1136/1/012052

Nikolaou, G., Neocleous, D., Christou, A., Kitta, E., & Katsoulas, N. (2020). Implementing sustainable irrigation in water-scarce regions under the impact of climate change. *Agronomy (Basel)*, *10*(8), 1120. doi:10.3390/agronomy10081120

Nourani, V., Elkiran, G., & Abba, S. I. (2018). Wastewater treatment plant performance analysis using artificial intelligence - an ensemble approach. *Water Science and Technology: A Journal of the International Association on Water Pollution Research, 78*(10), 2064–2076. https://doi.org/. doi:10.2166/wst.2018.477

Otterpohl, R., Grottker, M., and Lange, J., (1997). Sustainable water and waste management in urban areas. (1997). *Water science and technology: a journal of the International Association on Water Pollution Research, 35*(9). . doi:10.1016/S0273-1223(97)00190-X

Passos, A. L. L., Muniz, D. H. de F., Rangel, L. P., & Oliveira-Filho, E. C. (2019). *Selection of variables in the definition of a water quality index for the Brazilian Federal District.* Ambiente e Agua - An Interdisciplinary. *Revista Ambiente & Água*, *14*(4), 1. doi:10.4136/ambi-agua.2385

Ramos, M.-H., Bartholmes, J., & Thielen-del Pozo, J. (2007). Development of decision support products based on ensemble forecasts in the European flood alert system. *Atmospheric Science Letters*, *8*(4), 113–119. doi:10.1002/asl.161

Rong, G., Alu, S., Li, K., Su, Y., Zhang, J., Zhang, Y., & Li, T. (2020). Rainfall induced landslide susceptibility mapping based on Bayesian optimized random forest and gradient boosting decision tree models—A case study of Shuicheng County, China. *Water (Basel)*, *12*(11), 3066. doi:10.3390/w12113066

Safder, U., Kim, J., Pak, G., Rhee, G., & You, K. (2022). Investigating machine learning applications for effective real-time water quality parameter monitoring in full-scale wastewater treatment plants. *Water (Basel)*, *14*(19), 3147. doi:10.3390/w14193147

Sarker, B., & Keya, N., K., I. Mahir, F., M. Nahiun, K., Shahida, S., & A. Khan, R. (. (2021). Surface and ground water pollution: Causes and effects of urbanization and industrialization in South Asia. *Scientific Review (Singapore)*, *73*, 32–41. doi:10.32861r.73.32.41

Shiri, N., Shiri, J., Yaseen, Z. M., Kim, S., Chung, I.-M., Nourani, V., & Zounemat-Kermani, M. (2021). Development of artificial intelligence models for well groundwater quality simulation: Different modeling scenarios. *PLoS One*, *16*(5), e0251510. doi:10.1371/journal.pone.0251510 PMID:34043648

Sinagra, M., Nasello, C., Tucciarelli, T., Barbetta, S., Massari, C., & Moramarco, T. (2020). A self-contained and automated method for flood hazard maps prediction in urban areas. *Water (Basel), 12*(5), 1266. doi:10.3390/w12051266

Singh, A., Krause, A., Guestrin, C., & Kaiser, W. J. (2009). Efficient Informative Sensing using Multiple Robots. *Journal of Artificial Intelligence Research, 34*, 707–755. doi:10.1613/jair.2674

Singh, N. K., Yadav, M., Singh, V., Padhiyar, H., Kumar, V., Bhatia, S. K., & Show, P.-L. (2023). Artificial intelligence and machine learning-based monitoring and design of biological wastewater treatment systems. *Bioresource Technology, 369*(128486), 128486. doi:10.1016/j.biortech.2022.128486 PMID:36528177

Singh, R. B. (Ed.). (2015). *Urban development challenges, risks and resilience in Asian mega cities.* Springer Japan. doi:10.1007/978-4-431-55043-3

Slashchova, O., Yalanskyi, O., Slashchov, I., Kurinnyi, V., & Kulbach, A. (2023). Fuzzy logic methods for risk management at mining enterprises. *IOP Conference Series. Earth and Environmental Science, 1156*(1), 012015. doi:10.1088/1755-1315/1156/1/012015

Sohail, M. T., Elkaeed, E. B., Irfan, M., Acevedo-Duque, Á., & Mustafa, S. (2022). Determining farmers' awareness about climate change mitigation and wastewater irrigation: A pathway toward green and sustainable development. *Frontiers in Environmental Science, 10*, 900193. doi:10.3389/fenvs.2022.900193

Srinivasu, P. N., SivaSai, J. G., Ijaz, M. F., Bhoi, A. K., Kim, W., & Kang, J. J. (2021). Classification of skin disease using deep learning neural networks with MobileNet V2 and LSTM. *Sensors (Basel), 21*(8), 2852. doi:10.339021082852 PMID:33919583

Strokal, M., Bai, Z., Franssen, W., Hofstra, N., Koelmans, A. A., Ludwig, F., Ma, L., van Puijenbroek, P., Spanier, J. E., Vermeulen, L. C., van Vliet, M. T. H., van Wijnen, J., & Kroeze, C. (2021). Urbanization: An increasing source of multiple pollutants to rivers in the 21st century. *Npj Urban Sustainability, 1*(1), 24. Advance online publication. doi:10.103842949-021-00026-w

Sun, C., Parellada, B., Puig, V., & Cembrano, G. (2019). Leak localization in water distribution networks using pressure and data-driven classifier approach. *Water (Basel), 12*(1), 54. doi:10.3390/w12010054

Thierer, A. D., Castillo, A., & Russell, R. (2017). *Artificial intelligence and public policy.* SSRN Electronic Journal. doi:10.2139/ssrn.3021135

Thornton, P. K., & Herrero, M. (2010). *The inter-linkages between rapid growth in livestock production, climate change, and the impacts on water resources, land use, and deforestation.* The World Bank. . doi:10.1596/1813-9450-5178

Tien Bui, D., Pradhan, B., Lofman, O., Revhaug, I., & Dick, O. B. (2012). Landslide susceptibility assessment in the Hoa Binh province of Vietnam: A comparison of the Levenberg–Marquardt and Bayesian regularized neural networks. *Geomorphology, 171–172*, 12–29. doi:10.1016/j.geomorph.2012.04.023

Van Dijk, A. I. J. M., Renzullo, L. J., Wada, Y., & Tregoning, P. (2014). A global water cycle reanalysis (2003–2012) merging satellite gravimetry and altimetry observations with a hydrological multi-model ensemble. *Hydrology and Earth System Sciences, 18*(8), 2955–2973. doi:10.5194/hess-18-2955-2014

Vesović, M., & Jovanović, R. (2022). Adaptive neuro fuzzy Inference systems in identification, modeling and control: The state-of-the-art. *Tehnika, 77*(5), 439–446. doi:10.5937/tehnika2204439V

Williams, M. W. (2013). The status of glaciers in the Hindu Kush–Himalayan region. *Mountain Research and Development, 33*(1), 114. doi:10.1659/mrd.mm113

World Bank. (1999). *Pollution prevention and abatement handbook 1998: Toward cleaner production.* World Bank Publications.

World Health Organization(WHO). (1989). *Guidelines for the safe use of wastewater and excreta in agriculture and aquaculture: Measures for public health protection.* World Health Organization.

Wu, J., & Wang, Z. (2022). A hybrid model for water quality prediction based on an artificial neural network, wavelet transform, and long short-term memory. *Water (Basel), 14*(4), 610. doi:10.3390/w14040610

Xie, Y., Chen, Y., Lian, Q., Yin, H., Peng, J., Sheng, M., & Wang, Y. (2022c). Enhancing real-time prediction of effluent water quality of wastewater treatment plant based on improved feedforward neural network coupled with optimization algorithm. *Water (Basel), 14*(7), 1053. doi:10.3390/w14071053

Yan, J., Chen, X., Yu, Y., & Zhang, X. (2019). Application of a parallel particle swarm optimization-long short term memory model to improve water quality data. *Water (Basel), 11*(7), 1317. doi:10.3390/w11071317

Yang, J., Shi, Y., Yu, C., & Cao, S.-J. (2020). Challenges of using mobile phone signaling data to estimate urban population density: Towards smart cities and sustainable urban development. Indoor + Built Environment. *The Journal of the International Society of the Built Environment, 29*(2), 147–150. doi:10.1177/1420326X19893145

Yang, S., Liu, W., & Zhang, Z. (2022). The dynamic value of China's high-tech zones: Direct and indirect influence on urban ecological innovation. *Land (Basel), 11*(1), 59. doi:10.3390/land11010059

Yassin, M. M., Amr, S. S. A., & Al-Najar, H. M. (2006). Assessment of microbiological water quality and its relation to human health in Gaza Governorate, Gaza Strip. *Public Health, 120*(12), 1177–1187. doi:10.1016/j.puhe.2006.07.026 PMID:17034823

Yu, X., Ma, S., Cheng, K., & Kyriakopoulos, G. L. (2020). An evaluation system for sustainable urban space development based in green urbanism principles—A case study based on the Qin-Ba mountain area in China. *Sustainability (Basel), 12*(14), 5703. doi:10.3390u12145703

Chapter 13
Artificial Intelligence (AI) in the Sustainable Energy Industry

Cagla Ozen
https://orcid.org/0000-0003-1817-9806
Yeditepe University, Turkey

Ahmet Gedikli
Yeditepe University, Turkey

ABSTRACT

This chapter offers a comprehensive study on the impact of artificial intelligence (AI) in the sustainable energy industry. It aims to provide a detailed analysis of the potential applications, challenges, and opportunities that AI presents in the energy sector. To be able to accomplish this goal, a literature review was conducted on twelve papers directly or indirectly related to the subject. Their aims, methods, and main findings were included in the fourth section. A conclusion was reached by examining these contents. The findings indicate that AI has demonstrated significant advantages in the sustainable energy industry. It increased the efficiency of sustainable energy systems and had been used to improve their performance in different ways and tasks. Future opportunities of AI in this sector and a guideline for better use of AI were also included in the contents of this paper. Lastly, the limitations of this study and recommendations for future research were shared in the discussion.

INTRODUCTION

The mainstay of the global energy production has long been traditional energy sources like coal and oil. However, the environmental consequences of these sources have become increasingly evident, and the search for cleaner and more sustainable alternatives has intensified. "Sustainable energy can be defined as a form of energy that can be utilized again and again without putting a source in danger of getting depleted, expired, or vanished "(Junejo et al., 2018). Sustainable energy sources such as solar, wind, and hydro power have emerged as viable alternatives that can help reduce greenhouse gas emissions

DOI: 10.4018/979-8-3693-0373-3.ch013

and combat climate change. However, the implementation of these energy sources on a large scale is not without its challenges, which is where Artificial Intelligence (AI) can play a significant role.

AI is "the ability of a machine to perform cognitive functions that we associate with human minds, such as perceiving, reasoning, learning, interacting with the environment, problem solving, and even exhibiting creativity" (Collins et al., 2021). While doing such things, AI systems can operate independently without human intervention. AI technologies can be applied to various fields, including natural language processing, robotics, image and speech recognition, and decision-making systems. AI has the potential to transform many industries and improve human life in numerous ways, from healthcare to transportation and beyond. In this book chapter, uses of AI in the sustainable energy industry will be discussed.

ARTIFICIAL INTELLIGENCE (AI)

What is AI?

Artificial Intelligence (AI) refers to "the simulation of human intelligence by a system or a machine" (Xu et al., 2021). The goal of AI is to develop a machine that can think like humans and mimic human behaviors, such as perceiving, reasoning, learning, planning, predicting, and so on. The term AI was coined by John McCarthy in 1956 at a conference at Dartmouth College, which marked the birth of the AI research field (Toosi et al., 2022). Since then, AI has gone through several periods of progress and stagnation, known as summers and winters, depending on the availability of funding, data, and computing power. Some of the milestones of AI include the development of logic-based systems, expert systems, neural networks, natural language processing, computer vision, speech recognition, machine learning, and deep learning. Today, AI is widely used in various domains and applications that affect our daily lives. For example, AI powers the face ID feature on our smartphones that allows us to unlock our devices with biometrics. AI also enables smart assistants like Siri, Alexa, and Cortana to understand our voice commands and provide us with information and services. AI also helps us find relevant information on the web using search engines like Google and Bing that use sophisticated algorithms to rank and display results. AI also affects our preferences and decisions by making individualized recommendations for us on e-commerce websites like Amazon and Netflix as well as social networking sites like Facebook, Twitter, and Instagram. Along with changing individual industries, AI is also enhancing consumer experience, enhancing decision-making, and opening new prospects. For instance, AI is used in healthcare to identify illnesses, recommend treatments, track patients' states, and find novel medications. To give pupils adaptable learning alternatives, evaluate their performance, and provide feedback, AI is also applied in education. In cybersecurity, AI is also used to spot vulnerabilities, stop malicious attacks, and respond to incidents. AI is also used in entertainment to create realistic graphics, animations, and sounds for games and movies (Daley, 2023). In summary, AI is a powerful paradigm for scientific research that has a profound impact on various aspects of our society and culture. As AI continues to evolve and advance, it will offer more benefits and challenges for humanity.

Areas of Use

AI is a multipurpose technology with a big range of applications in different industries and areas. AI can complete tasks such as perception, reasoning, education, planning, prediction and so on, which requires a person's intelligence. Furthermore, AI can be used to simplify processes, analyze information, optimize systems, and create new opportunities. We can see examples of AI usage in the following areas.

- **Healthcare:** AI is being used in healthcare in various crucial areas such as living assistance, biomedical information processing, biomedical research, disease diagnostics and prediction and seizure and stroke prediction (Rong et al., 2020).
- **Finance:** AI applications in finance to mention are increasing each day. Fraud detection and compliance, banking chatbots and robot-advisory services, algorithmic trading, real estate business models and corporate governance contexts are the ones that are currently being used (Buchanan, 2019).
- **Education:** AI is becoming a very beneficial especially in education. The applications of AI in education are automatic writing evaluation, learning network orchestrators, language learning apps, AI collaborative learning, continuous assessment, AI learning companions, AI teaching assistants and AI research tools (Holmes et al., 2023).
- **Other:** It is highly challenging to restrict the applications of AI in a few domains since AI is being used in so many different parts in our lives. "We see the high-profile examples of AI including autonomous vehicles (such as drones and self-driving cars), medical diagnosis, creating art, playing games (such as Chess or Go), search engines (such as Google search), online assistants (such as Siri), image recognition in photographs, spam filtering, predicting flight delay etc." (Tai, 2020).

These are just some of the examples of how AI is applied in various domains. As AI continues to evolve and advance, it will offer more benefits and challenges for different industries and areas.

Benefits and Challenges

As indicated in the previous section AI has many applications and benefits for various domains and sectors in the modern world. AI can improve productivity, efficiency, innovation, and quality of life by automating processes, optimizing solutions, generating insights, and enhancing experiences. AI can also address some of the major challenges that humanity faces, such as climate change, poverty, health care, education, and security. AI can also create new possibilities for entertainment, communication, and expression.

AI also poses some significant challenges for our society and legal system, such as how to deal with social dilemmas where individual and collective interests are in conflict, how to assign legal liability and responsibility for the actions and outcomes of AI systems, and how to ensure that AI systems are transparent, accountable, fair, safe, and respectful of human dignity and autonomy. These challenges require moral, ethical, and legal reasoning and innovation, which may not be easy or consistent in AI systems or the current legal frameworks (Perc et al., 2019).

Perc et al. (2019) also provides this guideline about developing and using AI systems in a productive way:

- Ensure transparency and explain ability of AI systems, so that their functioning and decision making can be understood and verified by humans.
- Ensure accountability and oversight of AI systems, so that their actions and outcomes can be monitored and controlled by humans.

- Ensure human dignity and autonomy of AI systems, so that they respect and protect the rights and values of humans.
- Ensure fairness and justice of AI systems, so that they do not discriminate or harm any group or individual.
- Ensure safety and security of AI systems, so that they do not pose any physical or cyber risks to humans or other systems.

SUSTAINABLE ENERGY

What is Sustainable Energy?

Sustainable energy is a term that describes the energy sources that can meet the current and future needs of humanity without compromising the environment or the availability of resources. Sustainable energy sources are those that can be used repeatedly and are not in danger of expiring or being depleted (Raillani et al., 2022). Some examples of sustainable energy sources are solar, wind, hydro, geothermal, and biomass. These sources have low or zero greenhouse gas emissions and can reduce the dependence on fossil fuels that contribute to climate change and air pollution. Sustainable energy is essential for achieving the goals of the Paris Agreement and the United Nations Sustainable Development Goals (SDGs), which aim to ensure access to affordable, reliable, and clean energy for all people while protecting the planet and promoting social and economic development.

Benefits and Challenges

One of the many benefits of sustainable energy is that energy may be generated from it for free. As the sector expands, many new employments are being provided by the design and installation of tomorrow's renewable energy solutions. Renewable energy sources also make it easier for countries that are developing to access energy, which could result in lower energy prices. Indeed, one of the main benefits of renewable energy is that an important portion of it is recognized as clean and green energy. Therefore, the usage of renewable energy has increased with wind and solar power becoming especially popular. However not only renewable energy sources can offer these environmental benefits. Nuclear power also has no or very little carbon dioxide emissions, making it a carbon-free energy source. Some individuals prefer nuclear power to sources like solar and wind because it is a dependable source that is not reliant on the weather. This brings up a negative aspect of renewable energy (Jain, 2020).

As previously stated, it is not always possible to rely on the many renewable energy sources that exist. When the sun sets or is blocked by clouds, we cannot generate solar or wind power, and the opposite happens when there is no wind. As a result, some countries continue to use fossil fuels as a backup for their renewable energy resources. Because of the varying production capacity, large-scale storage mechanisms for energy are needed to ensure that there is always enough electricity available when the production of renewable energy decreases. Another option is to integrate a variety of renewable technologies to create a more flexible supply chain that can make up for drops in a specific source's production. Biomass and hydropower are two examples of renewable energy sources that don't have these supply problems, even though both resources have environmental problems. Additionally, neighbors who do not want to live next to some renewable energy sources, such as solar and wind farms, conflict with them (Jain, 2020).

AI IN SUSTAINABLE ENERGY INDUSTRY

Previous Work

This section reviews the existing literature about AI in the sustainable energy industry. It summarizes the aims, methods and the main findings of the previous papers that have contributed to the current state of knowledge in this field (See Table 1).

Table 1. Previous work on the existing literature about AI in the sustainable energy industry

Article	Aim(s)	Method(s)	Finding(s)
"Artificial intelligence in sustainable energy industry: Status Quo, challenges and opportunities" (Ahmad et al., 2021)	The aim of the paper is to offer a broad and detailed study of the effect of AI on the energy industry, including its potential applications, challenges, and opportunities. The paper also discusses the previous background of AI and the global energy industry, as well as the ethical applications of AI in the energy sector. The authors hope that this study will provide a general understanding of AI's potential significance and implementations in the sustainable energy industry and build the framework for identifying new strategic possibilities.	The article does not provide a detailed description of the methodology used in the study. However, it mentions that the authors conducted a broad and detailed study of the effect of AI in the energy industry, including its potential applications, drawbacks, and opportunities. The authors also identified key drivers and obstacles for AI, discussed the influence of AI in the energy sector, and delivered a critical viewpoint on the development of AI and its potential significance for the energy industry.	- AI has the potential to transform the energy industry by improving efficiency, reducing costs, and increasing sustainability. - AI can be used to optimize energy generation, distribution, and usage, as well as to improve energy storage and grid management. - AI can help to reduce energy waste and improve energy efficiency in buildings and transportation. - The integration of AI in the energy sector faces several challenges, including data quality, cybersecurity, and regulatory barriers. - The ethical implications of AI in the energy sector need to be carefully considered, including issues related to privacy, bias, and job displacement. - There are lots of opportunities for additional research and innovation in the field of AI and energy, including the development of new algorithms, the integration of AI with other technologies such as blockchain and IoT, and the exploration of new business models.
"Artificial intelligence for sustainable energy: A contextual topic modeling and content analysis" (Saheb et al., 2022)	The aim of this paper is to recognize the major academic subjects, sub-themes, and cross-topic issues in the scientific literature on sustainable AI in energy. The paper proposes a novel approach to modeling of contextual topics and content analysis achieve this aim. Additionally, the paper seeks to provide information regarding the productivity of science, draw attention to the problems requiring for more AI-based solutions, and encourage policymakers to create AI regulations that encourage the creation of sustainable algorithms and tools while minimizing the unintended consequences of non-sustainable energy sources and AI solutions.	The study uses a mixed-methodologies strategy which combines both quantitative and qualitative research methods. In their study, the authors drew from and used four complementary sets of research approaches. BERT, LDA topic modeling, and clustering are three of them that have ties to text mining methods. They included a qualitative topic-based content analysis to these quantitative findings as well. The mixed methods approach used by the authors is novel in three ways. Through a subject-based content analysis technique that includes examining the most pertinent papers within each topic, they conducted a qualitative review of the publications. They used computational techniques including BERT, LDA, and clustering to identify the important themes in the literature on sustainable AI in the energy sector. Finally, they combined these quantitative and qualitative findings to ensure that their results complemented one another.	- AI can boost the financial viability of new energy sources like solar and wind power. - By establishing distributed storage, processing, and analysis of data from renewable energy technologies, AI can offer answers to the issues brought on by the irregular nature of data on renewable energy. - AI can be used to evaluate renewable energy options in terms of their carbon footprint, cost of energy production, affordability of renewable resources, and efficiency of energy conversion. This ensures the most effective use of these resources while also promoting improved management and distribution networks. -By balancing the supply and demand of energy in real-time, AI can improve energy consumption and storage allocation. -The paper discusses the potential uses of sustainable AI in the energy sector, including energy management and optimization, renewable energy systems, energy storage systems, energy efficiency, energy policy and regulation, smart grid and microgrid systems, energy forecasting, and energy demand-side management. --In order to facilitate the development of environmentally friendly tools and algorithms and to lessen the unintended negative consequences of AI solutions and non-sustainable energy sources, the paper urges politicians to develop AI rules.

Continued on following page

Table 1. Continued

Article	Aim(s)	Method(s)	Finding(s)
"Quantum computing and quantum artificial intelligence for renewable and sustainable energy: A emerging prospect towards climate neutrality" (Ajagekar & You, 2022)	The aims of this article are to introduce quantum computing (QC) and quantum artificial intelligence (QAI) to the community of renewable and sustainable energy systems and to explore their possible applications in this area. The paper also analyzes the drawbacks of traditional computing methods for designing sustainable energy materials and proposes potential applications for energy sources that are clean and renewable that could use performance enhancements that are provided by quantum algorithms. The paper's authors believe that it will make it easier for users to fully understand and develop new quantum solutions to the challenging issues related to the establishment of macro-energy systems and sustainable energy sources.	As a review article, this paper does not have a specific methodology in the traditional sense. Instead, they gathered pertinent research on QC and QAI, examined their computational benefits, and offered potential uses for quantum algorithms in green and sustainable energy. The authors created their manuscript after conducting a literature review, summarizing the quantum techniques, and evaluating their computing advantages.	- Quantum computing and quantum AI have the potential to offer creative and scalable solutions for energy production and storage, which could assist in our efforts to become climate neutral. - The two fields where quantum computing approaches can be useful are quantum chemical computations and AI. - The efficiency of large-scale applications of classical quantum chemistry computations may be enhanced by quantum computing techniques in some circumstances due to their significant computational performance advantages. - The development of materials for sustainable energy generation and storage, as well as the adoption of renewable energy systems on a broader scale have been supported by improvements in quantum hardware and software, which have also sped up the development of quantum computing algorithms. - The drawbacks of quantum computing for bigger energy systems may be difficult to realize because of the limitations of current quantum devices.
"The Recent Development of Artificial Intelligence for Smart and Sustainable Energy Systems and Applications" (Lytras & Chui, 2019)	The aim of this paper is to bring insights into recent developments and emergent topics in the field of "Artificial Intelligence for Smart and Sustainable Energy Systems and Applications". It includes 11 papers and a review article that cover various topics and methodologies in this field. The guest editors have highlighted four types of newly emerging energy industry topics while summarizing the specifics of each effort.	The paper is a collection of 11 papers and a review article that cover various topics and methodologies in the field of "Artificial Intelligence for Smart and Sustainable Energy Systems and Applications". The methodologies used in the individual papers include support vector machines, genetic algorithms, bacterial foraging optimization, non-intrusive load monitoring techniques, flower pollination, long short-term memory, multiple kernel learning, decision tree models, and distributed genetic algorithms.	As an editorial paper, the main findings of this paper are not based on original research but rather on the insights and summaries provided by the guest editors of the 11 papers and the review article included in this special issue. The paper provides a quick review of each work and highlights four groups of emergent topics in the energy industry.
"Artificial Intelligence-Driven Circular Economy as a Key Enabler for Sustainable Energy Management" (Jose et al., 2020)	The purpose of this article is to promote the use of AI-related digital technologies to improve energy efficiency, enable carbon trading, and actualize governments' visions for a circular economy that would reduce extreme weather events and climate change.	There's no information about the methodology of the paper. Although, it provides information from various scientific articles. It can be stated that a literature review have been used.	Implementing AI-related digital technologies can assist in boosting energy efficiency, facilitating carbon trading, and realizing governments' circular economy visions to reduce extreme weather events and climate change. The paper argues that these solutions are necessary to address energy gaps and eliminate the challenging environmental consequences of energy supply chains to guarantee a high standard of living and sustainability.
"Application of Artificial Intelligence Methods for Hybrid Energy System Optimization" (Zahraee et al., 2016)	This paper's goal is to examine the research on several AI methods for hybrid energy system optimization, including genetic algorithms (GAs), simulated annealing (SA), and particle swarm optimization (PSO). The report also analyzes the features of all methods to help researchers in making efficient and economical use of them.	There's no information about the methodology used in the paper. However, it is mentioned that the paper reviews the literature related to the subject.	The study offers an overview of the literature relating to various AI methodologies for hybrid energy systems optimization. - To assist researchers in using each technique efficiently and successfully, the paper compares its features. - According to the review, problems involving renewable energy are typically solved using heuristic optimization techniques, particularly GAs and PSOs. - There is also usage of more conventional optimization methods as Nelder-Mead simplex search, Lagrangian relaxation, mixed-integer and interval linear programming, and quadratic programming. - Hybrid optimization approaches have been put out to integrate two or more methodologies to enhance them and speed up their convergence. -The paper concludes that additional study may open the door to hybridization and multi-objective applications of bio-inspired solutions.

Continued on following page

Table 1. Continued

Article	Aim(s)	Method(s)	Finding(s)
"Latest avenues and approaches for biohydrogen generation from algal towards sustainable energy optimization: Recent innovations, artificial intelligence, challenges, and future perspectives" (Zhang et al., 2023)	The paper aims to provide a comprehensive review of the latest approaches and innovations in biohydrogen generation from algal sources, with a focus on sustainable energy optimization and a greener environment. The authors also discuss the challenges faced in this field and the potential future applications of biohydrogen as a sustainable energy source. Additionally, the paper explores the use of AI in optimizing biohydrogen production.	There's no information about the methodology of the paper. Although, it provides information from various scientific articles. It can be stated that a literature review has been conducted.	AI models are among the simplest and most reliable mathematical models for predicting the results of the process of producing biohydrogen from algae. With the use of these models, AI promises to greatly boost the amount of green hydrogen production. The successful estimation of hydrogen generation using artificial neural network (ANN) models is also covered in the paper; the estimation of hydrogen generation has a correlation coefficient of 0.989.
"Artificial intelligence for planning of energy and waste management" (Huang & Koroteev, 2021)	This paper's goal is to present a machine learning-driven predictive analytical framework (MLDPAF) for waste management and energy planning. The authors contend that reliable data collection is necessary to support planning procedures in the efficient planning of waste management and that effective environmental protection depends on the quality of the information available for sound decision-making. The MLDPAF is designed to predict waste output and improve waste collection and energy costs through the use of machine learning.	The authors review related works and study findings to support the development of the MLDPAF. They then analyze the applicability of the MLDPAF beyond waste management systems and compare it to other methods. The authors also provide statistical analysis and graphs to illustrate the effectiveness of the proposed method.	- The proposed Machine learning-driven Predictive Analytic framework (MLDPAF) is effective in predicting waste output and improving waste collection and energy costs through the use of machine learning. - The MLDPAF significantly increases the waste analysis of results compared to related works. - The MLDPAF gives a higher percentage of waste quantities calculated compared to other methods. - The MLDPAF gives a complete simulation analysis of a wide range of features on recognizing several difficulties in energy and waste management and has been verified by multiple voting techniques.In-depth modeling and analysis are crucial for developing and validating both new and existing structures. The authors claim that reliable data collection is crucial to facilitating planning procedures in the effective planning of waste management and that effective environmental protection depends on the quality of information available for proper decision-making.
"Artificial intelligence on economic evaluation of energy efficiency and renewable energy technologies" (Chen et al., 2021)	The purpose of this research is to suggest the Artificial Intelligence-based Useful Evaluation Model (AIEM) for predicting the financial impacts of renewable energy sources and energy efficiency. The AIEM model assesses, examines, and develops a model centered on AI and economic indicators required for the economic projection for renewable energy sources. The research also introduces AIEM as a practical assessment model for forecasts of energy saving and efficiency.	The methodology of this paper involves the use of AIEM to accurately quantify renewable energy and life-saving practices in order to forecast the economy. Economic evaluation rate and energy efficiency are used to validate the AIEM model. The paper also includes a literature study to provide insights into the background studies and a discussion of the AIEM model's architecture and requirements. Finally, the paper concludes with a validation of the results and a summary of the research.	- The proposed AIEM model is an effective evaluation model for forecasts of energy saving and efficiency. - When compared to other existing methodologies, AIEM obtains the highest energy efficiency rate based on economic evaluation rate. - The AIEM model compares, evaluates, and enhances a model that employs AI and economic metrics pertinent to the economic projection for renewable energy sources. - The life cycle prices, scale investment, and the present total price for an investment rate over the product lifecycle make up the economic analysis. - The proposed model can lead to an increase in renewable energy utilization and a 97.32% improvement in energy efficiency.

Continued on following page

Table 1. Continued

Article	Aim(s)	Method(s)	Finding(s)
"Renewable energy: Present research and future scope of Artificial Intelligence" (Jha et al., 2017)	The aim of this paper is to summarize the current state-of-the-art research outcomes related to various renewable energy sources and the role of AI in achieving the future goals of renewable energy. The paper also discusses the potential of AI approaches in the control, decision, simulation, and optimization of renewable energy systems.	The paper is a review article that provides an overview of the present state of research and development in both single and hybrid renewable energy systems. The authors have conducted a comprehensive literature review of various research reports, case studies, and articles related to renewable energy and AI. The paper presents a critical analysis of the existing literature and highlights the potential of AI approaches in improving the effectiveness of renewable energy systems.	- The paper provides a comprehensive overview of various renewable energy sources, including bioenergy, solar energy, hydrogen energy, hydro energy, geothermal energy, wind energy, ocean energy, and hybrid RE. - The paper highlights the potential of AI approaches in improving the performance of renewable energy systems. The authors discuss the role of AI in control, decision, optimization and simulation of renewable energy systems. - The paper presents case studies and real-world examples of the successful implementation of AI approaches in renewable energy systems. - The authors suggest that there is a need for further research to investigate the potential of AI approaches in novel and hybrid renewable energy sources. - The paper concludes that the effective utilization of AI approaches can significantly improve the performance of renewable energy systems, leading to a more sustainable future.
"An artificial intelligence-based solar radiation prophesy model for green energy utilization in energy management system" (Alassery et al., 2022)	The aim or goal of this paper is to propose an AI-based solar radiation prediction model for green energy usage in energy management systems. The paper discusses the challenges of assuring reliable, cheap, and secure management of power in solar energy systems and how AI can help overcome these challenges.	The paper proposes a stochastic technique for solar radiation forecasting that utilizes AI algorithms such as the artificial neural network (ANN) and the support vector regression (SVR) model. The proposed technique is based on the integration of the ANN and SVR models to create a hybrid model that can provide more accurate solar radiation forecasts. The paper also discusses the data used in the study, which was obtained from the National Renewable Energy Laboratory (NREL) and covers a period of one year.	The proposed AI-based solar radiation prophesy model can significantly improve the accuracy of solar radiation forecasting. The results showed that the ANN algorithm outperformed the SVR and random forest (RF) algorithms, with an MAE of 0.9558 (training phase) and 1.7853 (testing phase) and an MFE of 0.4456 (training phase) and 0.5621 (testing phase). The paper also suggests that the proposed technique can be applied to other renewable energy sources such as wind, thermal, and hydropower generation.
"Artificial Intelligence Techniques in Smart Grid and Renewable Energy Systems—Some Example Applications" (Bose, 2017)	The aim of this paper is to discuss the applications of AI techniques in smart grid (SG) and renewable energy systems (RESs). The paper provides specific examples of how AI can be used for automated design, simulation, and control of wind generation systems, health monitoring of wind generation systems, fault pattern identification of SG subsystems, and master control of SG based on real-time simulation.	The methodology of the paper involves reviewing the basic features of AI relevant to smart grid and renewable energy systems, and providing specific examples of AI applications in these systems.	- The paper discusses the applications of AI techniques in SG and RESs. - Specific examples of AI applications in these systems are provided, including automated design, simulation, and control of wind generation systems, health monitoring of wind generation systems, fault pattern identification of SG subsystems, and master control of SG based on real-time simulation. - The basic AI characteristics that are relevant to various applications are briefly reviewed in the paper. - The results suggest that AI has the potential to revolutionize power electronics and power engineering, and can be used for design, simulation, control, estimation, fault diagnostics, and fault-tolerant control in modern industrial systems.

Future Opportunities

As mentioned in the findings of the papers that have been reviewed, AI is currently being used for different tasks and improvements in the sustainable energy industry. Ahmad et al. (2021) argues that there are many future opportunities for AI to keep improving and enhancing the sustainable energy industry to help increase sustainability of humans. The authors identify several areas where AI can be used to improve energy efficiency, reduce costs, and increase sustainability, including:

- The development of new algorithms and models to optimize energy production, distribution, and consumption.
- The integration of AI with other technologies such as blockchain and IoT to create more efficient and secure energy systems.
- The exploration of new business models that leverage AI to create new value propositions and revenue streams.
- The use of AI to improve energy storage and grid management, including the development of predictive maintenance and control systems.
- The application of AI to reduce energy waste and improve energy efficiency in buildings and transportation.

In another paper (Jha et al., 2017), the authors suggest that there is a need for further research to explore the potential of AI approaches in novel and hybrid renewable energy sources. They also highlight the importance of developing new AI-based tools and techniques for the control, decision, simulation, and optimization of renewable energy systems. They conclude that the effective utilization of AI approaches can significantly improve the performance of renewable energy systems, leading to a more sustainable future.

CONCLUSION

This book chapter aimed to discuss the current and possible future uses of AI in the sustainable energy industry by reviewing 12 scientific papers, examining their aims, methods, and findings.

Upon the findings from the literature review, it can be indicated that AI has demonstrated significant advantages in the sustainable energy industry. It increased the efficiency of sustainable energy systems and had been used to improve their performance in different ways and tasks. This argument is based on the results of the literature review that had been conducted. The reviews also revealed that AI can be used to optimize energy production, distribution, and consumption, as well as to improve energy storage and grid management. AI can improve the cost-effectiveness of new sources of energy such as solar and wind electricity. Quantum computing and quantum AI have the potential to provide innovative and scalable solutions for energy production and storage, which can help us achieve climate neutrality. The reviews also revealed the remarkable effectiveness of AI supported models and frameworks in various energy-related applications. The reviews showed that AI models and frameworks can provide accurate and reliable predictions, forecasts, and analyses of the outputs of different systems or processes that are involved in energy production, distribution, consumption, and storage. Some of the examples of these systems or processes are biohydrogen generation from algae, waste output prediction and management, energy efficiency and energy conservation assessment, solar radiation forecasting for renewable energy generation, and smart grid and renewable energy system optimization and control.

Despite the benefits, the reviews revealed that the implementation of AI in the sustainable energy sector can face some possible challenges. These challenges include data quality, cybersecurity, and regulatory barriers and ethical concerns. One of the papers suggest that the ethical implications of AI in the energy sector need to be carefully considered, including issues related to privacy, bias, and job displacement.

In conclusion, all the reviews showed that AI is being used to increase efficiency and improve performance in sustainable energy systems. Some of the findings stated the current and possible challenges of the implementation of AI in the sustainable energy industry. However, it was significantly clear that the current benefits and possible future uses of AI was way more prominent when compared to the concerns. It is also possible to argue that the usage areas and rates of AI in the sustainable or renewable energy industry will continue increasing as AI technologies improve in time.

The results indicate that AI has the potential to transform the sustainable energy industry by improving effectiveness and performance. Many results from the literature review that had been conducted can be used to support this argument. However, there were a few limitations during the development of this book chapter. One limitation of this literature review was the number of papers reviewed. Due to time and resource constraints, all the relevant studies on the topic could not be included in the reviews. That is to say, the generalizability of this research could be considered as a discussion. Recommendations for the future studies include increasing the generalizability by using more resources and looking into the most recent uses of AI in the sustainable energy industry since the AI technologies are improving notably fast.

REFERENCES

Ahmad, T., Zhang, D., Huang, C. C., Zhang, H., Dai, H., Song, Y., & Chen, H. (2021). Artificial intelligence in sustainable energy industry: Status Quo, challenges and opportunities. *Journal of Cleaner Production, 289*, 125834. doi:10.1016/j.jclepro.2021.125834

Ajagekar, A., & You, F. (2022). Quantum computing and quantum artificial intelligence for renewable and sustainable energy: A emerging prospect towards climate neutrality. *Renewable & Sustainable Energy Reviews, 165*, 112493. doi:10.1016/j.rser.2022.112493

Alassery, F., Alzahrani, A. I., Khan, A., Irshad, K., & Kshirsagar, S. R. (2022). An artificial intelligence-based solar radiation prophesy model for green energy utilization in energy management system. *Sustainable Energy Technologies and Assessments, 52*, 102060. doi:10.1016/j.seta.2022.102060

Bose, B. K. (2017). Artificial Intelligence Techniques in Smart Grid and Renewable Energy Systems—Some Example Applications. *Proceedings of the IEEE, 105*(11), 2262–2273. doi:10.1109/JPROC.2017.2756596

Buchanan, B. (2019). Artificial intelligence in finance. In Zenodo *(CERN European Organization for Nuclear Research)*. European Organization for Nuclear Research. https://doi.org/ doi:10.5281/zenodo.2626454

Chen, C., Yuhan, H., Karuppiah, M., & Kumar, P. M. (2021). Artificial intelligence on economic evaluation of energy efficiency and renewable energy technologies. *Sustainable Energy Technologies and Assessments, 47*, 101358. doi:10.1016/j.seta.2021.101358

Collins, C. M., Dennehy, D., Conboy, K., & Mikalef, P. (2021). Artificial intelligence in information systems research: A systematic literature review and research agenda. *International Journal of Information Management, 60*, 102383. doi:10.1016/j.ijinfomgt.2021.102383

Daley, S. (2023). 36 Artificial Intelligence Examples Shaking Up Business Across Industries. *Built In.* https://builtin.com/artificial-intelligence/examples-ai-in-industry

Holmes, W., Bialik, M., & Fadel, C. (2023). Artificial intelligence in education. *Data Ethics : Building Trust : How Digital Technologies Can Serve Humanity.*, 621–653. doi:10.58863/20.500.12424/4276068

Huang, J., & Koroteev, D. (2021). Artificial intelligence for planning of energy and waste management. *Sustainable Energy Technologies and Assessments*, *47*, 101426. doi:10.1016/j.seta.2021.101426

Jain, D. (2020). Renewable Energy: Powering a Safer Future. *Renewable Energy*, *1*(3).

Jha, S. K., Bilalovic, J., Jha, A., Patel, N., & Zhang, H. (2017). Renewable energy: Present research and future scope of Artificial Intelligence. *Renewable & Sustainable Energy Reviews*, *77*, 297–317. doi:10.1016/j.rser.2017.04.018

Jose, R., Panigrahi, S. K., Patil, R. A., Fernando, Y., & Ramakrishna, S. (2020). Artificial Intelligence-Driven Circular Economy as a Key Enabler for Sustainable Energy Management. *Mater Circ Econ*, *2*(1), 8. doi:10.100742824-020-00009-9

Junejo, F., Saeed, A., & Hameed, S. (2018). 5.19 Energy Management in Ocean Energy Systems. In *Elsevier eBooks* (pp. 778–807). Elsevier BV. doi:10.1016/B978-0-12-809597-3.00539-3

Lytras, M. D., & Chui, K. T. (2019). The Recent Development of Artificial Intelligence for Smart and Sustainable Energy Systems and Applications. *Energies*, *12*(16), 3108. doi:10.3390/en12163108

Perc, M., Ozer, M., & Hojnik, J. (2019). Social and juristic challenges of artificial intelligence. *Palgrave Communications*, *5*(1), 61. doi:10.105741599-019-0278-x

Raillani, B., Mezrhab, A., Amraqui, S., Moussaoui, M. A., & Mezrhab, A. (2022). Regression-based spatial GIS analysis for an accurate assessment of renewable energy potential. *Energy for Sustainable Development*, *69*, 118–133. doi:10.1016/j.esd.2022.06.003

Rong, G., Mendez, A., Assi, E. B., Zhao, B., & Sawan, M. (2020). Artificial Intelligence in Healthcare: Review and Prediction Case Studies. *Engineering (Beijing)*, *6*(3), 291–301. doi:10.1016/j.eng.2019.08.015

Saheb, T., Dehghani, M., & Saheb, T. (2022). Artificial intelligence for sustainable energy: A contextual topic modeling and content analysis. *Sustainable Computing: Informatics and Systems*, *35*, 100699. doi:10.1016/j.suscom.2022.100699

Tai, M. C. (2020). The impact of artificial intelligence on human society and bioethics. *Tzu-Chi Medical Journal*, *32*(4), 339. doi:10.4103/tcmj.tcmj_71_20 PMID:33163378

Toosi, A., Bottino, A., Saboury, B., Siegel, E., & Rahmim, A. (2022). A brief history of AI: How to prevent another winter (a critical review). *PET Clinics*, *16*(4), 449–469. doi:10.1016/j.cpet.2021.07.001 PMID:34537126

Xu, Y., Liu, X., Cao, X., Huang, C., Liu, E., Qian, S., Liu, X., Wu, Y., Dong, F., Qiu, C., Qiu, J., Hua, K., Su, W., Wu, J., Xu, H., Han, Y., Fu, C., Yin, Z., Liu, M., & Zhang, J. (2021). Artificial intelligence: A powerful paradigm for scientific research. *Innovation (Cambridge (Mass.))*, *2*(4), 100179. doi:10.1016/j.xinn.2021.100179 PMID:34877560

Zahraee, S. M., Assadi, M. K., & Saidur, R. (2016). Application of Artificial Intelligence Methods for Hybrid Energy System Optimization. *Renewable & Sustainable Energy Reviews*, *66*, 617–630. doi:10.1016/j.rser.2016.08.028

Zhang, G., Liu, J., Pan, X., Abed, A. M., Le, B. N., Ali, H. E., & Ge, Y. (2022). Latest avenues and approaches for biohydrogen generation from algal towards sustainable energy optimization: Recent innovations, artificial intelligence, challenges, and future perspectives. *International Journal of Hydrogen Energy*. Advance online publication. doi:10.1016/j.ijhydene.2022.10.224

Chapter 14
Comprehensive Environmental Management System Report in Specific Sugar Mill, India:
A Case Study Using SWOT Analysis – Road Map and Diffusion of EMS, Classification of the Environmental Management System

X. Agnello J. Naveen
Thanthai Roever Institute of Agriculture and Rural Development (TRIARD), India

C. Parameswari
Thanthai Roever Institute of Agriculture and Rural Development (TRIARD), India

Arivoli
Government Arts College, Bharathidasan University, India

Saratha
Thanthai Roever Institute of Agriculture and Rural Development (TRIARD), India

M. Prashanthi Devi
Bharathidasan University, India

Rajkumar
https://orcid.org/0000-0001-7605-2577
V.O. Chidambaram College, India

ABSTRACT

The sugar industry's contribution towards the production level is a substantial negative externality and "trade-off" caused by the industrial sector due to trade-off on the environmental front and genuine concern. This chapter is application-oriented to a precise environmental management system in a simple way of demonstration in a combination of enhancing management systems like recycling, reusing, green chemistry, energy and quality management system, acceptable housekeeping practices. This environmental management system reinforces a holistic approach with different data survey cross-check list in the manufacturing industry. Methods used are in a qualitative and quantitative to: 1. Interview schedule method, and 2. Calculate net savings and payback, saving cost, and environment advantages per year. EMS in developed countries like India is still in the rudimentary stage.

DOI: 10.4018/979-8-3693-0373-3.ch014

INTRODUCTION

Environmental Management System (EMS) was started in 1996 to achieve a holistic approach in production, update new technology, Accountability, and understand the ecological sustainability towards the annual target, This has been classified into many dimensions with different techniques from every sector, starting from smaller, medium and large firm depends on productivity, size, and finance (Miles 1999: Ammenberg and Hjelm 2003: Viranda et al. 2020). This paper focuses on the Manufacturing firms/Corporates (Sector) (Melnyk et al. 2003; Wu and Chang 2020) has given a more significant focus on the implementation of system-based criteria like a plan, do, check, and act (PDCA) framework with stringent regulation policy (Pacana and Ulewicz 2017; Căpuşneanu et al. 2020), which is a known fact envisage all the dimension and connects every factor like Top-level management, Accountability, like productivity, operational inputs and outputs, cost-Advantages analysis, environmental sustainability, record documentation, and review. It also includes proactive structures like LCA (Life cycle assessment) (Gallego-Schmid and Tarpani 2019). Furthermore, total quality management (Abbas 2020) in all manufacturing sectors is less than 40,000, including manufacturing sectors, Educational institutions, research and development sectors, hospitals, construction sites, and companies worldwide. To bring sustainable growth in every aspect. This approach changes the negative aspects of positive aspects and makes the productivity trend higher. It also focuses more on the account's grassroots problems and always makes diffusion and different road maps. It also adds to the energy management system (EnMS), Quality Management system (QMS) (Ann et al. 2006; Purwanto et al. 2020), occupational health and safety of the laborers (working committee), Good housekeeping practices, insurances, fire, and safety, material (resources) and energy flows, and corporate social responsibility (CSR). For adoption of EMS, variables are considered like Firm size, sunk costs, Foreign customers, economic opportunities, newer technology, crafted regulation may generate, environmental commitment, cutting costs, Incentives for certification, Environmental regulations to maintain Eco-balance in the right way this is called Integrated management strategy (IMS) or multiple management (Bernardo et al. 2009: Purwanto et al. 2020; Putri et al. 2020: Naveen et al. 2022j) this for Environmental sustainable and management accounting (Albelda 2011:Agnello et al. 2015: Sands et al. 2015; da Rosa et al. 2020) concept of adaptive control (Allan and Stankey, 2009) brings a proactive corporate environmental management system (Berry and Rondinelli, 1998; Amir et al. 2020) to mitigate the climate change (Mishra 2020).

ROAD MAP AND DIFFUSION OF EMS

The environmental management system was founded in 1992 by a British standards institution (technical standard guidelines/guidance) with international organization standards ISO-14000 series. These were followed around 171 countries to improvise their management; the application objective has a successful process with a balanced raw material used to create a sustainable environment in raw material consumption, training, and environmental perspective on credibility, transparency, Validation, verification, administration reporting, expansion, enrichment, upgrading technology on self-determination and self-declaration with a competitive advantage to improve public perception in business and reduce trade barriers by controlling internal goals Alberti et al. 2000: Hui et al. 2001: Johnstone 2020). There are multiple elementary audits on handling 14000 series standards enlisted into 13 categories. EMS is given 14001 and been revised version from the year 1996, 2004, 2015, 2016, 2019 in 300,000 company

(Tatoglu et al. 2020) has certifications, connection to this there are additional tools to provide like Environmental management information system (EMIS) (Chaudhry et al. 2020) and Environmental database system management (EDMS) (Warner 1993).

Statement of Problem

The case study is pilot research that focuses on the environmental management system to determine the different dimensions and perspectives like Socio-ecological, evidence, Providing valuable insights, Continuous improvement, Long-term and short-term goals, high turnover. Still, manufacturing firms have a different focus on pollution control issue that damages the environment like the trade-off concepts by polluting air, water, soil, hazardous and solid waste disposal, risk assessment, disaster management Odor, noise which are the factors that include government regulation changes time to time and this has to be tested with precision and error (Calibrated), record and documented for future insight, Providing with less manufacturing technology at low cost by an EMS-audit model in the manufacturing industry.

Figure 1 Aerial view of select sugar industry

Materials and Methods

The prepared environmental management system (EMS) 14001:2015 is a framework on Multi- criteria decision support system, making a sustainable future, a systematic approach like compiling data sheet for Environmental management was prepared depending on variables and factors on Audit. Table 2 discusses five main components on general identification, road map, and EMS diffusion, 2. They are finding the gaps and analyzing EMS, 3. Cost-Advantages, advantage, and finding critical gaps in technology adoption. 4. Review and feedback, 5. Adaptation of new technology. The data are a secondary source retrieved from Energy Engineers, Financial Auditor, Electricity board (EB), and environmental Managers. The data have two parts; qualitative analysis is done by giving scores Note-Yes (✔), No (✗), Survey- based research (Exploratory methodology) Considering accurate secondary data collected from the Third-party, and Central pollution control board, annual management report. The survey questionnaire and Data analysis are done on the essential criteria of Planning, Evaluation, Feasibility and implementing, on doing qualitative survey analysis - Strongly Agree, Agree, Neutral, Strongly disagree, Disagree, and quantitative analysis like cross-checking with older reports, cost analysis, calculation of cost and loss, environmental advantages (Sroufe 2003: Hughey et al. 2005; Ashley and Boyd 2006; Dahlmann et al. 2008; Nawrocka and Parker 2009; Molina-Azorín et al. 2015: Guerrero-Baena et al. 2015; Hutter and bailey 2020).

Cost Analysis Parameter

The cost variables involve Initial investment (Maintaiance+ Service+ Operation+ Building cost) = Operating Cost, LCA-life cycle assessment of a mechanism in years, Savings, Advantages (Benefits gained), Feldman et al. 1996; Kleindorfer 1997; Steger 2000; Alberti et al. 2000; Kwak, and Ibbs 2000; Bartolomeo et al. 2000, Hui et al. 2001)

Methods

The Method adopted is Simple net saving per year (Venkatesan and Kundu 2020). Moreover, Payback in months (Gorgulu and Kocabey 2020) has given below.

A net profit per annum in ₹ = Yearly savings- yearly operating cost Payback in months = (Initial Investment /net profit/ year) * 12

They can conclude this by using a SWOT qualitative analysis method (Pesce et al. 2018: Mucunguzi et al. 2021: Hwang 2022: Voukkali and Zorpas 2022).

Table 1. Roadmap and diffusion of technological changes in the specific sugar industry

S. no	Description	Date
1	The started sugars and chemicals supplying raw materials M/S SPB	1982
2	The pith from depicting bagasse is used as fuel along with other Energy to meet the steam requirement	1984
3	Sugar mill installs capacity to crush 1250 tonnes per MT	1984
4	These expanded the capacity to 2500 TCD	1994
5	4750 TCD, crushing consistently 100% and crushing ranges from 6.0 to 6.5 lakhs	2012
6	New company in Pooni sugar	1999
7	QMS:ISO:9002, Up-gradation QMS:ISO 9001:2008	1999
8	Installed ETP for processing	1999
9	Installed 15 MW, Co-gen power plant, using 100 percent Biomass	1999
10	ETP water used for irrigation inside the factory and adjacent colony	2001
11	Green Belt TNPCB in 3522 and targeted 8522 trees to be planted	2003
12	ESP for sugar mill	2003
13	The specific sugar mill got EMS-ISO:14001:2004 in	2004
14	SPM and SPB bring under irrigation about 1000 acres of lift irrigation(waste getting converted sludge)	2005
15	10 percent of production supplied as levy sugar to a govt agency	2005
16	Molasses are supplied to cattle fields, Ethanol, and the alcohol industry	2005
17	Reduction ETP water, freshwater consumption, and recycling of ETP water	2006
18	ESP field 3 installed joining with Co-generation	2009
19	ETP sludge and press muds (organic matter, NPK, and micronutrient	2009
20	Best technical efficiency of using energy conversion	2009
21	RO (UF) (MF) membrane to recycle the water	2010
22	Fully semi-automated the industry	2011
23	Waste cane seeding project to enhance the production capacity	2013

EMS-14001 Procedures

The datasheet of the EMS sheet is prepared in a step-by-step process in critical reviewing criteria. There are a variety of variables present in the study. Every single piece of data is taken into account. These factors were classified into four major components: grass root for decision- making related to green marketing, manufacturing, and production. The Input production level compares with the output pollution level, and a benchmark is set by norm (standard), A). The mandatory requirements, B). Classification of the Environmental management system (EMS), C). Legal framework and Logical necessity, D). Audit result. PDCA assessment gives a holistic process of EMS Audit.

Mandatory Requirement

The Verity of the required information is collected, as shown in the table: 1 shows (25 variables) with different elements required like an auditor, production capacity, time, date, decision- making, etc., every record is essential is documented. These are considered cross-checked in a trial and error method because this is an original dataset for further and future audit requirements/reference. This Sugar industry has been found operational since 1984 in Erode District, Tamil Nadu has a capacity of 2750 TCD to 4750 TCD from 2010 given in Table:1 And also falls in the Ultra-red categories industry (Most polluting) (Agnello et al. 2019c), So to this industry case study is done by conducting Environmental Management system (EMS).

Table 2. Interview data schedule in Environmental management system (EMS) in the specific sugar industry

S.no	Factors and variables	Elements or present status
A. Mandatory requirement		
1	Name of the factory	Special Sugar industry
2	Location and Mapping of Industry	Map figure.1, Tamil Nadu, India
3	The company started, capacity	1984-2500 TCD, 2011-4750, Road map of technology changes Table;1
4	The total area of the plant	3.4976 hectares, Building area-0.80 hectares, Vacant land-1.53hectres, Solid waste storage- 0.0076,
5	Green belt area	1.16 hectares
6	Product manufactured	Sugar, Bagasse, Molasses, Press muds Energy
7	Date of Operation	21-01-2020
8	Date of Audit reporting	22-01-2020
9	The time of the Audit started.	10.30 A.M.
10	Industrial pollution categories	Ultra-Red (most poLluting industry, Large scale, EIA- Annexure B,
11	Capacity in Tonne per day	4750
12	Environmental management budget	50,00,000 per annum
13	Stakeholder	1200 framers
14	Total population	Around the industrial zone
15	Total investment cost	37,00,000
16	Pollution control investment	Rs.2 crores
17	Number of operating days	170-210 depending on raw material usage of sugar cane yield
18	Average crushing rate	2595
19	Sugar produced	43030
20	List of products/by-products manufactured.	Sugar recovered (%) 09.76,Bagasse-27.85,Filter cake (%)-12.86,Molasses (%)-04.69
21	The quantity of sugar Bagged	443405
22	Number of cultivators	7475
23	Employee	Skilled, unskilled workers 600 shift-1, shift-2
24	Auditing of QMS, EMS	$_{8}$ 2004, 2008
25	Environmental management audit	--
B. Classification of the Environmental management system (EMS)		

S.no	Factors and variables	Elements or present status			
1	Year of certification, Environmental Management system	2005			
2	Environmental + Energy	-			
3	Envionmental+Energy+Quality	**Yes**			
4	Mandatory requirement Fire and Safety or Occupational health and safety	- -			
5	Has the organization defined an Environmental Management System accordingly, by ISO 14000?	Yes			
6	Are the specialized skills, human, financial, and technological resources necessary for energy management identified and provided By the Board?	Yes			
7	Environmental management regulation	Yes			
8	Environmental policy by CPCB/SPCB/PCB	Yes			
9	Energy Saving potential in the industry	Energy 16.2 GJ per year TNEB gird and Water to Sugar cane farmer			
10	Approval and completion	Yes			
11	Audit Mandatory regulation	Yes			
	Task (Internal Auditing report)	**Professionals**	**Initial date**	**Final date**	**Comments**
12	Internal Audit report	Auditor	07-11-2020	08-11-2020	Verified, non-compliance
13	Suitable Machinery	Technical engineer	09-11-2020	10-11-2020	Verified, non-compliance
14	Budgeting	Financial Auditor	09-11-2020	10-11-2020	Verified, non-compliance
15	Energy-saving potential technology	Operational engineer	09-11-2020	10-11-2020	Verified, non-compliance
16	Target update	Environmental engineer	10-11-2020	11-11-2020	Verified, non-compliance
17	New baseline	Executive committee	10-11-2020	11-11-2020	Verified, non-compliance
18	Timeline of technological up-gradation	Operational engineer	12-11-2020	13-11-2020	Verified, non-compliance

C. Legal framework and Logical requirement

	Variables	Mandatory Qualitative checklist							Remarks
		Y	**N**	**5**	**4**	**3**	**2**	**1**	
1	Classification of State of Art Pollution control technology	✔		✔					Non- compliance
2.	Capacity TCD/TPD/KWh/Units/MLD/KL/m^3 per day	✔		✔					Non-compliance

S.no	Factors and variables	Elements or present status							
3.	Air pollution control technology and Effluent treatment plant (ETP)	✔		✔					Non-compliance
4.	Energy management report	✔		✔					Non-compliance
5.	Cost analysis factors for pollution control technology								
6.	Methods of cost analysis, Documentation	✔			✔				Non-compliance
7.	Operation of the mechanism	✔			✔				Non-compliance
8.	Quality Management system	✔		✔					Non-compliance
9.	Occupational Health and safety report	✔		✔					Non-compliance
10.	Fire and safety report	✔		✔					Non-compliance
11.	Environmental factors Air, water, Soil and Solid (Hazardous waste) parameter with permissible limits: Reports	✔		✔					Non-compliance
12.	Corporate social responsibility (CSR)	✔			✔				Non-compliance
13.	Barriers and Driver	✔		✔					Non-compliance
14.	Management perspective, Report, and records	✔		✔					Non-compliance
D. External Audit report (Panel members)									
1	PDCA-Assessment	Non-compliance, Strongly agree							
2.	Compliance /Non-compliance verification	Has given by the auditor present and past reports for verification							
3.	Detailed Management, Budgeting	Ergonomics, Management, Cost-analysis							
4.	Environmental Management, Budgeting	Still to improve and rely on CT							
5.	Reporting/Documentation	Detailing, I Strongly agree.							
6.	Cross-check with all the records	Yes, it has been Verified.							
7.	Any other specific suggestion from the committee members (remark)	Odor in CSR, Green-house gas (carbon footprint) Calculation, compliance							
8.	Benchmarking setting	Resources management (raw material), Verified, non-compliance							
9.	EMS-Certification, review, planning, and Budgeting								
Note-Yes (✔), **No (✗)**, Checked or tested Verified – compliance, Non-compliance, Reasons: Flexibility, Reliability, Quality, 5-Very satisfied, 4- Satisfied, 3-Neutral, 2-Unsatisfied 1- Very Unsatisfied.									

Classification of the Environmental Management System (EMS)

An audit has classified into many patterns on the company's primary requirement. It considers the required elements, like regulation, policy, production capacity, and an environmental impact report. The Audit can be done individually or by grouping. These are structural models for small and medium-scale firm audits that can proceed just by accounting for a single audit like QMS. But in large-scale industries, Plan-Do-Check-Act (PDCA) has a procedure framework for investigations in an Integrated, holistic process that connects every single detail like EMS, EnMS, QMS, OSHS, CSR gives a clear picture of the firm's present situation from the past eco- technology, Resource-material balance analysis, and energy flow (Wilkinson and Dale 1999; Arda et al. 2019).

Logical Requirement

The Operational instruments for production like Screening, Washing, extraction, Purification, Evaporation Boiler (95 TPH) Crytillation pan were checked internally and externally; specification technology has been studied in Qualitative and Quantitative testing of the Classification enlists from the effluent treatment technology. This industry water management has a Closed-loop system connecting the Primary (Screening), Secondary (Activated sludge processing), and advanced treatment process (RO). Factors used air pollution control PM2.5, PM10, RSPM, NO2, SO2, CO, Testing, Advanced level adsorption technology, Inbuilt tech (Scrubbers) system. So in this industry, this parameter is periodically checked by calibrating in automatic sensors with flew meter (Digitalized) water parameters connected to CPU, Cooling tower, ETP closed-loop system, water is limited by Physico-chemical parameter. Air pollution control is checked and compared with permissible given by India's Third-party and SPCB/CPCB. Environmental aspects in product standards State pollution control board, online, continuous emission/ effluent, the pipes, and the machine's technical part are checked (LCA). Dust collector (2 available) odor pollution control (Compliance), Industrial Ecology (Scarp items), Solid waste management (Co-processing), Molasses and Co-generation Bagasse technology 119970 T/y has used inbuilt technology, Fertilizer is composting (Substitution Solid waste management system) Reducing, reusing and recycling the Organic waste Filter or press mud's 28728 T/y, Sludge from ETP-42 T/y, cane cutting-148,725 T/y, Soil- Soil profile, Characteristics, soil type, texture, NKP value Reducing, Rebuild, Remanufacturing, Consume Internally, Prolonging use, Returnable package, Waste incineration, Relocation are classified into reverse logistics which are not used in this industry. Green supply chain management (GSCM) 3 acres of trees on the campus to reduce pollution. Three Rainwater harvesting pits are built around the industrial location to save water. The Total quality management and life cycle assessment in advance. The environmental labeling, the product works under the standards of Food safety and the standard Authority of India.

Energy (EnMS) Report 50001 or Energy Report

In this Sugar plant energy consumption is 3.5 – 4 mega watt (stepped down from 11kilo volt to 440 Volts) Power export to Tamil nadu electricity board Grid – 8 to10 MW, 85 percent biomass has raw materials, only 15 percent of coal is used as per government norms Power transfer to grid (Paper board mill), Power supply to sugar process, ETP,WTP, VFD, ETP, Molasses filling, Falling film evaporator (FFE), Igni-fluid Turbine with alternator 15 to 20 percent coal in the boiler along with biomass 14.5 MW to 17.0 Mega watt Integrating tech used, Product redesign, Process redesign (customized redesign), Disassembly Standard operation procedure (SOP) Testing, Process flow chart, Automated monitoring system, Equipment availability, steam, pressure, and the temperature is calculated Furnace efficiency (Boiler), condensate polishing unit, cooling tower, Input and output, upgrading technology, research, and development on energy facility, improvised Cost, Employee training, Qualitative specification, Audit review (Energy reporting), Cross-check with EnMS or Energy report past report, Carbon footprint account, Energy Efficiency, EMS has all the requirements like adding into EMS with submitting the policy amended by the respective CPCB/SPCB, an essential requirement like saving potential, Approval, and completion of mandatory regulatory requirements. About the technical auditor, financial auditors target the baseline road map of the regulatory system. The working system combines the Auditor (Internal and

External Audit) required information to have committed (Calibration, testing, change in controlling the design, record, precision, and accuracy testing). It's verified and non-compliance and given strongly agree.

LEGAL FRAMEWORK (REGULATORY POLICY)

There are two types of regulatory norms. Local and international laws are essential for EMS auditors to assess the problem with mandatory regulation and policy. US-EPA (P2-Pollution prevention) and EU (BAT) have made a standard system of rules on (Environmental standards). The Central Pollution Control Board (CPCB) has been constituted under section (3) of the Water Act, 1974 water act with acceptable means. CPCB, earlier known as the Central Board for the Prevention and Control of Water Pollution (CBPCWP), has made it a mandate to restore the air and water quality. In 1981, the Board was made responsible for implementing the Air Act, 1981 to maintain, preserve, and check the ambient air quality like setting National Ambient air quality standards (NAAQs) Permissible standards and Since issues relating to prevention and control of pollution are linked with the overall maintenance of environmental management and quality, CPCB has been mandated to collect, perform, execute, inspect and co-ordinate all relevant provisions of the Environment Act, 1986 and Rules framed thereunder. Under its schedule VI- Annexure 1, it states that the State Pollution Control Boards (SPCB) should encourage industries to go in for waste minimization and waste utilization by the EU-IPPC, Best Available Technologies (BAT) (The Environment Act and Rules, 1986). Cleaner technology cell division by (MoEFCC) has a scheme called development and promotion of clean technology and waste minimization demonstration project, or the result of cleaner technologies to facilitate access to clean technology and its adoption by the small and medium scale collaboration with industries in setting up pilot projects. For new technology available technology/Creating institutional background, research, and development which compiles to the Sugar industry. Regulation of Co- generation and auxiliary mechanism Energy Conservation, Co-Processing, Recycling and reusing technology, Green Belt, Auditing of Cleaner technology in the large scale industry, Mandatory functions of large scale Industry (Ultra-red industry), Zero liquid discharge (ZLD) like closed-loop system (Condensate polishing unit, Cooling tower, ETP) (Agnello et al. 2019b) which is connected to CEMs reported to CPCB/SPCB. EMS has certain norms (international), but some developed countries use inbuilt technology combining conventional and cleaner technologies. It is verified and non-compliance and given strongly agree.

Cost Analysis Variables

There is a variety of cost models in determining the EMS datasets. Still, the feasibility and reliability are the total investment of the firm, Initial investment, Land cost, Construction cost, Operation cost, Buyback cost (Letmathe and doost 2000: Hilson and Nayee 2002: Carr 2005; Antonaras et al. 2011; Ahmed 2012: Khezek, and Olszewski 2017), Payback cost, Maintenance cost, (Socio-economic status) Social cost, Saving Cost, Subsidy, Research, and development expenditure. Return on investment, contingent valuation method (CVM), simple percentage, and simple statistical tools (Vanclay 2010: Joshi and Vinod 2015). It is verified and non-compliance and given strongly agree.

Documentation of the Cost Report

Computing models (online database management system) using excel sheet, tally are used, like using the data sets on Advantages amount (Rs.), the financial auditor carries out capacity improvement, Raw material savings, Energy savings, Water-savings, Improved recovery from waste, Operation, Monitoring, Testing, Maintenance, Reduction in abatement costs, which shows are a trend in Improvised price, Improved productivity for this year the operations. The cane is supplied by 1200 sugar cane farmers (stakeholders) in the Select sugar industry. There are 6 to 37 species of sugar cane from five different villages, 35,000 acres of sugar cane cultivated, and the highest cane crush of 22.35 Lakh MT. This industry runs over 210 days a year. Has per norms given by CPCB to control air pollution by using greenbelt? It's verified and non- compliance and provided strongly agree.

Table 3. Comparison between cleaner production and end-of-pipe technology using net saving per year and payback per month in the specific sugar mill

S. no	Technological equipment used	Cost details	Cost elements		Net profit ₹. In lakh Per annum		Payback amount per month	
			EOPT	CPT	EOPP	CPT	EOP	CPT
1.	Heat water Recycling	1. Initial Investment 2. Indirect cost 3. LTAE 4. Cost reduction 5. Merits	₹. 5,500,000 ₹. 733,000 per year 120 months ₹.3,370,000 per year 225 KL per year	₹.70,000,000 ₹.1,050,000 per year 240 months ₹.8,100,000 per year 540 KL per year	26.2	70.4	22.8 (1.10)	5.9
2.	Cooling system	1. Initial Investment 2. Indirect cost 3. LTAE 4. Cost reduction 5. Merits	₹.2,000,000 ₹.170,000 per year 96 months ₹.10,800,000 per year 720 KL per year	₹.3,000,000 ₹.706,000 per year 240 months ₹.20,250,000 per year 1,350 KL per year	106.3	195.4	0.2	0.10
3.	ETP	1. Initial Investment 2.Indirect cost 3.LTAE 4. Cost reduction 5. Merits	₹.43,500,000 ₹.2,470,000 per year 300 months ₹.28,350,000 per year 189,000 KL per year	₹.125,000,000 ₹.9,730,000 per year 120 months ₹.20,888,000 per year 52,200,000 KL per year	258.7	111.5	0.8	13.4
4.	Energy- conserve technology-1	1. Initial Investment 2. Indirect cost 3. LTAE 4. Cost reduction 5. Merits	₹.55,000,000 ₹.700,00 48 months ₹.924,000 per year N.A	₹.950,000,000 ₹.15,600,000 per year 240 months ₹.18,245,000 per year 12312 GJ	2.24	26.4	736.3	214.8
5.	Energy-saving technology 2 inbuilt	1. Initial Investment 2. Indirect cost 3. LTAE 4. Cost reduction 5. Merits	₹.2,000,000 ₹.10,000 per year 60 months ₹.110,250 per year 25.2 GJ	₹.4,500,000 ₹.50,000 per year 120 months ₹.50,000 per year 195.48 GJ	1	2.0	48	25.2
6.	Energy Saving technology	1. Initial Investment 2. Indirect cost 3. LTAE 4. Cost reduction 5. Merit	₹.2,000,000 ₹.125,000 per year 60 months ₹.200,000 per year 28.8 GJ	NA*	0.7	NA*	63.8	NA*
7.	Air pollution control monitoring	1. Initial Investment 2. Indirect cost 3. LTAE 4. Cost reduction 5. Merits	₹.15,000,000 ₹.1,055,000 per year 120 months ₹.1,152,000 per year 39.6 GJ	NA*	0.9	NA*	185.5	NA*

Continued on following page

Table 3. Continued

S. no	Technological equipment used	Cost details	Cost elements		Net profit ₹. In lakh Per annum		Payback amount per month	
			EOPT	CPT	EOPP	CPT	EOP	CPT
8.	Waste raw material re- processing	1. Initial Investment 2. Indirect cost 3. LTAE 4. Cost reduction 5. Merits	₹3,500,000 ₹30,000 48 months ₹308,000 per year 2299.392 GJ	NA*	2.7	NA*	37.2	NA*
9.	Recycling process	1. Initial Investment 2. Indirect cost 3. LTAE 4. Cost reduction 5. Merits	NA*	₹2,200,000 ₹555,000 per year 360 months ₹710,000 per year 17 lakh cane cutting p.a.	NA*	1.55	NA*	5.6
Note- NA*-Not Available, CPT-Cleaner production technology, EOPT- End of pipe technology, ₹-Rupees, LTAE* – Lifetime equipment assessment.								

Comparison Between Conventional and Cleaner Technology by an Explanation of Net Saving Per Year and Pay Back Per Month

EMAS gives a different perspective of audit cost analysis/production level output/input (Morrow and Rondinelli 2002). And environmental performance indicator, the Sugar industry has a different holistic approach to management scenario depending upon agricultural yield has per capita performance level. The hierarchy sets on certain criteria a step by step process, stakeholders-Yield performance level-raw material supply-operational performance-regulation- maintenance and service-pollution compliance-production level-customers satisfaction-feedback- review-planning to implement. Sugar pollution management can be classified into water, air, solid waste management, and Table 3. Shows Water management (Recycling of water plays a vital role in raw material in the sugar industry, so recycling and reusing technology is essential in this industry closed-loop system has been used, direct reuse of water connecting the Condensate polishing unit (CPU) steam unit for the boiler (water recycling) which is operated by 2 in 1 process recycle and reuse the water, Net savings amount Before CT (Rs.26.25 lakh p.a) and After using CT (Rs.70.45 lakh p.a) in this CT has a higher cost-saving value of (Rs.44.2 lakh p.a) Payback shows in Before CT (48 months) after using CT (5.9 months) in this also CT offers the lowest Payback with a difference of 43 months, the advantages are 54,000,000 liters p.a, 2. Cooling tower systems is used to cool the heated water and enhance the dissolved oxygen, maintain temperature and pH, Net savings amount Before CT (Rs.106.3 lakh p.a) and After using CT (195.44 lakh p.a) in this CT has a higher cost-saving value of (Rs.89.4 lakh) Payback shows Before CT (0.2 months) after using CT (0.10 months) conventional technology has the lowest period and different between 0.8 months advantages,135,000,000 liters p.a, 3.Effluent treatment plant (ETP), is used to recycle/reuse by Conventional technology combining two type technologies, classified into Primary (Screening) debris cleaner, Secondary (secondary clarifier) and activated sludge process (ASP) to remove suspendable solids and connecting cleaner technology (Advanced technology is classified into three different operational process, Multigrade filter (MGF) optimize DO, pH,reduce turbidity and TSS (<5ppm), Reverse Osmosis (RO) remove ions,larger particles and molecules, Ultra-filtration (UF) turbidity removal,in addition to microbes like pathogens, bacteria etc., by this end process is recycled and reused for sugarcane operation; net savings amount Before CT (Rs.258.7 lakh p.a) and After using CT (111.44 lakh p.a) in this Conventional Technology has a higher cost-saving value and the difference between the cost value is (147.3 lakh p.a) Payback shows Before CT (0.8 months) after using CT (13 months) conventional technology has the lowest period and different between 12.6 months advantages-189,000,000 liters p.a. Four systems in a combining operation CPU, Cooling tower, ETP and advance treatment process is called has a closed-loop water management system (Agnello et al. 2019e). Energy-saving technology-1 (Co-generation technology) (Agnello et al. 2021g) Igni-fluid boiler operation using turbine with alternator, low pressure/High-pressure steam is used in a ratio of 25 percent of coal and 75 percent of biomass, is used (Bagasse)(Agnello et al. 2021h), The Net savings amount Before CT (Rs.2.2 lakh p.a) and After using CT (Rs.26.45 lakh p.a) in this CT Have a higher cost-saving value and difference is (Rs.24.2 lakh p.a) Payback shows in Before CT (736 months) after using CT (214 months) in this also CT shows the lowest Payback, advantages-3,420,000 (KWh) p.a, Energy-saving technology inbuilt Variable frequency drive (VFD), Net savings amount Before CT (Rs.1 lakh p.a) and After using CT (Rs.2.08 lakh p.a) in this CT has a higher cost-saving value and difference is (Rs.1.08 lakh p.a) Payback shows in Before CT (48 months) after using CT (25.2 months) in this also C.T. Shows the lowest Payback, advantages 54,340 (kWh) p.a. Energy Saving technology Net savings amount Before CT (Rs.0.7 lakh p.a) and After using CT (NA.) Payback shows in Before CT (63.8 months) after using CT (NA) in this also C.T. Shows the lowest Payback, advantages 7,000 (kWh) p.a. Air pollution control (Two-stage Electrostatic precipitator (ESP), has a net savings amount Before CT (Rs.0.9 lakh p.a) and After using CT (NA.) Payback shows in Before CT (185.5 months) after using CT (NA) in this also C.T. Shows the lowest Payback, advantages 11,000 (kWh) p.a. Recycling process Co-processing (Soda) works as a catalyst, Net savings amount Before CT (Rs.2.7 lakh p.a) and After using CT (NA.) Payback shows in Before CT (37.2 months) after using CT (NA) in this also CT Has the lowest Payback, advantages 638,720 (kWh) p.a., Recycling Net savings amount Before CT (NA) and After using CT (Rs.1.55 lakh p.a) payback shows in Before CT (NA) after using CT (5.6 months) in this also C.T. Shows the lowest Payback, advantages 1,700,000 Cane cutting p.a. Lime stone grits - 04.70 tons p.a, Boiler ash-3955.3 tons p.a. Molasses (%) - 04.69 (Agnello et al. 2020f). It's verified and non-compliance and given strongly agree, but the odor is verified in this industry, and compliance is reported.

Green Belt

About 10,400 trees were planted tree are Coconut, Plantain, Teak, Palm, Ashoka, Neem, Banana, Sobibul, Casurina, Pungan Polyalthiya longifolia ficusreligiosa, and Tamarindus induce around the industry towards to control air pollution have per CPCB norms of Green belt regulation is verified has non-compliance.

Quality Management System (QMS)

An overall housekeeping process aided with QMS, Quality check-in material resources, in a Quality lab, Food safety and legal authority of India (FASSI) and National quality assurance standard (NQAS), operation with Standard operating procedure (SOP), like Labeling the product,5s system on process handling using Equipment availability, maintenance and service in right time towards machinery's (LCA), Improvised cost-cutting, Third party-Consultant, Quality Research, and development lab team towards (TQM), Employee training, Technical up- gradation, Documentation, and record, cross-check with the past report in 1 year, But this can be twice in a year, Employee feedback or opinion are an essential suggestion. Safety is an important priority; In this industry, it has been verified and given non-compliance given strongly agreed.

Occupational Health, Fire, and Safety Report

Labors are given a periodic Health check-up in three months intervals ones strictly following the regulation of the labour regulations like providing them with personal protective equipment (PPEs), helmets to ensure the employee's safety for identifying the grade from the helmet in different batch color Office staff-Yellow, Safety-Green, another contract-Blue color, Visitors White, Shoe, helmet, gloves, goggles, uniform. Critical area identification, Labeling Chemical handling assessment, First Aid kit, Audit review, Employee Training, Employee relation, Employees satisfaction, Human resources management Communication, Employee participation, Teamwork, Following labor law, Employee appraisal, reward, and recognition, Labor regulation and insurance policy, Employees feedback. Fire and safety report is classified into hazards areas identification, Standard operation procedure (SOP), Personal protective equipment availability (PPE), Employee Training, Motivations class, Communication, Institutional background, Technical up-gradation, Maintenance and service, Fire and damage insurance, Communication Record and Documentation, Audits review, Cross-check with the past report, Risk assessment, Employee feedback or opinion, Environmental, social Accountability, Implication cost. Are verified and reported as non-compliance given agree.

Environmental Factors Air, Water, Soil, and Solid (Hazardous Waste) Parameter Permissible Limits: Reports

Every report has been cross-checked with the older reports (annual) to maintain a consistent accountability note on EnMS, EMS, technology, and financial audit reports (Line et al. 2002, Agnello et al. 2019d) with Post and pre EIA, ESR, SPCB, and industrial third party consultant reports have been cross-checked in three months ones this is verified and reported as non- compliance given agree.

Corporate Social Responsibility (CSR)

Environmental standards about pollution are affected by the industrial pollution CSR, Livestock, Crops, Human beings, Periodic health check-up like camp (Loew et al. 2004: Agnello et al. 2021h). A disease is affected by the industrial pollution CSR; Advantages by Industry given to CSR. Are verified and reported as non-compliance given agree.

Advantage by Industry Given to CSR

CSR are given Educational institutes, Entertainment, Employment opportunities, Providing water facilities, Health care, Awareness program. CSR feedback of pollution, Public perception of this sugar industry.

Advantages for Labours

Labors have to be given many legal compliments. It has been mandatory in the system has labors organization/labors law/regulations like Improved Health standards, Improved Safety standard, Improved quality of air, Improved quality of water, Reduction in noise, Demonstration effect, Preempting peoples' resistance industrialization. Is verified and recorded non compliance are given as agreed.

Management Perspective

Management is classified into Top-level and medium management commitment, and this has been classified into the image of the firm, Improves environmental quality's, Reduce operational Cost, Meet the demands of the customers, Use marketing concepts, Meet company requirement, Staffs and labors training, risk aversion, Feedback of laborers, market image, Government regulation, Government subsidiaries, supply chains, sustainable network-level pavement management, Sustainable closed-loop supply chain, Environmental planning, Industry association, Environmental Business network, a comprehensive framework for environmental management accounting, differences in effectively improving ecological performance, Quality drive, Quantitative drive, dynamics modeling for sustainable environmental management, Various departments Human resources department, Safety department, Quality department, Process department, Sales department, Finance department in this industry are verified and recorded non-compliance given strongly agree. Still, the stakeholder's framers are given more value because of the raw material (Sugar cane). This aspect is essential in this industry (Schaltegger and Figge 2000).

Human Resource Department

The HR department is an act of public relation officer (PRO) is the outsourcing management system to conduct training and development for laborers, career research, Bonus Attentive maintenance, Wages and Salary administration, Grievance handling, Performance appraisal, career development and training, interview scheduling, Guest base, and the public Occupation. Finance Department: routine check-up of Assets and liabilities, property rights, market creation, fiscal instruments, charge system, financial Audit, liability performance of bond, Arrangement of borrowing, Auditing reports, Employees Attendance of the monthly salary, production capacity (Output/input) operations. This is verified and as recorded non- compliance.

Research and Development

The research and development is a team of operational engineers/environmental/Auditors/Quality assessment cell to evaluate/calibrate/calculate/assess the quality management system with operation/service/maintenance and to identify the gaps in production levels, risk assessment, Hazardous waste management system design, and to innovate new pollution control technology in energy management, (Update/upgrade) water management facility in this industry are verified and recorded has non-compliance agree. Due to the difficulty, the barrier and driver in the sector are verified and recorded has non-compliance given strongly agree.

Management Review, Report, and Record

Top-level to labour level management has reporting/ recording the in Production level, improvised Production level, Environmental Accountability, Total net saving cost, Advantages, new tariff, Corrective measures, gaps consistency in production range, New Environmental implementation, Validation and consolidation, eco-labeling, total audit review, and feedback is continuously monitored. Specific implications are made in practical this act is continuously implementing/reported in this industry; this is verified and recorded has non-compliance given strongly agree.

Table 4. Findings of EMS using SWOT analysis

Strength	Weakness
1. Decision-making advantage 2. Comprehensive approach 3. Holistic approach 4. Integrated strategy 5. Sustainable finance practices 6. Precision and accuracy	1. The cost is high 2. Small and medium scale industries cannot afford it. 3. Purchasing in Global trend 4. Can not understand the regulation policy.
Opportunities 1. Innovation 2. Institutional background (R and D) 3. Combined Organizational setup 4. Training 5. Supply chain 6. Material logistics 7. Circular economy 8. Depends on capacity	**Threatens** 1. Understanding between the international and local regulation policy 2. The cost is high because every report has been classified 3. Targets cannot be achieved due to international standards 4. Verity of updates in regulatory policy 5. Time delay

EMS Future Scope

Digital sensors are connected with a continuous monitoring system based on a software data analysis like Big data analytics (datasheet is given computing algorithm software like Flux Analyzer and Meta tool, excel sheet is connected to a storage facility (hardware) based to the EMS computing algorithm. There are research and development. This firm started this research in 2012 (Developer are working around the globe to enhance Performance, practice, and planning output in great precision and error testing manner in the domain (Hardware storage hub) by automated embedded technology tool the efficiency of automatic repairing, artificial intelligence domain, calibration, testing, updating the software sensing Quantitative and Qualitative data analysis (Quazi, 1999; To and lee 2014; Sun et al. 2020; Carvalho et al. 2020: Naveen et al. 2022i) and to innovate phytoremediation in natural effluent cleaning water technology can be introduced (Arivoli et al. 2021a and Arivoli et al. 2021b).

Report Specification

The Audit specifies the comments of the lead auditor classified the factors on assessment and combining in a format towards PDCA-assessment, Detailed compliance/ non-compliance verification, finance, supply chain, raw material logistics has strongly agreed, cross-check records verified, committee members odor in CSR (no adaptation of odor technology, GHG has compliance (no proper calibration and calculation is adopted), benchmarking (Resource management) and EMS, examining, technology finance is verified as non-compliance by the Audit.

CONCLUSION

The organization follows a strict standard operating procedure by regulation norms on management perspective by Maintaining labors in providing them with good health and safety, quality of goods, preventing pollution, managing resources, and productivity. Focus is given more to environmental management. This sugar industry installed different clean application energy-conserve technology, recycling, reusing the molasses for the co-generation process, Forward drive fans, Cooler tower (Recycling the water), and Reverse Osmosis (RO) in EMS, QMS, energy reporting by towards sustainable industrial, technological optimization development.

REFERENCES

Abbas, J. (2020). Impact of total quality management on corporate green performance through the mediating role of corporate social responsibility. *Journal of Cleaner Production, 242*, 118458. doi:10.1016/j.jclepro.2019.118458

Adams, C. A., Larrinaga-González, C., Pérez, E. A., Ruiz, C. C., & Fenech, F. C. (2007). Environmental management systems as an embedding mechanism: A research note. *Accounting, Auditing & Accountability Journal, 20*(3), 403–422. doi:10.1108/09513570710748562

Agnello J. Naveen. X, Ravichandran, M., & Balamurugan, J. (2015a). Clean Technology and its Efficacy: Strategies of Environmental Management. *Journal of Environmental and Social Sciences, 2*, 1-6.

Agnello, J. & Arivoli, A. (2019d). Case Study To Understand The Benefits Of Cleaner Technology By The Assessment Of Water, Air And Soil Quality Around The Sugar Industry In Erode, Tamil Nadu. *International Journal of Scientific & Technology Research* 8(9).

Agnello J. Naveen. X and Arivoli. A, (2021h) Corporate Social Responsibility in Environmental Protection of Specific sugar factory in Tamil Nadu: A case study. *Journal The New Horizon & Emerging Challenges In post COVID - 19 Business Scenario, 1*, 232-249.

Agnello, J., Naveen, X., Arivoli, A., Boopathi, S., & Balamurugan, J. (2019c). A Review On Cleaner Technology In Pollution Control At Ultra-red Industry In Tamil Nadu, India, Tamil Nadu. *International Journal of Scientific & Technology Research* 8(9), 1892-1898.

Agnello, J., Naveen, X., Boopahti, S., & Arivoli, A. (2019b). Efficacy of Cleaner technology in wastewater treatment and Energy conservation using (UASB-R) Anaerobic Digester at Bagasse-Based Pulp and Paper Mill in Tamil Nadu, ISSN: 2455-3085 (Online), Issue-06 Research Review. *International Journal of Multidisciplinary*.

Agnello J. Naveen.X, Boopathi. S & Arivoli. A, (2019e). Efficacy of Cleaner Technology in Recycling of Wastewater Treatment Process Using Add-on Applications at Sugar Industry In Tamil Nadu. *Poll Res., 38.*

Agnello, J., Naveen, X., Boopathi, S., & Arivoli, A. (2021g). Case Experience on WIN- WIN Approach Towards Industrial Pollution Control-Economic and Environmental Efficacy of Cleaner Technology in Select Cement Industry in Tamil Nadu. In *Bioremediation and Green Technologies* (pp. 209–234). Springer. doi:10.1007/978-3-030-64122-1_15

Agnello, J., Naveen, X., Boopathi, S., Arivoli, A., & Balamurugan, J. (2020f). Win-Win strategy of cleaner technology-environmental and economic scores of Sugar Industry in Tamil Nadu [IJEP]. *Indian Journal of Environmental Protection, 40*(2), 186–191.

Agnello, J., Naveen, X., Boopathi, S., Arivoli, A., & Kannan, A. (2021h). Economic and Environmental Benefits of Cleaner Technology in Industrial Pollution Control: Case Study of Select Sugar Industry in Tamil Nadu. In *Bioremediation and Green Technologies* (pp. 185–207). Springer. doi:10.1007/978-3-030-64122-1_14

Ahmed, A. C. A. (2012). Social and Environmental Auditing; Some Basic Concept. *Some Basic Concept (October 25, 2012)*.

Albelda, E. (2011). *The role of management accounting practices as facilitators of environmental management*. Sustainability Accounting, Management and Policy Journal. doi:10.1108/20408021111162137

Alberti, M., Caini, L., Calabrese, A., & Rossi, D. (2000). Evaluation of the costs and benefits of an environmental management system. *International Journal of Production Research*, *38*(17), 4455–4466. doi:10.1080/00207540050205226

Alberti, M., Caini, L., Calabrese, A., & Rossi, D. (2000). Evaluation of the costs and benefits of an environmental management system. *International Journal of Production Research*, *38*(17), 4455–4466. doi:10.1080/00207540050205226

Allan, C., & Stankey, G. H. (2009). *Adaptive environmental management* (Vol. 351). Springer. doi:10.1007/978-1-4020-9632-7

Amir, M., Rehman, S. A., & Khan, M. I. (2020). Mediating role of environmental management accounting and control system between top management commitment and environmental performance: A legitimacy theory. *Journal of Management Research*, *7*(1), 132–160.

Ammenberg, J., & Hjelm, O. (2003). Tracing business and environmental effects of environmental management systems—A study of networking small and medium-sized enterprises using a joint environmental management system. *Business Strategy and the Environment*, *12*(3), 163–174. doi:10.1002/bse.357

Ann, G. E., Zailani, S., & Abd Wahid, N. (2006). A study on the impact of environmental management system (EMS) certification on firms' performance in Malaysia. *Management of Environmental Quality*.

Antonaras, A., Iacovidou, M., & Memtsa, C. (2011). Measuring social return on investment using the EBEN GR Business Ethics Excellence Model. *Current Issues of Business and Law*, *6*(1), 69–89. doi:10.5200/1822-9530.2011.04

Arda, O. A., Bayraktar, E., & Tatoglu, E. (2019). How do integrated quality and environmental management practices affect firm performance? Mediating roles of quality performance and environmental proactivity. *Business Strategy and the Environment*, *28*(1), 64–78. doi:10.1002/bse.2190

Arivoli, A., Naveen, X. A. J., & Thangavelu, S. (2021a). Impact of Sugar Mill Effluent on the Quality of Groundwater in Cuddalore District, Tamil Nadu, India. In *Bioremediation and Green Technologies* (pp. 41–52). Springer. doi:10.1007/978-3-030-64122-1_4

Arivoli, A., Thangavelu, S., & Naveen, X. A. J. (2021b). Influence of Sugar Mill Effluent on Germination and Growth of Fenugreek (Trigonella foenumgraecum) and Mustard (Brassica nigra). In *Bioremediation and Green Technologies* (pp. 271–281). Springer. doi:10.1007/978-3-030-64122-1_19

Ashley, P., & Boyd, B. W. (2006). Quantitative and qualitative approaches to research in environmental management. *Australasian Journal of Environmental Management, 13*(2), 70–78. doi:10.1080/14486563.2006.10648674

Bartolomeo, M., Bennett, M., Bouma, J. J., Heydkamp, P., James, P., & Wolters, T. (2000). Environmental management accounting in Europe: Current practice and future potential. *European Accounting Review, 9*(1), 31–52. doi:10.1080/096381800407932

Bernardo, M., Casadesus, M., Karapetrovic, S., & Heras, I. (2009). How integrated are environmental, quality, and other standardized management systems? An empirical study. *Journal of Cleaner Production, 17*(8), 742–750. doi:10.1016/j.jclepro.2008.11.003

Berry, M. A., & Rondinelli, D. A. (1998). Proactive corporate environmental management: A new industrial revolution. [Competitive requirement]. *The Academy of Management Perspectives, 12*(2), 38–50. doi:10.5465/ame.1998.650515

Căpuşneanu, S., Topor, D. I., Constantin, D. M. O., Manole, A. L., & Hint, M. S. (2020). Environmental Management Accounting: A Business Perspective on the Policies, Analyses, and Benefits of Its Implementation. In Management Accounting Standards for Sustainable Business Practices (pp. 27-51). IGI Global.

Carr, H. S. (2005). *US Patent No. 6,968,295.* Washington, DC: US Patent and Trademark Office.

Carvalho, F., Santos, G., & Gonçalves, J. (2020). Critical analysis of information about integrated management systems and environmental policy on the Portuguese firms' website towards sustainable development. *Corporate Social Responsibility and Environmental Management, 27*(2), 1069–1088. doi:10.1002/csr.1866

Chaudhry, N. I., Asad, H., & Hussain, R. I. (2020). Environmental innovation and financial performance: Mediating role of environmental management accounting and firm's environmental strategy. [PJCSS]. *Pakistan Journal of Commerce and Social Sciences, 14*(3), 715–737.

da Rosa, F. S., Lunkes, R. J., & Mendes, A. C. (2020). Environmental management accounting and innovation in water and energy reduction. *Environmental Monitoring and Assessment, 192*(10), 1–15. doi:10.100710661-020-08586-7 PMID:32889603

Dahlmann, F., Brammer, S., & Millington, A. (2008). Environmental management in the United Kingdom: New survey evidence. *Management Decision, 46*(2), 264–283. doi:10.1108/00251740810854159

Feldman, S. J., Soyka, P. A., & Ameer, P. (1996). *Does improving a firm's environmental management system and environmental performance result in a higher stock price?* ICF Kaiser.

Gallego-Schmid, A., & Tarpani, R. R. Z. (2019). Life cycle assessment of wastewater treatment in developing countries: A review. *Water Research, 153*, 63–79. doi:10.1016/j.watres.2019.01.010 PMID:30690219

Gorgulu, S., & Kocabey, S. (2020). An Energy Saving Potential Analysis of Lighting Retrofit Scenarios in Outdoor Lighting Systems: A Case Study for a University Campus. *Journal of Cleaner Production, 260*, 121060. doi:10.1016/j.jclepro.2020.121060

Guerrero-Baena, M. D., Gómez-Limón, J. A., & Fruet, J. V. (2015). A multicriteria method for environmental management system selection: An intellectual capital approach. *Journal of Cleaner Production, 105*, 428–437. doi:10.1016/j.jclepro.2014.07.079

Hennink, M., Hutter, I., & Bailey, A. (2020). *Qualitative research methods*. SAGE Publications Limited.

Hilson, G., & Nayee, V. (2002). Environmental management system implementation in the mining industry: A key to achieving cleaner production. *International Journal of Mineral Processing, 64*(1), 19–41. doi:10.1016/S0301-7516(01)00071-0

Hughey, K. F., Tait, S. V., & O'Connell, M. J. (2005). Qualitative evaluation of three 'environmental management systems in the New Zealand wine industry. *Journal of Cleaner Production, 13*(12), 1175–1187. doi:10.1016/j.jclepro.2004.07.002

Hui, I. K., Chan, A. H., & Pun, K. F. (2001). A study of the environmental management system implementation practices. *Journal of Cleaner Production, 9*(3), 269–276. doi:10.1016/S0959-6526(00)00061-5

Hwang, S. I. (2022). EMSO Technology Development by SWOT Analysis. *The Journal of Korean Institute of Electromagnetic Engineering and Science, 33*(1), 58–68. doi:10.5515/KJKIEES.2022.33.1.58

Johnstone, L. (2020). A systematic analysis of environmental management systems in SMEs: Possible research directions from a management accounting and control stance. *Journal of Cleaner Production, 244*, 118802. doi:10.1016/j.jclepro.2019.118802

Joshi, K. K., and Vinod, K. (2015). Environmental Valuation and Green Accounting for the future.

Kleindorfer, P. R. (1997). Market-based environmental audits and environmental risks: Implementing ISO 14000. *The Geneva Papers on Risk and Insurance. Issues and Practice, 22*(2), 194–210. doi:10.1057/gpp.1997.16

Kluczek, A., & Olszewski, P. (2017). Energy audits in industrial processes. *Journal of Cleaner Production, 142*, 3437–3453. doi:10.1016/j.jclepro.2016.10.123

Kwak, Y. H., & Ibbs, C. W. (2000). Calculating project management's return on investment. *Project Management Journal, 31*(2), 38–47. doi:10.1177/875697280003100205

Letmathe, P., & Doost, R. K. (2000). Environmental cost accounting and auditing. *Managerial Auditing Journal, 15*(8), 424–431. doi:10.1108/02686900010354709

Line, M., Hawley, H., & Krut, R. (2002). The development of global environmental and social reporting. *Corporate Environmental Strategy, 9*(1), 69–78. doi:10.1016/S1066-7938(01)00159-2

Loew, T., Ankele, K., Braun, S., & Clausen, J. (2004). *Significance of the CSR debate for sustainability and the requirements for companies. Institute for Ecological Economy Research GmbH.* IÖW.

Mangra, M. G., Cotoc, E., & Dumitru, A. (2014). Sustainable economic development through environmental management systems implementation. *Journal of Studies in Social Sciences, 6*(1), 1–14. PMID:25530938

Melnyk, S. A., Sroufe, R. P., & Calantone, R. (2003). We are assessing the impact of environmental management systems on corporate and environmental performance. *Journal of Operations Management, 21*(3), 329–351. doi:10.1016/S0272-6963(02)00109-2

Miles, M. P., Munilla, L. S., & McClurg, T. (1999). The impact of ISO 14000 environmental management standards on small and medium-sized enterprises. *Journal of Quality Management, 4*(1), 111–122. doi:10.1016/S1084-8568(99)80098-4

Mishra, M. K. (2020). *Application of Operational Research in Sustainable Environmental Management and Climate Change.*

Molina-Azorín, J. F., Tarí, J. J., Pereira-Moliner, J., Lopez-Gamero, M. D., & Pertusa-Ortega, E. M. (2015). The effects of quality and environmental management on competitive advantage: A mixed-methods study in the hotel industry. *Tourism Management, 50*, 41–54. doi:10.1016/j.tourman.2015.01.008

Morrow, D., & Rondinelli, D. (2002). Adopting corporate environmental management systems: Motivations and results of ISO 14001 and EMAS certification. *European Management Journal, 20*(2), 159–171. doi:10.1016/S0263-2373(02)00026-9

Mucunguzi, P., Tugume, P., & Ogola, L. (2021). Environmental Management by Faith Based Organizations in Uganda: A SWOT Analysis. *International Journal of Environmental Protection and Policy, 9*(1), 5. doi:10.11648/j.ijepp.20210901.12

Naveen, X. A. J., Arivoli, A., Boopathi, S., & Rajkumar, V. (2022i). A Case Study on Evaluation of Energy Management System by Implication of Advanced Technology in Typical Cement Factory Tamil Nadu, India. In *Smart Technologies for Energy and Environmental Sustainability* (pp. 245–265). Springer. doi:10.1007/978-3-030-80702-3_15

Naveen, X. A. J., Arivoli, A., Malarmannan, V. C., & Boopathi, S. (2022j). A Review on Cleaner Technology for Sustainable Industrial Practices: Global and Indian Scenario Genesis of Technologies to Control Pollution. In *Computational Modelling in Industry 4.0* (pp. 91–116). Springer. doi:10.1007/978-981-16-7723-6_8

Nawrocka, D., & Parker, T. (2009). Finding the connection: Environmental management systems and environmental performance. *Journal of Cleaner Production, 17*(6), 601–607. doi:10.1016/j.jclepro.2008.10.003

Pacana, A., and Ulewicz, R. (2017). Research of determinants motiving to implement the environmental management system. *Polish Journal of Management Studies, 16.*

Pesce, M., Shi, C., Critto, A., Wang, X., & Marcomini, A. (2018). SWOT analysis of the application of international standard ISO 14001 in the Chinese context. A case study of Guangdong Province. *Sustainability (Basel), 10*(9), 3196. doi:10.3390u10093196

Purwanto, A., Asbari, M., and Santoso, P. B. (2020). Effect of integrated management system of ISO 9001: 2015 and ISO 22000: 2018 implementation to packaging industries quality performance at Banten Indonesia. *Jurnal Ilmiah MEA (Manajemen, Ekonomi, and Akuntansi), 4*(1), 17-29.

Purwanto, A., Putri, R. S., Ahmad, A. H., Asbari, M., Bernarto, I., Santoso, P. B., & Sihite, O. B. (2020). The effect of implementation integrated management system ISO 9001, ISO 14001, ISO 22000, and ISO 45001 on Indonesian food industries performance. *TEST Engineering and Management*, *82*, 14069.

Purwanto, A., Putri, R. S., Ahmad, A. H., Asbari, M., Bernarto, I., Santoso, P. B., & Sihite, O. B. (2020). The effect of implementation integrated management system ISO 9001, ISO 14001, ISO 22000, and ISO 45001 on Indonesian food industries performance. *TEST Engineering and Management*, *82*, 14069.

Quazi, H. A. (1999). Implementation of an environmental management system: The experience of companies operating in Singapore. *Industrial Management & Data Systems*, *99*(7), 302–311. doi:10.1108/02635579910262526

Sands, J., Lee, K. H., and Gunarathne, N. (2015). Environmental Management Accounting (EMA) for environmental management and organizational change. *Journal of Accounting and Organizational Change.*

Schaltegger, S., & Figge, F. (2000). Environmental shareholder value: Economic success with corporate environmental management. *Eco-Management and Auditing*, *7*(1), 29–42. doi:10.1002/(SICI)1099-0925(200003)7:1<29::AID-EMA119>3.0.CO;2-1

Sroufe, R. (2003). Effects of environmental management systems on environmental management practices and operations. *Production and Operations Management*, *12*(3), 416–431. doi:10.1111/j.1937-5956.2003.tb00212.x

Steger, U. (2000). Environmental management systems: Empirical evidence and further perspectives. *European Management Journal*, *18*(1), 23–37. doi:10.1016/S0263-2373(99)00066-3

Sun, C., Romero, L., Joseph-Duran, B., Meseguer, J., Muñoz, E., Guasch, R., Martinez, M., Puig, V., & Cembrano, G. (2020). Integrated pollution-based real-time control of sanitation systems. *Journal of Environmental Management*, *269*, 110798. doi:10.1016/j.jenvman.2020.110798 PMID:32561007

Tatoglu, E., Frynas, J. G., Bayraktar, E., Demirbag, M., Sahadev, S., Doh, J., & Koh, S. L. (2020). Why do emerging market firms engage in voluntary environmental management practices? A strategic choice perspective. *British Journal of Management*, *31*(1), 80–100. doi:10.1111/1467-8551.12351

To, W. M., & Lee, P. K. C. (2014). Diffusion of ISO 14001 environmental management system: Global, regional and country-level analyses. *Journal of Cleaner Production*, *66*, 489–498. doi:10.1016/j.jclepro.2013.11.076

Vanclay, F. (2010). The triple bottom line and impact assessment: how do TBL, EIA, SIA, SEA, and EMS relate to each other? Tools, Techniques, And Approaches For Sustainability: Collected Writings in Environmental Assessment Policy and Management (pp. 101-124).

Venkatesan, T. M. I., & Kundu, G. K. (2020). An empirical study of Kaizen events in Indian small and medium enterprises. *International Journal of Services and Operations Management*, *37*(2), 197–219. doi:10.1504/IJSOM.2020.110338

Viranda, D. F., Sari, A. D., Suryoputro, M. R., & Setiawan, N. (2020, January). 5S Implementation of SME Readiness in Meeting Environmental Management System Standards based on ISO 14001: 2015 (Study Case: PT. ABC). [). IOP Publishing]. *IOP Conference Series. Materials Science and Engineering*, *722*(1), 012072. doi:10.1088/1757-899X/722/1/012072

Voukkali, I., & Zorpas, A. A. (2022). Evaluation of urban metabolism assessment methods through SWOT analysis and analytical hierocracy process. *The Science of the Total Environment, 807*, 150700. doi:10.1016/j.scitotenv.2021.150700 PMID:34606858

Warner, J. W. (1993, January). Environmental data management system. In *SPE Annual Technical Conference and Exhibition*. Society of Petroleum Engineers. 10.2118/26363-MS

Wilkinson, G., & Dale, B. G. (1999). Integrated management systems: An examination of the concept and theory. *The TQM Magazine, 11*(2), 95–104. doi:10.1108/09544789910257280

Wu, J., & Chang, I. S. (2020). Environmental planning. In *Environmental Management in China* (pp. 17–34). Springer. doi:10.1007/978-981-15-4894-9_3

Chapter 15
Mobility Management in Smart Cities:
Exploratory Analysis in Mexico

Myrna Hortencia Lezama León
https://orcid.org/0000-0001-8181-3705
Universidad Politécnica Metropolitana de Hidalgo, Mexico

Rafael Ordoñez Gutierrez
https://orcid.org/0000-0001-7129-266X
Universidad Politécnica Metropolitana de Hidalgo, Mexico

Eduardo Cruz Aldana
Universidad Politécnica Metropolitana de Hidalgo, Mexico

Hugo Villeda Cuellar
Universidad Politécnica Metropolitana de Hidalgo, Mexico

Hector Armando Figueroa Urrea
Universidad Politécnica Metropolitana de Hidalgo, Mexico

ABSTRACT

To speak of smart cities is interpreted as the exclusive use of information technologies for the development of the daily activities of a population, however, this chapter develops the analysis of a smart city in the area of mobility and the factors involved for an efficient development of the existing relationship of society-infrastructure-sustainability, so that they converge within a single space that positively impact the quality of life of people. Through different international organizations, evaluation metrics for smart cities are established, where key indicators are valued for the development of a city with the perception of its inhabitants, emphasizing sustainable, safe and intelligent mobility. Therefore, data from 2019 to 2023 are rescued with the exception of 2022 (due to the Covid-19 pandemic), for the analysis of Mexico City regarding quality of life-technology-sustainability, directing its resources to the development of smart mobility, through an efficient management of its resources so that there is a permanent interconnectivity and care for the environment. In this sense, a proposal for improvement is made by taking advantage of communication technologies and the existing infrastructure for the implementation of means that allow connectivity between means of transportation and resources to collect data and thus manage them according to the needs of users.

DOI: 10.4018/979-8-3693-0373-3.ch015

INTRODUCTION

As technology has entered daily life, many of the daily activities have become more comfortable, efficient and safe to perform, in such a way that they favor the growth of the society in which we develop. Because of this, the need arises to name this emerging relationship of society-infrastructure-technology and the impact it generates in the inhabitants of a society in different aspects of their routine in the short and long term. This relationship has been named as "Smart Cities", which arise as a concept to identify those that apply information and communication technologies to improve the quality of life of their inhabitants, as well as to generate sustainable economic growth through the prudent management of resources (Moreno et al., 2016), in order to care for the environment and reduce social inequality (Alvarado, 2018).

It is worth mentioning that, within this relationship, the term mobility arises, i.e., the movement of people from one point to another meeting conditions such as equity, environmental responsibility and safety, to mention a few. Within the analysis of Smart cities, Mobility is one of the six axes of focus (Giffinger, 2007, as cited in Moreno et al., 2016). this due to the environmental impact and the development of the economy, as well as the welfare of the community; being its objective to improve mobility and housing through the promotion of the efficient management of resources and having as a priority the coexistence and interaction of people with their environment. This is possible through the implementation of sensors, information and communication technologies (ICT) and the Internet of Things (IoT).

According to Bibri (2017) the functions of a smart mobility, within a smart city, should be:

- Accessibility, both spatial and non-spatial
- Virtual mobility
- Balance between mobility and accessibility
- Sharing between motorized and non-motorized vehicles
- Safe and innovative transportation systems
- Diversity of travel modes
- Proximity of facilities and services

Thus, smart mobility not only seeks to reduce pollution and traffic, but as mentioned above, it also seeks the interconnectivity of the population to streamline their movement and have greater accessibility.

Automated security recognizes how to improve the quality of life and living conditions of all members of society, especially the less favored, integrating elements of continuous development and modifying the use of different modes of transportation aimed at an intelligent and integral mobility of these concepts.

The objective of this chapter is to analyze the current status of the case of Mexico City, which is moving towards becoming an intelligent and sustainable city in the area of mobility through the evaluation generated by the United Nations (UN), in order to finally make proposals for improvement.

The organization and structure of this chapter consists, first of all, in defining the importance and scope of smart and sustainable mobility in the management of smart cities, as well as establishing the metrics for the evaluation of smart cities and with this, briefly reviewing success stories of smart cities in the world. Identify the mobility practices that characterize them, as well as some of the challenges they faced for their implementation. The current benefits and their future projection, allowing to recognize those bases that are implemented to improve the quality of life of its inhabitants and daily activities.

Subsequently, the current case of Mexico City is reviewed through an exploratory study with documented information, which seeks to identify the applications of IoT together with the technological advances that the city currently has in terms of urban mobility. The above to identify the benefits obtained by its application and by the interaction of the elements of the system such as: users, transportation systems, infrastructure and external agents. Likewise, the strategic vision of the governments (federal, state and municipal) is identified, to move towards the management of smart cities in the aspect of urban mobility and thus achieve an efficient and sustainable operation. Mention is made of the impact of the implementation of an efficient public policy to move urban mobility towards smart management and a comparison is made with the policies implemented in smart cities with integrated mobility and development solutions. Finally, recommendations are established to achieve these objectives, integrating the main aspects of mobility, development, technology and quality of life.

SMART AND SUSTAINABLE CITY

Smart cities emerged as a new paradigm to establish the advantage acquired by certain cities that make use of technology to achieve better management of their resources and operations. This in different areas of city management, generating greater benefits for citizens such as quality services, safe, reliable, systematized; greater connectivity and environmental care to mention a few. Being pioneers some European cities in the development of this modality Barcelona and Helsinki, for example.

Alvarado (2018), cites that a Smart and Sustainable City model is based on the evolution of ICT's with the interrelation of the actors: society, government, economy and environment, which in turn are present in the following physical and service infrastructures:

- Mobility
- Real estate and services
- Industrial and manufacturing
- Utilities
- Waste management
- Safety and security
- Health care
- Education

Likewise, (as cited in Alvarado, 2018) Smart Cities place the citizen at the center of development, i.e., decisions revolve around the benefit of the population, as shown in Figure1.

Figure 1. Axes of a smart city
Source: based on Alvarado (2018).

Based on the development of cities for the benefit of citizens, mobility is one of the dimensions managed by smart cities, with an efficient and sustainable approach, where the aim is to reduce the problems generated by the increase of the population in cities and that have a direct impact on mobility, such as: high vehicle traffic density, accidents and pollution, which have a significant economic impact, as mentioned by Pérez et al. (2015). In Europe, road congestion costs 1% of the Gross Domestic Product (GDP) each year, in addition to the fact that 69% of road accidents occur in cities and 25% of CO2 emissions in urban areas are generated by transport, all of which are classified as key factors to be resolved due to their significant impact on the degradation of the quality of life in cities.

The European Union (EU) has funded research and innovation projects to develop mobility strategies, such as the Horizon 2020 program, which prioritizes urban mobility, such as sustainable and environmentally friendly transport through the use of non-motorized vehicles and reduction of combustion vehicles, so that transport is competitive worldwide improving mobility and reducing congestion and safety problems in transport (Pérez et al., 2015).Con esto se observa cómo los países desarrollados van a la vanguardia en la gestión de ciudades inteligentes. Sin embargo, los países en vías de desarrollo como lo es México pueden implementar prácticas de gestión de ciudades inteligentes que les ayuden a mejorar la calidad de vida de sus ciudadanos, siendo esto muy relevante, ya que tan solo en la República Mexico

has the sixth most populated city in the world, Mexico City, which together with the metropolitan area, accumulates more than 20 million inhabitants, which generates a very complex and specific urban planning where information technologies play a crucial role in improving the performance of urban mobility systems. Likewise, in the country, there are other important cities such as Monterrey, Guadalajara and Puebla, which also have a complexity in their operation. According to the Diario Oficial de la Federación [DOF] (2014), 77% of investments in mobility in Mexico have been destined for the construction of road infrastructure, which has encouraged a greater use of automobiles, which increases traffic and travel times, decisions that do not lead to intelligent mobility management. This research seeks to identify the current situation in Mexico City with respect to smart mobility management, and also, through comparison with successful cases, to propose ways to direct the management in Mexico towards smart cities in the aspect of mobility, according to current needs.

TECHNOLOGICAL APPLICATIONS FOR MOBILITY IN SMART CITIES (EVALUATION SCALES)

Based on the United Nations (UN) definition of smart and sustainable cities (CIS), it refers to these as "an innovative city that uses information and communication technologies (ICTs) and other means to improve the quality of life, efficiency and performance of urban services, as well as its competitiveness, while ensuring that it meets the needs of present and future generations with respect to economic, social, environmental and cultural aspects" (UNECE, 2023).

Transportation and mobility are critical services within any community nowadays; high urbanization implies the search for improvement in the interaction of infrastructure, users, vehicles and different modes of transportation in a harmonious way reducing the negative externalities that transportation can generate (pollution, accident rate, stress levels) and increasing the positive externalities (economic competitiveness, state-of-the-art technology). The efficient use of ICTs, as part of an integral project in the context of smart cities, will allow for coordination and management activities that would be impossible to achieve without technological support.

Based on the definition of the United Nations, which is considered the most comprehensive for promoting the concept of "people-centered smart cities", it involves not only the application of the latest technology but also social, environmental and even cultural aspects; all this aligned to the objectives of the 2030 Agenda, which allows identifying a comprehensive roadmap reducing the biases of other indexes that are remarkable in their analysis but with a clear bias towards a specific item such as economic or technological, leaving limited social and environmental items. Since this index is published annually only with a significant sample, where the leading countries are listed, it is not possible to verify the ranking of Latin American cities, so we will use the Smart Cities Index 2023 published by the World Competitiveness Institute (IMD) and the Singapore University of Technology and Design, which is published from 2019 on an annualized basis, as shown in Table 1.

Table 1. List of smart city evaluation indixes

Evaluation Framework	Year of publication	Main evaluation criteria	Developed by
IMD-SUTD Smart City index	2021	It evaluates aspects such as: infrastructure and technology applied to health, safety, mobility, as well as governance activities.	IMD World Competitiveness Center y Universidad de Tecnología y diseño de Singapur (SUTD)
Global Cities Index	2021	Business, Human Capital, Information Exchange, Cultural Experiences Cultural and Governance	Kearney
United 4 Smart Sustainable Cities KPIs	2021	Sustainable Development Goals (Target 11 "Make cities and human settlements inclusive, safe, resilient and sustainable.	ITU, UNECE, UN-Habitat
What Works Cities	2021	Data-driven governance	Bloomberg filantropía
Global Power City Index	2022	Multidimensional	Mori Memorial Foundation, Institute of Urban Strategies. Japan
Smart city Government	2021	Smart city governance and preparedness	Instituto Eden Strategy, Singapur
Innovation Cities Index	2021	Emphasis on innovative economics	2thinknow y socios
Research structures in smart cities Juniper.	2021	Smart solutions related to mobility, healthcare, public safety and productivity	Juniper Research
Index of cities on the move (CIMI)	2020	Multidimensional	Center for Strategic Globalization. Business School (IESE), Navarra University
Easy park	2020	Focus on mobility	Grupo Easy park
Austrian Digital Cities Index	2019	Based on the European Digital Cities Index	Center for industrial and economic innovation
Smart Cities Council Tools (Smart Cities Council's tools and frameworks)	2018	Multiple dimensions of intelligence	Australia and New Zealand Smart Cities Council
India Smart Cities Index	2017	Multiple dimensions	Indian School of Business
CityKeys	2017	Multiple dimensions	Netherlands Organization for Applied Scientific Research, Austrian Institute of Technology (AIT), Finnish Center for Technical Research (VTT)
European Digital Cities Index	2016	Digital entrepreneurship	NESTA

Source: WeGo Smart Cities Index 2022, Research on ESG Perspectives in Smart Cities Assessment.

This index published by IMD, in conjunction with the World Organization for Sustainable Smart Cities (WEGO), consists of the following methodology:

1.- The IMD Smart Cities Index evaluates perceptions from the residents about issues related to the infrastructures available in their city.

2.- For the 2023 edition of the CSI, it ranks 141 cities around the world by collecting the opinions of 120 residents in each city. The final score for each city is calculated using perceptions from the last three years of the survey, with a 3:2:1 weighting for 2023:2021:2020.

3.-There are two core elements in the perception gathered from residents: The first refers to the infrastructure that cities have; and the second key element is technology and its availability to residents.

4.- Each principle is evaluated in five key areas: health and safety, mobility, activities, opportunities and governance.

5.- Cities are distributed into four groups according to the Human Development Index (HDI) score [1] of the United Nations Global Data Lab. of the city to which they belong. With the HDI weighting, the comparison is more appropriate and equitable by weighting cities with similar characteristics, thus reducing the gap between cities in developed countries and cities in developing countries, which have different resources and different challenges.

6.- Within each HDI group, cities are assigned a “rating scale” (from AAA to D) based on the score of a given city’s perceptions compared to the scores of all other cities in the same group; of all other cities in the same group with similar characteristics.

Table 2. Description of the IMD-WeGo rating scale

Group 1 (highest quartile of the HDI human development scale)				
AAA	AA	A	BBB	BB
Group 2 (Second quartile of the HDI human development scale)				
A	BBB	BB	B	C
Group 3 (Third quartile of the HDI human development scale)				
BB	B	CCC	CC	C
Group 4 (lowest quartile of the HDI human development scale)				
CCC	CC	C	D	

Source: Based on Smart Index Report 2023

7.- Finally, the ranking is presented in two formats:

- Overall evaluation of the global ranking (1 to 141).
- Evaluation for each individual item, and overall evaluation.

In recent years, environmental, social and governance (ESG) items have been integrated into the weighting factors, to achieve this goal, the development of indicators is key and allows continuous and efficient monitoring of the performance of these issues, a fundamental tool is the human development index proposed by the united nations; which complements the multi-actor and multi-criteria approach required in this complex evaluation.

-Human Development Index (HDI, United Nations)

Figure 2. Human development index
Source: Human development reports United Nations for development programme (n.d.), https://hdr.undp.org/data-center/human-development-index#/indicies/HDI

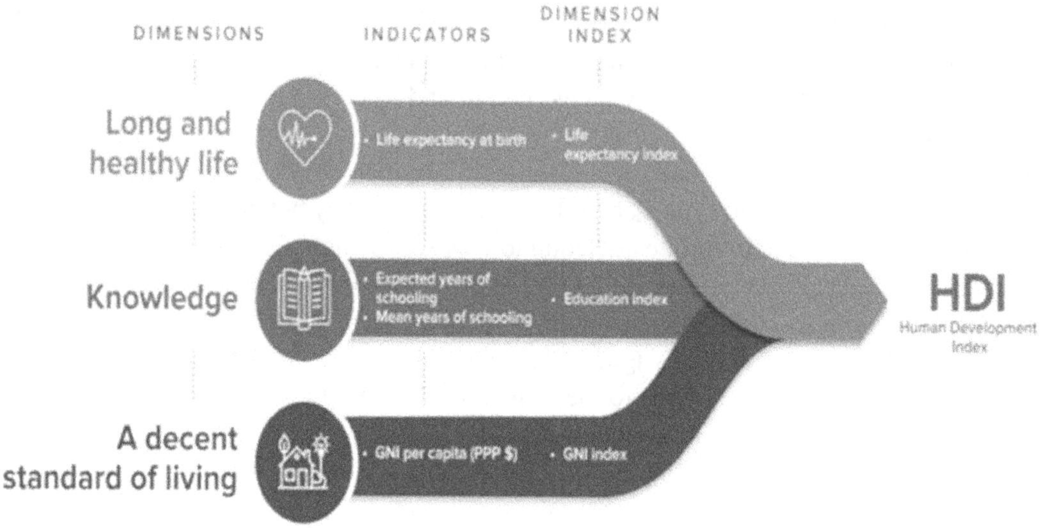

According to the The Human Development Index web page (n.d.): (HDI) "*is an indicator that considers the main dimensions of human development: life expectancy and health, functional educational level within society, and an average income level that allows satisfying an acceptable standard of living*". Thus, the HDI is the geometric mean of the normalized indexes of each of the three dimensions, as shown in Figure 2.

Within the life expectancy and health dimension, it is measured by life expectancy at birth; the education dimension is measured by the average years of schooling for adults over 25 years of age or older, as well as the expected years of schooling for school-age children; and the standard of living is measured by the gross domestic product (GDP).

The HDI is used in a variety of issues to support decision making, contrast and analyze between countries, identifying differences and similarities according to similar criteria. The HDI is considered one of the most standardized indicators. For this reason, it serves as support in the smart cities index, helping to compare the indexes between cities and recognizing those innovative proposals to implement within a smart city, specifically smart and sustainable mobility.

The HDI simplifies and captures only a part of what human development entails. It does not reflect inequalities, poverty, human security, empowerment, etc. The United Nations through its Human Development Reports Branch provides other composite indices as a broader approach to some key human development issues such as inequality, gender disparity and poverty, giving a comprehensive picture of all the characteristics involved in a city's development.

CDMX ANALYSIS

According to the exploratory study with documentary information oriented to the case of Mexico City (CDMX), for this chapter, and in addition to the aforementioned characteristics; the IMD World Competitiveness, in the Index Report issued for 2023, in relation to Smart Cities, within which 141 cities were reviewed. A previously described index called Human Development Index (HDI), proposed by the United Nations Development Programme (UNDP), is used.

In this HDI index, life expectancy, schooling and per capita income, among other data, are analyzed for each year reviewed. In addition to the data issued by Global Data Lab, thus allowing a comparison of the performance of the 141 cities mentioned above as Smart Cities.

The work methodology analyzed two general variables: city infrastructure and technology (technological benefits and services available to residents). In turn, each main variable is subdivided into five internal variables: health and safety, mobility, activities, opportunities and governance. Each of these variables has specific indicators for each subdivision.

Thus, the analysis has a temporal scope from 2019 to 2023, (with the exception of 2022, due to the COVID-19 pandemic). And in the case of the CDMX, it is analyzed for the year 2023, which has a population of 22,085,139 people; currently occupying 121st place out of 141 countries. It is worth noting that it had a setback from the 90th place, obtained in 2019, as shown in Table 3.

Table 3. Rankings 2019-2023

City	HDI city	Year			
		2019	2020	2021	2023
México city	0.815	90	103	110	121

Source: Modified from IMD *World Competitiveness, 2023.*
Note: data reflected in 2022 analysis didn´t count for the pandemic COVID-19.

Table 1 shows a significant decline from 90th place in 2019 to 121st place in 2023.

This regression is analyzed on the basis of five general indicators, which identify the urbanization prospects up to 2021. The regression is understood by analyzing indicators such as HDI, life expectancy, schooling, and National Income per capita (GNI) in detail in Table 4.

Tabla 4. Rankings 2019-2023

KPI´s CDMX	2018	2019	2020	2021	Changes 2018-2021
HDI	0.767	.779	0.756	0.758	-0.009
Life expectancy at birth	75	75.1	70.1	70.2	-4.6
Expected years of schooling	14.3	14.8	14.9	14.9	0.6
Average years of schooling	8.6	8.8	9.2	9.2	0.6
Gross National Income (GNI) per capita (PPP $)	17,628	19,160	17,235	17,896	268

Source: Modified from IMD *World Competitiveness, 2023.*

It can be observed the setback of 4.6 years in the indicator life expectancy in the comparative 2021 to 2018, as well as the increase of 268 dollars in the indicator Gross National Income (GNI) per capita (PPP $) in the same time comparative.

Within the first group of variables (health and safety indicators), of the so-called general variable CDMX Infrastructure, it can be seen in Table 5.

Table 5. Health and safety indicators

Health and safety indicators	Average value	CDMX value
Basic sanitation meets the needs of poorer areas	62	38.8
Recycling services are satisfactory	60	41.9
Citizen security is not a problem	43	20.6
Air pollution is not a problem	39	18.5
The provision of medical services is satisfactory	61	35.6
Finding housing with rents equal to or less than 30% of a monthly salary is not a problem Mobility	39	26.1

Source: Modified from IMD *World Competitiveness, 2023.*

It can be observed that the six health and safety indicators of the CDMX are lower than the average value obtained in the analysis of the 141 countries analyzed. The lowest being the indicator regarding air pollution.

The second group of infrastructure indicators focused on mobility are detailed in Table 6.

Table 6. Mobility indicators

Mobility Indicators	Average value	CDMX value
Traffic congestion is not an issue. Car sharing applications have reduced congestion.	25	20.1
Public transportation is satisfactory.	30	28.9

Source: Modified from IMD *World Competitiveness, 2023.*

It is observed that both indicators are lower than the average obtained in the analysis of the 141 countries analyzed. The lowest indicator is the one related to vehicular traffic congestion.

With respect to the third group of infrastructure indicators focused on outdoor activities, Table 7 shows the following details.

Table 7. Outdoor activities

Outdoor activity indicators	Average value	CDMX value
Green spaces are satisfactory	60	57.1
Cultural activities (shows, bars and museums) are satisfactory	72	70.4

Source: Modified from IMD *World Competitiveness, 2023.*

It is observed that both indicators are lower than the average obtained in the analysis of the 141 countries analyzed. The lowest is the green spaces indicator.

With respect to the fourth group of infrastructure indicators focused on opportunities (work and school), they are detailed in Table 8.

Table 8. Opportunities (work and school)

Indicators Opportunities (work and school)	Average value	CDMX value
Job search services are available	60	46.8
Most children have access to a good school.	62	35.5
Local institutions provide lifelong learning opportunitie	60	35.9
Companies are creating new jobs	59	46.7
Minorities feel welcome	59	36.6

Source: Modified from IMD *World Competitiveness, 2023.*

It can be seen that all six indicators are below the average obtained in the analysis of the 141 countries analyzed. The lowest indicator is access to a good school for children.

Regarding the fifth and last group of Governance indicators, they are detailed in Table 9.

Table 9. Governance

Governance Indicators	Average value	CDMX value
Information on local government decisions is easily accessible	60	49.3
Corruption of city officials is not a concern	39	16.2
Residents contribute to local government decision making	40	36.3
Residents give their opinion on local government projects	50	37.6

Source: Modified from IMD *World Competitiveness, 2023.*

It is observed that the four indicators are lower than the average obtained in the analysis of the 141 countries analyzed. The lowest indicator with respect to concern about corruption among city officials stands out.

With respect to the second general variable called technology (technological benefits and services available), the five groups of indicators are detailed below.

Within the first group of CDMX technology variables, the first six health and safety indicators were analyzed as shown in Table 10.

Table 10. Health and safety indicators

Health and safety indicators	Average value	CDMX value
Online reporting of city maintenance issues provides a quick fix	50	38.8
A website or app allows residents to easily give away unwanted items	52	44.0
Free public wifi has improved access to city services	58	59.6
CCTV cameras have made residents feel safer and more secure	60	51.3
A website or app allows residents to effectively monitor air pollution	48	48.7
Arranging medical appointments online has improved access	62	56.9

Source: Modified from IMD *World Competitiveness, 2023.*

It is observed that four indicators are lower than the average obtained in the analysis of the 141 countries analyzed; however, the free public wifi indicator has improved access to city services, it is the only one that has been able to be higher than the above-mentioned average.

With respect to the second group of infrastructure indicators focused on mobility, which are detailed in Table 11.

Table 11. Mobility indicators

Mobility Indicators	Average value	CDMX value
Car-sharing applications have reduced congestion	50	41.8
Apps that direct you to an available parking space have reduced travel time	52	42.8
Bike rentals have reduced congestion	52	52.2
Online scheduling and ticketing have made public transportation easier to use.	61	51.9
City offers traffic congestion information via app´s	60	60.5

Source: Modified from IMD *World Competitiveness, 2023.*

Of the five indicators, three are below the average obtained in the analysis of the 141 countries analyzed. However, the indicators "bicycle rental has reduced congestion" and "the city provides information on traffic congestion through cell phones" are above the average.

The third group of infrastructure indicators focused on outdoor activities are detailed in Table 12.

Table 12. Outdoor activities

Activity indicators	Average value	CDMX value
The online purchase of tickets for shows and museums has made it easier for people to attend.	80	72.1

Source: Modified from IMD *World Competitiveness, 2023.*

It can be seen that the only indicator is below the average obtained in the analysis of the 141 countries analyzed.

The fourth group of infrastructure indicators focused on opportunities (work and school) are detailed in Table 13.

Table 13. Opportunities (job and school)

Indicators Opportunities (job and school)	Average value	CDMX value
Online access to job offers has made it easier to find a job.	72	81.9
IT skills taught well in schools.	59	72.7
Online services provided by the city have made it easier to start a new business.	60	80.3
Today's Internet speed and reliability meet connectivity needs.	62	78.3

Source: Modified from IMD *World Competitiveness, 2023.*

With respect to this group of indicators, it can be observed that they are the only ones that are all above the average obtained in the analysis of the 141 countries analyzed.

With respect to the fifth and last group of infrastructure indicators focused on governance, they are detailed in Table 14.

Table 14. Governance

Governance Indicators	Average value	CDMX value
Online public access to city finances has reduced corruption	70	65.1
Online voting has increased participation	70	65.7
An online platform where residents can propose ideas has improved city life	79	72.8
The online processing of Identity Documents has reduced waiting times.	81	78.9

Source: Modified from IMD *World Competitiveness, 2023.*

It is observed that the four indicators are lower than the average obtained in the analysis of the 141 countries analyzed. The lowest indicator is access to public finances to reduce corruption through electronic means.

According to the above, it is observed that for this analysis, the CDMX presents a better development in the general variable called technology (technological benefits and available services), specifically, in the group of Indicators Opportunities (work and school), where the five indicators are above the above mentioned average and the general variable called Infrastructure of the cities. Each of these indicators identifies areas of opportunity for improvement and continued growth for one of the most important cities in Mexico, where a significant number of inhabitants and their development in different aspects are concentrated.

IMPROVEMENT PROPOSAL FOR THE CASE OF MEXICO CITY

The Smart City concept is focused on the use of information and communication technologies for the creation and improvement of services that impact the quality of life of people in a city. It allows the management of growth by taking advantage of both existing and new infrastructure under criteria of sustainability and inclusion. It also considers the reduction of energy and resource consumption, as well as waste generation. In addition, it focuses on obtaining an open government for the harmonized implementation of public policies. In short, a smart city prioritizes the care of the environment and the quality of life of its inhabitants through technology.

According to the KPMG portal, Mexico has made great efforts to develop smart cities, for which the Inter-American Development Bank (IDB) recognizes Guadalajara after the implementation of the Ciudad Creativa Digital (CCD) project, Chihuahua for its wireless internet coverage, as well as Mexico City for its innovative use of data in the public policy cycle. In addition, Aguascalientes, Mérida, Morelia and Xalapa seek to be promoted to this category for their initiatives and processes to improve their infrastructure and services for the benefit of their inhabitants and main activities for the state.

As previously mentioned, the International Institute for Management Development (IMD) has ranked Mexico City 108th out of 118 cities in 2021; and 121st out of 141 cities in 2023. The cities are distributed in four groups based on the Human Development Index (HDI), placing Mexico City in Group 3, positioned in Group C in structures, and in Group CC in technology, with all the rankings in this group being AAA to D. The indicators analyzed are the Human Development Index, life expectancy, school expectancy, years of schooling and Gross Domestic Product per capita.

Mexico City is considered one of the 5 smart cities in the Mexican Republic. It stands out for its sustainable mobility, which incorporates various platforms such as Ecobici, which shares the use of bicycles to move to different parts of the city in order to decongest traffic. Another of the achievements of this city is to be recognized as the second city in the world with more free public Internet, with 14 thousand C5 poles with 100 megabytes of speed, 96 connectivity points in public squares and hospitals, and 154 pillars with 200 megabytes of speed. It also has intelligent lighting, multimodal transportation, sensors, electronic payment cards, in addition to the growing use of mobile devices and a 5G network.

According to Guzmán (2023), "the spaces required today are modern buildings that can adapt to people and their needs, made with more sustainable materials, resistant to natural disasters and, above all, with more dynamic designs. There is a need for more spaces with a mixed approach, more people-oriented and with elements integrated with the environment to live, work and have fun, integrating technological elements in view of the growing need for interconnection.

Zapata mentions (2021), "In addition to the technology that can be used in smart cities, the space inhabited by the inhabitants must be taken into account in order to provide a good quality of life". In other words, a smart city does not only make use of technology. The very definition of smart city implies making life more friendly for all people, allowing an organic development according to present and future elements.

According to Cortés (2016), a study sponsored by Nokia places Mexico City in three different areas: Smart Safety, where Internet of Things applications aim to help prevent or minimize the risks and impact of adverse events such as crime, accidents, environmental pollution and natural disasters; Smart Sustainability, where applications aimed at reducing the environmental impact of the city, its businesses and its citizens are used; and Smart Quality of Life, where use is made of applications that are aimed at improving the quality of life of its citizens and providing economic support by making cities more attractive places to live by allowing the integration of the three elements in favor of the comfort of a city's inhabitants.

According to Cortés (2016), one of the most important points in Mexico City refers to the traffic and incident management system initiatives, where more than 20,000 cameras and sensors are in place, generating information in five control branches, monitored in a general control, communications, computers and intelligence center called C4, known locally as the CAEPCCM. This solution includes gunshot sensors, license plate number recognition software, panic buttons for emergency calls placed on guard posts, and aerial surveillance drones. This enables the collection of safety and road safety data as a consequence of implementing appropriate and tailored measures to reduce unfortunate events, or mismanagement of services offered.

In terms of human mobility, intelligent transportation and urban traffic management are revolutionizing the way in which mobility and emergency care must be addressed, reducing congestion on the streets through sensors, automation, advanced communication systems and high-speed networks. Giving way to proper management and, if necessary, the implementation of other means of transportation where appropriate to improve the level of service for the mobility of the inhabitants.

For Mazur (2020), intelligent transportation is about management, efficiency and safety. In other words, smart transportation uses new and emerging technologies to make getting around a city more convenient, more cost-effective (for both the city and the individual), and safer. It is not just a theory for the future; it is being applied today in several cities, and its successes and failures are being used to improve systems in new places. As is the case here, by studying the current way in which public and private transportation is managed, recognizing what factors do or do not help to make it efficient for its users.

As Mazur (2020) said, the benefits of smart technology and the advantages they bring to transportation within a smart city include the following: Safer smart transportation, which by combining machine learning from the Internet of Things and autonomous transportation systems reduce the human factor in accidents. Smart transportation has better management, as it allows for better monitoring of operations, better tracking of maintenance needs, as well as identifying the sources of problems to be fixed. Intelligent transportation is more efficient, since the data obtained helps identify areas for improvement to increase efficiency. Intelligent transportation is cost-effective, since it makes better use of available resources, reducing costs through preventive maintenance, lower energy consumption and fewer resources allocated to accidents. Intelligent transportation provides timely information; since traffic management centers can obtain quick visibility of problem points in order to take action and communicate more effectively with other agencies or emergency personnel, developing a mechanism for rapid action and continuous improvement to increase the use of this, allowing an integrated development with the different axes that make up a city of such magnitude.

Based on the above, the recommendations for Mexico City in terms of intelligent transportation would be as follows:

- **Security:** Intelligent transportation can make public transport more secure by reducing the possibility of both physical and cyber attacks through appropriate software upgrades, encrypted communications through virtual private networks (VPNs), and multi-layered systems that can mitigate the risk of cyber attacks.
- **Environmental considerations:** The use of mass transit is demonstrably better for the environment than private vehicles, so its use can be more lucrative for more sectors of the population,

using monthly prepaid cards that allow unlimited use, improving both household economy and quality of service.

- **Supply chain resilience:** the use of autonomous transportation for moving critical goods such as food and medicine without human intervention, using automation, robotics and artificial intelligence.
- **Intelligent highways:** through messaging panels placed on highways that send real-time information on traffic conditions, such as fog banks, road accidents, infrastructure failures such as potholes or water leaks, providing greater safety during travel. This option is also applicable to railways to improve Mexico City's public transportation system, which consists of the subway and suburban trains.
- **Traffic counting systems** would provide information on the number of vehicles and when the most traffic occurs so that authorities can better plan infrastructure projects such as lane widening and alternate route planning. Allowing optimal use of time and resources, in turn improving the level of service for users.
- **Improved toll booths:** payment systems can be implemented by transfers or through barcodes or QR codes to speed up waiting time at toll booths and reduce travel time.

The use of technologies can improve people's lives in many ways, as they can be applied to any field of work, leisure and life in general, to generate mobility solutions in a safer and more economical way, mobility considerations can not only be for a means of transport, and can even be applied to air transport, making not only roads and trains intelligent, but also intelligent airports. In this way, not only users but also governments benefit from being able to better plan communication routes to make them more efficient and reduce both manufacturing and maintenance costs.

This chapter explained the basis of a smart city and how mobility can also be smart with the appropriate resources and measures for the inhabitants, improving in three essential areas to the development of the city; time-sustainability-interconnectivity. The importance of collecting relevant information and data to make efficient use of them and propose efficient solutions to the use of roads, resources and direct users (those who make use of any means of transportation) or indirect users (sharing infrastructure and impacting their quality of life) was explained.

REFERENCES

Alvarado, L., R. A. (2018). Ciudad inteligente y sostenible: hacia un modelo de innovación inclusiva. *PAAKAT: revista de tecnología y sociedad, 7*(13).

Cortés, M. (2016). *Porque la ciudad de México es una de las más inteligentes del mundo*. CIO México https://cio.com.mx/la-ciudad-mexico-una-las-mas-inteligentes-del-mundo/

De Evaluación Modernización Y Desarrollo Administrativo. C. G. (s. f.). *Delegaciones*. Coordinación General de Evaluación, Modernización Y Desarrollo Administrativo. https://www.cgma.cdmx.gob.mx/temas-de-modernizacion/resultados-avance-aac/delegaciones

Guzman, A. (2022, 13 octubre). Smart Cities en México. *Magnet Mexico*. https://www.magnetmex.com/industria-4-0/smart-cities-en-mexico/

Human Development Index (HDI). (2023). *UNDP*. HDR. https://hdr.undp.org/data-center/human-development-index#/indicies/HDI

IMD. (2023). *Smart City Index Report 2023*. IMD. https://www.imd.org/wp-content/uploads/2023/06/SmartCityIndex-2023-V8.pdf

Inegi. (2020, 4 marzo). *México en cifras*. Inegi. https://www.inegi.org.mx/app/areasgeograficas/?ag=07000009#collapse-Resumen

Mazur, S. (n.d.). *An Introduction to Smart Transportation: Benefits and Examples*. Digi. https://es.digi.com/blog/post/introduction-to-smart-transportation-benefits

Millán, C. (s.f.) *Smart cities en México: factoresde éxito*. KPMG. https://kpmg.com/mx/es/home/tendencias/2021/10/ao-smart-cities-en-mexico-factores-de exito.html#:~:text=En%20el%20caso%20de%20M%C3%A9xico,%2C%20Puebla%2C%20Guadalajara%20y%20Monterrey

Moreno, A. C., Baucells, A. N., & Arce, R. R. M. (2016). *Smart mobility in smart cities*. En: XII Congreso de Ingeniería del Transporte (CIT 2016), Valencia.. 10.4995/CIT2016.2016.3485

Pérez, P. F., Velázquez, R. G., Fernandez, A. M. V., & Dorao, S. J. (2015). Movilidad Inteligente. *Economía Industrial*, (395), 111–121.

World Smart Sustainable Cities Organization (WeGo). (2022). Smart City Index 2022 Research on ESG perspectives in smart cities assessment. WeGo.

Zapata, E. (2021). Redensificación y construcción: claves para hacer de la CDMX una smart city. *Expansión*. https://expansion.mx/inmobiliario/2021/12/20/ciudad-de-mexico-lejos-de-convertirse-ciudad-inteligentehttps://cio.com.mx/la-ciudad-mexico-una-las-mas-inteligentes-del-mundo/

Chapter 16
Use of an Intelligent Voice Recognition Device to Monitor and Mitigate Children With Anxiety–Induced Asthma Attacks

Leticia Ortiz
Doctorado en Tecnología, Universidad Autónoma de Ciudad Juárez, Mexico

Alberto Ochoa-Zezzatti
https://orcid.org/0000-0002-9183-6086
Doctorado en Tecnología, Universidad Autónoma de Ciudad Juárez, Mexico & CADIT, Facultad de Ingeniería, Universidad Anáhuac, Mexico

Alexandra Juanes
Doctorado en Tecnología, Universidad Autónoma de Ciudad Juárez, Mexico

Erick Olguin
Doctorado en Tecnología, Universidad Autónoma de Ciudad Juárez, Mexico

Luis Vidal
Doctorado en Tecnología, Universidad Autónoma de Ciudad Juárez, Mexico

Víctor López
CADIT, Facultad de Ingeniería, Universidad Anáhuac, Mexico

ABSTRACT

In this research, the use of Alexa for monitoring patients with asthma anxiety attacks was evaluated. Twenty-seven dates in the current year were randomly selected and the duration of anxiety attacks in seconds was recorded, as well as their severity on a Likert scale ranging from 1.00 to 7.00. The results showed that the duration of anxiety attacks ranged from 47 to 287 seconds, with a mean of 163.7 seconds. In addition, a positive correlation was found between the duration of anxiety attacks and severity according to the Likert scale. These findings suggest that Alexa monitoring could be a useful option for the evaluation and treatment of patients with asthma anxiety attacks. Based on these findings and suggestions, the authors propose the integration of a mechatronic system that uses the conjunction of

DOI: 10.4018/979-8-3693-0373-3.ch016

mechanical, computer, electronic, and electrical systems to monitor the possible most recurrent symptoms of anxiety-induced asthma, in addition to the analysis of ergonomic factors that contemplate the satisfaction of the people to whom the proposal is addressed. This monitoring is aimed at reducing the frequency of attacks and improving the quality of life. However, future studies with larger and more diversified samples are needed to confirm these results and evaluate the effectiveness of the intervention in improving patients' quality of life. Different reactive levels are proposed to identify a real time solution of a possible massive anxiety attack for children between eight and 12 years old.

1. INTRODUCTION

Today, the term "Smart Life" refers to the ability of smart cities to improve the quality of life of their inhabitants through the application of innovative and sustainable technologies. The Smart City focuses on the integration of information and communication systems to offer more efficient and effective public services, optimizing natural resources and reducing costs. In this context, the Smart Life concept becomes a tool for improving the quality of life of citizens, allowing greater efficiency and time reduction in services such as transportation, health, education and security. (Rezvani, M., Fanaei, S., & Hassankhani, H.; 2019)

In addition, the implementation of smart technologies can improve resource management, minimize environmental impacts and ensure a better quality of life for citizens. One of the main objectives of smart cities is to improve the quality of life of their inhabitants, and this requires comprehensive planning, good resource management and effective integration of technologies. In this sense, Smart Life becomes an indispensable tool to achieve this goal, as it allows for a better management of natural resources and a reduction in the costs associated with the provision of public services. In short, the idea of a Smart City with an integrated Smart Life is a unique opportunity for the improvement of citizens' quality of life. It is an innovative and sustainable approach that can significantly improve the efficiency and effectiveness of public services and improve the overall quality of life. Therefore, it is essential to continue advancing in the research and development of smart technologies that enable a more efficient and effective management of cities, for the benefit of all their inhabitants.

2. CASE STUDY: ASTHMA IN CHILDREN WITHIN A SMART CITY

Asthma is a common respiratory disease that can be caused or made worse by psychological factors, such as stress and anxiety. Anxiety-induced asthma attacks are a particularly difficult way to treat the disease, as symptoms can come on suddenly and without warning. In this article, we present a case study of a child with anxiety-induced asthma who was monitored with an Alexa device to help prevent asthma attacks and improve the quality of life for the child and her family. Asthma is a chronic disease that affects millions of people around the world. It is characterized by inflammation of the airways, which can lead to shortness of breath, coughing, wheezing, and chest tightness. While most people with asthma can control their disease with medication and lifestyle changes, some patients may experience more severe asthma attacks, which can be triggered by psychological factors such as stress and anxiety.

Anxiety-induced asthma attacks can be particularly difficult to treat, as symptoms can come on suddenly and without warning. In addition, these attacks can be very distressing for patients and their families, which can further exacerbate anxiety and worsen asthma symptoms. In recent years, home assistive devices such as Amazon Alexa smart speakers have gained popularity for their ability to control the home and help with everyday tasks. In this article, we present a case study of a child with anxiety-induced asthma who was monitored with an Alexa device to help prevent asthma attacks and improve the quality of life for the child and her family.

Methods The study boy was 10 years old and had been diagnosed with anxiety-induced asthma. The boy's parents installed an Amazon Alexa device in her bedroom and programmed the device to monitor the following asthma indicators:

- The temperature and humidity in the child's room
- The air quality in the child's room
- The child's sleep patterns
- The frequency and duration of coughing and wheezing episodes
- The frequency and duration of asthma attacks

The parents also programmed the device to alert them when significant changes were detected in any of these indicators. In addition, the device was connected to a mobile app that allowed parents to monitor data in real time and receive alerts when necessary.

Results During the three-month study period, the child experienced a significant decrease in the frequency and duration of attacks.

The use of home health assistive devices is constantly evolving and improving [11]. One of the most popular devices is Alexa, a voice assistant developed by Amazon. Alexa has been used for a variety of tasks around the home, from home automation to cooking. In this essay, we will explore how Alexa can be used to monitor a child having anxiety-related asthma attacks. Anxiety is one of the main causes of asthma attacks in children. Asthma attacks can be caused by a variety of factors, including exercise, allergies, and stress. Anxiety can cause asthma attacks because it causes the muscles in the airways to tighten, making it hard to breathe. Monitoring anxiety and asthma symptoms is essential to treat and prevent asthma attacks. Alexa can be used to monitor a child with anxiety-related asthma attacks by providing reminders to take medication, intelligent analytics to predict attack intensity and duration, and a reactive model that can determine future action for the attack. type of attacks.

3. PROPOSED METHODOLOGY

To assess the effectiveness of an Alexa device in monitoring a child with anxiety asthma attacks, a pilot study was conducted. Three children diagnosed with asthma and anxiety participated in the study. The children's parents installed an Alexa device in their children's room and received training on how to use the device to monitor asthma symptoms. Parents used the Alexa device to monitor their children's asthma symptoms for a month. They recorded their children's asthma symptoms, including the frequency of attacks, the duration and severity of symptoms. Parents also recorded their children's anxiety level using an anxiety scale. Since in a Smart City it is common for an infant to be left alone in his room or at home and when suffering from this disease, it is important to determine that the IoT model works as a vital support to mitigate the effects and consequences of anxiety in children, in Figure 1, we show a different level of connectivity with diverse sensors to different applications in a Smart City. (Chen, X., Huang, X., Zhang, J., & Liu, J.; 2020)

To develop this study on the use of smart technology to monitor asthma anxiety attacks, the following components of the Internet of Things (IoT) could be used:

- Sensors: IoT sensors could be used to detect and monitor various environmental factors that can trigger asthma attacks, such as humidity, temperature, air quality, and pollen levels.
- Wearable devices: Wearable devices, such as smartwatches or fitness trackers, could be used to monitor patients' physical activity and vital signs, such as heart rate, blood pressure, and oxygen saturation levels.
- Smart home devices: Smart home devices, such as smart thermostats or air purifiers, could be used to create a comfortable and healthy indoor environment for asthma patients.
- Smart inhalers: Smart inhalers are devices that can be attached to traditional inhalers to monitor medication usage and provide feedback to patients and doctors on adherence and effectiveness. (Kocaballi, A. B., Berkovsky, S., Quiroz, J. C., & Quiroz, V,; 2020)
- Voice assistants: Voice assistants, such as Amazon Alexa or Google Assistant, could be used to allow patients to report their symptoms and receive personalized recommendations on how to manage their condition.
- Cloud computing: Cloud computing could be used to store and process large amounts of data generated by IoT devices, allowing for real-time monitoring and analysis of patients' condition and treatment effectiveness. (Liu, W., Li, L. y Su, Q.; 2019)
- Mobile apps: Mobile apps could be used to provide patients with access to their medical records, medication reminders, and personalized recommendations on managing their condition.
- Machine learning algorithms: Machine learning algorithms could be used to analyze data collected from IoT devices and predict patients' asthma attacks, allowing for early intervention and prevention. (Ye, Y., Hu, J., Sun, Z., & Guo, Y.; 2020)
- Blockchain: Blockchain technology could be used to secure and share medical data between patients, doctors, and other stakeholders involved in the treatment process.
- Augmented reality: Augmented reality could be used to provide patients with visual instructions on how to use their inhalers correctly and manage their condition effectively.
- Telemedicine: Telemedicine could be used to allow patients to connect with their doctors remotely, reducing the need for in-person visits and improving access to medical care.
- Data analytics: Data analytics could be used to identify patterns and trends in patients' condition and treatment effectiveness, allowing for continuous improvement of the treatment process.

Figure 1. Different layers associated with the connectopy in a project of IoT

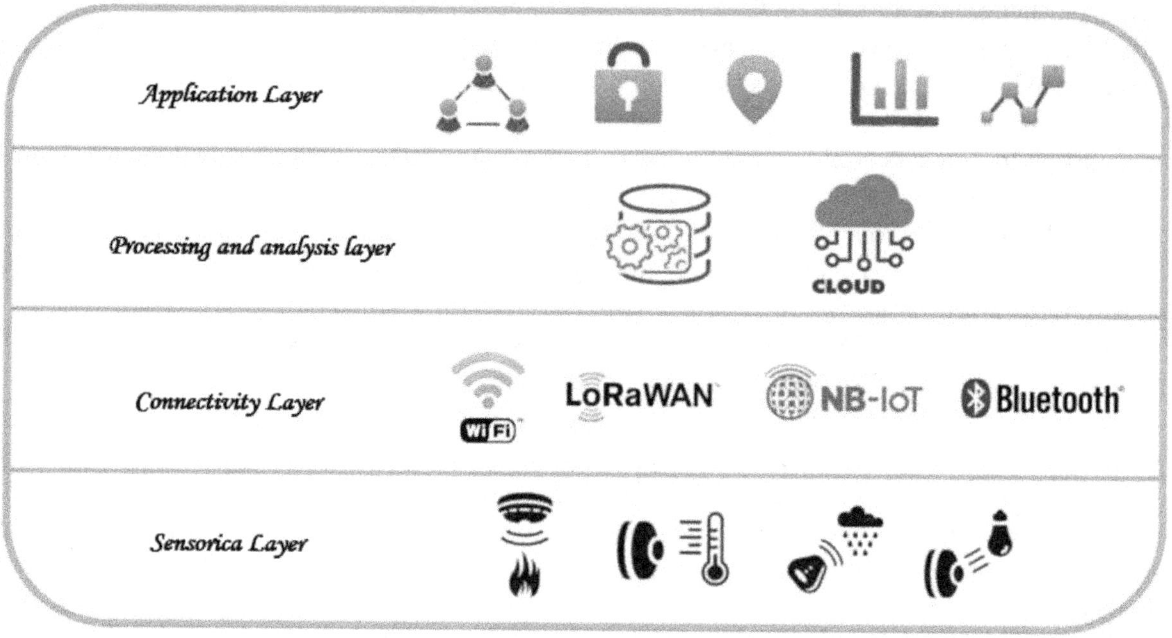

Broadly speaking, the operating principle of IoT is based on the following layers:

- Sensorics associated with the Dispositive: Congregates devices with the capacity to take measurements of certain physical magnitudes or parameters (temperature, humidity, etc.). Their energy consumption must be very low, since their power supply will depend on a battery. In addition, some of them may have capabilities to perform actions and interaction.
- Connectivity: Establishes a communication channel between sensors or devices and a platform or gateway, which can be implemented in a concentrated machine or under a cloud architecture, through a wide range of wireless technologies (Wi-Fi, NB-IoT, Zigbee, Bluetooth, LPWAN, etc.).
- Analysis and processing: Enable the collection of data from sensors, so that they can be analyzed and processed in real time (or near real time) in order to use them to create efficient business intelligence.
- Application or User Interface: Enables device management, helping companies to integrate, organize, monitor and remotely manage devices, while providing critical features to maintain system health, connectivity and security throughout their lifecycles.

Finally, there are a number of challenges that can hinder the successful implementation of an IoT-based solution, including issues related to security, interoperability, processing capabilities, power, scalability and availability.

4. DISCUSSION OF RESULTS

The results of the pilot study indicate that the use of an Alexa device to monitor a child with anxiety asthma attacks may be effective. Parents were able to record their children's asthma symptoms effectively and take preventive measures to avoid an asthma attack. Parents were also able to monitor their child's anxiety level and take steps to reduce anxiety. Parents reported that the Alexa device was easy to use and gave them a greater sense of control over their child's health. Children also reported that they liked using the Alexa device and that they felt more secure and comfortable knowing that their parents could effectively monitor their health. These results are very encouraging, as they indicate that remote monitoring technology can be effective in child health care. The ease of use of the device and the sense of control it gives parents are important factors in the successful adoption of remote monitoring technology. Additionally, the ability to monitor children's anxiety level may have additional benefits in terms of mental health and well-being. Anxiety can be a trigger for asthma attacks, so taking steps to reduce anxiety can help prevent future asthma attacks. We compiled a list of the seven most recurrent possible symptoms of anxiety-induced asthma, which are: Shortness of Breathing, Wheezing, Chest Tightness, Dry Cough, Fatigue, Palpitations and Sweating, which were characterized for a group of attacks to be able to consider close relationships between them, as can be seen in Figure 2.

Figure 2. Representation of a sample of asthma attacks and the correlation with specific symptoms.

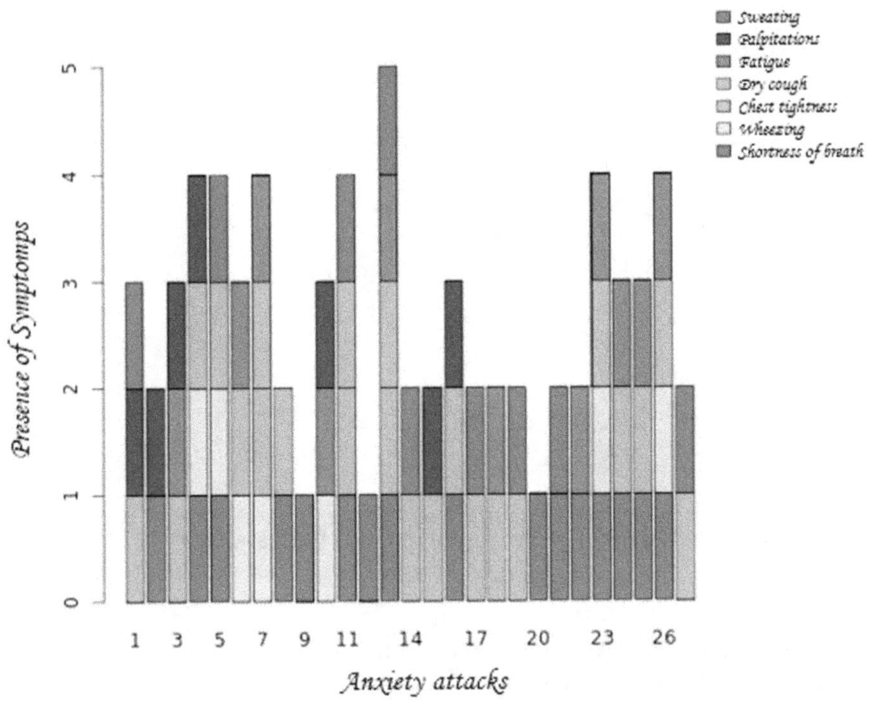

However, it is important to note that this study was a pilot and larger, controlled studies are needed to confirm the results. It is also important to consider the privacy and security of the data collected by the Alexa device and to ensure that applicable privacy policies and regulations are followed. In summary, the results of the pilot study indicate that the use of remote monitoring devices such as Alexa may be effective in child health care, especially in managing asthma and anxiety. More research is needed to confirm these results and to ensure the privacy and security of the data collected, which is presented in figure 3.Principio del formulario

Figure 3. Analysis of anxiety attack tracking by IoT monitoring of a speech recognition device adapted with concentric type wheels to be able to interact with the node on a table or smooth surface

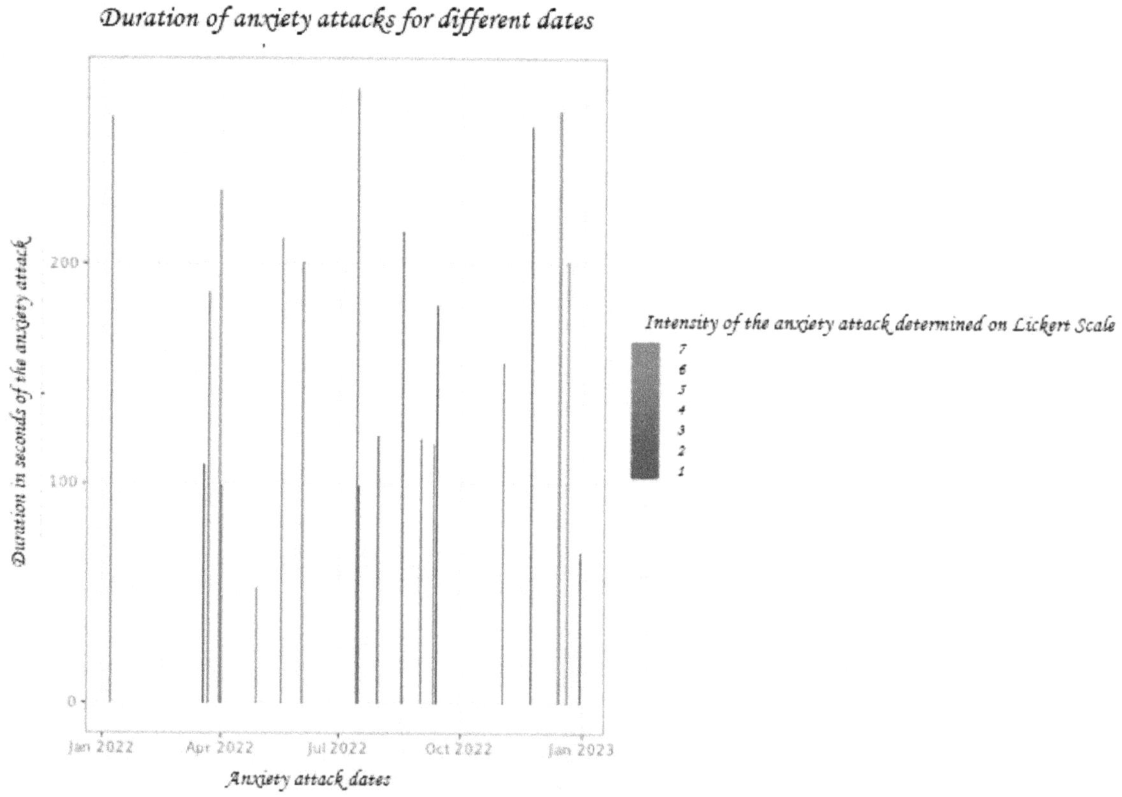

Here are some possible pros and cons of the research described above:

Pros:

- Contributes to knowledge about the use of technology to monitor patients with anxiety disorders associated with asthma, which could improve the quality of medical care that patients receive.
- Provides useful information on the duration of anxiety attacks in an Alexa monitoring context and its relationship to the Likert scale, which could help healthcare professionals bet-

ter understand symptom severity and make more informed decisions. informed about the treatment.

- The results of the research could serve as a basis for future studies in the field of psychology and mental health, particularly in the application of technology for monitoring anxiety disorders.

Cons:

- The sample of patients analyzed in the research was limited (27 random dates) and no information was provided on the ethnic, cultural and socioeconomic diversity of the patients included in the sample. This limits the generalizability of the results.
- The study focused only on the duration of anxiety attacks and its relationship to the Likert scale, which could limit understanding of the impact of other factors on symptom severity, as mentioned above.
- Although the use of Alexa to monitor patients can be an innovative and convenient option, it is not accessible to all patients due to factors such as availability, cost, and accessibility of technology, which could limit the applicability of the results.

In summary, although this research may contribute to knowledge about the use of technology for monitoring patients with anxiety disorders associated with asthma, there are some aspects that could be improved in future research.

Here are some future recommendations that could be derived from this research:

1. Expansion of the sample: This research focused on the analysis of data from 27 random dates, so it would be interesting to expand the sample to include a greater number of dates and patients with asthma anxiety attacks. In this way, more precise and generalizable results could be obtained.
2. Multivariate analysis: This study analyzed the duration of anxiety attacks and its relationship with the Likert scale, but it would also be interesting to explore other variables that may influence the severity of anxiety attacks. For example, the patient's age, general anxiety level, or the presence of other psychological disorders could be considered.
3. Evaluation of the impact of the intervention: In this research, the duration of anxiety attacks was analyzed in a context of monitoring with Alexa, but it would be interesting to evaluate the impact of the intervention on asthma control and the patient's quality of life. A pilot study could be conducted comparing the use of Alexa with other interventions and evaluating the results in terms of severity of asthma attacks, medication use, and quality of life. In Figure 4 is shown our proposal of a special kind of concentric and geodesic rims

Figure 4. Special kind of concentric and geodesic rims were proposed in order to have more mobility within the flat space where school activities take place

4. Validation of the results: Finally, it would be important to validate the results of this research in other samples and clinical contexts to determine their applicability and generalization in other healthcare settings. This would make it possible to confirm whether the conclusions obtained in this study are replicable in other settings and with other groups of patients.
5. Exploration of other remote monitoring technologies: While this study focused on the use of Alexa, it would be interesting to explore other remote monitoring technologies such as mobile applications or wearable devices. Comparing the effectiveness and ease of use of different technologies could help identify the best tools for monitoring asthma and anxiety in children.
6. Involvement of healthcare professionals: In future studies, it would be important to involve healthcare professionals in the use of remote monitoring technologies. This would allow for a more comprehensive approach to care, with healthcare professionals providing guidance and support to parents and children in the use of these tools.
7. Long-term follow-up: This study analyzed data from a short period of time, but it would be important to conduct long-term follow-up studies to evaluate the sustainability of the effects of remote monitoring on asthma and anxiety control. This would help determine whether the benefits observed

in this study are maintained over time and whether the use of remote monitoring technologies is a viable long-term solution for managing asthma and anxiety in children. In Figure 5, we propose the use of a Sankey Diagram to establish reactive actions associated with the medium- and long-term effects of an asthma attack due to anxiety associated with excessive homework.

Figure 5. Sankey diagram of symptomatology and how IoT can help through different reactive levels from trying to reassure the child, seeking alternative therapy solutions, calling their parents or alerting 911

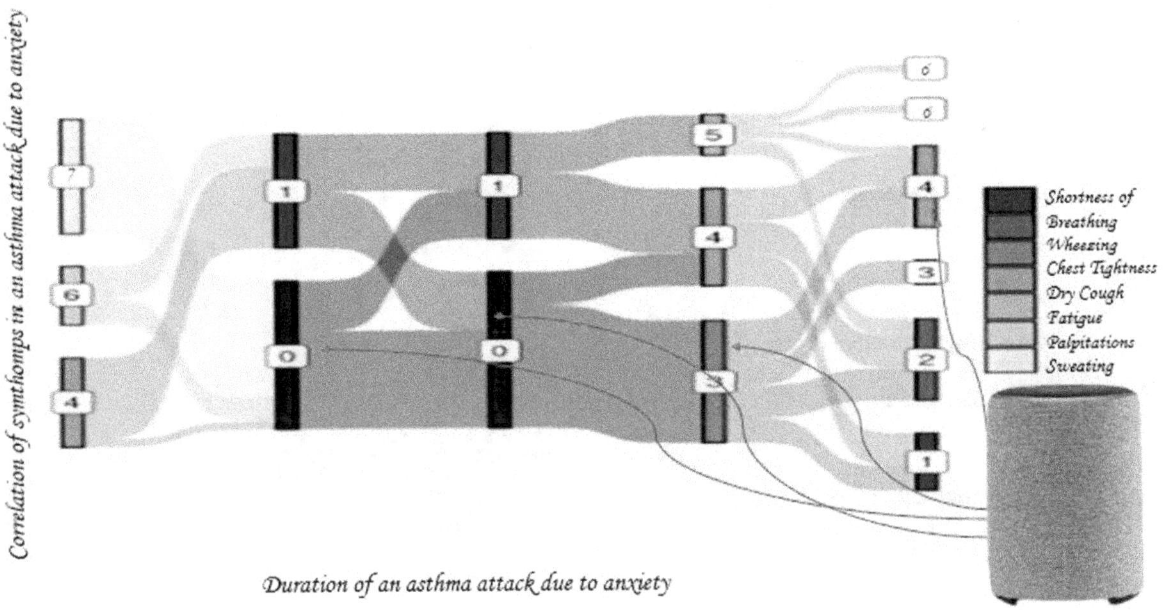

5. IMPLEMENTATION OF THE PROPOSED METHODOLOGY

Application layer: the final application will be presented in Alexa, so that the parameters that are being monitored in real time of the child can be visualized, and through four significant reagents Alexa can help and assist the child in case of starting to present symptoms that can be triggers for an anxiety attack and in turn trigger an asthma attack.

Processing and analysis layer: working with database and Arduino IoT cloud will enable the collection of data from sensors so that they are being stored in real time or as accurate as possible.

Connectivity layer: for our communication channel between sensors and platform the following microcontroller will be used:

- Arduino Nano RP2040 Connect: development board with a raspberry Pi SoC (integrated circuit with components of a computer), thus being a microcontroller with multiple connectivity capabilities, audio and more.

Sensory layer: will be responsible for determining the necessary measures to collect information to help us detect symptoms that usually occur in an anxiety or asthma attack.

- Max30102: pulse, heart rate and oxygen concentration sensor. The measurement of these parameters will help us to identify some of the seven main symptoms that occur in an anxiety or asthma attack, visualizing palpitations, as well as detecting if the child is having difficulty breathing.
- Adafruit Htu21d-f: humidity and temperature sensor. It will allow us to analyze the humidity of the child's forehead and thus determine if the child is sweating, as well as monitoring the temperature of the room.
- MP34DT05 (microphone integrated in Arduino Nano RP2040): has the ability to detect certain sounds and thus will be useful to identify if the child is having a dry cough constantly.

Figure 6. Different layers associated with the connectopy in this project of IoT

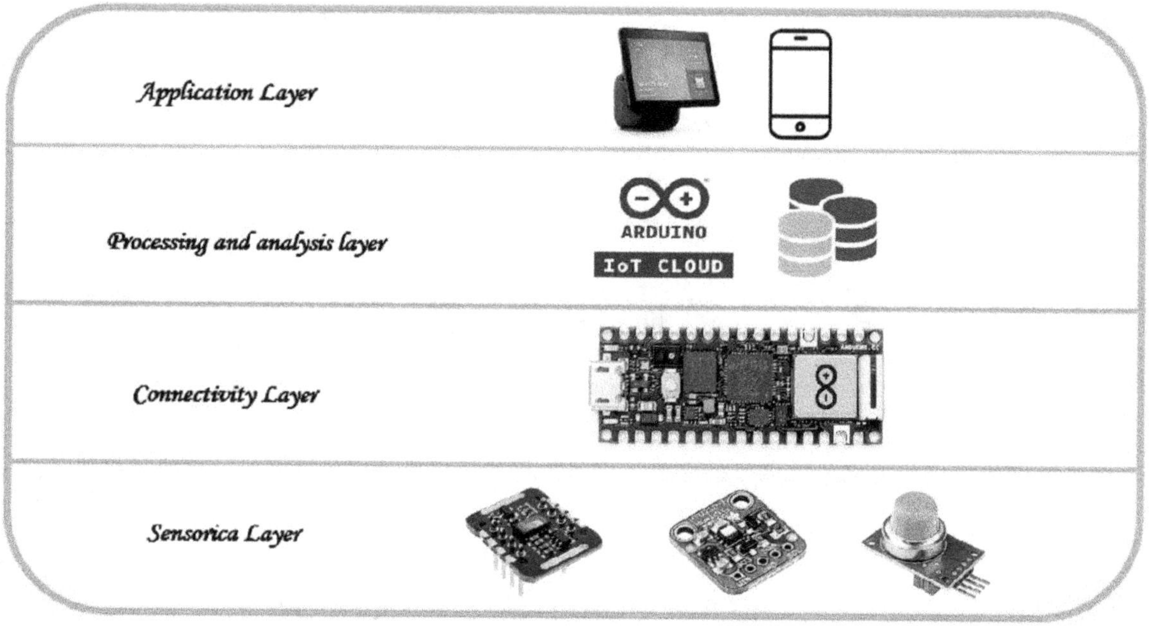

5.1.-Diagram of Connections

The diagram presents the conjunction of all the elements previously collected, creating a monitoring system, thinking about having at hand the ease of use, maintenance and spare parts, in addition to this thinking about the weight that can support a child without generating neck pain in the long term.

Figure 7. Intelligent band showing the electronic components that integrate it

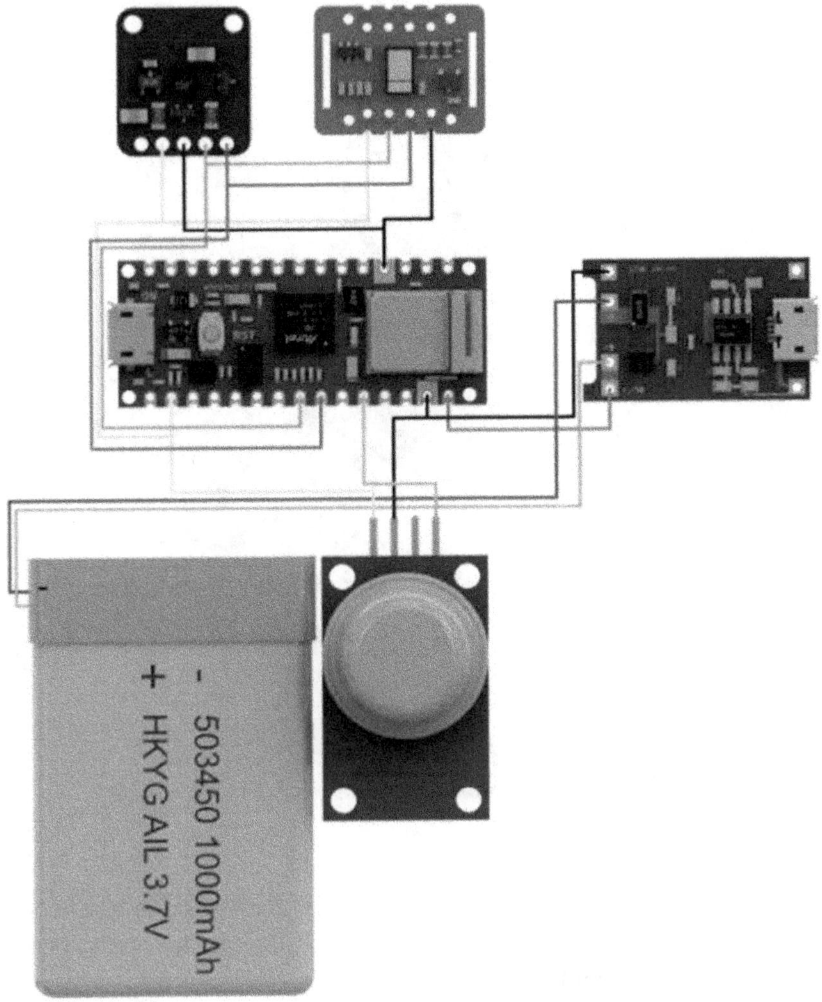

5.2.-Design of a Functional Prototype

By means of the elements described in the proposed methodology, a 3D model has been designed which tries to propose a solution to the data collection in an ergonomic way, such that it does not represent a nuisance for the child during the time he/she is performing his/her daily tasks where an anxiety attack can develop, also taking into account where each component necessary for the prevention of the attacks would work in the best way, as shown below:

Figure 8. Model developed for taking temperature, air quality, humidity, and heart rate

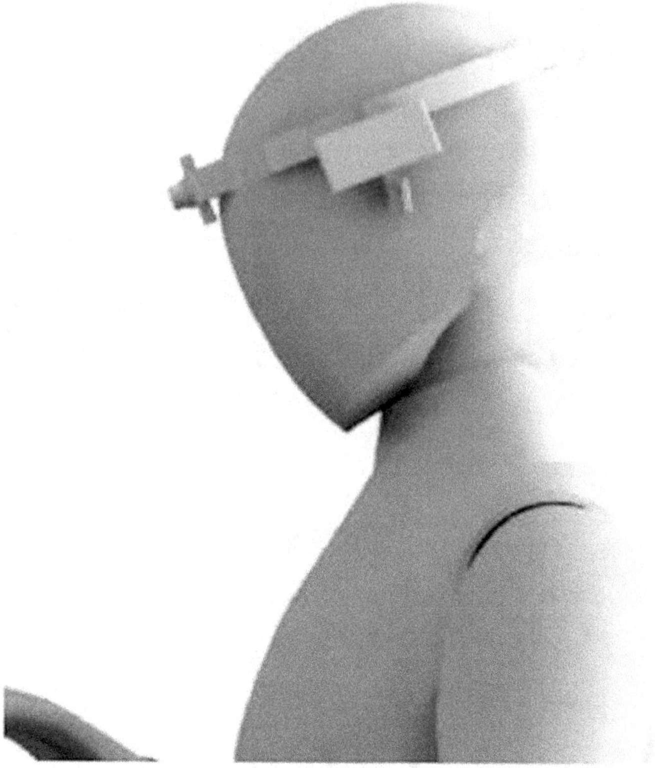

In this other image you can see how the sensors have been distributed to have good readings, in addition to this it should be mentioned that the smart band would have internet connection, as well as a gyroscope to know if the child has fainted.

Figure 9. Smart band for sensing environmental and physical factors in children with asthma attacks

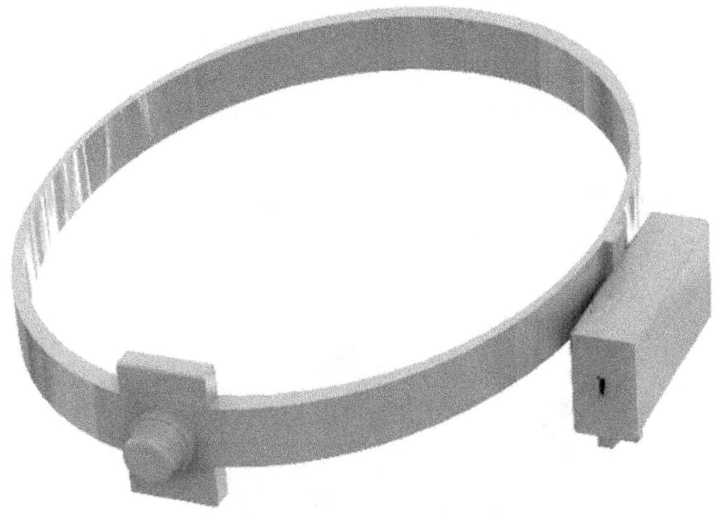

A closer view of what the device looks like without a casing would give us a good idea of where the sensors, power supply, microcontroller and link to the cloud had to be placed:

Figure 10. Smart band showing the electronic components that integrate it

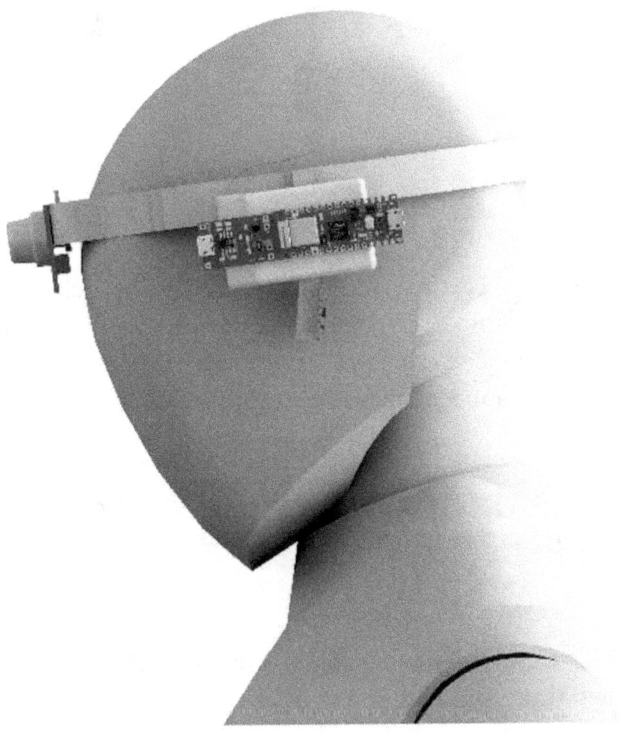

5.3.-Mobile Cart for Alexa Echo Show

We thought about the design of a mobile car that can move through small surfaces and that were omni-directional in order to allow the Alexa device to move through obstacles in a straight line, diagonally or perpendicular to the direction of the tires. As shown in the following image:

Figure 11. Directions in which the mobile with mecanum wheels can move forward

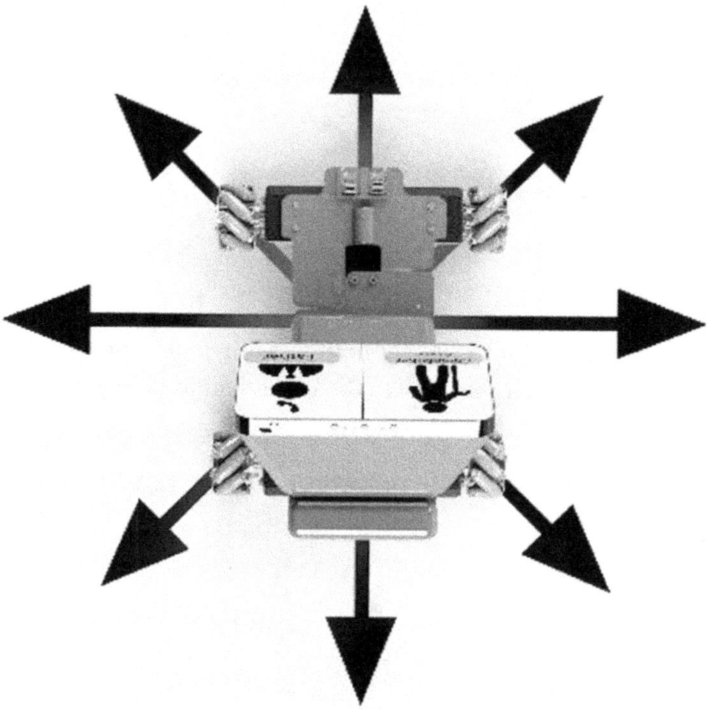

Talking about the structure of the cart we would be talking about a chassis of easy acquisition because it is commercial, uses quite accurate, efficient and good quality motors, in addition to a structure of robust materials, which from the mechatronic point of view is very striking to be able to manipulate an intelligent system that integrates a mechanical, electronic and IOT system.

6. KEY REACTIVE LEVELS OF GRAVITY IDENTIFICATION AND REACTIVITY OF OUR PROJECT

First reactive:

It covers the reminder of his medication to be able to guarantee that the child does not forget to take his medication at the indicated time, in addition it is in charge of monitoring the progress he is having in his daily tasks in a way that ensures greater concentration by the child, in turn it is responsible for assigning breaks between tasks to prevent him from over-stressing and can trigger an anxiety attack.

Second reactive:

This second reactive falls on the moment when the child begins to present at least one symptom of the seven most characteristic at the time of presenting an anxiety attack. As soon as the monitoring detects the presence of these symptoms, Alexa warns the child that he/she can take a break from his/her tasks to relax, as well as asking him/her to locate his/her inhaler and keep it nearby in case he/she starts presenting more symptoms. Another option is for Alexa to start playing soothing music or music based on the infant's preferences.

Third reagent:

If the monitoring starts to present more than two characteristic symptoms it means that the child is starting to suffer an anxiety attack, and the Alexa has to follow a process so that the child can cope in the best way. First, the Alexa activates an avatar of the child's grandfather that has a pre-recorded audio and begins to play to the child in order to reassure him. If the symptoms persist and the times that the infant was tried to be reassured did not work, the Alexa begins to establish communication with the parent through a call, so that someone responsible for the child can verify that he/she is well.

Fourth reagent:

Once the first three reagents have been presented and the objective of reducing or controlling the symptoms present in the child has not been achieved, the Alexa goes into alert mode and begins to focus on the sounds it is detecting to find out if the child is unconscious. If during 4 minutes the child does not respond and no sound is detected, the Alexa establishes communication with the emergency services and an ambulance is requested where, by geolocation, the parent will be notified so that they know which hospital the child has been taken to.

In next figure is possible show these levels of reaction.

Figure 12. Reaction representation levels associated with our research

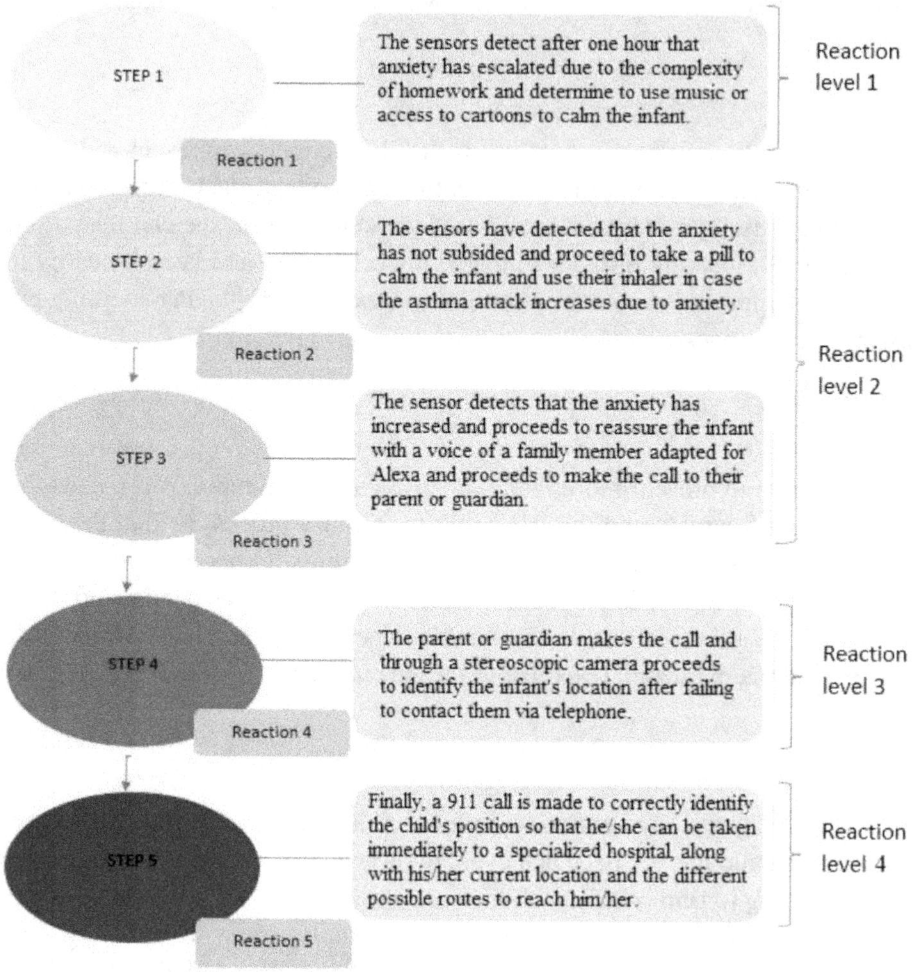

7. CONCLUSION

The study has demonstrated that using smart technologies like Alexa to monitor asthma anxiety attacks can have a positive impact on patients' health and quality of life. Smart Health is a promising concept that can significantly contribute to disease prevention, treatment, and management, as well as promote healthy lifestyles and improve access to quality health services. The personalized and real-time care enabled by smart technologies can prevent serious complications, and the systematic and detailed data collected can inform the development of more effective and personalized treatments. The research on the use of an Alexa to monitor asthma anxiety attacks is a concrete example of the potential of Smart Health, and further research and development in this field are crucial for improving people's health and well-being.

8. FUTURE RESEARCH

Expanding the sample to include more dates and patients with asthma anxiety attacks would yield more precise and generalizable results. Multivariate analysis could explore other variables that may influence the severity of anxiety attacks, such as the patient's age, general anxiety level, or the presence of other psychological disorders. Evaluating the impact of the intervention on asthma control and the patient's quality of life could involve a pilot study comparing the use of Alexa with other interventions. Validating the results in other samples and clinical contexts would determine their applicability and generalization in other healthcare settings. In Figure 6, we can see an avatar associated with the deceased grandfather of the child who, after several attempts to reassure the child with asthma, the voice recognition application decides to call his father to verify that everything is all right since he is not in Alexa's field of vision.

Figure 13. Intelligent system for monitoring the infant's location since it does not respond to voice commands, asking how he/she is so a direct call to the parent or guardian can be made

Exploring other remote monitoring technologies like mobile applications or wearable devices could identify the best tools for monitoring asthma and anxiety in children. Involving healthcare professionals in the use of remote monitoring technologies would allow for a more comprehensive approach to care. Conducting long-term follow-up studies would evaluate the sustainability of the effects of remote monitoring on asthma and anxiety control. In Figure 7, you can visualize the last reactive level that will affect if after not detecting any sound for more than 4 minutes, an ambulance will be called and it will indicate its geolocation so that the parents of the infant are informed and can arrive at the hospital as soon as possible.

Figure 14. Last reactive level of our proposed investigation associated with the infant fainting and generating an entire on-call protocol to take the infant as soon as possible to a respiratory specialty hospital

REFERENCES

Bibault, J. E., Chaix, B., & Guillemassé, A. (2020). Digital health and cancer care: The era of smart and connected systems. *Medical Oncology (Northwood, London, England)*, *37*(9), 78. PMID:32748212

Chen, J., Wang, Z., Xu, W., & Zhang, X. (2020). Smart Inhalers for Asthma Management: A Systematic Review and Meta-Analysis of Adherence Outcomes. *Journal of Medical Systems*, *44*(3), 54.

Chen, X., Huang, X., Zhang, J., & Liu, J. (2020). Internet of Things (IoT) in healthcare: A comprehensive literature review. *Journal of Healthcare Engineering*, *2020*, 1–15. doi:10.1155/2020/6660160

Dufour, M. A., Légaré, F., & Dubois, C. A. (2017). Smart technology, artificial intelligence, and the future of health care. *Journal of General Internal Medicine*, *32*(1), 86–90.

Eysenbach, G. (2018). The potential of AI in healthcare is immense. *The Lancet. Digital Health*, *1*(1), e1–e2.

Kim, K., & Lee, J. (2019). Development of a Smart Inhaler for Asthma Management. *Sensors (Basel)*, *19*(14), 3131. PMID:31315234

Kocaballi, A. B., Berkovsky, S., Quiroz, J. C., & Quiroz, V. (2020). Personalized Asthma Management Using Smart Inhalers: A Systematic Review. *Sensors (Basel)*, *20*(21), 6295. PMID:33167373

Liu, W., Li, L., & Su, Q. (2019). Smart Health-Care System Based on IoT and Cloud Computing. *Wireless Personal Communications*, *104*(2), 859–873.

Patel, R. B., Patel, N. M., & Thakkar, M. H. (2021). Design and Development of a Smart Inhaler: A Review. *Current Drug Delivery*, *18*(1), 36–48.

Rezvani, M., Fanaei, S., & Hassankhani, H. (2019). Smart Homecare Monitoring System Based on Internet of Things (IoT). *Journal of Medical Systems*, *43*(10), 326.

Uddin, M., & Mahmud, M. (2021). IoT-Based Asthma Management System: A Review. *IEEE Access : Practical Innovations, Open Solutions*, *9*, 15679–15692.

Ye, Y., Hu, J., Sun, Z., & Guo, Y. (2020). Smart asthma management system using machine learning and internet of things technologies. *Future Generation Computer Systems*, *110*, 415–423.

Compilation of References

Abbas, J. (2020). Impact of total quality management on corporate green performance through the mediating role of corporate social responsibility. *Journal of Cleaner Production*, *242*, 118458. doi:10.1016/j.jclepro.2019.118458

Abella, A., Ortiz-De-Urbina-Criado, M., & De-Pablos-Heredero, C. (2015). Informatio n reuse in smart cities ecosystems. *El Profesional de la Información*, *24*(6), 838–844. doi:10.3145/epi.2015.nov.16

Adams, C. A., Larrinaga-González, C., Pérez, E. A., Ruiz, C. C., & Fenech, F. C. (2007). Environmental management systems as an embedding mechanism: A research note. *Accounting, Auditing & Accountability Journal*, *20*(3), 403–422. doi:10.1108/09513570710748562

Adib, J., Abdelouahid, R. A., Marzak, A., & Moutachaouik, H. (2022). Ontological user profile for E-orientation platforms. *Procedia Computer Science*, *198*, 417–422. doi:10.1016/j.procs.2021.12.263

Adomavicius, G., & Tuzhilin, A. (2005). Toward the next generation of recommender systems: A survey of the state-of-the-art and possible extensions. *IEEE Transactions on Knowledge and Data Engineering*, *17*(6), 734–749. doi:10.1109/TKDE.2005.99

Afzaal, H., Farooque, A. A., Abbas, F., Acharya, B., & Esau, T. (2020). Computation of evapotranspiration with artificial intelligence for precision water resource management. *Applied Sciences (Basel, Switzerland)*, *10*(5), 1621. doi:10.3390/app10051621

Agarwal, S. M. (2023). Go-Brown, Go-Green and smart initiatives implemented by the University of Delhi for environmental sustainability towards futuristic smart universities: Observational study. *Heliyon*, *9*(3), e13909. doi:10.1016/j.heliyon.2023.e13909 PMID:36967932

Agnello J. Naveen. X and Arivoli. A, (2021h) Corporate Social Responsibility in Environmental Protection of Specific sugar factory in Tamil Nadu: A case study. *Journal The New Horizon & Emerging Challenges In post COVID - 19 Business Scenario, 1,* 232-249.

Agnello J. Naveen. X, Ravichandran, M., & Balamurugan, J. (2015a). Clean Technology and its Efficacy: Strategies of Environmental Management. *Journal of Environmental and Social Sciences, 2,* 1-6.

Agnello J. Naveen.X, Boopathi. S & Arivoli. A, (2019e). Efficacy of Cleaner Technology in Recycling of Wastewater Treatment Process Using Add-on Applications at Sugar Industry In Tamil Nadu. *Poll Res., 38.*

Agnello, J. & Arivoli, A. (2019d). Case Study To Understand The Benefits Of Cleaner Technology By The Assessment Of Water, Air And Soil Quality Around The Sugar Industry In Erode, Tamil Nadu. *International Journal of Scientific & Technology Research 8*(9).

Agnello, J., Naveen, X., Arivoli, A., Boopathi, S., & Balamurugan, J. (2019c). A Review On Cleaner Technology In Pollution Control At Ultra-red Industry In Tamil Nadu, India, Tamil Nadu. *International Journal of Scientific & Technology Research 8*(9), 1892-1898.

Agnello, J., Naveen, X., Boopahti, S., & Arivoli, A. (2019b). Efficacy of Cleaner technology in wastewater treatment and Energy conservation using (UASB-R) Anaerobic Digester at Bagasse-Based Pulp and Paper Mill in Tamil Nadu, ISSN: 2455-3085 (Online), Issue-06 Research Review. *International Journal of Multidisciplinary.*

Agnello, J., Naveen, X., Boopathi, S., & Arivoli, A. (2021g). Case Experience on WIN- WIN Approach Towards Industrial Pollution Control-Economic and Environmental Efficacy of Cleaner Technology in Select Cement Industry in Tamil Nadu. In *Bioremediation and Green Technologies* (pp. 209–234). Springer. doi:10.1007/978-3-030-64122-1_15

Agnello, J., Naveen, X., Boopathi, S., Arivoli, A., & Balamurugan, J. (2020f). Win-Win strategy of cleaner technology-environmental and economic scores of Sugar Industry in Tamil Nadu [IJEP]. *Indian Journal of Environmental Protection, 40*(2), 186–191.

Agnello, J., Naveen, X., Boopathi, S., Arivoli, A., & Kannan, A. (2021h). Economic and Environmental Benefits of Cleaner Technology in Industrial Pollution Control: Case Study of Select Sugar Industry in Tamil Nadu. In *Bioremediation and Green Technologies* (pp. 185–207). Springer. doi:10.1007/978-3-030-64122-1_14

Agrawal, P., Sinha, A., Kumar, S., Agarwal, A., Banerjee, A., Villuri, V. G. K., Annavarapu, C. S. R., Dwivedi, R., Dera, V. V. R., Sinha, J., & Pasupuleti, S. (2021). Exploring artificial intelligence techniques for groundwater quality assessment. *Water (Basel), 13*(9), 1172. doi:10.3390/w13091172

Aguilera, U., Peña, O., Belmonte, O., & López-de-Ipiña, D. (2017). Citizen-centric data services for smarter cities. *Future Generation Computer Systems, 76*, 234–247. doi:10.1016/j.future.2016.10.031

Ahmad, T., Zhang, D., Huang, C. C., Zhang, H., Dai, H., Song, Y., & Chen, H. (2021). Artificial intelligence in sustainable energy industry: Status Quo, challenges and opportunities. *Journal of Cleaner Production, 289*, 125834. doi:10.1016/j.jclepro.2021.125834

Ahmed, A. C. A. (2012). Social and Environmental Auditing; Some Basic Concept. *Some Basic Concept (October 25, 2012).*

Ajagekar, A., & You, F. (2022). Quantum computing and quantum artificial intelligence for renewable and sustainable energy: A emerging prospect towards climate neutrality. *Renewable & Sustainable Energy Reviews, 165*, 112493. doi:10.1016/j.rser.2022.112493

Akkem, Y., Biswas, S. K., & Varanasi, A. (2023). Smart farming using artificial intelligence: A review. *Engineering Applications of Artificial Intelligence, 120*, 105899. doi:10.1016/j.engappai.2023.105899

Alam, M. S., Sasaki, N., & Datta, A. (2017). Waterlogging, crop damage and adaptation interventions in the coastal region of Bangladesh: A perception analysis of local people. *Environmental Development, 23*, 22–32. doi:10.1016/j.envdev.2017.02.009

Alassery, F., Alzahrani, A. I., Khan, A., Irshad, K., & Kshirsagar, S. R. (2022). An artificial intelligence-based solar radiation prophesy model for green energy utilization in energy management system. *Sustainable Energy Technologies and Assessments, 52*, 102060. doi:10.1016/j.seta.2022.102060

AlAwadhi, S., & Scholl, H. J. (2013, January). Aspirations and realisations: The smart city of Seattle. In *2013 46th Hawaii international conference on system sciences* (pp. 1695-1703). IEEE.

Albelda, E. (2011). *The role of management accounting practices as facilitators of environmental management*. Sustainability Accounting, Management and Policy Journal. doi:10.1108/20408021111162137

Alberti, M., Caini, L., Calabrese, A., & Rossi, D. (2000). Evaluation of the costs and benefits of an environmental management system. *International Journal of Production Research, 38*(17), 4455–4466. doi:10.1080/00207540050205226

Albino, V., Berardi, U., & Dangelico, R. M. (2015). Smart Cities: Definitions, Dimensions, Performance, and Initiatives. *Journal of Urban Technology, 22*(1), 1, 3–21. doi:10.1080/10630732.2014.942092

Alcock, R., & Lenihan, D. G. (2001). Opening the e-government file: Governing in the 21st Century. *Changing Government, 2001*, 2.

Aldhyani, T. H. H., Al-Yaari, M., Alkahtani, H., & Maashi, M. (2020). Water quality prediction using artificial intelligence algorithms. *Applied Bionics and Biomechanics, 2020*, 1–12. doi:10.1155/2020/6659314 PMID:33456498

Alfoudari, A. M., Durugbo, C. M., & Aldhmour, F. M. (2023). Exploring quality attributes of smart classrooms from the perspectives of academics. *Education and Information Technologies*. Advance online publication. doi:10.100710639-022-11452-3 PMID:37361782

Alirio González-Bustamante, R., Ferro-Escobar, R., & Vacca-González, H. (2020). Smart cities in collaboration with the internet of things Ciudades inteligentes en colaboración con internet de las cosas. *VISIÓN ELECTRÓNICA, 14*(2). https://doi.org/ doi:10.14483/issn.2248-4728

Alison.com. (2023, 2023). Alison: Free Online Courses With Certificates & Diplomas. *AWS IoT*. https://aws.amazon.com/iot/?nc1=h_ls

Al-Jawad, J. Y., Al-Jawad, S. B., & Kalin, R. M. (2019). Decision-making challenges of sustainable groundwater strategy under multi-event pressure in arid environments: The Diyala River Basin in Iraq. *Water (Basel), 11*(10), 2160. doi:10.3390/w11102160

Al-Kodmany, K. (2018). The vertical farm: A review of developments and implications for the vertical city. *Buildings, 8*(2), 24. doi:10.3390/buildings8020024

Allaire, J. J. (2018). *Deep learning with R*. Manning Publications.

Allan, C., & Stankey, G. H. (2009). *Adaptive environmental management* (Vol. 351). Springer. doi:10.1007/978-1-4020-9632-7

Allwinkle, S., & Cruickshank, P. (2011). Creating smarter cities: An overview. *Journal of Urban Technology, 18*(2), 1–16. doi:10.1080/10630732.2011.601103

Al-Mefleh, N. K., AlAyyash, S. M., & Bani Khaled, F. A. (2019). Water management problems and solutions in a residential community of Al-Mafraq city, Jordan. *Water Science and Technology: Water Supply, 19*(5), 1371–1380. doi:10.2166/ws.2019.003

Alvarado López, R. A. (2018). Ciudad inteligente y sostenible: hacia un modelo de innovación inclusiva. *PAAKAT: revista de tecnología y sociedad, 7*(13).

Alvarado, L., R. A. (2018). Ciudad inteligente y sostenible: hacia un modelo de innovación inclusiva. *PAAKAT: revista de tecnología y sociedad, 7*(13).

Amir, M., Rehman, S. A., & Khan, M. I. (2020). Mediating role of environmental management accounting and control system between top management commitment and environmental performance: A legitimacy theory. *Journal of Management Research, 7*(1), 132–160.

Ammenberg, J., & Hjelm, O. (2003). Tracing business and environmental effects of environmental management systems—A study of networking small and medium-sized enterprises using a joint environmental management system. *Business Strategy and the Environment, 12*(3), 163–174. doi:10.1002/bse.357

Anagnostopoulos, T., Zaslavsy, A., Medvedev, A., & Khoruzhnicov, S. (2015). Top — k Query Based Dynamic Scheduling for IoT-enabled Smart City Waste Collection. *16th IEEE International Conference on Mobile Data Management.*

Angelaki, M. E., Karvounidis, T., & Douligeris, C. (2022). Towards a Smart Classroom Enabled Sustainability Education: A Conceptual Model. In M. E. Auer & T. Tsiatsos, New Realities, Mobile Systems and Applications Cham. doi:10.1007/978-3-030-96296-8_45

Ann, G. E., Zailani, S., & Abd Wahid, N. (2006). A study on the impact of environmental management system (EMS) certification on firms' performance in Malaysia. *Management of Environmental Quality.*

Anthopoulos, L. G. (2017). *Understanding Smart Cities: A Tool for Smart Government or an Industrial Trick?* (Vol. 22). Springer. doi:10.1007/978-3-319-57015-0

Anthopoulos, L., & Fitsilis, P. (2010). From digital to ubiquitous cities: Defining a common architecture for urban development. *2010 Sixth International Conference on Intelligent Environments.* 10.1109/IE.2010.61

Antonaras, A., Iacovidou, M., & Memtsa, C. (2011). Measuring social return on investment using the EBEN GR Business Ethics Excellence Model. *Current Issues of Business and Law, 6*(1), 69–89. doi:10.5200/1822-9530.2011.04

An, Y., Zhang, F., He, J., Shi, F., Han, S., & Li, X. (2010). Saltwater intrusion analysis and trend forecast in the coastal plain of Laizhou Bay. 2010 International Conference on Computer Application and System Modeling (ICCASM 2010). IEEE. doi:10.100712665-018-7866-8

Apple Inc. (2023, 2023). *HomeKit.* Apple. https://developer.apple.com/documentation/homekit

Arda, O. A., Bayraktar, E., & Tatoglu, E. (2019). How do integrated quality and environmental management practices affect firm performance? Mediating roles of quality performance and environmental proactivity. *Business Strategy and the Environment, 28*(1), 64–78. doi:10.1002/bse.2190

Aria, M., & Cuccurullo, C. (2017). Bibliometrix : An R-tool for comprehensive science mapping analysis. *Journal of Informetrics, 11*(4), 959–975. doi:10.1016/j.joi.2017.08.007

Arivoli, A., Naveen, X. A. J., & Thangavelu, S. (2021a). Impact of Sugar Mill Effluent on the Quality of Groundwater in Cuddalore District, Tamil Nadu, India. In *Bioremediation and Green Technologies* (pp. 41–52). Springer. doi:10.1007/978-3-030-64122-1_4

Arivoli, A., Thangavelu, S., & Naveen, X. A. J. (2021b). Influence of Sugar Mill Effluent on Germination and Growth of Fenugreek (Trigonella foenumgraecum) and Mustard (Brassica nigra). In *Bioremediation and Green Technologies* (pp. 271–281). Springer. doi:10.1007/978-3-030-64122-1_19

Armanda, D. T., Guinée, J. B., & Tukker, A. (2019). The second green revolution: Innovative urban agriculture's contribution to food security and sustainability – A review. *Global Food Security, 22*, 13–24. doi:10.1016/j.gfs.2019.08.002

Arturo, A.-L. R. (2020a). Ciudades inteligentes y sostenibles: Una medición a cinco ciudades de México. *Estudios Sociales (Santo Domingo, Dominican Republic), 1*, 2–28. doi:10.836/es.v30i55.860

Arup. (2010). *Smart Cities: Transforming the 21st-century city via the creative use of technology.* Arup.

Ashley, P., & Boyd, B. W. (2006). Quantitative and qualitative approaches to research in environmental management. *Australasian Journal of Environmental Management, 13*(2), 70–78. doi:10.1080/14486563.2006.10648674

Ashton, K. (2009). That 'Internet of things' thing. *RFID Journal, 22*(7), 97–114.

Athabasca University. (2023a). *FreudBot*. Athabasca University. https://psych.athabascau.ca/html/Freudbot/Freudbot.html

Athabasca University. (2023b). *PiagetBot*. Athabasca University. https://psych.athabascau.ca/html/Piagetbot/Piagetbot.html

Avila Bula, M. A. D. (2019). *Sistema de votaciones con blockchain*. Uniandes. https://repositorio.uniandes.edu.co/handle/1992/44085

Awogbemi, O., & Kallon, D. V. V. (2022, October 18). Valorization of agricultural wastes for biofuel applications. *Heliyon, 8*(10), e11117. doi:10.1016/j.heliyon.2022.e11117 PMID:36303926

AWWA. (2012). Water Treatment Plant Design. Second Edition. Cap 5. USA: Coagulation and Flocculation-American Water Works Association (AWWA).

Axelsson, K., & Granath, M. (2018). Stakeholder's stake and relation to smartness in smart city development: Insights from Swedish city planning project. *Government Information Quarterly, 35*(4), 693–702. doi:10.1016/j.giq.2018.09.001

Badami, M. G., & Ramankutty, N. (2015). Urban agriculture and food security: A critique based on an assessment of urban land constraints. *Global Food Security, 4*, 8–15. doi:10.1016/j.gfs.2014.10.003

Baidu. (2023, 2023). *Ernie Bot*. Baidu. https://yiyan.baidu.com/

Bailey, D., Southam, A., & Costley, J. (2021). Digital storytelling with chatbots: Mapping L2 participation and perception patterns. *Interactive Technology and Smart Education, 18*(1), 85–103. doi:10.1108/ITSE-08-2020-0170

Baird, V. (1999). Green cities. *New Internationalist, 313*. Retrieved March 19, 2018, from https://newint.org/features/1999/06/05/keynote

Bajaj, R., & Sharma, V. (2018). Smart Education with artificial intelligence based determination of learning styles. *Procedia Computer Science, 132*, 834–842. doi:10.1016/j.procs.2018.05.095

Bajer, L., & Krejcar, O. (2015). Design and Realization of Low Cost Control for Greenhouse Environment with Remote Control. *IFAC-PapersOnLine, 48*(4), 368–373. doi:10.1016/j.ifacol.2015.07.062

Bakupa Mbombo, A., & Nadire, C. (2021). Smart University: A University In the Technological Age. *TEM Journal, 10*(1). https://doi.org/Doi:10.18421/TEM101-02

Barad, M. (2019). Implementing Quality Function Deployment for improving cybersecurity in the healthcare industry: A structured framework. *Journal of Healthcare Informatics Research, 3*(2), 145–162. doi:10.100741666-019-00042-9

Barn, B. S. (2020). The Digital Enterprise as an Emerging Landscape for Universities and Their Operation. In V. Kulkarni, S. Reddy, T. Clark, & B. S. Barn (Eds.), *Advanced Digital Architectures for Model-Driven Adaptive Enterprises* (pp. 287–304). IGI Global. doi:10.4018/978-1-7998-0108-5.ch013

Barone, R. E., Giuffrè, T., Siniscalchi, S. M., Morgano, M. A., & Tesoriere, G. (2013). Architecture for parking management in smart cities. *IET Intelligent Transport Systems, 8*(5), 445–452. doi:10.1049/iet-its.2013.0045

Barry, M., & Fourie, C. (2002). Wicked problems, soft systems and cadastral systems in periods of uncertainty: South African experience. *Survey Review, 36*(285), 483–496. doi:10.1179re.2002.36.285.483

Bartolomeo, M., Bennett, M., Bouma, J. J., Heydkamp, P., James, P., & Wolters, T. (2000). Environmental management accounting in Europe: Current practice and future potential. *European Accounting Review, 9*(1), 31–52. doi:10.1080/096381800407932

Bartram, J., Brocklehurst, C., Fisher, M. B., Luyendijk, R., Hossain, R., Wardlaw, T., & Gordon, B. (2014). Global monitoring of water supply and sanitation: History, methods and future challenges. *International Journal of Environmental Research and Public Health, 11*(8), 8137–8165. doi:10.3390/ijerph110808137 PMID:25116635

Bartram, J., & Cairncross, S. (2010). Hygiene, sanitation, and water: Forgotten foundations of health. *PLoS Medicine, 7*(11), e1000367. doi:10.1371/journal.pmed.1000367 PMID:21085694

Bătăgan, L. (2011). Smart cities and sustainability models. *Informações Econômicas, 15*(3), 80–87.

Bayu, T., Kim, H., & Oki, T. (2020). Water governance contribution to water and sanitation access equality in developing countries. *Water Resources Research, 56*(4), e2019WR025330. Advance online publication. doi:10.1029/2019WR025330

Bell, D. (1999). The Coming of Post-industrial Society (Reissue edition). Basic Books.

Bellon, M., Aligishiev, Z., & Massetti, E. (2022). Macro-fiscal implications of adaptation to climate change. *Staff Climate Notes, 2022*(002), 1. doi:10.5089/9798400201608.066

Benis, K., & Ferrão, P. (2018). Commercial farming within the urban built environment – Taking stock of an evolving field in northern countries. *Global Food Security, 17*, 30–37. doi:10.1016/j.gfs.2018.03.005

Benke, K., & Tomkins, B. (2017). Future food-production systems: Vertical farming and controlled-environment agriculture. *Sustainability, 13*(1), 13–26. doi:10.1080/15487733.2017.1394054

Berke, A. (2020). Crypto Voting + US Elections: Reality. *MIT Media Lab.* https://www.media.mit.edu/posts/crypto-voting-us-elections-reality/

Bernardo, M., Casadesus, M., Karapetrovic, S., & Heras, I. (2009). How integrated are environmental, quality, and other standardized management systems? An empirical study. *Journal of Cleaner Production, 17*(8), 742–750. doi:10.1016/j.jclepro.2008.11.003

Berry, M. A., & Rondinelli, D. A. (1998). Proactive corporate environmental management: A new industrial revolution. [Competitive requirement]. *The Academy of Management Perspectives, 12*(2), 38–50. doi:10.5465/ame.1998.650515

Bhujel, A., Basak, J. K., Khan, F., Arulmozhi, E., Jaihuni, M., Sihalath, T., Lee, D., Park, J., & Kim, H. T. (2020). Sensor Systems for Greenhouse Microclimate Monitoring and Control: A Review. *Journal of Biosystems Engineering, 45*(4), 341–361. doi:10.100742853-020-00075-6

Bibault, J. E., Chaix, B., & Guillemassé, A. (2020). Digital health and cancer care: The era of smart and connected systems. *Medical Oncology (Northwood, London, England), 37*(9), 78. PMID:32748212

Biswas, S., Deka, B., Dash, S., & Rout, K. (2022). IoT-based fuzzy logic-controlled novel and multilingual mobile application for hydroponic farming. In *AI* (pp. 31–42). Edge and IoT-based Smart Agriculture, Intelligent Data-Centric Systems. doi:10.1016/B978-0-12-823694-9.00027-X

Błaziak, M., Urban, S., Wietrzyk, W., Jura, M., Iwanek, G., Stańczykiewicz, B., Kuliczkowski, W., Zymliński, R., Pondel, M., Berka, P., Danel, D., Biegus, J., & Siennicka, A. (2022). An artificial intelligence approach to guiding the management of heart failure patients using predictive models: A systematic review. *Biomedicines, 10*(9), 2188. doi:10.3390/biomedicines10092188 PMID:36140289

Bloomberg. (2009). *Age-friendly NYC: Enhancing our city's livability for older New Yorkers.* The City of New York Office of the Mayor.

Boes, K., Buhalis, D., & Inversini, A. (2016). Smart tourism destinations: Ecosystems for tourism destination competitiveness. *International Journal of Tourism Cities, 2*(2), 108–124. doi:10.1108/IJTC-12-2015-0032

Bolívar, M. P. R., & Meijer, A. J. (2016). Smart governance: Using a literature review and empirical analysis to build a research model. *Social Science Computer Review, 34*(6), 673–692. doi:10.1177/0894439315611088

Bonola, M., Bracciale, L., Loreti, P., Amici, R., Rabuffi, A., & Bianchi, G. (2016). Opportunistic communication in smart city: Experimental insight with small-scale taxi fleets as Data Carriers. *Ad Hoc Networks, 43*, 43–55. doi:10.1016/j.adhoc.2016.02.002

Borozdukhin, A., Dolinina, O., & Pechenkin, V. (2016). Approach to the garbage collection in The "smart clean city" project. *2016 4th IEEE International Colloquium on Information Science and Technology (CiSt)*. 10.1109/CIST.2016.7805019

Bose, S., & Rashel, M. R. (2007). Implementing e-governance using OECD model (Modified) and Gartner model (modified) upon agriculture of Bangladesh. *2007 10th International Conference on Computer and Information Technology*. 10.1109/ICCITECHN.2007.4579410

Bose, B. K. (2017). Artificial Intelligence Techniques in Smart Grid and Renewable Energy Systems—Some Example Applications. *Proceedings of the IEEE, 105*(11), 2262–2273. doi:10.1109/JPROC.2017.2756596

Botello-Peñaloza, H. A. (2015). Determinantes del acceso al internet: Evidencia de los hogares del Ecuador. *ENTRAMADO, 11*(2), 12–19. doi:10.18041/entramado.2015v11n2.22205

Bouloukakis, M., Partarakis, N., Drossis, I., Kalaitzakis, M., & Stephanidis, C. (2019). Virtual Reality for Smart City Visualization and Monitoring. In A. Stratigea & D. Kavroudakis (Eds.), *Mediterranean Cities and Island Communities: Smart, Sustainable, Inclusive and Resilient* (pp. 1–18). Springer International Publishing. doi:10.1007/978-3-319-99444-4_1

Bouskela, M., Casseb, M., & Bassi, S. (2016). *La ruta hacia las Smart Cities Migrando de una gestión tradicional a la ciudad inteligente*.

Bragagnolo, S., Rocha, H., Denker, M., & Ducasse, S. (2018). SmartInspect: solidity smart contract inspector. *International Workshop on Blockchain Oriented Software Engineering (IWBOSE)*, Campobasso, Italy. 10.1109/IWBOSE.2018.8327566

Brandt, S. A. (2016). Modeling and visualizing uncertainties of flood boundary delineation: Algorithm for slope and DEM resolution dependencies of 1D hydraulic models. *Stochastic Environmental Research and Risk Assessment, 30*(6), 1677–1690. doi:10.100700477-016-1212-z

Briassoulis, H. (2000). Environmental impacts of tourism: a framework for analysis and evaluation. In *Tourism and the Environment* (pp. 21–37). Springer. doi:10.1007/978-94-015-9584-1_2

Brovko, A., Dolinina, O., & Pechenkin, V. (2017). Method of the management of garbage collection in The "smart clean city" project. *Communications in Computer and Information Science, 718*, 432–443. doi:10.1007/978-3-319-59767-6_34

Brown, R. R., Keath, N., & Wong, T. H. (2009). Urban water management in cities: Historical, current and future regimes. *Water Science and Technology, 59*(5), 847–855. doi:10.2166/wst.2009.029 PMID:19273883

Buchanan, B. (2019). Artificial intelligence in finance. In Zenodo *(CERN European Organization for Nuclear Research)*. European Organization for Nuclear Research. https://doi.org/ doi:10.5281/zenodo.2626454

Bueermann, J. (2012). Being smart on crime with evidence-based policing. *NIJ Journal, 269*, 12–15.

Buhalis, D. (2003). eTourism: Information technology for strategic tourism management. Pearson Education.

Buhalis, D., & Amaranggana, A. (2013). Smart tourism destinations. In *Information and communication technologies in tourism 2014* (pp. 553–564). Springer. doi:10.1007/978-3-319-03973-2_40

Buhalis, D., & Deimezi, O. (2004). E-tourism developments in Greece: Information communication technologies adoption for the strategic management of the Greek tourism industry. *Tourism and Hospitality Research*, *5*(2), 103–130. doi:10.1057/palgrave.thr.6040011

Burd, P., Leslie, J., & Wilton, N. (2016). *Cruciform Water Distribution Valve for Aircraft Galley Plumbing System* [Patent]. https://patentscope.wipo.int/search/es/detail.jsf?docId=EP222931358&_cid=P12-L9MVZJ-64483-1

C3.ai. (2023). *C3 IoT platform*. c3. https://c3.ai/c3-ai-platform/

Cacho, A., Mendes-Filho, L., Estaregue, D., Moura, B., Cacho, N., Lopes, F., & Alves, C. (2016). Mobile tourist guide supporting a smart city initiative: A Brazilian case study. *International Journal of Tourism Cities*, *2*(2), 164–183. doi:10.1108/IJTC-12-2015-0030

California Institute. (2001). http://smartcommunities.org/concept.php

Camacho, D., Borrajo, D., & Molina, J. M. (2001). Intelligent travel planning: A multiagent planning system to solve web problems in the e-tourism domain. *Autonomous Agents and Multi-Agent Systems*, *4*(4), 387–392. doi:10.1023/A:1012767210241

Camboim, G. F., Zawislak, P. A., & Pufal, N. A. (2019). Driving elements to make cities smarter: Evidences from European projects. *Technological Forecasting and Social Change*, *142*, 154–167. doi:10.1016/j.techfore.2018.09.014

Căpuşneanu, S., Topor, D. I., Constantin, D. M. O., Manole, A. L., & Hint, M. S. (2020). Environmental Management Accounting: A Business Perspective on the Policies, Analyses, and Benefits of Its Implementation. In Management Accounting Standards for Sustainable Business Practices (pp. 27-51). IGI Global.

Caragliu, A., Del Bo, C., & Nijkamp, P. (2011). Smart cities in Europe. *Journal of Urban Technology*, *18*(2), 65–82. doi:10.1080/10630732.2011.601117

Carpenter, R. (2023, 2023). *CleverBot*. Cleverbot. https://www.cleverbot.com/

Carr, H. S. (2005). *US Patent No. 6,968,295*. Washington, DC: US Patent and Trademark Office.

Carrera, J., & Ramírez-Hernández, D. (2018). Innovative Education in MOOC for Sustainability: Learnings and Motivations. Sustainability, 10(9), 2990. https://www.mdpi.com/2071-1050/10/9/2990

Carvalho, F., Santos, G., & Gonçalves, J. (2020). Critical analysis of information about integrated management systems and environmental policy on the Portuguese firms' website towards sustainable development. *Corporate Social Responsibility and Environmental Management*, *27*(2), 1069–1088. doi:10.1002/csr.1866

Casamayou, A., & Morales González, M. J. (2018). Personas mayores y tecnologías digitales: desafíos de un binomio Elderly people and digital technologies: a dual challenge Idosos e tecnologias digitais: desafios duplos. *Conocimiento y Sociedad*, *7*(2), 199–226.

Castañeda-Miranda, A., & Castaño-Meneses, V. M. (2020). Internet of things for smart farming and frost intelligent control in greenhouses. *Computers and Electronics in Agriculture*, *176*, 105614. doi:10.1016/j.compag.2020.105614

Castillo, L., Armengol, E., Onaindía, E., Sebastiá, L., González-Boticario, J., Rodríguez, A., Fernandez, S., Arias, J. D., & Borrajo, D. (2008). samap: An user-oriented adaptive system for planning tourist visits. *Expert Systems with Applications*, *34*(2), 1318–1332. doi:10.1016/j.eswa.2006.12.029

Castro Álvarez, U., González Rodríguez, J. Á., & Maldonado Duarte, L. M. (2017). Destinos Turísticos Inteligentes: ¿Estrategia para el Desarrollo Local en Países Pobres? *Revista Turydes: Turismo y Desarrollo, 22*. https://www.eumed.net/rev/turydes/22/destinos-turisticos-inteligentes.html

Cats-Baril, W., & Thompson, R. (1995). Managing information technology projects in the public sector. *Public Administration Review, 55*(6), 559. doi:10.2307/3110347

Cea, L., & Costabile, P. (2022). *Flood risk in urban areas: Modelling, management and adaptation to climate change.* A review. *Hydrology, 9*(3), 50. doi:10.3390/hydrology9030050

Celani, G., Sperling, D. M., & Franco, J. M. S. (Eds.). (2015). Computer-Aided Architectural Design: The Next City–New Technologies and the Future of the Built Environment. *16th International Conference, CAAD Futures 2015, São Paulo, Brazil, July 8-10, 2015. Selected Papers* (*Vol. 527*). Springer.

Celdran-Bernabeu, M. A., Mazon, J. N., & Sanchez, D. G. (2018). Open Data and tourism. Implications for tourism management in Smart Cities and Smart Tourism Destinations. *Investigaciones Turísticas*, (15), 49–78. doi:10.14198/INTURI2018.15.03

Center for Sustainable Systems, University of Michigan (CSS). (2010) U.S. water supply and distribution fact sheet. *Pub No. CSS05-17*. CSS. http://css.snre.umich.edu/css_doc/CSS05-17.pdf

CEPAL. (2010). *Gobierno electrónico: indicadores. Comisión Económica para América Latina y el Caribe (CEPAL).* Instituto Latinoamericano y del Caribe de Planificación Económica y Social (ILPES). https://www.cepal.org/ilpes/noticias/paginas/0/40660/alejandra_naser_INDICADORES.pdf

Chakraborty, B., Hashimoto, T., & Chakraborty, G. (2012, November). Fuzzy-PSO based route recommendation for user aware pedestrian navigation system. In *TENCON 2012 IEEE Region 10 Conference* (pp. 1–6). IEEE. doi:10.1109/TENCON.2012.6412292

Chang, D.-L., Yang, S.-H., Hsieh, S.-L., Wang, H.-J., & Yeh, K.-C. (2020). Artificial Intelligence methodologies applied to prompt pluvial flood estimation and prediction. *Water (Basel), 12*(12), 3552. doi:10.3390/w12123552

Chang, Y., Li, G., Yao, Y., Zhang, L., & Yu, C. (2016). Quantifying the Water-Energy-Food Nexus: Current status and trends. *Energies, 9*(65), 65. doi:10.3390/en9020065

Character.ai. (2023). *Character.ai.* Character.AI. https://beta.character.ai/

ChatCompose. (2019). *ChatCompose Chatbot Platform for Sales and Support Automation.* Chatcompose. https://www.chatcompose.com

Chaudhry, N. I., Asad, H., & Hussain, R. I. (2020). Environmental innovation and financial performance: Mediating role of environmental management accounting and firm's environmental strategy. [PJCSS]. *Pakistan Journal of Commerce and Social Sciences, 14*(3), 715–737.

Checkland, P. B. (1989). Soft systems methodology. *Human Systems Management, 8*(4), 273–289. doi:10.3233/HSM-1989-8405

Chen, M., Wang, C., Wang, X., Fu, J., Gong, P., Yan, J., Yu, Z., Yan, F., & Nawab, J. (2019). Release of perfluoroalkyl substances from melting glacier of the Tibetan plateau: Insights into the impact of global warming on the cycling of emerging pollutants. *Journal of Geophysical Research Atmospheres*, 2019JD030566. . doi:10.1029/2019JD030566

Chen, C., Yuhan, H., Karuppiah, M., & Kumar, P. M. (2021). Artificial intelligence on economic evaluation of energy efficiency and renewable energy technologies. *Sustainable Energy Technologies and Assessments, 47*, 101358. doi:10.1016/j.seta.2021.101358

Cheng, H., & Hu, Y. (2010). Municipal solid waste (MSW) as a renewable source of energy: Current and future practices in China. *Bioresource Technology, 101*(11), 3816–3824. doi:10.1016/j.biortech.2010.01.040 PMID:20137912

Chen, J., Wang, Z., Xu, W., & Zhang, X. (2020). Smart Inhalers for Asthma Management: A Systematic Review and Meta-Analysis of Adherence Outcomes. *Journal of Medical Systems*, *44*(3), 54.

Chen, M., Huang, Z., & Li, X. (2020). Augmented reality in tourism: A review of literature. *Journal of Travel Research*, *59*(1), 3–19.

Chen, X., Huang, X., Zhang, J., & Liu, J. (2020). Internet of Things (IoT) in healthcare: A comprehensive literature review. *Journal of Healthcare Engineering*, *2020*, 1–15. doi:10.1155/2020/6660160

Cheshmehzangi, A. (2022). The Application of ICT and Smart Technologies in Cities and Communities: An Overview. In ICT, Cities, and Reaching Positive Peace (pp. 1-16). Springer Nature Singapore. doi:10.1007/978-981-19-3167-3_1

ChillonP. S. (2012). *Urban 360*. http://urban360.me

Chou, L., Dai, J., Qian, X., Karimipour, A., & Zheng, X. (2021). Achieving sustainable soil and water protection: The perspective of agricultural water price regulation on environmental protection. *Agricultural Water Management*, *245*, 106583. doi:10.1016/j.agwat.2020.106583 PMID:33100487

Chourabi, H., Nam, T., Walker, S., Gil-Garcia, J. R., Mellouli, S., Nahon, K., Pardo, T. A., & Scholl, H. J. (2012, January). Understanding smart cities: An integrative framework. In *2012 45th Hawaii international conference on system sciences* (pp. 2289-2297). IEEE.

Coates, B. E. (2001). SMART government on Line, not in line: Opportunities, challenges, and Concerns for Public Leadership. *Public Management*, *30*(4), 37–40.

Coe, A., Paquet, G., & Roy, J. (2001). E-governance and smart communities. *Social Science Computer Review*, *19*(1), 80–93. doi:10.1177/089443930101900107

Cohen, L. (1995). *Quality function deployment: How to make QFD work for you*. Addison-Wesley.

Collins, C. M., Dennehy, D., Conboy, K., & Mikalef, P. (2021). Artificial intelligence in information systems research: A systematic literature review and research agenda. *International Journal of Information Management*, *60*, 102383. doi:10.1016/j.ijinfomgt.2021.102383

CONAGUA. (n. d.). *Manual de Agua Potable, Alcantarillado y Saneamiento. Evaluación Rápida de Plantas Potabilizadoras. Comisión Nacional del Agua*. CONAGUA.

Connell, J. (2006). Medical tourism: Sea, sun, sand and… surgery. *Tourism Management*, *27*(6), 1093–1100. doi:10.1016/j.tourman.2005.11.005

Cook, D., & Das, S. K. (2004). *Smart Environment: Technology, protocols and applications* (Vol. 43). John Wiley&Sons. doi:10.1002/047168659X

Coro, Y., & Elizabeth, S. (2016). *Diseño e implementación de un prototipo inalámbrico IPv6 que permita comprobar la calidad de agua en smartcities*. Bachelor'sthesis, Escuela Superior Politécnica de Chimborazo.

Corp, N. H. N. (2023). *Naver*. Naver. https://www.naver.com/

Cortés, M. (2016). *Porque la ciudad de México es una de las más inteligentes del mundo*. CIO México https://cio.com.mx/la-ciudad-mexico-una-las-mas-inteligentes-del-mundo/

Cory Albers & Bernard Amell. (2018). *System and Method for Producing Potable Water from Stormwater* [Patent]. https://patentscope.wipo.int/search/es/detail.jsf?docId=US213379733&_cid=P12-L9MVZJ-64483-1

Cosgrave, E., Doody, L., & Walt, N. (2014). Delivering the smart city–governing cities in the digital age. *Arup, Liveable Cities, UCL, Smart City Expo, London.*

Cosgrove, W. J., & Rijsberman, F. R. (2014). *World water vision: Making water everybody's business.* Routledge. doi:10.4324/9781315071763

Couclelis, H. (2004). The construction of the digital city. *Environment and Planning. B, Planning & Design, 31*(1), 5–19. doi:10.1068/b1299

Coursera Inc. (2023, 2023). *Degrees, Certificates, & Free Online Courses.* Coursera. https://www.coursera.org/

Coutinho, S. M. V., Abilio, C. C. C., Da Penha Vasconcellos, M., & Netto, C. A. A. (2019). Smart cities indicators: The emergence of a new cliché. *Revista de Gestao Ambiental e Sustentabilidade, 8*(2), 386–402. doi:10.5585/geas.v8i2.13574

Crini, G., & Lichtfouse, E. (2019). Advantages and disadvantages of techniques used for wastewater treatment. *Environmental Chemistry Letters, 17*(1), 145–155. doi:10.100710311-018-0785-9

Czyczula Rudjord, Z., Reid, M. J., Schwermer, C. U., & Lin, Y. (2022). Laboratory development of an AI system for the real-time monitoring of water quality and detection of anomalies arising from chemical contamination. *Water (Basel), 14*(16), 2588. doi:10.3390/w14162588

D'Amore, G., Di Vaio, A., Balsalobre-Lorente, D., & Boccia, F. (2022). Artificial intelligence in the water–energy–food model: A holistic approach towards Sustainable Development Goals. *Sustainability (Basel), 14*(2), 867. doi:10.3390u14020867

da Rosa, F. S., Lunkes, R. J., & Mendes, A. C. (2020). Environmental management accounting and innovation in water and energy reduction. *Environmental Monitoring and Assessment, 192*(10), 1–15. doi:10.100710661-020-08586-7 PMID:32889603

Daelman, M. R., van Voorthuizen, E. M., van Dongen, U. G., Volcke, E. I., & van Loosdrecht, M. C. (2012). Methane emission during municipal wastewater treatment. *Water Research, 46*(11), 3657–3670. doi:10.1016/j.watres.2012.04.024 PMID:22575155

Dahlmann, F., Brammer, S., & Millington, A. (2008). Environmental management in the United Kingdom: New survey evidence. *Management Decision, 46*(2), 264–283. doi:10.1108/00251740810854159

Daley, S. (2023). 36 Artificial Intelligence Examples Shaking Up Business Across Industries. *Built In.* https://builtin.com/artificial-intelligence/examples-ai-in-industry

Dalton, J. (1802). Experiments and observations to determine whether the quantity of rain and dew is equal to the quantity of water carried off by rivers and raised by evaporation; with an inquiry into the origin of the springs. *Manchester Philosophical Society Memories, 5,* 346–372.

Dameri, R. P. (2013). Searching for smart city definition: A comprehensive proposal. *International Journal of Computers and Technology, 11*(5), 2544–2551. doi:10.24297/ijct.v11i5.1142

Dameri, R. P., & Benevolo, C. (2016). Governing smart cities: An empirical analysis. *Social Science Computer Review, 34*(6), 693–707. doi:10.1177/0894439315611093

Danziger, J. N., & Dutton, W. H. (1983). *Computers and politics: High technology in American local governments.* Columbia University Press.

Daramola, O., & Thebus, D. (2020). Evaluación centrada en la arquitectura del voto electrónico por contrato inteligente basado en blockchain para elecciones nacionales. *Informatica (Vilnius), 7*(2), 16. doi:10.3390/informatics7020016 de Abreu, M. C. S., & de Andrade, R. D. J. C. (2019). Dealing with wicked problems in socio-ecological systems affected by industrial disasters: A framework for collaborative and adaptive governance. *The Science of the Total Environment, 694*, 133700. doi:10.1016/j.scitotenv.2019.133700 PMID:31398643

De Evaluación Modernización Y Desarrollo Administrativo. C. G. (s. f.). *Delegaciones*. Coordinación General de Evaluación, Modernización Y Desarrollo Administrativo. https://www.cgma.cdmx.gob.mx/temas-de-modernizacion/resultados-avance-aac/delegaciones

De la Mata, A. (2021). *Visión estratégica del ecosistema digital., Apuntes del módulo 5 Innovación y emprendimientos digitales, Conferencia "El ecosistema Blockchain"*. Faculty Led Verano Universidad Politécnica de Madrid.

Dehghani, M. H., Salari, M., Karri, R. R., Hamidi, F., & Bahadori, R. (2021). Process modeling of municipal solid waste compost ash for reactive red 198 dye adsorption from wastewater using data driven approaches. *Scientific Reports, 11*(1), 11613. doi:10.103841598-021-90914-z PMID:34078966

Demirkol, E. C. (2022). Impacts of modern agriculture on environment and sustainable agriculture. *Journal of Life Economics, 9*(3), 171–182. doi:10.15637/jlecon.9.3.05

Deng, L., Guo, S., Yin, J., Zeng, Y., & Chen, K. (2022). Multi-objective optimization of water resources allocation in Han River basin (China) integrating efficiency, equity and sustainability. *Scientific Reports, 12*(1), 798. doi:10.103841598-021-04734-2 PMID:35039583

Deshpande, Y., & Unhelkar, B. (2011). Information Systems for a Green Organisation. In B. Unhelkar (Ed.), *Handbook of Research on Green ICT: Technology, Business and Social Perspectives* (pp. 116–130). IGI Global. doi:10.4018/978-1-61692-834-6.ch008

Dewitte, S., Cornelis, J. P., Müller, R., & Munteanu, A. (2021). Artificial Intelligence revolutionises Weather Forecast, Climate Monitoring and Decadal Prediction. *Remote Sensing (Basel), 13*(16), 3209. doi:10.3390/rs13163209

Di Virgilio, M. M., & Serrati, P. (2022). Smart Cities, Digital Divide, and Space. Evidence from the Case of the Greater Buenos Aires Agglomerate. *Territorios, 47*. doi:10.12804/revistas.urosario.edu.co/territorios/a.11635

Dill, S. David (2016). Stanford *INGENIERÍA: Por qué votar en línea es un peligro para la democracia*. Seguridad, Tecnología y Sociedad. https://engineering.stanford.edu/magazine/article/david-dill-why-online-voting-danger-democracy

Diogo, R. A., dos Santos, N., & Loures, E. F. R. (2023). 13 - Digital Transformation of Engineering Education for Smart Education: A systematic literature review. In M. Ram & L. Xing (Eds.), *Reliability Modeling in Industry 4.0* (pp. 407–438). Elsevier. doi:10.1016/B978-0-323-99204-6.00002-9

Djahel, S., Doolan, R., Muntean, G. M., & Murphy, J. (2014). A communications-oriented perspective on traffic management systems for smart cities: Challenges and innovative approaches. *IEEE Communications Surveys and Tutorials, 17*(1), 125–151. doi:10.1109/COMST.2014.2339817

Domínguez-Bolaño, T., Campos, O., Barral, V., Escudero, C. J., & García-Naya, J. A. (2022). An overview of IoT architectures, technologies, and existing open-source projects. *Internet of Things, 20*, 100626. https://doi.org/https://doi.org/10.1016/j.iot.2022.100626

Dondeynaz, C., Carmona Moreno, C., & Céspedes Lorente, J. J. (2012). Analysing inter-relationships among water, governance, human development variables in developing countries. *Hydrology and Earth System Sciences, 16*(10), 3791–3816. doi:10.5194/hess-16-3791-2012

Dong, H., Singh, G., Attri, A., & Saddik, A. E. (2017). Open Data-Set of Seven Canadian Cities. *IEEE Access : Practical Innovations, Open Solutions, 5*, 529–543. doi:10.1109/ACCESS.2016.2645658

Dorcic, J., Komsic, A., & Markovic, I. (2019). Mobile technologies and applications in smart tourism: A systematic literature review. *Journal of Hospitality and Tourism Technology, 10*(2), 343–367.

Dorcic, J., Komsic, J., & Markovic, S. (2019). Mobile technologies and applications towards smart tourism–state of the art. *Tourism Review, 74*(1), 82–103. doi:10.1108/TR-07-2017-0121

Douligeris, C. (1993). Intelligent Home Systems. *IEEE Communications Magazine, 31*(10), 52–61. doi:10.1109/35.237984

Drucker, P. F. (2011). *Landmarks of tomorrow: A report on the new*. Transaction Publishers.

Dufour, M. A., Légaré, F., & Dubois, C. A. (2017). Smart technology, artificial intelligence, and the future of health care. *Journal of General Internal Medicine, 32*(1), 86–90.

Du, J., Wen, Y., Wang, L., Zhang, P., Fei, M., & Pardalos, P. M. (2022). An adaptive human learning optimization with enhanced exploration–exploitation balance. *Annals of Mathematics and Artificial Intelligence*. doi:10.100710472-022-09799-x

Du, M., Chen, Q., & Ma, X. (2020). MBFT: A new consensus algorithm for consortium blockchain. *IEEE Access : Practical Innovations, Open Solutions, 8*, 87665–87675. doi:10.1109/ACCESS.2020.2993759

Dumitrascu, O., Dumitrascu, M., & Dobrotă, D. (2020). Performance evaluation for a sustainable supply chain management system in the automotive industry using artificial intelligence. *Processes (Basel, Switzerland), 8*(11), 1384. doi:10.3390/pr8111384

Dunleavy, P., Margetts, H., Tinkler, J., & Bastow, S. (2006). *Digital era governance: IT corporations, the state, and e-government*. Oxford University Press. doi:10.1093/acprof:oso/9780199296194.001.0001

Dutton, W. H., Blumler, J. G., & Kraemer, K. L. (1987). *Wired Cities: Shaping the future of communications*. GK Hall &Co.

Ebinger, F., Buttke, L., & Kreimeier, J. (2022). Augmented and virtual reality technologies in education for sustainable development: An expert-based technology assessment. *TATuP - Zeitschrift für Technikfolgenabschätzung in Theorie und Praxis, 31*(1), 28-34. https://doi.org/ doi:10.14512/tatup.31.1.28

Eclipse Foundation. (2023, 2023). *Eclipse sensiNact*. Eclipse Foundation. https://projects.eclipse.org/projects/technology.sensinact

Edmondson, V., Cerny, M., Lim, M., Gledson, B., Lockley, S., & Woodward, J. (2018). A smart sewer asset information model to enable an 'Internet of Things' for operational wastewater management. *Automation in Construction, 91*, 193–205. doi:10.1016/j.autcon.2018.03.003

edX LLC. (2023, 2023). *edX Build new skills. Advance your career*. EDX. https://www.edx.org

Election Commission of India. (2018). *Electronic Voting Machines and the Election Process*. ECI. https://eci.gov.in/faqs/election-machinery/faqs-election-machinery-r13/

Emaldi, M., Pena, O., Lazaro, J., & Lopez-de-Ipina, D. (2015). Linked Open Data as the Fuel for Smarter Cities. In F. Xhafa, L. Barolli, A. Barolli, & P. Papajorgji (Eds.), *Modeling and Processing for Next-Generation Big-Data Technologies: With Applications and Case Studies* (Vol. 4, pp. 443–472). Springer Int Publishing Ag. doi:10.1007/978-3-319-09177-8_18

Embarak, O. H. (2022). Internet of Behaviour (IoB)-based AI models for personalized smart education systems. *Procedia Computer Science, 203*, 103–110. doi:10.1016/j.procs.2022.07.015

Enerlis, E., & Young, F. (2012). *Libro Blanco. Smart cities. Madrid Network.*

Enguehard, C. (2008). *Transparency in Electronic Voting : the Great Challen*ge. IPSA International Political Science Association Conference on "E-democracy - State of the art and future agenda, Stellenbosch , South Africa. https://www.researchgate.net/publication/32221266_Transparency_in_Electronic_Voting_the_Great_Challenge

Enrique, H.-W. J., & Enrique, G. G. (2013). Concentración y diversidad de los medios de comunicación y las telecomunicaciones en México. *Comunicación y Sociedad, 19*, 113–152. https://www.scielo.org.mx/scielo.php?script=sci_arttext&pid=S0188-252X2013000100006

EOI. (2015). *El ecosistema SMART en Andalucía. Retos y oportunidades para la colaboración público-privada*. Escuela de Organización Industrial. Madrid. http://a.eoi.es/andalsmart

Ergazakis, K., Metaxiotis, K., & Ergazakis, E. (2010). Exploring Paths Towards Knowledge Cities Developments: A Research Agenda. Encyclopedia of Knowledge Management, 288–297. doi:10.4018/978-1-59904-931-1.ch028

Esposito, C., & Choi, C. (2023, March). Design and Implementation of a Blockchain-based e-Voting system by using the Algorand platform. *In Proceedings of the 38th ACM/SIGAPP Symposium on Applied Computing* (pp. 715-723). ACM. 10.1145/3555776.3577750

Estévez, E.C., and Janowski, T. (2016). Gobierno digital, ciudadanos y ciudades inteligentes. *Bit & Byte, 2.*

Estévez-Ortiz, F. J., García-Jiménez, A., & Glösekötter, P. (2016). An application of people's sentiment from social media to smart cities. *El Profesional de la Información*, *25*(6), 851–858. doi:10.3145/epi.2016.nov.02

European Commission. (2010). *Europa 2020: Una estrategia para un crecimiento inteligente, sostenible e integrador, COM(2010) 2020final, Bruselas, 3.3.2010.* https://eurlex.europa.eu/legal-content/en/ALL/?uri=CELEX:52010DC2020

Eurostat, E. E. (2023, April). Electricity price statistics. https://ec.europa.eu/eurostat/statistics-explained/index.php?title=Electricity_price_statistics

EVoting communications. (2021). *Evoting 2021: Entering the big league field.* Evoting. https://www.evoting.com/2021/12/30/z-evoting-2021-entrando-a-la-cancha-de-las-grandes-ligas/

Eynon, R. (2007). Breaking Barriers to eGovernment: Overcoming obstacles to improving European public services. DG Information Society and Media. European Commission.

Eysenbach, G. (2018). The potential of AI in healthcare is immense. *The Lancet. Digital Health*, *1*(1), e1–e2.

Famiglietti, J. S. (2014). The global groundwater crisis. *Nature Climate Change*, *4*(11), 945–948. doi:10.1038/nclimate2425

FAO (Food and Agriculture Organization of the United Nations). (2011). The state of the world's land and water resources for food and agriculture (SOLAW) – Managing systems at risk. Food and Agriculture Organization of the United Nations and London, Earthscan.

Farsani, N. T., Ghotbabadi, A. R., & Altafi, A. (2019). Agri-tourism as a sustainable form of rural tourism: A systematic literature review. *Journal of Hospitality and Tourism Management*, *41*, 218–232.

Farsani, N. T., Ghotbabadi, S. S., & Altafi, M. (2019). Agricultural heritage as a creative tourism attraction. *Asia Pacific Journal of Tourism Research*, *24*(6), 541–549. doi:10.1080/10941665.2019.1593205

Fasciolo, B., Awouda, A., Bruno, G., & Lombardi, F. (2023). A smart aeroponic system for sustainable indoor farming. *30th CIRP Life Cycle Engineering Conference, 116*, (pp. 636-641). CIRP. 10.1016/j.procir.2023.02.107

Feldman, S. J., Soyka, P. A., & Ameer, P. (1996). *Does improving a firm's environmental management system and environmental performance result in a higher stock price?* ICF Kaiser.

Feng, Z. (2011). *Research on water-saving irrigation automatic control system based on internet of things. 2011 International Conference on Electric Information and Control Engineering*. IEEE. do10.1109/ICEICE.2011.5778297

Fereidooni, Z., Tahayori, H., & Bahadori-Jahromi, A. (2021). A hybrid model-based method for leak detection in large scale water distribution networks. *Journal of Ambient Intelligence and Humanized Computing, 12*(2), 1613–1629. doi:10.100712652-020-02233-2

Fernandes, R. P. A. (2012). *Towards a collaborative tourist system using serious games*. UNIVERSIDADE DOPORTO.

Fernandez-Anez, V., Fernández-Güell, J. M., & Giffinger, R. (2018). Smart City implementation and discourses: An integrated conceptual model. The case of Vienna. *Cities (London, England), 78*, 4–16. doi:10.1016/j.cities.2017.12.004

Finkelstein, R., Garcia, A., Netherland, J., & Walker, J. (2008). *Toward an age-friendly New York City: A findings report*. New York Academy of Medicine.

Firfiris, V. K., Fragos, V. P., Kotsopoulos, T. A., & Nikita-Martzopoulou, C. (2020). Energy and environmental analysis of an innovative greenhouse structure towards frost prevention and heating needs conservation. *Sustainable Energy Technologies and Assessments, 40*, 100750. doi:10.1016/j.seta.2020.100750

Focus Group on Smart Sustainable Cities. (2015, Octuber, 2015). *Smart Sustainable City*. Retrieved April 27, 2023 from

Foster, L., Szilagyi, K., Wairegi, A., Oguamanam, C., & de Beer, J. (2023). Smart farming and artificial intelligence in East Africa: Addressing indigeneity, plants, and gender. *Smart Agricultural Technology, 3*, 100132. doi:10.1016/j.atech.2022.100132

Fritts, C.E. (1883). On a new form of selenium cell, and some electrical discoveries made by its use. *American Journal of Science, s3-26*(156), 465–472. . doi:10.2475/ajs.s3-26.156.465

Frutos, E., Ruiz, M., Belén, A., Sánchez, M., & Escarbajal Frutos, A. Belén Mirete Ruiz, A., Maquilón Sánchez, J. J., Izquierdo Rus, T., Isabel López Hidalgo, J., Orcajada Sánchez, N., & Sánchez Martín, M. (2012). La atención a la diversidad: la educación inclusiva. *REIFOP, 15*(1), 135–144. https://www.redalyc.org/articulo.oa?id=217024398011

Fu, G., Jin, Y., Sun, S., Yuan, Z., & Butler, D. (2022). The role of deep learning in urban water management: A critical review. *Water Research, 223*(118973), 118973. doi:10.1016/j.watres.2022.118973 PMID:35988335

Fujdiak, R. (2016). Using genetic algorithm for Advanced Municipal Waste Collection in smart city. *2016 10th International Symposium on Communication Systems, Networks and Digital Signal Processing (CSNDSP)*. 10.1109/CSNDSP.2016.7574016

Gagliardi, D., Schina, L., Sarcinella, M. L., Mangialardi, G., Niglia, F., & Corallo, A. (2017). Information and communication technologies and public participation: Interactive maps and value added for citizens. *Government Information Quarterly, 34*(1), 153–166. doi:10.1016/j.giq.2016.09.002

Gallego-Schmid, A., & Tarpani, R. R. Z. (2019). Life cycle assessment of wastewater treatment in developing countries: A review. *Water Research, 153*, 63–79. doi:10.1016/j.watres.2019.01.010 PMID:30690219

Gao, L., Pan, B., Li, X., & Wang, D. (2020). Chatbots in tourism: A review of recent studies. *Journal of Hospitality and Tourism Management, 44*, 154–163.

Garcia, A., Linaza, M. T., Gutierrez, A., & Garcia, E. (2019). Gamified mobile experiences: Smart technologies for tourism destinations. *Tourism Review, 74*(1), 30–49. doi:10.1108/TR-08-2017-0131

Gascó, M. (2005). Exploring the e-government gap in South America. *International Journal of Public Administration, 28*(7-8), 683–701. doi:10.1081/PAD-200064235

Gavalas, D., Konstantopoulos, C., Mastakas, K., & Pantziou, G. (2014). A survey on algorithmic approaches for solving tourist trip design problems. *Journal of Heuristics*, *20*(3), 291–328. doi:10.100710732-014-9242-5

Gaya, M. S., Abba, S. I., Abdu, A. M., Tukur, A. I., Saleh, M. A., Esmaili, P., & Wahab, N. A. (2020). Estimation of water quality index using artificial intelligence approaches and multi-linear regression. *IAES International Journal of Artificial Intelligence (IJ-AI)*, *9*(1), 126. . doi:10.11591/ijai.v9.i1.pp126-134

Gebremichael, S. G., Yismaw, E., Tsegaw, B. D., & Shibeshi, A. D. (2021). Determinants of water source use, quality of water, sanitation and hygiene perceptions among urban households in North-West Ethiopia: A cross-sectional study. *PLoS One*, *16*(4), e0239502. doi:10.1371/journal.pone.0239502 PMID:33886565

Geissbühler, A., Demongeot, J., Mokhtari, M., Abdulrazak, B., & Aloulou, H. (2015). *Inclusive Smart Cities and e-Health*. In Lecture Notes in Computer Science. Springer. doi:10.1007/978-3-319-19312-0

Geller, A. L. (2003). Smart growth: A prescription for livable cities. *American Journal of Public Health*, *93*(9), 1410–1415. doi:10.2105/AJPH.93.9.1410 PMID:12948954

Gharaibeh, A., Salahuddin, M. A., Hussini, S. J., Khreishah, A., Khalil, I., Guizani, M., & Al-Fuqaha, A. (2017). Smart cities: A survey on data management, security, and enabling technologies. *IEEE Communications Surveys and Tutorials*, *19*(4), 2456–2501. doi:10.1109/COMST.2017.2736886

Gharehgozli, A. H., Mileski, J., Adams, A., & von Zharen, W. (2017). Evaluating a "wicked problem": A conceptual framework on seaport resiliency in the event of weather disruptions. *Technological Forecasting and Social Change*, *121*, 65–75. doi:10.1016/j.techfore.2016.11.006

Gholami, V., Khaleghi, M. R., Pirasteh, S., & Booij, M. J. (2022). Comparison of self-organizing map, artificial neural network, and co-active neuro-fuzzy inference system methods in simulating groundwater quality: Geospatial artificial intelligence. *Water Resources Management*, *36*(2), 451–469. doi:10.100711269-021-02969-2

Giffinger, R., Fertner, C., Kramar, H., Kalasek, R., Pichler-Milanovic, N., & Meijers, E. (2007). *Smart cities – Ranking of European medium-sized cities*. Centre of Regional Science. https://www.smart-cities.eu/download/smart_cities_final_report.pdf

Giffinger, R., & Pichler-Milanović, N. (2007). *Smart cities: Ranking of European medium-sized cities*. Centre of Regional Science, Vienna University of Technology.

Gil-García, J. R. (2007). Exploring e-government benefits and success factors. In *Encyclopedia of digital government* (pp. 803–811). IGI Global. doi:10.4018/978-1-59140-789-8.ch122

Gil-Garcia, J. R. (2012). *Enacting electronic government success: An integrative study of government-wide websites, organisational capabilities, and institutions* (Vol. 31). Springer Science & Business Media. doi:10.1007/978-1-4614-2015-6

Gil-Garcia, J. R., Helbig, N., & Ojo, A. (2014). Being smart: Emerging technologies and innovation in the public sector. *Government Information Quarterly*, *31*, I1–I8. doi:10.1016/j.giq.2014.09.001

Ginting, A., Napitupulu, A., Tumanggor, R., & Lumbanraja, P. (2020). Quality function deployment and its application in public services. *Journal of Physics: Conference Series*, *1567*(2), 022038. doi:10.1088/1742-6596/1567/2/022038

Giraldo, F. D., Milton, B., & Gamboa, C. E. (2020). Electronic Voting Using Blockchain And Smart Contracts: Proof Of Concept. IEEE Latin America Transactions, 18(10). https://doi:10.1109/TLA.2020.9387645

Giustolisi, O., Savage, D. A., & Capellan, Z. (2009). Pressure-Driven Demand and Leakage Simulation for Water Distribution Networks. *Journal of Hydraulic Engineering*, *134*(5), 383–391. doi:10.1061/(ASCE)0733-9429(2009)135:5(383)

Glaeser, E., Kourtit, K., & Nijkamp, P. (2021). New urban challenges: Shared spaces in smart places – Overview and positioning. *Land Use Policy*, *111*, 105672. doi:10.1016/j.landusepol.2021.105672

Global University Systems. (2023). *FutureLearn: Online Courses and Degrees from Top Universities*. Future Learn. https://www.futurelearn.com/

Godart, J. M. (2001). Combinatorial optimisation for trip planning. *Belgian Journal of Operations Research, Statistics and Computer Science*, *41*(1-2), 59–68.

Goldstein, B., Hauschild, M., Fernandez, J., & Birkved, M. (2016). Testing the environmental performance of urban agriculture as a food supply in northern climates. *Journal of Cleaner Production*, *135*, 984–994. doi:10.1016/j.jclepro.2016.07.004

Góngora, G. P. M., & Bernal, W. N. (2017). Gestión de tecnología de información para gobiernos inteligentes: Un enfoque de arquitectura empresarial. *Gestion*, *38*(42), 14–24.

Góngora, G. P., & Nieto Bernal, W. (2015). Factores Clave en la Gestión de Tecnología de Información para Sistemas de Gobierno Inteligente. *Journal of Technology Management & Innovation*, *10*(4), 109–117. doi:10.4067/S0718-27242015000400012

Google. (2023). *bard*. Google. https://bard.google.com/?hl=en

Goralski, M. A., & Tan, T. K. (2020). Artificial intelligence and sustainable development. *International Journal of Management Education*, *18*(1), 100330. doi:10.1016/j.ijme.2019.100330

Gorgulu, S., & Kocabey, S. (2020). An Energy Saving Potential Analysis of Lighting Retrofit Scenarios in Outdoor Lighting Systems: A Case Study for a University Campus. *Journal of Cleaner Production*, *260*, 121060. doi:10.1016/j.jclepro.2020.121060

Grady, D. (2012). Exercising an aging brain. *New York Times*.

Grande, J. I. C. (2016). Las administraciones públicas en la era del gobierno abierto. Gobernanza inteligente para un cambio de paradigma en la gestión pública. *Revista de Estudios Políticos*, (173), 245–275.

Grbčić, L., Kranjčević, L., & Družeta, S. (2021). Machine learning and simulation-optimization coupling for water distribution network contamination source detection. *Sensors (Basel)*, *21*(4), 1157. doi:10.339021041157 PMID:33562175

Green, B. (2019). *The Smart Enough City: Putting Technology in Its Place to Reclaim Our Urban Future*. MIT Press. doi:10.7551/mitpress/11555.001.0001

Greene, W. H. (2003). *Econometric analysis*. Prentice Hall. chrome-extension://efaidnbmnnnibpcajpcglclefindmkaj/http://www.mim.ac.mw/books/William%20H.%20Green%27s%20Econometric.pdf

Gretzel, U., Sigala, M., Xiang, Z., & Koo, C. (2015). Smart tourism: Foundations and developments. *Electronic Markets*, *25*(3), 179–188. doi:10.100712525-015-0196-8

Grigoras, G., Bizon, N., Enescu, F. M., Lopez Guede, J. M., Salado, G. F., Brennan, R., O'Driscoll, C., Dinka, M. O., & Alalm, M. G. (2018). ICT based smart management solution to realize water and energy savings through energy efficiency measures in water distribution systems. *2018 10th International Conference on Electronics, Computers and Artificial Intelligence (ECAI)*. IEEE. 10.1109/ECAI.2018.8679012

GrowSpan. (2018, May 24). *Understanding Greenhouse Lighting*. GrowSpan. https://www.growspan.com/news/understanding-greenhouse-lighting/

Guerrero-Baena, M. D., Gómez-Limón, J. A., & Fruet, J. V. (2015). A multicriteria method for environmental management system selection: An intellectual capital approach. *Journal of Cleaner Production*, *105*, 428–437. doi:10.1016/j.jclepro.2014.07.079

Gujarati Damodar, N., & Porter Dawn, C. (2009). *Econometría*. Word Press. chrome-extension://efaidnbmnnnibpcajpcglclefindmkaj/https://fvela.files.wordpress.com/2012/10/econometria-damodar-n-gujarati-5ta-ed.pdf

Gul, S., & Topcu, I. (2015). A Multi-Attribute Decision Support Model for the Selection of Touristic Activities. *International Journal of the Analytic Hierarchy Process*, *7*(3). Advance online publication. doi:10.13033/ijahp.v7i3.354

Guo, L., Wu, H., Li, Z., Wu, W., & Zhang, C. (2019). An IoT-based intelligent tourist attraction framework: Concepts, technologies, and applications. *IEEE Access : Practical Innovations, Open Solutions*, *7*, 10458–10467.

Guzman, A. (2022, 13 octubre). Smart Cities en México. *Magnet Mexico*. https://www.magnetmex.com/industria-4-0/smart-cities-en-mexico/

Haase Richard Alan. (2007). *Potable water treatment system and apparatus*. Australia, Patent. OMPI. https://patentscope.wipo.int/search/es/detail.jsf?docId=US40239475&_cid=P12-L9MVZJ-64483-1

Haase, R. A. (2001). Potable water treatment system and method of operation thereof (Australia, Patent). OMPI. https://patentscope.wipo.int/search/es/detail.jsf?docId=AU180922058&_cid=P12-L9MVZJ-64483-1

Halgamuge, M., Bojovschi, A., Fisher, P. M. J., Le, T. C., Adeloju, S., & Murphy, S. (2021). Internet of Things and autonomous control for vertical cultivation walls towards smart food growing: A review. *Urban Forestry & Urban Greening*, *61*, 127094. doi:10.1016/j.ufug.2021.127094

Hall, P. (2000). Creative cities and economic development. *Urban Studies (Edinburgh, Scotland)*, *37*(4), 633–649. doi:10.1080/00420980050003946

Harsh, A., & Ichalkaranje, N. (2015). Transforming e-government to smart government: A South Australian perspective. *In Intelligent Computing, Communication and Devices: Proceedings of ICCD 2014,* Volume 1 (pp. 9-16). Springer India.

Harsh, A., & Ichalkaranje, N. (2015). Transforming e-government to smart government: A South Australian perspective. In *Intelligent Computing, Communication and Devices* (pp. 9–16). Springer. doi:10.1007/978-81-322-2012-1_2

Hassan, A. G., Fullen, M. A., & Oloke, D. (2019). Problems of drought and its management in Yobe State, Nigeria. *Weather and Climate Extremes*, *23*, 100192. doi:10.1016/j.wace.2019.100192

Hateffard, F., Balog, K., Tóth, T., Mészáros, J., Árvai, M., Kovács, Z. A., Szűcs-Vásárhelyi, N., Koós, S., László, P., Novák, T. J., Pásztor, L., & Szatmári, G. (2022). High-Resolution Mapping and Assessment of Salt-Affectedness on Arable Lands by the Combination of Ensemble Learning and Multivariate Geostatistics. *Agronomy (Basel)*, *12*(8), 1858. https://www.mdpi.com/2073-4395/12/8/1858. doi:10.3390/agronomy12081858

Haub, C., & Kaneda, T. (2011). *PRB's 2011 World Population Data Sheet*. PRB. https://www.prb.org/resources/2011-world-population-data-sheet/

Hauber-Davidson, G., & Idris, E. (2006). Smart water metering. *Water (Basel)*, *33*(3), 38–41.

Hauser, J. R., & Clausing, D. (1988). The house of quality. *Harvard Business Review*, *66*(3), 63–73.

Head, B. W. (2008). Wicked problems in public policy. *Public Policy*, *3*(2), 101.

Heddam, S., Sanikhani, H., & Kisi, O. (2019). Application of artificial intelligence to estimate phycocyanin pigment concentration using water quality data: A comparative study. *Applied Water Science*, *9*(7), 164. doi:10.100713201-019-1044-3

He, L., Fu, L., Gravano, L., Fang, W., Sun, X., Suo, R., Li, G., Zhao, G., Yang, R., & Li, R. (2022). IoT-based urban agriculture container farm design and implementation for localized produce supply. *Computers and Electronics in Agriculture, 203*, 107445. doi:10.1016/j.compag.2022.107445

Hennink, M., Hutter, I., & Bailey, A. (2020). *Qualitative research methods.* SAGE Publications Limited.

Hilson, G., & Nayee, V. (2002). Environmental management system implementation in the mining industry: A key to achieving cleaner production. *International Journal of Mineral Processing, 64*(1), 19–41. doi:10.1016/S0301-7516(01)00071-0

Himeur, Y., Elnour, M., Fadli, F., Meskin, N., Petri, I., Rezgui, Y., Bensaali, F., & Amira, A. (2023). AI-big data analytics for building automation and management systems: A survey, actual challenges and future perspectives. *Artificial Intelligence Review, 56*(6), 4929–5021. doi:10.100710462-022-10286-2 PMID:36268476

Hiramatsu, K., & Ishida, T. (2001). An augmented web space for digital cities. In *Applications and the Internet, 2001. Proceedings. 2001 Symposium on* (pp. 105-112). IEEE. 10.1109/SAINT.2001.905173

Hivon, J., & Tita, R. (2017). Conceptualising citizen participation in open data use at the city level. *Transforming Government: People. Process and Policy, 11*(1), 99–118. doi:10.1108/TG-12-2015-0053

Hjálmarsson, F. Þ., Hreiðarsson, G. K., Hamdaqa, M., & Hjálmtýsson, G. (2018). Blockchain-Based E-Voting System. *2018 IEEE 11th International Conference on Cloud Computing (CLOUD), EUA*, (pp. 983-986). IEEE. 10.1109/CLOUD.2018.00151

Hmoud Al-Adhaileh, M., & Waselallah Alsaade, F. (2021). Modelling and prediction of water quality by using artificial intelligence. *Sustainability (Basel), 13*(8), 4259. doi:10.3390u13084259

Holmes, W., Bialik, M., & Fadel, C. (2023). Artificial intelligence in education. *Data Ethics : Building Trust : How Digital Technologies Can Serve Humanity.*, 621–653. doi:10.58863/20.500.12424/4276068

Hou, G., Li, Z., Jing, W., & Jiang, Y. (2012). *Solar potable water preparation system and method for preparing potable water by using solar potable water preparation system* [China, Patent]. https://patentscope.wipo.int/search/es/detail.jsf?docId=CN85324013&_cid=P12-L9MVZJ-64483-1

Howard, E. (1965). *Garden cities of tomorrow* (Vol. 23). MIT Press. https://northstream.se/white-paper/archive

Huang, J., & Koroteev, D. (2021). Artificial intelligence for planning of energy and waste management. *Sustainable Energy Technologies and Assessments, 47*, 101426. doi:10.1016/j.seta.2021.101426

Huang, L.-S., Su, J.-Y., & Pao, T.-L. (2019). A Context Aware Smart Classroom Architecture for Smart Campuses. *Applied Sciences (Basel, Switzerland), 9*(9), 1837. https://www.mdpi.com/2076-3417/9/9/1837. doi:10.3390/app9091837

Huang, Z., Li, X., Xiang, Z., & Huang, D. (2020). Smart tourism destination competitiveness and tourist satisfaction: An empirical study. *Journal of Travel Research, 59*(6), 1090–1107.

Huerta-Wong, E. & Gómez García, R. (2013). Concentración y diversidad de los medios de comunicación y las telecomunicaciones en México. *Comunicación y Sociedad, 19*(0188–252x), 113–152.

Hugging Face, I. (2023, 2023). *HuggingChat.* Huffing Face. https://huggingface.co/chat/

Hughey, K. F., Tait, S. V., & O'Connell, M. J. (2005). Qualitative evaluation of three 'environmental management systems in the New Zealand wine industry. *Journal of Cleaner Production, 13*(12), 1175–1187. doi:10.1016/j.jclepro.2004.07.002

Hui, I. K., Chan, A. H., & Pun, K. F. (2001). A study of the environmental management system implementation practices. *Journal of Cleaner Production, 9*(3), 269–276. doi:10.1016/S0959-6526(00)00061-5

Human Development Index (HDI). (2023). *UNDP*. HDR. https://hdr.undp.org/data-center/human-development-index#/indicies/HDI

Hunter, W. C., Chung, N., Gretzel, U., & Koo, C. (2015). Constructivist research in smart tourism. *Asia Pacific Journal of Information Systems*, *25*(1), 105–120. doi:10.14329/apjis.2015.25.1.105

Hwang, S. I. (2022). EMSO Technology Development by SWOT Analysis. *The Journal of Korean Institute of Electromagnetic Engineering and Science*, *33*(1), 58–68. doi:10.5515/KJKIEES.2022.33.1.58

Hyandye, C. B., Worqul, A., Martz, L. W., & Muzuka, A. N. N. (2018). The impact of future climate and land use/cover change on water resources in the Ndembera watershed and their mitigation and adaptation strategies. *Environmental Systems Research*, *7*(1), 7. doi:10.118640068-018-0110-4

Iacob, V. S. (2013). The wastewater–a problem of integrated urban water management. *Procedia Economics and Finance*, *6*, 436–443. doi:10.1016/S2212-5671(13)00160-3

IBM. (2010). *Smarter thinking for a smarter planet*. IBM.

IBM. (2023, 2023). *IBM Watson IoT Platform*. IBM. https://internetofthings.ibmcloud.com/

Icke, O., van Es, DM, de Koning, MF, Wuister, JJG, Ng, J., Phua, KM, Koh, YKK, Chan, WJ y Tao, G. (2020). Mejora del rendimiento de los procesos de tratamiento de aguas residuales mediante la aplicación de aprendizaje automático. *Water Science and Technology: A Journal of the International Association on Water Pollution Research, 82*(12), 2671–2680. . doi:10.2166/wst.2020.382

IMD. (2023). *Smart City Index Report 2023*. IMD. https://www.imd.org/wp-content/uploads/2023/06/SmartCityIndex-2023-V8.pdf

Inegi. (2020, 4 marzo). *México en cifras*. Inegi. https://www.inegi.org.mx/app/areasgeograficas/?ag=07000009#collapse-Resumen

Instructure. (2023, 2023). *CANVAS by Instructure*. Instructure. https://www.instructure.com/canvas

IoTivity. (2023, 2023). *IoTivity*. IoTivity. http://iotivity.org/

Iqbal, H. M. N., Parra-Saldivar, R., Zavala-Yoe, R., & Ramirez-Mendoza, R. A. (2020). Smart educational tools and learning management systems: Supportive framework. [IJIDeM]. *International Journal on Interactive Design and Manufacturing*, *14*(4), 1179–1193. doi:10.100712008-020-00695-4

Isakova Mukhlisa Fakhriddin, D., & Fayzullayev Sayfiddin Bakhadir, S. (2022). SMART LEARNING TECHNOLOGY. *British Journal of Global Ecology and Sustainable Development*, *10*, 178–183. https://journalzone.org/index.php/bjgesd/article/view/160

Islam, SMD-U., Mondal, PK, Ojong, N., Bodrud-Doza, M., Siddique, MAB, Hossain, M. y Mamun, MA (2021). Prácticas de agua, saneamiento, higiene y eliminación de desechos como estrategia de respuesta al COVID-19: perspectivas de Bangladesh. *Desarrollo y sustentabilidad ambiental, 23*(8), 11953–11974. . doi:10.1007/s10668-020-01151-9

ISSN. 1988-5261

IUIT. (2015). *Destinos Turísticos Inteligentes. Manual operativo para la configuración de destinos turísticos inteligentes. Universidad de Alicante, Instituto Universitario de Investigaciones Turísticas*. IUIT.

Iza, X. C., Zumba, X., & Cardoso, S. M. (2021). *Análisis comparativo de Métodos de Consenso sobre plataformas Blockchain Comparative analysis of Consensus Methods on Blockchain platforms* (Vol. 33). Revista Tecnológica Espol–RTE.

Jain, D. (2020). Renewable Energy: Powering a Safer Future. *Renewable Energy, 1*(3).

Jamei, E., Mortimer, M., Seyedmahmoudian, M., Horan, B., & Stojcevski, A. (2017). Investigating the Role of Virtual Reality in Planning for Sustainable Smart Cities. *Sustainability (Basel), 9*(11), 2006. https://www.mdpi.com/2071-1050/9/11/2006. doi:10.3390u9112006

Janowski, T. (2015). *Digital government evolution: From transformation to contextualisation.*

Jaramillo, F., & Destouni, G. (2015). Local flow regulation and irrigation raise global human water consumption and footprint. *Science, 350*(6265), 1248–1251. doi:10.1126cience.aad1010 PMID:26785489

Javed, A. R., Faheem, R., Asim, M., Baker, T., & Beg, M. O. (2021). A smartphone sensors-based personalized human activity recognition system for sustainable smart cities. *Sustainable Cities and Society, 71*, 102970. doi:10.1016/j.scs.2021.102970

Jawad, J., Hawari, A. H., & Javaid Zaidi, S. (2021). Artificial neural network *modeling of wastewater treatment and desalination using membrane processes: A review. Chemical Engineering Journal (Lausanne, Switzerland: 1996), 419*(129540), 129540. https://doi.org/. doi:10.1016/j.cej.2021.129540

Jeong, K. H. (2006). *E-government, the road to innovation; Principles and Experiences in Korea*. Gil-Job-E Media.

Jessop, B. (1990). Regulation theory in retrospect and prospect. *Economy and Society, 19*(2), 153–216. doi:10.1080/03085149000000006

Jha, S. K., Bilalovic, J., Jha, A., Patel, N., & Zhang, H. (2017). Renewable energy: Present research and future scope of Artificial Intelligence. *Renewable & Sustainable Energy Reviews, 77*, 297–317. doi:10.1016/j.rser.2017.04.018

Jimenez, C. E., Solanas, A., & Falcone, F. (2014). E-government interoperability: Linking open and smart government. *Computer, 47*(10), 22–24. doi:10.1109/MC.2014.281

Jin, P., Fang, D., & Chen, B. (2019, February). Water-energy nexus based on modified multiregional input-output model within China. *Energy Procedia 158*, 4092-4098.

Jin, M., Bekiaris-Liberis, N., Weekly, K., Spanos, C. J., & Bayen, A. M. (2016). Occupancy detection via environmental sensing. *IEEE Transactions on Automation Science and Engineering.*

Ji, Z., & Anwen, Q. (2010, November). The application of Internet of things (IOT) in emergency management system in China. In *2010 IEEE International Conference on Technologies for Homeland Security (HST)* (pp. 139-142). IEEE.

Johnston, E. (2010). Governance infrastructures in 2020. *Public Administration Review, 70*(s1), s122–s128. doi:10.1111/j.1540-6210.2010.02254.x

Johnstone, L. (2020). A systematic analysis of environmental management systems in SMEs: Possible research directions from a management accounting and control stance. *Journal of Cleaner Production, 244*, 118802. doi:10.1016/j.jclepro.2019.118802

Jones, J. A. A., Vardanian, T. G., & Hakopian, C. (Eds.). (2009). *Threats to global water security*. Springer Netherlands., doi:10.1007/978-90-481-2344-5

Jordan, B. (2011). *Corbin ball associates*. www.corbinball.com

Jose, R., Panigrahi, S. K., Patil, R. A., Fernando, Y., & Ramakrishna, S. (2020). Artificial Intelligence-Driven Circular Economy as a Key Enabler for Sustainable Energy Management. *Mater Circ Econ, 2*(1), 8. doi:10.100742824-020-00009-9

Joshi, K. K., and Vinod, K. (2015). Environmental Valuation and Green Accounting for the future.

Jouhara, H., Czajczyńska, D., Ghazal, H., Krzyżyńska, R., Anguilano, L., Reynolds, A. J., & Spencer, N. (2017). Municipal waste management systems for domestic use. *Energy, 139*, 485–506. doi:10.1016/j.energy.2017.07.162

Junejo, F., Saeed, A., & Hameed, S. (2018). 5.19 Energy Management in Ocean Energy Systems. In *Elsevier eBooks* (pp. 778–807). Elsevier BV. doi:10.1016/B978-0-12-809597-3.00539-3

Jury, W. A., & Vaux, H. Jr. (2005). The role of science in solving the world's emerging water problems. *Proceedings of the National Academy of Sciences of the United States of America, 102*(44), 15715–15720. doi:10.1073/pnas.0506467102 PMID:16249337

Kadenge, J., Mandel, N., Mkandawile, M., & Grace Masanja, V. (2020). Multi-criteria decision making and numerical optimization approaches for optimizing water loss management strategies in water distribution system - A case of urban water supply and sanitation authorities in Tanzania. *International Journal of Mathematical Sciences and Computing, 6*(1), 10–24. doi:10.5815/ijmsc.2020.01.02

KamelBoulos, M.N., Tsouros, A.D., & Holopainen, A. (2015). Social, innovative and smart cities are happy and resilient: insights from the WHO EURO 2014 International Healthy Cities Conference. *Int J Health Geogr., 14*(3). 10.1186/1476-072X-14-3

Kamel-Boulos, M. N., & Al-Shorbaji, N. M. (2014). On the Internet of Things, smart cities and the WHO Healthy Cities. *International Journal of Health Geographics, 13*(1), 10. doi:10.1186/1476-072X-13-10 PMID:24669838

Kamel-Boulos, M. N., Rocha, A., Martins, A., Vicente, M. E., Bolz, A., Feld, R., Tchoudovski, I., Braecklein, M., Nelson, J., Laighin, G. O., Sdogati, C., Cesaroni, F., Antomarini, M., Jobes, A., & Kinirons, M. (2007). CAALYX: A new generation of location-based services in healthcare. *International Journal of Health Geographics, 6*(1), 9. doi:10.1186/1476-072X-6-9 PMID:17352802

Kamel-Boulos, M. N., & Yang, S. P. (2013). Exergames for health and fitness: The roles of GPS and geosocial apps. *International Journal of Health Geographics, 12*(1), 18. doi:10.1186/1476-072X-12-18 PMID:23561306

Kamruzzaman, M. M., Alanazi, S., Alruwaili, M., Alshammari, N., Elaiwat, S., Abu-Zanona, M., Innab, N., Mohammad Elzaghmouri, B., & Ahmed Alanazi, B. (2023). AI- and IoT-Assisted Sustainable Education Systems during Pandemics, such as COVID-19, for Smart Cities. *Sustainability (Basel), 15*(10), 8354. doi:10.3390u15108354

Kanyangarara, M., Allen, S., Jiwani, S. S., & Fuente, D. (2021). Access to water, sanitation and hygiene services in health facilities in sub-Saharan Africa 2013-2018: Results of health facility surveys and implications for COVID-19 transmission. *BMC Health Services Research, 21*(1), 601. doi:10.118612913-021-06515-z PMID:34172045

Karam, A., Zaher, K., & Mahmoud, A. S. (2020). Comparative studies of using nano zerovalent iron, activated carbon, and green synthesized nano zerovalent iron for textile wastewater color removal using artificial intelligence, regression analysis, adsorption isotherm, and kinetic studies. *Air, Soil and Water Research, 13*, 117862212090827. doi:10.1177/1178622120908273

Karaouzas, I., Theodoropoulos, C., Vardakas, L., Kalogianni, E., & Th. Skoulikidis, N. (2018). A review of the effects of pollution and water scarcity on the stream biota of an intermittent Mediterranean basin. *River Research and Applications, 34*(4), 291–299. doi:10.1002/rra.3254

Kasprzyk, M., Szpakowski, W., Poznańska, E., Boogaard, F. C., Bobkowska, K., & Gajewska, M. (2022). Technical solutions and benefits of introducing rain gardens – Gdańsk case study. *The Science of the Total Environment, 835*, 155487. doi:10.1016/j.scitotenv.2022.155487 PMID:35483461

Kassab, M., DeFranco, J., & Laplante, P. (2020). A systematic literature review on Internet of things in education: Benefits and challenges. *Journal of Computer Assisted Learning, 36*(2), 115–127. doi:10.1111/jcal.12383

Kasztelewicz, A., Tomaszewska, B., Rahner, S., Winter, I., & Voss, V. (2022). MOOC education for sustainable development. The Erasmus+ project experience [journal article]. *Polityka Energetyczna – Energy Policy Journal, 25*(4), 165-180. https://doi.org/ doi:10.33223/epj/156341

Kaur, A., & Bhatia, M. (2021, 4-5 Dec. 2021). Smart Education: A Systematic Survey and Future Research Directions. *2021 International Conference on Computing Sciences (ICCS).* ICCS. 10.1109/ICCS54944.2021.00042

Kaur, A., Bhatia, M., & Stea, G. (2022). A Survey of Smart Classroom Literature. *Education Sciences, 12*(2), 86. https://www.mdpi.com/2227-7102/12/2/86. doi:10.3390/educsci12020086

Kawai, Y., Zhang, J., & Kawasaki, H. (2009, June). Tour recommendation system based on web information and GIS. In *2009 IEEE International Conference on Multimedia and Expo* (pp. 990-993). IEEE. 10.1109/ICME.2009.5202663

Kawamura, S. (2000). Integrated Design and Operation of Water Treatment Facilities. United States of America: Second Edition; John Wiley & Sons, Inc.

Kayhomayoon, Z., Milan, S. G., Arya Azar, N., Bettinger, P., Babaian, F., & Jaafari, A. (2022). A simulation-optimization modeling approach for conjunctive water use management in a semi-arid region of Iran. *Sustainability (Basel), 14*(5), 2691. doi:10.3390u14052691

Kemp, R. (2020). The Future Of Farming Is Inside This Bomb Shelter. Ten Stories Underneath London, Thousands Of Plants Are Growing. Popular Mechanics. https://www.popularmechanics.com/science/a34618094/future-farming-underground/

Khan, M. R., Voss, C. I., Yu, W., & Michael, H. A. (2014). Water resources management in the Ganges basin: A comparison of three strategies for conjunctive use of groundwater and surface water. *Water Resources Management, 28*(5), 1235–1250. doi:10.100711269-014-0537-y

Khudoyberdiev, A., Ahmad, S., Ullah, I., & Kim, D. (2020). An optimization scheme based on fuzzy logic control for efficient energy consumption in hydroponics environment. *Energies, 13*(2), 289. doi:10.3390/en13020289

Kickbusch, I., & Sakellarides, C. (2006). Flu City—Smart City: Applying health promotion principles to a pandemic threat. *Health Promotion International, 21*(2), 85–87. doi:10.1093/heapro/dal014 PMID:16714297

Kim, J., Lee, J., & Park, M. (2022). Identification of smartwatch-collected lifelog variables affecting body mass index in middle-aged people using regression machine learning algorithms and SHapley additive explanations. *Applied Sciences (Basel, Switzerland), 12*(8), 3819. doi:10.3390/app12083819

Kim, K., & Lee, J. (2019). Development of a Smart Inhaler for Asthma Management. *Sensors (Basel), 19*(14), 3131. PMID:31315234

King, D. A. (2004). The scientific impact of nations. *Nature, 430*(6997), 311–316. doi:10.1038/430311a PMID:15254529

Kiss, M., & Muha, L. (2018). The Cybersecurity Capability Aspects of Smart Government and Industry 4.0 Programmes. *Interdisciplinary Description of Complex Systems: INDECS, 16*(3, 3-A), 313–319. doi:10.7906/indecs.16.3.2

Kleindorfer, P. R. (1997). Market-based environmental audits and environmental risks: Implementing ISO 14000. *The Geneva Papers on Risk and Insurance. Issues and Practice, 22*(2), 194–210. doi:10.1057/gpp.1997.16

Kluczek, A., & Olszewski, P. (2017). Energy audits in industrial processes. *Journal of Cleaner Production, 142*, 3437–3453. doi:10.1016/j.jclepro.2016.10.123

Kocaballi, A. B., Berkovsky, S., Quiroz, J. C., & Quiroz, V. (2020). Personalized Asthma Management Using Smart Inhalers: A Systematic Review. *Sensors (Basel), 20*(21), 6295. PMID:33167373

Kohad, H. W., Kumar, S., & Ambhaikar, A. (2023). Design of a Novel Side Chaining Model for Improving the Performance of Security Aware E-Voting Applications. In *Mobile Radio Communications and 5G Networks: Proceedings of Third MRCN 2022* (pp. 13-28). Singapore: Springer Nature Singapore.

Komninos, N. (2006, July). The architecture of intelligent cities. In *Conference Proceedings Intelligent Environments* (*Vol. 6*, pp. 5-6). Academic Press.

Komninos, N. (2002). *Intelligent Cities: Innovation, knowledge systems and digital spaces.* Taylor and Francis.

Komninos, N. (2008). *Intelligent cities and globalisation of innovation networks.* Routledge. doi:10.4324/9780203894491

Komninos, N. (2009). Intelligent cities: Towards interactive and global innovation environments. *International Journal of Innovative Research and Development, 1*(4), 337–355. doi:10.1504/IJIRD.2009.022726

Koop, S. H. A., & van Leeuwen, C. J. (2017). The challenges of water, waste and climate change in cities. *Environment, Development and Sustainability, 19*(2), 385–418. doi:10.100710668-016-9760-4

Koppes, S. (2023, February 20) New LED strategies could make vertical farming more productive, less costly. *Newsroom.* https://www.purdue.edu/newsroom/releases/2023/Q1/new-led-strategies-could-make-vertical-farming-more-productive,-less-costly.html

Kovačević, A., & Kečo, D. (2023, June). VoteChain-A Blockchain-Based Voting Platform. In *2023 XXIX International Conference on Information, Communication and Automation Technologies (ICAT)* (pp. 1-6). IEEE.

Krajčovič, M., Gabajová, G., Matys, M., Furmannová, B., & Dulina, Ľ. (2022). Virtual Reality as an Immersive Teaching Aid to Enhance the Connection between Education and Practice. *Sustainability (Basel), 14*(15), 9580. https://www.mdpi.com/2071-1050/14/15/9580. doi:10.3390u14159580

Krishnan, S. R., Nallakaruppan, M. K., Chengoden, R., Koppu, S., Iyapparaja, M., Sadhasivam, J., & Sethuraman, S. (2022). Smart water resource management using Artificial Intelligence—A review. *Sustainability (Basel), 14*(20), 13384. doi:10.3390u142013384

Kristanto, S., Yashiro, T., Koshizuka, N., & Sakamura, K. (2016, May). Dynamic Polling Algorithm for Low Energy Garbage Level Measurement in Smart Trash Bin. In *Proceedings of the Second International Conference on IoT in Urban Space* (pp. 92-94). ACM. 10.1145/2962735.2962748

Kuecker, G. D., & Hartley, K. (2019). How Smart Cities Became the Urban Norm: Power and Knowledge in New Songdo City. In *Annals of the American Association of Geographers, 110*(2). https://www.tandfonline.com/doi/abs/10.1080/24694452.2019.1617102

Kullu, P., Majeedullah, S., Pranay, P. V. S., & Yakub, B. (2020). Smart urban farming (Entrepreneurship through EPICS). *Procedia Computer Science, 172*, 452–459. doi:10.1016/j.procs.2020.05.098

Kuppusamy, P. (2019). Smart Education Using Internet of Things Technology. In Z. Ma & L. Yan (Eds.), Emerging Technologies and Applications in Data Processing and Management (pp. 385-412). IGI Global. doi:10.4018/978-1-5225-8446-9.ch017

Kurata, Y. (2009, June). Challenges in user-adaptive tour planning systems. In *AGILE Workshop on Adaptation in Spatial Communication* (pp. 19-26).

Kwak, Y. H., & Ibbs, C. W. (2000). Calculating project management's return on investment. *Project Management Journal, 31*(2), 38–47. doi:10.1177/875697280003100205

Langendahl, P. A., Tunberg, M., & Kokko, S. (2022). Smart urban agriculture – Exploring its development in Sweden. *Future Food Reports, 18.*

Lawrence, D., Lansing, J. R., Lawrence, D., & Lansing, P. E. (2019) Water Production Employing a Hydrogen Cycle. https://patentscope.wipo.int/search/es/detail.jsf?docId=US279855441&_cid=P12-L9MVZJ-64483-1

Leadaki, S.A. (2023, 2023w). *Chatbot.* Cliengo. https://www.cliengo.com/chatbot

Leahy, S. (2018, June 7). Carbon Engineering Liquid Fuel Carbon Capture Neutral Science. *National Geographic.* https://www.nationalgeographic.com/science/article/carbon-engineering-liquid-fuel-carbon-capture-neutral-science

Lee, W. Froemke (2019). Air temperature control using potable water [Patent]. https://patentscope.wipo.int/search/es/detail.jsf?docId=US238727825&_cid=P12-L9MVZJ-64483-1

Lee, C. S., Chang, Y. C., & Wang, M. H. (2009). Ontological recommendation multi-agent for Tainan City travel. *Expert Systems with Applications, 36*(3), 6740–6753. doi:10.1016/j.eswa.2008.08.016

Lee, J., Kang, E., & Park, G. L. (2007, August). Design and implementation of a tour planning system for telematics users. In *International Conference on Computational Science and Its Applications* (pp. 179-189). Springer, Berlin, Heidelberg. 10.1007/978-3-540-74484-9_16

Leonidis, A., Korozi, M., Margetis, G., Grammenos, D., & Stephanidis, C. (2013, December). An intelligent hotel room. In *International Joint Conference on Ambient Intelligence* (pp. 241-246). Springer, Cham. 10.1007/978-3-319-03647-2_19

Letmathe, P., & Doost, R. K. (2000). Environmental cost accounting and auditing. *Managerial Auditing Journal, 15*(8), 424–431. doi:10.1108/02686900010354709

Li, B., Li, G., Xu, J., Li, X., Liu, X., Wang, M., & Lv, J. (2023). A personalized recommendation framework based on MOOC system integrating deep learning and big data. *Computers & Electrical Engineering, 106*, 108571. doi:10.1016/j.compeleceng.2022.108571

Li, K. C., Chen, X., Jiang, H., & Bertino, E. (Eds.). (2019). *Essentials of blockchain technology.* CRC Press. doi:10.1201/9780429674457

Li, L., Li, X., Chong, C., Wang, C. H., & Wang, X. (2020). A decision support framework for the design and operation of sustainable urban farming systems. *Journal of Cleaner Production, 268*, 121928. doi:10.1016/j.jclepro.2020.121928

Li, L., Pan, C., Ling, S., & Li, M. (2022). Ecological efficiency of urban industrial land in metropolitan areas: Evidence from China. *Land (Basel), 11*(1), 104. doi:10.3390/land11010104

Li, M., Jia, N., Lenzen, M., Malik, A., Wei, L., Jin, Y., & Raubenheimer, D. (2022). Global food-miles account for nearly 20% of total food-systems emissions. *Nature Food, 3*(6), 445–453. doi:10.103843016-022-00531-w PMID:37118044

Lim, C., Kim, K. J., & Maglio, P. P. (2018). Smart cities with big data: Reference models, challenges, and considerations. *Cities (London, England), 82*, 86–99. doi:10.1016/j.cities.2018.04.011

Line, M., Hawley, H., & Krut, R. (2002). The development of global environmental and social reporting. *Corporate Environmental Strategy, 9*(1), 69–78. doi:10.1016/S1066-7938(01)00159-2

Lin, F., Weng, Y., Chen, H., & Zhuang, P. (2021). Intelligent greenhouse system based on remote sensing images and machine learning promotes the efficiency of agricultural economic growth. *Environmental Technology & Innovation, 24*, 101758. doi:10.1016/j.eti.2021.101758

Lin, J., Niu, J., Li, H., & Atiquzzaman, M. (2019). A secure and efficient location-based service scheme for smart transportation. *Future Generation Computer Systems, 92*, 694–704. doi:10.1016/j.future.2017.11.030

Lin, L., Yang, H., & Xu, X. (2022). Effects of water pollution on human health and disease heterogeneity: A review. *Frontiers in Environmental Science, 10*, 880246. doi:10.3389/fenvs.2022.880246

Lin, Y. P., & Yu, Z. G. (2023). A bibliometric analysis of artificial intelligence chatbots in educational contexts. *Interactive Technology and Smart Education*. Advance online publication. doi:10.1108/ITSE-12-2022-0165

Li, Q., Chen, L., & Xu, Y. (2022). Drought risk and water resources assessment in the Beijing-Tianjin-Hebei region, China. *The Science of the Total Environment, 832*, 154915. https://doi.org/https://doi.org/10.1016/j.scitotenv.2022.154915. doi:10.1016/j.scitotenv.2022.154915 PMID:35364182

Li, Q., Shi, Y., Lin, R., Qiao, W., & Ba, W. (2022). *A novel oil pipeline leakage detection method based on the sparrow search algorithm and CNN*. Measurement. *Measurement, 204*(112122), 112122. doi:10.1016/j.measurement.2022.112122

Liu, H., Li, X., & Wang, D. (2020). Big data analytics in tourism and hospitality: A literature review. *Tourism Management, 74*, 103961.

Liu, W., Li, L., & Su, Q. (2019). Smart Health-Care System Based on IoT and Cloud Computing. *Wireless Personal Communications, 104*(2), 859–873.

Liu, Y., Ramin, P., Flores-Alsina, X., & Gernaey, K. V. (2023). *Transforming data into actionable knowledge for fault detection, diagnosis and prognosis in urban wastewater systems with AI techniques: A mini-review*. Process Safety and Environmental Protection : Transactions of the Institution of Chemical Engineers. *Process Safety and Environmental Protection, 172*, 501–512. doi:10.1016/j.psep.2023.02.043

Livingstone, S. J., Li, Y., Rutishauser, A., Sanderson, R. J., Winter, K., Mikucki, J. A., Björnsson, H., Bowling, J. S., Chu, W., Dow, C. F., Fricker, H. A., McMillan, M., Ng, F. S. L., Ross, N., Siegert, M. J., Siegfried, M., & Sole, A. J. (2022). Subglacial lakes and their changing role in a warming climate. *Nature Reviews. Earth & Environment, 3*(2), 106–124. doi:10.103843017-021-00246-9

Li, X., Liu, H., Song, H., & Chen, J. (2020). Blockchain in tourism and hospitality: A systematic review. *Journal of Travel Research, 59*(7), 1244–1263.

Li, X., Pan, B., Xie, K., & Liang, Z. (2020). Internet of things and smart tourism: A systematic review of literature and future directions. *Journal of Travel Research, 59*(2), 215–231.

Li, X., Xiang, Z., Wang, D., & Du, Q. (2021). Geospatial technologies in smart tourism destinations: A systematic review. *Journal of Travel Research, 60*(2), 436–453.

Llorca Abad, G. (2012). Exclusión digital y límites de la comunicación mediada Digital exclusion and the limits of mediated communication. *Trípodos, 31*(1138–3305), 111–123. https://www.google.com/search?q=Llorca+Abad%2C+G.+(2012).+Exclusi%C3%B3n+digital+y+l%C3%ADmites+de+la+comunicaci%C3%B3n&oq=Llorca+Abad%2C+G.+(2012).+Exclusi%C3%B3n+digital+y+l%C3%ADmites+de+la+comunicaci%C3%B3n+&aqs=chrome.69i57.18327425j0j15&sourceid=chrome&ie=UTF-8

Loew, T., Ankele, K., Braun, S., & Clausen, J. (2004). *Significance of the CSR debate for sustainability and the requirements for companies. Institute for Ecological Economy Research GmbH*. IÖW.

Loftus, T. J., Tighe, P. J., Filiberto, A. C., Efron, P. A., Brakenridge, S. C., Mohr, A. M., Rashidi, P., Upchurch, G. R. Jr, & Bihorac, A. (2020). Artificial intelligence and surgical decision-making. *JAMA Surgery, 155*(2), 148–158. doi:10.1001/jamasurg.2019.4917 PMID:31825465

Lombardi, F., Rinaldi, C., Cirillo, F., & Russo, D. (2020). Applying Quality Function Deployment to Security Engineering: The House of Security (HoS). *Proceedings of the 15th International Conference on Availability, Reliability and Security (ARES)*, (pp. 1-10). ACM. 10.1145/3407023.3409231

Lombardi, P., Giordano, S., Farouh, H., & Yousef, W. (2012). Modelling the Smart City Performance. *Innovation (Abingdon)*, *25*(2), 137–149. doi:10.1080/13511610.2012.660325

Lorenzo, S., and César, C. (2010). *Open government: gobiernoabierto*. Jaén, España: AlgónEditrores MMX, 2010.

Lotti, T., Kleerebezem, R., van Erp Taalman Kip, C., Hendrickx, T. L. G., Kruit, J., Hoekstra, M., & van Loosdrecht, M. C. M. (2014). Anammox growth on pretreated municipal wastewater. *Environmental Science & Technology*, *48*(14), 7874–7880. doi:10.1021/es500632k PMID:24927034

Lovell, S. T. (2010). Multifunctional urban agriculture for sustainable land use planning in the United States. *Sustainability (Basel)*, *2*(8), 2499–2522. doi:10.3390u2082499

Lowe, M., Qin, R., & Mao, X. (2022). A review on machine learning, artificial intelligence, and smart technology in water treatment and monitoring. *Water (Basel)*, *14*(9), 1384. doi:10.3390/w14091384

Lozoya, S. V. M., Guirado, M. A. Z., Zapata Gonzalez, A., & Lopez, A. B. M. (2022). Use of Technologies and Self-Efficacy in Older Adults. *IEEE-RITA*, *17*(2), 125–130. doi:10.1109/RITA.2022.3166870

Lucia, P., & Ana, R. (2012). Ceibal Uruguay. *Edición Especial Bilingüe: Investigación Sobre TIC4D En Latinoamérica*, *8*(4), 161–175. https://itidjournal.org/index.php/itid/article/view/962.html

Lu, J., Wu, D., Mao, M., Wang, W., & Zhang, G. (2015). Recommender system application developments: A survey. *Decision Support Systems*, *74*, 12–32. doi:10.1016/j.dss.2015.03.008

Luna-Reyes, L. F. (2013). Trust and Collaboration in Interorganizational Information Technology Projects in the Public Sector. *Gestión y Política Pública*, 22.

Lv, M., Niu, X., Zhang, D., Ding, H., Lin, Z., Zhou, S., & Zhu, Y. (2023). A data-driven framework for spatiotemporal analysis and prediction of river water quality: A case study in Pearl River, China. *Water (Basel)*, *15*(2), 257. doi:10.3390/w15020257

Lv, Z., Li, X., Wang, W., Zhang, B., Hu, J., & Feng, S. (2018). Government affairs service platform for smart city. *Future Generation Computer Systems*, *81*, 443–451. doi:10.1016/j.future.2017.08.047

Lyapina, I., Sotnikova, E., Lebedeva, O., Makarova, T., & Skvortsova, N. (2019). Smart technologies: Perspectives of usage in higher education. *International Journal of Educational Management*, *33*(3), 454–461. doi:10.1108/IJEM-08-2018-0257

Lytras, M. D., & Chui, K. T. (2019). The Recent Development of Artificial Intelligence for Smart and Sustainable Energy Systems and Applications. *Energies*, *12*(16), 3108. doi:10.3390/en12163108

Madon, S., Reinhard, N., Roode, D., & Walsham, G. (2009). Digital inclusion projects in developing countries: Processes of institutionalization. *Information Technology for Development*, *15*(2), 95–107. https://onlinelibrary.wiley.com/doi/abs/10.1002/itdj.20108. doi:10.1002/itdj.20108

Mageira, K., Pittou, D., Papasalouros, A., Kotis, K., Zangogianni, P., & Daradoumis, A. (2022). Educational AI Chatbots for Content and Language Integrated Learning. *Applied Sciences (Basel, Switzerland)*, *12*(7), 3239. https://www.mdpi.com/2076-3417/12/7/3239. doi:10.3390/app12073239

Mahbooba, B., Timilsina, M., Sahal, R., & Serrano, M. (2021). Explainable Artificial Intelligence (XAI) to enhance trust management in intrusion detection systems using decision tree model. *Complexity*, *2021*, 1–11. doi:10.1155/2021/6634811

Main, H. C., & O'Connor, P. (1998). The use of smart card technology to develop a destination based loyalty/affinity scheme for SMES in tourism and hospitality. In *Information and communication technologies in tourism 1998* (pp. 7–15). Springer. doi:10.1007/978-3-7091-7504-0_2

Malinauskaite, J., Jouhara, H., Czajczyńska, D., Stanchev, P., Katsou, E., Rostkowski, P., Thorne, R.J., Colón, J., Ponsá, S., Al-Mansour, F., Anguilano, L., Krzyżyńska, R., López, I.C., Vlasopoulos, A., Spencerk, N. (2017). Municipal solid waste management and waste-to-energy in the context of a circular economy and energy recycling in Europe. *energy, 141*, 2013-2044.

Malinauskaite, J., Jouhara, H., Czajczyńska, D., Stanchev, P., Katsou, E., Rostkowski, P., Thorne, R. J., Colon, J., Ponsa, S., Al-Mansour, F., Anguilano, L., Krzyzynska, R., Lopez, I. C., Vlasopoulos, A., & Spencer, N. (2017). Municipal solid waste management and waste-to-energy in the context of a circular economy and energy recycling in Europe. *Energy, 141*, 2013–2044. doi:10.1016/j.energy.2017.11.128

Mangra, M. G., Cotoc, E., & Dumitru, A. (2014). Sustainable economic development through environmental management systems implementation. *Journal of Studies in Social Sciences, 6*(1), 1–14. PMID:25530938

Manyika, J., Lund, S., Chui, M., Bughin, J., Woetzel, J., Batra, P., Ko, R., & Sanghvi, S. (2017). *Jobs lost, jobs gained: Workforce transitions in a time of automation*. McKinsey Global Institute. http://hdl.voced.edu.au/10707/444873

Maqsood, T., Finegan, A. D., & Walker, D. H. (2003). A soft approach to solving hard problems in construction project management. Digital Connections. https://digitalcollections. qut. edu. au/1661/.

Marquez, G. P. B., Takeuchi, H., Montaño, M. N. E., & Hasegawa, T. (2020). Performance of rice straw as mono- and co-feedstock of Ulva spp. for thalassic biogas production. *Heliyon, 6*(9), e05036. doi:10.1016/j.heliyon.2020.e05036 PMID:33015390

Marquez, G. P. B., Yuan, G. N., Deng, H., Iu, A., Fabella, M., Salonga, R. B., Ashardiono, F., & Cartgena, J. A. (2022). A review on urban agriculture: Technology, socio-economy, and policy. *Heliyon, 8*(11), e11583. doi:10.1016/j.heliyon.2022.e11583 PMID:36406682

Marshall, R. E., & Farahbakhsh, K. (2013). Systems approaches to integrated solid waste management in developing countries. *Waste Management (New York, N.Y.), 33*(4), 988–1003. doi:10.1016/j.wasman.2012.12.023 PMID:23360772

Martinez Silva, A. (2022). *Análisis y presentación de información para el área de población y desarrollo del Fondo de Población de las Naciones Unidas (UNFPA)*. Universidad de los. *Andes (Salta)*.

Martin, S., & Guarneros-Meza, V. (2013). Governing local partnerships: Does external steering help local agencies address wicked problems? *Policy and Politics, 41*(4), 585–603. doi:10.1332/030557312X655819

Maruyama, A., Shibata, N., Murata, Y., Yasumoto, K., & Ito, M. (2004, March). A personal tourism navigation system to support traveling multiple destinations with time restrictions. In *18th International Conference on Advanced Information Networking and Applications, 2004. AINA 2004.* (Vol. 2, pp. 18-21). IEEE. 10.1109/AINA.2004.1283747

Masanet, M. J., Gómez-Puertas, L., & Pires, F. (2021). The risks of the gender digital divide among teenagers. *El Profesional de la Información, 30*(1), 1–15. doi:10.3145/epi.2021.ene.12

Mashhadi, N., Shahrour, I., Attoue, N., El Khattabi, J., & Aljer, A. (2021). Use of machine learning for leak detection and localization in water distribution systems. *Smart Cities, 4*(4), 1293–1315. doi:10.3390martcities4040069

Mason, B., Rufí-Salís, M., Parada, F., Gabarrell, X., & Gruden, C. (2019). Intelligent urban irrigation systems: Saving water and maintaining crop yields. *Agricultural Water Management, 226*, 105812. doi:10.1016/j.agwat.2019.105812

Matchaya, G. C., Tadesse, G., & Kuteya, A. N. (2022). Rainfall shocks and crop productivity in Zambia: Implication for agricultural water risk management. *Agricultural Water Management, 269*, 107648. https://doi.org/https://doi.org/10.1016/j.agwat.2022.107648. doi:10.1016/j.agwat.2022.107648

Matsuda, Y., Fedotov, D., Takahashi, Y., Arakawa, Y., Yasumoto, K., & Minker, W. (2018). EmoTour: Estimating Emotion and Satisfaction of Users Based on Behavioral Cues and Audiovisual Data. *Sensors (Basel), 18*(11), 3978. doi:10.339018113978 PMID:30445798

Matsuda, Y., Sugiyama, O., & Yagi, Y. (2018). EmoTour: A tourist emotion- and satisfaction-estimation system using multimodal sensing and machine learning. *IEEE Transactions on Multimedia, 20*(12), 3307–3319.

Mazur, S. (n.d.). *An Introduction to Smart Transportation: Benefits and Examples*. Digi. https://es.digi.com/blog/post/introduction-to-smart-transportation-benefits

McCorry, P., Shahandashti, S. F., & Hao, F. (2017). A smart contract for boardroom voting with maximum voter privacy. In *Financial Cryptography and Data Security: 21st International Conference, FC 2017*, (pp. 357-375). Springer International Publishing. 10.1007/978-3-319-70972-7_20

Mechant, P., & Walravens, N. (2018). E-Government and Smart Cities: Theoretical Reflections and Case Studies. *Media and Communication, 6*(4), 119–122. doi:10.17645/mac.v6i4.1848

Mehdipour, S., Nakhaee, N., Khankeh, H., & Haghdoost, A. A. (2022). Impacts of drought on health: A qualitative case study from Iran. *International Journal of Disaster Risk Reduction, 76*, 103007. https://doi.org/https://doi.org/10.1016/j.ijdrr.2022.103007. doi:10.1016/j.ijdrr.2022.103007

Mehmood, F., Ullah, I., Ahmad, S., & Kim, D. H. (2019). Object detection mechanism based on deep learning algorithm using embedded IOT devices for smart home appliances control in CoT. *Journal of Ambient Intelligence and Humanized Computing*. doi:10.100712652-019-01272-8

Mehra, M., Saxena, S., Sankaranarayanan, S., Tom, R. J., & Veeramanikandan, M. (2018). IoT based hydroponics system using Deep Neural Networks. *Computers and Electronics in Agriculture, 155*, 473–486. doi:10.1016/j.compag.2018.10.015

Melnyk, S. A., Sroufe, R. P., & Calantone, R. (2003). We are assessing the impact of environmental management systems on corporate and environmental performance. *Journal of Operations Management, 21*(3), 329–351. doi:10.1016/S0272-6963(02)00109-2

Memos, V. A., Psannis, K. E., Ishibashi, Y., Kim, B. G., & Gupta, B. B. (2018). An efficient algorithm for media-based surveillance system (EAMSuS) in IoT smart city framework. *Future Generation Computer Systems, 83*, 619–628. doi:10.1016/j.future.2017.04.039

Mena, M. (2016). *Diseño de la Red De Distribución De Agua Potable De La Parroquia El Rosario Del Cantón San Pedro De Pelileo,Provincia De Tungurahua.". Tesis de Ingeniería. UNIVERSIDAD TÉCNICA DE AMBATO*. AMBATO.

Menardo, S., Bauer, A., Theuretzbacher, F., Piringer, G., Nilsen, P. J., Balsari, P., Pavliska, O., & Amon, T. (2012). Theuretzbacher, F.; Piringer, G.; Nilsen, P.J.; Balsari, P.; Pavliska, O.; Amon, T. Biogas Production from Steam-Exploded Miscanthus and Utilization of Biogas Energy and CO2 in Greenhouses. *BioEnergy Research, 6*(2), 620–630. doi:10.100712155-012-9280-5

Mens, M., Minnema, B., Overmars, K., & van den Hurk, B. (2021). Dilemmas in developing models for long-term drought risk management: The case of the National Water Model of the Netherlands. *Environmental Modelling & Software, 143*, 105100. https://doi.org/https://doi.org/10.1016/j.envsoft.2021.105100. doi:10.1016/j.envsoft.2021.105100

Meta A. I. (2023, Feb 24, 2023). *Introducing LLaMA*. Meta AI. https://ai.facebook.com/blog/large-language-model-llama-meta-ai/

Micera, R., & Crispino, R. (2017). Destination web reputation as “smart tool” for image building: The case analysis of naples city-destination. *International Journal of Tourism Cities*, *3*(4), 406–423. doi:10.1108/IJTC-11-2016-0048

Michael, A. R. (2016). *Título: Electronic Elections: The Perils and Promises of Digital Democracy*. Editorial Princeton University Press.

Microsoft. (2023a, March 30, 2023). *Azure FarmBeats*. Microsoft. https://learn.microsoft.com/en-us/azure/industry/agriculture/overview-azure-farmbeats

Microsoft. (2023b, 2023). *Azure IoT*. Microsoft. https://azure.microsoft.com/en-us/solutions/iot/

Microsoft. (2023c, 2023). *Bing Chat*. Microsoft. https://www.bing.com/search?form=MA13FJ&q=Bing+AI&showconv=1

Miles, B., Bourennane, E., Boucherkha, S., & Chikhi, S. (2020). A study of LoRaWAN protocol performance for IoT applications in smart agriculture. *Computer Communications*, *164*, 148–157. doi:10.1016/j.comcom.2020.10.009

Mileski, J., Clott, C., & Galvao, C. B. (2018). Cyberattacks on ships: A wicked problem approach. *Maritime Business Review*, *3*(4), 414–430. doi:10.1108/MABR-08-2018-0026

Miles, M. P., Munilla, L. S., & McClurg, T. (1999). The impact of ISO 14000 environmental management standards on small and medium-sized enterprises. *Journal of Quality Management*, *4*(1), 111–122. doi:10.1016/S1084-8568(99)80098-4

Millán, C. (s.f.) *Smart cities en México: factoresde éxito*. KPMG. https://kpmg.com/mx/es/home/tendencias/2021/10/ao-smart-cities-en-mexico-factores-de exito.html#:~:text=En%20el%20caso%20de%20M%C3%A9xico,%2C%20Puebla%2C%20Guadalajara%20y%20Monterrey

Miller-Robbie, L., Ramaswami A., & Amerasinghe, P. (2017, July 4). Wastewater treatment and reuse in urban agriculture: exploring the food, energy, water, and health nexus in Hyderabad, India. *Environmental Research Letters, 12*(7). doi:10.1088/1748-9326/aa6bfe

Minaei, N. (2022). Critical review of smart agri-technology solutions for urban food growing. In *Digital Agritechnology* (pp. 199–217). Robotics and Systems for Agriculture and Livestock Production. doi:10.1016/B978-0-12-817634-4.00006-9

Mishra, M. K. (2020). *Application of Operational Research in Sustainable Environmental Management and Climate Change.*

Moghayedi, A., Richter, I., Owoade, F. M., Kapanji-Kakoma, K. K., Kaliyadasa, E., Francis, S., & Ekpo, C. (2022). Effects of urban smart farming on local economy and food production in urban areas in African cities. *Sustainability (Basel)*, *14*(17), 10836. doi:10.3390u141710836

Mohammed, F., Idries, A., Mohamed, N., Al-Jaroodi, J., & Jawhar, I. (2014, May). UAVs for smart cities: Opportunities and challenges. In *2014 International Conference on Unmanned Aircraft Systems (ICUAS)* (pp. 267-273). IEEE. 10.1109/ICUAS.2014.6842265

Moher, D., Liberati, A., Tetzlaff, J., & Altman, D. G. (2009). Preferred reporting items for systematic reviews and meta-analyses: The PRISMA statement. *Annals of Internal Medicine*, *151*(4), 264–269. doi:10.7326/0003-4819-151-4-200908180-00135 PMID:19622511

Molina-Azorín, J. F., Tarí, J. J., Pereira-Moliner, J., Lopez-Gamero, M. D., & Pertusa-Ortega, E. M. (2015). The effects of quality and environmental management on competitive advantage: A mixed-methods study in the hotel industry. *Tourism Management*, *50*, 41–54. doi:10.1016/j.tourman.2015.01.008

Montesinos-López, O. A., Montesinos-López, A., Pérez-Rodríguez, P., Barrón-López, J. A., Martini, J. W. R., Fajardo-Flores, S. B., Gaytan-Lugo, L. S., Santana-Mancilla, P. C., & Crossa, J. (2021). A review of deep learning applications for genomic selection. *BMC Genomics*, *22*(1), 19. doi:10.118612864-020-07319-x PMID:33407114

MOOC4ALL. (2023, 2023). *MOOC4ALL*. MOOC4ALL. https://platform.mooc4all.eu/

Moorkattil, X. (2022). Blockchain White Paper. *SSRN*. doi:10.2139/ssrn.4176506

Morales Romo, N. (2016). El reto de la brecha digital y las personas mayores en el medio rural español. El caso de Castilla y León. *Fonseca. Journal of Communication*, *13*(13), 165. doi:10.14201/fjc201613165185

Moreno, A. C., Baucells, A. N., & Arce, R. R. M. (2016). *Smart mobility in smart cities*. En: XII Congreso de Ingeniería del Transporte (CIT 2016), Valencia.. 10.4995/CIT2016.2016.3485

Morrow, D., & Rondinelli, D. (2002). Adopting corporate environmental management systems: Motivations and results of ISO 14001 and EMAS certification. *European Management Journal*, *20*(2), 159–171. doi:10.1016/S0263-2373(02)00026-9

Motiwalla, J., Yap, M., & Ngoh, L. H. (1993). Building the intelligent island. *IEEE Communications Magazine*, *31*(10), 28–34. doi:10.1109/35.237979

Moturi, C., Ochieng, D., & Chepkoech, I. (2016). *An Assessment of Green ICT Effect on Sustainable Environment in Institutions of Higher Learning in Kenya.*

Mucunguzi, P., Tugume, P., & Ogola, L. (2021). Environmental Management by Faith Based Organizations in Uganda: A SWOT Analysis. *International Journal of Environmental Protection and Policy*, *9*(1), 5. doi:10.11648/j.ijepp.20210901.12

Munawar, H. S., Ullah, F., Qayyum, S., Khan, S. I., & Mojtahedi, M. (2021). UAVs in disaster management: Application of integrated aerial imagery and Convolutional Neural Network for flood detection. *Sustainability (Basel)*, *13*(14), 7547. doi:10.3390u13147547

Musso, J., Weare, C., & Hale, M. (2000). Designing web technologies for local governance reform: Good management or good democracy? *Political Communication*, *17*(1), 1–19. doi:10.1080/105846000198486

Muyunda, N., & Ibrahim, M. (2017, November). Arduino-based smart garbage monitoring system: Analysis requirement and implementation. In *Computer and Drone Applications (IConDA), 2017 International Conference on* (pp. 28-32). IEEE.

Myers, A. (2022, February 9). Stanford engineers create a catalyst that can turn carbon dioxide into gasoline 1,000 times more efficiently. *Stanford News*. https://news.stanford.edu/2022/02/09/turning-carbon-dioxide-gasoline-efficiently/#:~:text=captured%20co2%20can%20be,1%2c000%20times%20over%20existing%20methods

Naik, M. B., Kumar, P., & Majhi, S. (2019). Smart public transportation network expansion and its interaction with the grid. *International Journal of Electrical Power & Energy Systems*, *105*, 365–380. doi:10.1016/j.ijepes.2018.08.009

Najwa Mohd Rizal, N., Hayder, G., Mnzool, M., Elnaim, B. M. E., Mohammed, A. O. Y., & Khayyat, M. M. (2022). Comparison between regression models, support vector machine (SVM), and artificial neural network (ANN) in river water quality prediction. *Processes (Basel, Switzerland)*, *10*(8), 1652. doi:10.3390/pr10081652

Nakamoto, S. (2008). Bitcoin: A peer-to-peer electronic cash system. *Decentralized business review*. https://assets.pubpub.org/d8wct41f/31611263538139.pdf

Nandal, N., Singh, A., Kumar, M., & Tanwar, R. (2022). Healthcare based financial decision making system using artificial intelligence. [IJHS]. *International Journal of Health Sciences*, 11255–11267. doi:10.53730/ijhs.v6nS2.8025

Nanda, M., & Randhawa, G. (2019). Smart Cities Project: Some Lessons for Indian Cities. In K. Saravanan, G. Julie, & H. Robinson (Eds.), *Handbook of Research on Implementation and Deployment of IoT Projects in Smart Cities* (pp. 80–95). IGI Global. doi:10.4018/978-1-5225-9199-3.ch006

Nasiri, H., Mohd Yusof, M. J., & Mohammad Ali, T. A. (2016). An overview to flood vulnerability assessment methods. *Sustainable Water Resources Management*, *2*(3), 331–336. doi:10.100740899-016-0051-x

Naveen, X. A. J., Arivoli, A., Boopathi, S., & Rajkumar, V. (2022i). A Case Study on Evaluation of Energy Management System by Implication of Advanced Technology in Typical Cement Factory Tamil Nadu, India. In *Smart Technologies for Energy and Environmental Sustainability* (pp. 245–265). Springer. doi:10.1007/978-3-030-80702-3_15

Naveen, X. A. J., Arivoli, A., Malarmannan, V. C., & Boopathi, S. (2022j). A Review on Cleaner Technology for Sustainable Industrial Practices: Global and Indian Scenario Genesis of Technologies to Control Pollution. In *Computational Modelling in Industry 4.0* (pp. 91–116). Springer. doi:10.1007/978-981-16-7723-6_8

Nawrocka, D., & Parker, T. (2009). Finding the connection: Environmental management systems and environmental performance. *Journal of Cleaner Production*, *17*(6), 601–607. doi:10.1016/j.jclepro.2008.10.003

Negm, A., Ma, X., & Aggidis, G. (2023). Review of leakage detection in water distribution networks. *IOP Conference Series. Earth and Environmental Science*, *1136*(1), 012052. doi:10.1088/1755-1315/1136/1/012052

Newman, P., & Kenworthy, J. (1999). *Sustainability and Cities: Overcoming Automobile Dependency*. Island Press.

Nieves, V. (2017). *Economista*. elEconomista.es. https://www.eleconomista.es/economia/noticias/8128422/02/17/Donde-la-maquina-sustituira-al-hombre-los-empleos-mas-amenazados-en-Espana-por-la-automatizacion.html

Nikolaou, G., Neocleous, D., Christou, A., Kitta, E., & Katsoulas, N. (2020). Implementing sustainable irrigation in water-scarce regions under the impact of climate change. *Agronomy (Basel)*, *10*(8), 1120. doi:10.3390/agronomy10081120

Nitoslawski, S. A., Galle, N. J., Van Den Bosch, C. K., & Steenberg, J. W. N. (2019). Smarter ecosystems for smarter cities? A review of trends, technologies, and turning points for smart urban forestry. *Sustainable Cities and Society*, *51*, 101770. doi:10.1016/j.scs.2019.101770

Nogales, B. (2019). ¿Qué es un ataque de 51% de la Blockchain? *Bitcoin.es*. https://bitcoin.es/criptomonedas/que-es-un-ataque-de-51-de-la-blockchain/

NOM. (1994). Norma Oficial Mexicana Nom-127-SSA1-1994, Salud Ambiental, Agua para Uso y Consumo Humano-Límites Permisibles de Calidad y Tratamientos a que Debe Someterse el Agua para su Potabilización. http://www.agrolab.com.mx/sitev002/sitev001/assets/nom-127-ssa1-1994.pdf

Nourani, V., Elkiran, G., & Abba, S. I. (2018). Wastewater treatment plant performance analysis using artificial intelligence - an ensemble approach. *Water Science and Technology: A Journal of the International Association on Water Pollution Research*, *78*(10), 2064–2076. https://doi.org/. doi:10.2166/wst.2018.477

Oberascher, M., Kinzel, C., Kastlunger, U., Kleidorfer, M., Zingerle, C., Rauch, W., & Sitzenfrei, R. (2021). Integrated urban water management with micro storages developed as an IoT-based solution – The smart rain barrel. *Environmental Modelling & Software*, *139*, 105028. doi:10.1016/j.envsoft.2021.105028

OECD Observed. (1999). *Learning cities: the new recipe in regional development*. OECD.

OECD. (2010). *Green Cities Programme*. https://www.oecd.org/gov/regional-policy/49318965.pdf

Ogie, R. I., Clarke, R. J., Forehead, H., & Perez, P. (2019). Crowdsourced social media data for disaster management: Lessons from the PetaJakarta.org project. *Computers, Environment and Urban Systems*, *73*, 108–117. doi:10.1016/j.compenvurbsys.2018.09.002

Oh, S., & Lu, C. (2023). Vertical farming - Smart urban agriculture for enhancing resilience and sustainability in food security. *The Journal of Horticultural Science & Biotechnology*, *98*(2), 133–140. doi:10.1080/14620316.2022.2141666

Omidinia, S., Masrom, M., & Selamat, H. (2013). *An Examination of the Concept of Smart School: An Innovation to Address Sustainability*. CSE. doi:10.2991/cse.2013.73

Ontiveros, E., Vizcaíno, D., & López Sabater, V. (2016). *Las Ciudades del Futuro: inteligentes, digitales y sostenibles*. Ariel.

ONU. (2015). Organización de las Naciones Unidas. Retrieved 08 21, 2019, from: http://www.onu.org.mx/wp-content/uploads/2017/07/180131_ODS-metas-digital.pdf

Open A. I. (2023, 2023). *Chatgpt*. Open AI. https://openai.com/blog/chatgpt

OpenupEd. (2023). *OpenupEd*. https://www.openuped.eu

Oralhan, Z., Oralhan, B., & Yiğit, Y. (2017). Smart City Application: Internet of Things (IoT) Technologies Based Smart Waste Collection Using Data Mining Approach and Ant Colony Optimization. *The International Arab Journal of Information Technology*, *14*(4).

Oreon. (n.d.) *Water-Cooled Led Grow Lights*. Oreon. https://www.oreon-led.com/en/water-cooled-led-grow-lights

Otterpohl, R., Grottker, M., and Lange, J., (1997). Sustainable water and waste management in urban areas. (1997). *Water science and technology: a journal of the International Association on Water Pollution Research, 35*(9). . doi:10.1016/S0273-1223(97)00190-X

Pacana, A., and Ulewicz, R. (2017). Research of determinants motiving to implement the environmental management system. *Polish Journal of Management Studies, 16*.

Padmapriya, V., & Sujatha, D. N. (2023). Impact of blockchain technology on the urban environment and climate change. In S. Krishnan, R. Kumar, & V. E. Balas (Eds.), *Green Blockchain Technology for Sustainable Smart Cities* (pp. 97–117). Elsevier. doi:10.1016/B978-0-323-95407-5.00016-5

Palm Joseph, M., & Semler Loren, H. (2005). Automatic Flushing System and Method for a Potable Water Station [Patent]. https://patentscope.wipo.int/search/es/detail.jsf?docId=US40921905&_cid=P12-L9MVZJ-64483-1

Pal, S., Bhattacharya, S., Mustafi, S., & Mitra, S. (2023). Smart Green Classroom and Machine Learning to Promote Green Awareness for Sustainable Livings. *International Journal of Instructional Technology and Educational Studies*, *4*(1), 7–15. doi:10.21608/ihites.2021.107726.1081

Panizo, A. Luis (2007). *Aspectos tecnológicos del voto electrónico*. Oficina Nacional de Procesos Electorales (ONPE) Perú Editor. https://www.researchgate.net/publication/259668840_Aspectos_tecnologicos_del_voto_electronico

Paquet, G. (2001). Smart communities. *LAC Carling Government's Review*, *3*(5), 28–30.

Parysek, J., & Mierzejewska, L. (2016). Spatial structure of a city and the mobility of its residents: Functional and planning aspects. *Bulletin of Geography. Socio-Economic Series*, *34*(34), 91–102. doi:10.1515/bog-2016-0037

Passos, A. L. L., Muniz, D. H. de F., Rangel, L. P., & Oliveira-Filho, E. C. (2019). *Selection of variables in the definition of a water quality index for the Brazilian Federal District.* Ambiente e Agua - An Interdisciplinary. *Revista Ambiente & Água*, *14*(4), 1. doi:10.4136/ambi-agua.2385

Patel, R. B., Patel, N. M., & Thakkar, M. H. (2021). Design and Development of a Smart Inhaler: A Review. *Current Drug Delivery*, *18*(1), 36–48.

Patentcope. (2022). *Patentscope search engine*. Patentcope. https://patentscope.wipo.int/search/es/search.jsf

Pathmudi, V. R., Khatri, N., Kumar, S., Abdul-Qawy, A. S. H., & Vyas, A. K. (2023). A systematic review of IoT technologies and their constituents for smart and sustainable agriculture applications. *Scientific African*, *19*, e01577. doi:10.1016/j.sciaf.2023.e01577

Perc, M., Ozer, M., & Hojnik, J. (2019). Social and juristic challenges of artificial intelligence. *Palgrave Communications*, *5*(1), 61. doi:10.105741599-019-0278-x

Pereira, G.V., Parycek, P., Falco, E., and Kleinhans, R. Smart governance in the context of smart cities: A literature review. *Information Polity*, 1-20.

Pérez, P. F., Velázquez, R. G., Fernandez, A. M. V., & Dorao, S. J. (2015). Movilidad Inteligente. *Economía Industrial*, (395), 111–121.

Perveen, S., Yigitcanlar, T., Kamruzzaman, M., & Hayes, J. (2017). Evaluating transport externalities of urban growth: A critical review of scenario-based planning methods. *International Journal of Environmental Science and Technology*, *14*(3), 663–678. doi:10.100713762-016-1144-7

Pesce, M., Shi, C., Critto, A., Wang, X., & Marcomini, A. (2018). SWOT analysis of the application of international standard ISO 14001 in the Chinese context. A case study of Guangdong Province. *Sustainability (Basel)*, *10*(9), 3196. doi:10.3390u10093196

Petit, E. P. (2022). Smart City Technologies plus Nature-Based Solutions: Viable and valuable resources for urban resilience. In *Smart Cities Policies and Financing* (pp. 377–398). Approaches and Solutions. doi:10.1016/B978-0-12-819130-9.00001-2

Pfister, S., Bayer, P., Koehler, A., & Hellweg, S. (2011, September). agriculture: Scenarios and related impacts. *The Science of the Total Environment*, *409*(20), 4206–4216. doi:10.1016/j.scitotenv.2011.07.019 PMID:21840571

Pingale, S. M., Jat, M. K., & Khare, D. (2014). Integrated urban water management modeling under climate change scenarios. *Resources, Conservation and Recycling*, *83*, 176–189. doi:10.1016/j.resconrec.2013.10.006

Pino Juste, M. R., Soto Carballo, J. G., & Rodríguez López, B. (2015). Las personas mayores ante las Nuevas Tecnologías de la Información y Comunicación. Un compromiso para reducir la brecha digital social. *Pedagogia Social Revista Interuniversitaria*, *26*(26), 337. doi:10.7179/PSRI_2015.26.13

Podder, A. K., Al Bukhari, A., Isalm, S., Mia, S., Mohammed, M. A., Kumar, N. M., Cengiz, K., & Abdulkareem, K. H. (2021). IoT based smart agrotech system for verification of Urban farming parameters. *Microprocessors and Microsystems*, *82*, 104025. doi:10.1016/j.micpro.2021.104025

Polèse, M., & Stren, R. E. (Eds.). (2000). *The social sustainability of cities: Diversity and the management of change*. University of Toronto Press. doi:10.3138/9781442682399

Pollack, J. (2009). Multimethodology in series and parallel: Strategic planning using hard and soft OR. *The Journal of the Operational Research Society*, *60*(2), 156–167. doi:10.1057/palgrave.jors.2602538

Popli, S., Jha, R. K., & Jain, S. (2021). Green NOMA assisted NB-IoT based urban farming in multistory buildings. *Computer Networks*, *199*, 108410. doi:10.1016/j.comnet.2021.108410

Porat, M. U. (1978). Global Implications of the Information Society. *Journal of Communication, 28*(1), 70–80. doi:10.1111/j.1460-2466.1978.tb01565.x

Praharaj, S., Han, J. H., & Hawken, S. (2018). Towards the right model of smart city governance in India. *International Journal of Sustainable Development and Planning, 13*(2), 171–186. doi:10.2495/SDP-V13-N2-171-186

Priynka, B. H. D. D., Udayaraju, P., Koppireddy, C. S., & Neethika, A. (2023). Developing a region-based energy-efficient IoT agriculture network using region-based clustering and shortest path routing for making sustainable agriculture environment. Measurement. *Sensors (Basel), 27*, 100734.

PTC. (2023). *ThingWorx IIoT Platform.* PTC. https://www.ptc.com/en/products/thingworx

Puiu, D., Barnaghi, P., Tonjes, R., Kumper, D., Ali, M. I., Mileo, A., Parreira, J. X., Fischer, M., Kolozali, S., Farajidavar, N., Gao, F., Iggena, T., Pham, T. L., Nechifor, C. S., Puschmann, D., & Fernandes, J. (2016). Citypulse: Large scale data analytics framework for smart cities. *IEEE Access : Practical Innovations, Open Solutions, 4*, 1086–1108. doi:10.1109/ACCESS.2016.2541999

Purón-Cid, G., & Gil-García, J. R. (2012). Gobierno abierto, tecnologías de información y análisis de políticas públicas: oportunidades y retos para América Latina y el Caribe. In *XVII Congreso Internacional del clad.* Cartagena de Indias.

Purwanto, A., Asbari, M., and Santoso, P. B. (2020). Effect of integrated management system of ISO 9001: 2015 and ISO 22000: 2018 implementation to packaging industries quality performance at Banten Indonesia. *Jurnal Ilmiah MEA (Manajemen, Ekonomi, and Akuntansi), 4*(1), 17-29.

Purwanto, A., Putri, R. S., Ahmad, A. H., Asbari, M., Bernarto, I., Santoso, P. B., & Sihite, O. B. (2020). The effect of implementation integrated management system ISO 9001, ISO 14001, ISO 22000, and ISO 45001 on Indonesian food industries performance. *TEST Engineering and Management, 82*, 14069.

Qi, L., & Shaofu, L. (2001). Research on digital city framework architecture. In *Info-tech and Info-net, 2001. Proceedings. ICII 2001-Beijing. 2001 International Conferences on* (Vol. 1, pp. 30-36). IEEE.

Qin, S., Man, J., Wang, X., Li, C., Dong, H., & Ge, X. (2019). Applying Big Data Analytics to Monitor Tourist Flow for the Scenic Area Operation Management. *Discrete Dynamics in Nature and Society, 2019*, 2019. doi:10.1155/2019/8239047

Qin, X., Liu, Z., Chen, Y., Li, Z., Wang, Z., & Li, Z. (2019). Monitoring tourist flow and travel behavior in scenic areas using big data and CDR data. *Tourism Management, 75*, 345–357.

Quazi, H. A. (1999). Implementation of an environmental management system: The experience of companies operating in Singapore. *Industrial Management & Data Systems, 99*(7), 302–311. doi:10.1108/02635579910262526

Ragini, J. R., Anand, P. M. R., & Bhaskar, V. (2018). Big data analytics for disaster response and recovery through sentiment analysis. *International Journal of Information Management, 42*, 13–24. doi:10.1016/j.ijinfomgt.2018.05.004

Raillani, B., Mezrhab, A., Amraqui, S., Moussaoui, M. A., & Mezrhab, A. (2022). Regression-based spatial GIS analysis for an accurate assessment of renewable energy potential. *Energy for Sustainable Development, 69*, 118–133. doi:10.1016/j.esd.2022.06.003

Ramaswami, A., Boyer, D., Singh Nagpure, A., Fang, A., Bogra, S., Bakshi, B., Cohen, E., & Rao-Ghorpade, A. (2017). An urban systems framework to assess the trans-boundary foodenergy-water nexus: Implementation in Delhi, India. *Environmental Research Letters, 12*(2), 025008. doi:10.1088/1748-9326/aa5556

Ramaswami, A., Russell, A. G., Culligan, P. J., Sharma, K. R., & Kumar, E. (2016). Meta-principles for developing smart, sustainable, and healthy cities. *Science, 352*(6288), 940–943. doi:10.1126cience.aaf7160 PMID:27199418

Ramirez Montoya, M. S., Martínez-Pérez, S., Rodriguez-Abitia, G., & Lopez-Caudana, E. (2022). Digital accreditations in MOOC-based training on sustainability: Factors that influence terminal efficiency. *Australasian Journal of Educational Technology*, *38*(2), 162–180. doi:10.14742/ajet.7082

Ramos, M.-H., Bartholmes, J., & Thielen-del Pozo, J. (2007). Development of decision support products based on ensemble forecasts in the European flood alert system. *Atmospheric Science Letters*, *8*(4), 113–119. doi:10.1002/asl.161

Randed. (2018, 05 11). randed.com. Retrieved 08 23, 2019, from https://randed.com/smart-city-riesgos-y-beneficios/

RED GEALC, S.-O. I. (2008, 10). De la teoría a la práctica: cómo implementar con éxito el gobierno electrónico.

Reddy, P. S. N., Naik, R. N., Kumar, A. A., & Kishor, S. N. (2017, February). Wireless dust bin monitoring and alert system using Arduino. In *Electrical, Computer and Communication Technologies (ICECCT), 2017 Second International Conference on* (pp. 1-5). IEEE. 10.1109/ICECCT.2017.8117960

Rezvani, M. H., & Khani, H. (2019). e-Voting over Blockchain Platforms: A Survey. *Journal of Network Security and Data Mining*, *2*(3), 1–14. doi:10.5281/zenodo.3463190

Rezvani, M., Fanaei, S., & Hassankhani, H. (2019). Smart Homecare Monitoring System Based on Internet of Things (IoT). *Journal of Medical Systems*, *43*(10), 326.

Rico-Bautista, D., Guerrero, C., Collazos, C., Maestre, G., Sanchez, M., & Medina-Cárdenas, Y. (2022). *Universidad inteligente una mirada desde la adopción de tecnologías emergentes.*

Rivera Urrutia, E. (2006). Concepto y problemas de la construcción del gobierno electrónico Una revisión de la literatura. *Gestión y Política Pública*, *15*(2), 259–305.

Rivest, L. Ronald (2009). *A Method for Obtaining Digital Signatures and Public-Key Cryptosystems.* ACM. https://dl.acm.org/doi/abs/10.1145/359340.359342

Rocha, A. . (2019). *2019 14th Iberian Conference on Information Systems and Technologies (CISTI) : proceedings of CISTI'2019 - 14th Iberian Conference on Information Systems and Technologies : 19 to 22 of June 2019, Coimbra, Portugal (Vol. 19)*. Associação Ibérica de Sistemas e Tecnologias de Informação, & Institute of Electrical and Electronics Engineershttps://sigarra.up.pt/reitoria/pt/pub_geral.editora_view?pi_editora_id=378

Rogerson, S. (1997). *A prospectus for the electronic delivery of government services.* Centre for Computing and Social Responsibility.

Rokhman, A. (2016). The Case of Indonesia. *Journal of Computing E-Government Adoption in Developing Countries.* https://jurnal.asian.or.id/index.php/JIANA/article/download/44/37/Viewproject

Roller, L., & Waverman, L. (2001). Telecommunication Infrastructure and Economic Development: A Simultaneous Approach. *The American Economic Review*, *91*(4), 909–923. doi:10.1257/aer.91.4.909

Rong, G., Alu, S., Li, K., Su, Y., Zhang, J., Zhang, Y., & Li, T. (2020). Rainfall induced landslide susceptibility mapping based on Bayesian optimized random forest and gradient boosting decision tree models—A case study of Shuicheng County, China. *Water (Basel)*, *12*(11), 3066. doi:10.3390/w12113066

Rong, G., Mendez, A., Assi, E. B., Zhao, B., & Sawan, M. (2020). Artificial Intelligence in Healthcare: Review and Prediction Case Studies. *Engineering (Beijing)*, *6*(3), 291–301. doi:10.1016/j.eng.2019.08.015

Ruhlandt, R. W. S. (2018). The governance of smart cities: A systematic literature review. *Cities (London, England)*, *81*, 1–23. doi:10.1016/j.cities.2018.02.014

Rus, A. (2022). Ataque del 51%. *Economipedia.* https://economipedia.com/definiciones/ataque-del-51.html

Safder, U., Kim, J., Pak, G., Rhee, G., & You, K. (2022). Investigating machine learning applications for effective real-time water quality parameter monitoring in full-scale wastewater treatment plants. *Water (Basel), 14*(19), 3147. doi:10.3390/w14193147

Safe cities index. (2021). Safe Cities. https://safecities.economist.com

Saheb, T., Dehghani, M., & Saheb, T. (2022). Artificial intelligence for sustainable energy: A contextual topic modeling and content analysis. *Sustainable Computing: Informatics and Systems, 35*, 100699. doi:10.1016/j.suscom.2022.100699

Sahin, E., & Demirtas, E. A. (2020). Utilizing the Quality Function Deployment technique and a proportional House of Quality for determining customer and technical requirements in the banking sector: A case study on credit card services for university students. *Journal of Business Economics and Finance, 9*(4), 203–218. doi:10.13189/jbef.2020.090401

Salomon, M. J., & Cavagnaro, T. R. (2022). Healthy soils: The backbone of productive, safe and sustainable urban agriculture. *Journal of Cleaner Production, 341*, 130808. doi:10.1016/j.jclepro.2022.130808

Sands, J., Lee, K. H., and Gunarathne, N. (2015). Environmental Management Accounting (EMA) for environmental management and organizational change. *Journal of Accounting and Organizational Change.*

Sangki, J. (2018). Vision of future e-government via new e-government maturity model: Based on Korea's e-government practices. *Telecommunications Policy, 42*(10), 860–871. doi:10.1016/j.telpol.2017.12.002

Sarker, B., & Keya, N., K., I. Mahir, F., M. Nahiun, K., Shahida, S., & A. Khan, R. (. (2021). Surface and ground water pollution: Causes and effects of urbanization and industrialization in South Asia. *Scientific Review (Singapore), 73*, 32–41. doi:10.32861r.73.32.41

Sarker, T., Kibler, K., & Reinhart, D. (2016). Concept mapping of food waste management alternatives within the food-energy-water nexus. *Proceedings of the World Environmental and Water Resources Congress.*

Sayeed, S., & Marco-Gisbert, H. (2019). Assessment of Blockchain consensus and security mechanisms against the 51% attack. *Applied Sciences (Basel, Switzerland), 9*(9), 1788. doi:10.3390/app9091788

Schaltegger, S., & Figge, F. (2000). Environmental shareholder value: Economic success with corporate environmental management. *Eco-Management and Auditing, 7*(1), 29–42. doi:10.1002/(SICI)1099-0925(200003)7:1<29::AID-EMA119>3.0.CO;2-1

Schiewe, J., Krek, A., Peters, I., Sternberg, H., & Traub, K. P. (2008). HCU research group "Digital City": developing and evaluating tools for urban research. Digital earth summit on geoinformatics.

Schomakers, E.-M., Biermann, H., & Ziefle, M. (2021). Users' Preferences for Smart Home Automation – Investigating Aspects of Privacy and Trust. *Telematics and Informatics, 64*, 101689. doi:10.1016/j.tele.2021.101689

Schuler, D. (2001, October). Digital cities and digital citizens. In *Kyoto Workshop on Digital Cities* (pp. 71-85). Springer.

Scott, N., Zhang, R., Le, D., & Moyle, B. (2017). A review of eye-tracking research in tourism. *Current Issues in Tourism*, 1–18.

Sebastia, L., Garcia, I., Onaindia, E., & Guzman, C. (2009). e-Tourism: A tourist recommendation and planning application. *International Journal of Artificial Intelligence Tools, 18*(05), 717–738. doi:10.1142/S0218213009000378

Semiat, R. (2008). Energy issues in desalination processes. *Environmental Science & Technology, 42*(22), 8193–8201. doi:10.1021/es801330u PMID:19068794

Sen, A. (1992b). Pobreza: identificación y agregación. In L. Beccaria y otros (Ed.), *América Latina: el reto de la pobreza. Conceptos, métodos, magnitud, características y evolución.* Programa de las Naciones Unidas para el Desarrollo (PNUD).

SENAGUA. (2012). *Normas para Estudio y Diseño de Sistemas de Agua Potable y Disposición de Aguas Residuales para Poblaciones Mayores a 1000 Habitantes (Norma CO 10.07 SENAGUA)*. Código Ecuatoriano de la Construcción de Parte IX Obras Sanitarias.

Setis-Eu. (2012). setis.ec.europa.eu/implementation/technology-roadmap/European-initiative-on-smart-cities

Sharholy, M., Ahmad, K., Mahmood, G., & Trivedi, R. C. (2008). Municipal solid waste management in Indian cities– A review. *Waste Management (New York, N.Y.)*, *28*(2), 459–467. doi:10.1016/j.wasman.2007.02.008 PMID:17433664

Shim, J. (2023). Investigating the effectiveness of introducing virtual reality to elementary school students' moral education. *Computers & Education: X Reality*, *2*, 100010. https://doi.org/https://doi.org/10.1016/j.cexr.2023.100010

Shim, E., Kim, D., Woo, H., & Cho, Y. (2016). Designing a sustainable noise mapping system based on citizen scientists smartphone sensor data. *PLoS One*, *11*(9), e0161835. doi:10.1371/journal.pone.0161835 PMID:27626273

Shin, D. H. (2009). Ubiquitous city: Urban technologies, urban infrastructure and urban informatics. *Journal of Information Science*, *35*(5), 515–526. doi:10.1177/0165551509100832

Shiraishi, T., Nagata, M., Shibata, N., Murata, Y., Yasumoto, K., & Ito, M. (2005). A personal navigation system with functions to compose tour schedules based on multiple conflicting criteria. *IPSJ Digital Courier*, *1*, 528–536. doi:10.2197/ipsjdc.1.528

Shiri, N., Shiri, J., Yaseen, Z. M., Kim, S., Chung, I.-M., Nourani, V., & Zounemat-Kermani, M. (2021). Development of artificial intelligence models for well groundwater quality simulation: Different modeling scenarios. *PLoS One*, *16*(5), e0251510. doi:10.1371/journal.pone.0251510 PMID:34043648

Si, F., Huang, T., Li, N., Li, K., Wen, G., Li, Y., & Zhang, H. (2022). Effects of flood discharge on the water quality of a drinking water reservoir in China – Characteristics and management strategies. *Journal of Environmental Management*, *314*, 115072. https://doi.org/https://doi.org/10.1016/j.jenvman.2022.115072. doi:10.1016/j.jenvman.2022.115072 PMID:35452880

Sikora-Fernández, D. (2017). Factores de desarrollo de las ciudades inteligentes. *Revista Universitaria de Geografía*, *26*(1), 135–152.

Sikora-Fernandez, D. (2018). Smarter cities in post-socialist country: Example of Poland. *Cities (London, England)*, *78*, 52–59. doi:10.1016/j.cities.2018.03.011

Silva, B., Khan, M., & Han, K. (2018). Towards sustainable smart cities: A review of trends, architectures, components, and open challenges in smart cities. *Sustainable Cities and Society*, *38*, 697–713. doi:10.1016/j.scs.2018.01.053

Sinagra, M., Nasello, C., Tucciarelli, T., Barbetta, S., Massari, C., & Moramarco, T. (2020). A self-contained and automated method for flood hazard maps prediction in urban areas. *Water (Basel)*, *12*(5), 1266. doi:10.3390/w12051266

Singh, A. (2018). Assessment of different strategies for managing the water resources problems of irrigated agriculture. *Agricultural Water Management*, *208*, 187–192. doi:10.1016/j.agwat.2018.06.021

Singh, A., Krause, A., Guestrin, C., & Kaiser, W. J. (2009). Efficient Informative Sensing using Multiple Robots. *Journal of Artificial Intelligence Research*, *34*, 707–755. doi:10.1613/jair.2674

Singh, D. K., & Sobti, R. (2022). Long-range real-time monitoring strategy for Precision Irrigation in urban and rural farming in society 5.0. *Computers & Industrial Engineering*, *167*, 107997. doi:10.1016/j.cie.2022.107997

Singh, N. K., Yadav, M., Singh, V., Padhiyar, H., Kumar, V., Bhatia, S. K., & Show, P.-L. (2023). Artificial intelligence and machine learning-based monitoring and design of biological wastewater treatment systems. *Bioresource Technology*, *369*(128486), 128486. doi:10.1016/j.biortech.2022.128486 PMID:36528177

Singh, R. B. (Ed.). (2015). *Urban development challenges, risks and resilience in Asian mega cities*. Springer Japan. doi:10.1007/978-4-431-55043-3

Slashchova, O., Yalanskyi, O., Slashchov, I., Kurinnyi, V., & Kulbach, A. (2023). Fuzzy logic methods for risk management at mining enterprises. *IOP Conference Series. Earth and Environmental Science*, *1156*(1), 012015. doi:10.1088/1755-1315/1156/1/012015

SMART Technologies ULC. (2009, 2019). *SMART Classroom Suite*. SMART. https://usermanual.wiki/m/0f5b7918aaa470a4cf118a8a208988be8d6263b84e27f1b85cf058d93af5d7db.pdf

SMART Technologies ULC. (2023, 2023). *SMART Technologies*. SMART. https://www.smarttech.com/en/education

Smith, J. (2020). The safe city concept: Utilizing technology for crime reduction and enhanced safety. *Journal of Urban Safety*, *7*(2), 45–58.

Sohail, M. T., Elkaeed, E. B., Irfan, M., Acevedo-Duque, Á., & Mustafa, S. (2022). Determining farmers' awareness about climate change mitigation and wastewater irrigation: A pathway toward green and sustainable development. *Frontiers in Environmental Science*, *10*, 900193. doi:10.3389/fenvs.2022.900193

Song, S., Cheong, J. C., Lee, J. S. H., Tan, J. K. N., Chiam, Z., Arora, S., Png, K. J. Q., Seow, J. W. C., Leong, F. W. S., Palliwal, A., Biljecki, F., Tablaba, A., & Tan, H. T. W. (2022). Home gardening in Singapore: A feasibility study on the utilization of the vertical space of retrofitted high-rise public housing apartment buildings to increase urban vegetable self-sufficiency. *Urban Forestry & Urban Greening*, *78*, 127755. doi:10.1016/j.ufug.2022.127755

Souffriau, W., & Vansteenwegen, P. (2010, July). Tourist trip planning functionalities: State–of–the–art and future. In *International Conference on Web Engineering* (pp. 474-485). Springer, Berlin, Heidelberg. 10.1007/978-3-642-16985-4_46

Spasova, E., & Raiu, I. (2022). Evaluating quality in software engineering using the House of Quality method. *Informatics (MDPI)*, *9*(2), 31. doi:10.3390/informatics9020031

Spasova, V., & Raiu, O. (2022). Implementation of House of Quality Method for software tools evaluation. *Mathematical and Software Engineering*, *8*(1-2), 10–18.

Srinivasu, P. N., SivaSai, J. G., Ijaz, M. F., Bhoi, A. K., Kim, W., & Kang, J. J. (2021). Classification of skin disease using deep learning neural networks with MobileNet V2 and LSTM. *Sensors (Basel)*, *21*(8), 2852. doi:10.339021082852 PMID:33919583

Sroufe, R. (2003). Effects of environmental management systems on environmental management practices and operations. *Production and Operations Management*, *12*(3), 416–431. doi:10.1111/j.1937-5956.2003.tb00212.x

Stanford University. (2023, 2023). *Stanford Online*. Stanford University. https://online.stanford.edu

Steger, U. (2000). Environmental management systems: Empirical evidence and further perspectives. *European Management Journal*, *18*(1), 23–37. doi:10.1016/S0263-2373(99)00066-3

Strokal, M., Bai, Z., Franssen, W., Hofstra, N., Koelmans, A. A., Ludwig, F., Ma, L., van Puijenbroek, P., Spanier, J. E., Vermeulen, L. C., van Vliet, M. T. H., van Wijnen, J., & Kroeze, C. (2021). Urbanization: An increasing source of multiple pollutants to rivers in the 21st century. *Npj Urban Sustainability*, *1*(1), 24. Advance online publication. doi:10.103842949-021-00026-w

Su, K., Li, J., & Fu, H. (2011). Smart city and the applications. *IEEE International Conference on Electronics, Communications and Control (ICECC)*, 1028-1031. 10.1080/13604810802479126

Sukhbaatar, U. (2016). *A model simulation for trip planning recommendation system in Tourism* [Doctoral dissertation, Université Grenoble Alpes].

Sullivan, L. P. (1986). Quality function deployment: A system to assure that customer needs drive the product design and production process. *Quality Progress*, *19*(9), 39–50.

Sunao, I. (2012). Potable Water Remote Automatic Supply Control Unit and Potable Water Remote Automatic Supply Control System [Patent]. https://patentscope.wipo.int/search/es/detail.jsf?docId=JP273350066&_cid=P12-L9MVZJ-64483-1

Sun, C., Parellada, B., Puig, V., & Cembrano, G. (2019). Leak localization in water distribution networks using pressure and data-driven classifier approach. *Water (Basel)*, *12*(1), 54. doi:10.3390/w12010054

Sun, C., Romero, L., Joseph-Duran, B., Meseguer, J., Muñoz, E., Guasch, R., Martinez, M., Puig, V., & Cembrano, G. (2020). Integrated pollution-based real-time control of sanitation systems. *Journal of Environmental Management*, *269*, 110798. doi:10.1016/j.jenvman.2020.110798 PMID:32561007

Su, Y. L., Wang, Y. F., & Ow, D. W. (2020). Increasing effectiveness of urban rooftop farming through reflector-assisted double-layer hydroponic production. *Urban Forestry & Urban Greening*, *54*, 126766. doi:10.1016/j.ufug.2020.126766

Tabasová, A., Kropáč, J., Kermes, V., Nemet, A., & Stehlík, P. (2012). Waste-to-energy technologies: Impact on environment. *Energy*, *44*(1), 146–155. doi:10.1016/j.energy.2012.01.014

Tai, M. C. (2020). The impact of artificial intelligence on human society and bioethics. *Tzu-Chi Medical Journal*, *32*(4), 339. doi:10.4103/tcmj.tcmj_71_20 PMID:33163378

Taş, R., y Özgür Tanrıöver, Ö. (2020). A Systematic Review of Challenges and Opportunities of Blockchain for E-Voting. *208 MDPI Journals Awarded Impact Factor*. doi:10.3390/sym12081328

Tatoglu, E., Frynas, J. G., Bayraktar, E., Demirbag, M., Sahadev, S., Doh, J., & Koh, S. L. (2020). Why do emerging market firms engage in voluntary environmental management practices? A strategic choice perspective. *British Journal of Management*, *31*(1), 80–100. doi:10.1111/1467-8551.12351

Ten Hagen, K., Kramer, R., Hermkes, M., Schumann, B., & Mueller, P. (2005). Semantic matching and heuristic search for a dynamic tour guide. In *Information and Communication Technologies in Tourism 2005* (pp. 149–159). Springer. doi:10.1007/3-211-27283-6_14

Terzieva, V., Ilchev, S., & Todorova, K. (2022). The Role of Internet of Things in Smart Education. *IFAC-PapersOnLine*, *55*(11), 108–113. doi:10.1016/j.ifacol.2022.08.057

Teslya, N. N., Ryabchikov, I. A., Petrov, M. V., Taramov, A. A., & Lipkin, E. O. (2019). Smart City Platform Architecture for Citizens' Mobility Support. *Procedia Computer Science*, *150*, 646–653. doi:10.1016/j.procs.2019.02.041

Thakare, V., & Khire, G. (2014). Role of emergency technology for building smart hospital information system. *Procedia Economics and Finance*, *11*, 583–588. doi:10.1016/S2212-5671(14)00223-8

Thakur, A. (2022). Sensor-Based Technology in the Hospitality Industry. In A. B. Waluyo & L. Tan (Eds.), *Mobile Computing and Technology Applications in Tourism and Hospitality* (pp. 24–43). IGI Global., doi:10.4018/978-1-7998-6904-7.ch002

Thierer, A. D., Castillo, A., & Russell, R. (2017). *Artificial intelligence and public policy*. SSRN Electronic Journal. doi:10.2139/ssrn.3021135

ThingsBoard. I. (2023). *ThingsBoard IoT Platform*. ThingsBoard. https://thingsboard.io/

Thornton, P. K., & Herrero, M. (2010). *The inter-linkages between rapid growth in livestock production, climate change, and the impacts on water resources, land use, and deforestation*. The World Bank. . doi:10.1596/1813-9450-5178

Tien Bui, D., Pradhan, B., Lofman, O., Revhaug, I., & Dick, O. B. (2012). Landslide susceptibility assessment in the Hoa Binh province of Vietnam: A comparison of the Levenberg–Marquardt and Bayesian regularized neural networks. *Geomorphology*, *171–172*, 12–29. doi:10.1016/j.geomorph.2012.04.023

Tong, Y., Yang Q. C., Shimamura S. (2013, October). Analysis of Electric-Energy Utilization Efficiency in a Plant Factory with Artificial Light for Lettuce Production. *Acta Horticulturae 1037*(1037). . doi:10.17660/ActaHortic.2014.1037.32

Toosi, A., Bottino, A., Saboury, B., Siegel, E., & Rahmim, A. (2022). A brief history of AI: How to prevent another winter (a critical review). *PET Clinics*, *16*(4), 449–469. doi:10.1016/j.cpet.2021.07.001 PMID:34537126

To, W. M., & Lee, P. K. C. (2014). Diffusion of ISO 14001 environmental management system: Global, regional and country-level analyses. *Journal of Cleaner Production*, *66*, 489–498. doi:10.1016/j.jclepro.2013.11.076

Townsend, A. M. (2013). *Smart cities: Big data, civic hackers, and the quest for a new utopia*. WW Norton & Company.

Tranos, E., & Gertner, D. (2012). Smart networked cities? *Innovation (Abingdon)*, *25*(2), 175–190. doi:10.1080/13511610.2012.660327

Tripathy, A. K., Tripathy, P. K., Ray, N. K., & Mohanty, S. P. (2018). iTour: The future of smart tourism: An IoT framework for the independent mobility of tourists in smart cities. *IEEE Consumer Electronics Magazine*, *7*(3), 32–37. doi:10.1109/MCE.2018.2797758

Turner, A. J., Willetts, J. R., Fane, S. A., Giurco, D., Chong, J., Kazaglis, A., & White, S. (2010). *Guide to demand management and integrated resource planning* (Update on Original 2008 Guide). Academic Press.

Tüzünkan, D. (2017). The Relationship between Innovation and Tourism: The Case of Smart Tourism. *International Journal of Applied Engineering Research: IJAER*, *12*(23), 13861–13867.

Tzezana, R. (2017). High-probability and wild-card scenarios for future crimes and terror attacks using the Internet of Things. *foresight, 19*(1), 1-14.

Uddin, M., & Mahmud, M. (2021). IoT-Based Asthma Management System: A Review. *IEEE Access : Practical Innovations, Open Solutions*, *9*, 15679–15692.

UNESCO, & Commonwealth of Learning. (2016). *Making Sense of MOOCs: A Guide for Policy-Makers in Developing Countries*. https://doi.org/10.56059/11599/2356

UNESCO. (2018). *Global Education Meeting 2018: Brussels Declaration*. UNESCO. https://unesdoc.unesco.org/notice?id=p:usmarcdef_0000366394_spa

United Nations Educational. (2015). *Qingdao Declaration, 2015: Seize Digital Opportunities, Lead Education Transformation*. International Conference on Information and Communication Technology (ICT) and Post-2015 Education, Qingdao, China. https://unesdoc.unesco.org/notice?id=p:usmarcdef_0000233352

United Nations Educational. S. a. C. O. (2019). *Beijing Consensus on Artificial Intelligence and Education*. International Conference on Artificial Intelligence and Education 'Planning education in the AI era: Lead the leap', Beijing, Republic of China. https://unesdoc.unesco.org/notice?id=p:usmarcdef_0000368303

United Nations Educational. S. a. C. O. (2021). *Recommendation on the Ethics of Artificial Intelligence*. UN. https://unesdoc.unesco.org/notice?id=p:usmarcdef_0000381137

United Nations. (2015). *Transforming our world: the 2030 Agenda for Sustainable Development.* UN. https://documents-dds-ny.un.org/doc/UNDOC/GEN/N15/291/89/PDF/N1529189.pdf?OpenElement

United Nations. (2018). *E-Government Survey. Department of Economic and Social Affairs.* UN. publicadministration.un.org

University of China. (2023, 2023). *icourse163-org.* University of China. https://www.icourse163.org/

Van Bastelaer, B. (1998, October). Digital Cities and transferability of results. In *4th EDC Conference on digital cities* (pp. 61-70). Academic Press.

Van der Meer, A., & Van Winden, W. (2003). E-governance in cities: A comparison of urban information and communication technology policies. *Regional Studies, 37*(4), 407–419. doi:10.1080/0034340032000074433

Van Dijk, A. I. J. M., Renzullo, L. J., Wada, Y., & Tregoning, P. (2014). A global water cycle reanalysis (2003–2012) merging satellite gravimetry and altimetry observations with a hydrological multi-model ensemble. *Hydrology and Earth System Sciences, 18*(8), 2955–2973. doi:10.5194/hess-18-2955-2014

Vanclay, F. (2010). The triple bottom line and impact assessment: how do TBL, EIA, SIA, SEA, and EMS relate to each other? Tools, Techniques, And Approaches For Sustainability: Collected Writings in Environmental Assessment Policy and Management (pp. 101-124).

Vanolo, A. (2016). Is there anybody out there? The place and role of citizens in tomorrow's smart cities. *Futures, 82*, 26–36. doi:10.1016/j.futures.2016.05.010

Vansteenwegen, P., & Van Oudheusden, D. (2007). The mobile tourist guide: an OR opportunity. *OR insight, 20*(3), 21-27.

Varfolomeyev, A., Kozun, D., Ivanovs, A., Soms, H., & Petrina, O. (2015). Smart space based recommendation service for historical tourism. *Procedia Computer Science, 77*, 85–91. doi:10.1016/j.procs.2015.12.363

Vasagade, T. S., Tamboli, S. S., & Shinde, A. D. (2017, March). Dynamic solid waste collection and management system based on sensors, elevator and GSM. In *Inventive Communication and Computational Technologies (ICICCT), 2017 International Conference on* (pp. 263-267). IEEE. 10.1109/ICICCT.2017.7975200

Vegara, A. (2009). Territorios inteligentes. *Ambienta*, (89), 34-58. https://www.revistaambienta.es/WebAmbienta/marm/Dinamicas/secciones/articulos/Vegara.htm

Velasco, M. (2016). Tourism Policy. In A. Farazmand (Ed.), *Global Encyclopedia of Public Administration, Public Policy, and Governance.* Springer. doi:10.1007/978-3-319-31816-5_2674-1

Venkatesan, T. M. I., & Kundu, G. K. (2020). An empirical study of Kaizen events in Indian small and medium enterprises. *International Journal of Services and Operations Management, 37*(2), 197–219. doi:10.1504/IJSOM.2020.110338

Vesović, M., & Jovanović, R. (2022). Adaptive neuro fuzzy Inference systems in identification, modeling and control: The state-of-the-art. *Tehnika, 77*(5), 439–446. doi:10.5937/tehnika2204439V

Villarejo Galende, H. (2015). Smart cities: una apuesta de la Unión Europea para mejorar los servicios públicos urbanos. *Revista de estudios europeos*, (66), 25-51.

Viranda, D. F., Sari, A. D., Suryoputro, M. R., & Setiawan, N. (2020, January). 5S Implementation of SME Readiness in Meeting Environmental Management System Standards based on ISO 14001: 2015 (Study Case: PT. ABC). []. IOP Publishing]. *IOP Conference Series. Materials Science and Engineering, 722*(1), 012072. doi:10.1088/1757-899X/722/1/012072

Vlacheas, P., Giaffreda, R., Stavroulaki, V., Kelaidonis, D., Foteinos, V., Poulios, G., Demestichas, P., Somov, S., Biswas, A. R., & Moessner, K. (2013). Enabling smart cities through a cognitive management framework for the Internet of things. *IEEE Communications Magazine, 51*(6), 102–111. doi:10.1109/MCOM.2013.6525602

VomBrocke, J., Simons, A., Niehaves, B., Riemer, K., Plattfaut, R., & Cleven, A. (2009, June). Reconstructing the giant: On the importance of rigour in documenting the literature search process. In ECIS (Vol. 9, pp. 2206-2217). Academic Press.

Voukkali, I., & Zorpas, A. A. (2022). Evaluation of urban metabolism assessment methods through SWOT analysis and analytical hierocracy process. *The Science of the Total Environment, 807*, 150700. doi:10.1016/j.scitotenv.2021.150700 PMID:34606858

Vu, D. D., & Kaddoum, G. (2017). *A Waste City Management System for Smart Cities Applications*. IEEE. doi:10.1109/RTUWO.2017.8228538

Wang, D., Li, X., & Zhang, J. (2021). Gamification in tourism: A review of literature. *Journal of Travel Research, 60*(1), 104–124.

Wang, D., Li, X., & Zhang, J. (2021). Smart destination and sustainable tourism development: A review of literature. *Journal of Sustainable Tourism, 29*(3), 291–309.

Wang, D., Xiang, Z., Zhang, J., & Li, X. (2021). Social robots in tourism and hospitality: A review of current research. *Journal of Hospitality and Tourism Management, 48*, 139–151.

Wang, D., Zhang, J., & Li, X. (2020). Virtual reality for tourism: A systematic review. *Tourism Management, 82*, 104202.

Wang, S., Cao, T., & Chen, B. (2017). Urban energy–water nexus based on modified input–output analysis. *Applied Energy, 196*, 208–217. doi:10.1016/j.apenergy.2017.02.011

Wang, X., Li, X., Zhen, F., & Zhang, J. (2016). How smart is your tourist attraction?: Measuring tourist preference of smart tourism attractions via FCEM-AHP and IPA approach. *Tourism Management, 54*, 309–320. doi:10.1016/j.tourman.2015.12.003

Warner, J. W. (1993, January). Environmental data management system. In *SPE Annual Technical Conference and Exhibition*. Society of Petroleum Engineers. 10.2118/26363-MS

Washburn, D., Sindhu, U., Balaouras, S., Dines, R. A., Hayes, N., & Nelson, L. E. (2009). Helping CIOs understand "smart city" initiatives. *Growth, 17*(2), 1–17.

WaterModels. (n.d.). *Mathematical models in Watermodels*. Water Models. https://lanl-ansi.github.io/WaterModels.jl/latest/math-model.html

Weidner, T., & Yang, A. (2020). The potential of urban agriculture in combination with organic waste valorization: Assessment of resource flows and emissions for two european cities. *Journal of Cleaner Production, 244*(1), 118490. doi:10.1016/j.jclepro.2019.118490

Weidner, T., Yang, A., & Hamm, M. W. (2019). Consolidating the current knowledge on urban agriculture in productive urban food systems: Learnings, gaps and outlook. *Journal of Cleaner Production, 209*, 1637–1655. doi:10.1016/j.jclepro.2018.11.004

Werthner, H., & Klein, S. (1999). *Information technology and tourism: a challenging relationship*. Springer-VerlagWien. doi:10.1007/978-3-7091-6363-4

Wickramasuriya, R., Ma, J., Berryman, M., & Perez, P. (2013). Using geospatial business intelligence to support regional infrastructure governance. *Knowledge-Based Systems, 53*, 80–89. doi:10.1016/j.knosys.2013.08.024

Widmer-lliescu, R., Cristina, B., Simao, C. N., Mythili, M., & Chirs, L. (2023). El papel de las tecnologías digitales en el envejecimiento y la salud. In *El papel de las tecnologías digitales en el envejecimiento y la salud* (Vol. 1). Pan American Health Organization., doi:10.37774/9789275326558

Wilkinson, G., & Dale, B. G. (1999). Integrated management systems: An examination of the concept and theory. *The TQM Magazine*, *11*(2), 95–104. doi:10.1108/09544789910257280

Williams, M. W. (2013). The status of glaciers in the Hindu Kush–Himalayan region. *Mountain Research and Development*, *33*(1), 114. doi:10.1659/mrd.mm113

Williamson, B. (2015). Educating the smart city: Schooling smart citizens through computational urbanism. *Big Data & Society*, *2*(2), 2053951715617783. doi:10.1177/2053951715617783

Windapo, A. O., & Moghayedi, A. (2020). Adoption of smart technologies and circular economy performance of buildings. *Built Environment Project and Asset Management*, *10*(4), 585–601. doi:10.1108/BEPAM-04-2019-0041

Witanto, J. N., Lim, H., & Atiquzzaman, M. (2018). Smart government framework with geo-crowdsourcing and social media analysis. *Future Generation Computer Systems*, *89*, 1–9. doi:10.1016/j.future.2018.06.019

Woebot Health. (2023). *Woebot*. Woebot. https://woebothealth.com/

Wooldridge, J. M. (2012). Introductory Econometrics. *Economics*. https://economics.ut.ac.ir/documents/3030266/14100645/Jeffrey_M._Wooldridge_Introductory_Econometrics_A_Modern_Approach__2012.pdf

World Bank. (1999). *Pollution prevention and abatement handbook 1998: Toward cleaner production*. World Bank Publications.

World Health Organization(WHO). (1989). *Guidelines for the safe use of wastewater and excreta in agriculture and aquaculture: Measures for public health protection*. World Health Organization.

World Smart Sustainable Cities Organization (WeGo). (2022). Smart City Index 2022 Research on ESG perspectives in smart cities assessment. WeGo.

Wright, G., Cairns, G., O'Brien, F., & Goodwin, P. (2018). Scenario analysis to support decision making in addressing wicked problems: Pitfalls and potential. *European Journal of Operational Research*, *278*(1), 3–19. doi:10.1016/j.ejor.2018.08.035

WSO2 LLC. (2023, 2023). *WSO2 Iot*. WS02LLC. https://wso2.com/iot/

Wu, H. C., & Cheng, C. C. (2018). Relationships between technology attachment, experiential relationship quality, experiential risk and experiential sharing intentions in a smart hotel. *Journal of Hospitality and Tourism Management*, *37*, 42–58. doi:10.1016/j.jhtm.2018.09.003

Wu, J., & Chang, I. S. (2020). Environmental planning. In *Environmental Management in China* (pp. 17–34). Springer. doi:10.1007/978-981-15-4894-9_3

Wu, J., & Wang, Z. (2022). A hybrid model for water quality prediction based on an artificial neural network, wavelet transform, and long short-term memory. *Water (Basel)*, *14*(4), 610. doi:10.3390/w14040610

Xiang, Z., Zhang, D., Du, Q., & Li, G. (2019). Understanding social media data for smart tourism destination: An integrated approach. *Journal of Travel Research*, *58*(9), 1656–1670.

Xie, K., Li, X., Li, X., & Liu, H. (2021). Machine learning in smart tourism recommendation systems: A systematic review. *Journal of Travel Research*, *60*(4), 933–952.

Xie, Y., Chen, Y., Lian, Q., Yin, H., Peng, J., Sheng, M., & Wang, Y. (2022c). Enhancing real-time prediction of effluent water quality of wastewater treatment plant based on improved feedforward neural network coupled with optimization algorithm. *Water (Basel), 14*(7), 1053. doi:10.3390/w14071053

Xu, Y., Liu, X., Cao, X., Huang, C., Liu, E., Qian, S., Liu, X., Wu, Y., Dong, F., Qiu, C., Qiu, J., Hua, K., Su, W., Wu, J., Xu, H., Han, Y., Fu, C., Yin, Z., Liu, M., & Zhang, J. (2021). Artificial intelligence: A powerful paradigm for scientific research. *Innovation (Cambridge (Mass.)), 2*(4), 100179. doi:10.1016/j.xinn.2021.100179 PMID:34877560

Yandex. (2023, 2023). *YadexGPT*. Yandex. https://cloud.yandex.ru/services/yandexgpt

Yang, J., Shi, Y., Yu, C., & Cao, S.-J. (2020). Challenges of using mobile phone signaling data to estimate urban population density: Towards smart cities and sustainable urban development. Indoor + Built Environment. *The Journal of the International Society of the Built Environment, 29*(2), 147–150. doi:10.1177/1420326X19893145

Yang, Q., & Lee, Y.-C. (2021). The Critical Factors of Student Performance in MOOCs for Sustainable Education: A Case of Chinese Universities. *Sustainability (Basel), 13*(14), 8089. https://www.mdpi.com/2071-1050/13/14/8089. doi:10.3390u13148089

Yang, S., Liu, W., & Zhang, Z. (2022). The dynamic value of China's high-tech zones: Direct and indirect influence on urban ecological innovation. *Land (Basel), 11*(1), 59. doi:10.3390/land11010059

Yan, J., Chen, X., Yu, Y., & Zhang, X. (2019). Application of a parallel particle swarm optimization-long short term memory model to improve water quality data. *Water (Basel), 11*(7), 1317. doi:10.3390/w11071317

Yassin, M. M., Amr, S. S. A., & Al-Najar, H. M. (2006). Assessment of microbiological water quality and its relation to human health in Gaza Governorate, Gaza Strip. *Public Health, 120*(12), 1177–1187. doi:10.1016/j.puhe.2006.07.026 PMID:17034823

Ye, Y., Hu, J., Sun, Z., & Guo, Y. (2020). Smart asthma management system using machine learning and internet of things technologies. *Future Generation Computer Systems, 110*, 415–423.

Yigitcanlar, T., & Dizdaroglu, D. (2014). Ecological approaches in planning for sustainable cities: A review of the literature. *Global journal of environmental science and management, 1*(2), 159-188.

Yigitcanlar, T., & Kamruzzaman, M. (2018). Smart cities and mobility: Does the smartness of Australian cities lead to sustainable commuting patterns? *Journal of Urban Technology*. Advance online publication. doi:10.1080/10630732.2018.1476794

Yigitcanlar, T., Kamruzzaman, M., Buys, L., Ioppolo, G., Sabatini-Marques, J., Costa, E., & Yun, J. (2018). Understanding 'smart cities': Intertwining development drivers with desired outcomes in a multidimensional framework. *Cities (London, England), 81*, 145–160. Advance online publication. doi:10.1016/j.cities.2018.04.003

Yovanof, G. S., & Hazapis, G. N. (2009). An architectural framework and enabling wireless technologies for digital cities and intelligent urban environments. *Wireless Personal Communications, 49*(3), 445–463. doi:10.100711277-009-9693-4

Yu, C. C., & Chang, H. P. (2009, September). Personalized location-based recommendation services for tour planning in mobile tourism applications. In *International Conference on Electronic Commerce and Web Technologies* (pp. 38-49). Springer, Berlin, Heidelberg. 10.1007/978-3-642-03964-5_5

Yu, Tong & Kozai, T. & Nishioka, N. & Ohyama, Katsumi. (. (2012). Reductions in Energy Consumption and CO2 Emissions for Greenhouses Heated with Heat Pumps. *Applied Engineering in Agriculture, 28*, 401–406. doi:10.13031/2013.41488

Yu, X., Ma, S., Cheng, K., & Kyriakopoulos, G. L. (2020). An evaluation system for sustainable urban space development based in green urbanism principles—A case study based on the Qin-Ba mountain area in China. *Sustainability (Basel), 12*(14), 5703. doi:10.3390u12145703

Zahraee, S. M., Assadi, M. K., & Saidur, R. (2016). Application of Artificial Intelligence Methods for Hybrid Energy System Optimization. *Renewable & Sustainable Energy Reviews, 66*, 617–630. doi:10.1016/j.rser.2016.08.028

Zapata, E. (2021). Redensificación y construcción: claves para hacer de la CDMX una smart city. *Expansión.* https://expansion.mx/inmobiliario/2021/12/20/ciudad-de-mexico-lejos-de-convertirse-ciudad-inteligentehttps://cio.com.mx/la-ciudad-mexico-una-las-mas-inteligentes-del-mundo/

Zecchin, A. C., Simpson, A. R., Maier, H. R., Leonard, M., Roberts, A. J., & Berrisford, M. J. (2006, September). Application of two ant colony optimisation algorithms to water distribution system optimisation. *Mathematical and Computer Modelling, 44*(5–6), 451–468. doi:10.1016/j.mcm.2006.01.005

Zeunert, J., & Court, T. (2023). Translating unique agricultural precedents into public urban agriculture design. In *Urban and Regional Agriculture* (pp. 431–456). Building Resilient Food Systems. doi:10.1016/B978-0-12-820286-9.00002-9

Zhang, D. Q., Tan, S. K., & Gersberg, R. M. (2010). Municipal solid waste management in China: Status, problems and challenges. *Journal of Environmental Management, 91*(8), 1623–1633. doi:10.1016/j.jenvman.2010.03.012 PMID:20413209

Zhang, G., Liu, J., Pan, X., Abed, A. M., Le, B. N., Ali, H. E., & Ge, Y. (2022). Latest avenues and approaches for biohydrogen generation from algal towards sustainable energy optimization: Recent innovations, artificial intelligence, challenges, and future perspectives. *International Journal of Hydrogen Energy*. Advance online publication. doi:10.1016/j.ijhydene.2022.10.224

Zhang, J., Wang, D., Li, X., & Zhang, W. (2020). Artificial intelligence in smart tourism: A review. *Journal of Hospitality and Tourism Management, 44*, 103–116.

Zhang, J., Xiang, Z., Du, Q., & Li, X. (2021). Adoption of smart tourism technologies by destination management organizations: A systematic review. *Journal of Travel Research, 60*(3), 674–690.

Zou, W., Lo, D., Kochhar, P. S., Le, X. B. D., Xia, X., Feng, Y., Chen, Z., & Xu, B. (2019). Smart contract development: Challenges and opportunities. *IEEE Transactions on Software Engineering, 47*(10), 2084–2106. https://ieeexplore.ieee.org/abstract/document/8847638. doi:10.1109/TSE.2019.2942301

Zvobgo, L., & Do, P. (2020). COVID-19 and the call for 'Safe Hands': Challenges facing the under-resourced municipalities that lack potable water access - A case study of Chitungwiza municipality, Zimbabwe. *Water Research X, 9*, 100074. doi:10.1016/j.wroa.2020.100074 PMID:33089132

About the Contributors

Jorge A. Ruiz-Vanoye was born in D.F. Mexico in 1975. He obtained his Ph.D. degree in Computer Science in 2008 from CENIDET. He has worked at Electric Research Institute of Mexico government (IIE) and in diverse companies more. He has given classes in diverse Mexican Universities since 1996. He is reviewer of Computers & Security, Neural Computing & Applications journal, Journal of Computer Information Systems, Computers & Electrical Engineering, Journal of Computational and Applied Mathematics and others journals and conferences.

***

Jaime Aguilar-Ortiz has a Ph.D. in mathematics.

Ricardo Barrera-Cámara has a Ph.D. in Computer Systems from the Universidad del Sur. Master in Informatics from the Universidad Autónoma of Carmen. Research professor at the Autonomous University of Carmen in Mexico. National System of Researchers level candidate. Leader of the academic group of scientific and technological computing. Leader of the Academy of Administration and information processing. His research areas are Scientific Computing, Data Science, Optimization, Quality and Information Technology.

Marìa Beatriz Bernábe was born in the city of Puebla, Mexico. She received the B.S.degree in Computer Science from Benemérita Universidad Autónoma de Puebla (BUAP), Mexico in 1993 and the M.I. degree in quality engineering from Universidad Iberoamericana (UIA), Mexico in 2003. In January 2010, she received the Doctorate degree in Operations Research from the Universidad Nacional Autónoma de México (UNAM.). Since 1995, she has been a professor at the School of Computer Science of BUAP, where she works in statistics.and operations research. Her research interests are combinatorial optimization, territorial design and multiobjective techniques. She belongs to "Sistema Nacional de Investigadores" Conacyt - México.

Ricardo Calderón-Suarez is a Doctor in Optomechatronics.

Brenda Eguiluz-Ruiz has a Bachelor's degree in Administration and Head of the Social Service Department at the Office of Community Engagement.

Alejandro Fuentes Penna. has a Ph.D. on Strategic Planning and Technology Directorate.

Ahmet Gedikli is a recent graduate from the department of Information Systems and Technology, Yeditepe University.

Sandra Luz Hernández Mendoza is a professor of the Department of Information Technology at the Universidad Autónoma del Estado de Hidalgo. ORCID -0000-0002-2022-3135

Zeus Salvador Hernández Veleros is a research professor in the Academic Area of Economics at the Instituto de Ciencias Económico Administrativas. He is in the National System of Researchers with the Level I. He is a consultant in quantitative and simulation issues, and has worked on port, fiscal, environmental and cluster issues. He worked at the Unidad de Análisis Económico y Apoyo Técnico de la Subsecretaría de Ingresos del Gobierno del Estado de México and was Deputy Director of Quantitative Methods at the Instituto Nacional de Migración. He began his teaching activities at the Universidad Anáhuac in 1997 and that same year at the Universidad Autónoma del Estado de Hidalgo. He has been a professor at institutions such as El Colegio Mexiquense, the Economics Faculty of the Universidad Autónoma del Estado de México, the Instituto de Administración Pública del Estado de Hidalgo, the Instituto Tecnológico de Monterrey, the Centro Universitario Hidalguense, and the Universidad Autónoma de Quintana Roo. He works on growth models with aspects of econometric measurement, time series and simulation, in this sense his most recent co-authored publication is "Gasto público y crecimiento en un modelo con dos sectores: tasas impositivas óptimas" (2022).

Evangelina Lezama-León is a research professor in the department of information technology at the Universidad Autónoma del Estado de Hidalgo.

Marco Marquez-Vera is a full time professor in the Machatronics Engineering department. The PhD is in Computational Science. He is associated editor in the International Journal on Robotics and Control Systems.

Cagla Ozen has taken her PhD from Computer Science Department of University of York, UK. She has more than 30 publications and one of her publications awarded as Outstanding Paper Award Winner at the Literati Network Awards for Excellence 2011. Her research interests are user experience, user interface, technology adoption and IoT.

C. Parameswari, M.Sc., (Ag) is an Assistant Professor. Qualifications: M.Sc. (Ag.); Specialization: Soil Science and Agricultural Chemistry.

Edgar Pineda has a Master's degree in Strategic Planning and Technology Management from the Universidad Popular Autónoma del Estado de Puebla, and CEO of ALFASistemas TI, a technology company.

José Ramírez Rosas holds a degree in Public Accounting and Auditing from the Benemérita Universidad Autónoma de Puebla. They have also obtained Master´s degrees in Taxation and Organizational Management from BUAP. Furthermore, they hold a Doctorate in Administration, They have a specialization in Digital Teaching from the Universidad Popular Autónoma del Estado de Puebla (UPAEP) and are a candidate member of the National System of Researchers (SNI)

Evelyn V. Tafoya-Rivera studied Mechatronic Engineering at Universidad Politécnica de Pachuca (UPP), Mexico, graduating with an average grade of 9.5, the highest in her class. She is currently pursuing a Master's degree in Mechatronics at UPP, focusing on heuristic algorithms, artificial intelligence, and mobile robotics at the "Laboratorio Nacional en Vehículos Autónomos y Exoesqueletos" (LANAVEX).

Miguel Ángel Torres González has a bachelor's degree in computer science from the Universidad Autónoma del Estado de Hidalgo, Master in Economic and Financial Engineering from the Universidad La Salle Pachuca, PhD. in Strategic Planning and Technology Management from the Universidad Popular Autónoma de Puebla, Professor at the Graduate School of the Universidad La Salle Pachuca, External advisor to the Consultoría en Economía, Inversiones y Proyectos (CEIP), Leader of the Academic Body of Strategies, Knowledge Management, Competitiveness and Technological Innovation and Full Time Research Professor for the Universidad Politécnica de Pachuca under the research lines "Design of knowledge management strategies and technology promotion" and "Analysis of the drinking water sector through simulation models and data imputation", Director of the Financial Engineering Educational Program of the Universidad Politécnica de Pachuca, National Financial Engineering Coordinator of the Sistema de Universidades Tecnológicas y Politécnicas, Member of the Technical Advisory Committee for the Preliminary Electoral Results Program. (COTAPREP) from Instituto Nacional Electoral (INE).

Francisco R. Trejo-Macotela received the PhD. Degree in Electronics from the National Institute of Astrophysics, Optics and Electronics, Puebla, Mexico. Currently he is professor in the Master's in Mechatronics and Master's in ICT programs at the Polytechnic University of Pachuca, Mexico. His main research interests are Integrated Circuit Design, Analog and Digital Design, Embedded Systems, RF Electronics, Telecommunications Systems, Precision Agriculture, Internet of Things, among others.

Index

W

Ensure Quality Research is Introduced to the Academic Community

Become an Evaluator for IGI Global Authored Book Projects

The overall success of an authored book project is dependent on quality and timely manuscript evaluations.

Applications and Inquiries may be sent to:
development@igi-global.com

Applicants must have a doctorate (or equivalent degree) as well as publishing, research, and reviewing experience. Authored Book Evaluators are appointed for one-year terms and are expected to complete at least three evaluations per term. Upon successful completion of this term, evaluators can be considered for an additional term.

If you have a colleague that may be interested in this opportunity, we encourage you to share this information with them.

www.ingramcontent.com/pod-product-compliance
Lightning Source LLC
LaVergne TN
LVHW062136300926
849161LV00010B/2550